Practising Self-Government

Autonomy is an important constitutional concept allowing for regions within countries to exercise self-government. This book presents detailed case studies of thirteen such autonomies from around the world, in which noted experts on each outline the constitutional, legal and institutional frameworks as well as how these arrangements have worked in practice to protect minority rights and prevent secession of the territories in question. The volume's editors draw on the case studies to provide a comparative analysis of how autonomy works and the political and institutional conditions under which it is likely to become a workable arrangement for management of the differences that brought it into being.

Yash Ghai is Professor Emeritus at the University of Hong Kong and Director of the Katiba Institute, Nairobi. For the past thirty years, he has been involved in the study of autonomy as a scholar and as a framer of constitutional arrangements that use autonomy as a device for resolving conflict.

Sophia Woodman is a postdoctoral research fellow at the University of British Columbia, Vancouver. She is a sociologist who studies Chinese politics, including the politics of autonomy and minorities in contemporary China.

The Law in Context Series

Editors: William Twining (University College London), Christopher McCrudden (Queen's University Belfast) and Bronwen Morgan (University of Bristol).

Since 1970 the Law in Context series has been at the forefront of the movement to broaden the study of law. It has been a vehicle for the publication of innovative scholarly books that treat law and legal phenomena critically in their social, political and economic contexts from a variety of perspectives. The series particularly aims to publish scholarly legal writing that brings fresh perspectives to bear on new and existing areas of law taught in universities. A contextual approach involves treating legal subjects broadly, using materials from other social sciences, and from any other discipline that helps to explain the operation in practice of the subject under discussion. It is hoped that this orientation is at once more stimulating and more realistic than the bare exposition of legal rules. The series includes original books that have a different emphasis from traditional legal textbooks, while maintaining the same high standards of scholarship. They are written primarily for undergraduate and graduate students of law and of other disciplines, but will also appeal to a wider readership. In the past, most books in the series have focused on English law, but recent publications include books on European law, globalisation, transnational legal processes, and comparative law.

Books in the Series

Anderson, Schum & Twining: *Analysis of Evidence*
Ashworth: *Sentencing and Criminal Justice*
Barton & Douglas: *Law and Parenthood*
Beecher-Monas: *Evaluating Scientific Evidence: An Interdisciplinary Framework for Intellectual Due Process*
Bell: *French Legal Cultures*
Bercusson: *European Labour Law*
Birkinshaw: *European Public Law*
Birkinshaw: *Freedom of Information: The Law, the Practice and the Ideal*
Brownsword & Goodwin: *Law and the Technologies of the Twenty-First Century*
Cane: *Atiyah's Accidents, Compensation and the Law*
Clarke & Kohler: *Property Law: Commentary and Materials*
Collins: *The Law of Contract*
Collins, Ewing & McColgan: *Labour Law*
Cowan: *Housing Law and Policy*
Cranston: *Legal Foundations of the Welfare State*
Darian-Smith: *Laws and Societies in Global Contexts: Contemporary Approaches*
Dauvergne *Making People Illegal: What Globalisation Means for Immigration and Law*
Davies: *Perspectives on Labour Law*
Dembour: *Who Believes in Human Rights?: The European Convention in Question*
de Sousa Santos: *Toward a New Legal Common Sense*
Diduck: *Law's Families*
Fortin: *Children's Rights and the Developing Law*
Ghai & Woodham: *Practising self-government: A Comparative Study of Autonomous Regions*
Glover-Thomas: *Reconstructing Mental Health Law and Policy*
Gobert & Punch: *Rethinking Corporate Crime*
Goldman: *Globalisation and the Western Legal Tradition: Recurring Patterns of Law and Authority*
Harlow & Rawlings: *Law and Administration*
Harris: *An Introduction to Law*

Harris, Campbell & Halson: *Remedies in Contract and Tort*
Harvey: *Seeking Asylum in the UK: Problems and Prospects*
Hervey & McHale: *Health Law and the European Union*
Holder & Lee: *Environmental Protection, Law and Policy*
Jackson & Summers: *The Internationalisation of Criminal Evidence*
Kostakopoulou: *The Future Governance of Citizenship*
Lewis: *Choice and the Legal Order: Rising above Politics*
Likosky: *Transnational Legal Processes*
Likosky: *Law, Infrastructure and Human Rights*
Maughan & Webb: *Lawyering Skills and the Legal Process*
McGlynn: *Families and the European Union: Law, Politics and Pluralism*
Moffat: *Trusts Law: Text and Materials*
Monti: *EC Competition Law*
Morgan: *Contract Law Minimalism*
Morgan & Yeung: *An Introduction to Law and Regulation: Text and Materials*
Norrie: *Crime, Reason and History*
O'Dair: *Legal Ethics*
Oliver: *Common Values and the Public–Private Divide*
Oliver & Drewry: *The Law and Parliament*
Picciotto: *International Business Taxation*
Probert: *The Changing Legal Regulation of Cohabitation, 1600–2010*
Reed: *Internet Law: Text and Materials*
Richardson: *Law, Process and Custody*
Roberts & Palmer: *Dispute Processes: ADR and the Primary Forms of Decision-Making*
Rowbottom: *Democracy Distorted: Wealth, Influence and Democratic Politics*
Scott & Black: *Cranston's Consumers and the Law*
Seneviratne: *Ombudsmen: Public Services and Administrative Justice*
Stapleton: *Product Liability*
Stewart: *Gender, Law and Justice in a Global Market*
Tamanaha: *Law as a Means to an End: Threat to the Rule of Law*
Turpin and Tomkins: *British Government and the Constitution: Text and Materials*
Twining: *Globalisation and Legal Theory*
Twining: *Rethinking Evidence*
Twining: *General Jurisprudence: Understanding Law from a Global Perspective*
Twining: *Human Rights, Southern Voices: Francis Deng, Abdullahi An-Na'im, Yash Ghai and Upendra Baxi*
Twining & Miers: *How to Do Things with Rules*
Ward: *A Critical Introduction to European Law*
Ward: *Law, Text, Terror*
Ward: *Shakespeare and Legal Imagination*
Wells & Quick: *Lacey, Wells and Quick: Reconstructing Criminal Law*
Zander: *Cases and Materials on the English Legal System*
Zander: *The Law-Making Process*

International Journal of Law in Context: A Global Forum for Interdisciplinary Legal Studies

The *International Journal of Law in Context* is the companion journal to the Law in Context book series and provides a forum for interdisciplinary legal studies and offers intellectual space for ground-breaking critical research. It publishes contextual work about law and its relationship with other disciplines including but not limited to science, literature, humanities, philosophy, sociology, psychology, ethics, history and geography. More information about the journal and how to submit an article can be found at http://journals.cambridge.org/ijc.

Practising Self-Government

A Comparative Study of Autonomous Regions

Edited by

YASH GHAI AND SOPHIA WOODMAN

CAMBRIDGE
UNIVERSITY PRESS

CAMBRIDGE
UNIVERSITY PRESS

University Printing House, Cambridge CB2 8BS, United Kingdom

Published in the United States of America by Cambridge University Press, New York

Cambridge University Press is part of the University of Cambridge.

It furthers the University's mission by disseminating knowledge in the pursuit of education, learning and research at the highest international levels of excellence.

www.cambridge.org
Information on this title: www.cambridge.org/9781107018587

First published 2013

Printed in the United Kingdom by Clays, St Ives plc

A catalogue record for this publication is available from the British Library

Library of Congress Cataloguing in Publication data
Practising self-government : a comparative study of autonomous regions / edited by Yash Ghai and Sophia Woodman.
pages cm. – (The law in context series)
Includes bibliographical references and index.
ISBN 978-1-107-01858-7 (hardback)
1. Autonomy – Case studies. 2. Self-determination, National – Case studies.
I. Ghai, Yash P., 1938–
JC327.P73 2013
320.1′5 – dc23 2013009530

ISBN 978-1-107-01858-7 Hardback

Contents

Tables

Contributors

Paulo Cardinal has been a legal adviser to the Macau Legislative Assembly since 1992, and is an invited lecturer at the Faculty of Law, University of Macau. He has published widely on public law issues. Besides autonomy systems and fundamental rights, his main areas of research include the *amparo* writ, constitutional justice, comparative constitutional law and some international law areas such as human rights and international personality.

Jill Cottrell taught law at university level for many years, with research interests mainly in the areas of tort, environmental law and human rights. She has also written several articles on aspects of Indian law. Over the last decade she has advised on constitution making in a number of countries, and is now mostly involved in helping with the implementation of the constitution of Kenya through engagement with civil society.

Carlos Flores Juberías is Professor of Constitutional Law at the University of Valencia Law School. He has been a Fulbright scholar at the University of California San Diego, and received a Doctor *honoris causa* from the St. Francis Xavier University in Sucre, Bolivia.

Chris Himsworth is Emeritus Professor of Administrative Law at the University of Edinburgh. He has written widely on devolution (especially in relation to Scotland and the United Kingdom), human rights, local government and administrative law, as well as general constitutional law.

Helen Irving is Professor in the Faculty of Law, The University of Sydney, where she teaches Australian and comparative constitutional law. Her research focuses on constitutional citizenship, including its historical relationship with gender. She is the author and editor of many publications, including *Gender and the Constitution: Equity and Agency in Comparative Constitutional Design* (Cambridge University Press, 2008).

Joseph Marko is Dean of the Faculty of Law and professor of public law and political science at the Institute of Austrian, European and Comparative Public Law and Political Science at the University of Graz. Since 1998 he has been director of the Minority Rights Institute at the European Academy Bolzano/Italy. He is also the scientific co-ordinator of the Joint Ph.D. Program in 'Diversity Management and European Governance'. From May 1997 to May 2002 he served as an international judge of the Constitutional Court of Bosnia and Herzegovina, acting as its vice-president from 1999 to 2001.

Oskar Peterlini has represented South Tyrol in the Italian Senate since 2001. For twenty years he held a seat in the Regional Parliament of Trentino-South Tyrol and served as its President for ten years. He is an expert on autonomies and the Italian Constitution at the Free University of Bozen Bolzano. He has published several books on constitutional reforms in Italy, on federalism and electoral systems, on protection of minorities and the Special Statute of South Tyrol. He has also written on pension funds in Italy, and created an innovative complementary pension system.

Anthony J. Regan is a Fellow in the State, Society and Governance in Melanesia Program, College of Asia and the Pacific at The Australian National University. A constitutional lawyer who has lived and worked for twenty years in Papua New Guinea and Uganda, his main field of research concerns the use of constitution-making processes and constitutional arrangements as part of conflict resolution processes. He has been involved in such processes in relation to a number of countries, including Papua New Guinea, Uganda, Solomon Islands, Timor L'este, Fiji, India and Sri Lanka. He has been an adviser to the Bougainville parties in the peace process there since the late 1990s.

Efrén Rivera-Ramos is a former Dean and full professor at the School of Law of the University of Puerto Rico, where he teaches Constitutional Law, Jurisprudence and Law and Culture. He is a recognised expert on the legal and political relationship between the United States and Puerto Rico. He has been a visiting professor at Yale University, the University of Ottawa, Pompeu Fabra University and the Autonomous University of Barcelona and has lectured widely in the United States, Europe and Latin America.

Richard Simeon is Emeritus Professor of Political Science and Law, University of Toronto. He is a Fellow of the Royal Society of Canada and a recent recipient, of the Daniel Elazar award of the American Political Science Association for a lifetime contribution to the study of federalism and intergovernmental relations. His current focus is on how, whether, and when federalism and related ideas can contribute to accommodation in divided societies.

Markku Suksi is Professor of Public Law at Åbo Akademi University, Finland. He has edited or authored several autonomy-related books.

Luc Turgeon is an Assistant Professor at the School of Political Studies at the University of Ottawa. His main fields of research are federalism, nationalism and social policies. He is currently working on a manuscript on the politics of representative bureaucracy in Belgium, Canada and Switzerland.

Sophia Woodman is a sociologist who studies Chinese politics, including the politics of autonomy and minorities in contemporary China. She is currently a postdoctoral fellow at the University of British Columbia in Vancouver. Her wider research interests are in citizenship, human rights and social movements.

Acknowledgements

The genesis of this book was in an April 2005 conference held at Hong Kong University, on Comparative National Experiences of Autonomy: Purpose, Structures and Institutions. The conference was held under the auspices of the Hong Kong University Faculty of Law's Centre for Comparative and Public Law, which also provided support to this event. The stimulating conversations at this conference generated an enthusiasm that kept the project alive in the many years since then. As well as hearing papers by some of the authors in this book, we were lucky enough to have many other fascinating contributions at this conference, including from Lord David Steel, first presiding officer of the Scottish Parliament; the Rt. Hon. Robert Rae, currently acting leader of the Canadian Liberal Party; Ao Junde, an eminent scholar on China's system of ethnic regional autonomy; Benedicto Bacani, an expert on autonomy in Mindanao; and Stephen Lam, then Secretary for Constitutional Affairs in Hong Kong. We are grateful to all those who participated in this conference, and especially to those who contributed to its organisation, in particular Lison Harris, Monnie Leung and Flora Leung.

Some of the papers from the conference became chapters in this book; others were commissioned subsequently to fill perceived gaps in the geographical coverage and thematic range of the book. We offer our sincere thanks to all our contributors for their patience and willingness to update their chapters, in some cases many years after the original papers had been delivered.

The background work for the project formed part of Yash Ghai's research as Sir Y. K. Pao Professor of Public Law at the University of Hong Kong. It was supported by his 2001 Distinguished Researcher Award from Hong Kong University, without which the book would not have been brought to completion. A grant from the Centre of Comparative and Public Law at the later stages of editing the manuscript enabled us to finish the project.

We are grateful for the patience of our editors at Cambridge, who have put up with many delays in finishing the book.

For his careful copy-editing work and many hours inputting proofreading corrections, as well as his support to Sophia in completing this project when it seemed it would never be done, we would like to thank Alex Carr.

This book has been a long time in the making, and in the process we have become indebted to many people. We would like to thank them all, even if we have not listed their names here.

Yash Ghai and Sophia Woodman
January 2013

Introduction: Nature and origins of autonomy

Yash Ghai

This introduction examines the purposes for which autonomy has been used and aims to place it within the norms and structures of the state. It identifies dimensions of autonomy which are critical to its operation and fortunes and also issues central to the understanding of the success and failures of autonomies, which are analysed in succeeding chapters. In the concluding chapter, some of these issues are addressed in comparative perspective, drawn from these case studies.

The focus of the book is on institutions and procedures: negotiations for autonomy, the mechanisms through which self-government is exercised, internally in the autonomous area, and in the relations between that area and the central authorities of the state. The term *institutions* is understood more in the sense that lawyers would give it than would economists: power, structures and processes of the state, including political parties. The principal issues of autonomy are examined in the context of its legal foundations, particularly the entrenchment of these institutions and procedures, at both international and national levels. Among the factors examined in this volume are the scope of the autonomous region to make and adopt its own constitution; the relationship of the constitution of the autonomous region to the national constitution; the broad scheme for the division of powers between national and autonomous governments; the participation of residents or institutions of the autonomous region at national level; the structure and composition of government institutions at the autonomous level; the relations between institutions at national and autonomous levels; methods of co-operation and consultation between different levels of government; modes of dispute resolution; and the interpretation and implementation of autonomy provisions. These issues, and others, are placed in the specific context of the country concerned, such as notions of state or parliamentary sovereignty, the purposes of autonomy (ethnic, administrative, economic), the relative size of the autonomous region compared to the rest of the country and differing legal traditions between the state and autonomous regions. These then provide the basis in the final chapter for the exploration of a number of common elements regarding the origin, nature and functioning of autonomy systems.

The book contains studies of thirteen autonomous areas, which are examined within a broadly common framework. The introductory and concluding chapters attempt to enhance understanding of the purposes, structures and institutions of autonomy by comparing the formation and operation of these autonomous areas. Is this a useful – even feasible – exercise? There may be problems of definition to start with, to be sure that we are dealing with the same phenomenon, that it is sufficiently distinguishable from other constitutional concepts and arrangements, that there are both sufficient commonalities and differences that justify comparisons, and that causation can confidently be ascribed to the structures and institutions of autonomy, albeit in the broader political, economic and social context.

Markku Suksi, a leading scholar of autonomy, provides a word of caution: 'No solid theory underpins autonomy, because autonomy arrangements are often very pragmatic ad hoc solutions that escape generalisations'.[1] There are many purposes of autonomy and the arrangements for it vary a great deal, such as in terms of powers transferred or institutional relationships. If there is no core understanding of autonomy, is there any prospect of a comparative study? There are fruitful comparative studies of federalism, but few of autonomy (although there are collections of essays on individual countries). The assumption of this book is that autonomy is distinctive as regards both its purposes and institutions (from both federal and unitary states), and that there are sufficient commonalities and differences among autonomies to justify a comparative approach.

There appears to be a core understanding of the definitional and institutional meaning of autonomy. Often the purpose is the accommodation of ethnic diversity ('ethnic' used to refer to various kinds of distinction among people: religion, language, culture, history); but there can be other purposes, as in the arrangements between Tanganyika and Zanzibar, and those between China and Hong Kong and Macau, which are discussed in this volume. To some extent, an understanding of the different purposes and histories of autonomy can be gained through comparing the origin and mechanism of autonomy: autonomy as the result of decentralising a state (the more common instance) and autonomy by the coming together of previously separate territories or sovereignty. The latter is seldom driven by ethnic considerations.

However, in some instances the distinction is blurred, especially as the system of one country may owe itself to both decentralisation and unification of territories, of which India is a good example: at independence it absorbed a number of 'princely states' over which the British had no sovereignty, and re-organised the original state into provinces and autonomous areas (discussed in Chapter 5). The joining of territories is much less common, Kashmir/India and Zanzibar/Tanzania being the two examples studied in this volume.

[1] This statement was made at a conference on autonomy at Hong Kong University in 2005.

The precise purposes and structures may vary but the essence of autonomy is clear. Precisely because there is such a variation, there are advantages in comparing dissimilar cases, to understand the variety of purposes served by autonomy and to see what works and what does not. Of course this implies that there is a common core and broadly similar context; the volume shows that the political and constitutional context for Chinese 'autonomy'/'autonomies' is so different from other autonomies studied here that they are not broadly comparable, yet there are points on which a comparison is illuminating. Comparison of such dissimilar cases may also help us to get a better grasp of the essence of autonomy.

It is significant that when the Finnish government was preparing the autonomy law for Åland in the 1930s, it looked at various examples of autonomy including the British Isles and Danzig, but concluded that none was suitable for Åland. It is interesting that the fundamental principles of the Åland autonomy were put together by an international committee of jurists appointed by the League of Nations, and that the final arrangements had to obtain the approval of both the Finnish and Swedish governments (see Suksi's Chapter 2 and references therein). These linkages between international and domestic norms, and between the international community and kin states, have continued to characterise the origin and functioning of autonomies.

Origins of autonomy

With the rise of identity politics based on race, caste, gender, religion, language or ethnicity, the traditional structures of power, particularly in relation to the state, are being challenged across the globe. The easy recruitment of dissidents and the ready availability of arms pose horrendous threats to the classical conception and practice of the state. Throughout history the state, often annexing the territory of others, has been the principal means of regulating relations among communities. At first the state was identified with a ruling dynasty and in due course with the majority community. Then most states were exclusionary, on the basis of caste, religion or ethnicity; large sections of the people had no entitlements to franchise, public office or even occupations. Gradually the state began to be invested with emotions and symbols, connected to those of the majority or the ruling community.

After the Westphalian settlement,[2] political and legal concepts, developed under the sovereignty of the state, reflected the essential principles of the modern state. Gradually the concept of citizenship, based on the rights and duties of the individual, became central to membership in the political community constituted by the state. With the growth of the notion of human rights and

[2] There are different understandings of the Westphalian doctrine. I refer here to related notions of a dominant ideology (then of the religion of the ruler), the location and centralisation of sovereignty in the state, and the predominance of the 'nation-state'. These elements produce a degree of rigidity and inflexibility and are unable properly to accommodate diversity. See the following footnote for references.

democracy, members of excluded communities were given the right to citizenship. This did not imply the political inclusion of these communities, as such; instead citizenship became a means towards their assimilation into the wider political community.

From the eighteenth century onwards, as the political map of Europe was re-drawn, the homogeneity of the people, defined by their cultural, particularly linguistic, affiliation, became the basis of the creation of new states. Congruence between a cultural community and the boundaries of the state became the major principle of the re-organisation of states ('nation-state'). This approach was justified on the grounds of the preservation of both culture and democracy, and subsequently social welfare (arguing that redistribution of resources implicit in welfare programs is possible only if there is social solidarity, dependent on a common history and culture). The position of communities different from the dominant one was ameliorated through the recognition of rights of minorities.

The state in Asia and Africa has not followed this trajectory. At least in Asia the state accommodated considerable diversities of people; demanded loyalty and taxes, but accepted different religions, languages and customary practices, with limited disruption of lifestyles, and a certain porosity of borders.[3] All this changed with colonialism, which brought with it firm and rigid boundaries, the inter-mixing of communities adhering to different religions and speaking different languages, and above all, the imposition of the Western type of state. Colonial peoples, with a few exceptions, became independent within the integument of this state. The imposition and centrality of the state, with the logic of the 'nation state', changed relationships between the diverse communities from both the pre-colonial and colonial periods. The unifying tendencies of state sovereignty (in values, policies, laws and institutions), buttressed by aspirations of development and modernisation, became a straitjacket, under which the smaller communities suffered considerable discrimination, and some exclusion. As previously in Europe, the state has attempted to inculcate 'nationalism' through assimilating minorities to the religion, language and mores of the majority.

As a consequence of identity politics, some key principles and components of the liberal state – sovereignty as vested in the entire people as a collectivity and manifested in the centralisation of the state; common citizenship with equal rights and obligations; equality; uniformity of law and legal institutions; majoritarian democracy; the nature of rights; and the distinction between the public and the private,[4] have been critically examined, found wanting and are being

[3] Bhikhu Parekh, 'Cultural diversity and the modern state' in Martin Doornbos and Sudipta Kaviraj (eds.), *Dynamics of State Formation* (New Delhi: Sage Publications, 1997); Rajni Kothari, 'Ethnicity' in his *Rethinking Development: In Search of Humane Alternatives* (Delhi: Ajanta Publications, 1988).

[4] I have discussed the rise of and challenge to the liberal state form in my chapter, 'Constitutionalism and the challenge of diversity', in Heckman, Nelson and Cubbington (eds.), *Contemporary Reflections on the Rule of Law* (Routledge: London, 2009) and in my chapter

re-defined. The challenge to these norms of the modern state has frequently involved violence, which has forced world attention on the discontent of ethnic groups. The response to the challenge has taken several forms: empowerment and participation of smaller ethnic groups, special types of representation in the legislature, executive and other public agencies, affirmative action and promotion of minority cultures. Short of secession, one of the most far reaching of such responses is autonomy. It has significantly re-configured the state, redistributed state power and resources, changed the basis of relations between communities, modified the concept and form of citizenship and the bearing of rights and obligations and introduced new dynamics in state politics.

Defining autonomy

Although the idea of autonomy is clear, there are some difficulties in defining it. Autonomy is used in a number of different contexts and senses, and often connotes a state of being rather than a legal category. Autonomy is used, predominantly, to protect a cultural, national or ethnic community, but there are other uses too which are briefly explored in this introduction. Autonomy sometimes refers to the choices of an individual, and sometimes of a community. It is also connected to the conceptualisation of the state and to tendencies towards decentralisation, away from monopolisation of power at the centre. Autonomy takes many forms and is espoused by many groups. In particular there is confusion between autonomy and federation as legal concepts – because both attempt to define a space where different values and aspirations can be pursued. Autonomy also sometimes involves the idea of periphery: the accommodation of the unusual, the recalcitrant, almost the outsider (such as in Åland, South Tyrol, the Nagas, Hong Kong and Wales). Nor is autonomy merely a device to reconcile the citizenry to the state or its form of democracy: it is also about the celebration of diversity, identity and spaces. It recognises the importance of sub-national communities and collectives, their values, cultures and institutions. Autonomy refers not only to specific constitutional arrangements, but also to practices and attitudes to politics, dialogue, openness and so on – a framework of mind and national orientation.

For the purposes of this book, autonomy connotes self-government, the ability of a region or community to organise its affairs without interference from the central government or neighbouring regions or communities. In an earlier publication, I defined autonomy as a device to allow ethnic or other groups claiming a distinct identity to exercise direct control over affairs of special concern to them while allowing the larger entity to exercise those powers which cover common interests (a definition which has been adopted by some

'Ethnicity and competing notions of rights' in Harvey and Schwartz (eds.), *Human Rights in Divided Societies* (Oxford: Hart Publishers, 2012). See also James Tully, *Strange Multiplicity: Constitutionalism in an Age of Diversity* (Cambridge University Press, 1995).

scholars).[5] When negotiations on the oldest surviving autonomy, Åland,[6] were underway, the Finnish government defined autonomy in the following way: 'to secure for the Åland islanders the possibility of arranging their existence as freely as possible for a territory which does not itself constitute a state'.[7] (The original instruments do not use the term autonomy, but self-government.)

Autonomy is often seen as a sort of deviation from the normal principles, institutions and processes of a state, though sanctioned by the state, for the specific purpose of enabling a community to pursue a lifestyle justified on grounds of its values and culture. There are, as a rule, no generally prescribed objectives, powers or institutions at the international level that constitute autonomy. There are certain norms under international law or emerging practices concerning autonomy, but they say little about powers or structures, and only a bit more about entitlement. At the national level, only a few constitutions provide for entitlement to autonomy – exceptions include China and Spain. The first of these sets out in considerable detail rules governing one kind of autonomy, the nationalities' regional autonomy, but for another, 'Special Administrative Region', there is only the simple and short article authorising its establishment, leaving the details to the National People's Congress (as discussed by Ghai in Chapter 10 on Hong Kong). The Spanish Constitution establishes both potential powers of autonomous areas and the process for negotiating specific powers and structures (as discussed by Flores Juberías in Chapter 7). When there is no constitutional entitlement to autonomy, autonomy arrangements are generally negotiated ad hoc, to suit particular objectives and circumstances, including the necessity to amend the constitution.

Autonomy usually takes territorial forms, but some sort of autonomy can also be exercised through cultural councils or other limited forms of self-government, such as the regimes of personal laws. These devices are essentially ways of overcoming the limits of territory – when the community in question is dispersed over a wide area or, if concentrated, is not the majority there. There are also alternatives to autonomy: various forms of minority rights, special systems of representation, affirmative action, recognition of culture, languages, proportionality principle, freedom of religion and so on. Sometimes these are combined with autonomy (and may be designed to protect the interests and promote the participation of minorities within the autonomous area). Belgium is an interesting example of two forms of autonomy: one geared towards culture, and the other connected to territory as an administrative unit. In this volume, Bosnia-Herzegovina comes closest to the combination of autonomy

[5] Yash Ghai, 'Ethnicity and autonomy: a framework for analysis' in Yash Ghai (ed.), *Autonomy and Ethnicity: Negotiating Competing Claims in Multi-Ethnic States* (Cambridge University Press, 2000), 8–11.

[6] This claim is often made for Åland, but, depending on how one defines autonomy, Québec can justifiably make that claim.

[7] Government Bill 73/1919, 2.

with other devices, while South Tyrol combines autonomy with power sharing. This volume concentrates on territorial autonomy.[8]

Although autonomy has become common in recent decades, its origins are much older. One of the entities discussed in this book, Macau, was autonomous for centuries under Portuguese rule (see Chapter 12 by Cardinal). The Francophones in Québec have enjoyed autonomy in Canada since the nineteenth century. Finland, another country discussed in this book (Chapter 2), was an autonomous Grand Duchy of the Russian Empire between 1809 and 1917, with its own constitution and legal order. Article 2 of the 1906 Constitution of Russia stated that '(t)he Grand Duchy of Finland, while it constitutes an indivisible part of the Russian State, is governed in its domestic affairs by special institutions on the basis of a special legislation'.[9] The example of the creation of the Free City of Danzig under the Treaty of Versailles in 1919 was another precedent for the recognition of Ålandic autonomy. The loose structures and character of some Asian empires, including India under the Mughals, and the millet system of the Ottoman Empire, facilitated forms of self-government.

An even older instance of spatial organisation of government are 'reserves', which were first used by European settlers in the Americas to isolate and dominate indigenous peoples, and were subsequently adopted in Australia, Africa and parts of Asia. The apartheid policy of Bantustans was a modern version of this. However, in recent years the aspirations and historical claims of indigenous peoples have been recognised through the transformation of reserves into self-governing areas, particularly in Canada and the Philippines, although the extent to which they can opt out of national laws, which may be necessary for the preservation of their political and cultural practices, is variable.

But autonomy, on the present wide scale, is essentially the product of the twentieth century, for historical reasons outlined previously (and examples given later). As a form of limited self-government, it has become fashionable as a solution to some problems of multi-ethnic states. It has come to be seen as a mid-way or compromise solution between a unitary state and secession. It is often more popular with the international community than either the state or the ethnic group in relation to which autonomy is proposed (many recent autonomies have been conceded and accepted under international/regional pressure). Sometimes the suspension of a civil war is secured by the offer to negotiate autonomy, as in Sri Lanka, Sudan and many other places.

Autonomy is no longer an aberration. Operating at the intersection of international and constitutional laws, it is now widespread. Today it would be difficult to study most countries' constitutional and political system without addressing

8 For cultural autonomy, see Asbjorn Eide, 'Cultural autonomy: concept, content, history, and role in the world order' in Markku Suksi (ed.), *Autonomy: Applications and Implications* (The Hague: Kluwer, 1998); and Yash Ghai, *Public Participation and Minorities* (London: Minority Rights Group, 2001).

9 Marc Szeftel, *The Russian Constitution of April 23, 1906: Political Institutions of the Duma Monarchy* (Bruxelles: Les éditions de la librairie encyclopédique, 1976), 84.

autonomy. Some constitutions have recognised the right to autonomy (Spain and China, previously Papua New Guinea). This book has studies of autonomy in large states (China, India, the United States, the United Kingdom, Italy and Canada), medium-sized states (Finland, Tanzania, Australia) and small states (Papua New Guinea) whose constitutional and political systems are hard to understand without an understanding of systems of autonomy. Russia, not studied here, used autonomy extensively during the Soviet period to deal with minorities, as does the present somewhat more democratic system (though some minority regions could not be so accommodated and were allowed to secede). Some countries have had to deal with demands for autonomy on a frequent, extended, or even continuous basis, such as India, Sri Lanka, Indonesia, Sudan, Canada, Spain and France. Even if autonomy is not granted, the very agitation for it is of considerable interest to constitutional scholars. Other instances of autonomy are discussed in this chapter. Autonomy has become an integral part of contemporary constitutions, but there are few studies of its origins, structures and operation – and both its influence and dependence on constitutional and political orders.

Purposes and varieties of autonomy

Autonomy became important during the period of decolonisation following World War I and particularly World War II. It was used principally for two purposes. The first was to accommodate communities within former colonies which because of their distinct ethnicity wanted to secede on independence (such as Åland in Finland, the Buganda in Uganda, the Maasai and other minority communities in Kenya, Bougainville in Papua New Guinea, Banabans in Kiribati). The second purpose was to re-organise the relationship between the colonial authorities and the colonies, short of independence (Cook Islands and Niue in relation to New Zealand, Puerto Rico and American Micronesia in relation to the United States, New Caledonia in relation to France and various British colonies in the Caribbean).[10] In a similar vein, decolonisation also led to some re-organisation of territory, for example in relation to Italian colonies in Africa, in the Horn of Africa where Eritrea was joined to Ethiopia in a sort of federal relationship and Italian, British and French possessions

[10] The closely connected concept of association was defined in 1959 by the UN General Assembly (distinguishing it from internal self-government as follows):

'(a) Free association should be the result of a free and voluntary choice by the peoples of the territory concerned expressed through informed and democratic processes. It should be one which respects the territory and its peoples, and retains for the peoples of the territory which is associated with an independent State the freedom to modify the status of that Territory through the expression of their will by democratic means and through constitutional processes.'

'(b) The associated territory should have the right to determine its internal constitution without outside interference, in accordance with due constitutional processes and the freely expressed wishes of the people. This does not preclude consultations as appropriate or necessary under the terms agreed upon'.

in North Africa were brought together in the new federation of Libya. Perhaps the most striking example was the way in which India became independent, where a number of states not fully incorporated within British India ('princely states') were encouraged or forced to join India on independence, with significant autonomy (of which Kashmir is examined by Cottrell in this volume, Chapter 5). In more recent times the manner in which the British handed back Hong Kong, and the Portuguese handed over Macau, to China also shows the utility of autonomy. Its utility was evident also in the post-colonial period (twice the attempt to keep the southern part of Sudan within that country led to autonomy for the south, and to major re-organisations of India). Autonomy played a critical role also in the re-organisation of states and territory in the cataclysmic events during the breakup of the Yugoslav republic in the 1990s, particularly in Bosnia-Herzegovina (examined in this volume by Marko, Chapter 9), Montenegro and Kosovo.

Autonomy has also placed a role in the settlement of disputes between states. After World War I the dispute between Germany and Poland over the ownership of the city of Danzig was settled by giving the city an autonomous status, as was that between Germany and Lithuania over Memel. The dispute between Austria and Italy over Alto Adige (also known as Südtirol in German, or more commonly in English as South Tyrol), annexed by Italy from Austria during World War I in 1918, was settled by agreeing on autonomy for the territory within Italy only in 1946 after World War II in an agreement between Italy and Austria (known as the Paris Agreement and discussed by Peterlini in this volume, Chapter 4). The same approach was adopted over Åland in the dispute between Finland and Sweden. And the differences between China on the one hand and Britain and Portugal on the other over Hong Kong and Macau were resolved through negotiations over the status and scope of their autonomy. The dispute between Indonesia and Portugal over East Timor was resolved by offering autonomy to its people (though in the end Indonesia also offered the choice of independence which East Timor gladly accepted).

For these reasons, the international community has played a critical role in the grant and sometimes even the management of autonomy – contradictory as that seems – especially in Bosnia-Herzegovina and Kosovo. The European Union has been particularly active, especially as many conflicts have taken place in Europe. The United States has, as is its style, played a general role as a somewhat biased sheriff of the globe and has intervened in several negotiations on autonomy. Inevitably the objectives of the EU and the US have played as important a role as those of the people and governments concerned (for example in regard to Israel/Palestine, Bosnia-Herzegovina, Sudan and the Kurdish autonomy during the last years of Saddam Hussein in Iraq, enforced by European and US aircraft).

On longevity of autonomy: permanent or transitional

Most studies focus on autonomy as a permanent arrangement, but some autonomies are, or have been, transitional. In some cases the transition is to full integration with the state: as in the case of Hong Kong and Macau, in which the autonomous area has no choice. The transitory nature of autonomy served several purposes. It enabled the British to claim that they had left Hong Kong with significant self-government (reference to the fifty-year limit was seldom made); it provided assurance to Hong Kong people that life would go on as before; and it guaranteed China the full recovery of Hong Kong.

Another type of transitory autonomy involves the promise of independence, as in the Sudan and New Caledonia,[11] leading to separation, at the choice of the autonomous area (perhaps this was also the Irish perception of Home Rule in the nineteenth century). Bougainville is another example, but here the referendum on the subject in which only members of the autonomous people vote, is 'advisory' (see Chapter 13 in this volume), and, if passed, would open a process of negotiations on separation. The Oslo agreement on the future of Palestine (Declaration of Principles on Interim Self-Government Arrangements 1993) also provided for transitional autonomy for five years during which time a permanent agreement would be negotiated. The notion of what we might call conditional autonomy is to test whether autonomy sufficiently meets the demands and expectations of the autonomous part (although in the Oslo agreement separate status of Palestine was the ultimate objective). In the case of Palestine, continued progress towards a settlement was made conditional on the good behaviour of the Palestinians. Sometimes the agreement is reached because one or both sides want the easing of foreign pressure. In all these cases the option of independence, not now but maybe in the future, is a powerful factor in reaching an agreement – and thus the perceptions and motivations of the two sides are often very different.

Sometimes autonomy may be transitional to something yet to be worked out: a holding operation (proposed Palestine autonomy, renewed autonomy of Kosovo, de facto autonomy of Montenegro and settlements in Sudan, Bougainville and New Caledonia). In some ways this is true of the autonomy in an associated state; here effectively and morally, the choice is of the associated state, for whose benefit the autonomy option is adopted, whether it wants increased powers and responsibilities or independence. Under the dynamics of autonomy, situations change: Puerto Rico is now making a claim for statehood and is likely to get it as the mainland is becoming more amenable to multiculturalism, and Scotland where a referendum for yet another change in status is scheduled to take place in 2014.

A particular advantage of autonomy is that, based on territory, it enables ethnic problems to be solved without 'entrenching' ethnicity, although some forms of autonomy may indeed entrench ethnicity, as with reservations where cultural dimensions and the need to preserve the identity of the group may serve to sharpen boundaries against outsiders, or the claims of the

[11] D. Chappell, 'The Noumea Accord: decolonization without independence in New Caledonia?' in *Pacific Affairs*, 72:3, 373–91.

Francophones in Québec. Autonomy often provides a basis for a compromise as it is a mid-point of competing claims, that of a separate statehood/sovereignty and a unitary state – examples being Kosovo; devolution proposals in Sri Lanka; current negotiations between China and Taiwan; Russia and Chechnya; and the Sudan. Autonomy can thus fudge the thorny issue of sovereignty, which has been so troublesome in conflicts around the world. Self-government and self-determination can be accommodated within the confines of autonomy (with substantial devolution of powers, and the paraphernalia of 'statehood' such as a flag, postal stamps and even an anthem) while retaining intact the boundaries of the state. Various forms of autonomy are also linked to consociationalism, which, as political form of power sharing, has been gaining popularity in recent years, as in Bosnia, Belgium and Italy). Autonomy enables a region to exercise substantial self-government without assuming all the functions of the state or losing the benefits of metropolitan nationality. Equally, autonomy has been used when a region of a state does not want to join a bigger union (e.g. Greenland and Faroe when Denmark joined the EU; and special provisions could be negotiated for Åland when Finland joined the European Union because of its pre-existing autonomy). This observation illustrates the flexibility of autonomy, which can comprise a wide variety of arrangements regarding structure and powers. Consequently it allows considerable flexibility in negotiations and permits a gradual transfer of powers, giving time for adjustment to both sides.

Territorial autonomy can increase the political integration of ethnic groups with the rest of the country by accentuating intra-group differences and leading to the fragmentation of previously monolithic ethnic parties. The proliferation of parties enables coalitions of similarly situated ethnic parties, as in Nigeria and India, across the state. Local problems which might otherwise have created a national crisis are dealt with by the locality itself. Territorial asymmetrical arrangements encourage demands for similar arrangements by other groups, as we see later, in India, Nigeria, Papua New Guinea and China. The proliferation of these arrangements increases the prospects of national unity as it diffuses state power and enables central authorities to balance regional with national interests.

Because autonomy arrangements divide power, they also contribute to constitutionalism. The guarantees for autonomy and the modalities for their enforcement show the reliance on the rule of law and the role of independent institutions. The operation of the arrangements, particularly those parts governing the relationship between the centre and the region, being dependent on discussions, mutual respect and compromise, frequently serve to strengthen these qualities.

But there are also drawbacks to autonomy. The first is not so much a criticism as a delineation of its limits: it is possible only if there is geographical concentration of a group in a defined territory where there are few members of other ethnic groups. A major criticism is that the cleavages which are meant to be transcended by autonomy may instead be sharpened and the concept of equal citizenship compromised. Autonomy arrangements are likely to create new minorities within the autonomous areas. And autonomy may allow free rein to the culture of the dominant groups, often to the detriment of the status and rights of women. Autonomy may become the vehicle for domination by previous warring factions which are undemocratic and without legitimacy (and may lead to long transition periods without elections, etc.). Autonomy can be fragmenting, pigeonholing and divisive to societies. Sometimes in an attempt to preserve the integuments of a state, autonomy is so structured that it is difficult to find the common ground on which communities can find a moral or political basis for co-existence. The demand for, and resistance to, autonomy may itself become the cause of conflict. Negotiations can be long and protracted, during which there is no real peace, security, or normality. Negotiations on autonomy are extremely complicated, and due to the complexity of issues, the transitional arrangements, hostility, multiplicity of parties, intervention of outside parties, diversity of interests, both within the autonomous area and between the state and the autonomous entity and disputes on boundaries, may break down soon after autonomy is established or agreed upon.

Negotiating autonomy

Negotiating autonomy is seldom easy. Neither under international law or national law are the rules entitling a group to autonomy clear or convenient to states. Getting a state to discuss autonomy often requires a group to disrupt the normal rhythm of civil life, mostly through force and violence, and through the destruction of property and loss of life. There is little doubt that today's easy availability of arms and the eagerness of the global media to broadcast scenes of violence has shifted the balance in favour of would be secessionists or autonomists. Perhaps a statistician exploring the exponential growth in autonomy type arrangements could trace it to the easy availability of arms and the ease with which civil life can be disrupted. Violence is more often addressed to the international community than the home government.

The interest and role of the international community arises from various considerations, such as global security and stability; the near impossibility of resolving the conflict internally; the high cost in human suffering and lives; and most of all, the interests of the intervening states, economic and political. Domestic strategic interests can lead a major power or a consortium of states to intervene in the dispute. Only major powers like China, India and Russia, all with secessionist or autonomist movements, can ward off foreign intervention and establish their own rules. We talk of the international community but the intervenors (sometimes called mediators) are mostly the United States and Europe, even if under UN auspices. Because of the strategic interests of the big powers in the decision to intervene (despite the emerging doctrine of the obligation to protect), no clear international or regional rules have emerged to govern entitlement to autonomy or the principles of intervention. For example,

China's accumulation of foreign reserves has silenced the previous support the US and EU gave to Tibetan autonomy, justified in many pious declarations.

Foreign intervention, in the form of 'contact groups' and other modalities, immediately narrows the groups at the negotiating table, mostly to the warring factions, with the complete exclusion of civil society,[12] as well as limiting the agenda. The West is in a hurry to leave, and negotiations, supported by promises of great bounty, assume speed, as if in a hothouse (the exception may be the Balkan autonomies fashioned by the US, EU and NATO, where they stay on as imperial powers to administer the 'autonomy'), a Nobel Prize or two awarded. Agreements signed in these circumstances, with the speedy withdrawal of the West, often fail to deliver what they promise. Some have built in self-destruct mechanisms, though some do survive.

The resistance to autonomy

Despite the theoretical advantages of autonomy and developing norms, there has been considerable resistance to it on the part of governments. In numerous cases, a settlement on autonomy has eluded negotiators, or one party has escalated its demands beyond autonomy. Sudan and Sri Lanka are obvious examples. Questions of territory can arouse deep emotions: such as motherland versus homeland, and other historical associations. There can also be disputes about the precise boundaries of the territory in question, as in Palestine, Sri Lanka, India (in relation to the division of the Punjab in the 1960s) and the Philippines.

Occasionally a minority may reject autonomy because it is seen as compromising the fundamental goal of separate statehood, as has been the case for the Turks in Cyprus and the Tamil Tigers in Sri Lanka. In such cases a solution may be to make autonomy a temporary expedience, pending further negotiations, or a referendum after a specified period allowing for time to see if autonomy provides an acceptable measure of self-government, such as in the Israel-Palestine agreement or the agreement between France and the Kanaks in New Caledonia; a similar procedure has been adopted as a way forward in Bougainville. On the other hand, and more rarely, the state may prefer that the minority secede rather than be granted autonomy. A case in point was the decision of President Habibie of Indonesia in respect of East Timor, due to his fear that its autonomy might be seen by other groups as a precedent; nor was he comfortable with the notion that East Timorese, having chosen autonomy, had a continuing right to self-determination whereby they could later claim secession.[13]

The establishment of autonomy involves a major, or at least a significant re-organisation of the state. For a long time autonomy was seen to clash with

[12] In one such negotiation when I suggested that civil society groups might be included, even if only as observers, I was asked, 'How many AK47s do they have?', with both sides nodding their heads.

[13] Iain C. Martin, *Self-Determination in East Timor: The United Nations, the Ballot, and International Intervention* (Boulder: Lynne Rienner Publishers, 2001).

the project of 'nation' and 'state' building which underlay much modernisation theory – and with the ambitions of 'nationalist' leaders. It upsets long held views of the sacredness of territory and the unity of 'motherland' and it necessitates a significant re-allocation of resources, including that of political power.

The leaders of the majority community may be reluctant to concede autonomy fearing the loss of electoral support among their own community (a problem that has bedevilled Sri Lanka). Majority leaders, even if well-disposed to autonomy, may not have the confidence that they would be able to implement the autonomy agreement, especially if it requires an amendment to the constitution, a referendum or even merely new legislation. There may be fears that autonomy will be merely a springboard to secession. This is seen to be a serious problem when the group demanding autonomy is related to a neighbouring kin state with continguous territory. Autonomy granted to a minority in its 'homeland' may in turn create new minorities (as with Muslims in Eastern District of Sri Lanka, which the Tamil Tigers want under their control, or Christians in Mindanao, the re-organisation of states in Nigeria and India, or the fear that Malaysian Borneo states may get too close to Indonesia). This may trigger demands for autonomy by the 'new minorities' and lead to further fragmentation of the state.

Connected with the preceding point is the fear that if autonomy can be justified on ethnic grounds, the rationalisation and rules justifying the grant of autonomy (identity, a sense of discrimination or injustice) may encourage the mobilisation of other communities along ethnic lines, indeed the manufacture of 'ethnic communities'. Autonomy may be resisted for another reason: the unpredictability of its consequences. The adoption of the federal device changes the context of ethnic relations. Territorial or corporate federal arrangements are not purely instrumental; merely by providing a framework for inter-ethnic relations, they affect and shape these relations; they may fashion new forms of identity or reinforce old identities; they may enhance or decrease the capacity of particular groups to extract resources from the state; and they may provide new forms of contention and dispute. Equally, autonomy may break up the internal unity of a community, leading to intra-community conflicts (as has been seen in Mindanao, Sri Lanka and Bougainville), and jeopardize autonomy.

There may also be a concern with economic and administrative efficiency, which is frequently seen to be jeopardised by complex autonomy arrangements, both upwards in relations to the centre, and downwards to local authorities. Because autonomy arrangements are frequently negotiated involving different political parties, ministries and other actors, rather than planned, there may be a mismatch between powers, institutions and resources. Even if there are in fact efficiency gains, autonomy inevitably adds to the costs of government, as much of the theory of decentralisation claims.[14] Autonomy also affects the operation

[14] See for example, Brian E. Dollery and Lorenzo Robotti, *The Theory and Practice of Local Government Reform* (Cheltenham: Edward Elgar, 2008); and World Bank, 'Administrative

of the economy, especially as there may be regional taxes and restrictions on the mobility of labour or preferences for local capital or labour. A related difficulty can arise from the unequal regional distribution of resources, giving a particularly sharp edge to ethnic differences. Autonomy may be interpreted merely as a way to ensure for the richer region (and community) an unequal share of that wealth. If it is a minority which resides in the rich region, it may create resentment, and possible retaliation, from the majority group, and if it is the majority group which lives in the richer region, it may lead to the ghettoisation of the other. Secessionist groups or those demanding internal autonomy are frequently accused of greed and the unwillingness to share their resources with others, as in Katanga, Biafra and Bougainville.

A further limitation, connected to the need for habits of tolerance and compromise, is that autonomy may be unable to accommodate communities with very different ideas, beliefs and practices. There is sometimes fear that the fundamental values of the state may be compromised by the recognition through autonomy of different cultural or religious values. A classic, although simplified case of this was the US Civil War, when Abraham Lincoln justified the stance of the northern states by saying that 'This country cannot endure permanently half slave and half free'. In more recent times, this was one (although not the fundamental) reason for the rejection of a federal solution to the Jewish-Arab problem in Palestine under the Mandate or the UN schemes.[15] The Muslim League in colonial India rejected a federal solution for Muslims for the same reason, and it has been claimed that this was also why an Ethiopian-Eritrean federation was deemed impossible.[16] The position of the French in Québec is not dissimilar.

Even when granted, autonomy may not survive, due to continuing questioning of its legitimacy by the state, or difficulties of managing it (examples are Chittagong autonomy in Bangladesh under the Chittagong Hill Tracts Accord 1997, Southern Sudan under the 1971 Addis Ababa Agreement and the repeal of Eritrea's autonomy under the United Nations in 1962).[17] In numerous cases, a settlement on autonomy has eluded negotiators, or one party has escalated its demands beyond autonomy (Sudan and Sri Lanka are obvious examples). The breakup of the former Yugoslavia and the Soviet Union are often seen as spectacular failures of ethnic federation or autonomy.

In order to understand two key aspects of autonomy, I discuss first its similarities with and differences from federalism (a much better understood

decentralization', available at: www1.worldbank.org/publicsector/decentralization/admin.htm (accessed 30 November 2012).

15 Connor O'Brien, *The Siege: The Saga of Israel and Zionism* (New York: Simon & Schuster, 1986), 228.

16 A. Tekle, 'Another Ethiopian-Eritrean federation? An Eritrean view', *World Today* 47 (1991), 47–50.

17 See for example Miek Boltjes (ed.), *Implementing Negotiated Agreements: the Real Challenge of Intrastate Peace* (Hague: TMC Asser Press, 2007).

phenomenon) and then its relationship to human rights, in view of the fact that contemporary justifications of autonomy by those claiming it are generally framed in terms of human and collective rights.

Autonomy and federalism

Comparing autonomy and federalism is not easy, as they have many similarities of objectives and methods. Federalism is occasionally a response to geography and distance, dictated by the difficulty of managing places far from the capital (the United States is partly an example, as are the island autonomies in France and Spain). More often the reasons have been defence, nationalism, or modalities of independence (India or the British Caribbean). Classical federalism was seldom based on ethnicity (despite the partial exception of Switzerland and Canada). Autonomy on the other hand has often been based on ethnicity (from the time of the Ottoman Empire, although there are exceptions, as Hong Kong and Macau illustrate). It is interesting that while South Tyrol was annexed by Italy against the principle of 'nationality' (ethnicity), its autonomy under the Italian constitutional system was granted on the principle of ethnicity.

The origins of federalism are on the whole more consensual than those of autonomy, and therefore less a question of entitlement, while the claim of autonomy has often required a legal justification – and long negotiations, involving external actors. International intervention tends to be less critical in the case of federations, though here too there are exceptions: the formation of the Libyan Federation after World War II and Bosnia-Herzegovina after the collapse of the Yugoslav federation.

Both federation and autonomy can arise either from the coming together of previous separate entities (the United States, Switzerland and Canada exemplify this for federation; and India, Tanzania and Eritrea's joining Ethiopia, for autonomy) or the disaggregation of an entity (Germany and partially India for federation; and Finland, Australia/Norfolk, US/Puerto Rico, Papua New Guinea and Spain for autonomy). However, some countries exemplify both types: India and Canada, for example. And it is hard to know where to place Hong Kong and Macau, over which China claims never to have abandoned its sovereignty. Spain's post-Franco history shows the difficulty of distinguishing federation from autonomy: what started as a species of autonomy rapidly assumed the form of federation, so that one can say that Spain has the form of autonomy but the appearance of federation.

Compared with autonomy, which often wants to be left alone, federalism places greater emphasis on 'shared rule', that is, all the units are represented at the national level, especially the legislature – for example, Puerto Rico has almost no participation or influence in Washington. This and the earlier factors make it hard to categorise countries that are both a federation and have autonomous areas, for example Canada, India, the United States, Russia and Bosnia-Herzegovina. Given the dominance of the federal in these states, they are usually considered as federations, though the dominance of autonomy in Bosnia-Herzegovina means it is more accurate to think of it in terms of autonomy. And how should one designate or analyse a system that has a number of autonomies? China may end up with three types (if Taiwan joins China) with some variations; Italy has five somewhat varying autonomous units; and Canada is adding First Nations' self-government to Québec's somewhat distinctive status. Will this lead to some kind of federal type strategies – with autonomous areas forming something of a trade union? – Or will the interests be diverse, or will they compete for this purpose (on this see Peterlini's interesting discussion of recent constitutional changes in Italy, Chapter 4)? Is there a lesson from Spain? Too much asymmetry in a federal system, as in Québec and Kashmir, can blur the distinction between federation and autonomy. If asymmetry in a unit in the federation is too marked, the unit might be seen as example of autonomy (Québec and Kashmir in our case studies, and arrangements in Spain in their original form).

If the need is to accommodate only one or two minority groups, the federal model may be regarded as unnecessary. In these situations, special powers may be devolved to only a part of the country where the minority constitutes a majority, to be exercised by regional institutions. In practice federations involving two units tend not to work well, as shown by the collapse of the federations between Malaya and Singapore; East and West Pakistan; the Czech Lands and Slovakia; and the failure to agree on a federation in Cyprus after years of negotiations. On the other hand, federalism where all regions have equal powers may not be sufficiently sensitive to the peculiar cultural and other needs of a particular community, which may require a greater measure of self-government. Asymmetry may fill the need. Most multi-ethnic federations are in fact asymmetrical, as with Canada and Switzerland; other examples are India, Spain, Russia and Malaysia – but relationships are not easy. On the other hand, it may be difficult to give autonomy only to one or two regions, as shown in Sri Lanka; and autonomous arrangements tend towards proliferation of autonomous units.

Autonomy clearly is more flexible than federalism. Federalism normally means universalising self-government on certain national principles, while the rationale of autonomy is the desirability, even necessity, of a special form of self-government for a particular group different from other parts of the country. Asymmetry acknowledges the unevenness of diversity and opens up additional possibilities of awarding recognition to specific groups with special needs or capacities, such as indigenous peoples whose traditional culture is central to their way of life, or a minority linguistic group. Examples of asymmetry abound: China has at least four types (special economic zones, metropolitan cities, ethnic minorities and special administrative regions) responding to different imperatives;[18] as does India, with its 'standard provinces', special arrangements for Kashmir, and provinces in the northeast,

[18] Yash Ghai, 'Autonomy regimes in China: coping with ethnic and economic diversity' in Ghai (ed.), *Autonomy and Ethnicity*.

tribal areas and union territories, each enjoying a different relationship with the centre.

This distinctiveness, which comes with the type of autonomy, has a particular attraction for the group concerned, not only for practical reasons but also psychological ones: the satisfaction that their special status is thus recognised. Bougainville was acutely disappointed that in the earlier stage of autonomy, in 1976, the autonomy it had negotiated was granted to all provinces, though this in no way affected its own powers. The Naga people are seeking special powers and a special relationship with New Delhi, in part because they want recognition of their distinctiveness; but that very factor may become a source of complaints for other minorities, at least those who consider that they are similarly situated, who feel left out.

Yet autonomy may be seen to have an advantage over federalism, especially if it is restricted to a smallish community in a part of the country that is not central to national politics or economy (as reserves for indigenous peoples in Canada or the United States), as this threatens the national ethos less than federalism. Puerto Rico was denied federal status because it was fundamentally different from other states and would thus affect the culture and political basis of the United States, but autonomy was feasible due to the notion of separation. Greenland too was denied federation (the choice was independence or autonomy as 'home rule'). So 'separation' or autonomy can also serve the purpose of the state, not only the 'minority'. On the other hand, in Canada federalism is such a defining characteristic of the state that it is difficult to discuss autonomy except in the federal context. This is also becoming the case in Italy, as the discussion on the dialectics of autonomy and federalism by Peterlini (see Chapter 4) shows.

Asymmetry arises in various ways. Sometimes it is the result of a constitutional provision enabling regions to negotiate separately with the centre for autonomy and establishing a menu of which powers may be devolved (Spain, Papua New Guinea, Russia). Regions may make different use of concurrent powers and may be endowed with the power to determine their own structures for the exercise of autonomy, leading to differences in constitutional arrangements. National laws may apply differentially for other reasons, the outstanding example being the 'notwithstanding' clause in Canada that enables a province to opt out of most provisions of the Charter of Rights under prescribed conditions and another provision that limits the application of the Charter in aboriginal areas by the supremacy of treaties between indigenous groups and the Crown. Asymmetry can also be used as a general technique for opting out of a scheme, or for a phased entry to full membership, as has happened frequently with the European Union. Other forms of asymmetry include special representation for a region at the centre (Québec's entitlements to seats in the Senate and the Supreme Court), or special voting power given to the region at the centre (double voting or vetoes). Residents of a region may have special rights, at least in the region, that are not available to other citizens, as in the concept of permanent resident of the Hong Kong Special Administrative Region. The viability of the Russian federation depends on the acceptance and successful operation of autonomy: eighty-eight units have differing relationships with Moscow.

The dynamics of relations between the centre and the sub-national unit in a federation are likely to be different than in an autonomy, more fluid and changing, especially in federations built on 'co-operation'. This is well recognised by Ålanders, who have had considerable success in fighting off the consequences that would occur in a federation as a result of Finland joining the EU.

There is no point in driving home the differences between federalism and autonomy. They often serve similar objectives and have similar provisions: division of powers, institutions that define the relationship of the centre to the sub-national units, judicial review and other modes of dispute settlement, and the importance of legality. Both work well when there is effective entrenchment of the status and powers of the sub-national units. And both depend significantly on protection by the judiciary.

Autonomy and human rights

Åland's autonomy was justified on grounds of self-determination, a principle of collective rights that finds support in the UN Charter, despite the shift from collective to individual rights after World War II. Internal conflicts of the last few decades, based largely on claims of ethnic groups, have highlighted collective rights. The rise of ethnic consciousness and its political mobilisation (for which phenomenon I use the term 'ethnicity') have forced the re-conceptualisation of rights.[19] Ethnicity presents its claims as imperatives of identity. Charles Taylor defines identity as 'a person's understanding of who they are, of their fundamental characteristics as a human being'. Identity is achieved through an individual's search for their inner soul. At another point, he writes, 'There is a certain way of being that is *my* way. I am called upon to live my life in this way [. . .] If I am not true [to myself], I miss the point of my life'.[20] According to Taylor, this consciousness of the uniqueness of one's identity is the result of the breakdown of social hierarchies, which defined our roles and gave us the understanding of our place in society. But with democracy and the re-ordering of society, our identity comes from self-reflection and contemplation and has become essential to the sense of our dignity, as an attribute of being human. Thus dignity is closely related to equality. And equality in turn depends on recognition by others, in the form of demands for the equal status of cultures and genders.

[19] Yash Ghai, 'Ethnicity and competing notions of human rights' in Colin Harvey and Alex Schwartz (eds.), *Rights in Divided Societies* (Oxford: Hart Publishers, 2012).

[20] Charles Taylor, 'The politics of recognition' in Amy Gutmann (ed.), *Multiculturalism* (Princeton University Press, 1994).

Although identity understood in this sense is an intensely personal affair, achieving a satisfactory understanding of oneself and one's potential, and of determining one's direction in life, it is dependent on our contacts with others. Kymlicka says that our orientation, the way we negotiate values and make choices, comes from our membership of a cultural community.[21] Thus in their different ways, Taylor and Kymlicka place the individual securely within a cultural context and interactions within a community. In an earlier period, Herder and other German philosophers[22] had emphasised the uniqueness of each community, with its singular, historically, even ethnically derived identity being expressed as the nation. Thus Kant's emphasis on individual autonomy had firm roots in the community. The politics of recognition in public and private spheres has become central to our quest for just political and social orders.

Ethnicity both invokes and undermines human rights. The fundamental dilemma of rights and diversity is well captured by Charles Taylor when he writes,

> Now underlying the demand [for recognition of diversity] is a principle of universal equality. The politics of difference is full of denunciations of discrimination and refusals of second class citizenship. This gives the principle of universal equality a point of entry within the politics of dignity. But once inside, as it were, its demands are hard to assimilate to that politics. For it asks we give acknowledgement and status to something that is not universally shared. Or, otherwise put, we give due acknowledgment only to what is universally present – everyone has an identity – through recognizing what is peculiar to each. The universal demands powers and acknowledgement of specificity.[23]

Human rights as basis of autonomy

While there is no general right to autonomy under domestic or international law, there is an increasing recognition internationally and regionally that in some circumstances there is at least a strong moral case for autonomy. There are currently several bases for autonomy. The first is minority rights, involving positive interpretations of Article 27 of the International Covenant on Civil and Political Rights, which recognises that a measure of autonomy and group rights may be necessary for the protection of cultural rights of minorities. This broader approach is reflected in the UN Declaration on the Rights of Minorities adopted by the General Assembly in 1992, which places positive obligations on the state to protect the identity of minorities and encourage 'conditions for the promotion of that identity'.[24] At the regional level the greatest advance

[21] Will Kymlicka, *Liberalism, Community and Culture* (Oxford University Press, 1989).

[22] F. M. Barnard, *Herder's Social and Political Thought: From Enlightenment to Nationalism* (Oxford: Clarendon Press, 1967).

[23] Taylor, 'The politics of recognition', p. 39.

[24] Art. 1.

has been made by the Organisation for Security and Co-operation in Europe (OSCE), which favours autonomy regimes in its various declarations as well as practice. The 1990 Copenhagen Declaration of the Conference for Security and Co-operation in Europe (the predecessor of OSCE) recognises the central importance of human rights, stating that 'appropriate local or autonomous administrations' could be 'one of the possible means' for the promotion of the 'ethnic, cultural, linguistic and religious identity of certain minorities'.[25] The principal instrument of the Council of Europe is the Framework Convention for the Protection of National Minorities (1994), which protects various rights of minorities, obliges the state to facilitate the enjoyment of these rights and recognises many rights of 'identity'.[26] The EU played a key role in the establishment of autonomies in Bosnia-Herzegovina (see Marko, Chapter 9), in the spirit of the OSCE and EU instruments.

The second source of support for autonomy is the 1991 International Labour Organisation (ILO) Convention on the rights of indigenous peoples, which recognised the 'aspirations of these peoples to exercise control over their own institutions, ways of life and economic development and to maintain and develop their identities, languages and religions, within the framework of the States in which they live'.[27] More explicitly the UN Declaration on the Rights of Indigenous Peoples proclaims their right to self-determination, under which they have the 'right to autonomy or self-government in matters relating to their internal and local affairs', which include social, cultural and economic activities, and the right to control the entry of non-members.[28] However, this volume does not deal with autonomies for indigenous peoples.

The third and broadest basis is the right to self-determination, in itself a difficult and controversial concept, but one which is increasingly being analysed in terms of the internal, democratic organisation of a state rather than secession or independence. The contemporary source for autonomy lies in the notion of self-determination. As long ago as the 1920s, the legal basis of autonomy was discussed by the League of Nations when it dealt with the claims of the people of Åland for secession from Finland. After concluding that the protection

[25] Art. 35.

[26] A. Bloed, 'The OSCE and the issue of national minorities' in A. Phillips and A. Rosas (eds.), *Universal Minority Rights* (Abo: Abo Akademic University Press, 1995); J. Packer, 'Autonomy with the OSCE: the case of Crimea' in Markku Suksi (ed.), *Autonomy: Applications and Implications* (The Hague: Kluwer, 1998); P. Thornberry, 'Images of autonomy and individual and collective rights in international instruments on the rights of minorities' in Suksi, *Autonomy: Applications and Implications.*

[27] ILO Convention 169 concerning Indigenous and Tribal Peoples in Independent Countries, entered into force 5 Sept. 1991.

[28] Art. 31. See C. M. Brolmann and M. Y. A. Zieck, 'Indigenous Peoples' in C. Brolman et al. (eds.) *Peoples and Minorities in International Law* (Dordecht: M. Nijhoff, 1993); G. Alfredson, 'Indigenous peoples and autonomy' in Suksi, *Autonomy: Applications and Implications*; and B. Kingsbury, 'The application of the international legal concept of indigenous peoples in Asia' in J. Bauer and D. Bell (eds.), *The East Asian Challenge for Human Rights* (Cambridge University Press, 1999).

of minorities was already provided for in many constitutions and that the body of international law under the League of Nations had resulted in the creation of special legal regimes for certain sections of the population of a state, a commission appointed by the League suggested that there could be a middle ground between the formation of a new and independent state and choosing between two existing states: 'Under such circumstances, a solution in the nature of a compromise, based on an extensive grant of liberty to minorities, may appear necessary according to international legal conception and may even be dictated by the interests of peace.'[29] Although the League upheld the principle of the territorial integrity of the state as a fundamental principle of international law as necessary to prevent anarchy, it declared that if the minority was oppressed, it would support Åland's secession. Perhaps anticipating such an outcome, Finland had already proposed an autonomy law.

Many years ago the UN General Assembly resolved that autonomy is a manifestation of self-determination. The greater involvement of the UN or a consortium of states in the settlement of internal conflicts has also helped to develop the concept of self-determination as it implies autonomy in appropriate circumstances.[30]

In addition, the right to autonomy can be based on specific agreements or treaties for particular communities, or, exceptionally, on a country's constitution. Many of the autonomies discussed in this volume fall within these categories (Hong Kong, Macau, South Tyrol, Bosnia-Herzegovina, Kashmir, Bougainville and Spain). Other examples include first the autonomy and then the independence of Southern Sudan and East Timor.

Rights are not only a possible basis for autonomy but should, as some scholars argue, at least shape the structure of autonomy itself. The early autonomies discussed in this volume were designed before the full articulation of human rights as we understand them today. Self-determination came before rights. We can compare the influence of human rights on autonomy by tracing it at different phases of the development of regimes of human rights. In an interesting paper, Suksi compares the role of human rights in autonomies in Åland and Kosovo.[31] Suksi reaches the following conclusion:

> The Kosovo Resolution of 1999 illustrates how international human rights are implemented in a statute for an area plagued by violence. Through that Resolution, the grant of human rights on a non-discriminatory basis is extended with a number of provisions that create special protection for some categories of individuals and their national communities in the area. In Kosovo, the point of departure is that human rights are there for everyone. With its grant of special rights in

[29] *Official Journal of the League of Nations, Special Supplement No. 3*, October 1920, 6.

[30] T. Franck, 'Postmodern tribalism and the right to secession', and R. Higgins, 'Comments', both in C. Brolman et al., *Peoples and Minorities in International Law.*

[31] Markku Suksi, 'The protection of the rights of minorities by means of autonomy: the cases of the Åland Islands and Kosovo' in Zelim A. Skurbaty (ed.), *Beyond a One-Dimensional State: An Emerging Right to Autonomy?* (Leiden: Martinus Nijhoff Publishers, 2005).

> the areas of participation through elections, property, and language, the Åland Islands Settlement of 1921 may go beyond what would be possible without greater difficulty at the eve of the twentieth century and against the background of international human rights. Comparing the two decisions and their actual or projected outcome in a very rough way, it seems as if Kosovo had more autonomy but less special or exclusive rights for the total body of inhabitants, while the Åland Islands would have somewhat less autonomy but more exclusive rights for the total body of inhabitants that qualify for the right of domicile.[32]

In the case of both Kosovo and Bosnia-Herzegovina, comprehensive human rights were binding from the very beginning. Suksi argues that if human rights were as developed in the 1920s as today, specific features of Åland's autonomy such as special citizenship rights and a separate educational policy protecting a minority language and restricting use of the national language would have been impossible.

Though based on human rights, autonomy can put rights at risk. A specific objection to autonomy regimes comes from those who espouse an individual-oriented view of human rights. The notion of group rights that is the basis of some autonomy regimes is considered problematic from that point of view. But even those who are less committed to an individualist conception of rights have problems with some kinds of autonomy systems. Steiner, valuing the diversity and richness of ethnic groups, has cautioned against autonomy regimes that hermetically divide one community from another. He writes,

> Rights given ethnic minorities by human rights law to internal self-determination through autonomy regimes could amount to authorisation to them to exclude 'others', in the manner of states exercising their sovereign power to control crossings of their frontiers within a territorially fragmented world. Ethnic groups could be empowered to erect and enforce cultural, political, ideological and (if they were geographically concentrated) physical boundaries.

As several chapters show, in some autonomies there is differentiation of rights between different residents. Steiner goes on to say that, 'Enforced ethnic separation both inhibits intercourse among groups, and creative development within the isolated communities themselves. It impoverishes cultures and peoples'.[33]

Some autonomy regimes have indeed raised these difficulties (notoriously in North East India[34] and Nigeria),[35] but in most states fundamental rights are protected against regional violations. Certainly Steiner's anxieties point to the need to draft the instruments of autonomy with care. Today there is

[32] Ibid., 395–6.

[33] H. Steiner, 'Ideals and counter-ideals in the struggle over autonomy regimes for minorities', *Notre Dame Law Review* 66:5 (1991), 1551 and 1554 respectively.

[34] Ranabir Samaddar (ed.), *The Politics of Autonomy: Indian Experiences* (New Delhi: Sage Publications, 2005).

[35] See the report of the International Crisis Group, *Nigeria's Faltering Experiment*, Africa Report, 119, 25 October 2006.

considerable concern about discrimination against minorities within regions. In most countries a national Bill of Rights applies to the regions and would thus protect minorities within them, but unfortunately in the face of local political forces not averse to using violence, the national authorities may not be able to do much to protect these minorities.

A particular form of opposition to autonomy is in the form of group rights. Autonomy does not always take the form of group rights; as traditionally understood, it is more like corporate rights. Many autonomies do not have a notion of local citizenship, and if they do it is no different from citizenship of a state in a federation. But clearly some do, especially those oriented towards ethnic groups, and also in Hong Kong and Macau, though for different reasons. A well-known example is Bosnia-Herzegovina, which is tightly structured around its ethnic communities. But it is also bound by the European Convention of Human Rights, which the Constitutional Court has used to mitigate the discriminatory aspects of its constitution (see Marko, Chapter 9).

There are of course ways to deal with these new minorities through special representation in the region, special consultative councils, local government and by vesting special responsibilities in the central institutions for their welfare and protection (for example, in Canada minorities in a province can appeal to the centre against provincial discrimination; the constitutions of states that emerged out of the former Yugoslavia have similar protections as do the 2000 constitutional proposals of the Sri Lanka government), but these methods have seldom been effective. Sometimes the need to protect minorities leads to a layering of sub-autonomies producing complex systems, most prominently in India, especially the North East, and in South Tyrol, Bosnia-Herzegovina and in the proposals of the Muslim community in Sri Lanka. Many countries today would grant autonomy only on the acceptance by the autonomous area of the basic principles of human rights and state policies (India, for example).

There are many situations when the conflict between human rights and group rights becomes an issue. These represent different paradigms of rights: one deriving from the nation/state, the other from the ethnic community. With group rights, there may be problems of both exclusion and 'locking in' (locking persons into a community when their desire is to move out to a more cosmopolitan lifestyle – the rule of self-identity deals with the latter of these problems, and perhaps the former as well). This has sometimes happened when indigenous peoples are granted autonomy, based particularly on cultural grounds. This can disadvantage women within the community,[36] as indeed can

[36] *Sandra Lovelace v. Canada*, Communication No. 24/1977: Canada 30/07/81, UN Doc. CCPR/C/13/D/24/1977. Sandra Lovelace, a Maliseet Indian, lived on the Tobique Reservation with her parents until she married a non-Indian man. The marriage ended, and Ms. Lovelace returned to the reservation to live with her parents, however, she could not purchase a home on the reserve because the council prioritised housing for members of the group. The Canadian Indian Act stated that an Indian woman who married a non-Indian man loses her Indian status, which also means a loss of access to federal programs for Indians in education,

happen when the primary reason for autonomy is the unfettered profession of a religion. Another instance of discrimination against a group is when the autonomy is seen to be granted to a community with traditional links to the area; they are then seen as the principal beneficiaries of autonomy ('sons of the soil'), with political, social and economic discrimination against those who do not satisfy membership of that community. Some groups can suffer discrimination because the autonomous area adopts only the language of the majority.

Today a fundamental justification for autonomy is the recognition and promotion of diversity. Steiner's point is that exclusionary forms of autonomy amount in fact to the denial of diversity – a country dotted with exclusive cultural zones, jealously preserving particular values and institutions, neither intermingling nor accessible to all. In this way, as some might ask, is autonomy different from secession?

Institutions of autonomy: implementing and operating autonomy

We now turn to the constitutional and political framework for implementing and operating autonomy. Negotiations on autonomy are extremely complicated and long drawn out, and autonomy may break down soon after it is established or agreed upon. Sometimes the autonomy group may have taken on more than it can cope with, such as a panoply of powers beyond its capacity or resources. The transitional arrangements for the establishment of the autonomy and its operations, requiring lengthy negotiations at various levels with experts, bureaucrats and politicians, are often complex. In many cases boundaries may need to be negotiated, or at least drawn up. Diversity of interests is likely to emerge soon, both within the autonomous area and within the state. Autonomy is often granted after a conflict, so negotiations become part of conflict resolution, and can be difficult and complex. Autonomy is seldom granted because it is considered to be a good thing in itself, so it may come bundled with suspicions and resentments.

The principal focus of this book is on the operation of autonomies, and in particular the role of institutions. The institutions that we discuss here are for the most part formal, rooted in the authority of the state, purposive, have a clear structure, membership, functions and procedures. They are underpinned by law and often by sanctions. Public institutions are consciously created, but sometimes informal institutions arise through informal understandings or practice to meet some contingency (as well as the role of constitutional conventions or understandings). These institutions and the accompanying rules for the

housing and social assistance, as well as losing the right to own a home or live on a reserve; to borrow funds from the Band Council for housing; to traditional hunting and fishing rights; and cultural benefits that come with living among family and friends on the reserve. The Canadian courts held that the Act was valid (this was before the Charter of Human Rights) but the UN Committee on Human Rights held that it violated her rights under Art. 27 of the ICCPR, which guaranteed her rights as a member of a minority community.

most part affect state and public authorities; but formal institutions, even with detailed rules and procedures, operate within social, political and economic contexts and are invariably affected by them. So similar institutions can operate quite differently in different countries (the outstanding example in this book is the contrast between the Åland Delegation and the Basic Law Committee in Hong Kong).

Autonomy is principally about the norms and structures of the state, which are largely manifested in institutions and their relationship to each other, and between people at different levels of government. Autonomy is a process, with its own dynamics and it is through institutions that autonomy is sustained and moves forward. Differences and tensions are inevitable in any system of divided powers. An advantage of devolution is the flexibility in the ways that it can be designed and structured, which can facilitate the designing of devolution to the circumstances of the particular country – and within the country. But the very openness can lead to complex structures, especially when more than one type of autonomy exists within a country, then the task of managing diversity becomes even more complicated (as amply demonstrated by Peterlini, Chapter 4).

Institutions serve a number of purposes. At the most general level, they are the concretisation of theory, aspirations and compromises. They provide a guide to the objectives of autonomy and to the democratic nature of autonomy. They distribute powers and resources between the national government and the autonomous area. Institutions mediate between different levels of government, particularly in resolving differences. They are often burdened with the lack of trust between the parties, but they are required to help build and maintain consensus; balance predictability with flexibility; establish autonomous government; develop capacity and manage the transition to autonomy. Given the fragility of the autonomous area and the likely resistance to autonomy, what can be done to ensure its implementation and operation?

There is not a great deal about the norms and structures of autonomy institutions in regional or international law, or in the few national constitutions that promise or authorise autonomy. Institutional arrangements thus have to be negotiated. They do not receive as much attention as they deserve, despite the fact that the operation and success of the autonomy are greatly dependent on them.

The following are the key institutional factors that influence the functioning of autonomy.

- A clear understanding of the purposes and limits of devolution. It is not of course unusual for parties to the agreement to have different expectations: the group asking for it expects a degree of self-rule, the government conceding it hopes to preserve the integrity of the state and the external groups may count on regional stability. The important thing is that the powers, institutions and the manner of their exercise are understood and accepted by all.

- The degree and method of entrenchment of the agreement is critical. The principal mode of entrenchment is through the national constitution (though autonomies founded merely on statute have endured in Puerto Rico and Greenland). Sometimes international guarantees or engagement can be significant (as in Bosnia-Herzegovina). The presence of constitutional or statutory underpinning provides the basis for judicial supervision, which in many cases has been central to the protection and development of autonomy.
- An important consideration is the extent of the powers of the region. If significant powers are vested in a region of significant size, the ability of the national government to regulate the economy, distribute resources and even safeguard national security may be seriously affected. The region might have little interest in participation in national affairs or even in a share in national government. On the other hand, if only a few matters are vested in the regional government, the centre will continue to dominate affairs in the region.
- Another aspect of the distribution of powers, applicable where there is more than one autonomous region, is whether regional powers are uniform or asymmetrical. It can be hypothesised that in the case of uniformity, especially when all the regions are similar in size or resources, the system may work smoothly, but when they are asymmetrical (the Northern State in the original Nigerian federation, Québec in Canada, Kashmir in India or Zanzibar in Tanzania), tensions may arise. Yet degrees of asymmetry may sometimes be better suited to addressing the accidents and circumstances of ethnic distribution or history.
- The method for the distribution of powers has a major effect on the relationship between the centre and regions. When certain powers are vested exclusively in the centre and others exclusively in regions, there is a clear separation between the two levels of government, but where a significant number of powers are 'concurrent', that is, both the centre and regions may use these powers, the centre and regions have to regularly consult and co-operate. In this case institutions for inter-level co-ordination and co-operation make a critical contribution, as in the system described in the following paragraph.
- Another method to distribute powers is to separate legislative from executive powers, and instead of, as is usual, giving both legislative and executive responsibility to one level of government in respect of specified matters, to give, for example, legislative responsibility over certain matters to one level of government, normally the centre, and the executive responsibility to another. In this way most policies are nationally determined and apply uniformly throughout the country, but their implementation takes account of local

circumstances. Germany and South Africa follow this system, as to a lesser extent do India, Switzerland, Austria and Malaysia.

- Financial arrangements include the division of powers to raise and spend public revenue and the transfer of funds from one level of government to another (usually from the centre to the region). Financial arrangements touch on some fundamental issues, such as whether the region receives special grants from the centre to ensure that its inhabitants enjoy the same level of amenities and social services as other parts of the country, or indeed whether a better endowed region should contribute to the national fund.
- There are various other elements to inter-level or inter-government relations. Some autonomy systems provide for powers of the national government to monitor, intervene in or direct, or even suspend the regional government (as in India). This type of rule can cause extreme tension between the different levels of government and revive fears in the region that led to demands for autonomy in the first instance.
- Often an autonomous region will have minorities within it. Autonomy arrangements sometimes include provisions for the protection of minorities. Sometimes the national government may have supervening powers to safeguard their rights.
- Where parties exist at both national and regional level, party structures often play a key role in bringing people together. Hardly any constitutions mention political parties, but they are important institutions that need to be looked at and understood. Where there are no national parties, as in Belgium, or where national parties do not have an effective regional base, as is partly the case in Canada, the parties do not function well as institutions of integration and articulation. Parties then reinforce tendencies of separateness, as in Belgium. China is a one party state; ultimately no authority is higher, as Hong Kong and Macau have realised, though the communist party has no formal role in these autonomies. However, on the whole, the linkages between national and regional parties are not as strong in autonomies as in federations (Åland's parties have always been distinct from those on the Mainland).
- There are diverse mechanisms to deal with inter-level relations, such as consultations, co-ordination of policies and adjustments in fiscal relations. These mechanisms compensate for divided authority, inevitable in autonomy systems.
- Supplementing these mechanisms are those that focus on dispute resolution: negotiations, mediation, arbitration, administrative (such as a commission of enquiry) and judicial adjudication. Of these the most important is the last. This assumes that the judiciary is independent and has the ultimate authority for the interpretation of the constitution and laws. Often this would be the final court in the country. The supremacy of the constitution, the entrenchment of the autonomy and tradition of the rule of law provide the basis of the jurisdiction and authority of the courts. The Chinese system, which has none of these qualities, means that disputes between Beijing and

Hong Kong or Macau are more likely to be dictated by the directives from the centre than by a legal or judicial process.

Contextual factors

How the institutions and procedures described previously function depends on a number of contextual factors identified here, which vary, sometimes greatly, from one case study to another. I mention some key points in the differences that affect their functioning. To begin with, there is considerable difference in the circumstances that lead to autonomy. Some arise in the aftermath of wars (such as in South Tyrol and Bosnia-Herzegovina); some on the grant of independence (Åland/Finland); some as part of post–World War II decolonisation (for example, Kashmir and Puerto Rico); some after internal struggles for secession (Bougainville/Papua New Guinea). Two autonomies, Hong Kong and Macau, resulted from the transfer of sovereignty to China by Britain and Portugal.

There are two types of circumstances under which an autonomy can come about: by carving it out of an existing state (Åland from Finland, Catalonia in Spain), or by the merger of two distinct entities (Tanganyika and Zanzibar). Their logic and dynamics are different, but often this dichotomy proves too simplistic. China may think that Hong Kong and Macau were merely returned to the 'motherland'; but the people of these entities may regard them as distinct entities forced into a merger with China. Québec's status in Canada has varied, at first a forced merger as a separate unit, then a merger with another unit and finally its own separate entity. Similarly South Tyrol was annexed by Italy from Austria, but its present status can be understood as moving within Italy to a distinct status. Scotland, once an independent entity, was absorbed into Britain and centuries later granted autonomy within the UK. It may be poised on a greater measure of self-government, if not independence, in a forthcoming referendum.

Motivations for autonomy vary. The most common reason is the pressure from ethnic, religious linguistic or cultural minorities for self-government in areas of special significance to them (Åland, Bougainville, Norfolk Island). Other reasons include strengthening regional defence and security (Tanzania) or preserving an economic and social system inconsistent with the national system (Hong Kong and Macau). There is generally a degree of convenience in respect of small and distant islands (Spain/Majorca; Australia/Norfolk). In some countries secession autonomy is claimed, but accepted as the second best (Bougainville, Kashmir, South Tyrol, Québec and, possibly, Scotland). More rarely, the initiative for autonomy may come from the central government because it suits its strategy (Finland/Åland; US/Puerto Rico; China/Hong Kong and Macau).

The most common legal basis for autonomy is self-determination – at least so far as international law is concerned (the foundation for the earliest autonomy in this volume is Åland). The doctrine has been refined since then, gaining momentum after World War II. An emerging principle is that an oppressed minority has a right to autonomy, if not actually secession, a position endorsed by the Canadian Supreme Court.[37] Some national constitutions provide for autonomy under special circumstances, the outstanding example in this volume being Spain.

The mode of, and participation in, negotiations for autonomy are often critical factors. Except for autonomy discussions in the big powers (the United States, India, China, Canada), there is usually a degree of foreign involvement. This involvement varies, but is often necessary to a settlement. The greater the degree of local control of negotiations, the more likely is it that it will address local issues in some detail. And also perhaps that the agreement will be more durable, especially if the local people, as opposed to merely local leaders, have some participation.

The degree to which the autonomy agreement and its resulting legal form are entrenched is another important consideration. The greater the degree of entrenchment in the national constitution, and the involvement of the autonomous region in it, the more secure is autonomy likely to be. A good example of this is Papua New Guinea, where the lack of regional involvement facilitated the dismantling of autonomy. Some autonomies in this volume are part of a broader scheme of federalism, which gives them considerable security (Kashmir, Québec, Bosnia-Herzegovina).

The size of the autonomous region vis-à-vis the state is likely to affect the operation of autonomy – the significance of Norfolk Islands to Australia is of a different dimension than Québec to Canada, Catalonia to Spain, or Kashmir to India. So is the strategic role of the region. This factor is to some extent connected with the presence of a 'kin state' in the vicinity. India's relationship with Kashmir is complicated both by Kashmir's size and its critical situation along the borders of Pakistan and China. Size has not been Finland's problem with Åland but in the early nineteenth century its strategic position in the Baltic was, though the relatively good understanding with Sweden, the 'kin state', was a factor in the happy conclusion. Kin state factor has been important also in South Tyrol with Austria's role in securing autonomy, and it continues to be a major issue in Bosnia-Herzegovina.

The operation of autonomy depends a great deal on the political traditions of the country, in particular its commitment to democracy and human rights. The precise nature of the formal relationship between the centre and the region become less important given these traditions, as do constitutional guarantees. In a curious way, legal guarantees also become less important in practice if these traditions do not exist. Canada is an example of the former and China of the latter. Closely connected to these factors is the method for the resolution of disputes between the centre and the region. Differences in size and clout of the

[37] *Reference re Secession of Québec*, [1998] 2 S.C.R. 217.

centre and the region are likely to be less critical if there is a strong commitment to the rule of law and judicial review.

The number of autonomous regions can influence centre-region relations. This is perhaps most evident in Spain, and to some extent in India where the centre has to negotiate a host of issues common to the autonomies and federal units. But in China, despite its multiplicity of autonomies, the centre has had a firm grip, principally through the Communist Party, though with the introduction of a sort of market economy, the relations between Beijing and the provinces, even if not ethnic autonomies, are being redefined.

Perhaps the most important of all factors are the variations in the structures of the state and the region. The relationship between the centre and the region is influenced not only by the division of powers and responsibilities but also the structure of institutions at both levels; for example, how democratic and inclusive they are, the role of political parties and the ability to negotiate binding settlements. In this sense, for example, a major problem in Tanzania is structural. Hong Kong has similar problems – institutions at both levels were devised by the Chinese authorities, who managed to keep their principles and structures out of the Joint Declaration with Britain. Another factor is whether the region is intended to have a government and policies largely separate from the centre, or to be bound to the centre by requiring the development of common policies and the mechanisms of co-ordination.

The concluding chapter considers these institutional factors and contextual factors in comparative perspective, to deepen our understanding of the dynamics of autonomy regimes, as well as providing insights on the transferability of institutions.

1

Seeking autonomy in a decentralised federation

The case of Québec

Richard Simeon and Luc Turgeon

Canada and Québec are a puzzle for those seeking a deeper understanding of the implications of federal institutions for the management of conflict in divided or multinational societies. On the one hand, Canada is one of the world's longest-lived and most decentralised federations. Few would dispute that historically federalism has been an important institutional device for managing linguistic and regional conflicts. On the other hand, in recent years many Québec nationalists have rejected federalism and struggled to achieve an independent, sovereign Québec state. In October 1995, they came within a few thousand votes of winning a referendum calling for the secession of Québec, albeit on a basis of continuing economic and political 'partnership' with Canada. More generally, Canada illustrates the Janus-faced quality of federalism. It is at once a vehicle for accommodation, a way of reconciling the minority nations and groups to the larger whole; and at the same time, a device for perpetuating and institutionalising the very cleavages it is designed to manage, one which may provide the institutional resources from which to launch a successful secession movement. Canada adopted federalism in large measure as a means to accommodate its linguistic duality and regional differences; but the capacity of federalism to continue to provide a framework for accommodation remains in question. Support for federalism or independence continues to fluctuate within Québec in light of shifting issues, just as support for symmetrical or asymmetrical responses fluctuates within the rest of Canada.

But in a comparative context, perhaps what is most remarkable is that Canadians have been able to debate the possibility of secession and break up openly, democratically and peacefully. Very few federal leaders have argued that secession, were it to be chosen by Québécois, should be opposed by force. All have accepted, either implicitly or explicitly, that a clear decision by Québécois for independence would have to be accommodated. None have challenged the legitimacy of a sovereignist[1] Parti Québécois (PQ) governing Québec, or of

[1] This word comes from the Canadian French *souverainiste* and means an advocate for Québec's independence.

its federal counterpart, the Bloc Québécois, holding (briefly) a majority of the Québec seats in the federal House of Commons. With a relatively brief exception in the late 1960s, culminating in the 'October crisis' of 1970, when a radical movement, the Front de la Libération du Québec, kidnapped a British diplomat and killed a Québec cabinet minister, the sovereignist movement has also been completely peaceful and democratic. It has embraced the democratic rules of the game both in Québec and in national politics. This must be counted as an enormous success for Canada, perhaps with lessons for other countries.[2]

The purpose of this chapter is to provide an overview of the principles and institutional mechanisms that have allowed a predominantly Francophone population to survive and flourish in North America, despite constituting less than 2 per cent of the population of that continent. As Peter Russell aptly puts it, 'No other country in the world today has been engaged so intensively, so passionately, or for so long in searching for the constitutional conditions of its continuing unity'.[3] In this chapter, we focus on the role of Québec in Canada, but no such analysis can ignore the other dimensions of diversity in Canada: regional and provincial identities and interests; relations between indigenous 'First Nations' and 'European' Canada; and the increasingly multicultural Canada evident throughout the country. The Canadian challenge has been to find ways to accommodate all four of these dimensions of diversity simultaneously.[4]

In this chapter, we understand 'autonomy' to refer to the degree of freedom of choice that a sub-state unit in a federation has in order to make its own policy according to its values, interests and preferences, and to resist central government policies that it finds inimical. Federalism is one important set of instruments that can ensure that autonomy is guaranteed in the constitution. However, federal systems vary widely in the autonomy accorded to their constituent units, and in the extent to which sub-state authorities are distributed equally or differently across the units. The Canadian case, largely but not only because of the presence of predominantly French-speaking Québec, falls among the relatively autonomous and relatively asymmetrical variants of federalism.

Historical legacies cast a long shadow over contemporary events. So we begin with some history.

[2] See Richard Simeon, 'Debating secession peacefully and democratically', paper presented at III General Assembly, Club de Madrid. http://archivo.clubmadrid.org/cmadrid/fileadmin/6-Simeon.pdf (accessed 26 March 2013).

[3] Peter Russell, *Constitutional Odyssey: Can Canadians Become a Sovereign People?* (University of Toronto Press, 1992), 193.

[4] Will Kymlicka, *Finding Our Way: Rethinking Ethnocultural Relations in Canada* (Toronto: Oxford University Press, 1997).

The historical foundations of autonomy

The Québec Act[5]

France and Britain were the contending powers in North America in the eighteenth century. The British prevailed on the Plains of Abraham in 1759. But how were the British to deal with French-speaking and Catholic Québec, especially in the face of growing restiveness in their American colonies to the south? In order to retain support among the Francophone community, the British decided to recognise its legitimacy. The Québec Act of 1774[6] stands out as a defining moment that allowed the survival of a French-speaking society in North America.

The Québec Act was enacted eleven years after the Royal Proclamation of 1763,[7] which had constrained the rights of the French-speaking population (while according important recognition to Aboriginal rights). The Québec Act was the first imperial statute to create a constitution for a British colony.[8] It recognised the right of *Canadiens* (the self-named people of Québec) to enjoy the free exercise of their religion, to use the French language and to maintain both the seigniorial (basically feudal) system of land ownership, and the customary civil law from the French period.

The Act may have been motivated by the desire to maintain stability in the colony when the American colonies were rebelling, and it was opposed by many Whig politicians because it did not guarantee a parliament. But there is ample evidence to suggest that such recognition was consistent with the intellectual context of late eighteenth century Britain (and therefore not solely motivated by military imperatives). As Hilda Neatby argues, many provisions of the Act confirmed previous legislation such as the principle enunciated in 1765 by the law officers that 'Roman Catholics in colonies abroad ceded to the King were not subject to the disabilities imposed on Roman Catholics in the United Kingdom'.[9]

Moreover, as James Tully discusses in his book *Strange Multiplicity*,[10] the Québec Act, though a Tory initiative, was also defended by Whig partisans such as William Knox on the basis of the doctrine of the Ancient Constitution.[11] The philosophy of the Ancient Constitution was centred on the idea of continuity,

[5] This section and the next two draw on Alain G. Gagnon and Luc Turgeon, 'Managing diversity in eighteenth and nineteenth century Canada: Québec's constitutional development in light of the Scottish experience', *Commonwealth and Comparative Politics*, 41:1 (March 2003), 1–23.

[6] The Québec Act 1774, 14 Geo III, c. 83.

[7] Royal Proclamation of 1763, R.S.C. 1985, App. II, no. I.

[8] Hilda Neatby, *The Québec Act: Protest and Policy* (Scarborough: Prentice Hall Canada, 1972), 1.

[9] Ibid., 140–1.

[10] James Tully, *Strange Multiplicity: Constitutionalism in an Age of Diversity* (Cambridge University Press, 1995).

[11] On the Whig philosophy of the Ancient Constitution, see John Pocock, *The Ancient Constitution and the Feudal Law: A Study of English Historical Thought in the Seventeenth Century* (Cambridge University Press, 1989).

which posited that fundamental laws were based on customs that could not be displaced by a conqueror without altering the liberty of the people. It was on such terms that Knox supported the maintenance of the laws of the French regime in his argument for the Québec Act:

> [W]e shall cease to wonder, that the Canadians are not in raptures with the English laws of arrest; and be less amazed at the obstinate prejudice they entertain for their own laws and customs. The truth is, our laws of arrests are innovations upon our constitution; and the good of trade has superseded the regard our ancients showed for the personal liberty of the subject. And, at this day, there is no country under heaven, where the recovery of debt is attended with more cruelty, misery, and slavery than in our own.[12]

The Québec Act was thus a defining moment in the relation of *Canadiens* with the British Crown, since it legitimised the maintenance of their established customs, laws and traditions. Maurice Séguin, the *éminence grise* behind the neo-nationalist Montreal School of History, aptly expresses the importance of the Québec Act for subsequent generations of French Canadians:

> Whether they were seigneurs or men of the legal profession, the repeal of the Royal Proclamation and later the Québec Act of 1774 provided Canadian leaders with a constitutional text, a 'grand charter' that they later exploited to the benefit of the French-Canadian collectivity. The Québec Act legalized survival. It encouraged those Canadians to continue to consider themselves as a people of the colony.[13]

Following the Conquest, the British established two separate colonies: Upper Canada (today, Ontario), predominantly British and Protestant, and settled chiefly by United Empire Loyalists fleeing the American Revolution, and later by Scottish and Irish immigrants; and Lower Canada, in what is now Québec. But tensions ran high in both areas. In 1837 and 1838, failed rebellions in Upper and Lower Canada led to the appointment of a British Royal Commissioner, Lord Durham, to sort things out.

He found 'two nations warring in the bosom of a single state'. His solution to this problem was to assert the primacy of the British heritage. The two colonies would be combined, and eventually, he believed, British values and cultures would prevail, subordinating, if not eliminating, the Francophone identity. The Act of Union[14] joined Upper and Lower Canada and abolished French as an official language.

But this assimilationist project failed. Almost immediately French was restored as an official language. Separate Francophone and Anglophone ministers and bureaucracies were established. Double majorities were required on major issues; and Members of Parliament from each region decided matters of

[12] William Knox, *The Justice and Policy of the Late Act of Parliament for Making More Effective the Provision for the Government of the Province of Québec* (London: n.p., 1774), 15–16.

[13] Maurice Séguin, *Une Histoire du Québec* [A History of Québec] (Montréal: Guérin, 1995), 36.

[14] 3 and 4 Victoria c.35.

local significance. The experience closely modelled Arend Lijphart's model of consociational democracy. But tensions increased as the population of Upper Canada rapidly grew, leading to calls for 'Representation by Population', which would have further diminished Francophone influence.

How could this deadlock be broken? And how to do so in the context of American expansionism, declining British interest in the North American colonies, and the presence of other colonies in Nova Scotia, New Brunswick, Prince Edward Island and British Columbia, each with its own history and identity? The result was a series of conferences, beginning in 1864, that led to the British North America Act, 1867, which created modern Canada.[15]

Alfred Stepan has distinguished between federation as 'coming apart' and 'coming together'.[16] In Canada, it was both. It was a 'coming apart' in the sense that it was a solution to the political impasse in the united provinces of Canada, leading to the new provinces of Ontario and Québec. It was a 'coming together' in the sense that the other British North American colonies also joined the union, and in the subsequent century that union was expanded to create a Canada 'from sea to sea to sea'.

The British North America Act

The result of all these debates was the British North America Act (BNA Act, since re-named the Constitution Act, 1867),[17] passed by the UK Parliament. It established the 'Dominion of Canada', substantially independent from Britain, but with remaining colonial ties, some of the vestiges of which remain in today's fully independent Canada.[18] Unlike the United States, Canada was not a product of revolution.[19]

Two impulses shaped the Confederation debates, and the tensions among them are clearly reflected in the BNA Act itself.[20] The first was the pan-Canadian nation-building imperative, represented by the first Prime Minister, Sir John A. Macdonald. His preferred vision was of a unitary state, endowed with the jurisdictional and fiscal levers to create a new political and economic entity on the northern half of the continent. He believed that with the passage of time, the

15 See P. B. Waite, *The Confederation Debates in the Province of Canada, 1865: A Selection* (Toronto: McClelland and Stewart, 1963).

16 Alfred Stepan, 'Federalism and democracy: beyond the US model', *Journal of Democracy*, 10, no. 4 (1999), 19–34.

17 Constitution Act, 1867 (UK), 30 and 31 Victoria, Ch. 3.

18 Such as a 'Governor-General' as head of state, nominally appointed by the British monarch, but only on the advice of the Canadian Prime Minister.

19 For a broad explanation of the consequences of this for Canada in contrast to the United States, see Seymour M. Lipset, *Continental Divide: The Values and Institutions of the United States and Canada* (London: Routledge, 1990).

20 In Canada the term confederation notes not so much the final institutional settlement enshrined in the BNA Act, but the process by which the former British Colonies came together to negotiate the creation of a federal political system.

provinces would become less and less important, ending up as little more than municipalities. In order to achieve this vision, the BNA Act assigned Ottawa the primary tools for building the Canadian political and economic union.[21]

But Macdonald knew that his preferred model could never be accepted, and in an historic partnership with Québec Conservative Georges-Etienne Cartier, a compromise was reached. As a result, the second major thrust of the BNA Act reflected the argument most frequently made by French Canadians. As A. I. Silver observed, the forced union of 1840 would be revisited and French Canadians would be granted control over a province of their own, with a substantial degree of autonomy.[22] French Canadians viewed confederation as a compromise allowing them to control the institutions and practices that were essential to maintaining Québec's identity: Québec's Legislative Assembly, later named the National Assembly; Québec's distinct legal system and its Civil Code; the official status accorded to the French language and Catholic institutions; and its exclusive jurisdiction over important sectors, such as education, that were considered essential for the preservation of Québec as a distinct political community.

Provincial powers, set out in Schedule 92, were primarily those necessary to ensure autonomy in cultural and social matters. The Act created a new political entity, Canada, based on 'an agglomeration of communities' according to one of its founding fathers, Georges-Étienne Cartier, or a 'community of communities' according to a future Prime Minister, Joe Clark, in which both French and English agreed to live together yet also apart. But, as Samuel LaSelva argues, 'the Fathers of Confederation did not merely believe that nationalities could co-exist under the same state; they also sought to create a great and single nation, united by a strong central government and a strong nationality'.[23]

Yet, in many ways, the BNA Act also constituted what Janet Azjenstat has called a 'procedural constitution', that is, a constitution as the rulebook for the game of politics, detached as much as possible from specific ideologies and political interests.[24] The constitution contained no grand aspiration of the sort expressed in the American or French constitutions. Yet, it is precisely this lack of a clear 'We the People' statement that allowed different interpretations of the Canadian constitution to co-exist over the next century.[25] Federalism, then, was less a 'solution' than a formula for continuous negotiation.

[21] See Richard Simeon and Ian Robinson, *State, Society and the Development of Canadian Federalism* (University of Toronto Press, 1990), Chapter 3.

[22] A. I. Silver, *The French-Canadian Idea of Confederation, 1864–1900* (Toronto University Press, 1997, 2nd edn), 41.

[23] Samuel LaSelva, *The Moral Foundation of Canadian Federalism* (Montreal-Kingston: McGill-Queen's University Press, 1996), 46–7.

[24] Janet Ajzenstat, 'Decline of Procedural Liberalism: the Slippery Slope to Secession', in J. Carens (ed.), *Is Québec Nationalism Just?* (Montreal-Kingston: McGill-Queen's University Press, 1995).

[25] Various attempts to write a 'Canada' clause into the constitution that would define Canada's fundamental values have all failed. The closest Canada has come to such a statement in constitutional law is the Supreme Court of Canada's judgment in the Secession Reference (see

The first major challenge to Macdonald's vision of a strong central government was the emergence of the 'compact theory' towards the end of the nineteenth century. The most refined articulation of this theory was put forward by Justice Loranger in his 1884 *Lettres sur l'interprétation de la constitution fédérale* [Notes on interpretation of the Federal Constitution]. Widely accepted in Québec, Anglophone scholars were deeply critical of the theory. The elements of the doctrine are that:[26]

Firstly, the confederation of the British provinces was the result of a compact entered into by the provinces and the United Kingdom.

Secondly, the provinces entered into the federal union with their corporate identity, former constitutions and all their legislative powers intact. A portion of these powers was ceded to the federal parliament, which was to exercise them in the common interest of the provinces. The powers not ceded were retained by the provincial legislatures, which continued to act within their own sphere according to their former constitutions, with certain modifications of form established by the compact.

And finally, far from having been conferred upon them by the federal government, the powers of the provinces are the residue of their former colonial powers. Therefore, the federal government is the creation of the provinces, the result of their association and of their compact.

This confederal idea gained political momentum when Québec Premier Honoré Mercier, strongly supported by his Ontario counterpart, Oliver Mowat, convened the first inter-provincial conference in 1887, which mounted a strong challenge to federal dominance. In later years, this political challenge was reinforced by a series of decisions of the British Judicial Committee of the Privy Council, until 1949 Canada's highest court. These judgments, which continued into the 1930s, radically reduced federal authority. Examples include: a narrow interpretation of the 'peace, order and good government' clause,[27] a similarly restrictive interpretation of the trade and commerce clause and a limitation on the federal power to implement treaties that touch on provincial powers.[28] Thus, by the 1920s the Canadian governing model had become fully federal.

There was, however, one other question about the compact theory. Was Canada a compact between several provinces (eventually ten, together with three 'Territories' that were gradually approaching full provincial status); or was it a compact between two linguistic groups? Was it dualist federalism; or territorial/provincial federalism? The Québec government could use the former

later). It defined democracy, federalism, constitutionalism and the rule of law, and respect for minorities as Canada's fundamental values.

26 Quoted in Alain G. Gagnon, 'Québec's constitutional odyssey', in James Bickerton and Alain G. Gagnon (eds), *Canadian Politics* (Peterborough: Broadview Press, 1999, 3rd edn), 282.

27 See section on division of powers later.

28 Richard Simeon and Martin Papillon, 'Canada', in Akthar Majeed, Ronald L. Watts and Douglas M. Brown (eds.), *Distribution of Powers and Responsibilities in Federal Countries* (Montreal and Kingston: McGill-Queen's University Press, 2006), 91–122.

model to legitimise its claim to provincial autonomy and asymmetry in the federation. But French-speaking Canadians also found out that this doctrine could be used by other provinces to limit the rights of French-speaking minorities outside Québec. Rights to denominational schooling and the use of the French language were challenged in Ontario; and when new western provinces – Manitoba, Saskatchewan and Alberta – were added they quickly reneged on linguistic guarantees contained in their acts of accession.[29] It is in this context that one of Québec's leading intellectuals, Henri Bourassa, developed the 'double compact' interpretation of confederation. According to this perspective, the Canadian federation is both a compact among provinces and a contract between French and English Canadians. He argued that since the Québec Act, French Canadians had been guaranteed the right to use their language throughout Canada. Bourassa attempted a difficult balancing act, like many Québec nationalists in later years: defending provincial autonomy while at the same time ensuring that other provinces would not use this argument to infringe on the rights of French-Canadian minorities outside of Québec.

Active discrimination against Francophones (and Catholics) in Ontario and in the new western provinces had profound consequences for the politics of language in Canada. Had French-speakers populated the west, then all Canadian provinces would have had significant Francophone minorities; as it was, French-speakers remained largely confined to Québec, ensuring that over time they would become smaller and smaller minorities elsewhere, while at the same time, Francophone identity would shift from *Canadiens*, to 'French Canadians' (a cultural-religious community), to 'Québécois' (a political identity, focused on the Québec state).

The rise of modern Québec nationalism

Despite the powers provided to Québec by the BNA Act, more than one hundred years after the 1867 settlement, nationalist ideas continued to develop in Québec, and increasingly came to be framed in constitutional language. This was not so much the result of a profound dissatisfaction with the content of the BNA Act, but rather of growing resentment about the persistent decline in the socio-economic status of French-speakers and the discrimination they faced in the institutions of the federal government, which was increasingly oriented to the interests of the English-speaking majority.[30]

It was also a result of the changing policy agenda. As a result of the Great Depression of the 1930s and World War II, Canada, along with all other Western

[29] Manitoba Act, 1870, R.S.C. 1985, App.II, No. 8; Saskatchewan Act, Statutes of Canada 1905, 4–5 Ch. 42 1905; Alberta Act, Statutes of Canada 4–5 Edward VII c.3.

[30] These disadvantages were fully documented in the three volumes of the Royal Commission on Bilingualism and Biculturalism, *Report* (Ottawa: Queen's Printer, 1965). By the 1980s, as a result of policy development both in Québec and Ottawa, almost all these indicators of Francophone disadvantage had been reversed.

democracies, constructed a modern welfare state. The problem for Canada was that under the 1867 constitution most of the tools necessary for this project lay in provincial hands. The post-war version of Macdonald's nation-building came to be expressed through federal leadership in building the welfare state, partly through a few constitutional amendments placing social security (unemployment insurance and old age pensions) in federal hands, and partly through the use of the federal spending power, using federal conditional grants to influence provincial priorities.[31]

This project was strongly supported in English Canada, but bitterly resisted by the Québec government.[32] The resistance stemmed both from the dominant Québec view of the federation, hostile to federal expansion, and from the anti-statist, conservative ideology of the provincial government of the time.[33] This changed in 1960, with the election of a new provincial government, committed to modernisation and secularisation of the Québec state, and to the embrace of the modern social policy agenda, in the so-called 'Quiet Revolution'.[34] But now it was Québec, not Ottawa, that should lead the change, as '*maîtres chez nous*' [masters in our own house]. Political modernisation was accompanied by a renewed secular nationalism. A new government elected in 1966 adopted the slogan, *égalité ou indépendance* (equality or independence). In 1968, a group of dissident Québec Liberals formed the Parti Québécois, whose goal was a sovereign Québec with a continued 'association' with the rest of the country.[35] Indeed, association, or partnership, between a sovereign Québec and the rest of the country has been a consistent theme in Québec sovereignist proposals; it has been met by Anglophone reactions that ask how does one develop a new relationship after a divorce, and how can a two-unit confederation operate as equals when the two differ so greatly in population and economic weight?[36]

Partly in response to these developments, the federal Liberals recruited a group of leading Québec intellectuals, led by Pierre Trudeau, to bolster the federalist cause. Trudeau became Prime Minister in 1968. With his election, modern Canadian constitutional politics begins.[37] Trudeau was deeply opposed to nationalism in all its forms. He came to Ottawa, he said, to arrest what he saw as a drift towards secession manifested in growing de facto asymmetry. He

[31] The definitive work on this period is Keith Banting, *Federalism and the Welfare State in Canada* (Montreal-Kingston: McGill-Queen's University Press, 1987, 2nd edn).

[32] Simeon and Robinson, *State, Society and the Development of Canadian Federalism*, 137–40.

[33] The fullest expression of this view is found in Québec, *Royal Commission of Enquiry on Constitutional Problems* (The Tremblay Report, 1954).

[34] See Kenneth McRoberts and Dale Posgate, *Québec: Social Change and Political Crisis* (Toronto: McClelland and Stewart, 1980); Simeon and Robinson, *State, Society and the Development of Canadian Federalism*, 186–7.

[35] Québec, *Québec-Canada: A New Deal* (Québec: Conseil Exécutif, 1979).

[36] See Richard Simeon, 'The Limits of Partnership', in David Cameron (ed.), *The Referendum Papers: Essays on Secession and National Unity* (University of Toronto Press, 1999), 384–428.

[37] The most authoritative scholarly account is Peter Russell, *Constitutional Odyssey: Can Canadians Become a Sovereign People?* (University of Toronto Press, 2004, 3rd edn).

accepted the idea of linguistic duality, but his was a pan-Canadian vision, a bilingual Canada from sea to sea. His most important legacy was the Official Languages Act, 1969,[38] which sought to enhance the provision of services to linguistic minorities (French-speaking outside Québec, English-speaking within Québec), to ensure that Anglophone and Francophone Canadians could interact with federal agencies in their mother tongue, and to ensure full representation of Francophones within the central administration.

The Québec nationalist position – both federalist and sovereignist – saw Québec as a sociological nation, and Canada as a partnership between two equal 'founding peoples'. The provincial government was the primary political expression of the French-Canadian people; Ottawa was the primary government of English Canada. The constitution must reflect this fundamental asymmetry if not by according Québec a 'special status' within the federation, then by independence itself.

Indeed, the Parti Québécois came to power in 1976 with a promise to hold a referendum on Québec sovereignty. In 1980, the Québec government held its first referendum. It called for a mandate to negotiate a new relationship with the rest of Canada, sovereignty with continued association, *d'égal a l'égal* (between equals). It was defeated by a 60 per cent to 40 per cent margin, though it is probable that a narrow majority of Francophone Québécois voted 'yes'.

The Constitution Act of 1982

The result of the 1980 referendum prompted a new round of constitutional negotiations. During the campaign, Trudeau had promised that rejection of sovereignty would be followed by a commitment to a 'renewed federalism'. The content of this promise was never spelled out. For many Québécois it meant greater recognition of Québec as the primary political expression of the Québec nation within Canada. Trudeau, of course, had an alternative vision.[39] An elaborate series of federal-provincial conferences were held in the summer of 1979, culminating in a first ministers' conference in September. At this conference, the conflicting visions of Canadian federalism – Canada-centred, Québec-centred, provincialist – were laid out in stark clarity, and once again no agreement was possible. Many of the other provinces had now begun to generate their own constitutional demands for enhanced provincial powers and a reduction of federal power, partly in response to the deep regional cleavages provoked by the energy crises of the decade, which sharply divided central and western Canada.

[38] Official Languages Act, RSC 1970, c. O-2.

[39] For a critique of Trudeau's actions during that period, see André Burelle, *Pierre Elliott Trudeau: L'intellectuel et le politique* [Pierre Elliot Trudeau: The Intellectual and the Politics] (Montréal: Fides, 2006).

The federal government responded to this failure by undertaking an act of *force majeure*. Faced with the impossibility of intergovernmental agreement on constitutional change, Ottawa would act unilaterally: to strengthen national unity by 'patriating' the constitution to make it a fully Canadian document, thus cutting the last colonial ties with Britain; to constitutionalise a 'Charter of Rights and Freedoms', embodying values all Canadians held in common, to be enforced by a national institution, the Supreme Court; and to impose a formula for future amendment of the constitution. In the face of provincial intransigence, argued Trudeau, Ottawa had no alternative but to exercise its right to request that Britain amend the British North America Act, 1867, one last time.[40]

All but two of the provinces (Ontario and New Brunswick) joined with Québec in the 'gang of eight' to oppose this initiative. They argued that it failed to respond to provincial demands for constitutional change, and that unilateral action violated an established convention that provincial consent was necessary before any amendment affecting them was proposed to the British Parliament. The ensuing battle was played out in many political arenas. Eventually the provinces convinced the federal government to submit a Reference to the Supreme Court of Canada to ascertain whether or not provincial assent to change was constitutionally required. In a politically astute judgment, the Court replied that according to black letter law, Ottawa did have the right to seek the amendment, but that a constitutionally enforceable convention requiring 'substantial provincial consent' was also in force.[41] Hence the parties were forced back to the negotiating table. When talks restarted in the fall of 1981, the provincial alliance broke down. Ultimately the English-speaking provinces could not sustain their alliance with a separatist Québec government. In a late night agreement, Ottawa and the other provinces agreed on a compromise that left Québec out.

The compromise, embodied in the Constitution Act, 1982, reflected the blend of Canada- and province-centred visions of federalism. It did patriate the constitution,[42] along with a Charter of Rights and Freedoms. But it also adopted some limitations on the scope of the Charter advocated by provinces (for example, a 'notwithstanding clause' permitting any government to set aside certain sections of the Charter for a limited period); and it adopted a highly provincialist formula for constitutional amendment. It would require the

[40] The Canadian constitution had remained an Act of the British Parliament, a result of Canadians' inability to agree on a domestic amending formula. But Britain would only amend the BNA Act if Canada requested it. So the issue was: who had the power to make the request? Was it the government of Canada, acting unilaterally, or the government of Canada only after having achieved consensus among the Canadian provinces? Trudeau argued the former position.

[41] Reference re: a Resolution to amend the Constitution, [1981] 1 S.C.R. 753 [Patriation Reference].

[42] Until 1982, the Canadian constitution could only be changed by an Act of the British Parliament. Patriation refers, therefore, to the adoption of a Canadian amending formula.

approval of the federal Parliament and seven of the ten provincial legislatures, comprising 50 per cent of the population, for most amendments, and unanimity for some others.

What the agreement did not include was any recognition of or increased powers for Québec, or a Québec veto over future constitutional change. It was thus an enormous defeat, not only for Québec sovereignists, but also for Québec federalists who had pinned their hopes on a renewed federalism recognising Québec's distinct status in Canada. Québec made a last appeal to the courts, arguing that the constitutional convention for provincial consent also required the assent of Québec, but the Court rejected the argument.[43]

Thus Canada had achieved major constitutional change, which would have important effects on Canadian politics. The Charter added a third pillar to the Canadian institutional structure of parliamentary government and federalism. It meant that the constitution was now as much about the relations of citizens to governments as it was about federal-provincial relationships. But the absence of Québec was a gaping hole. Many Québec analysts argued that the new Constitution Act limited the powers of Québec, especially with regard to education and language rights (see later text on the Supreme Court judgments on education and language rights). Moreover, they questioned the legitimacy of a constitution that was adopted without the support of a province representing the largest minority group in Canada, and that could be modified in the future without its consent.[44] What long-term legitimacy could the settlement have if Québec were excluded? Could not the 'imposition' of a new constitution supply a potent weapon for Québec sovereignists in the future?

The potential foundation for a sovereign Québec

In the aftermath of the exclusion of Québec from the Constitution Act of 1982, a new federal government led by Brian Mulroney proposed a constitutional package to bring Québec back into the constitutional family 'with honour and dignity'. The Meech Lake Accord of 1987 proposed to add to the constitution an interpretative clause recognising Québec as a 'distinct society' within the Confederation; a veto for Québec over any future constitutional amendments; a constitutional guarantee of Québec representation on the Supreme Court; a limitation on the federal government's power to spend in areas of provincial jurisdiction through an 'opting-out' provision; and a constitutionalising of

43 Québec Veto Reference (Reference re: Amendment of the Canadian Constitution, [1982] 2 S.C.R. 793.

44 For a trenchant critique of the patriation from the point of view of Québec, see Guy Laforest, *Trudeau and the End of a Canadian Dream* (Montreal-Kingston: McGill-Queen's University Press, 1995). For a critical perspective from Canada outside of Québec, see Keith Banting and Richard Simeon (eds.), *And No One Cheered: Federalism, Democracy and the Constitution Act* (Toronto: Methuen, 1983) and Kenneth McRoberts, *Misconceiving Canada: The Struggle for National Identity* (Oxford University Press, 1997).

existing informal arrangements giving Québec a greater voice in immigration. The Accord was rejected when the Mulroney government was unable to obtain the support of two provinces, Manitoba and Newfoundland, before the compulsory three-year deadline for final passage set out in the 1982 Constitution expired.[45]

A subsequent attempt to address constitutional issues beyond Québec's concerns (such as Senate reform and Aboriginal self-government), the Charlottetown Accord, was defeated in a national referendum in 1992. Thus Canadians had failed to create a formula that could reconcile the competing models of federalism. Moreover, the middle ground was disappearing. Québec opinion was now distributed along a continuum from recognition of its distinct society and special status to outright independence; opinion outside Québec increasingly rejected any departure from provincial equality.

Meanwhile, the Parti Québécois (PQ) had regained power in Québec. It called a second referendum on sovereignty for October 1995. Premier Jacques Parizeau was an avowed separatist, impatient both with a gradualist approach to sovereignty (*étapisme*), and with the idea of political partnership with the rest of Canada. However, others in the PQ argued that Québécois retained a strong attachment to Canada, and would reject a clear break. Following intense negotiations within Québec, the question posed asked Québécois to support sovereignty, along with a proposed economic and political 'partnership' with the rest of the country. If it passed, and the rest of Canada refused to negotiate partnership, then Québec could decide to go it alone. The referendum came within a hair's breadth of passage, losing by less than 1 per cent of the vote, in a very high turnout.[46]

The shock of this result led the federal government to re-think its approach. It had two elements, the carrot and the stick. The carrot was to convince Québécois that federalism could be responsive to their interests through 'non-constitutional renewal'.[47] Accordingly, Ottawa adopted a non-constitutional resolution recognising Québec as a distinct society in Canada. This resolution has had little impact on the working of Canadian federalism.

The stick was the attempt to convince Québécois that sovereignty could not be achieved easily, or without cost. Secession could not be achieved unilaterally; it would be a fundamental constitutional change in which all Canadians would have a stake.

The most important element of the federal post-referendum strategy was a Reference by the federal government to the Supreme Court of Canada in 1996. It asked whether Québec has a right to unilateral secession either under existing

[45] Constitution Act, 1982, s. 39(2).

[46] The 'yes' option obtained 49.4 per cent of the vote and the 'no' option 50.4 per cent, a difference of less than 50,000 votes. The turnout was around 94 per cent.

[47] For various assessments, see Harvey Lazar (ed.), *Non-Constitutional Renewal. Canada: The State of the Federation, 1997* (Kingston: Institute of Intergovernmental Relations, 1998).

Canadian law, or under international law; and if these differ, which should prevail?

The Court determined that neither Canadian nor international law provides for such a right.[48] The Canadian Constitution is silent on the matter; and Québec does not fall under the category of oppressed or colonial peoples that would justify self-determination under international law. A secession in Canada, the court concluded, would be a constitutional change of profound importance to all; it could only be achieved in accordance with the Canadian Constitution, and within the rule of law. The court also asserted a set of broad principles that underpin Canadian constitutionalism, and that would have to be respected in any secession exercise. These include: constitutionalism and the rule of law, federalism, democracy and respect for minorities.

But having rejected the 'black letter' legality of unilateral secession, the court went on to level the playing field. It said that if Québécois were to vote for secession according to a 'clear question' and with a 'clear majority', then other Canadian political actors would have a *constitutional* obligation to negotiate the matter, taking into account the fundamental principles and the questions that would be on the table – including debts, borders and the like. Canada was divisible. Canada, as a result of this judicial decision, thus became one of the few countries in the world with an explicit secession provision.

Following the Supreme Court decision, the federal government introduced Bill C-20, 'An Act to give effect to the requirement for clarity as set out in the opinion of the Supreme Court of Canada in the Québec Secession Reference'. Dubbed the 'Clarity Act',[49] this acknowledged in the preamble that any province is free to put any question to its people. But at the same time it asserted that 'the House of Commons as the only political institution elected to represent all Canadians, has an important role in identifying what constitutes a clear question and a clear majority sufficient for the Government of Canada to enter into negotiations in relation to the secession of a province from Canada'. The Act then specified that within thirty days after its promulgation, the national Parliament would determine whether or not a question put to the voters of a province is clear.[50] It further declared that any question that asked merely for a 'mandate' to negotiate rather than a direct intention to separate is to be deemed unclear, as is any question that ties the idea of secession to continued economic or political arrangements with Canada.[51] If the proposed question does not meet these tests, then the government of Canada can refuse to enter into any negotiations on secession.

The Act also states that the government will only enter negotiations if it is satisfied that there has been 'a clear expression of a will by a clear majority of the population' of the seceding province. Yet it does not set out how high the bar should be. Instead, the House should take into account the size of

[48] Reference re: The Secession of Québec (1998), 161 D.L.R. (4th).
[49] Parliament of Canada, Clarity Act 2000, C. 26. Assented to 29 June 2000. [50] S.1. [51] S.4.

the majority achieved, the percentage of the electorate that had voted and 'any other' relevant circumstances.[52] Fifty per cent plus one, it clearly implied, would not be sufficient.

Finally, the Act states that no constitutional amendment bringing about secession can be considered unless it has addressed the terms of secession, including 'the division of assets and liabilities, any changes in the borders of the province, the rights, interests and territorial claims of the Aboriginal peoples of Canada, and the protection of minority rights'.[53] Each of these issues is enormously contentious within the Canadian context.

The PQ government retaliated with its own legislation, asserting the right of Québécois alone to decide their future, the sanctity of the 50 per cent plus one majority principle, the inviolability of Québec's current boundaries and Québec's respect for diversity.[54] The Clarity Act was said to deny the basic right of Québecers and Québecers alone to determine the choice between sovereignty and a reformed federalism. 'We subscribe, of course, to the obligation of clarity, but we maintain it is a responsibility that only the (Québec) National Assembly can and must assume'.[55]

Thus positions about the basic rules that might determine Canada's future remain starkly polarised. The irony is that to avoid chaos and uncertainty in the event that there were a 'yes' vote for sovereignty, both sides would have an enormous interest in prior agreement on the rules of the game, and the consequences that would flow from different outcomes. The politics of the situation, however, render such a priori agreement on the rules impossible.

But the intensity of this debate varies. Québec, while exerting its special role, continues to be a vigorous participant in intergovernmental affairs. Since 1976 Québec has alternated between federalist liberal and sovereignist governments. Public support for sovereignty rises when Québec's interests are seen to be neglected, and declines when accommodation appears to work. It also responds to the vicissitudes of politics. Thus, in 2005, federalist forces in Québec seemed decimated by political scandal that discredited the governing Liberals and by the rise of the Bloc Québécois as the strongest party representing Québec on a federal level.

52 S.2(2). Québec sovereignists have consistently argued that in a democracy '50 per cent plus one' is the magic number. Opponents have argued that constitutional amendments – not to mention change as profound as secession – normally require some form of 'super-majority' for passage.

53 S.3. In 1995 Aboriginal peoples in Québec, asserting their constitutional link to the federal government, held their own informal referendum, resulting in a huge majority for federalism. Some non-Francophone groups argued that if Québec had a right to secede from Canada, then they too should have a right to secede from an independent Québec.

54 Québec, National Assembly, Bill 99. An Act respecting the exercise of the fundamental rights and prerogatives of the Québec people and the Québec State.

55 Government of Québec, 'Notes for a Statement by the Premier of Québec upon the Tabling of a Bill Respecting the Exercise of the Fundamental Rights and Prerogatives of the People of Québec and the State of Québec', 15 December 1999.

But in the federal election of 2011, the Bloc suffered a massive and unexpected defeat. It was reduced to only four of Québec's seventy-five seats in the Commons. At the same time, the provincial Parti Québécois was experiencing deep internal tensions. Support for sovereignty in the polls remains at around 40 per cent, and is unlikely to wane. However, modernisation and renewal will be essential if the sovereignty movement is to appeal to younger Québécois, who have grown up in a province where historic grievances do not have the same resonance as in the past and where the Québec nation-building project, in culture and policy, has been highly successful within the federation. In 2006, Parliament passed a motion recognising Québec as a nation within Canada.[56]

The constitutional and institutional sources of Québec's autonomy

Constitutional provisions for autonomy

Section 71 of the BNA Act states 'there shall be a Legislature for Québec consisting of the Lieutenant Governor and of Two Houses, styled the Legislative Council of Québec and the Legislative Assembly of Québec'. The re-establishment of a legislature in Québec was seen as a key victory by the political leaders of the time. The province was also granted exclusive control over a number of significant policy areas (see section on the division of powers). Because of the principle of non-subordination associated with federalism, sub-national units have historically had a right to adopt their own constitutions without interference from the federal parliament, so long as they are not inconsistent with the national constitution.[57] Such constitutions establish the principles and rules guiding the working of their autonomous institutions. This is unlike the autonomous communities in Spain or the Scottish Parliament and the National Assembly of Wales in the United Kingdom, for which the powers and rules have been set by acts of the national parliament.

In Canada, however, provincial constitutions are largely unwritten. As F. L. Morton puts it, 'any attempts to "define" a province's constitution produces a lengthy list of statutes, orders-in-council, the rules of order and procedure of the legislatures, and constitutional conventions'.[58] Among the main acts comprising the unwritten constitution of Québec are: the National Assembly Act, the Election Act, the Referendum Act, the Executive Council Act, the Department Act and the Québec Charter of Human Rights and Freedoms. Thus Canada has the distinction, with India, of being one of few federations where the constituent units do not have their own written constitutions, the

56 Hansard, 39th Parliament, First Session; No. 087, 27 November 2006.

57 On this topic, see Nelson Wiseman, 'Clarifying Provincial Constitutions', *National Journal of Constitutional Law*, 6 (1996), 269–93.

58 F. L. Morton, 'Provincial constitutions in Canada,' Paper presented at the Conference on Federalism and Sub-national Constitutions: Design and Reform, Center for the Study of State Constitutions, Rockefeller Center, Bellagio, Italy, 22–26 March 2004.

sole exception being British Columbia, which adopted a provincial constitution in 1871 that was consolidated in 1979.[59]

Sections 58 to 90 of the BNA Act give the provinces the right to modify their constitutions, although they may not alter the executive office of Lieutenant Governor (the Queen's representative in each province). This allowed Québec, for example, to abolish its Legislative Council in 1968, the last of the provinces to do so. The exclusive right of provinces to modify their respective constitutions was reaffirmed in the Constitution Act, 1982. Section 45 states that, 'subject to section 41, the legislature of each province may exclusively make laws amending the constitution of the province'. This would permit, for example, a province like Québec to alter its electoral system. Indeed, several provinces are now considering electoral reform, suggesting that, once again, innovation in federal systems often takes place at the local/regional level.

The structure of Québec institutions

Like the federal government and the other provinces, Québec follows the Westminster model of parliamentary government with a single legislature, the National Assembly.

It is composed of 125 members, elected by single-member constituencies on the 'first past the post system', for no more than five years.[60] The current main political parties of Québec (the federalist Liberal Party of Québec and the sovereignist Parti Québécois) are not affiliated with any federal party, reinforcing the autonomous nature of Québec's political life.[61] Moreover, Section 58 of the Act Respecting the National Assembly explicitly forbids a member of the National Assembly from holding office or employment with the government of Canada. This underlines the 'separated' rather than 'integrated' character of Canadian federalism.

Following an election, by convention, the leader of the party that has gained the most parliamentary seats is appointed by the Lieutenant Governor as the Premier of the Province. But following the Westminster model, the Premier is responsible to the legislature.

As with the federal government and other provincial governments, numerous independent commissions exist in Québec to ensure the rule of law in Québec's public institutions. These include the *Commission des droits de la personne et des droits de la jeunesse* (Commission on Human Rights and Rights of the Child, charged with upholding the Québec Charter of Human Rights and Freedoms) and the Commission de la représentation électorale [Commission on Electoral Representation].

59 See Campbell Sharman, 'The strange case of a provincial constitution: the British Columbia Constitution Act', *Canadian Journal of Political Science*, 17 (1984), 87–108.

60 *An Act Respecting the National Assembly*, R.S.Q., c. A-23.1. s.6.

61 However, the Bloc Québécois, advocating sovereignty within the Canadian parliament, is closely associated with the PQ.

As with other Westminster parliamentary systems, Canadian governments, federal and provincial, are strongly executive-centred. This profoundly affects the conduct of intergovernmental relations in Canada, which is conducted almost entirely among executives, ensuring that provinces speak as single actors in negotiations.

Broad scheme for the division of powers

The Constitution Act, 1867, sets out clear lists of federal and provincial powers with few areas of concurrency. The model is one of divided federalism, in sharp contrast to the more integrated model represented, for example, by Germany. Powers and responsibilities are divided into two sets of watertight compartments; constitutionally, at least, there are few areas of concurrent jurisdiction (only agriculture and immigration initially; pensions were added later, but with provincial paramountcy).[62]

In general, the federal government was given the powers necessary to build a national polity and economy, and to make laws for 'peace, order and good government of Canada'. Section 91 of the BNA Act specified twenty-nine items as exclusively the domain of the federal government, including trade, commerce, banking, credit, currency, navigation, citizenship, Aboriginal affairs and defence. The federal government was also granted the unlimited power to tax. Section 92 of the Act delineated sixteen specific areas of provincial jurisdiction, most related to social policy and to sub-national cultural and institutional matters. These include hospitals, prisons and municipal institutions. Unlike the federal government, provinces can only levy direct taxes, but this distinction has little relevance today. The wording of the Québec Act was transferred into the constitution, in a provision giving the provinces the exclusive right to make laws regarding 'property and civil rights in the province', constituting a second residual clause after the federal government's general power to make 'laws for peace, order and good government'. Section 93 made education a matter of provincial jurisdiction, but circumscribed that power by special rules setting up denominational schools in Ontario and Québec.[63] The distinct character of the Québec civil law system was also reflected in Section 94, which allowed the Parliament of Canada to make provision for the uniformity of laws in all federating provinces except for Québec, thus recognising an asymmetrical element in Confederation (see section on asymmetry).

Although the constitution does not grant specific direct powers over social policy, such as health care, to the federal government, it has played a very significant role in this area. A few constitutional amendments gave the central

62 Richard Simeon, 'Consideration on the design of federations: the South African constitution in comparative perspective', *SA Public Law*, 13, no. 1 (1998), 42–72.

63 Québec's obligation to provide denominational schools was abolished in 1997, Constitutional Amendment, 1997 (Québec).

government primary control over the basic elements of social security – old age pensions, employment insurance and tax benefits for those with young children. The federal government has engaged more deeply in social policy by transferring financial resources to the provinces, sometimes with conditions, to ensure national norms and 'standards'.

This is based on what has been interpreted as the federal government's 'spending power' – the ability to provide grants to the provinces with conditions attached. Technically, this power cannot be found in the Constitution. In many ways, it is simply the 'expansion of the taxing power to the point that the federal government has sufficient revenues to underwrite national programmes, in addition to fulfilling its more specific constitutional mandate'.[64] This federal spending power remains controversial in Canada. For some, especially in Québec, it is a licence for federal intervention into areas that are constitutionally the domain of the provinces. For others, it is a valuable instrument of policy flexibility, facilitating the development of countrywide standards in crucial areas, such as health care. All provinces, however, complain about the ways in which the use of this power by Ottawa can distort provincial priorities, and about the unpredictability of federal funding. Various constitutional proposals have attempted to place limits on the spending power. The conditions imposed on provinces by federal transfers remain much lower than in other federations, and over time, the number of conditions attached to federal transfers has been steadily falling.[65]

Canada has a unified judicial system, but authority for the administration of justice is divided between the federal and provincial governments. Article 92(14) of the BNA Act states that the provinces have power over 'the Administration of Justice in the Province, including the Constitution, Maintenance, and Organisation of Provincial Courts, both of Civil and of Criminal Jurisdiction, and including Procedure in Civil Matters in those Courts'. All superior courts, including the Supreme Court of Canada, are appointed by the federal government. According to the Supreme Court Act,[66] three of the nine justices are to be appointed from Québec. On occasion, Québec commentators have argued that the Supreme Court of Canada has favoured the federal position, but as the Patriation and Secession References demonstrate, the court has played an important balancing role in the recent evolution of the federation.

Relations between institutions at the national and autonomous level

Despite assigning important powers to the provinces, the Constitution Act, 1867 appeared to give the dominant powers to the central government. In

[64] Mollie Dunsmuir, *The Spending Power: Scope and Limitations* (Ottawa: Parliamentary Research Branch, Library of Parliament, 1991), 3.

[65] See Ronald Watts, *The Spending Power in Federal Systems: a Comparative Study* (Kingston: Institute of Intergovernmental Relations, 1999).

[66] Supreme Court Act (R.S.C., 1985, c. S-26).

addition to responsibility for the most important policy areas at the time, it included an unlimited power to 'disallow' or 'reserve' any provincial legislation. In the early years, the federal government used these powers over the provinces with little restraint. Indeed, K. C. Wheare described the 1867 constitution as only 'quasi-federal'.[67] However, this centralist model did not persist. By the early twentieth century, Canada had come to function as a fully federal polity. The pendulum shifted back to Ottawa between the 1930s and 1950s, the result of depression, war and the building of the welfare state. Since then, the predominant forces have been toward decentralisation.

There are many reasons for these shifts. First, they result from the fact that throughout much of Canadian history, Ottawa was unable to establish the hegemony of a national vision. Provincial and regional identities and interests remained strong. The most powerful of these were in Québec. Seeing itself as possessing a distinctive culture and identity, and its population as a minority on the national scene, it has consistently argued for greater provincial autonomy, and has resisted federal 'intrusions' into provincial jurisdiction. Ontario and the wealthier provinces in western Canada have also often argued for greater provincial autonomy. Provincial political and bureaucratic competence and self-confidence, together with their share of total government spending, grew in the 1950s and 1960s since most of the postwar expansion of government took place in areas of provincial jurisdiction, such as health, education and welfare.[68]

The disallowance and reservation powers, while remaining in the constitution, have long since fallen into disuse, and are now considered essentially defunct. The most important power to influence the provinces that remains in federal hands is the 'spending power' described previously, but even that plays a lesser role than it once did, especially in an era of fiscal restraint.

Judicial interpretation has also played a major role in the evolution of Canadian federalism. Until 1949, the Judicial Committee of the Privy Council (JCPC) in Britain remained Canada's final court of appeal. In a series of decisions, it sharply limited the scope of the 'peace, order and good government' clause, turning it into an emergency power. It narrowed federal powers over trade and commerce, and said that the treaty-making power could not breach the watertight compartments of the division of powers. The adoption of a Charter of Rights and Freedoms in 1982 greatly expanded the place of the courts in Canada's political system. Many Québec analysts argued that the Charter would 'work towards the unification of the nation by homogenising policies across the country'.[69] Analysts from outside of Québec, such as Alan Cairns, made similar predictions.[70] Although some Supreme Court decisions have stirred controversy, especially when striking down elements of Québec's language policy,

67 K. C. Wheare, *Federal Government* (Oxford University Press, 1949), 19–20.

68 See Simeon and Robinson, *State, Society and the Development of Canadian Federalism.*

69 Laforest, *Trudeau and the End of a Canadian Dream*, 134.

70 Alan Cairns, *Charter versus Federalism: the Dilemmas of Constitutional Reform* (Montreal-Kingston: McGill-Queen's University Press, 1992).

overall, on matters related to federalism, the Supreme Court of Canada has taken a balanced approach, sensitive to federalist values. In fact, the perceived activism of the Supreme Court over social matters, such as its decisions respecting the rights of gays and lesbians, women and drug users have been favourably received in Québec, where social norms are more liberal. In fact, although Québécois rejected the process by which the Charter was adopted, public opinion surveys show that they share the generally positive view of the Charter that prevails in the rest of Canada.[71]

Representation in national institutions

Québécois have played a significant role in national institutions. Article 51 of the BNA Act, which originally guaranteed Québec sixty-five seats in the House of Commons, was revised in the 1970s to guarantee Québec seventy-five seats. The overall proportion of Québec's seats in the House of Common has, however, declined over the years as Québec's share of the Canadian population has fallen. Québec currently accounts for slightly more than 24 per cent of the House total, while it was close to 28 per cent in 1949 when Newfoundland and Labrador joined the federation. The failed Charlottetown Accord of 1992 contained a clause guaranteeing Québec a minimum of 25 per cent of the seats in the House of Commons in order to compensate for its declining proportion of the Canadian population.

The Head of State of Canada is the British monarch, whose representative in Canada is the Governor General, appointed by the Queen on the instruction of the Prime Minister. The convention has been to alternate between a Francophone and an Anglophone Governor General. Politicians from Québec have held the role of Prime Minister for much of Canadian history. Québécois led the government with almost no interruption between 1968 and 2006, the sole exception being the very short tenures of Joe Clark in 1979–80, John Turner in 1984 and Kim Campbell in 1993. By convention, the federal cabinet includes representatives of the different regions of Canada, including Québec. Also by convention, any national party leader must be able to communicate in both national languages.

The Canadian Senate is structured along regional, rather than provincial lines. Equal numbers of senators come from the Atlantic provinces, Ontario, Québec and the west. They are appointed until age seventy-five by the national government; provinces have no formal role. Thus the Senate functions primarily as a patronage body for the federal government, and does not provide effective representation either for provincial governments, or their populations. As a result, unlike second chambers in other federations such as Germany, it is unable to play a bridging role between federal and provincial governments, or to provide effective representation of minority regions within the national

[71] Joseph Fletcher and Paul Howe, 'Public opinion and the courts,' *Choices*, 6, no. 3 (May 2000).

government.[72] Canadians have debated many proposals for 'Senate reform', but these have been much more oriented to the interests of smaller provinces and to those in the west which have felt excluded from power in Ottawa, than they have been to Québec.

The current federal government has introduced legislation that would limit Senators' terms to a non-renewable nine years; and would include provincial elections of Senators, who would still be formally appointed by the Prime Minister. Several provinces are opposed to the idea, and it remains unclear whether the proposals could survive a constitutional test in the Supreme Court.

The methods of autonomy

Intergovernmental relations and dispute resolution

In order to manage the interdependence of governments at national and provincial levels, a complex network of intergovernmental institutions – federal-provincial and interprovincial First Ministers' Conferences and Meetings, ministerial councils and conferences and meetings of federal and provincial officials – has been established. But this machinery is only weakly institutionalised. It does not appear in the constitution, and has no legislative basis, little bureaucratic support, few rules and procedures and cannot make binding decisions. It is an 'add-on' to the basic federal structure, rather than an integral part of it.[73]

The combination of federalism and Westminster-style parliamentary government, with a strong executive, has led to the predominance of 'executive federalism' or 'federal-provincial diplomacy' in Canada, limiting the participation of the legislatures or civil society in intergovernmental relations.

Relations among provinces and territories, bypassing the federal government, have grown in importance. Annual Premiers' Conferences were initiated by Québec in the 1960s, and have recently been further institutionalised in the Council of the Federation (2003). The main objective of the Council is to promote interprovincial co-operation on issues of common concern, and to co-ordinate strategy in relations with Ottawa. It has a small secretariat in Ottawa.

The Québec government has played an important role in intergovernmental relations, most often by leading coalitions in favour of greater fiscal transfers to the provinces or opposing federal intrusion into provincial jurisdiction. Despite playing a key role in asserting the rights of the provinces, however, Québec has from time to time been 'opted-out' of federal-provincial agreements, especially respecting social policy, on the grounds that such agreements violate the division of powers outlined in the Constitution and legitimise the spending power of

[72] See Donald Smiley and Ronald Watts, *Intrastate Federalism in Canada* (University of Toronto Press, 1985).

[73] See Richard Simeon, *Federal-Provincial Diplomacy* (University of Toronto Press, 1971, 1973, re-issued 2006).

the federal government, which the Québec government has always challenged. This has added a further dimension of asymmetry to Canadian federalism.

Asymmetrical arrangements

One of the most contentious methods used to ensure the autonomy of Québec in the Canadian federation has been asymmetrical federal arrangements, in which the constituent units of the federation are treated differently, to reflect their distinct character and priorities. In Canada, there are both de jure asymmetrical features, entrenched in constitutional law, and de facto features reflected in practice.[74]

The Canadian Constitution contains numerous clauses containing asymmetrical elements, some, but not all, related to Québec's distinctiveness.[75] The use of French and English is guaranteed in the provincial legislatures of Québec, New Brunswick and Manitoba, but not in those of other provinces.[76] With respect to education, Section 93(2) guarantees denominational education for Protestants and Catholics in Ontario and in Québec,[77] and Section 59 of the Constitution Act, 1982 allows Québec to restrict access to English schools to the children of parents who have received their elementary education in English in Canada for as long as it deems necessary in order to protect the French language.[78] Nonetheless, recent attempts to introduce more asymmetrical elements into the Canadian Constitution (such as recognising Québec as a 'distinct society' within Canada) have been rejected as the concept of 'equality of provinces' has gained ground among politicians and public opinion outside Québec. De facto asymmetry is widely accepted; formal asymmetry opposed.[79]

This was certainly the case in the 1960s during the leadership of Lester B. Pearson, a Prime Minister especially sensitive to Québec's demands.[80] Québec was permitted to opt out of certain national social programmes allowing it to go its own way in areas such as hospital insurance, welfare and education, with

[74] Douglas Brown, 'Who's afraid of asymmetrical federalism? A summary discussion', *Asymmetry Series* 17 (Institute of Intergovernmental Relations, Queen's University, 2005), 2. Available at www.iigr.ca.

[75] For an elaborate discussion and defence of asymmetrical constitutional arrangements in Canada, see Jeremy Webber, *Reimagining Canada: Language, Culture, Community and the Canadian Constitution* (Montreal-Kingston: McGill-Queen's University Press, 1994), 229–59.

[76] Constitution Act, 1867, s. 133; Constitution Act, 1982, ss. 16–22; Manitoba Act, s. 23.

[77] However, following Constitutional Amendment, 1997 (Québec), s. 93(a) now states that paragraphs (1) to (4) of s. 93 do not apply to Québec.

[78] Québec's language law makes it compulsory for French-speaking Québécois and the children of immigrants to attend French schools. Québec, Charter of the French language, S. Q. 1977, c. 5.

[79] For a full list, see David Milne, 'Asymmetry in Canada, past and present', *Asymmetry Series* 17 (Institute of Intergovernmental Relations, Queen's University, 2005). Available at www.iigr.ca. Recent examples include the September 2004, intergovernmental agreement on health care. Government of Québec, 'Asymmetrical federalism that respects Québec's jurisdiction,' press statement, 15 September 2004.

[80] For an analysis of this period, see Simeon, *Federal-Provincial Diplomacy*.

financial compensation.[81] The Québec government was allowed to operate its own student loans and youth allowances programme despite the existence of national programmes, and with financial compensation. Third, in the light of Section 94(a) (1951) of the constitution, which allows any province to operate its own contributory pension plan, Québec was able to establish its own contributory pension system (the Québec Pension Plan), while the federal government operates the Canada Pension Plan for the other nine provinces.[82]

Although Prime Minister Trudeau was hostile to 'special deals' for any province, under his premiership Québec signed an agreement with the federal government regarding immigration, a constitutionally concurrent area of jurisdiction. This agreement, the Cullen-Couture Agreement, allows the Québec government to select half of the immigrants coming to Québec. Again, the model seems to be that there can be widespread asymmetry in practice, but there is a strong reluctance to incorporate the principle into the constitution.

Fiscal federalism

After Switzerland, it is often said, Canada is the most decentralised federation in the world. This is especially the case with regard to fiscal matters. The federal share of total government spending is 37 per cent – compared with 61 per cent in the United States, 53 per cent in Australia, and 41 per cent in Germany.[83] Each level of government has a high degree of autonomy in raising and spending revenues. Each is constitutionally entitled to occupy all major tax fields.[84] Each is free to borrow on domestic and international markets. There are considerable financial transfers between federal and provincial governments, but these are remarkable for their largely unconditional nature, especially when compared with other federations, such as the United States, Germany and Australia.

The largest single transfer is for 'equalisation', designed, as s.36 of the Constitution Act, 1982, puts it, to ensure through unconditional federal payments that all provinces have the ability to provide 'comparable' levels of public service at 'comparable' levels of taxation.[85] Other transfers for health, post-secondary education and other matters have only very broad and general conditions attached. Transfers from Ottawa to the provinces represent only 13 per cent of provincial spending (though this varies considerably between richer and poorer provinces), compared with 31 per cent in the United States, and 41 per cent in

81 Canada, Established Programs (Interim Arrangements) Act, 1964.

82 In practice, the two plans are closely co-ordinated.

83 Data reported in George Anderson, 'Canadian fiscal federalism and fiscal pressures,' Presentation at the Conference Recovering Together? Fiscal Pressures, Federalism and Social Policy, Queen's University School of Policy Studies, Kingston, 17 August, 2010.

84 With the exception of 'indirect taxes' for the provinces.

85 Equalisation payments, of which Québec is the largest single recipient, primarily by virtue of its large population compared with other poorer provinces, have no conditions attached.

Australia.[86] Thus, since the high water mark of federal fiscal dominance in the 1950s, the trend – often led by Québec – has been towards fiscal decentralisation, both in terms of provincial revenues and spending, and in terms of fewer and weaker 'conditions' linked to the federal transfers that remain.

Nonetheless, there has been an important debate in Canada over the last decade about an alleged 'fiscal imbalance' in Canadian fiscal federalism. Again, the debate was initiated by Québec.[87] The debate suggests a fundamental mismatch between the policy responsibilities assigned to provinces (which include most of the growing areas of public expenditure) and the resources that are available to them. The alleged mismatch has two dimensions: the 'vertical' imbalance suggesting that the central government has revenues that exceed its needs, thus producing large surpluses, and providing an incentive to spend in areas of provincial jurisdiction, while the provinces collectively are running fiscal deficits. Ottawa has said this is illusory; there are no constitutional barriers to provinces raising their taxes to meet their needs. Two sets of solutions have been proposed: shifting additional taxing powers to the provinces (as happened in the 1960s and 1970s), or increasing federal transfers to the provinces in areas such as post-secondary education. The recent recession reduced the intensity of the debate, since now both orders of government face major fiscal problems.

The 'horizontal' fiscal imbalance refers to the economic disparities among Canadian provinces. The Canadian solution to this has been 'equalisation'. The principle is clear, and fundamental to the idea of Canada as a 'sharing community'. The concept has deep support in all sections of the Canadian community. But it has recently come under considerable strain. Partly this is because one province, energy-rich Alberta, has per capita revenues that now greatly exceed those of any other province. To 'equalise' provincial revenues to the level of Alberta (the ten-province standard) and to take full account of energy revenues would, as the program is designed, massively increase federal spending, much of it funded by Ontario taxpayers, who do not themselves benefit from resource revenues.[88] As economic activity has shifted to the resource rich west, Ontario and Québec, the seat of the Canadian manufacturing industry, are in relative decline. Ontario is now a recipient of equalisation payments.

While fiscal federalism is not a constitutional issue, it has become a central concern of the politics of Canadian federalism. Fundamental issues of public

86 See Simeon and Papillon, 'Canada', 103–6.

87 Québec, Commission sur le déséquilibre fiscal, *Pour un nouveau partage des moyens financiers au Canada. Rapport final* [Toward a New Division of Finances in Canada – Final Report], March 2002, at www.desequilibrefiscal.gouv.qc.ca. For the federal response, see Government of Canada, Department of Finance, 'The Fiscal Balance in Canada', October 2004, at www.fin.ca/facts/fbcfacts9_e.html (accessed 13 March, 2013).

88 Two reports, reaching slightly different conclusions, make recommendations for reform of equalisation. Finance Canada, Expert Panel on Equalisation and Territorial Formula Financing, *Achieving a National Purpose: Putting Equalisation Back on Track* (Ottawa: 2006), at www.eqtff-pfft.ca. Council of the Federation, Advisory Panel on Fiscal Imbalance, *Reconciling the Irreconcilable: Addressing Canada's Fiscal Imbalance*, (Ottawa, 2006).

policy – childcare, health care, the environment, global warming – become subordinated to wrangling over funding.

Language rights

Québécois have an acute sense of their status as a linguistic minority, not only in Canada, but also in the larger North American environment. Concern for the survival and the promotion of the French language has been a preoccupation of all Québec governments.

Québécois have wanted to make sure that French would remain the dominant language in Québec and that French-speakers outside Québec could use their language, especially in primary and secondary educational institutions. This concern was heightened by attempts by provinces such as Ontario and Manitoba at different points in their history to abolish French education, as well as by the difficulty of French-speaking Canadians to obtain federal government services in their language and the obstacles they faced in integrating into the federal bureaucracy. The federal government responded to growing discontent among Francophones in the 1960s with legislation to guarantee bilingual federal services throughout Canada and by entrenching the educational rights of French-speaking minorities outside Québec. The Québec government, on the other hand, adopted its own legislation to promote the French language that would later become a model for laws adopted by governments in Catalonia and Latvia.

The Federal 1969 Official Languages Act[89] established French and English as the official languages of Canada. It established in law the rights of public servants to use French or English in federal institutions and in crown corporations and of citizens to be served by the federal government in the language of their choice in the national capital. It also created the office of the Commissioner of Official Languages to ensure compliance with the Act, to investigate public complaints and to report annually to Parliament on the state of bilingualism in Canada.

The Constitution Act, 1982 entrenched a series of language rights in Sections 16 to 23. Besides reaffirming Canada's bilingual status (Section 16(1)), the Act also constitutionalised the right of citizens to receive services from the federal government in the language of their choice (other than English and French), when there is a sufficient demand, and made New Brunswick officially a bilingual province. For members of the French-speaking minority outside Québec (and for the English-speaking minority in Québec), the most important aspect of the Act was Section 23 on Minority Language Educational Rights. It gave these groups the right to have their children receive primary and secondary education in their own language and in a minority language educational facility, where numbers warrant.

[89] Official Languages Act, RSC 1970, c. O-2.

The 1988 Official Languages Act[90] added a requirement that the federal government provide services in both official languages not only in Ottawa, but anywhere there is a significant demand. It committed the federal government to providing equal employment opportunities for both French- and English-speaking Canadians in federal institutions and to setting policies to encourage the development of official minority language communities across Canada. Despite these efforts, powerful demographic forces perpetuate the declining role of Francophones outside Québec, except for in New Brunswick and a few parts of Ontario.[91]

While the objective of the Official Languages Act was to make Canada a bilingual country, at least institutionally, Québec's main language law, Bill 101, adopted in 1977 and also known as *la Charte de la langue française* (Charter for the French Language), aimed at ensuring the predominance of the French language in all aspects of Québec's political, economic and cultural life. The central component of the law was to make French-medium primary and secondary school compulsory for all children in Québec, except for those whose parents had received their education in English in Québec (later changed for Canada after a decision of the Supreme Court of Canada).[92] As a result, the children of immigrants, who in the past had overwhelmingly attended English schools (their parents wishing to assimilate to the dominant North American and Canadian linguistic majority), now had to attend Francophone schools. The law also banned any other language than French on commercial and public signs. This element of the law was struck down by the Court, and was replaced eventually by legislation requiring the *predominance* of French on all commercial signs.[93] Finally, in order to redress the discrimination that Francophones had historically experienced in the workplace, the law made it compulsory for employers, especially those working for corporations, to communicate with their employees in French.

In many ways, both the provincial and the federal legislation have been successful. The federal government is no longer perceived as an 'English' institution. Francophones are now fully represented in the senior levels of the public service; Anglophones who aspire to such positions must demonstrate bilingual capacity. Education in French is now generally available across the country, as is French language television and radio. The federal public service is generally able to provide services in French throughout the country. This is a major success, but it is under considerable strain. Native French-speakers constitute a small and rapidly declining proportion of the population outside Québec (except in New Brunswick). They are greatly outnumbered by recent immigrants speaking Chinese, Urdu and other languages. Where once parents told their children

90 Official Languages Act, R.S.C. 1985, c. 31 (4th Supp.).

91 See Graham Fraser, *Sorry, I don't Speak French: Confronting the Canadian Crisis that Won't Go Away* (Toronto: McClelland and Stewart, 2006).

92 A. G. (Que.) v. Québec Protestant School Boards [1984] 2 S.C.R. 66.

93 Devine v. Québec [1988] 2 S.C.R 790; and Ford v. Québec [1988] 2 S.C.R. 712.

that to be successful in Canada, they must be bilingual, today, many would say: yes, but in Chinese or Spanish.

In Québec, language policy in the schools has significantly increased the adaptation of immigrant groups to the French language, and in many cases to identification with the nation of Québec. But this is by no means complete; recent studies suggest that the economic and cultural pull of Anglophone North America remains a powerful attraction to immigrants in Québec, as well as elsewhere in Canada.

The autonomy of Québec's minorities

A critical issue when territorially concentrated minorities seek to enhance their political and cultural autonomy is how to treat what Alan Cairns has called the 'minorities within the minorities'. In Québec, this refers to English speakers within the province, to recent immigrants and to the Aboriginal peoples, which together constitute close to 18 per cent of the population.[94]

Diversity has become a growing reality for modern Québec, and its management has become a significant challenge for Québec governments. The government of Québec has a long track record of financing public schools for the English-speaking minority (until a recent change, defined in terms of religion, Catholic and Protestant, rather than on the basis of language). The English-speaking minority is well represented both in the National Assembly and in the cabinet of the current Liberal government.

Notwithstanding occasional tensions, often caused by the linguistic insecurity of the French-speaking population, the present situation in Québec can be described as one of relative linguistic peace. Anglophones, once the dominant elite of Québec, are today overwhelmingly bilingual.

Despite the recognition in 1985 by the government of René Lévesque of the existence in Québec of eleven Aboriginal nations, tensions between the government and these groups has often run very high. Yet relations have significantly improved over the last decade, especially following the adoption of what is referred to as '*La Paix des Braves*' (Peace of the Braves).[95] This 'nation to nation' agreement between the Québec government and the Cree Nation, one of the most important Aboriginal communities in the province, marked a new beginning in which the Québec government agreed to consult the community before starting any new hydro-electric projects on their territory, while ensuring that they benefit from the economic development of their region.

More broadly, Québec leaders have worked intensively to define their nationalism as a 'civic' nationalism rooted in a multicultural French-speaking Québec,

94 See the website of Québec's Office de la Langue Française for the most recent data, at www.oqlf.gouv.qc.ca (accessed 13 March 2013).

95 An Act to ensure the implementation of the Agreement Concerning a New Relationship Between le Gouvernement du Québec and the Crees of Québec (2002, c. 25; after consolidation: R.S.Q., c. M-35.1.2).

rather than as an 'ethnic' nationalism, open only to descendants of the original '*pure laine*' settlers from the French colony. In this they have been largely successful. It is true that 'Allophone'[96] Québécois tend to be federalists rather than supporters of sovereignty. But it is also true that Québec is itself a society as multi-culturally diverse as other cosmopolitan provinces such as Ontario and British Columbia. There is, for example, no 'nativist' anti-immigrant political movement in Québec equivalent to groups like the National Front in France.

Conclusion

Federal institutions have had a deep influence on conflict and its management in Canada. Language and regional differences ensured that the Canadian polity would be federal; but federalism, in turn has influenced the ways in which these divisions are structured and articulated, the nature of the discourse that surrounds them, the arenas and sites where they are played out and the solutions that are explored.

In many ways federal institutions have proved effective in managing the divisions. In Canada's highly decentralised model, Québec governments have had broad scope to engage in a successful nation-building project. It has also permitted a considerable degree of asymmetry – a separate Québec system of civil law, a separate provincial income tax system, a greater voice than other provinces in the concurrent area of immigration policy and separate Québec and Canadian pension plans. Ironically, perhaps federalism has also provided the institutional resources that make a final step towards sovereignty if not likely, at least plausible. Some politicians and analysts, such as Canada's former minister of intergovernmental affairs, Stéphane Dion, have argued that Québec may have the most powerful sub-national government in the world, though this is not an easy proposition to prove.

But there is another side to the balance sheet. In successive rounds of constitutional discussion, Québec's search for constitutional recognition as a distinct society within the federation and for a special status that would recognise the Québec government as having a special role within Canada as the primary government of the Francophone community, or nation, has been rejected. Recognition of Canadian duality in the constitution has been trumped by the ideas of the equality of the provinces, national bilingualism and Canada as a site of multiple diversities, of which Québec is only one. The declining proportion of French-speakers in the Canadian population, along with the changing demographic makeup of Canada outside Québec suggests that this is unlikely to change. Moreover, the failures of the Meech Lake and Charlottetown Accords demonstrate that constitutional amendment has become extraordinarily difficult in Canada; the dream of formally constitutionalising Québec's distinct

[96] This term refers to people whose first language is neither of the two official Canadian languages.

status remains remote. Hence the impasse, and the polarised choice between opting for the status quo or for sovereignty.

More generally, Québec nationalists have argued that the federal regime is a 'strait-jacket', limiting Québec's autonomy and leaving it subject to continuing federal intrusions into provincial jurisdiction. But on the other hand, it can be argued that Canadian federalism has provided the political and jurisdictional space for a highly successful Québec nation-building project. In arts and culture, in business and in public policy, it has allowed Québec to pursue distinctive paths. It has permitted Québec to define itself as a French-speaking, but non-ethnic, society; the Secession Reference has written into the constitution a right to secede under certain circumstances.

But the debate persists. For sovereignists, the old Westphalian model of one nation, one state remains the Holy Grail; they look forward to yet another referendum in which Québécois will make this choice. Others look forward to a post-modern Canada, in which 'state' and 'nation' are no longer synonymous; and in which different images of Canada – as a bi-national society, as a regionally diverse society, as a multi-cultural society and as a society that must reconcile the rights of its 'First Nations' – must continue to co-exist, not so much because of shared values (though there are many), but more because they share the same fate, as interdependent societies, bound together by their co-existence in the northern half of the North American continent.

2

Prosperity and happiness through autonomy

The self-government of the Åland Islands in Finland

Markku Suksi

The Åland Islands, situated in the Baltic Sea between mainland Finland and Sweden and inhabited by 28,000 mainly Swedish-speaking people, are often referred to as the oldest existing autonomy arrangement in the world. When the Åland autonomy was created in 1920 in the midst of the dispute between Finland and Sweden concerning the sovereignty over Åland, Finland had already expressed its intention in 1919 to secure for the inhabitants of Åland the possibility of arranging their existence as freely as is possible for a territory which does not constitute a state.[1] In 1921, the League of Nations decided the territorial dispute between Finland and Sweden over the Åland Islands in favour of Finland on condition that guarantees for the Islanders' prosperity and happiness would be established in an Autonomy Act. The autonomy of Åland was instituted more than ninety years ago, and today, the region is both prosperous and reasonably happy, but it has lost some of its powers after Finland's 1995 accession to the European Union. Therefore, the governmental institutions of the Åland Islands are seeking an enlargement of their legislative competences.

As early as August 1917, several months before Finland became independent from Russia, an unofficial assembly of the inhabitants of Åland proposed that the area secede from Finland and join Sweden. Soon after the Finnish Declaration of Independence, a petition campaign was launched in December 1917 to support the wish of the Åland inhabitants to secede. A majority of those with the right to vote was thus in favour of union with Sweden.[2] Soon thereafter, a dispute about the Islands arose between Finland and Sweden. Although Sweden was

[1] Government Bill 73/1919 concerning the Act on the Self-Government of the Åland Islands, 2.

[2] Y. de Geer-Hancock, *Åländskhet. Nationsbygge på fredens öar* [Being an Åland Islander. Nation-Building on the Islands of Peace] (Mariehamn: Ålands Tidnings-Tryckeri Abs förlag, 1986), 32–5; T. Modeen, *De folkrättsliga garantierna för bevarandet av Ålandsöarnas nationella karaktär* [The Guarantees in International Law for the Maintenance of the National Characteristics of the Åland Islands] (Åbo: Åbo Akademi, 1973), 14–16. For more sources and cases, see M. Suksi, *Ålands konstitution – en sammanställning av material och tolkningar i anslutning till självstyrelselag för Åland* [The Constitution of Åland – a Compilation of Materials and Interpretations in Relation to the Self-Government Act of the Åland Islands] (Åbo: Åbo Akademis Förlag, 2005) and M. Suksi, *Sub-state Governance Through Territorial Autonomy* (Berlin, Heidelberg: Springer-Verlag, 2011).

not a party to the 1856 treaty establishing the Åland Islands as a demilitarised area (see later), it brought the matter before the Paris Peace Conference in 1919 in the hope that a resolution similar to that of Denmark regarding Schleswig would be found, where a referendum resolved the border issue. This plan did not succeed, mainly because Finland and Sweden were not warring parties in World War I, although it was supported by another petition campaign in Åland, which was completed on 29 June 1919. In 1920, the League of Nations took the matter up following a proposal by Great Britain, which was a party to the 1856 treaty.

At this point, the Act on the Self-Government of the Åland Islands (hereinafter: the Autonomy Act)[3] was enacted by the Parliament of Finland, probably as a pre-emptive measure, although it had been initiated already in the fall of 1919. The governmental committee that prepared the Autonomy Act was originally commissioned with the task of developing a scheme of regional devolution or decentralisation for the whole country, but its work resulted only in a self-government act for one specific part of the country, because the particular regulation concerning the Åland Islands diminished the need for territorial solutions for the Swedish-speakers in mainland Finland. The committee made a comparative analysis of a number of cases of territorial self-government with law-making powers but concluded that none of these models was really suitable as a point of departure for the self-government of the Åland Islands.[4]

With the Autonomy Act of 1920, the province of Åland gained its own Legislative Assembly with general competence in fields that were not included in the enumeration of exclusive legislative powers of the Finnish Parliament. This meant that Åland then possessed residual powers, while the state (or the mainland) was vested with enumerated powers (with later Autonomy Acts, Åland's residual powers were changed to enumerated powers). The reason for the change was that state competence in the area of matters regulated through international treaties, on the one hand, and state competence concerning new matters that did not exist in 1920, on the other, pre-empted Ålandic legislative competence and led to 'leakage' of competence from Åland to Finland. However, because the Åland inhabitants felt that the autonomy legislation had been imposed upon them, the Assembly did not convene until 1922.[5]

Specific guarantees

When the matter came up in the League of Nations, Sweden requested that the future of the Åland be decided by their inhabitants through a plebiscite.[6]

3 Statutes of Finland (henceforth SoF) 124/1920.

4 See the report of the so-called Tulenheimo Committee, kommittébetänkande 24/1919, 19.

5 The Åland political leaders who had advocated secession were charged with treason, but on the basis of a special Act of Parliament (SoF 310/1921), the charges were dropped.

6 Modeen, *De folkrättsliga garantierna för bevarandet av Ålandsöarnas nationella karaktär*, 14, 16, 26.

Although plebiscites were fashionable in resolving such questions after World War I, no popular vote was ever organised. After a Commission of Jurists concluded that the League had jurisdiction over the Åland Islands issue, a Commission of Rapporteurs investigated the facts of the case and proposed the solution that Åland should remain under the sovereignty of Finland.

The negotiation process did not actually involve the local population or their representatives to a significant extent (although the Committee of Rapporteurs visited the Åland Islands and the Council of the League of Nations heard the representatives of the Åland Islanders).[7] The main negotiations were conducted between the representatives of Finland, Sweden and the Council of the League of Nations. The option of secession was quickly ruled out by the League, although the Commission of Jurists had concluded that the

> principle recognising the rights of peoples to determine their political fate may be applied in various ways; the most important of these are, on the one hand the formation of an independent State, and on the other hand the right of choice between two existing States.

The principle of self-determination, it said, must 'be brought into line with that of the protection of minorities; both have a common object – to assure to some national Group the maintenance and free development of its social, ethnical or religious characteristics'. The Commission suggested that there could be a middle ground between the formation of a new and independent state and choosing between two existing states: 'Under such circumstances, a solution in the nature of a compromise, based on an extensive grant of liberty to minorities, may appear necessary according to international legal conception and may even be dictated by the interests of peace'.[8]

Considering the historical background and Finland's transformation after 1917, the Commission concluded that the 'fact that Finland was eventually reconstituted as an independent State is not sufficient to efface the conditions which gave rise to the aspirations of the Aaland Islanders and to cause these conditions to be regarded as if they had never arisen'.[9] It was therefore necessary to take into consideration the factual situation on the Islands, such as the fairly homogeneous nature of the inhabitants; the geographical location of the Islands; the racial, linguistic and traditional links between the Islands and Sweden; and the forcible separation of the Islands from Sweden in 1808–9. Accordingly, the Commission concluded that, under public international law, the Åland Islands question should not be left entirely to the domestic jurisdiction of Finland, and that the Council of the League of Nations was competent, on the basis of

[7] J. Barros, *The Aland Islands Question: Its Settlement by the League of Nations* (New Haven and London: Yale University Press, 1968), 276, 310, 324, 328–9.

[8] *Official Journal of the League of Nations*, Special Supplement No. 3, October 1920, 6.

[9] Ibid., 12.

paragraph 4 of Article 15 of the Covenant of the League of Nations, to make any recommendations that it deemed just and proper in the case.[10]

The League of Nations' Commission of Rapporteurs on the Åland Islands question concluded that the

> right of sovereignty of the Finnish State over the Aaland Islands is [. . .] incontestable and their present legal status is that they form part of Finland. To detach the Aaland Islands from Finland would therefore be an alteration of its status, in depriving this country of a part of that which belongs to it.[11]

The Commission stated that a linguistic or religious minority or 'any fraction of a population' does not per se have the right to secede, as it would 'destroy the order and stability within the state' and 'inaugurate anarchy in international life'. It would also 'uphold a theory incompatible with the very idea of a state as a territorial and political unity'.[12] The Commission formulated what has become the established position:

> separation of a minority from the State of which it forms a part and its incorporation in another State can only be considered as an altogether exceptional solution, a last resort when the State lacks either the will or the power to enact and apply just and effective guarantees.[13]

Because the Commission of Rapporteurs could not find evidence of any gross violations of the rights of the Åland Islanders and because the application of the Wilsonian principle of self-determination for deciding on the national affiliation of a population group was not a rule of positive public international law, the Commission did not find any immediate reason to recommend either secession or a referendum on the issue in the Åland Islands. Instead of a transitional arrangement for about five years, which would ease tension, and then a referendum, the Commission, supported by Finland and the Åland Islanders,[14] recommended a comprehensive solution, based on the conditional maintenance of the sovereignty of Finland. If Finland acted against the expectations of the Commission and refused to grant the guarantees recommended, it proposed an outcome it clearly considered undesirable:

> The interest of the Aalanders, the interests of a durable peace in the Baltic, would then force us to advise the separation of the islands from Finland, based on the wishes of the inhabitants which would be freely expressed by means of a plebiscite.[15]

The Åland Islands question was ultimately resolved along the lines recommended by the Commission of Rapporteurs. Finland and Sweden agreed to the terms of the settlement, prior to discussion in the Council, which endorsed the

[10] Ibid., 14.

[11] *The Aaland Islands Question*, Report submitted to the Council of the League of Nations by the Commission of Rapporteurs, Document du Conseil B7, 21/68/106, of 16 April 1921, 25.

[12] Ibid., 28. [13] Ibid., 28. [14] Ibid., 32. [15] Ibid., 34.

principles of the Settlement on 24 June 1921.[16] The Åland Islands Settlement, agreed to by the two parties on 27 June 1921, confirmed the then existing autonomy of Åland as a self-governing territory with its own law-making powers in Finland and supplemented the arrangement with some additional guarantees. Thus the autonomy of Åland received international recognition and guarantee, albeit not in the form of a formal treaty under public international law. After the transformation of the Åland Islands Settlement into domestic law in the Guaranty Act of 1922, which was more or less an exact translation of the Settlement, the inhabitants of Åland were persuaded to begin using the institutional structures established by the Autonomy Act of 1920, aimed at the preservation of the Swedish character of Åland. The final arrangements for autonomy added other rights. These material rights now are the right to participation in regional and municipal elections, including eligibility for office,[17] the right to acquire real estate in the manner provided for under the Land Acquisition Act[18] and the right of trade,[19] as well as exemption from the general duty to perform military service.[20]

[16] Decision by the Council of the League of Nations, 24 June, 1921, 7 League of Nations O.J., 697–702 (1921). See also Barros, *The Aland Islands Question*.

[17] According to Section 67 of the Autonomy Act, an act enacted by a two-thirds majority in the Legislative Assembly may stipulate that a citizen of Finland without the right of domicile and citizens of Iceland, Norway, Sweden and Denmark shall be granted suffrage and be eligible for office in municipal elections provided they meet certain requirements and that the same rights may be given to citizens of other states. The latter part of the Section is a reaction to the exception that remained unrealised in the Accession Treaty and to Article 8b of the Treaty on the European Union, which grants these rights to citizens of member states in respect of municipal elections in any member state, albeit on the basis of a Council Directive, which may contain derogations that follow from 'problems specific to a Member State'. See Council Directive 94/80/EC of 19 December 1994. In an Explanatory Memorandum to a Proposal for a Council Directive (COM(95) 499 Final/11.01.1996) amending the previously mentioned Council Directive on municipal elections, the European Commission points out that '(s)ince a period of residence, irrespective of nationality, is required of all those that do not have the right of domicile it can be concluded that there is no discriminatory treatment incompatible with article 8b (1) of the EC Treaty, between Finnish citizens and other EU nationals as regards to the right to vote and to stand in municipal elections. No specific conditions are therefore necessary to apply article 8b (1) to the Åland islands'. In 1997, such an Act, the Ålandic Act on the right to vote and the right to stand as candidates in municipal elections for persons who lack the right of domicile (Statutes of Åland [SoÅ] 63/1997), was passed. The Act first required a residency of three years, later lowered to one year. Through the Act, the Åland Islanders themselves have chosen to open up one central element in the Åland Islands Settlement of 1921. Note that the elections to the Legislative Assembly are not covered by provisions of the EU Treaties.

[18] SoF 3/1975. It is likely that the idea for an exclusive property regime stems from among the Swedish-speakers in mainland Finland after 1917, when such a regime was contemplated for the coastal regions. See G. von Bonsdorff, *Självstyrelsetanken i finlandssvensk politik åren 1917–1923* [The Idea of Self-Government in the Politics of Finland-Swedes during 1917–1923] (Helsingfors: Finska Vetenskaps-Societeten, 1950), 41–6.

[19] Under Section 11 of the Autonomy Act, the right of trade is not exclusively tied to the right of domicile, but is dependent on an act of Åland, which, however, shall not limit the right of trade of a person residing in Åland, if no staff except his spouse and minor children are employed in the trade and if the trade is not practiced in business premises, an office or another special place of business.

[20] See generally Modeen, *De folkrättsliga garantierna för bevarandet av Ålandsöarnas nationella karaktär*, 25–40.

Although the Åland Islands Settlement is *not* a formal treaty under public international law, Finland enacted the Act containing Certain Provisions concerning the Inhabitants of the Åland Islands, the so-called Guaranty Act, in 1922.[21] This Act, amending and adding to the Autonomy Act of 1920, was enacted in the manner prescribed for constitutional amendments. It made the appointment of the Governor of Åland by the President dependent on the assent of the Chairman of the Legislative Assembly[22] and stipulated that the Legislative Assembly and the Ålandic municipalities were not obliged to maintain or support schools other than those in which Swedish was the language of instruction (thus excluding the teaching of Finnish in state or municipal schools without the consent of the municipality).[23]

The Guaranty Act specifies that a citizen of Finland who moves to the Åland Islands acquires the municipal and regional right to vote only after he or she has been legally resident there for five years.[24] Finally, if a piece of real property had been sold to somebody whose legal residence was not in the Åland Islands, the Åland Government, the municipality within which the property was situated or a private person legally resident in the Åland Islands has the right to redeem the piece of property at a fair price.[25] None of these laws created a right of domicile that was limited to the inhabitants of Åland, but the regulations concerning the right to vote contained the roots of such a concept.

The League of Nations Settlement gave the rights granted under this autonomy arrangement a collective character. Under the Guaranty Act the Legislative Assembly of the Åland Islands could submit complaints to the Finnish Government about the implementation of the Autonomy Act and the Guaranty Act for presentation to the Council of the League of Nations.[26] If the matter were judicial, the Council could obtain an opinion from the Permanent Court of International Justice. Although the procedure lapsed with the collapse of the League of Nations system, it was not eliminated from Finnish legislation until 1951, when the new Autonomy Act repealed the 1920 and 1922 Acts.[27]

Relevant international and regional law

Prior to the Åland Islands Settlement, a treaty on security issues existed for more or less the same geographical area. The 1856 Convention on the Demilitarisation of the Åland Islands was concluded between Russia, Great Britain and

21 SoF 189/1922. 22 Section 1. 23 Section 2.
24 Section 3. 25 Section 5. 26 Section 6.
27 There were plans, recorded in committee proceedings and in a government proposal to the Parliament in 1946, to establish a similar procedure under the United Nations. However, the Soviet Union was opposed to such arrangements, and thus the 1951 Autonomy Act made no reference to international guarantees. On this, see Modeen, *De folkrättsliga garantierna för bevarandet av Ålandsöarnas nationella karaktär*, 61–76; L. Hannikainen, *Ahvenanmaan itsehallinnon ja ruotsinkielisyyden kansainoikeudelliset perusteet* [The Basis in International Law of the Self-Government and of the Status of the Swedish Language of the Åland Islands] (Turku: Åbo Akademin Ihmisoikeusinstituutti, 1993), 41–8.

France and annexed to the 1856 Peace Treaty of Paris after the Crimean war.[28] When the Council of the League of Nations dealt with the Åland Islands issue, it recommended that the conflict be resolved on two tracks, first, the autonomy and special rights of the inhabitants and second, the continued demilitarisation of the area. For the latter, a conference of states, in 1921, replaced the 1856 Convention by the 1921 Convention concerning the Non-fortification and Neutralisation of the Åland Islands to which Finland (but, of course, not the Åland Islands) was a party.[29] Russia (or the Soviet Union) was not party to this Convention, and in the aftermath of the so-called Winter War of 1939–1940 between Finland and the Soviet Union, the 1940 Treaty between Finland and Soviet Union concerning the Åland Islands was concluded, confirmed in another treaty after World War II.[30] Under this bilateral treaty, Finland was to demilitarise the Islands.

As these treaties demonstrate, the Åland Islands have been at the centre of security concerns in the Baltic Sea area. However, the Commission of Rapporteurs was clear that issues of autonomy and security should be kept separate, concluding that '[t]he question of sovereignty does not need to be intermingled with that of disarmament and neutralisation'.[31] Nonetheless, some have argued that the two different regimes for the Åland Islands, the autonomy arrangement, on the one hand, and the demilitarisation and neutralisation, on the other, form one package.[32]

The Åland autonomy arrangement is now regarded as customary international law in the relationship between Finland and Sweden, with obligations undertaken by Finland and with a potential (albeit not manifested) Swedish interest in implementation.[33] For instance, during the negotiations for the Finnish accession to the European Union (EU), the exclusive rights of Islanders to vote and stand as a candidate, acquire real estate and trade (involving the freedoms of establishment and services) were preserved, despite Finnish membership, and recognised in Protocol No. 2 of the Finnish accession treaty and

[28] See M. Björkholm and A. Rosas, *Ålandsöarnas demilitarisering och neutralisering* [The Demilitarisation and Neutralisation of the Åland Islands] (Åbo Academy Press, 1990), 19–25; Modeen, *De folkrättsliga garantierna för bevarandet av Ålandsöarnas nationella karaktär*, 14.

[29] Finnish Treaty Series (henceforth FTS) 1/1922. The states parties to the 1921 Convention are Germany, Denmark, Estonia, Finland, France, Great Britain, Italy, Latvia, Poland and Sweden.

[30] FTS 24/1949. Björkholm and Rosas, *Ålandsöarnas Demilitarisering och Neutralisering*, 22–5.

[31] *The Aaland Islands Question*, 36–7.

[32] N. Fagerlund, *Ålands folkrättsliga status och EG* [The Status of the Åland Islands under Public International Law in Relation to the EC] (Mariehamn: Ålands Högskola, 1993), 112–19.

[33] A. Rosas, 'Mot en partikulär Östersjörätt' [Towards a Particular Law of the Baltic Sea Area], in P. Joenniemi and U. Vesa (eds.), *Säkerhetsutveckling i Östersjöområdet: tendenser, läge, framtidsperspektiv* [The Security Development in the Baltic Sea Region: Tendencies, Status, and Future Perspectives] (Tampere Peace Research Institute, 1988), 142; Hannikainen, *Ahvenanmaan itsehallinnon ja ruotsinkielisyyden kansainoikeudelliset perusteet*, 79–102. The demilitarisation and neutralisation of Åland can be classified as an arrangement based on both treaty law and customary international law, and could be regarded as an 'objective regime' under international law in the Baltic Sea area. See ibid., 103–30.

thereby became a part of the primary law of the European Union (EU) (see later). This was done both because it was considered that the exclusive rights, previously protected under international law, could not be touched and because of political considerations regarding Åland's support for its membership in the EU and its continued viability as a part of the EU.

Without successful EU membership negotiations concerning a protective system for some dimensions of the Åland Islands arrangement, the assent of the Åland Legislative Assembly could not be taken for granted, and the Åland Islands might have remained outside the European Union. Apart from maintaining the rights exclusive to locally domiciled inhabitants, the EU allowed a permanent exemption from EU tax harmonisation legislation for Åland and the ferry traffic passing through the Islands. Although the EU did not accept Finland's proposal to include provision for the Åland Islands' legislative power under the 1991 Autonomy Act to regulate the right to vote and to stand as a candidate in elections to the Legislative Assembly and to municipal councils, this was recognised by other means.[34] In other respects the EU required equal treatment of all EU citizens.

The final arrangement, currently Article 355(4) of the Treaty on the Functioning of the European Union, states that the 'provisions of the Treaties shall apply to the Åland Islands in accordance with the provisions set out in Protocol 2 to the Act concerning the conditions of accession' of, *inter alia*, Finland. One effect of the arrangements is a special tax regime that makes Åland comparable to a third country concerning indirect taxation in relation to Finland and the EU thus drawing a tax boundary between Åland and mainland Finland in the east and Åland and Sweden in the west.

The local foundations of autonomy

Historical and political background

The autonomy of Åland is explained by a number of historical circumstances. Finland and Sweden formed one single kingdom until 1808–9, when Finland was conquered by Russia, leaving a substantial Swedish-speaking population in the coastal areas of southern, western, and southwestern Finland (including Åland). Until the twentieth century, some Swedish-speakers retained a longing for a reunification with Sweden. Finland itself provided a model of autonomy: it had been an autonomous Grand Duchy of the Russian Empire between 1809 and 1917 with its own legal order and constitution, from 1906 on under Article 2 of the 1906 Constitution of Russia.

Finnish independence at the end of 1917 resulted in the separation of Finland from the multi-ethnic Russian Empire and in the creation of Finland as an

[34] In Declaration No. 32 on the Åland Islands of the Final Act on the Accession by the current member states, the Union recalls that, in respect of municipal suffrage and eligibility, Article 8b Treaty on the European Union (TEU) makes it possible to agree with the requests of Finland.

independent state with one dominant linguistic group, the Finnish-speaking population, parts of which aimed at the creation of a nation state with one single language. This development was probably perceived quite negatively on Åland, where the population was predominantly Swedish-speaking, with only a 5 per cent minority of Finnish-speakers. Finland, seeking to establish independence and sovereignty and to become a fully fledged member of the League of Nations, had an interest in being seen to be respectful of a key concern behind the establishment of the League: the rights of minorities. Partly therefore, in the Form of Government (Constitution) Act of 1919, a nation with two equal languages, Finnish and Swedish, was established.

The inhabitants of Åland were at that time hardly viewed as a separate linguistic minority, but as part of the Swedish-speaking population of Finland. Nevertheless, because of its geographically separate position (the area was quite difficult to reach before twentieth century methods of communication were available) the population of the Islands developed the characteristics of a community and displayed distinct political aspirations, but whether the Islanders constituted a separate minority is debatable.[35] Currently they display a strong 'Ålandic' identity in comparison with the Swedish-speaking population in Finland, which in general strongly identifies itself with Finland. Of a total population of 5.3 million in Finland, some 294,000 (5.5 per cent) speak Swedish. The population of Åland amounts to 28,000 inhabitants, of which 25,200 are Swedish-speaking and 1,400 Finnish-speaking. Hence the Åland Islanders make up 0.53 per cent of the total population and 8.6 per cent of the Swedish-speaking population.

Purposes of autonomy: creation of some special rights

The purpose of the Åland Islands Settlement was and is the preservation of the language, culture and the local Swedish traditions in Åland. Hence the purpose of the autonomy is primarily of a linguistic nature. The implication is that the mechanisms created for the protection of the Swedish-speaking character of Åland are aimed at preventing an influx of Finnish-speaking people. It should, however, be emphasised that the establishment in the Ålandic jurisdiction of special rights for those with the right of domicile does not directly affect the freedom of movement of persons between the mainland and Åland or the freedom to take up residence on the Islands.

[35] See for example Hannikainen, *Ahvenanmaan itsehallinnon ja ruotsinkielisyyden kansainoikeudelliset perusteet*, 124–7. and L. Hannikainen, *Cultural, Linguistic and Educational Rights in the Åland Islands – An Analysis in International Law* (Helsinki: Ministry of Foreign Affairs, 1993), 20, which concludes that the Swedish-speaking population of Åland forms a distinct national community which should be considered as qualifying for the status of a national minority or its equivalent in international law, although not all of the common criteria for minority status are fulfilled.

The 1991 Act on the Autonomy of Åland[36] spells out the details of Ålandic autonomy and creates, in line with its predecessor of 1951, an exclusive characteristic in respect of citizenship: only citizens of Finland may have the right of domicile in Åland.[37] The arrangement amounts to a special regional citizenship,[38] possessed by a person who at the time of the entry into force of this Act had the right of domicile according to the 1951 Autonomy Act or by a child under 18 years of age, who is a citizen of Finland and is resident in Åland, provided that the father or the mother of the child has the right of domicile. However, the right of domicile may be granted upon application to a citizen of Finland who has moved to the Åland Islands,[39] and who has, without interruption, been habitually resident in Åland for at least five years, and who is satisfactorily proficient in Swedish.

The rules concerning the acquisition of the right of domicile or regional citizenship in Åland may thus be viewed as exclusive in relation to citizens of other countries and restrictive as concerns the mainland citizens of Finland. Moreover, the right of domicile entitles the possessor of this right under Sections 9 to 12 of the Autonomy Act to some material rights that present themselves as exclusive compared with the persons who are not in the possession of the right of domicile. Under Section 8 of the Autonomy Act, the forfeiture of Finnish citizenship shall also mean the forfeiture of the right of domicile, while the forfeiture of the right of domicile of a person who moves permanently away from Åland shall be regulated in an act adopted by the Legislative Assembly.[40]

Provisions for autonomy in the Constitution of Finland

The provisions concerning Åland create an autonomous jurisdiction for a fairly peripheral archipelagic territory in what otherwise is a unitary state. The arrangement can be said to constitute a separate legal order of Åland which is, in its own areas of competence, parallel to the competences of the Parliament of Finland, effective in other areas of competence. Hence two different domestic legal orders apply in the jurisdiction of the Åland Islands, the Åland legal order according to Section 18 of the Autonomy Act and the legal order of Finland according to Section 27 and Section 29 of the Autonomy Act. While the overall structure of the arrangement has remained the same for almost a century, the constitutional provisions have undergone changes that specify the relationship between Åland and the rest of the country.

In addition, due to Finnish (and Ålandic) membership in the European Union since 1 January 1995, a third separate legal order applies on the Åland Islands,

36 SoF 1144/1991. 37 Section 6.

38 Since 1 January 1995, the term *regional citizenship* is equivalent to the right of domicile as mentioned in Article 1 of Protocol 2 on the Åland Islands attached to the 1994 Treaty of Accession of Finland to the European Union. Official Journal of the European Community 94/C241/08.

39 Section 7. 40 See Ålandic Act concerning the Right of Domicile (SoÅ 2/1993).

that of the European Union. While EU membership does not formally alter the allocation of legislative competence between Åland and the state according to the Autonomy Act, legislative competence from both legal orders has been transferred to the European Union to be exercised by the Union bodies.[41] As a consequence, an individual or a business enterprise in Åland is potentially subject to the norms of three different law-makers. Because the structures of the EU address themselves to the member states, sub-state entities like the Åland Islands have experienced a *de facto* loss of influence, in this case to Finland, and of competence to the EU. Nonetheless, the three legal orders can be understood as separate and exclusive in relation to each other and, as a consequence, as parallel legal orders based on a separation of competencies without any hierarchical ordering between them (although the EU legal order presents itself as a supra-national legal order, at least when looking at it from an EU law point of view). The parallel existence of three legal orders may be confusing: for the individual residing in Åland, it may be difficult to know exactly which law to obey.

In terms of the Åland legal order, deciding whether or not to enact an Ålandic act[42] and what sort of material rules to pass is in principle up to the Legislative Assembly. However, the Constitution of Finland, the Autonomy Act, and EU law contain a number of requirements concerning the enactment of rules in the Ålandic jurisdiction. The constitutional rights and liberties in Chapter 2 of the Finnish Constitution require legislative action in a multitude of fields, many of which are relevant within the Ålandic legislative competence.[43] The Autonomy Act itself pre-supposes the enactment of Ålandic legislation on a number of matters, such as the organisation of the bodies of government on the Åland Islands. Finally, although the EU has normative powers in a number of fields (through the European Union treaties), one main method the EU utilises in regulating different issues is the directive, which is a request to the national law-maker to implement at least the minimum level of rules indicated in the directive within a certain time-frame. Where the subject matter of such directives falls under the legislative competence of the Åland Islands, the Legislative Assembly is in many cases under a duty to enact Ålandic acts to implement the directives. Hence the law-maker of Åland does not have complete discretion in law-making, but is instead under a multitude of regulatory demands.

From the start, the President of Finland has had an absolute veto over the legislative enactments of the Legislative Assembly if an Ålandic act violated the exclusive legislative powers of the state, or if the act was in conflict with the good of the Republic, provided the Supreme Court gave an opinion

[41] On the EU issue, see N. Jääskinen, *EU's behörighet och Åland* [The Competences of the EU and Åland] (Helsingfors: Statsrådets Kansli, 2003). For Åland, the transfer of law-making powers to the EU is particularly important in the fields of agriculture and fisheries, transport policy and subsidies to business enterprises and industries.

[42] Act enacted by the Legislative Assembly of the Åland Islands.

[43] Section 18 of the Autonomy Act.

to that effect.[44] In addition, state courts were (and still are) in charge of interpreting acts of the Åland Legislative Assembly. As early as 1920, Åland was also given the right to use the proceeds of certain taxes and to levy some additional taxes and charges connected to these general state taxes. Many of these taxation powers subsequently diminished and became obsolete by the 1950s since the state abolished the relevant categories of taxes when restructuring its general taxation.[45] In the 1991 Autonomy Act, an amount of equalisation is determined at 0.45 per cent of annual state income (after deduction of the new loans the state has taken) as compensation for the transfer of the taxation to the state.[46] Today, the State of Finland collects income and property taxes on the Åland Islands under the ordinary national tax schemes, and if the taxes collected are proportionally higher than on the mainland, the Åland Islands shall, in addition to the fixed equalisation amount, be entitled to compensation. This extra compensation is determined by the Åland Delegation, which is a joint co-ordination body of the Government of Finland and the Government of the Åland Islands. If the Åland Islands should suffer from an unexpected incident causing an unreasonable financial burden, it is eligible for a special grant from the state budget.

Under the current Autonomy Act, Åland still has law-making powers concerning the so-called local government tax, which is a flat-rate tax imposed by the individual municipalities to cover their expenses. Thus the tax powers of the Åland Legislative Assembly are far from insignificant. Moreover, under the Åland Regional Tax Act,[47] an additional tax can be levied on the top of all other taxes (although it has not been used during the past forty years). The Autonomy Act also contains a provision allowing an Ålandic act imposing a one-time extra tax, which provision has never been used. In spite of the financial autonomy the equalisation amount and other compensation schemes allows, some believe that Åland does not have sufficient fiscal autonomy, and there have been calls for Åland to be accorded greater tax competence.

Entrenchment of Åland autonomy

The original Autonomy Act of 1920 was enacted on the basis of Section 60 of the 1906 Diet (Constitution) Act as an Act of Exception, following the formula for amendment of the Constitution. This method of enactment established the Ålandic autonomy arrangement as an exception to the constitutional structure, but without making the Autonomy Act a part of the formal Constitution of Finland or without declaring the Act constitutional. Section 36 of the Autonomy Act laid out the special features of this legislative arrangement, stating

[44] See later for more detail.

[45] When the Parliament of Finland abolished the old forms of taxation on the mainland, they remained in force in the Åland Islands until the Legislative Assembly itself abolished them.

[46] Sections 46 and 47. [47] SoÅ 58/1993.

that the Autonomy Act could be amended only in the manner established for the amendment of the Constitution and with the consent of the Legislative Assembly.

The 1951 Autonomy Act confirmed the basic elements of the original arrangement, but created at the same time a specific right of domicile, which defined the group of persons who were to be beneficiaries of the special features of autonomy, that is, the right to vote and stand as a candidate in municipal and regional elections, acquisition and possession of real estate,[48] the right to carry out 'regulated' branches of trade and exemption from military service. In this way, the definition of the right of domicile created a distinction between the inhabitants of the Åland Islands and those of mainland Finland that was more protective of the former than under the previous legislation, and served to discourage mainlanders from moving to Åland.

This Autonomy Act made the contours of autonomy more specific and provided more detailed regulations concerning the powers and functioning of autonomy. An enumerated list replaced the more general clause defining the competences of the Legislative Assembly. The boundaries of the law-making capacity of the Legislative Assembly could be efficiently supervised through the presidential veto procedure.[49] However, the authorities of Åland had no corresponding remedy if the legislature of the Republic of Finland interfered with the legislative powers of the Legislative Assembly.[50] This asymmetry is currently one element distinguishing the Ålandic arrangement from a federative arrangement.

The Åland Islands now has a special status in the formal Constitution, but this has undergone some changes over time. The Åland Islands used to be referred to only in Section 33 of the Parliament (Constitution) Act, which stated that '(s)eparate provisions shall apply on the right of the Åland Legislative Assembly to submit initiatives' to the Parliament of Finland. In amendments that entered into force on 1 March 1994, Åland has self-government (i.e., autonomy) in accordance with separate enactments,[51] while a provision was incorporated stating that the procedure for enactment of the Autonomy Act and the Act on Acquisition of Land on the Åland Islands should be that established in these laws. There is also a provision authorising separate legislation to establish the Legislative Assembly's right to present legislative initiatives to the Finnish Parliament.[52]

48 An Act on the Purchase of Real Estate (SoF 3/1975) was enacted for the first time in 1938 (SoF 140/1938) and amended in 1951. Under the 1975 Act, persons who do not have the right of domicile require an advance permit before they can purchase real property.

49 Discussed previously, and also further later. When an Ålandic act is presented for the President's competence review, it is always accompanied by an opinion of the Åland Delegation.

50 On this, see A. Jyränki, 'Autonomy of the Åland Islands: a federal element in the constitution of a unitary state?' in *Constitutionalism in Finland – Reality and Perspectives*, K. Pohjolainen (ed.) (Helsinki: the Finnish Society of Constitutional Law, 1995), 13–15.

51 Form of Government (Constitution) Act, Section 52a.

52 Parliament (Constitution) Act, Section 33.

Do these amendments mean that Åland enjoyed a very weak constitutional status before 1994? On the contrary, despite the fact that the Åland Autonomy Act and the Act on Acquisition of Land on the Åland Islands do not declare themselves to be constitutional laws, one could conclude that their status was, in practice, *stronger* than that of the other four constitutional laws of the time: both the Autonomy Act and the Land Acquisition Act[53] stipulate that amendments to these laws may only be made in the order established for the amendment of the Constitution[54] and with the consent of the Åland Legislative Assembly. However, the Finnish Constitution does not regard these two acts as of a formally higher order than the former constitutional acts or the current Constitution, but rather as acts of exception to the Constitution. As concerns Ålandic consent to amendments to the Autonomy Act, Section 69 of this Act requires materially identical decisions of the Finnish Parliament and the Legislative Assembly of Åland, so that the Ålandic decision is made by two-thirds qualified majority. The Land Acquisition Act does not require any super-majority in the Åland Legislative Assembly, but leaves its entrenchment and the raising of the decision-making threshold to the two-thirds level to be determined in an Ålandic Act (which itself must be enacted in that manner).[55]

Thus the constitutional setting of Åland before 1994 includes both special and regional entrenchment, special meaning here the requirement of the constitutional amendment formula with a two-thirds majority in Parliament for alterations of the Autonomy Act and regional meaning here the requirement of Ålandic consent for any modifications to the Autonomy Act. After the 1994 constitutional amendments, it now also includes a clear general entrenchment of the Åland arrangement. In this way, the constitutional setting of Åland has become even more fixed than it was before. Further amendments to the Constitution of Finland on 1 March 2000 meant that the features of general entrenchment of the Ålandic arrangement were strengthened. The generic provisions for the arrangement are currently included in Section 75 and Section 120 of the Constitution of Finland.[56] The special status of Åland is codified through the latter section as follows: 'The Åland Islands have self-government in accordance with what is specifically stipulated in the Act on the Autonomy of the Åland Islands'.[57]

53 Section 69 and Section 17, respectively.

54 A simple majority in favour of the amendment in one Parliament and a two-thirds majority in a new Parliament convening after elections or, a decision on urgency of the amendment with a five-sixths majority and adoption by two-thirds by the same Parliament.

55 Section 17. Such an entrenchment is included in Section 19 of the Ålandic Act concerning the Right to Acquire Real Property and the Permission to Acquire Real Property (SoÅ 68/2003).

56 SoF 731/1999.

57 The term 'autonomy' is not used in the original languages in which the phenomenon is described, but rather the term self-government. This choice of wording places the emphasis on the fact that the inhabitants of the area should participate in the government of the territory and make their own decisions. The term 'Autonomy Act' was, however, used by the League of Nations in the 1921 Åland Islands Settlement.

Admittedly, Section 120 does not say anything about the nature of the decision-making powers that the self-government should encompass, but leaves this to the Autonomy Act. The Autonomy Act, in turn, is an enactment of the Finnish Parliament, under the condition that it is adopted and amended in the qualified decision-making procedure prescribed for the adoption and amendment of the Constitution, supplemented with a similar adoption procedure by the Legislative Assembly of the Åland Islands (this is also the case for the Act on the Right to Acquire Real Estate in the Åland Islands). Thus the nature of Ålandic autonomy rests on the Autonomy Act, which provides that the legislative competences of the Åland Legislative Assembly and those of the Parliament of Finland are separate and exclusive in relation to each other.

However, Section 75, which deals with special legislation for the Åland Islands, also points in this direction. Sub-Section 1 has the function of underlining the exceptional character of the Ålandic arrangement under the Finnish Constitution. Although the two Acts mentioned in the Sub-Section do not identify themselves as constitutional laws in a formal sense, they clearly are drawn into the ambit of constitutional norms. This theme is sustained in Sub-Section 2, which contains two different issues, namely the right of the Legislative Assembly of the Åland Islands to submit proposals to the Parliament of Finland on the one hand (see later), and the enactment of acts passed by the Legislative Assembly. While again there is a reference to the Autonomy Act, it is indicated in the Constitution of Finland that the Legislative Assembly of the Åland Islands is empowered to pass acts that have the same normative force as the acts of the Parliament of Finland.

This is the reason the overall state jurisdiction has surprisingly limited formal connection with the jurisdiction of Åland. In addition, the existence of legislative competence for Åland implies at the same time the existence of administrative competence in the same substantive areas. However, Ålandic acts have to undergo a control of legislative competence that involves the Åland Delegation (which is a joint expert body composed of representatives from the Åland Islands and the Government of Finland under the chairmanship of the Governor of the Åland Islands), the Supreme Court of Finland and the President of Finland.[58] The Autonomy Act provides that when the Legislative Assembly adopts an Act, it is to be given to the Finnish Ministry of Justice and the Åland Delegation. The Ministry submits the Act to the President after receiving the opinion of the Delegation. The President may annul the Act in part or wholly, within four months of its submission to the Ministry, only after he or she has obtained the opinion of the Supreme Court on its validity.[59] If the Act is annulled in part, the Åland Government may decide whether to accept the Act so modified or to let it lapse entirely. The veto power can only be exercised if the Legislative Assembly has exceeded its legislative powers, or if the Ålandic act relates to the internal or external security of the state. A reference to the latter

[58] Sections 55 and 56. [59] Section 19, Sub-Sections 1–2.

has been used only once (in 1951, in relation to the flag issue) to veto an Ålandic act. Because of the introduction of the partial veto in the 1991 Autonomy Act, the use of the complete veto has almost ceased. The presidential control powers are not exercised in a political manner, but are without exception based on the legal interpretation of the Supreme Court. The President uses the veto powers only in very few cases per year (around 3–4 per cent; mainly the partial veto in relation to some provisions of an individual enactment of Åland), which means that most of the enactments of the Legislative Assembly are passed into law by publication of the enactment in the Statutes of Åland.

An amendment of the veto procedure in 2004 to create a special mechanism for budgetary legislation has introduced a presidential veto that is abstract and *post legem*.[60] The possibility of passing and promulgating budget legislation without a preliminary control was motivated by the wish of Åland to apply such legislation immediately on commencement of the new budgetary year on 1 January.[61] This move provoked serious criticism, because it could lead to legal uncertainty if a budget law were later repealed by the President.

On the basis of the Autonomy Act, the Finnish President declares the sessions of the Åland Legislative Assembly opened and closed. However, in practice, this function is almost always exercised by the Islands' Governor, who is the representative of the national government in the region and heads the provincial government. It is also the Governor who presents the proposals and statements of the President to the Åland Legislative Assembly.[62] This power of the President covers the domestic implementation acts of such international treaties for which the assent of the Legislative Assembly of the Åland Islands is necessary, as well as amendments to the Autonomy Act. These powers are not interpreted so that the President would be generally entitled to file proposals for the enactment of Ålandic Acts in the Legislative Assembly. Only the Government of the Åland Islands can do so. The President also has the formal power to participate in the dissolution of the Legislative Assembly and order new elections.[63] Such action, which can be activated only after consultation with the speaker of the Legislative Assembly, has never been taken and would probably be relevant only if the Legislative Assembly became incapacitated due to political stalemate.

The provincial government headed by the Governor of the Åland Islands is a state authority which, due to the broad competences of the Legislative Assembly, has much more limited administrative competencies than other provincial governments in mainland Finland. It should be emphasised that the Governor has almost no role at all in the daily politics of Åland, but has a function in the control of legislation because he is the chairperson of the Åland Delegation.[64]

60 Section 20, Sub-Section 2.

61 Under the previous procedure, the approval of ordinary legislation relevant for the budget could take up to four months.

62 Section 14. 63 Section 15. 64 Section 55.

The role of Åland in establishing constitutional guarantees

Although the Autonomy Act is passed by the Parliament of Finland, the Åland Legislative Assembly has an important role in its enactment or amendment.

The Åland Legislative Assembly may submit initiatives on matters within the legislative power of the state, and the Government of Finland shall present such initiatives for the consideration of the Parliament.[65] In principle, this looks like a general right of legislative initiative, but in practice it has been used mainly in relation to the Autonomy Act itself and also such legislation adopted by the Parliament that applies only or predominantly to the Åland Islands.

The Åland autonomy arrangement is entrenched in various ways. One is through regional entrenchment, with a provision that the Autonomy Act can be amended or repealed, or exceptions to it made, only by congruent decisions of the Parliament and the Åland Legislative Assembly.[66] In the Parliament, the decision shall be made as provided for the amendment and repeal of the Constitution, and in the Legislative Assembly, by a majority of at least two thirds of the votes cast. This means that although ultimately the Åland Legislative Assembly is in a sense in control of amendments to the Autonomy Act and can refuse any amendment it does not agree with and even block the repeal of the entire Autonomy Act, it cannot compel the Parliament to amend the Autonomy Act if there is resistance to such a measure in the Finnish Parliament. Thus the agreement of both parties is necessary for change.

The Parliament could, in theory, use its powers to amend the Constitution to vest significant legislative action in itself and in the other law-making body in Finland, the Åland Legislative Assembly, for instance, by re-formulating the provisions on constitutional rights and liberties (regardless of regional and special entrenchment) and making them very detailed. Therefore, there is a very remote possibility that the autonomy of Åland could be negatively affected by such amendments – how ever unrealistic this may seem at present. But insofar as they relate to the principles governing the right of a private person to own real property or business property in Åland, amendments to the Constitution or other acts of Parliament cannot enter into force in Åland without the consent of the Legislative Assembly.[67] Hence there is a specific area of law within which the Legislative Assembly of the Åland Islands can, in fact, block the entering into force on the Islands of an act of the Parliament even if it were passed as an amendment to the Constitution of Finland.

Under the Autonomy Act, an individual Ålandic act can be identified by the Legislative Assembly as one that can be enacted and amended only with a qualified majority, thus distinguishing between acts of an internal constitutional nature and ordinary acts.[68] This power has been used in a small number of cases,

[65] Section 22. [66] Section 69. [67] Section 28.

[68] Section 69, Sub-Section 2. In addition, Section 67, Sub-Section 1, of the Act (concerning eligibility in local government elections for persons not in the possession of the right of domicile) makes it possible to enact an Ålandic act on this issue according to the qualified procedure.

such as in the Ålandic Acts on the Organisation of the Legislative Assembly of the Åland Islands,[69] on the Government of the Åland Islands[70] and on Some Principles for the Economy of the Åland Islands.[71] The 'Constitution of Åland' thus comprises legislative enactments passed by the Parliament with the consent of the Åland Legislative Assembly and also acts that are indigenously Ålandic, adopted by way of qualified majority. In addition, the Constitution of Finland, that is, the formal constitutional Act, is a part of the broader 'Constitution of Åland', at least to the extent that no exceptions to the Constitution of Finland are made by the Autonomy Act and the Act concerning the Possession of Real Property on the Åland Islands.

The qualified procedure means that when the Legislative Assembly passes an Ålandic act with such an internal constitutional character, the proposal undergoes the ordinary readings and is decided upon in the final reading by a majority of two thirds of the votes cast instead of simple majority. In this manner, a layer of 'higher' legislation in Åland has been created. However, because the Legislative Assembly lacks a formal procedure for the internal control of the constitutionality of legislation *ante legem*, there is no organ to monitor legislative proposals and check whether a piece of proposed law should be enacted by simple majority or by two-thirds majority. Such a function could, in principle, be exercised by a Committee of the Legislative Assembly, but on at least one occasion, the enactment of the Act on the EU Referendum in 1994 (see later), the system failed to pick up the internal constitutional character of the matter and the referendum legislation was passed by a simple majority. According to the Referendum Act the purpose of the *advisory* referendum was to indicate how the Legislative Assembly *shall* vote on the EU membership issue. Thus it could be argued that the referendum was not actually advisory, but was to some extent intended to be binding and therefore was in violation of the decision-making powers of the Legislative Assembly.

Dispute resolution and implementation of constitutional and legal provisions

As mentioned previously, the presidential veto power over Ålandic legislation functions *ante legem* and is exercised on the basis of a judicial determination of the Supreme Court (see example following).[72] The presidential control of legislative competence is not symmetrical. The President has an absolute veto over Åland legislation, but in respect of enactments of the Finnish Parliament, her veto can be overridden by the Parliament. The Constitutional Committee of the Parliament has used its power of abstract review of the constitutionality of legislative proposals[73] to review constitutionality, not only in relation to the Constitution, but also in relation to the Autonomy Act, especially with a view to whether a government proposal stays within the boundaries of

[69] SoÅ 11/1972. [70] SoÅ 42/1971. [71] SoÅ 22/1983.

[72] Section 19, Sub-Section 2. See previously for details on the procedure.

[73] Constitution, Section 74.

Section 27. In 2001, the Parliament overruled a presidential veto that was based on an adverse opinion of the Supreme Court,[74] and the Constitutional Committee's version was passed into law. Adding to the constitutional convulsions caused by the event was a note from the Constitutional Committee stating that it has the supreme authority to interpret the Constitution and that it should not be bound by the opinions of the Supreme Court in legislative matters.[75]

This case demonstrates that there is no single body which interprets the Autonomy Act in a coherent and systematic manner. However, because the Supreme Court passes judgments on the legislative competencies of both Åland and the Finnish Parliament upon the request of the President, there are strong arguments to support the view that the Constitutional Committee should consider Supreme Court opinions as authoritative interpretations of the Autonomy Act.

The Parliament of Finland cannot veto laws of the Åland Legislative Assembly or pre-empt its competence. Instead, because the legislative competences are exclusive in relation to each other, their legislative enactments should in principle not conflict with each other. An act of the Legislative Assembly of the Åland Islands is perceived to be on the same hierarchical level as an act of the Parliament of Finland. Therefore, the acts of the Parliament do not displace acts of the Legislative Assembly. However, in the application of legislation in individual cases, the courts in Åland may have to make a choice of law when making a determination of an individual entitlement.

In the event of confusion as to how the law should be applied and what law should apply in Åland, administrative authorities (and also the courts) may apply for an opinion of the Supreme Court.[76] If a conflict of authority arises between Åland officials and state officials on a given administrative function, either party can ask the Supreme Court to give a decision. Before rendering the decision the Supreme Court shall obtain opinions from the appropriate official and the Åland Delegation.

Under Section 106 of the Finnish Constitution, courts of law can, in individual cases before them, conclude that the application of an act in the case is in evident conflict with the Constitution. If so, the court can, in concrete judicial review *post legem*, set aside the act and apply the relevant constitutional provision directly. So far, Section 106 has been used only a few times and only in relation to acts of the Parliament of Finland, but it has been argued that this section could also cover Ålandic acts. Undoubtedly, from the perspective of an individual, this position is justifiable. However, the different control mechanisms created in the Autonomy Act, which itself is of an exceptional nature, mean that it is not totally clear whether or not Section 106 is among the constitutional provisions

[74] Opinion of the Supreme Court of 29 August 2001/1625 (No. 2001:79).

[75] Opinion of the Constitutional Committee of the Parliament of Finland 36/2001.

[76] Section 60.

applicable on the Åland Islands. An amendment of the Autonomy Act clarifying this matter would be advisable.

The relationship between the Ålandic arrangements and the various human rights conventions binding on Finland has been the subject of some debate. It has been suggested that the 1921 Settlement of the League of Nations should be considered a *lex specialis* in those limited material areas it affects, but most legal experts give precedence to Finland's obligations under human rights conventions according to the principle of *lex posterior*.[77]

An example of the process of interpreting the law in relation to Åland emerged during the process of preparing Finland's accession to the European Union. The question arose whether the Åland Islands should hold an advisory referendum on the EU issue before the Legislative Assembly decided on its formal consent to the Islands' membership of the EU, particularly given that this involved the creation of a special status for Åland through Protocol 2 (see previously). The Autonomy Act does not provide for referendums, so the question was whether Åland was permitted to organise popular votes of any kind. A positive solution could be based on the right to self-determination: since EU regulations supersede and supplant Ålandic norms and interfere with Ålandic jurisdiction, especially within the area of trade, it could be argued that EU membership would have the effect of diminishing the autonomy.[78] Such arguments supported the holding of an advisory referendum,[79] especially as the conditions of accession had not been on the agenda during the Legislative Assembly elections of 20 October 1991.

In an Opinion to the President of the Republic, the Supreme Court of Finland emphasised the fact that the referendum was only advisory, so it did not constitute an infringement of the Legislative Assembly's decision-making procedures and thus did not deprive it of its right to represent Åland. Therefore, the Court found that regulations concerning an advisory referendum did not violate the Autonomy Act. The Court concluded that provisions concerning advisory referendums were not of a constitutional character in the sense that they would impinge on the competence of the state to enact laws at the constitutional level.[80] Thus the Supreme Court ruled that Ålandic legislation concerning an advisory referendum could be enacted under the Autonomy Act, because the matter fell under the competence of Åland.[81] Hence the President did not veto the Ålandic law on the advisory EU referendum.

[77] Hannikainen, *Cultural, Linguistic and Educational Rights in the Åland Islands*, 53–4.

[78] In the same vein, one could also argue for an Ålandic mandate in the European Parliament, although the inequality produced in the ratio of representation of the population would be unjustifiable.

[79] A decisive referendum would clearly require an amendment of the Autonomy Act.

[80] Section 27, paragraph 1.

[81] Opinion of the Supreme Court, 9 September 1994, Nr 3169 (Dnr OH 94/104).

Institutions of autonomy

The structure and composition of government institutions at the autonomous level

The Autonomy Act identifies governmental institutions at the autonomous level, but leaves their specific regulation to enactments of the Legislative Assembly. It vests the administration of Åland in the Government of Åland and its officials.[82] It further stipulates that the population of Åland is, in matters relating to autonomy, represented by the Legislative Assembly.[83] The members of this Legislative Assembly are elected by direct and secret ballot, through universal and equal suffrage,[84] although suffrage is restricted to those with domicile.[85] In addition, the Autonomy Act provides that the Legislative Assembly shall enact legislation for Åland.[86]

Thus the internal structures of government are determined by Ålandic legislation. The scope of the authority of the Åland Legislative Assembly to pass legislation on these issues is laid out in Section 18, according to which Åland shall have legislative powers in respect of, *inter alia*, establishment of governmental institutions, procedures and staff structures, but also in the areas of education, social affairs, health and the environment. The list of legislative powers of Åland comprises a total of twenty-seven paragraphs. Because most of these powers are in the sphere of so-called 'public law', they imply the existence of a relatively broad administrative machinery. In fact, the public sector of Åland appears greater than that of the mainland, proportionally speaking, partly because of this 'public law' orientation, partly because of the independent Ålandic control over the state grants to Åland.

Two Ålandic acts of an internal constitutional nature are essential for the creation of the structures of government, namely that on the Organisation of the Legislative Assembly of the Åland Islands and that on the Government of the Åland Islands.

The first determines that the Legislative Assembly is composed of thirty representatives and that they are elected by means of proportional representation from the single constituency of Åland. Various political groupings compete in elections; they are not political parties proper constituted on the basis of the Finnish Party Act,[87] but are registered under the Finnish Associations Act.[88] The Åland Government provides some subsidies for their political activities. The political system of Åland has almost no connection to the parties on the mainland; only the Ålandic Social Democrats have some contacts with the mainland

82 Section 3, Sub-Section 2. 83 Section 3, Sub-Section 1. 84 Section 13.

85 Section 9. See also *Py v. France*, European Court of Human Rights, application no. 66289/01, judgment of 11 January 2005; *Gillot v. France*, UN Human Rights Committee, Comm. 932/2000, UN Doc. CCPR/C/75/D/932/2000. Both cases deal with residency requirements in New Caledonia and no violation of the European Convention on Human Rights or the International Convenant on Civil and Political Rights was found.

86 Section 17. 87 SoF 10/1969. 88 SoF 503/1989.

Social Democratic Party. The Åland Government or a member of the Legislative Assembly may propose legislation to be adopted by the Legislative Assembly.

The Organisation of the Legislative Assembly Act specifies that the relationship between the Legislative Assembly and the Åland Government be based on the principle of parliamentarism, in other words, the Government must be accountable to and enjoy the confidence of the Legislative Assembly.[89] The confidence is both collective and individual in respect of the five to seven members of the Government. After elections, the Legislative Assembly elects the First Minister, who then proposes the composition of the Government, which requires the support of a simple majority of the Assembly. The Government can be removed by vote of no confidence by the absolute majority of sixteen members, which means that the parliamentary mechanism is not symmetrical. The Government of the Åland Islands Act contains corresponding provisions on accountability to parliament, supplemented by a provision allowing the Government itself to declare that it will consider a defeat in a vote on a legislative proposal a motion of no confidence.

Various government offices and administrative bodies[90] operate under the Åland Government. While the Government as a collective body is in charge of more political decision-making, individual members as heads of different departments participate in making administrative decisions on the basis of Ålandic acts.

The official language of the Åland Islands is Swedish,[91] but Swedish skills among central government officials in mainland Finland are in the decline and increasingly, central government documents, especially related to the EU, are often solely provided in Finnish. This has become a source of irritation in the relationship between Åland and mainland Finland. Although the Autonomy Act contains a number of provisions on the use of the Swedish language,[92] they are clearly not being properly implemented.

One of the salient features of the 1921 Åland Islands Settlement was the municipalities, which constitute an essential part of the autonomy scheme. Under Section 121 of the Constitution, they are based on the right of self-government of their inhabitants. At the moment, there are sixteen municipalities, many of them very small, counting their population in the hundreds. Mariehamn, the capital of Åland, is the largest with more than 10,000 inhabitants. The municipalities have their own constitutionally guaranteed power of taxation (although the competence to regulate municipal taxation in Åland rests with the Legislative Assembly). Compared with the municipalities on the mainland, the Åland municipalities have fewer functions, because the Åland

89 On parliamentary accountability, see also *Interpretation of the Statute of Memel Territory*, Permanent Court of International Justice of 11 August 1932, Series A/B-Fasc., No. 50.

90 These include the Åland Police, the Board of Environment, the Schools of Åland (except those of the municipalities, see later) and the Health Care of Åland.

91 Section 36.

92 Sections 36–42.

Government takes charge of such important functions as health care and education above primary level.

The competence regarding courts and the administration of justice is vested in the state,[93] and state courts exercise jurisdiction on the Åland Islands.[94] However, the courts try cases not only on the basis of acts of the Parliament of Finland, but also on the basis of acts of the Åland Legislative Assembly, because the two sets of acts are equally authoritative and judicially recognised.

There are two courts in Åland, the Court of First Instance for civil and criminal matters and the Administrative Court for administrative matters. The courts are situated in the town of Mariehamn. Appeals concerning decisions of the Court of First Instance are tried at the Court of Appeals in Turku/Åbo in the mainland, with the possibility of final review by the Supreme Court of Finland. Prosecution in criminal matters is a state function, but the criminal investigation is mainly a task of the Åland Islands Police. The cases of the Administrative Court originate in the administrative decision-making of the Ålandic municipalities or the bodies subordinate to the Åland Government. The decisions of the Administrative Court can be appealed to the Supreme Administrative Court of Finland. Decisions made by the Åland Government, such as on the right of domicile and right to possess real property, are generally appealed directly to the Supreme Administrative Court. In this respect, the Åland Government is the equal of the Government of Finland.

The division of powers

The current Autonomy Act was enacted in 1991 and served to strengthen the autonomy of Åland and restrict the state's supervision over its affairs.[95] The matters within the legislative and administrative competence of Åland are mainly in the sphere of public law (as the term 'public law' is understood in continental Europe). The Finnish Parliament has the competence to pass legislation in these areas, but only to the extent that the law is applied on the mainland. If the Åland Legislative Assembly chooses not to pass laws on a certain public law matter, the laws of the mainland on those matters are not applicable in Åland. However, insofar as the constitutional provisions concerning the rights and liberties of individuals contain references to the law and demand legislative action, then the Legislative Assembly is under a duty to pass legislation that fulfils their prescriptions. The same applies to regulatory demands imposed by the EU by way of directives.

The legislative powers of the Finnish Parliament applicable in Åland are numerous and range from enactment and amendment of the Constitution

93 Section 27. 94 Section 35.

95 Examples of powers vested with Åland in 1991 include: regulations concerning use of the flag of Åland, leasing, historical sites, social care, sub-soil resources (in respect of which there is a divided competence with the state), the sale of alcoholic beverages, archives, postal affairs, radio and telecommunications.

through the general provisions of criminal law to matters of private law or civil law (as these terms are understood in continental Europe).

The two lists of legislative competence are perceived as a complete demarcation of the respective legislative competencies, but reference is made to 'other matters' that are deemed to be within the legislative power of the Åland Islands or the state according to the principles underlying the Autonomy Act, indicating that for matters that are difficult to allocate through the listing of express competencies, the question of competence may be resolved on the basis of the principle of affinity.[96]

In addition to the two lists in the Autonomy Act, Section 29 lists a group of additional state competencies. Whereas changes to the competences listed in Sections 18 and 27 would necessitate amendment of the Autonomy Act following the complicated procedure of qualified majorities, the additional list in Section 29 identifies a set of state competencies that could be transferred to Åland through an ordinary act of the Parliament. This simplified mechanism of transfer of competences has so far not been used.

Åland representation at national level

The Constitution provides that for the parliamentary elections, the country shall be divided, on the basis of the number of Finnish citizens, into at least twelve, and at most, eighteen constituencies and that the Åland Islands shall, in addition, form their own constituency for the election of one Representative.[97] The Autonomy Act contains a similar provision, according to which Åland shall, in parliamentary and presidential elections, constitute an electoral district.[98] The Election Act creates the Åland Islands as one constituency from which one Minister Parliament shall be elected to the Finnish Parliament.[99]

The one Ålandic representative in the Finnish Parliament can be viewed as an example of so-called special representation. This arrangement was not a part of the Settlement before the League of Nations, but was incorporated into domestic legislation in 1947 without external pressure and put into effect in the elections of 1948. A mandate in the Finnish Parliament represents in mathematical terms approximately 25,600 citizens. Hence because the MP elected from Åland would represent approximately 25,000 citizens, the special representation does not result in any significant disproportionality. Because the Ålandic MP represents all citizens, not only persons domiciled in Åland, the MP is not prevented from participating in deliberation on national legislation which, according to the Autonomy Act, belongs to the legislative competence of the Åland Islands. In his or her task as a representative, the Ålandic parliamentarian should observe the

96 For an example, see the Opinion of the Supreme Court on the EU Referendum Issue, 9 September 1994.

97 Section 25, Sub-Section 2.

98 Section 68.

99 SoF 714/1998, Section 6, Sub-Section 1. In addition, a provision in the Parliamentary Procedure Act states that the Ålandic MP shall always have the right to be present in the meetings of the Grand Committee of Parliament, which is the EU integration committee.

prohibition of the imperative mandate in the Finnish Constitution[100] and try to avoid becoming an arm of the governmental institutions of the Åland Islands in the Finnish Parliament.

However, since the electoral system in Finland is based on the principle of proportional representation in multi-member constituencies,[101] the one MP elected from Åland is an anomaly. Instead of the regular first-past-the-post election in a single member constituency, the Ålandic representative to the Finnish parliament is actually returned by means of a modified proportional election which could be called the first-*list*-past-the-post system, provided that lists are used in a particular election. Thus the election of the Ålandic representative to the Finnish parliament can be described as partially proportional. No special seat exists for the Åland Islands in the European Parliament, although such representation has been requested by Åland in compensation for loss of competence to the EU.

The methods of autonomy

Methods of co-operation and consultation between different levels of government

There is a host of different co-operation procedures for resolving day-to-day issues, relevant especially to the administrative competencies in the Autonomy Act.[102] This requires that state authorities should undertake extensive co-ordination and consultation with the Ålandic authorities on administrative matters. This could imply anything from a phone call to the relevant Åland Government official to the appointment of a joint committee of civil servants to draw up principles for dealing with an issue.

In addition, as mentioned previously the Supreme Court can issue opinions concerning conflicts of competence in the application of legislation. To some extent, the Åland Delegation also has such responsibilities. Also, co-operation and consultation is practiced in relation to EU matters and treaty matters.

The Autonomy Act provides for a complex web of participation for Åland in decision-making concerning EU matters.[103] The Åland Government has the right to participate in the preparation of the national positions of Finland within the Council of State preceding decision-making in the European Union (this means that Åland is expected to participate in the forty relevant sector committees in the Finnish Government), if the matter would fall within the powers of Åland or otherwise have special significance for it, and to be notified

[100] Section 29. The prohibition of the imperative mandate is based on the principle that an MP is not bound by external instructions from his or her voters.

[101] Under the Election Act, Section 110, thirty persons with a right to vote in parliamentary elections may found an electoral association for the purpose of nominating a candidate in the parliamentary elections and two or more electoral associations may present a joint list, which may include a maximum of four candidates.

[102] Section 30. [103] Section 59a.

if such issues are pending.[104] If a decision to be made in the European Union pertains in full or in part to the application of a common EU policy in Åland, the Åland Government shall formulate the position of Finland insofar as the matter would in other respects fall within the powers of Åland. If the positions of Åland and the state cannot be harmonised regarding a matter falling within the powers of the former, the Åland Government can request that its view be declared when the Finnish position is being presented to EU institutions. A similar mechanism applies for the presentation of the position of the Finnish Government and the Åland Government to the European Court of Justice.[105]

There is a somewhat similar mechanism in the Autonomy Act with respect to treaties, which provides that the Åland Government may propose negotiations on a treaty or other international obligation to the appropriate state officials.[106] The Åland Government should be informed about negotiations on a treaty or another international obligation if the matter is subject to the competence of Åland, or otherwise relates to matters of special importance to it. The Åland Government shall have the opportunity to participate in the negotiations, if there is a special reason for this.

One post as a special adviser or councillor at the Finnish mission to the European Union in Brussels is reserved to an Åland Islander. A candidate selected by the Åland Government is to be among the Finnish representatives to the EU Committee of Regions.[107] The Åland Government is also allowed to make direct contact with the European Commission regarding matters falling within the powers of Åland and concerning the implementation of EU decisions there,[108] but it is expected to notify the Council of State of such contacts.

Sovereignty and Åland autonomy

In the 1920s, the whole Åland Islands question turned on the issue of the (external) sovereignty of the state: which state should have sovereignty over the Åland Islands and who should decide the matter, the League of Nations by peaceful means, or Finland and Sweden by war? The matter was resolved peacefully, and autonomy was established on the Åland Islands under Finnish sovereignty. In fact, the state of Finland has consented to two different peace projects that have meant transfer of law-making power from its Parliament, namely the autonomy of the Åland Islands in the 1920s and membership of the European Union in 1995.

The autonomy legislation created a second law-maker in Finland, but with competencies only in certain fields and a jurisdiction territorially limited to the Åland Islands. Nonetheless, this could be described as devolution of the

[104] The Ministry of Foreign Affairs should ensure that all EU proposals for new legislative acts are forwarded to the Åland Government, while specialised ministries should inform the Åland Government about matters that they are dealing with.

[105] Section 59c. [106] Section 58. [107] Section 59e. [108] Section 59b, Sub-Section 4.

internal sovereignty of Finland. While it may have been a matter of some debate in the 1920s and 1930s among academics whether Ålandic acts should assume a lower position than the acts of the Parliament of Finland, it is clear from the preparatory materials for the 1920 Autonomy Act that two spheres of legislation were being established that are exclusive in relation to each other. Since World War II, this has been unquestioned, and in the current Constitution, acts of the Parliament and acts of the Legislative Assembly are regarded as norms on the same hierarchical level. Thus there exist two different law-makers in Finland, but whether either can still be considered as sovereign after the conclusion of a multitude of treaties of international law and after membership in the European Union is a complicated matter. The Åland Islands are autonomous in relation to Finland, but equally non-autonomous as Finland in relation to the EU. However, on some occasions, a minister of the Åland Government has been empowered to represent Finland in the Council of Ministers of the EU.

The international relations of the Åland Islands are not exclusively regulated by the Autonomy Act. The so-called Helsinki Agreement, or the 1962 Co-operation Agreement between Denmark, Finland, Iceland, Norway and Sweden, actually creates two international organisations, the Nordic Council and the Nordic Council of Ministers. Originally, the Helsinki Agreement facilitated co-operation between the Nordic States only, but on the basis of amendments in 1970 and 1984 to the Helsinki Agreement, the Nordic Council also incorporates the Nordic self-governing entities, that is the autonomous areas of the Åland Islands, Faeroe Islands and Greenland. Åland participates in the work of the Nordic Council through its delegation, although under Finnish law,[109] the representatives of Åland to the Nordic Council constitute a separate part of the national delegation of Finland. The Åland Islands have the right to vote in the Nordic Council and to put questions to the members of the state governments on the basis of the reports given concerning the implementation of the recommendations. A representative of Åland has held the presidency of the Nordic Council and has also been chairperson of some committees of the Nordic Council, which means that the representatives of Åland are involved in the work of the Nordic Council on an equal footing with the representatives of the State of Finland.

The status of Åland is different in the Nordic Council of Ministers, which is empowered to make decisions binding on the five states. Åland has the right to have a representative present in the meetings of the Nordic Council of Ministers, and in practice, this delegate can also speak on the various issues, but Åland does not have the formal right to vote, which is reserved for the five member states. Although the decisions of the Nordic Council of Ministers are not binding on Åland, Åland may commit itself politically to abiding by them to the extent that the matter in question falls within its legislative competence, thus facilitating domestic implementation of the decisions.

[109] Act on the Finnish Delegation to the Nordic Council (SoF 170/1960).

From the point of view of international law, Finland as a state and as a subject of international law is liable also for the actions of the Åland Islands, despite their rather far-reaching autonomy.[110]

Conclusion

As the legislative powers of the Åland Islands have become broader, the entrenchment of the position of the Åland Islands in the Finnish Constitution is no longer solely dependent on a special and regional entrenchment, but features also a general entrenchment. The cogs of the Autonomy Act are fitted into the cogs of the Constitution in a multitude of ways, making the relationship a very complex matter, while the Åland Islands have their own legislative competence. With the membership in the European Union, a matrix of pluralistic sources of law has evolved, making it more difficult than before to know where sovereignty actually resides. The loss of power to the EU has certainly caused dissatisfaction in Åland, but nobody knows if the alternative that existed in 1994 (that is, remaining outside of the EU) would have been any better. As the legislative and administrative powers of Åland have expanded, so they now also have the opportunity of direct involvement in international and EU affairs. Thus the Ålandic autonomy arrangement has grown beyond the original frame laid down at the beginning of the 1920s, although the EU at the same time curtails the autonomy of Åland.

In the contemporary world, the appeal of the Åland arrangement seems to depend on its close relationship with the international law concept of self-determination. This concept has various interrelated dimensions, some of which are relevant for areas which form parts of a state. The narrow version of the concept of self-determination (in comparison to that common after World War II) had tremendous appeal in Åland at the end of the 1910s and the beginning of the 1920s and resulted in the organisation of two petition campaigns on the Islands advocating secession from Finland and accession to Sweden. However, after the consolidation of the position of Åland as an autonomous part of Finland, the question of their sovereignty has mainly ceased to be contentious.[111]

With territorial demarcation as a starting point, the autonomy of Åland has become ever stronger: the specially guaranteed high level of self-government, that is, autonomy, created in 1920 was supplemented, on the basis of the League of Nations' decisions of 1921, by a set of special features in the Guaranty Act of 1922. Here the position of Ålandic culture based on the Swedish language was entrenched at the same time as specific provisions concerning the right to vote and stand as a candidate in elections and the acquisition and possession of

[110] See *Ekholm v. Finland*, European Court of Human Rights, Judgment of 24 July 2007, regarding non-implementation of national court decisions by authorities of Åland.

[111] In the current Legislative Assembly, two out of thirty members is a representative of a political group that advocates independence.

real estate were created. Later amendments to this autonomy arrangement in 1951 and 1991 deepened the autonomy and the position of Åland by establishing a distinct regional citizenship to which a number of features were connected: the right to vote and stand as a candidate in regional and municipal elections; the acquisition and possession of real estate; the right of trade (which was *not* an element of the original Settlement, and which, along with the right of domicile, have been created through Finnish legislation); and exemption from military service (which already was an element of the Autonomy Act of 1920). Although this arrangement, which could be called a 'sandwich' of exclusive rights, contains elements of minority protection, the protection of the territory is a central theme.

Åland has managed to prosper during the past three decades and the financial provisions have evidently not been an impediment, because the GDP per capita and per year exceeded US$57,000 in 2007.[112] This figure places Åland among the wealthiest regions in the EU. When the level of health of the populations of Åland and adjacent regions in mainland Finland and Sweden has been compared, the higher level of self-perceived health in Åland (resulting, for example, in the relative longevity of the Ålanders) has been attributed to the 'sense of coherence' experienced by the population[113] and the positive effects of concomitant higher levels of social capital there.[114] Both characteristics are potentially linked to the empowering feeling of being truly self-governing and autonomous. It remains to be seen what the long-term impact of EU membership will be on that feeling. It is probably possible to further increase the autonomy of Åland within the EU frame to reach a level closer to near-independence,[115] although it seems that already today the inhabitants of Åland enjoy such prosperity and happiness as was intended by the League of Nations in 1921.

112 See *Åland i siffror* 2007, 15, where the GDP/capita is estimated in Euro. At www.asub.ax/files/alsiff10sv.pdf (accessed on 16 June 2011). One reason for the high figure is the important position of the shipping sector in the economy of Åland.

113 M. Eriksson, B. Lindström and J. Lilja, 'A sense of coherence and health. Salutogenesis in a societal context: Åland, a special case' in *J. Epidemiol. Community Health* 61 (2007), 684–7.

114 M. Hyyppä, *Livskraft ur gemenskap – om socialt kapital och folkhälsa* [Life Energy from Community – on Social Capital and National Health] (Lund: Studentlitteratur, 2007), 97–101.

115 See the report by a Finnish governmental committee that proposes the commencement of the drafting of a new self-government act which could enter into force at the beginning of the 2020s. *Ålands självstyrelse i utveckling* [The Evolving Self-Government of Åland], Betänkande 4/2013, (Helsingfors: Justitieministeriet), 2013.

3

Puerto Rico

Autonomy or colonial subordination?

Efrén Rivera-Ramos

Whether Puerto Rico's current political system can be characterised as a system of autonomy is subject to debate. Since the concept of autonomy does not have a set meaning and is thus ambiguous, it would be unproductive to try to give a conclusive answer to the question. In fact, throughout Puerto Rican history the autonomy debate has produced several strands of autonomism as a political proposition, including those who assert that 'true autonomy' would require a fundamental revision of the present political arrangement. Therefore, I think it would be more illuminating simply to describe the current characteristics of the prevailing structure, the normative understandings that support it and the key historical processes that have produced it. That is what I will try to do for the most part in this chapter. Of course, a certain degree of personal interpretation will inevitably enter into the account.

The geographical and historical context

Puerto Rico is the name given to a group of islands located between the Caribbean Sea and the Atlantic Ocean. Originally inhabited by several successive groups of indigenous peoples, the last of which were known as *taínos*, the islands were conquered by the Spaniards after they landed in the largest of the group in 1492. The ethnic configuration of the Puerto Rican people was the eventual product of the convergence of the indigenous inhabitants, European settlers, mostly Spaniards, Africans brought in as slaves by the latter and several waves of immigrants from the nearby Caribbean islands and South America, the majority of whom were fleeing from the revolutionary uprisings against Spain in their countries of origin. A considerable influx of Cubans and Dominicans in the twentieth century has added to the total population residing in Puerto Rico.

Puerto Rico covers an area of approximately 4,560 square miles. Its population is slightly over 3.7 million. Over four million people of Puerto Rican origin live in the United States or its other territories. Although English and Spanish have been made official languages, Spanish is the mother tongue of most Puerto Ricans living in Puerto Rico. Many of those living in the United States also speak Spanish.

Because of its geographic location at the entrance to the Caribbean Sea, Puerto Rico remained a military post for the Spaniards for most of the Spanish colonial period, which extended until 1898. That year, Spain ceded Puerto Rico to the United States as a result of the Spanish-American War. Upon occupying the islands, the United States established a military government that lasted two years. In 1900, the military government was replaced by a civilian government. Successive legislation approved by the US Congress, briefly described in the following sections, has further developed the contours of that civilian government, which has been gradually devolved important competencies without altering the fundamental relationship between the United States and Puerto Rico, as will become apparent from the discussion next.

During the 113 years that Puerto Rico has been under US jurisdiction, the country has evolved from a mostly rural, agrarian society of slightly less than a million people to a densely populated largely urban society. Its industrialised – and more recently service-oriented – economy depends significantly upon foreign, mostly American, investment and on substantial amounts of monetary transfers from the US government in the form of subsidies, social security and welfare benefits, and diverse types of grants to the central government, the municipalities and individuals. Puerto Rico has also served as an important military post for the United States, although that role has been reduced in recent years. These developments have conditioned the possibilities for change in the political relationship between the United States and Puerto Rico and weigh heavily on the debate about the future of that relationship.[1]

The constitutional basis of the current arrangement

As soon as the United States acquired Puerto Rico, along with Guam and the Philippines, as a result of the Spanish-American War, an intense debate began to rage throughout American society. The public discussion involved not only the political branches of government, but the popular press, the leading legal journals and, eventually, the courts, including the Supreme Court. Several important questions had to be settled. They included: under what constitutional authority did the United States acquire these territories and their peoples? What was the location of these new possessions in the constitutional system of the nation? What was the extent of the power of the US Congress, the federal executive and the federal courts over these lands? What rights extended to their inhabitants? What should their final political destiny be? Both Congress and the Supreme Court eventually provided the answers that have constituted the basic framework for the constitutional governance of Puerto Rico until this day.

[1] For a more detailed account of how those and other social and economic conditions weigh on the possibilities for change in the political status of Puerto Rico, see Efrén Rivera-Ramos, 'Self-determination and decolonisation in the society of the modern colonial welfare state', in William Twining, (ed.), *Issues of Self-Determination* (Aberdeen University Press, 1991).

The authoritative answers came mostly through a series of decisions of the United States Supreme Court known as the *Insular Cases*, rendered between 1901 and 1922.[2] The decisions addressed controversies arising from situations involving Puerto Rico, the Philippines and Hawaii and Alaska, then not yet states of the Union. They constitute a set of complex legal texts that meander through the posed questions in complicated, sometimes contradictory, ways. However, when taken as a whole, and following the trajectory of the main issues they gradually resolved, they do contain a number of conclusions that define the constitutional status of Puerto Rico and other US territories in a rather coherent fashion. In this chapter I will summarise the main tenets of the doctrine produced by the *Insular Cases* and their progeny.

The first group of cases was decided in 1901. Salient among them was *Downes v. Bidwell*.[3] The controversy involved the constitutional validity of the collection of duties on imports from Puerto Rico into the United States pursuant to a provision of the Foraker Act of 1900,[4] the first organic act passed by Congress to establish a civilian government in Puerto Rico.[5] The plaintiff had alleged that the special tax imposed on products travelling from Puerto Rico violated the Uniformity Clause of the US Constitution, which dictates that 'all duties, imposts and excises' laid by Congress 'shall be uniform throughout the United States'.[6] Puerto Rico, it was argued, was now a part of the United States. Therefore, the Uniformity Clause applied.

In a closely divided decision, the Court rejected these arguments and found that the special tax was constitutional. There was no majority opinion. Justice Henry Billings Brown delivered the conclusion and judgment of the Court and wrote his own opinion. Justice Edward Douglas White rendered what would prove to be a highly influential concurring opinion, adhered to in substance by three other justices. The main conclusion of Justice Brown's opinion was that the Uniformity Clause of the Constitution did not apply to Puerto Rico because Puerto Rico was 'a territory *appurtenant* and *belonging to* the United States, but not a *part* of the United States within the revenue clauses of the Constitution'.[7]

Justice Brown also addressed some of the larger issues raised by the situation of the new territories. He concluded that the United States had authority to

2 See *De Lima v. Bidwell*, 182 US 1 (1901); *Goetz v. United States*, 182 US 221 (1901); *Grossman v. United States*, 182 US 221 (1901); *Dooley v. United States*, 182 US 222 (1901); *Armstrong v. United States* 182 US 243 (1901); *Downes v. Bidwell*, 182 US 244 (1901); *Huus v. New York and Porto Rico Steamship Company*, 182 US 392 (1901); *Dooley v. United States*, 183 US 151 (1901); *Fourteen Diamond Rings v. United States*, 183 US 176 (1901); *Hawaii v. Mankichi*, 190 US 197 (1903); *González v. Williams*, 192 US 1 (1904); *Kepner v. United States*, 195 US 100 (1904); *Dorr v. United States*, 195 US 138 (1904); *Mendozana v. United States*, 195 US 158 (1904); *Rasmussen v. United States*, 197 US 516 (1905); *Trono v. United States*, 199 US 521 (1905); *Grafton v. United States*, 206 US 333 (1907); *Kent v. Porto Rico*, 207 US 113 (1907); *Kopel v. Bingham*, 211 US 468 (1909); *Dowdell v. United States*, 221 US 325 (1911); *Ochoa v. Hernández*, 230 US 139 (1913); *Ocampo v. United States*, 234 US 91 (1914); and *Balzac v. Porto Rico*, 258 US 298 (1922).

3 182 US 244 (1901). 4 Described later. 5 31 Stat. 77 (1900).

6 US CONST., Art. I, §8, cl. 1. 7 *Downes*, 182 US at 287 (emphasis added).

acquire new territory by virtue of its inherent powers as a sovereign nation as well as by the authority granted by several provisions of the Constitution, including the powers to make war and to enter into international treaties. From the power to acquire territories flowed the power to govern them. Such power is entrusted by the Constitution to Congress. The basis of that grant is found in the provision of the Constitution known as the Territorial Clause.[8] This reads: 'The Congress shall have power to dispose and make all needful Rules and Regulations respecting the Territory or other Property belonging to the United States . . . ' This reasoning was echoed in Justice White's concurring opinion and repeated in further opinions of the Court regarding the situation of the newly acquired territories.

The importance of Justice White's concurring opinion lies in its development of what soon was to become the settled doctrine of the Court. In order to determine what provisions of the Constitution apply to a specific territory, Justice White argued, the Court had to ascertain 'the situation of the territory and its relation to the United States'.[9] He then fashioned a distinction until then unknown in American constitutional jurisprudence: that between what he termed 'incorporated' territory and 'unincorporated' territory. Incorporated territory is territory that should be constitutionally considered part of the United States. Unincorporated territory, on the other hand, is territory *belonging to* but *not a part of* the United States. Not all provisions of the Constitution apply to unincorporated territory. To decide whether the Uniformity Clause was extended to Puerto Rico, it was necessary to determine whether the latter had been incorporated into the United States by the provisions of either the Treaty of Paris or the Foraker Act. He concluded that it had not. His conclusion was based, partly, on the provision made by Article IX of the Treaty of Paris that 'the civil rights and political status of the native inhabitants of the territories hereby ceded to the United States shall be determined by Congress',[10] and, partly, by his assessment that, taken as a whole, the Foraker Act showed that Congress had not manifested its intention to incorporate Puerto Rico into the nation.[11] In an often quoted passage of his opinion, Justice White concluded:

> The result of what has been said is that whilst in an international sense Porto Rico was not a foreign country, since it was subject to the sovereignty of and was owned by the United States, it was foreign to the United States in a domestic sense, because the island had not been incorporated into the United States, but was merely appurtenant thereto as a possession.[12]

Justice White's incorporation doctrine was accepted by only four members of the majority in *Downes*, including himself. But the doctrine was fully adopted

[8] Art. IV, Section 3, clause 2. [9] *Downes*, 182 US, at 293.
[10] Ibid., at 339–40. [11] Ibid., at 340.
[12] Ibid., at 341–42. Upon arriving in Puerto Rico, the Americans changed Puerto Rico's name to Porto Rico. In later decades the misspelling was corrected and the original Spanish form was restored.

by the majority in 1904 in *Dorr v. United States*,[13] a case arising from the Philippines, in which the Court held that the constitutional right to a trial by jury did not apply to the Philippines because those islands had not been incorporated into the United States. With the distinction between incorporated and unincorporated territories, the Court was in effect treating some of the new territories merely as property of the United States.

In *Kopel v. Bingham*, a case decided in 1909, the Supreme Court found that although it had not been incorporated, as that term was defined in those early cases, Puerto Rico should be considered a completely 'organised' territory of the United States.[14] Making reference to nineteenth-century cases referring to the territories, the Court defined organised territory as:

> that system of organized government[. . .]by which certain regions of the country have been erected into civil governments. These governments have an executive, a legislative and a judicial system. They have the powers which all these departments of government have exercised, which are conferred upon them by act of Congress, and their legislative acts are subject to the disapproval of the Congress of the United States. They are not in any sense independent governments; they have no Senators in Congress and no Representatives in the lower house of that body except what are called delegates, with limited functions. Yet they exercise nearly all the powers of government, under what are generally called organic acts passed by Congress conferring such powers on them.[15]

As a result of these cases, territories, then, could be either incorporated or unincorporated, organised or unorganised, in various combinations. Puerto Rico, it was determined, was an unincorporated, organised territory of the United States.

All members of the majority of the Court in *Downes* also found that the US Congress enjoyed *plenary* powers over unincorporated territories. They did clarify that plenary power did not mean absolute, arbitrary power. Some of the language of the later decisions seems to throw light on the meaning of the concept as related to the territories in question. For example, in *Grafton v. United States*,[16] Justice John Marshall Harlan explained that the relationship between a territory and the United States was not the same as that between a state and the US government. The main difference lies in the source of the authority to govern invested in the state or the territorial government. The government of a state derives its powers from the people of the state, whereas the government of the territory owes its existence wholly to the United States. Consequently, Justice Harlan added, the US government could exert over the territory power that it could not exercise over the states. The authority of the United States over the territories is 'paramount', he concluded. This, then, makes it clear that the normative sources of whatever autonomy states or territories may enjoy are quite different. The autonomy the territories may eventually gain, while

13 195 US 138 (2004). 14 211 US 468 (1909).
15 Ibid., at 475–76, quoting *In re Lane*, 135 US 443, 447 (1890). 16 206 US 333 (1907).

remaining territories, are the product of concessions made by the US Congress. In theory, those concessions may be revoked as Congress pleases. In *Grafton*, the Court seems to equate *plenary* with *exclusive* power. Not only is the power to govern the territories an exclusive power of the federal government, but also, within that government, it belongs exclusively to Congress.

The majority in *Downes* also agreed that there are limitations on the plenary power of Congress to govern the territories. According to the Court, those limitations are imposed by some then-undefined 'fundamental rights' enjoyed by those subject to the authority of the US government. In familiar common-law technique, the Court left the task of defining those fundamental rights to further case by case determinations. Over time, the Court has extended to the territories most of the fundamental personal rights enshrined in the US Constitution Bill of Rights. Thus, it has been decided that at least the following constitutional rights should be considered fundamental, and therefore extensive to Puerto Rico: freedom of expression,[17] due process of law,[18] equal protection of the laws,[19] the right to travel[20] and the protection against unreasonable searches and seizures.[21] Those residing in Puerto Rico may also claim against the US government rights created by federal legislative enactments made extensive to Puerto Rico expressly or implicitly. However, the general principle established in the *Insular Cases* was that the full constitution does not automatically apply to the peoples of the territories. In fact, some discrete rights are still held not to apply in the territories, such as the federal constitutional right to a trial by jury.[22] It is unclear, on the other hand, whether such a right as the right to bear arms, enshrined in the Second Amendment to the Constitution, is extensive to Puerto Rico.

A case that elaborated these understandings with reference to the status of the inhabitants of Puerto Rico was *Gonzalez v. Williams*.[23] The Court unanimously determined that Puerto Ricans should not be considered 'aliens' for purposes of entry into the US mainland. The case arose when a Puerto Rican woman arriving from Puerto Rico was detained in the port of New York as an alien under the US Immigration Act of 3 March 1891.[24] As someone who had come under the sovereignty of the United States, the Court reasoned, Ms. González owed

[17] *Balzac v. Porto Rico, 258 US 298 (1922); Posadas de Puerto Rico Associates v. Tourism Company of Puerto Rico*, 478 US 1046 (1986).

[18] *Bianchi v. Morales*, 262 US 170 (1923); *Secretary of Agriculture v. Central Roig*, 338 US 604 (1950); *Calero Toledo v. Pearson Yacht Leasing Co.*, 416 US 663 (1974); *Examining Board v. Flores de Otero*, 426 US 572 (1976).

[19] *Examining Board v. Flores de Otero*, 426 US 572 (1976); *Califano v. Torres*, 435 US 1 (1978); *Harris v. Rosario*, 446 US 651 (1980).

[20] *Califano v. Torres*, 435 US 1 (1978).

[21] *Segurola v. United States*, 275 US 106 (1927); *Torres v. Puerto Rico*, 442 US 465 (1979).

[22] See, for example, *Hawaii v. Mankichi*, 190 US 197 (1903) (the right to trial by jury did not apply to Hawaii, then a territory); *Dorr v. United States*, 195 US 138 (1904) (the right to a jury trial was not applicable in the Philippines); and *Balzac v. Porto Rico*, 258 US 298 (1922) (the right did not apply in Puerto Rico, either).

[23] 192 US 1 (1904).

[24] US Immigration Act, 3 March 1891, 26 Stat. 1084 (1891).

allegiance to that country and should, accordingly, be considered a national of the United States of America. As a national she could not be denied entry into the country.

As will be discussed next, in 1917 Congress extended US citizenship collectively to those born in Puerto Rico. Many residents of the island hoped that the extension of citizenship would be deemed to signal the intention of Congress to incorporate Puerto Rico. After all, in previous decisions the Supreme Court had expressed the notion that bestowing US citizenship to a given territory should be taken as an indication that the territory had been incorporated. Prominent among those decisions had been *Rasmussen v. United States*,[25] in which the Court had determined that Alaska had been constitutionally incorporated into the United States, based primarily on the fact that in the treaty of acquisition of that territory from Russia, Congress had manifested its desire to confer political and civil rights on its inhabitants as American citizens. Faced with the question of whether the transformation of the inhabitants of Puerto Rico into US citizens implied the incorporation of the territory, the Court answered in the negative in *Balzac v. Porto Rico*, decided in 1922.[26] It concluded that the law extending such citizenship contained no indication from which to infer the purpose of Congress to incorporate Puerto Rico into the Union. According to the Court, the realities surrounding the situation of the new territories required that incorporation be not lightly inferred from any act of Congress, but should be the result of 'a clear declaration of purpose'.[27] The Court stated:

> Had Congress intended to take the important step of changing the treaty status of Porto Rico by incorporating it into the Union, it is reasonable to suppose that it would have done so by the plain declaration, and would not have left it to mere inference. Before the question became acute at the close of the Spanish War, the distinction between acquisition and incorporation was not regarded as important, or at least it was not fully understood and had not aroused great controversy. Before that, the purpose of Congress might well be a matter of mere inference from various legislative acts; but in these latter days, incorporation is not to be assumed without express declaration, or an implication so strong as to exclude any other view.[28]

The incorporation of territory into the Union, as a constitutional matter, was thus declared to be a political decision to be made by Congress in the exercise of its plenary powers over the territories. This is still the prevailing understanding.

The doctrine of unincorporation in effect constituted a regime of political and legal subordination that granted the US Congress paramount powers over the territories. The system can cut several ways for the territories. It can be the basis for discriminatory legislation, as has often been the case, especially regarding social benefits for the population at large. Thus, for example, in 1978 the Supreme Court validated federal legislation that excluded Puerto Rico from a programme that provided aid to qualified aged, blind and disabled

[25] 197 US 516 (1905). [26] *Balzac v. Porto Rico*, 258 US 298 (1922).
[27] Ibid., 311. [28] Ibid., 306.

persons in the United States.[29] And in 1980 the Court asserted that, under its plenary powers over the territories, Congress can determine that Puerto Rico will receive less financial assistance than the states to provide aid to families with needy dependent children.[30] Both cases relied on the rationale of the *Insular Cases*, discussed earlier. But under that same paramount power Congress can also produce legislation deemed beneficial to the territories. That may be the case with the provision that allows the proceeds of United States excise taxes collected on articles produced in Puerto Rico and sent to the United States and those of customs collected on foreign products entering Puerto Rico to be returned to the government of Puerto Rico. Some have argued that equally beneficial have been the several programmes of tax exemption put in place by the US Congress for the benefit of individuals residing and US corporations doing business in the territories, including Puerto Rico. The delegation of power to Puerto Rico to draft its own internal constitution, as discussed later, may be considered another example of such benign exercise by Congress of its plenary power over the islands.

The validity of the doctrine fashioned in those early years of the twentieth century has been confirmed by the US Supreme Court on many occasions in a variety of contexts. One such recent reaffirmation occurred in a case dealing with the situation of the detainees in the US military base in Guantánamo, Cuba. The Court had to decide whether the prisoners held as enemy combatants in Guantánamo had a constitutional right to question the legality of their detention through the writ of habeas corpus in federal courts. In order to address the issue, the Court, in a divided decision in *Boumedienne v. Bush*,[31] first examined the extent of the extraterritorial application of the US Constitution. It relied expressly on the rationale of the *Insular Cases* to sustain the conclusion that wherever the United States of America exercised its sovereignty, whether *de jure* or *de facto*, at least some Constitutional guarantees had to apply. In Guantánamo, it held, the right to seek relief under the habeas corpus provisions of the Constitution was one of them.

One interesting comparison to make is that between the territories and the situation of the Native American tribes. The Supreme Court of the United States has exhibited significant variation in its normative treatment of indigenous peoples throughout US history. It has gone from recognising them as 'nations' in the early years of the Republic to their description as 'domestic' or 'dependent' sovereigns in more recent times.[32] As in the case of the territories, the Court has determined that Congress's power over Indian affairs is plenary. One basic difference, however, between the Indian tribes and the territories is the recognition that the tribes hold at least a residual inherent sovereignty that does not

[29] *Califano v. Torres*, 435 US 1 (1978). [30] *Harris v. Rosario*, 446 US 651 (1980).

[31] 553 US 723 (2008).

[32] See generally T. Alexander Aleinikoff, *Semblances of Sovereignty: The Constitution, The State, and American Citizenship* (Cambridge, MA: Harvard University Press, 2002), especially Ch. 5: 'The erosion of American Indian sovereignty', 95–122.

depend, at least theoretically, on a delegation of powers from Congress. The territories, on the other hand, enjoy only such powers as are delegated to them by Congress by virtue of its prerogatives under the Territorial Clause. A leading student of these questions has summarised some of the major differences in the following manner:

> Nor are tribes analogous to governments in US territories. Indian sovereignty is to some degree more expansive: it is deemed inherent, while territorial governmental power is a product of congressional delegation. Furthermore, the Constitution does not directly apply to tribal actions; under the Insular Cases, however, territorial residents receive the protection of some 'fundamental' constitutional rights. But tribal sovereignty is also less comprehensive than the power conferred on territorial governments, which are delegated authority to regulate all persons within their boundaries. [In general, Indian tribes may regulate only their members.] And territories are plainly outside the borders of US states[. . .]Reservations, however, may be subject to regulation by the states in which they are located.[33]

The statutory framework

Since 1900, the US Congress has passed a series of legislative acts to provide for the government of Puerto Rico. They constitute the basic statutory framework that supports the system of autonomy – however it may be characterised – under which the Puerto Rican political community is governed. The following is a brief account of the relevant legislation.

The Foraker Act, 1900

The United States of America replaced the military government installed in Puerto Rico after the 1898 occupation with a civilian government whose features were defined in an act of Congress known as the Foraker Act of 1900,[34] after the Senator from Ohio who sponsored the bill. At that point Puerto Rico did not have any representation, of any form, in Congress. Given this fact and the nature of its dispositions, the Foraker Act cannot be characterised except as a decidedly imperial piece of legislation designed to organise a colonial government in the newly acquired territory.

The Foraker Act established a civilian government constituted by a governor, appointed by the President of the United States; a legislative assembly made up of a House of Delegates, invested with traditional legislative powers; and an Executive Council, which exercised both legislative and executive functions. The assembly would exercise legislative power over vaguely defined local matters, including the power to modify and repeal any laws then in existence in Puerto Rico. The members of the House of Delegates were to be elected by qualified voters; whereas all Executive Council members were to be appointed by the

[33] Ibid., at 98. [34] 31 Stat. 77 (1900).

President of the United States. Only five of the eleven members of the Executive Council had to be native inhabitants of Puerto Rico. The US Congress retained the power to annul the acts of the Puerto Rican legislature. The Foraker Act vested the judicial power in the courts and tribunals already established by the military governors that ruled the country from 1898 to 1900. A much debated provision of the Foraker Act, which underlined its colonial character, automatically extended to Puerto Rico all statutory laws of the United States 'not locally inapplicable'. This final phrase has never had any practical consequences.

The Foraker Act initiated the practice of exempting Puerto Rico from the application of US internal revenue laws, although Puerto Rican residents do pay several federal taxes, such as those relating to social security. By generally exempting Puerto Rico from paying federal income taxes and federal duties on goods and services produced and merchandised in Puerto Rico, Congress created a sphere of fiscal autonomy in the island that would allow the territorial government to impose its own taxes internally. It is generally understood that this fiscal autonomy is subject to revision by the US Congress as it sees fit. For example, eventually Congress clarified that in the exercise of its tax prerogatives, the Puerto Rican government could not discriminate against products imported into the country from the United States or other foreign jurisdictions. This provision left the Puerto Rican government practically helpless to protect Puerto Rico's internal production from outside competition.[35]

The Jones Act, 1917

In 1917, in the exercise of its plenary powers over the territory of Puerto Rico, Congress passed the Jones Act.[36] The Act introduced certain changes in the structure of the government of the islands. It eliminated the Executive Council and created a second legislative chamber, the Senate, also to be elected by qualified voters residing in Puerto Rico. It provided for a statutory bill of rights largely modelled on the federal Bill of Rights. This new organic act to provide for the government of Puerto Rico did not alter in any fundamental way the relationship between the islands and the United States. It left unaltered several important provisions of the Foraker Act of 1900, including that providing for the automatic extension of US federal laws to the territory.

By far the most important provision of the Jones Act was the collective extension of United States citizenship to Puerto Rican residents. A series of successive legislative provisions have given shape to the statutory framework that governs the enjoyment of US citizenship by persons born in Puerto Rico.

[35] See Carlos Díaz Olivo, 'La autonomía de Puerto Rico y sus lecciones en términos fiscales y económicos' [Puerto Rico's autonomy and its fiscal and economic lessons], in *L'abast de l'autonomia politica de Puerto Rico/El alcance de la autonomía política de Puerto Rico: Jornades/Jornadas* [The scope of the political autonomy of Puerto Rico: Proceedings] (Barcelona: Parlament de Catalunya, 2005), 29–30.

[36] 39 Stat. 951 (1917), codified at 48 USC §731 (1987).

In another section, later, I will address briefly some of the constitutional, legal, political and cultural implications of this provision.

The Elective Governor Act, 1947

Since 1900, the authority to appoint the governor of Puerto Rico resided in the President of the United States. Until 1946, all governors appointed by the president were Americans. This had been a constant source of friction between the appointed chief executives and the political leadership of the legislative assembly, composed almost entirely of Puerto Rican natives. Finally, in 1946, President Harry S. Truman appointed a Puerto Rican to occupy the post. However, pressure persisted to move Congress to allow Puerto Ricans to choose their governor themselves. In 1947 Congress passed legislation authorising Puerto Rican residents to elect their governor in the forthcoming 1948 general elections.[37] On January 1949, fifty years after the American occupation, the first elected Puerto Rican governor took office. He was Luis Muñoz Marín, a charismatic leader who had been an independence advocate and a socialist in his early political career, and who had founded the Popular Democratic Party (PDP) in the mid 1940s with a platform that promised fundamental social and political reforms. The PDP and Muñoz Marín were able to benefit from the effects of President Franklin D. Roosevelt's New Deal policies and from post–World War II American economic prosperity. As a result, the PDP was to become the dominant political party in Puerto Rico for the next quarter of a century. Its successful social reform movement led to the passing of abundant progressive legislation and to an eventual transformation of Puerto Rican society from a largely rural, agrarian world to a modernised, increasingly urban, industrial-oriented community. With a solid popular base, the PDP was able to draw into its fold former supporters of independence and statehood for Puerto Rico as well as liberals, socialists, nationalists and even conservatives. This strong and ample base of support seemed auspicious for further political reforms.

Public Law 600 of 1950

From the executive mansion, Muñoz Marín led a drive to obtain greater autonomous powers from the United States government. Meanwhile, the nationalist movement and a newly founded pro-independence party pursued through various means their campaign for an independent Puerto Rico. Additionally, the worldwide post–World War II decolonisation movement placed international pressure on the United States to deal with the problem of Puerto Rico. These and other factors seem to account for the decision made in 1950 by the United States Congress to legislate again to further increase the limited sphere of autonomy of the Puerto Rican government.

[37] Elective Governor Act 1947, 48 USC §737 *et seq.*

Action came by way of a congressional enactment known as Public Law 600,[38] which authorised Puerto Ricans to draft their own internal constitution, without recognising their full sovereignty. Congress mandated that the new constitution provide a republican form of government and include a bill of rights. It repealed most of the provisions contained in the Foraker and Jones Acts relating to the internal structure of the government of the territory, but left intact other important provisions pertaining to such matters as Puerto Rico's economic relationship to the United States, the force and effect of federal laws and the form of representation in Washington. The surviving provisions were codified into a new statute known as the Puerto Rican Federal Relations Act.[39] The Puerto Rican electorate gave its consent to the provisions of Public Law 600 in a referendum to that effect. A constitutional convention was convened. All existing political parties, except the Puerto Rican Independence Party, participated in the convention's proceedings. The constitutional text drafted by the convention was submitted to the electorate and approved by a majority vote. As prescribed by Public Law 600, the constitution was sent to the US Congress for its approval. Congress approved the new constitution on condition that certain of its provisions were rescinded and others modified. The Puerto Rican Constitutional Convention accepted the modifications and the Constitution was proclaimed into effect on 25 July 1952 by Governor Muñoz Marín. It was not until the general elections of November of that year that the voters had the opportunity to ratify the amendments required by Congress. They did.

The Puerto Rican Constitution, 1952

It should be noted that Public Law 600's intent was only to authorise the adoption of a new constitution to govern the internal affairs of Puerto Rico. Accordingly, the new constitution adopted in 1952 provided for the structure of the government and for a bill of rights. This bill of rights is generally regarded as a limitation on the actions of the Puerto Rican government, not of the federal government. As explained previously, US courts have held that constitutional protections for the individual rights of Puerto Rican residents against the actions of the US federal government, including Congress, are grounded on the fundamental provisions of the Bill of Rights of the US Constitution.

The 1952 Constitution established the process by which its text could be amended. The amendment process requires that at least two thirds of the total number of members of each house of the legislature concur on the proposal. The amendments must be submitted to the people in a referendum and, in order to pass, must be ratified by a majority of the electors voting thereon. To comply with a requirement imposed by the US Congress, the Constitution further added that any amendment shall be consistent with the resolution

[38] 64 Stat. 319, 48 USCA A. 731b (1950).

[39] 75 Stat. at L. 245, 48 USCA. §745 (1950).

enacted by the Congress of the United States approving the Constitution, with the applicable provisions of the Constitution of the United States, with the Puerto Rican Federal Relations Act and with Public Law 600.

The Constitution adopted two new names for the political entity known as Puerto Rico, one in English and another in Spanish. The members of the constitutional convention resolved that the body politic of Puerto Rico would be henceforth known in Spanish as the 'Estado Libre Asociado de Puerto Rico' and, in English, as the 'Commonwealth of Puerto Rico'. These two expressions do not correspond to each other from a linguistic point of view. They were made, conventionally, to translate into each other by the fiat of the majority of the members of the constitutional convention, who determined that the meanings of those two terms properly defined

> a state which is free of superior authority in the management of its own local affairs but which is linked to the United States of America and hence is a part of its political system in a manner compatible with its federal structure.[40]

The description of the current system provided in this chapter clearly suggests that the members of the convention went too far in their characterisation of what the new relationship entailed.

Arguments and a substantial amount of wishful thinking to the contrary, the process that led to the adoption of the 1952 Constitution did not effect a fundamental change in the constitutional and political relationship between the United States and Puerto Rico. The latter continued to be subjected to many of the provisions of the US Constitution, especially its Territorial Clause, to the plenary powers of Congress and to federal laws extended to it under the provisions of the old Foraker Act still in effect. As stated previously, some of the most important provisions of the old colonial organic statutes, the Foraker and the Jones Acts, were kept in force under what is known as the Puerto Rican Federal Relations Act.

Perhaps the most distinctive feature of the 1952 Constitution is the progressive character of the Bill of Rights adopted by the Puerto Rican Constitutional Convention. The new text benefitted from developments in the human rights discourse then in circulation in the international community. In many ways, its provisions go much further in the protection of individual rights than the US Constitution. Thus, for example, the Puerto Rican Constitution proscribes the death penalty; expressly recognises the right to privacy; incorporates certain social rights, such as the right to education; contains prohibitions against discrimination based on sex and social condition, among other (more

40 Resolution 22, Approved by the Constitutional Convention of Puerto Rico in the plenary session held 4 February 1952, in Marcos Ramírez Lavandero (ed.), *Documents on the Constitutional Relationship of Puerto Rico and the United States* (Puerto Rico Federal Affairs Administration, 3rd edn., 1988), at 191.

traditional) categories; and extends certain constitutional protections to relationships among private actors (establishing important exceptions to the state action doctrine prevalent in US constitutional jurisprudence).

The international dimension

The international foundations of the current political arrangement in Puerto Rico may be described very succinctly.

Puerto Rico was ceded to the United States by virtue of the Treaty of Paris[41] entered into by that country and the Spanish government as a result of the Spanish-American War of 1898. Article IX of the treaty tersely stated, 'The civil rights and political status of the native inhabitants of the territories hereby ceded to the United States shall be determined by the Congress'. This broad concession of power, together with the provisions of the Territorial Clause of the US Constitution, has served as a basis for the 'plenary powers' element of the doctrine of unincorporation and as a justification for the great flexibility accorded Congress by the American courts in its dealings with the territories.

After the establishment of the United Nations, the United States began sending annual reports about Puerto Rico to the international organisation to comply with the obligations imposed upon colonial powers by Article 73(e) of the UN Charter.[42] However, after the adoption of the Puerto Rican Constitution of 1952, the United States notified the UN that it would no longer report on Puerto Rico, arguing that the latter had acquired a sufficient degree of self-government to justify its being removed from the list of territories about which the existing colonial powers had to report.[43] On 27 November 1953 the UN General Assembly noted the position taken by the United States and expressed its approval.[44]

[41] Treaty of Paris, December 10, 1898, US-Spain, 30 Stat. 1754.

[42] Article 73(e) of the UN Charter reads:

> Members of the United Nations which have or assume responsibilities for the administration of territories whose peoples have not yet attained a full measure of self-government recognize the principle that the interests of the inhabitants of these territories are paramount, and accept as a sacred trust the obligation to promote to the utmost, within the system of international peace and security established by the present Charter, the well-being of the inhabitants of these territories, and, to this end:
>
> ...
>
> e. to transmit regularly to the Secretary-General for information purposes, subject to such limitation as security and constitutional considerations may require, statistical and other information of a technical nature relating to economic, social, and educational conditions in the territories for which they are respectively responsible other than those territories to which Chapters XII and XIII apply.

[43] Memorandum by the Government of the United States of America Concerning the Cessation of Transmission of Information Under Article 73(e) of the Charter with Regard to the Commonwealth of Puerto Rico (1953), in *Documents on the Constitutional Relationship of Puerto Rico and the United States*, 616–24.

[44] United Nations General Assembly Resolution 748 (VIII): Cessation of the Transmission of Information Under Article 73(e) of the Charter in Respect to Puerto Rico, in *Documents on the Constitutional Relationship of Puerto Rico and the United States*, 614–15.

The Assembly expressed its recognition that the people of the Commonwealth of Puerto Rico had effectively exercised their right to self-determination and that, by virtue of the process leading to the promulgation of the Constitution of 1952, they had been invested with 'attributes of political sovereignty' which 'clearly' identified the status of self-government attained by the Puerto Rican people 'as that of an autonomous political entity'.[45] As a result, the United States ceased sending its annual reports to the UN regarding Puerto Rico.

Puerto Rico has very limited participation in international affairs. It is not a member of the United Nations, the Organisation of American States and many other international and regional institutions. Its foreign relations are handled generally by the United States. Whatever international participation Puerto Ricans have engaged in have been mostly through private individuals and entities who have managed to link themselves to international non-governmental organisations. One salient example is Puerto Rico's independent participation in the International Olympic Committee and other sports organisations and networks. Association with international institutions, however limited in scope, has had to rely on Washington's formal or informal consent. In that vein, Puerto Rico has been granted observer status in the Caribbean Community (CARICOM), associate membership in the World Health Organisation and participation in the World Tourism Organisation. The governor of Puerto Rico participated for the first time as an observer in the Second Ibero-American Summit of Heads of States and Governments held in Madrid, Spain, in 1992. The UN Secretary General invited Puerto Rico to take part in the World Summit on Sustainable Development in South Africa in 2002. Efforts to be admitted into UNESCO and other international bodies have been unsuccessful.[46]

On the other hand, barring an express provision to the contrary, all treaties signed by the United States bind Puerto Rico to the same extent as the states of the Union. Ordinarily, Puerto Rico does not play any significant role in negotiations over treaties that may have special relevance for Puerto Rico.

Resolution 1514 (XV) of the UN General Assembly, adopted in 1960, proclaimed the right to self-determination and independence of all colonial countries and peoples.[47] Its reference not only to Trust and Non Self-Governing Territories, but also to all those 'that had not yet attained independence', opened up a new debate about Puerto Rico. Upon the urging of independence advocates, in 1967 the UN Decolonisation Committee assumed jurisdiction over the Puerto Rican case and for several years has consistently asserted the right of the Puerto

45 Ibid.

46 For more detailed analysis of Puerto Rico's international activity, see Arnaldo J. Teissoniere Ortiz, 'Situación de Puerto Rico frente al Derecho Internacional, con especial referencia al Derecho Internacional del Trabajo y la participación en la OIT' [Puerto Rico in the light of international law, with special reference to international labour law and participation in ILO], *Cuadernos de Estudios Empresariales*, 12 (2002), 325–48.

47 United Nations General Assembly Resolution 1514 (XV) on the Granting of Independence to Colonial Countries and Peoples (1960).

Rican people to self-determination and independence under international law and has exhorted the United States to transfer the powers of sovereignty to Puerto Rico in accordance with Resolution 1514 (XV).[48]

The committee has recently called upon the General Assembly to review the case of Puerto Rico in all its aspects.[49]

Today most people in Puerto Rico – of all political persuasions – adhere to the belief that Puerto Rico has a right to self-determination. Even the US Congress has recognised the validity of the claim, at least rhetorically, and has included references to the right of self-determination of the Puerto Rican people in proposals that have come out of diverse congressional committees or that have been advanced by individual legislators to provide for a process by which Puerto Ricans may decide their future political status.[50] Similar language has been used by the President's office.[51] However, to date no federal legislation has been passed to achieve that purpose.

Conceptually, the recognition of the people of Puerto Rico's right to self-determination is a very important development. However one may characterise the current system of government in the islands, widespread support for the notion that Puerto Rico should be provided the opportunity to fully exercise its right to self-determination suggests that there is a high degree of dissatisfaction with the actual arrangement and that there is an urgent need to revise it.

Institutional framework

The institutional framework of Puerto Rico's relative autonomy has two basic dimensions: the institutions of the so-called 'federal' government, and those pertaining to the internal structure of the Puerto Rican government itself.

The basic structure of the federal system in the United States comprises two main components: the states and the central, or federal, government. Other units, such as Washington, DC (the capital), territories and Indian tribes, occupy peculiar locations in the constitutional scheme of things, as is illustrated by the status of the territory of Puerto Rico. The federal government, in turn, is constituted by three separate but interdependent branches of government: the

[48] See Ramirez Lavandero, 'Introductory note', *Documents on the Constitutional Relationship of Puerto Rico and the United States*, 613.

[49] See General Assembly, GA/COL/3160, Department of Public Information, News and Media Division, New York, Special Committee on Decolonization, 5th and 6th Meetings, 'Special Committee on Decolonization calls on United States to expedite Puerto Rico's self-determination process', 14 June 2007; Kevin Mead, 'UN decolonization committee eyes PR', *Caribbean Business*, Sunday, 26 June, 2011, online edition at www.caribbeanbusiness.com/news03.php?nt_id=58665&ct_id=1 (accessed 22 March 2013).

[50] See, for example, United States Congress, House Committee on Interior and Insular Affairs, Report Together with Additional Views on Puerto Rico Self-Determination Act, H.R. 4765, 101st Cong., 2nd Sess. (1990); United States Congress, H.R 1230: Puerto Rico Self-Determination Act, 112th Cong. (2007).

[51] See *Report by the President's Task Force on Puerto Rico's Status*, March 2011.

bicameral legislature known as the US Congress; the Executive, whose powers are vested in the President of the nation; and the judicial branch, led by the US Supreme Court. All three branches of the federal government have jurisdiction over Puerto Rico. The US Government exercises either exclusive or concurrent power over such areas of Puerto Rican life and society as communications, currency, postal service, citizenship, immigration, interstate and international commerce, labour relations, the environment, safety and health, among others, and controls all matters relating to foreign affairs and military defence.

Congressional legislation extends to Puerto Rico to the same extent that it does in the states, unless Puerto Rico is expressly exempted from its application. Congress may also legislate specifically for Puerto Rico by virtue of its plenary powers under the Territorial Clause of the US Constitution. The US President is the supreme executive authority and oversees a plethora of US administrative agencies that operate in Puerto Rico as in any other state of the Union. Federal social and welfare programmes have been extended, with limitations, to the residents of Puerto Rico. The United States possesses military installations and other property in Puerto Rico. In sum, for all practical purposes the Puerto Rican government's relationship to US federal executive agencies is very similar to that of the states. Puerto Rico is also inserted into the structure of the federal judiciary as if it were a state of the Union. Because of its special importance, the way the federal judiciary operates in Puerto Rico will be described separately later.

Puerto Rico is represented in the US federal government by way of a Resident Commissioner in Washington, DC, who is a member of the US House of Representatives with voice, but without full voting rights. The Commissioner is elected in Puerto Rico by popular vote during the general elections every four years. He or she may be appointed to House committees, where he or she can vote, but cannot cast a final vote on legislation proposed in the House, even if it applies to Puerto Rico. There is no representation in the Senate. In recent years the government of Puerto Rico has run an office for Puerto Rican affairs in Washington that carries on mostly lobbying activities on behalf of Puerto Rico. The office is a dependency of the Puerto Rican government and not a federal organ. Its relationship to the Resident Commissioner depends on whether the latter and the governor belong to the same or different political parties.

The internal structure and dynamics of the Puerto Rican government

The Constitution of 1952 established a government based on the principle of separation of powers and patterned on the structure of the US government. The Executive Branch is headed by a Governor, elected by popular vote for a four-year term. He or she is assisted by a constitutional cabinet whose members are appointed by the Governor and confirmed by the Senate, with the exception of the Secretary of State, whose appointment requires confirmation by both the Senate and the House of Representatives. There is a bicameral legislative branch. The upper house is the Senate, and the lower chamber is the House of Representatives, both of whose members are chosen by popular vote. All members of these bodies are elected for four-year terms that coincide with those served by the Governor.

Formally, the role of the Governor in the relationship with the United States of America is very similar to that of the governors of the states. But politically, his or her degree of influence and the dynamics of her or his relationship to the US President have varied over the years since the establishment of the Commonwealth government. During the years of the governorship of Luis Muñoz Marín, the head of the pro-Commonwealth Popular Democratic Party, he sought to relate to the presidents, especially Presidents Harry S. Truman and John F. Kennedy, in a way resembling the relationship among heads of states. He strove to serve as a liaison between the United States of America and the leaders of Latin American and Caribbean countries closely allied to the United States of America. Later governors, especially those belonging to the pro-statehood New Progressive Party, have preferred to link themselves to the organisations of state governors and to function as other state governors do within the political structure of the United States of America.

Besides the central government, there are seventy-eight municipal governments that oversee governance at the local level. They are typically headed by a mayor, as the chief executive, and a local legislative assembly. Mayors usually constitute a strong political force with the capacity to influence the results of general elections and, therefore, the composition of the central government's elective organs.

Puerto Rican politics is driven by a system of political parties whose ideological positions are generally defined by their stance regarding the political status of Puerto Rico vis-à-vis the United States. Thus, there is currently a political party that advocates statehood, that is, that Puerto Rico become the fifty-first state of the Union (the New Progressive Party or NPP); another that promotes independence (the Puerto Rican Independence Party or PIP); and yet another that prefers the current Commonwealth arrangement or some modified form of autonomy (the Popular Democratic Party or PDP).[52] Support for these political options has varied throughout the past century. It seems to hinge, among other things, on popular perceptions about their respective capacities to address three fundamental concerns: (1) economic well-being; (2) cultural survival; and (3) political empowerment. One can comfortably predict that whoever or whatever political organisation or movement is able to articulate the formula better adjusted to satisfy these common aspirations of the diverse sectors of the Puerto Rican people will eventually move a substantial majority in its favour.

[52] As of this writing there are also some minor parties seeking official recognition. One advocates 'sovereignty' for Puerto Rico; another one has not adopted a single stance about the status options, but supports a process of self-determination by which Puerto Ricans choose their own political future; and a third one has made workers' rights its main focus of attention.

The judicial system

The judicial system in Puerto Rico also has two levels: the Puerto Rican judiciary and the federal judicial system.

The Puerto Rican judicial system properly has several layers, including municipal judges, courts of first instance, intermediate courts of appeals and, at the apex of the system, a Supreme Court. Judges, including Supreme Court Justices, are appointed by the Governor with the consent of the Senate. Currently, all the members of the Puerto Rican judiciary are Puerto Rican natives. Inferior and appellate court judges are appointed for specified terms, while Supreme Court Justices may serve until they reach seventy years of age. The courts are tribunals of general jurisdiction and have the obligation to apply both Puerto Rican and US law. The administration of the entire system is entrusted by the Constitution to the President of the Supreme Court, with the assistance of the Office for the Administration of Courts, which, in turn, is overseen by an Administrative Director. This system of courts manages by far the majority of civil and criminal cases generated within the jurisdiction of Puerto Rico. Proceedings are conducted in Spanish.

Federal courts have consistently determined that the Supreme Court of Puerto Rico is to be considered the final arbiter in the resolution of disputes about the interpretation of the Puerto Rican Constitution and Puerto Rican laws. However, federal law is supreme, which means that, in case of conflict, the US Constitution, federal legislation and regulations, as well as treaties entered into by the US, supersede the Constitution, laws and regulations of Puerto Rico.

The federal judiciary operating in Puerto Rico is part of the federal judicial system in place in the United States. That system consists mainly of courts of first instance known as federal district courts, intermediate courts of appeals that operate in geographical divisions known as circuits and the US Supreme Court. There are also several specialised courts that have jurisdiction over such matters as taxes, bankruptcy, international trade and veterans' claims.

There is a federal district court for the district of Puerto Rico located in the capital city, San Juan. Like any other federal court in the United States, its jurisdiction is limited. It concentrates on resolving issues arising under federal law or involving citizens of diverse states or territories of the United States, including Puerto Rico. Presently, all active and senior judges of the district court for Puerto Rico are lawyers of Puerto Rican origin. Proceedings are conducted in English.

Decisions from the district court can be appealed to the Federal Court of Appeals for the First Circuit, located in Boston, Massachusetts. Revision of determinations of this Court of Appeals, in turn, may be sought in the United States Supreme Court. The US Supreme Court may also review certain final judgments and decrees of the Supreme Court of Puerto Rico.[53]

[53] Section 1258 of Volume 28 of the United States Code reads: 'Final judgments or decrees rendered by the Supreme Court of the Commonwealth of Puerto Rico may be reviewed by the Supreme Court by writ of certiorari where the validity of a treaty or statute of the United States is drawn in question or where the validity of a statute of the Commonwealth of Puerto Rico is

In appropriate cases and controversies properly brought before them, US federal courts may subject to scrutiny any actions of the Puerto Rican government allegedly in conflict with the Constitution, laws or treaties of the United States. This means that any competent US federal court may invalidate legislation passed by the Puerto Rican legislature, if it violates federal law. There are no specialised tribunals established specifically to address controversies between Puerto Rico and the United States regarding the exercise of powers by either government. Interpretations about the extent of federal power over Puerto Rico are, by definition, federal questions subject to ultimate determination by the United States Supreme Court.

On many occasions these prerogatives of federal courts have caused frictions between the federal judiciary, especially at the local level, and the government and sectors of the Puerto Rican people. These powers have also been the source of considerable controversy. Some view the federal court as a guarantor of the rights of US citizens residing in Puerto Rico. In fact, there have been periods in which advocates for the poor, civil rights, prison reform and other popular causes have resorted to federal court to seek relief from actions or omissions by officers and agents of the Commonwealth government under the belief that that court would be more inclined to favour their claims than its Puerto Rican counterparts. Others have regarded the court as an imperial imposition that should be abolished or, at least, strictly limited in its capacity to intervene in Puerto Rican affairs. Certain very controversial decisions by some of its judges that seemed to favour the pro-statehood movement have spurred accusations that the court has taken upon itself the promotion of a particular position in the never-ending debate about Puerto Rico's political future. An example of an especially ardent indictment of the court was provided by popular reaction to the willingness of its judges to punish harshly hundreds of people who engaged in civil disobedience as part of a massive movement to oust the US Navy from the small island of Vieques. This populated Puerto Rican municipality had lived for decades under the effect of live bombardment and other military exercises conducted by the US Armed Forces. The US Navy eventually withdrew from Vieques under local and international pressure. The federal court in Puerto Rico, however, remained tarnished by the experience. The federal district court's composition has also been cause for resentment. Although its members are appointed by the President of the United States, the appointment process has not been immune from the intervention of local politics, with contending sides vying to influence the designation of its judges.

drawn in question on the ground of its being repugnant to the Constitution, treaties, or laws of the United States, or where any title, right, privilege, or immunity is specially set up or claimed under the Constitution or the treaties or statutes of, or any commission held or authority exercised under, the United States. 28 USC. 1258.

The interaction of legal traditions

After over a century of US presence, Puerto Rico has developed what amounts to a mixed legal system that incorporates important elements of continental Europe's civil law tradition and of the Anglo-American common law tradition. This convergence of legal traditions has been the result of intentional efforts to adjust the Puerto Rican legal system to the US legal framework as well as the consequence of the transformation of Puerto Rico into a constitutional, partly democratic, colonial welfare state.

By the end of the nineteenth century, Puerto Rico had in place a legal system drawn principally from the Spanish Civil Law tradition. Spain had extended to Puerto Rico its Civil, Commercial and Penal Codes; the Codes of Civil and Criminal Procedure; the *Ley Hipotecaria* (a comprehensive body of norms regulating the registration of title and diverse proceedings concerning the protection of property-related rights); and the Organic Law for the Court System. A unified Bar Association was established in 1840. Provision was made for free legal assistance to the poor.

From the early years of the American occupation, the US government decided to undertake reform of the system. A Penal Code imported from California and a Code of Criminal Procedure brought from Ohio replaced the existing ones. Constitutional and administrative law evolved following the American paradigm. Eventually, legislation was adopted modelled on American law in areas such as environmental, labour, insurance, banking, consumer, corporate and commercial law. Currently, the Rules of Evidence and Criminal and Civil Procedure follow closely the analogous federal rules. In short, substantive public law and civil and criminal procedure are closely patterned on the American model.

Civil Law has evolved in a different direction. The early American administrators decided to allow the system of private law prevalent in Puerto Rico to remain essentially unchanged. Some modifications were introduced into the Civil Code originated in Spain, but it was largely left in effect. The Code was amended again in 1930, but its main structure and philosophy remained. Major reforms were introduced by the Puerto Rican legislature in 1976 in order to address discriminatory provisions on account of sex in family and commercial matters. But they were achieved predominantly by amending provisions of the existing code.

Puerto Rican judges, scholars and law students, therefore, are trained in the concepts and methods of US public law and procedure as well as in the modes of analysis and interpretation of codes of the Spanish legal tradition. The interaction between those two legal cultures has sometimes been extremely problematic. For example, for many years the Puerto Rico Supreme Court interpreted the terse provisions of the Civil Code relating to responsibility arising out of negligence or fault by hastily importing concepts and solutions from the Anglo-American common law of torts. This tended to create confusion among the members of the legal community. Calls were made by scholars and members of the court itself, with limited success, to reverse this course.[54] On other occasions the interaction has been more fruitful. One arguably beneficial effect has been the extent to which legal operators have been able to draw on the wider spectrum of methods and techniques of interpretation and analysis available to them because of the community's familiarity and exposure to both legal traditions. This has enhanced the system's capacity to address complex legal problems in more creative ways.[55]

A salient development must be noted: the incorporation of public law values into the process of interpretation of the Civil Code and other legislation relating to private transactions. This has been largely the product of the constitutionalisation of private law, a phenomenon common in legal systems in which the civil law has to operate in the context of a constitution deemed to be the supreme law of the land. For example, in 1963, the Supreme Court of Puerto Rico, making a direct application of the constitutional principle of equality found in the Puerto Rican Constitution, abolished the traditional distinctions between legitimate and illegitimate children that existed in Puerto Rican family law.[56] In 1978, the Court, on the basis of the right to privacy, determined that it was unconstitutional to deny to married couples the right to obtain a divorce by mutual consent and ordered the lower courts to fashion and grant the appropriate remedy in spite of the provision to the contrary found in the Civil Code.[57] Relying mostly on privacy and the right to dignity, expressly mentioned in the Constitution, the Court has declared that it is unconstitutional for an employer to require an employee to submit to a polygraph test.[58] These few examples – many more could be cited – illustrate how the general tendency of constitutionalisation of the so-called private sphere has found fertile ground in the Puerto Rican legal system, although, precisely because of the influence of the US constitutional tradition, this development has not been taken to its logical conclusion. There still remain many areas of private action that are deemed to escape constitutional scrutiny. On many of those areas, however, the values underlying specific constitutional human rights – such as the prohibitions against different forms of discrimination – have found expression in extensive civil rights legislation. The Supreme Court of Puerto Rico has expressly held that such legislation

[54] See José Trías Monge, *El choque de dos culturas jurídicas en Puerto Rico: el caso de la responsabilidad extracontractual* [The clash between two legal cultures in Puerto Rico: the example of tort law] (Hato Rey PR: Equity Publishing Company, 1991).

[55] For more detailed analyses of this interaction, see, Ennio Colón and Associates, 'Puerto Rico', in Vernon Valentine Palmer, *Mixed Jurisdictions Worldwide: The Third Legal Family* (Cambridge University Press, 2001), 364–424; Efrén Rivera-Ramos, *The Legal Construction of Identity: The Judicial and Social Legacy of American Colonialism in Puerto Rico* (Washington, DC: APA Books, 2001), 50–3; José Trías Monge, *Legal Methodology in Some Mixed Jurisdictions*, 78 Tulane L. Rev. 333 (2003–4).

[56] *Ocasio v. Díaz*, 88 DPR 673 (1963).

[57] *Figueroa Ferrer v. ELA*, 107 DPR 250 (1978).

[58] *Arroyo v. Rattan Specialties*, 117 D.P.R 35 (1986).

embodies the ideals contained in the Puerto Rican Constitution and must be so construed.[59]

Legal education and the legal profession closely follow the American model, although there still remain vestiges of how the profession operates in civil law countries. Law is taught at the postgraduate level, as in law schools throughout the United States. Puerto Rican law schools submit to the accreditation standards of the American Bar Association. The University of Puerto Rico School of Law is a member of the American Association of Law Schools. The Bar is unified and subject to regulation and discipline by the Supreme Court of Puerto Rico, as is the practice in the several states of the Union. Admission to the Bar requires passing a bar exam administered by the Supreme Court. As in many civil law countries, however, notaries public have to be lawyers. A separate exam is required for that purpose. Until very recently, in order to be able to practice, all lawyers had to join the *Colegio de Abogados de Puerto Rico* (the Puerto Rican Bar Association), an organisation whose roots went back to the Spanish colonial period. However, in 2009, the Puerto Rican legislature, dominated by the pro-statehood New Progressive Party, abolished the compulsory requirement and now membership in the Bar Association is voluntary.[60] There is a separate, voluntary organisation for judges and lawyers involved in federal practice, which is actually a chapter of the national Federal Bar Association of the United States. Legal ethics, both in the Puerto Rican and federal bars, are based on American Bar Association principles, standards and rules.

The most dramatic transformation in the legal system since the Spanish colonial period has had to do with the judicial system and the role of courts. Gradually Puerto Rican courts, especially the Supreme Court, came to resemble American courts in many respects. Judicial review and the precedential value of Supreme Court decisions became firmly established. The structure and style of US constitutional argument became the norm. And so it remains to this day.

Citizenship, voting rights and representation

Puerto Ricans have been US citizens since 1917. The decision by the US government to collectively extend US citizenship to residents of Puerto Rico aroused expectations among sectors of the Puerto Rican population that viewed it as an indication that the Unites States was committing itself to incorporating Puerto Rico into the federation. After close to a hundred years since that event, this expectation has not been met. In fact, in 1922, in *Balzac v. Puerto Rico*,[61] the United States Supreme Court expressly decided that the extension of citizenship to Puerto Rican residents did not alter in any fashion the condition of Puerto

[59] *Santini Rivera v. Serv. Air*, 137 DPR 1, 4–12 (1994); *García Pagán v. Shiley Caribbean*, 122 DPR 193, 197–204 (1988); *Rodríguez Meléndez v. Supermercado Amigo*, 126 DPR 117, 124 (1990).

[60] Puerto Rico Law No. 121 of 13 October, 2009.

[61] 258 US 298 (1922).

Rico as an unincorporated territory of the United States. Neither did it accord its residents any additional political rights. Federal appellate courts have rejected claims by some Puerto Rican statehood supporters that US citizenship entitles residents of Puerto Rico at least to vote for the President of the United States.[62] The current situation, then, is that residents of Puerto Rico do not vote for federal officials, including the President, nor have representation in Congress, except for a non-voting resident commissioner in Washington who sits in the lower house.

The differentiated status of US citizens born or residing in Puerto Rico has several dimensions. One of them has to do with the notion that the citizenship enjoyed by those born in Puerto Rico is of a statutory nature, as opposed to the constitutional citizenship acquired by those born in the United States by virtue of the provisions of the Fourteenth Amendment to the US Constitution.[63] Although of little practical effect in the ordinary course of things, this distinction is important when considering the extent of the power of the US Congress to deprive someone of his or her US citizenship. It is generally accepted that statutory citizenship, such as that extended to those born in Puerto Rico, has less constitutional protection than that enjoyed by Fourteenth Amendment citizens. This understanding is crucial when assessing the possibilities that US citizens born or naturalised in Puerto Rico or their descendants be required to relinquish their citizenship in case of a radical change in the status of Puerto Rico, such as that entailed in its becoming a sovereign nation.[64]

Another dimension refers to the fact that the limitations inherent in the status of a US citizen residing in Puerto Rico is a condition based more on considerations of territoriality than anything else. Thus, a person born in Puerto Rico who moves to one of the United States acquires the right to vote for federal officials in his new state of residence. Whereas a US citizen – regardless of her ethnic or national origin – who moves from one of the states to Puerto Rico automatically loses her right to vote for President of the United States or to elect members of the US Congress. Puerto Rico is thus akin to a black hole where federal voting rights are lost as soon as a US citizen becomes a resident there.[65]

[62] See, for example, *Igartúa de la Rosa v. United States* (Igartúa I), 842 F. Supp. 607 (D. Puerto Rico), aff'd, 32 F.3rd 8 (1st Cir. 1994), cert. denied, 514 US 1049 (1995); *Igartúa de la Rosa v. United States (Igartúa II)*, 229 F.3d 80 (1st Cir. 2000); *Igartúa de la Rosa v. United States (Igartúa III)*, 417 F.3d 145 (1st Cir. 2005).

[63] The relevant part of the Fourteenth Amendment to the US Constitution reads: 'All persons born or naturalized in the United States, and subject to the jurisdiction thereof, are citizens of the United States and of the State wherein they reside'.

[64] For an excellent discussion of this question, see José Julián Álvarez González, 'The empire strikes out: Congressional ruminations on the citizenship status of Puerto Rico', *Harv. J. Legis* 27, 309 (1990).

[65] See Efrén Rivera-Ramos, 'Puerto Rico's political status: the long-term effects of American expansionist discourse', in Sanford Levinson and Bartholomew H. Sparrow (eds.), *The Louisiana Purchase and American Expansion, 1803–1898* (Lanham, MD: Rowman & Littlefield Publishers, 2005), 173–5.

These and other facts have led many to assert that the US citizenship enjoyed by Puerto Rican residents is a second-class citizenship.

Regardless of its constitutional and legal consequences, the extension of US citizenship to Puerto Ricans has had important political, social and cultural effects. It has become a discursive instrument to justify reciprocal demands between the metropolitan state and the population of the territory. For example, based on the argument that Puerto Ricans are US citizens, the United States government has conscripted Puerto Rican nationals to serve in its military forces. The government of Puerto Rico, on the other hand, has consistently petitioned the federal government for the extension of social and economic benefits to the population based on the claim that it constitutes a community of US citizens. US citizenship has also become a contested terrain on which issues of individual and collective identity have been intensely played out. Debates about the political future of Puerto Rico have been traversed by the question of citizenship. Some contend that the issue relates to the location of a community of US citizens in the constitutional landscape of the nation, while others regard the problem as one of according respect to a distinctive national community called Puerto Rico that has a right to self-determination and sovereignty.[66]

Conclusion

This chapter has illustrated the complexity of the relationship between the United States and Puerto Rico. That relationship has been the product of a series of historical, international, normative, institutional, political, social and cultural developments that have shaped the experience of Puerto Ricans as a political community as they passed from the domain of the Spanish Crown to the sovereignty of the United States.

Over the years Puerto Rico has gained a degree of autonomy over internal matters, such as the adoption of its own Constitution, the organisation and election of its own government and the ability to legislate over important areas of its economic, social, cultural and political life. The extent and implications of this progress has been the object of considerable controversy within the Puerto Rican community itself.

On the other hand, the normative framework developed by the United States to govern Puerto Rico from the early days of the occupation has left the country in a condition of undeniable political subordination. That situation is reflected in the jurisprudential doctrine that the US Congress enjoys plenary powers to dispose of matters pertaining to Puerto Rico as an unincorporated territory; in the supremacy of federal over Puerto Rican law; in the faculty of Congress to

[66] For a more in-depth consideration of the political, social, cultural and ideological effects of the extension of US citizenship to Puerto Rico, see Rivera-Ramos, *The Legal Construction of Identity*, in particular, Ch. 7: 'Hegemony through citizenship'.

legislate unilaterally over Puerto Rico; and in the lack of voting rights of Puerto Rican residents regarding the election of members of Congress with full voting prerogatives and of the Chief Executive officer of the country that may send their young people to war.

This reality has convinced many people that Puerto Rico's right to self-determination is being negated on a daily basis. There is, however, no consensus about the best solution to the problem. The difficulty is compounded by the fact that throughout the twentieth century, a process of *de facto* assimilation has brought Puerto Rico closer to the United States economically, demographically and politically. The close economic links between Puerto Rico and the United States make it difficult for many people to conceive an alternative future disassociated from the United States. On the other hand, important cultural differences persist between the two communities. Although Puerto Ricans have been made US citizens, a majority of Puerto Ricans view themselves as members of a distinct national community, Puerto Rico, with a national identity of its own. The United States, in turn, while willing in the 1950s to accommodate some of Puerto Rico's demands for self-government, has been reluctant to initiate a process leading to a more definitive solution of Puerto Rico's political status question.

The formal solution to the problem may be found in the United Nations' normative framework for addressing questions of decolonisation. This framework calls for a process leading to the colonial people's choice of one of three options: full sovereignty as an independent state; free association with an independent state, which could be the former metropolis; and integration with another independent state, which could also be the former metropolitan power.[67] Nonetheless, as a practical matter, the realisation of this formal dimension requires a political and social process generated within the territory itself that may be able not only to mobilise the majority of its population behind a unified claim for decolonisation, but also to pressure the United States into effectively addressing the question.

After more than a century of US presence in Puerto Rico, the island has undergone important demographic, economic, social, cultural and political transformations. It has become a heavily populated country, with its people divided between Puerto Rico and the mainland United States. It is no longer an agrarian society. But its industrial and commercial activity has been seriously impaired by the recent world crisis and economic upheavals of its own making. It has high indexes of formal education and also unbearably high rates of unemployment. Culturally, it has adopted many of the features of American pop culture, but it has retained important elements of its Spanish, African and indigenous heritage. Its legal system is the result of the convergence of the legal traditions of the US and the European continent. Puerto Rico is, in many ways, a place of conflicting tensions and demands. Most of all, it is still deeply engaged

[67] UN General Assembly Resolution 1541 (XV) of 1960.

with, and considerably divided about, the fundamental question of its political condition vis-à-vis the United States and the rest of the world. Whether Puerto Rico will be able to confront effectively the challenges posed by the conditions described previously is still an open question.

4

Foundations and institutions of South Tyrol's autonomy in Italy

Oskar Peterlini

My native land high in the Alps is known in English as South Tyrol, in German as Südtirol, and in Italian as Alto Adige (the name given to it by the Fascists). Although now part of Italy, it has historically been part of 'Land Tirol', or *Land im Gebirge* ('country of the mountains') as it was originally called, and lies at the heart of Central Europe. The historical Tyrol stretched from the northern chain of the Alps (the Karwendel Mountains), along the Austrian border with Germany, to the southern foothills of the Alps, at Lake Garda. The Brenner Pass, the deepest cleft in the Alps, is the geographical pass linking the north with the south.

Tyrol, including South Tyrol, was an independent country from 1248 to 1363 when it became part of the Duchy of Austria, although it maintained many of its ancient rights. This relationship remained unchanged for more than 500 years, until 1918, when South Tyrol was transferred to Italy after World War I. North and East Tyrol still belong to Austria and make up 'Bundesland Tirol'. The southern part, South Tyrol and Trentino, is now part of Italy, and forms the Region Trentino-South Tyrol, known as Trentino-Alto Adige in Italian.[1]

Italy, with a population of nearly 61 million, covers a land area of 301,263 square kilometres. South Tyrol (Province of Bozen/Bolzano) covers 7,400 square kilometres and Trentino (Province of Trento), 6,200 square kilometres, respectively making up 2.5 per cent and 2.1 per cent of the national territory. As it is a mountainous region and not as densely populated as the rest of Italy, with approximately 512,000 inhabitants in South Tyrol and 533,000 in Trentino, each province represents less than one per cent of the country's population.[2]

Apart from the small settlement areas, the population of the province of Trento is mainly Italian. The population of South Tyrol is nearly two-thirds

[1] Given the multi-lingual character of this part of Europe, place names in South Tyrol are given in Italian and German and, in the Ladin valleys, also in Ladin. The German 'Bozen' is the Italian 'Bolzano'.

[2] Data from the end of December 2011 put Italy's population at 60,820,787, with a population of 511,750 in South Tyrol and 533,394 in Trentino. Available at ISTAT (Italian Institute of Statistics), http://demo.istat.it/bilmens2011gen/index.html (accesssed 13 August 2012).

German speaking and just one-quarter Italian speaking.[3] About 30,000 people in the entire region (21,000 in South Tyrol and 9,000 in Trentino) speak the ancient Ladin language. In South Tyrol the Ladins live in the valleys of Gardena and Badia, in Trentino in the Val di Fassa, and others live in the province of Belluno in the area of Ampezzo. A further 9,000 people of Ladin origin (but who do not speak the language) in Trentino live mostly in Val di Non and Val di Sole.[4]

This chapter aims to provide a comprehensive overview of the historical, political and legal aspects of the autonomy of Trentino-South Tyrol.[5] I discuss how different communities within a single autonomous area can live together in harmony and co-operation, and how the arrangements for this, based on consociation,[6] can contribute to dealing with past injustices.

The international foundations of autonomy: historical and political background

From an independent country to a part of Austria

South Tyrol is a land of mountain passes and an important thoroughfare in the heart of the Alps. Lying as it does to the south of their main ridge, it acts as a link between the central European and Mediterranean worlds, and is equidistant from Venice, Milan and Munich. Its location means that South Tyrol has always been an important intersection point for trade between Italy,

[3] South Tyrol's population, including immigrants and others, October 2011: 62.3 per cent German speakers, 23.4 per cent Italian, 4.1 per cent Ladin and 10.3 per cent others, ASTAT Institute for Statistics of the Province of Bozen: www.provincia.bz.it/astat/de/bevoelkerung/bevoelkerung.asp (accessed 13 August 2012).

[4] Development of the language groups in South Tyrol 1880–2011, in Oskar Peterlini, *Südtirols Autonomie und die Verfassungsreformen Italiens, Vom Zentralstaat zu föderalen Ansätzen: die Auswirkungen und ungeschriebenen Änderungen im Südtiroler Autonomiestatut* [South Tyrol's Autonomy and the Constitutional Reforms in Italy – The constitutional debate about new forms of democratic participation, Italy's long road from the centralised state to timid federal principles, and interference with the Autonomy Statute], (Wien: New Academic Press Braumüller, 2012), 180.

[5] It expands on and updates the account in Oskar Peterlini, *Autonomy and the Protection of Ethnic Minorities in Trentino-South Tyrol* (Vienna: Wilhelm Braumüller, Universitätsverlag, 1997), in English and German; and *Regione Autonoma Trentino Alto Adige* [The Autonomous Region of Trentino-Alto Adige] (Trento: Piazza Dante, 1996 and 2000). The 1996 edition is in English, Italian and German and the 2000 edition is in German, Italian and Ladin; see also Oskar Peterlini, *L'autonomia che cambia. Gli effetti della riforma costituzionale del 2001 sull'autonomia speciale del Trentino Alto Adige Südtirol e le nuove competenze in base alla clausola di maggior favore* [The changing autonomy: the effects of the constitutional reform of 2001 on the Special Autonomy of Trentino South Tyrol/Alto Adige and the new powers according to the clause providing for more favourable provisions] (Bolzano: Casa editrice Praxis 3, 2010), http://oskarpeterlini.it/145.html.

[6] The concept of consociation, in the context of multi-ethnic societies, in which entitlements are based on membership of a community, in a scheme of power-sharing, has been associated in recent times with Arend Lijphart, although the practice or advocacy of power-sharing has ancient roots. For further discussion of power-sharing see the Introduction to this volume and the chapter by Joseph Marko.

Austria and Germany. The Brenner Pass (1,370 m, 4,495 ft), the deepest cleft in the Alps, links South and North Tyrol and is undoubtedly the most important connection between Northern and Southern Europe. It currently marks the border between Austria and Italy.

As early as Roman times, the 'country of the mountains' was an area of strategic importance. At the time of Christ's birth the Romans used it for their campaigns to the north while the German kings went south through the Brenner Pass to be crowned as emperors by the Pope. Seven hundred years ago the counties of the 'country of the mountains' were politically fused and the year 1248 marked the official birth of the 'Land Tirol' when the Count of Tyrol succeeded in joining the dioceses of Brixen and Trento to his territory.

Because of its strategic location, Tyrol's inhabitants have repeatedly had to defend their territory from attack. Out of this has emerged a desire for freedom that is evident from the region's earliest history. This was first apparent in the claim for democratic participation rights for citizens and farmers in the Constitution Act, known as the *Großer Freiheitsbrief* (Major Declaration of Freedom), of 1342. While the rest of Europe was still deep in the Middle Ages, Tyrol, as well as Switzerland, had one of the first democracies of Europe. In 1363 Tyrol freely chose to be annexed to the Habsburg Empire and thus became, and remained part of, Austria until the last century. Under this annexation, guarantees of freedom were maintained and extended. For example, the 'Landlibell' military treaty of 1511, a cornerstone of Tyrol's democracy, exempted the Tyrolese from military service outside their region.

Whenever the area was threatened, or when the Tyrolese people were repressed by their sovereigns, the desire for freedom re-emerged. This was the situation in 1525 under Michael Gaismayr, the rebel leader of the farmers' wars in the sixteenth century, when the Tyrolese called for the abolition of the privileges of the aristocracy and the clergy. The same spirit of independence was rekindled even against the generally beloved ruling house of Vienna, when the empress Maria Theresia (1740–80), and her heir, Josef II (1780–90), reformed the national administration that resulted in restrictions on previously held liberties. At this time, the slogan going around Tyrol was 'Vienna – slaughterhouse of freedom' ('Wien – Schlachthof der Freiheit'). After fierce protests, the Tyrolese succeeded in regaining these liberties.

During the Napoleonic era, when the whole of Europe feared domination, Tyrolean farmers defended themselves with pitchforks, scythes and simple carbines against the French-Bavarian enemy. The Tyrolese, a deeply religious people, so valued their freedom that they also entered a symbolic 'pact with Jesus': at the most perilous moment of occupation, in 1796, long prayer meetings were held where the people's representatives called for God's help and vowed in return to remain eternally faithful to the 'Sacred Heart of Jesus'. Even today, on the Eve of the Sacred Heart in June, the inhabitants of Tyrol light bonfires on the mountains to commemorate the hard-won fight against Napoleon.

This same desire for freedom gave the Tyrolese south of the Brenner the strength to defend their own language and culture after the annexation by Italy and, under Fascism, to continue teaching their mother-tongue in schools hidden in 'catacombs'. History has inspired them in their efforts to achieve real autonomy within the Italian state.[7]

The division of Tyrol: South Tyrol passed to Italy

After World War I, this 'Land Tirol', in which three ethnic groups, the German, the Ladin (in the Dolomite valleys) and the Italian group (mostly in the Welschtirol, today's Trentino) had always lived peacefully together, was divided.[8] The Peace Treaty of Saint Germain in September 1919 mandated a readjustment of the frontiers not 'along clearly recognisable lines of nationality' – the aim set by President Woodrow Wilson – which would have been along the linguistic border of Salurn, but geographically along the Alpine crest.[9]

The Italian historian Gaetano Salvemini refutes the view propounded by Fascist Senator Ettore Tolomei that South Tyrol should be considered part of Italy. 'Before [Tolomei] created an Alto Adige inhabited by Italians, nobody had ever considered the possibility of the existence of such a place as Alto Adige'.[10]

Interestingly, a number of Italian politicians were highly critical of the 1919 adjustment of the frontiers. On 28 December 1918, Minister Leonida Bissolati resigned from the Cabinet to express his unbending opposition to the annexation. On 14 July 1919, the deputy Filippo Turati exhorted the House of Representatives to vote against the annexation 'of over a quarter million Germans, whose pride in their heritage, their homeland and their freedom would represent an eternal seed of discord and rebellion'.[11] Many years later, in 1988, Giuliano Amato, former Italian Prime minister said, 'South Tyrol was historically born with bent legs and until today we haven't succeeded in straightening them out. It started off badly, because the transfer to Italy after World War I

[7] Michael Forcher, *Tirols Geschichte in Wort und Bild* [The History of Tyrol in Words and Pictures] (Innsbruck: Haymon-Verlag, 1984).

[8] Theodor Veiter, *Die Rechtslage des Italieners in der Österreichisch-Ungarischen Monarchie (mit besonderer Berücksichtigung Tirols)* [The legal position of Italians in the Austro-Hungarian monarchy (with particular reference to Tyrol)], in *Südtirol – Eine Frage des europäischen Gewissens* [A question of European conscience] (Vienna: Verlag für Geschichte und Politik, 1965), 202.

[9] Alfons Gruber, *Südtirol unter dem Faschismus* [South Tyrol under Fascism] (Bozen/Bolzano: Athesia, 1975), second revised edition, 9–11. Point 9 of the Wilson's 14 points states: 'There should be a readjustment of the frontiers of Italy along clearly recognisable lines of nationality'.

[10] Gaetano Salvemini, *Mussolini diplomatico (1922–1932)* [Mussolini's diplomacy 1922–1932] (Bari: Laterza, 1952), 439.

[11] Renato Ballardini, Report of the Speaker of the Permanent Constitutional Committee of the Italian Parliament on the occasion of the presentation of the new Autonomy Statute, from Atti Parlamentari, Italian Parliament No. 2216–227 A, Roma 1970, 2.

did not represent the completion of the "Risorgimento" frontiers, but was an injustice, justified as being necessary for strategic reasons'.[12]

The first attempts at autonomy

In 1919, the Italian King Victor Emanuel III promised a generous and understanding policy towards minorities: 'The new territories connected to Italy are creating new problems that have to be solved', he declared before Parliament on 1 December 1919. 'Our tradition of freedom will show us the way to solve these problems, with the highest respect for the autonomies and the local traditions'.[13]

But in practice this approach was not followed.

> The history of South Tyrol did not begin well: after an initial intelligent period of tolerance, the Fascist rulers of Italy followed a consistent policy of denationalisation and assimilation, including the predominance of culture and language of the Italian group. This was a tragic mistake [. . .] Under this portent, the Republic inherited the problem, with all its emotions and vengefulness,

said Amato of this period.[14]

The Mussolini period

In an interview with the French newspaper *Petit Parisien* on 27 February 1926, the Duce declared his programme for the Region:

> I saw this danger in Alto Adige; everything was German there, employees, teachers, clergy, the post offices and the railroads. Only German was spoken. I just put things in order. [. . .] Now the Italian language is obligatory in the whole territory, all the post and railroad officials are now Italians, and Italian families have settled everywhere.[15]

In 1939 Hitler and Mussolini concluded the Options Agreement and confirmed the Brenner Pass as the border between the two countries. South Tyrol remained part of Italy and the people had the option of either emigrating to the German Reich or remaining in Italy and facing losing their culture and language. It was a difficult decision that divided many families. Due to Nazi

[12] Giuliano Amato, *Diario in Pubblico* [Public diaries], L'Espresso, Rome, 20 March 1988, 33.

[13] 'Le nuove terre unite all'Italia creano nuovi problemi da risolvere. La nostra tradizione di libertà ci indicherà la via per la soluzione che si confermerà al massimo rispetto per le autonomie e le tradizioni locali', cited in Renato Ballardini, Report of the Speaker of the Permanent Constitutional Committee of the Italian Parliament.

[14] 'E' cresciuta peggio perché, dopo una fase iniziale di intelligente tolleranza, subentra il Fascismo che volle imporre l'italianità all'insegna dell'intollerante predominio della cultura delle insegne e della lingua del gruppo etnico italiano. Fu un tragico errore [. . .]. Ed è in questi termini che la Repubblica ha ereditato il problema, ereditandone umori e rivalse'. In Amato, *Diario in Pubblico.*

[15] Salvemini, *Mussolini diplomatico*, 448.

propaganda, about 80 per cent of the South Tyrolese opted for Germany.[16] Subsequently, about 79,000 South Tyrolese left their native land, but the exodus of the remaining population was halted by the outbreak of World War II. Only a few of the emigrants returned after the war.

International guarantees: the Paris Agreement

Even before the end of World War II, and also immediately afterwards, South-Tyrolese representatives and the provisional government of Austria began working towards the return of South Tyrol to Austria in the coming peace negotiations. The Great Powers of the victorious Allies had, however, already rejected similar requests in the autumn of 1945 and, despite strong pressure from the South Tyrolese and Austria, the Allies decided at the end of April 1946 to leave the relevant national borders as they were. The only remaining avenue was for Austria and Italy to negotiate directly so that South Tyrol could secure some form of self-government.[17]

The two sides reached a basic agreement within the framework of the peace negotiations in Paris, and on 5 September 1946 the 'Paris Agreement' was signed by the representatives of the two countries, Italian Prime Minister Alcide Degasperi and Austrian Foreign Minister Karl Gruber. It was annexed to the Peace Treaty with Italy, thereby giving the South Tyrol question international standing.[18]

Article 1 of the Paris Agreement states: 'German-speaking inhabitants of the Bolzano Province and of the neighbouring bilingual townships of the Trento Province will be assured a complete equality of rights with the Italian-speaking inhabitants within the framework of special provisions to safeguard the ethnic character and the cultural and economic development of the German-speaking element'. Article 1 further specifically grants German-speaking citizens the right to primary and secondary teaching in their mother tongue; parity for the German and Italian languages in public offices and in bilingual topographic naming; the right to restore German family names that had been Italianised;

16 Gruber, *Südtirol unter dem Faschismus*, 215–31, and Leopold Steuerer, *Südtirol zwischen Rom und Berlin 1919/1939* [South Tyrol between Rome and Berlin 1919/1939], Dis. Vienna, 1975, Teil 1, 11 und III, 416–561. Different sources put the number of people who opted for Germany at between 69.4 per cent and 92.8 per cent.

17 Rolf Steininger, *Südtirol im 20. Jahrhundert* [South Tyrol in the Twentieth Century] (Innsbruck, Vienna: Studienverlag, 1997), and Autonome Provinz Bozen (ed.), *South Tyrol – An Introduction* (Bozen: Provincial Government Office for Press and Public Relations, November 1989).

18 The Peace Treaty was published on 24 September 1947 in the Gazette of the Republic No. 295. The Paris Agreement is therefore part of Italian legislation, even if after some decisions of the Constitutional Court it is to be considered as an ordinary state law. Its importance lies in the internationalisation of the South Tyrol problem and in the protective role of Austria. Austria, as a party to the Paris Agreement, can always appeal against non-implementation. In accordance with Art. 90 of the Peace Treaty, only the French, English and Russian versions are authentic; only the English version was signed.

and 'a more appropriate proportion of employment' between the two ethnic groups in public offices.

Article 2 provides that 'the population of the above-mentioned zones will be granted the right to exercise autonomous legislative and executive regional power', thus anchoring the existing autonomy for the Province of Bozen/Bolzano and 'the neighbouring bilingual townships of the Trento Province'. At the time of the Paris Agreement the neighbouring municipalities of South Tyrol's Unterland and the German-speaking part of Nonsberg also belonged to Trento Province.

In Article 3 Italy pledged to restore the citizenship of those who had opted for Germany and to provide for measures and agreements with Austria for the recognition of qualifications, the free passage of people and simplification of the exchange of goods.

The people of Tyrol and South Tyrol reacted to the results of the negotiations in Paris, and to the Treaty itself, with deep disappointment. To them, the Treaty effectively signified assent to Italy's annexation of South Tyrol.

The first Autonomy Statute of 1948

Italy believed it would fulfil its obligation to give the Province of South Tyrol autonomous legislative and executive power under the Agreement through the enactment of an Autonomy Statute. This was adopted by the Constituent Assembly on 31 January 1948. Despite strong opposition from the South Tyrolese representatives, the autonomy created in the 1948 Autonomy Statute included Trentino, creating the Region of Trentino-Alto Adige/Tiroler Etschland, although under the Paris Agreement the autonomy had been envisaged for South Tyrol and the neighbouring bilingual townships alone. This Region, which included the Provinces of Bozen/Bolzano and Trento, with its overwhelmingly Italian majority, was thereby endowed with far greater powers than the Province of Bozen. Even the few autonomous powers accorded solely to the Province could hardly be applied (partly because executive decrees for the Statute were not issued). Thus the impatience and disappointment of the South Tyrolese continued to grow.[19]

> Again, as had occurred in 1919, after a good start the trend was reversed[. . .] mistrust and suspicion gradually froze the relations between the central government and the South Tyrolese and produced a constant trickle of non-fulfilments, delays in the implementation of the Autonomy Statute's Executive Decrees and absurd interpretations of the regulations

wrote Renato Ballardini, the official spokesman for the Italian Parliament's Constitutional Committee.[20]

[19] Special Statute for Trentino-Alto Adige, Constitutional Law No. 5 of 26 February 1948, Italian and German version in the *Regional Gazette* No. 1 of 25 February 1949.

[20] Renato Ballardini, *Report of the Speaker of the Permanent Constitutional Committee of the Italian Parliament* 4–5: 'Un'altra volta, come già nel 1919, ad un buon avvio verso la soluzione

Unrest in South Tyrol and the UN Resolutions

The situation was worsening. In 1956 and 1957, disillusioned young South Tyrolese carried out several bomb attacks – single, but significant, isolated incidents – as a mark of protest against the apparent unwillingness of the government to implement the Paris Agreement.

The Italian Government then announced a public building programme in the city of Bolzano/Bozen. As feared by the South Tyrolese, this was effectively an incentive for Italian families to move to the area. These events together culminated in a large protest that took place on 17 November 1957 at the Castle of Sigmundskron. The protestors called for a separation of South Tyrol from Trentino in order to establish their own, completely autonomous region. They emphasised that this would fulfil the objectives of the Paris Agreement. 'The most effective means,' as the leader Magnago said in his rousing and unanimously applauded speech, 'that the Agreement provided to safeguard the rights of ethnic groups – the exercise of autonomous legislative and executive regional power for South Tyrol only – has been denied us'.[21]

In 1959 the Südtiroler Volkspartei (South Tyrolese People's Party, SVP) quit the regional government; in September 1959 the South Tyrol Question was raised for the first time at the United Nations in New York by the then Austrian Foreign Minister Bruno Kreisky.

Austria and other states finally took the problem to the UN General Assembly,[22] which in 1960 and 1961 passed two resolutions urging 'the two parties concerned to resume negotiations with a view to finding a solution for all differences relating to the implementation of the Paris agreement of 5 September 1946'.[23] But further efforts by the SVP and Austria met with no success.

The tension among the South Tyrolese continued to grow. On the night of 11–12 June 1961, the traditional Eve of the Sacred Heart, when the whole of South Tyrol remembers the long struggle for freedom against Napoleon by lighting bonfires on the hills, a new fire broke out in South Tyrol: thirty-seven

del problema ha fatto seguito un'inversione di tendenza[. . .] Diffidenza e sospetto raggelarono via via i rapporti fra potere centrale e sudtirolesi, produssero uno stillicidio di piccoli inadempimenti, di ritardi nell'emanazione delle norme di attuazione, di assurde astuzie nella cavillosa redazione dei testi' [. . .].

21 Quoted in Dolomiten, *Tagblatt der Südtiroler* [Dolomiten, South Tyrolean daily newspaper] (Bozen: Verlagsanstalt Athesia, 18 November 1957), 2; Silvius Magnago, *30 Jahre Pariser Vertrag* [Thirty Years of the Paris Agreement] (Bozen: Parteileitung der SVP, 1976), 33.

22 Wolfgang Strasser, *Österreich und die Vereinten Nationen* [Austria and the United Nations] (Vienna: Wilhelm Braumüller, 1967), 370–1.

23 Resolution 1497 (XV) of 31 October, 1960, based on the resolution project of the seventeen states A/SPC/L 50 of 27 October: Argentina, Bolivia, Brazil, Canada, Ceylon, Cyprus, Denmark, Equador, Ghana, India, Iraq, Ireland, Jordan, Mexico, Norway, Paraguay and Uruguay); Resolution 1661 (XVI) of 28 November 1961, resolution project A/SPC/L 77 REV 1 & ADD. 1 of the states: Argentina, Chile, Greece, Guatemala, India, Indonesia, Ireland, Yemen, Panama, Peru, Sweden, Uruguay, United Arabian Republics and Cyprus. In Peterlini, *Autonomy and Protection of Ethnic Minorities*, 97–8, http://oskarpeterlini.it/145.html.

electricity pylons were blown up. This Eve of the Sacred Heart has gone down in history as 'the Night of Fire' ('Feuernacht') and marked the beginning of hard years of violence, persecution, arrests and torture of local activists.[24]

The 'Commission of Nineteen' and the negotiations between Italy and Austria

On 1 September 1961 the Italian Government set up a commission of inquiry composed of nineteen members (eleven Italian and eight South Tyrolean). This was known as the 'Commission of Nineteen' and was created to find solutions to the problems of 'Alto-Adige'. Italy and Austria also began negotiations, which, after an unpromising start, led, on the basis of the work of the 'Commission of Nineteen', to a 'Package' of measures for South Tyrol, to put self-government into effect.

Specific treaty arrangements: the 'Package for South Tyrol'

It was with great difficulty that the South Tyrolese came to accept the compromises, as they did not contain all that they had expected on the basis of the Paris Agreement. The Package of 'Measures in Favour of the South Tyrol Population', as it was officially termed,[25] was accepted by a narrow majority of the Südtiroler Volkspartei (South Tyrolean People's Party), at its Congress on 23 November 1969.[26] It was finally agreed upon and signed by the Foreign Ministers of Italy and Austria, Aldo Moro and Kurt Waldheim, on 30 November 1969 in Copenhagen. Thereafter it was formally approved by the Italian House of Representatives, on 4 December, followed by the Senate, on 5 December 1969. The Austrian National Assembly approved the Package on 16 December of the same year.[27] The Package consisted of 137 measures: ninety-seven required implementation through amendment of the 1948 Autonomy Statute by constitutional law, eight through executive decrees related to the Statute,

[24] Hans Karl Peterlini, *Feuernacht, Südtirols Bombenjahre, Hintergründe, Schicksale, Bewertungen 1961–2011* [Night of fires, years of bombings in South Tyrol: background, stories, review] (Edition Raetia, Bozen 2011).

[25] Misure a favore delle popolazioni altoatesine, Repubblica Italiana, Presidenza del Consiglio dei Ministri, 1969. 'Maßnahmen zugunsten der Bevölkerung Südtirols', 'Das Paket', Bundesministerium für auswärtige Angelegenheiten, Wien, Österreichische außenpolitische Dokumente, Sonderdruck Südtriol Dokumentation (1946–69). In Peterlini, *Autonomie und Minderheitenschutz in Trentino-Südtirol*, 250–74. The text of the 'Package' is included only in the German and Italian editions, while the English edition contains the Autonomy Statute based on the Package, http://oskarpeterlini.it/145.html.

[26] At the SVP Congress, of the 1,112 persons eligible to vote, 1,104 (99.4 per cent) were present; 52.8 per cent voted for and 44 per cent against the Package; 2.6 per cent of the votes were left blank or were invalid. Magnago, *30 Jahre Pariser Vertrag*, 46.

[27] On 4 December 1969 by the Italian Camera dei Deputati, 5 December 1969 by the Senato della Repubblica and on 16 December by the Nationalrat der Republik Österreich.

fifteen through ordinary state laws, nine through administrative decrees and the rest through administrative regulations.

An 'operational calendar', a detailed timetable, laid down in eighteen points the concrete steps towards the implementation of the Package, as well as laying out a path towards settlement of the dispute before the United Nations to be finalised by the conclusion of a treaty of friendship.

The Package could not be qualified as an international law treaty, because Italy took the view that it exclusively concerned an internal Italian problem. In contrast the Austrian federal government understood it to be a process moving towards fulfilment of the Paris Agreement. However, there is no doubt about the international anchoring of the South Tyrolean Autonomy. In 1992 Italy communicated to Austria the fulfilment of the Package and asked for settlement of the disputes before the UN, as had been agreed. On 11 June 1992 the Austrian government communicated the following to the Secretary General of the UN:

> Taking into account the realization of the measures that were announced at that time by the Italian government in favour of the population of South Tyrol, as communicated to the Austrian Government in a note of April 22, 1992, which was replied to by a note of the same date, the Austrian Federal Government finally stated in a declaration of 11 June, 1992, that it considers as terminated the above-mentioned dispute.[28]

This settlement of the disputes originally taken to the UN in 1960 and 1961, clearly constitutes a 'later practice' relevant in international law in the terms set by the two subsequent UN resolutions.[29]

The purposes of autonomy

In his 1967 book *Diplomatic History of the South Tyrol Question* Mario Toscano, Italian Ambassador to the United Nations at the time of the negotiations, reveals the reasons behind Degasperi's decision to sign the Paris Treaty. He considered that an agreement with Austria would imply recognition of the Brenner border.

[28] Ministry for External Affairs, Austrian foreign policy documents, Vienna special issue South Tyrol documentation (1946–69), 48, and no. 4, October 1992, in Oskar Peterlini, *Autonomy and the Protection of Ethnic Minorities in Trentino-South Tyrol* (Vienna: Wilhelm Braumüller, Universitätsverlag, 1997), 205–22, http://oskarpeterlini.it/145.html.

[29] See Peter Hilpold, *Die völkerrechtliche Absicherung der Südtirolautonomie* [The international legal protection of the autonomy of South Tyrol], in Joseph Marko, Sergio Ortino, Francesco Palermo, Leonhard Voltmer and Jens Woelk (eds.): *Die Verfassung der Südtirol Autonomie* [The Constitution of South Tyrol autonomy] (Eurac Schriftenreihe, Band 7, Baden-Baden: Nomos Verlagsgesellschaft, 2005), 38–46. Karl Zeller, *Das Problem der völkerrechtlichen Verankerung des Südtirol-Pakets und die Zuständigkeit des internationalen Gerichtshofes* [The problem of the international legal anchoring of the the South Tyrol Package and the jurisdiction of the International Court of Justice] (Vienna: Ethnos 34, Wilhelm Braumüller, Universitätsverlag, 1989), 85.

Vienna could no longer speak of a dictate and would, indirectly, freely agree to sign the treaty. Thus the first purpose was political: conceding an autonomy rather than a change of border.[30]

The purpose of the autonomy itself was also recognition of the ethnic character of the area. On the basis of the Paris Agreement, the South Tyrol Autonomy Statute should 'safeguard the ethnic character and the cultural and economic development of the German-speaking element' (Article 1 of Paris Agreement) and of the Ladin ethnic group (not mentioned in the Paris Agreement) within the framework of the Italian State. At the same time the decision to support autonomy was territorial: the benefits of these increased powers of self-government apply to members of all three linguistic groups in South Tyrol. Degasperi also wanted a precedent to create protection for the 180,000 Italians living in the area that was to be assimilated into Yugoslavia.[31]

Constitutional provisions for autonomy

The new Autonomy Statute of 1972

The most important element of the Package for South Tyrol was the approval of a new Autonomy Statute (formally a fundamental amendment to the Statute of 1948) enacted in 1971, which came into force in 1972.[32] This contains 115 articles divided into twelve chapters, which include the establishment of the Region and Provinces of Trento and Bozen, the powers of the Region and Provinces, measures for the enactment of laws, local public bodies, public property, finance, establishment of posts in state offices in the Province of Bozen/Bolzano, legal bodies, the role of the Constitutional Court and the use of the German and Ladin languages. With this Statute, the powers of the Region were diminished and those of the two Provinces substantially expanded. The provisions for autonomy apply generally to both Provinces in the same way, but there are additional special provisions for South Tyrol regarding issues such as the use of the mother tongue, schools, culture, bilingualism and ethnic proportions in employment.

The Autonomy Statute has the status of constitutional law. Together with the Constitution the Autonomy Statute is consequently in the highest tier of legislation. Below it, there are executive decrees that implement constitutional

30 Mario Toscano, *Storia diplomatica della questione dell'Alto Adige* [Diplomatic history of the South Tyrol question] (Bari: Editore Laterza, 1967), 17.

31 Ibid., 17; Steininger, *Südtirol im 20. Jahrhundert*, 140.

32 This was effected by the adoption of Constitutional Law No. 1, 10 November 1971, effective 20 January 1972. A unified text, D. P. R. No. 670, 31 August 1972, incorporates provisions of the former Statute still in force, as GA No. 301, 20 November 1972, updated 2011, www.regione.taa.it/moduli/933_statuto_speciale.pdf. In English: Special-Statute for Trentino-Alto Adige/Südtirol, www.provinz.bz.it/en/.

laws (such as the executive decrees for the Autonomy Statute), followed by ordinary legislation (laws) and administrative decrees.[33]

Even though the Italian Constitution is the framework for the whole state and defines the legal principles for all regions, the Autonomy Statute of South Tyrol and Trentino is at the same juridical level. There are of course no contradictions between the two Constitutional laws, but the special provisions of the Autonomy Statute do establish some particular rules, following the Roman principle *lex specialis derogat generali* (specific rule prevails over general rule). In fact, the Constitutional Court, which can annul laws and provisions from the state, the regions and the provinces if they conflict with the Constitution or with constitutional laws, such as the Autonomy Statute, cannot touch the Statute itself.

The Italian Constitution

The autonomy and the protection of minorities are also anchored in the principles of the Italian Constitution. Article 3 mandates equality of rights for all citizens, 'without distinction of sex, race, language, religion, political opinion and personal and social condition'. Article 6 requires that the Republic protect linguistic minorities 'with special provisions'. Article 116 guarantees 'special forms and conditions of autonomy' for the two large islands of Sicily and Sardinia, as well as for the three border Regions of Aosta, Friuli-Venezia-Giulia and Trentino-Alto Adige/Südtirol. The 2001 constitutional reform specifies that 'The Region Trentino-Alto Adige/Südtirol is composed of the Provinces of Trento and Bolzano' (Bozen).[34]

Furthermore, the national Constitution protects autonomy in a variety of ways. Italy is divided into twenty regions; fifteen of these have limited competences, and the five which have a special statute have a relatively high degree of autonomy. Since the 2001 reform of the Italian Constitution, the autonomy of the fifteen ordinary regions has also increased. The state retains exclusive power over national questions such as foreign policy, immigration, defence, currency, public order, jurisdiction, education, social security and so on.[35] The other competences are passed to the regions, with the difference being that while ordinary regions are required to follow state guidelines in all the fields of concurrent competences, regions with special statutes have greater exclusive autonomy in the fields of economics, education and culture, social affairs and the environment.[36]

[33] Constitutional laws are provided for in Art. 138 of the Italian Constitution.

[34] Art 116. Costituzione della Repubblica Italiana, published in the 'Gazzetta Ufficiale' 27 December 1947 and in force since 1 January 1948. Last amendments through Constitutional Law No. 3, 18 October 2001, and No. 1, 23 October 2002.

[35] Italian Constitution 2001, Art. 117, para. 2. Ibid., para. 3.

[36] They are also entitled to retain most of the taxes collected in their regions.

The ordinary regions adopt their own statutes through deliberation in the *regional* Parliaments by a qualified majority. The five regions for which there are special statutes may not do so; their statutes are constitutional laws, a status that brings both advantages and disadvantages. The disadvantages are that the autonomous regions and the provinces can only propose changes to the statute, but they must be approved by the Parliament in Rome. Theoretically also the national Parliament could amend the statute to limit autonomy, but there would clearly be international consequences. The advantages are that the autonomous statutes of these five special regions, including Trentino-South Tyrol, are not just regional laws subject to the Italian Constitution, but constitutional laws.

The federal reform of 2001 – greater autonomy for all

Since the 1980s and 1990s several attempts have been made to reorganise the state along federal lines. After a series of failed attempts, in 2001 Italy succeeded in carrying through constitutional reforms,[37] which did not turn it into a federal state similar to the United States or Austria, Germany and Switzerland, but introduced some key federal principles. Regional and local authorities are no longer simply a part of the state. They have become key components of the Republic, as outlined in the revised Article 114 of the Constitution.

Limits have been set on the responsibilities of the state and a new general clause in favour of the regions has been introduced. Municipalities and provinces, metropolitan cities and regions have their own statutes, powers and functions and have financial autonomy with regard to their own resources and assets.

State control over regional legislation was reduced. The possibility of referral of regional laws back to the regional government by the government was abolished. Since the constitutional reform of 2001, regional laws come into effect without preventative testing and governmental approval. If it objects to regional legislation the government's only recourse is to appeal the matter to the Constitutional Court. Parliament's power to veto legislation on the grounds of national interest no longer exists.

The new fiscal federalism project that is being developed will have to strengthen the financial powers of these authorities and establish a solidarity fund for social welfare issues. Other constitutional reforms are being discussed with a view to reforming the Senate, turning it into a House of the Regions, thereby ensuring regional participation in the Parliament's decision-making process.

In a formal sense, the statutes of special-status regions have remained unchanged. The 2001 constitutional reform was not incorporated into the formal text of the statutes. Yet the reform has changed them significantly, introducing substantial new elements, which are not immediately apparent when

[37] Constitutional Law of 18 October 2001, No. 3, which came into force on 8 November 2001.

reading the text. Thanks to the so-called 'more favourable treatment clause', the provisions of the constitutional reform are also directly applied to special status regions and to the autonomous Provinces of Trento and Bozen/Bolzano for those areas 'for which more extensive autonomous rights and powers are envisaged than those already conferred'.[38]

Thus, thanks to Italy's federal development, the autonomous regions have obtained more extensive autonomous rights and powers than those conferred upon them in their respective statutes.[39] What were once absolute exceptions within a centralist state with which they are at odds, the autonomous regions are now forerunners of a new, more federal system.

Executive measures for implementation of the Autonomy Statute

For the actual implementation of the Autonomy Statute executive measures – decrees – are required. Two commissions were established to draft these, with representatives of South Tyrol among their membership, and are examples of how the law provides for 'parity' in representation. The 'Commission of Twelve', which draws up the executive measures to the Statute for the Region and for both Provinces, is made up equally of members representing the state on the one hand and the Region and Provinces on the other. Three members must belong to the German linguistic group. The 'Commission of Six', a sub-commission for the executive measures just for the Province of Bozen/Bolzano, is balanced in the same way: 'It is composed of six members, three of whom shall represent the State and three the Province'. The languages must also be similarly represented, with three Italian and three German speakers. Under the Package for South Tyrol, the government should have issued the executive decrees within two years, but in the end the process took twenty years, not being completed until 1992. The two Commissions are still in operation today, as they continue to be needed to formulate executive responses to new and changing situations, even if the Statute had provided for these bodies only as transitional measures. They have also been incorporated into various legal provisions, most recently in the reform of fiscal federalism, thus becoming a permanent feature of the arrangements.[40]

Governing institutions at the autonomous level

The Region of Trentino-South Tyrol

As mentioned previously, Italy is divided into twenty regions, five of which have special autonomy statutes.[41] Of the latter, the Autonomous Region of

[38] Article 10 Constitutional Law 3/2001. [39] Peterlini, *L'autonomia che cambia.*

[40] The state law on fiscal federalism provides for its application in the autonomous regions by means of these commissions (Law 5 May 2009, No. 42).

[41] Arts. 114, 116 and 131 of the Italian Constitution.

Trentino-South Tyrol provides the political framework for the Autonomous Provinces of Bozen/Bolzano (Südtirol/Alto Adige) and Trento (Trentino). These two provinces stretch from the Brenner Pass to Lake Garda. Whereas in the old Autonomy Statute of 1948 the Region, in comparison to the provinces, was provided with far-reaching legislative and executive powers, in the Autonomy Statute of 1972 the most important of these have been transferred to the two autonomous provinces, creating three autonomous bodies: the Region of Trentino-South Tyrol and the two provinces of Südtirol and Trentino, each with their own parliament and Government.

The Regional Parliament (Consiglio Regionale/Regionalrat) consists of seventy deputies, being composed of the thirty-five members of the Parliament of Bozen and the thirty-five members of the Trento Parliament. The five-year legislative period is the same as for the two provincial parliaments. The Regional Parliament sits in Trento in the first half of the legislative period and in Bozen during the second half. The President of the Regional Parliament must be a deputy of the Italian-speaking group during the first half of the legislative period and of the German-speaking group in the second, while the two Vice-Presidents may not belong to the language group of the President. With the agreement of the majority of the German and the Italian deputies, a Ladin may also be elected as President. The Regional Parliament enacts laws within the framework of the Region's powers and monitors the regional Government.[42]

The Regional Government (Giunta Regionale/Regionalausschuss) consists of the President, two Vice-Presidents and the regional 'Assessors', chosen from among its members every five years by the Regional Parliament. According to the Autonomy Statute, the Italian, German and Ladin language groups must be proportionally represented in the Regional Government, and one Vice-President must come from the German-speaking group and the other from the Italian-speaking group.[43] The Ladin linguistic group is guaranteed representation in the Regional Government, even if this means derogating from the rules governing proportional representation. The duties of the Regional Government are to implement regional laws, administer those subject matters falling within regional competence and give direction to subordinate regional bodies.[44]

The provincial parliaments (Consiglio provinciale/Landtag) are the legislative organs, and the highest-ranking bodies of the Provinces. Within the framework of the powers granted to them by the Statute, they are tasked with enacting provincial laws; electing the Provincial Government (the President and the Assessors; in the Province of Bolzano, and in the Province of Trento, where the President is directly elected, may convene a vote of no confidence); supervising the Provincial Government; discussing problems of public concern; and, if it falls within their competence, deciding upon their resolution.

Each Provincial Parliament consists of thirty-five deputies who are elected by universal suffrage using a secret ballot system.[45] A special provincial law,

[42] Autonomy Statute, Arts. 25–30. [43] Ibid., Art. 36.
[44] Ibid., Art. 44. [45] Ibid., Art. 48.

approved by an absolute majority of the members of the Provincial Parliament, determines the form of government of the Province and, specifically, the manner of election of the Provincial Parliament, the President of the Province and members of the Provincial Government. It also regulates the relationship between those organs. This reinforced law determines also the exercise of the right of popular initiative for provincial laws and the abrogative, propulsive or consultative referendum, for provincial laws.[46] In order to guarantee representation of all groups, the Autonomy Statute prescribes that in the Autonomous Province of Bozen/Bolzano the Provincial Parliament shall be elected using a proportional system. Provincial laws on the election of the President of the Province of Bolzano, provided they stipulate an election process involving universal and direct suffrage, can be enacted by a majority of two thirds of the members of the Provincial Parliament.

In South Tyrol's parliament, as with the Regional Parliament, the office of President is rotated among the linguistic groups. The Provincial Parliament of Bolzano elects a President, two Vice-Presidents and Secretaries from among its members. The Vice-Presidents are elected from among the members belonging to linguistic groups different to that of the President. The President designates which Vice-President will take over the office in the event of that official's absence or impediment. For the first thirty months of the term of the Provincial Parliament of Bolzano the President is elected from among the members of the German linguistic group; for the subsequent period the President is elected from among the Italian-speaking members. A member belonging to the Ladin linguistic group may be elected, subject to the approval of the German or Italian groups.[47]

Each provincial government (Giunta provinciale/Landesauschuss) implements the laws passed by the Provincial Parliament and governs the Province through its executive body. The composition of the Provincial Government of Bozen/Bolzano must reflect the numerical strength of the linguistic groups represented in the provincial Parliament. Members of the Provincial Government of Bozen/Bolzano, not members of the Provincial Parliament, are elected by the Provincial Parliament,[48] with a majority of two thirds of its members, on the proposal of one or more parliamentary groups. A consensus on the designated candidate is required among the members of the linguistic group they represent, and candidacy is limited to councillors who constitute the majority supporting the Provincial Government. One of the Vice-Presidents must belong to the German linguistic group and the other to the Italian linguistic group.

The Ladin linguistic group may be given representation in the Provincial Government of Bolzano, even if this means derogating from proportional representation. In the event there is only one Ladin representative in the Provincial Parliament who is elected to Government, that representative cannot hold the office of President or Vice-President of the Provincial Parliament.[49]

[46] Ibid., Art. 47. [47] Ibid., Art. 48c.
[48] Ibid., Art. 50, paragraph 2. [49] Ibid., Art. 50.

Table 4.1 Language groups in South Tyrol (total population and percentages)

Year	German	Italian	Ladins	Others	Total population
1910	223,913	7,339	9,429	10,770	251,451
	89%	2.9%	3.8%	4.3%	
1921	193,271	27,048	9,910	24,506	254,735
	75.9%	10.6%	3.9%	9.6%	
1961	232,717	128,271	12,594	281	373,863
	62.2%	34.3%	3.4%	0.1%	
1971	260,351	137,759	15,456	475	414,041
	62.9%	33.3%	3.7%	0.1%	
1981	279,544	123,965	17,736	9,593	430,568
	64.9%	28.7%	4.1%	2.2%	
1991	287,503	116,914	18,434	17,657	440,508
	65.3%	26.5%	4.2%	4%	
2001	296,461	113,494	18,736	34,308	462,999
	64%	24.5%	4%	7.4%	
2011*	314,604	118,120	20,548	51,795*	505,067*
	62.3%	23.4%	4.1%	10.3%*	

*Provisional data for 2011.
Source: Oskar Peterlini, *Autonomy and the Protection of Ethnic Minorities in Trentino-South Tyrol*, 163; ISTAT, Österreichisches Stat. Zentralamt, ASTAT.

Language groups and protection of group rights

The total population of the Region Trentino-Südtirol is a little over a million (around 1,045,000), with the population approximately equally divided between the two provinces. The population in the province of Trento is mostly Italian, but an estimated 18,000 people are of Ladin origin – 9,000 of whom live in the Ladin Fassa valley – and 3,000 who speak the ancient Germanic languages known as Mocheni and Cimbri.

In South Tyrol there are about 315,000 German speakers; taken together with the Germanic linguistic minorities of Trentino they make up one third of the regional population, but only 0.52 per cent of the national population.[50] A breakdown of the population of the Region by linguistic group over time is presented in Table 4.1.

The Ladins are the oldest inhabitants of the region; about 21,000 live in South Tyrol and 18,000 in Trentino. Only half of the Trentino Ladins, those in the Fassa valley, have Ladin as their first language. In total there are 39,000 declared Ladin

[50] Data from the end of December, available at ISTAT (Italian Institute of Statistics): http://demo.istat.it/bilmens2011gen/index.html (accessed 13 August 2012); ASTAT Institute of Statistics of the Province of Bozen, www.provincia.bz.it/astat/de/bevoelkerung/bevoelkerung.asp (accessed 13 August 2012).

speakers in the region, constituting 0.06 per cent of the national population. Historically, they were resident in Tyrol at the time of the Roman conquest of Raetia, but were increasingly pushed back by invading Germanic tribes in the sixth and seventh centuries, and eventually became partially Germanised. Today the Ladin language and culture are maintained in the Dolomiten valleys of Grödental (Val Gardena), Gadertal (Val Badia), Val di Fassa and Ampezzo,[51] as well as in some areas of Switzerland. As the smallest language group, the Ladins are the most endangered linguistic minority and are entitled to special protective measures.

The Italians in South Tyrol live mainly in the towns of Bozen and in the larger population centres. In the census of 1910, the last to be held before World War I and before Italy's annexation of South Tyrol, there were 7,339 Italian-speaking inhabitants, amounting to 2.9 per cent of the population. As a result of the fascist Italianisation of the province, the Italian population increased substantially during the 1930s, and also in the years after 1945, reaching its peak, 34.3 per cent, as revealed by the 1961 census. As subsequent censuses show, the Italian percentage of the population declined somewhat thereafter; the German language group now forms the majority, amounting to more than sixty per cent of the population in the Province of Bozen.[52]

In the 1920s and 1930s the Fascists, in a policy that included the elimination of the German language from public life, succeeded almost completely in forcing the South Tyrolese out of public employment in the province.[53] Mussolini, in his speech to Parliament in Rome in 1928, complained that there were still 376 native officials in the town of Bolzano and 664 in the Province: 'So now they will have to face the alternative: a transfer into another province of the state or dismissal'.[54] He referred to German-speakers as 'those of foreign origin'. Furthermore, during the Fascist dictatorship, and also in the years after World War II, public housing in South Tyrol was almost exclusively allocated to Italian-speaking tenants.[55]

51 There are also 16,000 Ladin speakers in Ampezzo in the Province of Belluno, but they do not enjoy as many special rights as they do in South Tyrol. Peterlini, *Autonomy and the Protection of Ethnic Minorities in Trentino-South Tyrol*, 161–2.

52 According to the 2011 Census, 62.3 per cent of the people in the Province of Bozen are German, 23.4 per cent Italian, 4.1 per cent Ladin, and 10.3 per cent others. To exercise proportional representation and rights, the 'others' had to declare the language group to which they wished to be affiliated, with these results: 69.41 per cent German, 26.06 per cent Italian and 4.53 per cent Ladin. ASTAT.

53 Some were forcibly transferred to other Provinces. Ettore Tolomei, *Archivio per l'Alto Adige XXIII*, [Archives of Alto Adige XXIII] Amministrazione dell'Archivio per l'Alto Adige, Roma and Glen (Montan), 1928.

54 Ibid., 13, and Salvemini, *Mussolini Diplomatico*, 448.

55 From 1935 to 1943 3,100 units of public housing built in South Tyrol were allocated to Italian families. From 1950 to 1959 the state built a further 5,500 units, of which only five per cent were allocated to German-speaking tenants. Oskar Peterlini, *Der ethnische Proporz in Südtirol* [Ethnic proportionality in South Tyrol] (Bozen: Athesia, 1980), 137–9.

In 1975, just before regulations on ethnic apportionment of the 6,000 posts in the state administration came into effect, only 800 – less than 14 per cent of the total – were filled by members of the German- and Ladin-speaking groups,[56] despite the 'equality of rights' and 'the more appropriate proportion of employment' provided for in the Paris Agreement.

Distribution of posts in the civil service and public housing

The introduction of a fair distribution of administrative posts and housing according to the numerical strength of the ethnic groups was essentially a form of reparation for Fascist injustice. The key to that redistribution is the principle of 'ethnic proportion', which is based on the numerical strength of the three linguistic groups living in the Province (not including 'others').

Public housing built since 1972 has been distributed according to ethnic proportions, but since 1988 a 'combined proportion' has been used, which takes into account not only the numerical strength of the three linguistic groups but also the separate needs of each.

With regard to *local* bodies in the province (the personnel employed by the province, the region, the municipalities, the health service, etc.), the equality of rights as regards entering into public office provided for in the 1946 Paris Agreement was gradually implemented in the 1950s and 1960s. Admission to civil service jobs according to their proportion of the population was first granted to German- and Ladin-speaking South Tyrolese in the new Autonomy Statute of 1972, which expressly stipulates that state posts in South Tyrol should be allocated in accordance with the proportion of the three language groups in the population.[57] This method was implemented with Presidential Decree no. 752 of 26 July 1976. The Decree provided that by the year 2002, employment in state and semi-state bodies in South Tyrol (such as the railways, the postal service, the state roads administration, the customs service and court administration) should reflect the proportions of the three language groups living in South Tyrol as enumerated in the census. This objective has now nearly been reached.[58]

Language group declaration

An important prerequisite for the protection of linguistic minorities is accurate data on the numerical size of each minority. In accordance with special measures of protection for linguistic minorities, in principle only a person who belongs to a linguistic minority can claim the relevant rights. In South Tyrol, the proportions are determined by the census, which is carried out every ten

[56] Ibid., 86 and 92.

[57] Art. 89. Certain state bodies, such as the military and the security services, are exempted from the principle of employment according to linguistic proportion.

[58] Peterlini, *Südtirols Autonomie und die Verfassungsreformen Italiens*, 148.

years at national level. In addition to other information required, persons in South Tyrol have to make a declaration as to which of the three language groups they belong.[59]

This declaration used to be valid for ten years and can only be changed at the following census, with the exception of minors. Since the reforms of 2005 came into effect,[60] the individual declaration is now separate from the census and valid for life, with the opportunity available to change it. Persons belonging to other linguistic groups can declare their own language and then choose which of the three official languages they wish to be assigned to for the purposes of ethnic proportionality.

Bilingualism as a requirement for public office

The Proportion Decree[61] also provides that for entry to a post in the public service an acceptable knowledge of German and Italian is required. The 'acceptable knowledge of the German and Italian languages' is determined by a special Commission through a bilingualism examination. The examination consists of written and oral components, and varying degrees of difficulty apply to four different career levels. Other proofs of language competence may also be admitted.[62] Candidates who do not speak both languages are excluded from public employment. The bilingualism examination applies to all candidates, but is undoubtedly an advantage for all those in South Tyrol seeking work, where candidates are more likely to speak both languages. As an incentive, all state employees in South Tyrol and employees of other public bodies who possess a certificate of bilingualism receive what is known as a bilingualism bonus.

The proportional and bilingual regulations represent not only reparation for one of Fascism's greatest acts of injustice against the South Tyrolese, but also at the same time are a real safeguard, a not uncontroversial but nevertheless justified means for achieving an agreed distribution of posts in public administration among applicants from the three language groups.

Language parity and rights

The 1946 Paris Agreement provided that, following the period of Fascist repression of the German language, through special provisions and legislation already enacted, 'German-speaking citizens' would be granted 'parity of the German and Italian languages in public offices and official documents, as well as in bilingual topographic naming'. This principle is laid down in the Autonomy Statute of 1972:

59 A separate form is provided in South Tyrol for this information.

60 Legislative decree 99/2005. 61 DPR 752/1976. 62 See section previously.

> In the Region the German language has parity with the Italian language, which is the official language of the State. In legislative acts and in all cases where this Statute provides for a bilingual text the Italian text is authoritative.[63]

However, it was not until 1988, after years of negotiations, that the Council of Ministers in Rome approved Executive Decrees giving parity to the German language in public administration, the courts and the police.[64]

The Autonomy Statute also provides for people in the Province to use the language of their choice:

> German-speaking citizens of the Province of Bozen have the right to use their language in relations with the organs and offices of the public administrations which are situated in the Province or which possess regional power, as well as with concessionaries who provide public services in the Province.
>
> In sittings of the collegial organs of the Region, of the Province of Bozen and of local bodies, the Italian or the German language may be used.
>
> The offices, the organs and the concessionaries have – in correspondence and in oral dealings – to use the language of the applicant and to reply in the language in which proceedings by another organ or office have been started; in cases where an office initiates correspondence it must use the presumed mother tongue of the citizen to whom it is directed.
>
> Except for cases expressly provided for – and except for the regulation through executive decrees of cases of joint use of the two languages in documents intended for the general public, in individual documents intended for public use and in documents intended for more than one office – the right to use the German or Italian language separately in other cases shall be recognized. The requirement to use only the Italian language in organizations of a military nature shall remain unchanged.[65]

Achieving bilingualism in the police and in the courts was particularly difficult. The so-called unilingual proceedings issue was a serious point of dispute for several years. According to the 'Language Decree'[66] legal proceedings and trials must be conducted in the declared mother tongue of the accused; in other words, proceedings against an accused person who has declared German to be their mother tongue must be conducted by all the participants – judge, court staff, lawyers – only in German, and likewise in Italian for an Italian-speaking defendant.

The executive decrees contain a special regulation providing for the use the Ladin language for Ladins in oral and written communications between organs and offices of the public administration and the courts.

63 Autonomy Statute, Art. 99.
64 Decree No. 574, 15 July 1988.
65 Autonomy Statute, Art. 100.
66 Decree No. 574, 1988.

Impact of EU principles and procedures

In contrast to other special internal laws, as for example the Åland Protocol,[67] South Tyrol autonomy was not included in the accession Treaty to the European Union.

> It was with a sense of dismay that having fought for and won the meaningful autonomy sought, the South Tyroleans should now see [. . .] the main pillars of the autonomy [. . .] challenged, not by the aggressive nationalism of the past, but by that very European internationalism they had for so long unswervingly supported.[68]

In contrast to the practice relating to the extension of the European Union to the north, as exemplified by the Åland Protocol in 1995, there was also no mention of measures for the protection of minority rights with the accession of countries to the east in 2004.[69]

Despite the lack of safeguard clauses in EU law, no dramatic judgments have been made that undermine the basic pillars of the autonomy and minority protection measures. But there have been some conflicts which Italy had to address in consultation with the representatives of South Tyrol. One example was the use of the German language in the courts that were reserved for 'German speaking citizens' (Article 100, Autonomy Statute). The question was: can a national of an EU member state rely on the principle of non-discrimination on grounds of nationality in order to be granted the right to have criminal proceedings against him in another member state conducted in a language other than the official language of that other state where that right is granted to certain nationals of that member state?[70] That was the issue raised in the Italian criminal proceedings against Bickel and Franz.[71] The conclusion was clear:

> Accordingly, the question referred by the Pretura Circondariale di Bolzano must in my opinion be answered as follows: Where a member state grants residents in part of its territory the right to use a language other than its official language in criminal proceedings against them, Article 6 of the EC Treaty must be interpreted as requiring it to afford the same right to nationals of other member states

67 The accession Treaty of Finland to the European Union came into force at the beginning of 1995, with Protocol No. 2 included in the accession Treaty. Gabriel N. Toggenburg, *Kapitel 27: Europas Integration und Südtirols Autonomie: Konfrontation – Kohabitation – Kooperation?* [Europe's integration and autonomy of South Tyrol: Confrontation – Cohabitation – Co-operation?], in Marko et al. (eds.), *Die Verfassung der Südtirol Autonomie*, 449–92.

68 Antony Alcock, 'The protection of regional cultural minorities and the process of European integration: the example of South Tyrol,' *International Relations*, 29 April 1992, 17–36.

69 Toggenburg, *Kapitel* 27, 452.

70 Peterlini, *L'autonomia che cambia*.

71 Judgment of the European Court of Justice 1999/C 20/08 in Case C-274/96, (reference for a preliminary ruling from the Pretura Circondariale di Bolzano, Sezione Distaccata di Silandro): Criminal proceedings against Horst Otto Bickel and Ulrich Franz, 24 November 1998, summary available at: http://eurlex.europa.eu/LexUriServ/LexUriServ.do?uri=OJ:C:1999:020:0006:0006:EN:PDF.

visiting that territory if those nationals have that other language as their mother tongue.[72]

Another example was the requirement that, to be eligible to apply for posts in public offices, societies and bodies that manage public services, individuals had to have passed an examination showing they had reached a certain level of competence in the German and Italian languages.[73] A Mr. Angonese applied for a position at a private bank and was rejected because he did not have an official certificate attesting to his knowledge of the two languages as required by the Commission in Decree DPR 752/1976.[74] A decision by the European Court of Justice found such an exclusive role for the Commission in setting standards for bilingualism to be discriminatory. The Court's judgment stated,

> 'Where an employer makes a person's admission to a recruitment competition subject to a requirement to prove evidence of his linguistic knowledge exclusively by means of one particular diploma, such as the Certificate, issued only in one particular province of a member state, that requirement constitutes discrimination on grounds of nationality contrary to Article 39 (ex-article 48) EC'.[75]

In response to these cases, ten years overdue, the Council of Ministers finally adopted a new set of executive measures to the autonomy Statute, allowing for other types of certification of bilingualism to be used in South Tyrol. These measures were adopted in Rome on 23 April 2010 on the recommendation of the Commission of Six.[76] The decree, which applies to all Italian and EU citizens, does not change the existing scheme, but adds more means whereby individuals can demonstrate their knowledge of the Italian and German languages.[77] Under the new rules, if you can prove that you have completed a certain level of schooling in either German or Italian, you are only required to pass the examination in the other language. And those who can prove they have completed high school in one language and tertiary education in the other are deemed to have achieved bilingualism.[78]

72 Opinion of Advocate General Jacobs, delivered on 19 March 1998, Case C-274/96, as in ibid.

73 Art. 1 Presidential Decree DPR 752/1976, based on Arts. 99 and 100 Autonomy Statute.

74 Peterlini, *L'autonomia che cambia*, 68–72.

75 Case C-281/98, *ECR*, 2000, p I-04139, Angonese, 06.06.2000, http://ec.europa.eu/internal_market/qualifications/docs/judgments/list_en.pdf, uploaded 2 October 2011 (accessed 26 March 2013).

76 See later for details on this body.

77 The measures thus contribute five additional paragraphs to Presidential Decree 752/1976.

78 D. lgs. 14 maggio 2010, No. 86, Norme di attuazione dello Statuto speciale per il Trentino-Alto Adige recanti modifiche al decreto del Presidente della Repubblica 26 luglio 1976, No. 752, in materia di equipollenza degli attestati di conoscenza delle lingue italiana e tedesca [Executive measure to the Special Statute for Trentino-Alto Adige containing amendments to the Decree of the President of 26 July 1976, No. 752, on the equivalence of certificates of knowledge of the Italian and German languages].

Relations between institutions at national and autonomous levels

Legislative competencies and the centralist principle

The legislative competencies of the Region Trentino Südtirol and of the autonomous provinces of Trento and Bozen are, for the main part, set out in Articles 4 to 19 of the Autonomy Statute, which enumerates all the areas of autonomy. This means that all subject matters not listed in these articles automatically come under national competence.

In federal states that are created by the coming together of former sovereign entities, the reverse happens. Based on the subsidiarity principle, the competencies are attributed first to the local communities, which then transfer part of their powers to federal institutions so that a common administration can be formed. Only with the most recent amendments to the Italian Constitution in 2001 were the competencies of the federal state accurately listed,[79] as they are in Austria and Germany. Since 2001, all the subject matters not listed now fall within the competence of the Regions (and indirectly the autonomous provinces) as defined in Article 117, paragraph 4 of the Italian Constitution. This new system, created in 2001, increases the competencies of all Italian Regions, including South Tyrol.

Despite the fact that the Autonomy Statute has not been amended, the new Constitution applies also to those Regions with special statutes and to the autonomous Provinces, 'for the areas of competency which provide greater autonomy than that currently held'.[80] The introduction of this new federal principle means that in Trentino-South Tyrol, all the subject matters not referred to in the Constitution as state competencies fall within the competence of the autonomous provinces, including matters that arise from new and unforeseen future developments, in addition to the matters listed in the Autonomy Statute.

However, in contrast to these efforts to reorganise the Italian State along federalist lines, a so-called 'authority of alignment and co-ordination' continues to operate, with the effect that the central government can, through guidelines, limit the autonomous power of the regions and provinces. The intention of this law, passed in 1988, was to safeguard national interests and strengthen uniformity.[81] It gives the central government general authority for the 'alignment and co-ordination' of administrative activities of the regions and 'within the regulations of the Autonomy Statute, also of the regions with special statutes and of the autonomous Provinces of Trento and of Bozen/Bolzano'. A special government decree,[82] enacted after protests from

79 Art. 117, paras 2 and 3.
80 Constitutional Law, 18 October 2001, No. 3, Art. 10.
81 Law 23, August 1988, No. 400, Art. 12; Leg. Decree, 16 December, 1989, No. 418 and Leg. Decree, 28 August 1997, No. 281.
82 Legislative decree, 16 March 1992, No. 266.

South Tyrol, somewhat moderated its impact on South Tyrol and Trentino. It stated that, in contrast to the situation in other regions, governmental authority would not automatically come into force in the region and the two provinces, but that the Regional Parliament and the Landtag, the Provincial Parliament, would be given a period of six months to adapt their laws accordingly. If they do not, the Italian Government would have three months to bring the offending regional and provincial laws before the Constitutional Court.

Legislation and the national veto of laws

The constitutional reforms of 2001 abolished the central government's power to veto regional legislation,[83] which had previously been used by the Italian Government to reject approximately one third of South Tyrol's laws.[84] Before this change, although regional and provincial bills had to be approved by the regional or provincial parliaments, they did not come into force until central government approval had been obtained. Firstly, each provincially or regionally approved bill had to be transmitted to the Government Commissioner (the highest representative of the central government in the province and in the region), then the central government reviewed it for legality and agreement with national interests. It had thirty days to endorse it or, should the bill be considered to be beyond the scope of regional or provincial competence or in conflict with national interests, to send it back. If no decision was taken by the central government within thirty days, the bill became law and came into force after publication.

Taking into account the objections of central government, regional or provincial parliaments could amend laws that had been rejected, or alternatively they could persist, approving the same version of the law by an absolute majority of its members (eighteen members of the Provincial Parliament and thirty-six from the Regional Parliament). Legislation passed in this way could not be rejected a second time by central government, but if the law was considered to be in conflict with the Constitution, it could be brought before the Italian Constitutional Court, or before Parliament in the event of it conflicting with the national interest. The central government had fifteen days to make such a referral, and if no action was taken within that time, the law would come into force.

Under the reformed Constitution, the central government only has the power to bring regional and provincial laws before the Constitutional Court. The laws

83 Autonomy Statute, Art. 55.

84 Oskar Peterlini, *I limiti dell'autonomia, Le leggi provinciali rinviate dal Governo central 1984–87* [The limits of autonomy, the provincial laws rejected by the Central Government 1984–87] (in German, *Grenzen der Autonomie, Die Rückverweisung der Landesgesetze durch die Zentralregierung 1984–87*), (Bozen Bolzano: Südtiroler Landtag, Bozen, Consiglio provinciale dell'Alto Adige, 1988).

remain in force unless, or until, the Court decides they are unconstitutional. However, a new round of constitutional reforms proposed by the right-wing Italian Government, the so-called Devolution, was approved by Parliament in October (Camera dei Deputati) and November (Senato) 2005.[85] Pressed by the federalist movement of the Northern League (*Lega Nord*), it attempted to transfer more competencies to the regions, but at the same time was pushed for more centralisation of power by the parties Alleanza Nazionale and Forza Italia. It aimed to reintroduce the review of regional and provincial legislation with regard to their compliance with 'national interest' and to reintroduce the possibility of bringing it before the national Parliament. A referendum held on 25 and 26 June 2006 rejected the constitutional law. Thus the legislative procedure remains as stipulated in the 2001 reform, with the only avenue for the Italian Government to pursue objections to provincial laws being to bring them before the Constitutional Court.

Regional and provincial laws are recorded by the President of the region or the President of the province, published in the Gazette of the Region in German and in Italian and, if not otherwise specified, come into force fifteen days after their publication. In the event of problems of interpretation, Italian is the authoritative language.[86]

Division of powers between national and autonomous governments

Legislative competences and their limitations

The main innovation of the constitutional reform of 2001 relates to the distribution of powers between central government and the regions. Article 117 of the 1948 Constitution assigned to the regions few responsibilities (only eighteen), which were not exclusive but were defined as competing. The federal law outlined the principles for the regions. As further limitation on their powers the regions had to respect, in their regional legislation, national interests and the interests of other regions. The first paragraph of Article 117 of the new Constitution now puts the legislative power of the regions on the same level (at least formally) as that of the central government. The division of power is no longer based on a hierarchy, but from the assigned competencies. 'The legislative power is exercised by the State and the regions', as stated in Article 117, paragraph 1 of the new Constitution.

The limits of legislative powers are also defined for both the state and for the regions. The powers of both must conform to the Constitution; the legal order of the European Community; and Italy's international obligations.

These limits apply to the so called exclusive competences of the state and of the regions. In paragraph 2 of Article 117, the exclusive powers of the state are

[85] Oskar Peterlini, *Südtirols Autonomie und die Verfassungsreformen Italiens*, 339.
[86] Autonomy Statute, Art. 57.

enumerated exhaustively. These include foreign policy, immigration, relations with other states, defence, currency and other classic powers of the state to protect the environment, the ecosystem and cultural resources, covering seventeen areas. Paragraph 3 outlines the concurrent competencies of the state and the regions, for which the state has to set the fundamental principles. When exercising their powers in these fields the regions (and the autonomous provinces) have to respect the fundamental principles of state laws, as well as the obligations outlined earlier.[87]

The real revolution in the distribution of powers is contained in paragraph 4 of Article 117.

Article 117 of the old Constitution reserved a total of eighteen legislative powers to the regions. All rights not expressly enumerated automatically fell within the jurisdiction of the state. Article 117 in the new Constitution reverses this principle in favour of the region, with the responsibilities of the state now exhaustively enumerated in paragraph 2, as are the concurrent competencies of the regions in paragraph 3. Paragraph 4 states that: 'For all matters that are not reserved expressly for the State legislation, the Regions shall have the power to legislate'. This is a key point in the federal context and is an essential step in the direction of federalism.[88]

Legislative competences and the Autonomy Statute

The Autonomy Statute of Trentino-South Tyrol adoped in 1972 enumerates the powers of the Region and the autonomous provinces. Everything else is the responsibility of the state. The Statute also sets the limits on legislation of the Region and the autonomous provinces. There are three levels of competences, with respective restrictions: exclusive legislative competence (the most extensive); secondary legislative competence (competitive); and integrative legislative competence the (most restrictive).

In the spheres where the regions and provinces exercising autonomy have *exclusive* legislative competence, regional and provincial legislation must stay within the following boundaries: it must be 'in harmony with the Constitution' and must consider 'the principles of the Italian legal order'. It must also 'respect international obligations', a very important limitation, given that more and more of the competences that fall directly within the powers of the provinces will be covered by European Union agreements.[89] Following the Statute, regional and provincial legislation also has to respect 'national interest'. According to Article 4 of the Autonomy Statute, the term 'national interest' includes also 'the protection of linguistic minorities'. The concept of national interest is

[87] Oskar Peterlini, *Die Föderalismusentwicklung in Italien und ihre Auswirkungen auf die Sonderautonomien* [The effects of federal development in Italy on special autonomies], Zeitschrift für Öffentliches Recht (ZÖR 63), (Wien/New York: Springer, 2008), 224–6.

[88] Peterlini, *Südtirols Autonomie und die Verfassungsreformen Italiens*, 227.

[89] Autonomy Statute, Arts. 4 and 5.

controversial in jurisprudence because it is essentially a subjective notion and can be used in an arbitrary fashion, but the central government has never overturned any law on these grounds. Such a conflict would not have been challenged before the Constitutional Court, as mentioned earlier, but would come before the Italian Parliament. The greatest limitation on the autonomy of South Tyrol and the Region lies in the requirement that legislative acts must be in accordance with 'the basic guidelines of economic and social reforms of the Republic'. This condition can also be applied whenever the state approves a law reforming the current arrangements.

Although these far more restrictive limits were reduced by the constitutional reform of 2001 and the limitation on the grounds of national interest has been removed from the Italian Constitution, they remain in the Statute and apply to the 'old' competences.[90] The spirit of 'national interest' still inspires some of the decisions made by the Constitutional Court.

In areas in which the Region and the provinces exercise *secondary* legislative competence, the competences are jointly held by the state (for the basic principles) and the Region or the Province respectively. In addition to the previously mentioned limitations on the exclusive competences, in this case legislation must comply with 'the principles contained in ordinary State laws'.[91]

For a small subset of subject matters, the Region and the provinces exercise *integrative* or *complementary* competence, which means they can legislate to incorporate state laws, without changing them. For the Region this covers (integrative) social insurance and social security,[92] and for the provinces it covers unemployment offices,[93] providing them with the power to introduce laws 'in addition to national laws'. Thus, national laws are enforceable on regional or provincial territory, but can be supplemented by local legislation.[94] With the constitutional reform of 2001 the competence for complementary social security, for example, pension funds, became a competitive one for all regions, consequently also for the Region of Trentino-South Tyrol.

Division of the fields of competences

The Region has *exclusive* competence to legislate in the following fields: organisation of regional authorities and their staff; organisation of semi-regional bodies; organisation of local bodies (municipalities and territorial boundaries); expropriation for purposes of common welfare, provided public works within the sphere of interest of the state or the relevant province are not affected; land registers and land registry offices; fire services; organisation of health bodies; organisation of chambers of commerce; and development and control

[90] See later on the Constitutional Court.
[91] Autonomy Statute, Art. 5. [92] Ibid., Art. 6. [93] Ibid., Art. 10.
[94] For example, the Italian pension laws are in force also in the region, but the Region has passed a complementary law on pension funds. See Oskar Peterlini, *Le nuovi pensioni* [The new pensions – experiences and strategies to avoid the pension crash] (Milano: FrancoAngeli 2003).

of co-operatives. After public consultation the Region can also establish new municipalities, change municipal boundaries and alter their names.[95]

The Region has *secondary (competitive)* competence in the organisation of public welfare bodies and the organisation of credit banks. It previously (and still now formally in the Statute) had *integrative/complementary* competence, but now has *competitive* competence for social welfare and can also establish autonomous social security institutions.

The most comprehensive lists of competences are those exercised at provincial level. Among the *exclusive* competences in education and culture, provinces may legislate on: place names, subject to the obligation of bilingualism in the Province of Bozen; the protection and care of historical, artistic and ethnic values; local usages and customs, as well as cultural institutions; local, artistic, educational and cultural events and activities (within the Province of Bozen, radio and television stations can be used to this end, but the right to establish radio and television stations is excluded); nursery schools; construction of schools; school welfare; and professional and vocational training.[96] In the cultural and educational field, provinces also have *competitive* (secondary) competence regarding teaching in primary and secondary schools.[97]

Provincial legislative powers over economy and administration are *exclusive* in the areas of the organisation of provincial authorities and their staff; planning and building directives; landscape conservation; common rights governing pasturage and timber; the organisation of small-holdings; crafts and handicrafts; inland harbours; fairs and markets; mining, including mineral and thermal waters, quarries and pits as well as peat cutting; hunting and fishing; alpine agriculture and the protection of fauna and flora; public works, roads and aqueducts within each province's sphere of interest; communication and transport services within the province's sphere of interest, including the technical regulation of cable cars and their operation; the use of public utilities for separate administration and their running by special undertakings; the tourism and catering industry; agriculture, forestry, livestock and wildlife; provincial expropriation for the purpose of common welfare in all areas of provincial competence; and certain types of waterworks.

In addition to this list of exclusive powers, provinces have *competitive* competence covering local police; trade and commerce; public performances; public enterprises; promotion of industrial production; and exploitation of public waters, with the exclusion of the main diversions for the production of energy. In the social field, provinces have *exclusive competence* in: subsidised housing; measures for disaster prevention and immediate aid; and social welfare. They exercise *competitive* competence in hygiene and health; apprenticeships and employment registers; control over unemployment offices; and sport and leisure. In addition, as mentioned earlier they have *integrative/complementary*

[95] Autonomy Statute, Art 7. [96] Ibid., Art. 8. [97] Ibid., Art. 9.

competence in employment, whereby unemployment offices in the Province of Bozen give priority to local jobseekers.[98]

Administrative competence

The provinces and the Region are also responsible for the administration and implementation of their laws. They hold the administrative powers that previously belonged to the state in all the fields for which they legislate, within the same limitations. Thus, alongside legislative autonomy there is also administrative autonomy.

In addition, by enacting laws the state can also transfer the administration of its own competences to the Region, to the provinces, or to other territorial bodies. For instance, the organisation of schools, including the employment of teachers, upkeep of the roads, the labour offices and inspectorates, the cadastral survey and the motor vehicles offices, have been delegated to the Provinces of Trento and Bozen.

The Region mainly exercises its administrative functions by transferring them to the provinces, for example: land registers; chambers of commerce; co-operatives; fire brigades; organisation of health bodies and hospitals. The Region also transfers some responsibilities to the municipalities, and to other territorial bodies, or by using their offices. The provinces can likewise transfer their administrative functions to the municipalities or other territorial bodies, or carry them out using their offices.[99]

Each municipality exercises administrative autonomy and, as an autonomous corporation, has its own organs: a mayor, as the head and the external representative of the municipality; a municipal council, as the decision-making body; and a municipal committee, which, with the mayor as its head, is responsible for implementing decisions. The municipalities have social, economic and cultural administrative functions.[100]

State administration in the autonomous areas

Two government Commissioners act as the senior representatives of the central government in the region: one for Trentino (responsible also for regional matters) and one for South Tyrol. According to the Autonomy Statute, their responsibilities are: firstly, to co-ordinate, in conformity with government directives, the exercise of state powers, and to supervise the activities of the respective offices, with the exception of those relating to the administration of justice, defence and the railways. Secondly, they are tasked with supervising the activities

[98] Ibid., Art. 10. [99] Ibid., Art. 18.

[100] Trentino has 226 municipalities and 11 districts. With approximately the same geographical area and population, South Tyrol has 116 communes or municipalities, making up the eight districts of the Province.

of the provinces and other local public bodies regarding the powers delegated to them by the state, and communicating possible objections to the Presidents of the provinces. In the case of the Commissioner of Trento, this also includes supervision of the Region and its institutions. And finally, they are to perform all the other duties normally required of the Prefect (the title equivalent to 'Commissioners' in all other Italian Regions), insofar as they have not been entrusted to organs of the Region, the provinces, or other state organs by the Autonomy Statute or other laws.[101]

The government Commissioner is responsible to the Minister of the Interior for the maintenance of public order. To this end the Commissioner can make use of the police forces and organs of the state and, within the limits of existing laws, can request deployment of the armed forces, particularly as they relate to public security.[102]

Several other powers – specifically relating to the tax system, foreign policy, the military, the police, justice, immigration, state pensions and work-related accidents, the postal system, public broadcasting, the rail service and others – remained under the control of the state even after the new Autonomy Statute became effective, and are dealt with mainly by departments of the various ministries in Rome or by independent entities, for example, railways and social security. Public broadcasting and rail and postal services, however, have been privatised, but still belong to the state.[103]

The proportion of posts in the various state administrations in South Tyrol reserved for the different language groups is decided upon by a Coordination Committee composed of the Government Commissioner and three members nominated by the South Tyrolese Parliament.[104]

Autonomous Region participation at national level

The population of the autonomous areas are represented at national level through the election of representatives to the national Parliament. In addition, a number of constitutional provisions and political conventions allow regional input into national politics.

The national Parliament is composed of the Senate (315 'Senatori della Repubblica' and a few life members) and the Chamber of Deputies (630 'Deputati'). Voters from South Tyrol and Trentino elect ten members to the Chamber of Deputies, a number set in proportion to the population of the Region. The new electoral law of 2005 abolished the former mixed preponderant majority system and the constituencies,[105] and reverted to a proportional system, with different thresholds (minimum percentages of votes) required for representation (which stands at 4 per cent at national level for the Chamber of Deputies)

101 Autonomy Statute, Art. 87. 102 Autonomy Statute, Art. 88.

103 Public broadcasting, along with the postal and rail services, are organised as joint stock companies (società per azioni), with the shares still belonging to the state.

104 The author has been a member of this Committee in the past.

105 Law No. 270, 21 December 2005.

and a premium of additional seats for the party or coalition with the largest proportion of votes. For the language minorities in autonomous Regions protected under the Statute, the minimum required is set at regional level and fixed at 20 per cent, otherwise the minorities, such as the Germans (the biggest group in Italy), who amount to approximately 0.5 per cent of the population at national level, would have no representation in the Chamber of Deputies.

The Senate in Italy is elected at regional level. Voters in the Region of Trentino-South Tyrol over the age of twenty-five also elect seven members to the Senate: three from each province and one at regional level. Although a proportional voting system was introduced at national level, for the Chamber and the Senate, with a threshold also for the Senate of 8 per cent applicable at regional level, South Tyrolean Senators succeeded in getting an exception to this system for Trentino South Tyrol, and were able to maintain – for the Senate – the former system, with six single-seat constituencies and one proportional seat.

Since the election of 1948, South Tyroleans have been represented at national level by three (sometimes two, sometimes four) deputies and two or three senators from the language minority, all from the Südtiroler Volkspartei (SVP), and, since 2001, one jointly supported by the SVP and the Italian left-wing Partito Democratico (PD).[106] In addition, in 2013 one additional German representative was elected from the left wing Sinistra ecologica e Libertà. During this same period, in the Italian group from the Province of Bolzano/Bozen there have been one to three (increased to four in 2008) members of Parliament.[107] In the 2013 elections, the Province elected two deputies from the Partito Democratico (PD) and one from the right wing Popolo della Libertà (PDL).[108]

Various modest arrangements exist for additional participation from the regions. For example, there is a special co-ordination committee, known as the 'State Regions Conference'. It is composed of the Presidents (or delegated members of the regional government) from the twenty regions and the two autonomous provinces and is under the chairmanship of the President of the Council of Ministers, or the Minister for Regional Affairs. The government must consult this Conference for all matters of regional competences. But their appraisals are not binding.[109]

There is also a 'Conference State-Cities and Local Autonomies' (Conferenza Stato-Città e autonomie locali). Together they form the 'United Conference' (Conferenza unificata). The State-Regions Conference has become a strong discussion partner for the state. By the direct election of regional presidents

[106] The author of this article held this office in the Senate from 2001–13.

[107] Oskar Peterlini, *Südtirols Vertretung am Faden Roms, Die Auswirkungen von Wahlsystemen auf ethnische Minderheiten am Beispiel Südtirols in Rom von 1921–2013* [South Tyrol representation in Rome, the impact of electoral systems on ethnic minorities on the example of South Tyrol in Rome], in Peter Hilpold (ed.), *Minderheitenschutz in Italien* [Protection of Minorities in Italy]. (Wien: Reihe Ethnos 70, Braumüller, 2009).

[108] Ministero degli Interni: http://elezionistorico.interno.it/index.php, accessed 16 May 2013.

[109] Conferenza Stato Regioni, Legislative Decree 28 August 1997, No. 281: www.statoregioni.it/home_UNI.asp?CONF=*UNI*, accessed 7 July 2010.

since 1999 these Conferences gained further weight, but has no legislative chamber, such as exists in the federal system, which can participate in the legislative process.[110]

The regions also participate in the election of the President of the Republic. When Parliament elects the President, three delegates from each region elected by the regional parliaments participate in the election.[111]

However, proposals made during discussions on constitutional reform in 2001 to turn the Senate into a Chamber of the Regions were not adopted. The constitutional reform of 2001 was limited to Title V of the second part of the Constitution and concerns the municipalities, provinces, metropolitan cities and the regions, as well as the state, which together form the Republic.[112]

After the 2001 parliamentary elections were won by Silvio Berlusconi and his right-wing coalition, a new attempt at constitutional reform was made. However, the work was split between various government forces: the Northern League, which advocated a federal State, and the centralist parties, Alleanza Nazionale and Forza Italia, which wanted to strengthen central government.

The result was a constitutional draft law, which favoured a tentative federalism (devolution),[113] transferring some new powers to the regions, but also the reintroduction of the principle of 'national interest', returning a series of powers of the regions to the state competences. The draft law also strengthened the position of the Prime Minister and weakened the power of Parliament.[114]

The proposed devolution reforms of 2005 also provided for a so-called Federal Senate consisting of directly elected Senators, as before, and new non-voting delegates from the Regions.[115] The constitutional draft law, however, was rejected at a referendum on 25 and 26 June 2006. Voter turnout was 52.3 per cent. Of the approximately 26 million votes cast there were 38.68 per cent in favour of the reform, with 61.32 per cent against.[116]

110 Augusto Barbera, *L'elezione diretta dei Presidenti delle Giunte regionali: meglio la soluzione transitoria?*, [The direct election of the presidents of regional governments: the best interim solution?] (Quaderni costituzionali, No. 3, 1999).

111 Constitution, Art. 83.

112 Constitution, Arts. 114–32.

113 The term devolution corresponds to decentralisation in the UK, see Sara Parolari, *Il regionalismo inglese* [English regionalism] (Milano: EURAC collana diretta da Sergio Ortino, CEDAM 2008); on decentralisation in Italy, France, Spain, UK and Belgium see Mario Caciagli, *Le Regioni d'Europa, Devoluzioni, regionalismi, integrazione europea* [The Regions of Europe, Devolution, Regionalism, European integration] (Bologna: Il Mulino 2006), 21–48.

114 Peterlini, *Südtirols Autonomie und die Verfassungsreformen Italiens*, Chapter 6.

115 Oskar Peterlini, *Föderalismus und Autonomien in Italien* [Federalism and autonomy in Italy] – *Die Auswirkungen der Föderalismusentwicklung in Italien auf die Sonderautonomien und im Besonderen auf das Autonomiestatut von Trentino Südtirol*, Dissertation, Leopold Franzens Universität, Faculty of Political Science and Sociology, Innsbruck, 2010.

116 Referendum 2006, www.referendum2006.interno.it, (accessed 15 February 2009). An analysis about the reasons for rejection see Martin J. Bull, 'La "grande riforma" del centro-destra alla prova del referendum' [The "major reform" of the center-right to the test of the referendum] in J. L. Briquet and Alfio Mastropaolo (eds.), *Politica in Italia, I fatti dell'anno e le interpretazioni* [Politics in Italy, The facts of the year, and interpretations], (Bologna: Istituto Carlo Cattaneo, Il Mulino Bologna 2007), 123–42.

Draft constitutional Law No. 24, unified with many subsequent laws, has been in Parliament since April 2012. The proposed changes include a reduction in the numbers of members of Parliament and separation of the competences of Chamber and Senate.[117] After an initially promising agreement between the parties of the left- and right-wing and the centre, who were supporting the Monti Government, the right-wing proceeded alone by instituting a semi-presidential system (with the direct election of the President) and a timid Federal Senate, as was done in 2005. The draft was approved by the Senate on a first reading on 25 July 2012 in the unified text and sent on to the Chamber of Deputies. However, the premature dissolution of Parliament and early elections in February 2013 brought this process to a halt. The new government of Enrico Letta wants to make a fresh start.

The regional parliament, and since 2001 also the autonomous provincial parliaments,[118] can approve draft proposals and bills to be presented in the national Parliament which cover subject matters that do not fall within the competence of the region, but which are of some interest to it.[119] The Italian Constitution also provides for the holding of a referendum, if the government is petitioned by not less than 500,000 electors or if it is requested by five regional parliaments.[120]

At the national level, the Presidents of autonomous regions and provinces are, based on their special statutes, entitled to participate in meetings of the Council of Ministers when questions concerning their respective jurisdictions are being considered.

Co-operation and consultation between different levels of government

The State Regions Conference becomes the focal point

As mentioned earlier, although the Italian Parliament is composed of two Chambers, it does not include a federal Chamber representing the regions, as is the practice in federal states. In the absence of such a Chamber, the role of the Conference of the Presidents of the Regions is crucial. This situation is similar to that which exists in Austria or Germany, where leaders of the Länder constituted an additional conference (of the presidents) to the Bundesrat (Chamber of the Regions) in which they are directly represented. The Conference of the Regions in Italy evolved out of a series of meetings between their respective Presidents during the 1980s. The 'State-Regions Conference' (Conferenza Stato Regioni) was launched by the Parliamentary Commission for Regional Affairs

[117] *Changes to Part II of the Constitution relating to the Houses of Parliament and the form of government.* Atto Senato No. 24, Iniziativa Parlamentare Oskar Peterlini (UDC-SVP-Aut) unified with other proposals and with the new title: 'Modifiche alla Parte seconda della Costituzione concernenti le Camere del Parlamento e la forma di governo', www.senato.it/leg/16/BGT/Schede/Ddliter/29633.htm.

[118] Constitutional law 31 January 2001, No. 2, Article 4.

[119] Autonomy Statute, Art. 35.

[120] Constitution, Art. 75.

in February 1980, functioning initially as the body connecting national and regional policies, and as a conduit for communication between the Government and the regions. Law No. 5 of 15 March 1997, called the Bassanini Law, changed their nature from the ground up: the State-Regions Conference became a focal point for co-ordination and dialogue between Government and the regions, a 'kind of embryo regional chamber in formation', writes Simona Piattoni.[121] The following Legislative Decree of 28 August 1997 No. 281 increased its role and provided compulsory expertise for all legislative initiatives of the government in the areas of regional legislation.[122]

The State Regions Conference became the focal point for co-ordination and dialogue between the Italian Government and the regions. As has been mentioned previously, the State-cities and Local Governments Conference, combined with the State Region Conference, forms the Joint Conference.

Aware of the lack of a regional Chamber, the constitutional reform of 2001 provided for a representation of the Regions in the joint parliamentary Bicameral Committee for Regional Affairs.

> Until the revision of the provisions of Title I of Part II of the Constitution, the Regulations of the Chamber of Deputies and the Senate may provide for the participation of representatives of the Regions, autonomous Provinces and local authorities to the Parliamentary Committee for Regional Affairs.[123]

The constitutional reform prescribes majority approval when a draft law contains provisions concerning the matters of regional competitive competences (foreseen in the third paragraph of Article 117 and Article 119 of the Constitution) on which the parliamentary Committee for Regional Affairs, integrated with the representatives of the Region and local authorities, has expressed a contrary or a favourable opinion with conditions. If the legislative Commission that carried out the examination has not taken the corresponding parts of the bill into account, the Assembly must vote with an absolute majority of its members. However, twelve years after the opportunity for it was constitutionally provided, the representatives of the regions and local authorities have not been able to participate in the Committee.

The Permanent Commission on the Province of Bozen

The final measure of the 'Package' for South Tyrol No. 137 requires the establishment of a 'permanent Commission for the problems of the Province of Bozen' (ständige Kommission für die Probleme der Provinz Bozen) at the Presidency

[121] Simona Piattoni, *Regioni a statuto speciale e politica di coesione. Cambiamenti interistituzionali e risposte regionali*, in Sergio Fabbrini (ed.), *L'europeizzazione dell'Italia* [The Europeanisation of Italy], (Roma/Bari Editori Laterza, 2003), 108–38.

[122] Vgl Conferenza Stato Regioni: www.statoregioni.it/home_UNI.asp?CONF=UNI, accessed 7 July 2010.

[123] Constitutional Law 18 October 2001, No. 3, Art. 11.

of the Council of Ministers.[124] The Commission is charged with examining 'the problems connected to safeguarding the rights of the linguistic minorities and the cultural, social and economic development of the population of South Tyrol'.[125] The Commission is important because it recognises that new developments related to the autonomy of the Province may arise and therefore adjustments to the Autonomy Statute will need to be made. Reports of the Commission are not binding on the government or parliament. Seeking its opinion is only obligatory if any changes are proposed in the Autonomy Statute.

The President of the Commission is an Undersecretary of State at the Presidency of the Council of Ministers. The Commission consists of seven members elected by the Provincial Parliament: four German speakers, two Italian speakers, and a Ladin speaker chosen from three candidates proposed by the Ladin mayors. In reality, the Commission has almost never convened because there has been minimal discussion about changing the Autonomy Statute. Indeed, the Statute should be adapted to the constitutional reforms of 2001, but the representatives of the linguistic minorities have been reluctant to do this because of the possibility of negative changes to it during the tenure of the right-wing government. The only amendment that they currently would like to see is the establishment of a consensus for amending the Statute to prevent unilateral changes being made to it through Parliament.

As the implementation of autonomy will need constant adjustment, the two other commissions, the so-called Commission of Twelve and the Commission of Six responsible for the implementation of the Autonomy Statute, are still active, despite having passed the date set for their discharge after implementation of the Package. As has been previously emphasised, newly promulgated laws, such as the introduction of fiscal federalism, are referred to these commissions for adaption to the situation of the autonomous regions.

Amendment of the Statute and the finance system

The Autonomy Statute of Trentino-South Tyrol is a constitutional law and, as with the Constitution, is at the highest level of legislation. It can, therefore, only be amended by a special procedure provided for in the Constitution and the Statute. The Constitution requires that constitutional laws must be approved twice by each Chamber of Parliament. The time between the two votes must be an interval of at least three months. In the second vote, the consent of an absolute majority of the members of each Chamber is required for approval of the amendment.[126]

[124] Package of South Tyrol: VII. Interne Garantien [Internal Guarantees], Measure (137), original wording: Mit Dekret des Ministerpräsidenten wird, gemäß nachstehender Bestimmungen, eine ständige Kommission für die Probleme der Provinz Bozen geschaffen.

[125] Package, Measure 137. [126] Constitution, Art. 138.

The Autonomy Statute further provides that after a proposal from the provincial parliaments, the Regional Parliament (in addition to the government and each Member of Parliament) is entitled to Submit official amendments to the Statute to the National Parliament.[127] Proposals for amendments initiated by the government or Parliament must be communicated by the government to the regional and provincial parliaments, which must express their opinion within two months. Approved amendments to the Statute cannot be subject to a national referendum.[128]

The regime for the financing of autonomy[129] and the concessions for large-scale diversions for hydro-electric purposes[130] are governed by Article 104 of the Autonomy Statute, which allows them to be altered by an ordinary state law.

However, special safeguards are provided. For the amendment to be achieved, a joint request is required of the government and, depending on the jurisdiction,of the Region or the two provinces. This agreement reinforces the bargaining power of the autonomous bodies, the Region and the provinces. Although the procedure is simpler than that for constitutional laws, the bargaining position of the autonomous bodies is stronger because no similar arrangement is provided for change to other parts of the Statute. Parliament can, for other parts, eventually proceed alone with the legislation.

In the event of refusal of consent to a financial agreement by the local bodies, the only way left to the state would be the possibility of changing the Autonomy Statute itself and removing this provision, although with predictable conflicts with Austria as a partner of the Paris Agreement.[131]

Taxation and finance

The Region and the provinces have autonomy in spending but practically none in taxation. With a few minor exceptions, the state is responsible for the setting and levying of taxes and duties; it makes the statutory arrangements for fixing tax rates and their collection and uses the relevant state offices to collect them. The funding system has been changed once: as distinct from other Italian Provinces and Regions, and on the basis of the Autonomy Statute and a 1989 law, the government guaranteed financing for the Region and Provinces through grants.[132]

More recently, a legislative reform package on fiscal federalism[133] was enacted to transfer a portion of taxes to local authorities, with the requirement, however,

[127] Autonomy Statute, Art. 103 paras 2 and 3.

[128] Art. 103, paragraph 4 of the Autonomy Statute, introduced with constitutional law 31 January 2001, No. 2, Art. 4.

[129] Ibid, Title VI. [130] Ibid, Art. 13.

[131] Peterlini, *Südtirols Autonomie und die Verfassungsreformen Italien.*

[132] Law No. 386 of 30 November 1989 amended Articles 69 to 82 of the Autonomy Statute to achieve this.

[133] Law No. 42 of 5 May 2009.

that 'solidarity contributions' be made to poorer Italian regions. In this spirit, a new regulation was agreed, involving an amendment to the Autonomy Statute, in Milan on 30 November 2009 between the Central Government, the Region of Trentino South-Tyrol and the two Provinces of Trentino and South Tyrol, which came into force on 1 January 2010.[134] Under this new arrangement, the state devolves 90 per cent of the tax yield collected in the Region to the provinces, and cancelled all other forms of contribution. A smaller portion of the tax yield goes to the Region, with the state retaining one tenth of the yield to cover the costs of tax collection and state administration. Almost all the grants are made unconditionally, thus the regional or provincial parliaments can act independently with regard to the distribution of this income in the provincial budget.[135]

The Milan Agreement provided for a saving of €1,500 million annually for the state. The annual budgets of the two provinces amount approximately to €5,000 million each, that of the Region around to €470 million.[136]

This was just the beginning of strict austerity measures imposed by the central government. One difficulty became apparent almost immediately after the Milan Agreement: in view of the Maastricht criteria, impending state bankruptcy and high public debt, radical cost-cutting measures were forced on the Italian government. In 2011 the public debt amounted to €1,900 billion, a ratio to the GDP of 120.1 per cent,[137] and climbing to over €2,000 million by June the end of 2012. In late 2011 Italy came to the brink of insolvency, which led to the ousting of the Berlusconi government and its replacement by the government of Mario Monti in November of that year.

The principles of consensus for amendment of the finance system and the procedures of the Autonomy Statute have been violated by the state in recent years, by the Berlusconi government in 2010[138] and 2011[139] and the Monti government when it cut the revenues of the autonomous regions of Northern Italy without attempting to reach any form of agreement with them.

Government cuts because of the financial crisis will affect provincial budgets up to 2013. South Tyrol's budget estimate for 2012, planned in November 2011, currently provides for a modest reduction in revenue of €102.9 million over the previous year. Planned revenue in 2011 declined from €5,227 million to

134 The amendment is to Part VI. Arts. 69–79 of the Autonomy Statute, amended by Art. 2, 107, Law 23 December 2009, No. 191 (legge finanziaria 2010).

135 Autonomy Statute, Arts. 83 and 84.

136 www.regione.taa.it/SchedaInfo.aspx?Id=420, accessed 17 December 2009.

137 ISTAT, Ministero dell'Economia e delle Finanze, Dipartimento del Tesoro, DEF 2012 (for perspective 2012). www.istat.it/it/files/2011/06/italiaincifre2011.pdf; ISTAT: www.marcostradiotto.org/wp-content/uploads/2011/12/ITALIA-spesa-9dic2011-11.pdf; www.dt.tesoro.it/it/debito_pubblico/_link_rapidi/debito_pubblico.html (downloaded 3 June 2012).

138 Decreto legge (DL), 31 May 2010, No. 78.

139 DL 6 July 2011, n 98, convertito in L 15 July 2011 n 111, DL 13 August 2011, n 138, convertito in L 14 September 2011 n 148.

€5,124 million. The more radical cuts made in 2012,[140] which will be followed by the austerity measures of the state, are difficult to predict. The Province of Bozen estimates the burden for the year 2012 at €611 million, mounting to €800 million in 2013.[141]

There are a number of Constitutional Court judgments pending on such unilateral decisions on budget cuts. The Court has repeatedly confirmed the necessity of agreements, and has disallowed conflicting standards.[142] How the financial crisis will affect its future decisions remains to be seen.[143]

On 2 February 2012 the Presidents of the Provinces of Trento and Bolzano, Lorenzo Dellai and Luis Durnwalder, handed a letter to the Prime Minister Monti, in which they confirmed their willingness to contribute to the fiscal consolidation and rehabilitation of the state and work towards finding a final, stable system. Within the meaning of Article 104 of the Autonomy Statute they argued that a new agreement should be concluded that would lead to the amendment of the financial regulation in Title VI of the Autonomy Statute. The autonomous provinces and the Region proposed that they take over all the expenses of the state on their territory, by delegation or transfer of state functions or by agreements. The responsibilities of the autonomous provinces in tax matters should be established and the relationships between the provincial laws and the state laws should be clearly defined.

The implementation of fiscal federalism in Italy was placed on ice because of the austerity measures. In the Monti and Letta governments, the Northern League, which had been the driving force for fiscal federalism, is no longer part of the governing coalition.[144] A new, centralising wind blows across Italy.

Methods of dispute resolution

Since the Italian Government's power to reject regional laws has been eliminated by the constitutional Reform of 2001, the Constitutional Court alone is responsible for the resolution of conflicts relating to autonomy legislation.

The Constitutional Court adjudicates disputes regarding the constitutionality of the laws of the state, regions, and the autonomous provinces. The central government may contest regional or provincial laws in the Court for violation of the Constitution or the Autonomy Statute, or the principle of equality among the language groups. Regional law may also be contested by one of the Provincial

[140] DL 6 July 2012, No. 95, disposizioni urgenti per la revisione della spesa pubblica con invarianza dei servizi ai cittadini (5389) [Urgent provisions for the review of public spending].

[141] Regione e Provincie Autonome Trento e Bolzano, Letter to Monti, Ridefinizione dei rapporti finanziari tra Provincie Autonome e Stato, Trento 2 febbraio 2012 [Redefinition of the financial relations between the State and Autonomous Provinces, Trento, 2 February, 2012].

[142] Constitutional Court rulings: 179/2012, 178/2012, 142/2012, 323/2011, 133/2010, 341/2009, 74/2009, 190/2008, 159/2008, 145/2008, 95/2008.

[143] Peterlini, *Südtirols Autonomie und die Verfassungsreformen Italien.*

[144] Regione e Provincie Autonome Trento e Bolzano, Letter to Monti.

Parliaments, and provincial law by the Regional Parliament, or by the other Provincial Parliament in the region.[145]

The Region and the provinces also have the power to ask the Court to review laws and acts of the Republic: 'for violation of the (present) Statute or of the principle of the protection of the German and Ladin language minorities'.[146]

Each year dozens of questions are brought to the Constitutional Court. Those questions concerning the linguistic and cultural protection of minorities are often decided in the plaintiff's favour, while those concerning areas of competency are more difficult to resolve.

With regard to elections to the national Parliament, the 1993 'Mattarellum Law'[147] stipulated that three quarters of the Chamber of Deputies must be elected from single-seat constituencies and the remaining quarter by a list system of proportional representation. To win seats in the proportional allocation, single lists must obtain at least 4 per cent of the national vote.

The Province of Bozen challenged the provisions of this electoral law[148] before the Constitutional Court because they made no provision for representation of linguistic minorities, who constitute only 0.5 per cent of the national population. Although the Court found the challenge justified, the appeal was rejected on the grounds that possible solutions to the problem were beyond the remit of the Court. The judges invited Parliament to make the necessary changes in the law deemed necessary to resolve the issue.[149] However, no changes were made until 2005, which led the President of the Republic to request that Parliament respect the rights of the linguistic minorities of Italy; currently the law is not in force.[150]

On 31 December 2005, a new electoral law went into effect[151] that changed the two texts for the election of the Chamber and the Senate, and introduced a new system of proportional representation.[152] To gain admission to a seat in the Chamber of Deputies, various restrictive clauses were introduced, also a 4 per cent hurdle for single lists. But the new law exempts the recognised linguistic minorities in autonomous regions from the 4 per cent rule and sets a threshold of 20 per cent for them, but only at regional level. A new reform has been under discussion since summer 2012.

145 Autonomy Statute, Art. 97. 146 Autonomy Statute, Art. 98.

147 Laws of 4 August 1993, No. 276 (Senate) and No. 277 (Chamber of Deputies).

148 Law of 4 August 1993, No. 277.

149 Constitutional Court, ruling No. 438 of 13 December 1993: www.cortecostituzionale.it/actionPronuncia.do (accessed 15 August 2012).

150 Peterlini, *Südtirols Vertretung am Faden Roms*, 103–6.

151 Law No. 270 from 21 December 2005, Gazzetta Ufficiale No. 303.

152 Unified text for Chamber DPR 30 March 1957, No. 361; for Senate Leg. D. 20 December 1993, No. 533.

Conflicts over constitutional reform

The reform of the Italian Constitution in 2001 enlarged the competencies of the ordinary regions. As previously mentioned, a clause contained in this reform states that for the autonomous regions, 'The provisions of this Constitutional law shall also apply to the Special Statute Regions and autonomous provinces of Trento and Bolzano insofar as they provide broader forms of autonomy than those already assigned'.[153] Only the more favourable parts of the reform therefore were applicable to the special Regions. Furthermore, until 2001, the few powers of the ordinary regions were, for tax purposes, listed in Article 117 of the Constitution; all other matters not listed came under the competences of the State.

As a result, in the first five years of application the Constitutional Court dealt with 500 cases of conflicts related to these issues.[154] The Court has ruled several times on the 'more favourable' clause, in particular how the 'broader forms of autonomy' could be extended to the Special Statute Regions and autonomous provinces. In 2003 the Court declared that the clause could be applied only when there was 'comparable content', as described next.[155]

The ruling was particularly addressed to the special process by which the laws of the Region of Sicily could be challenged. Unlike the laws for other regions with special status, the Statute of Sicily had, from the beginning, allowed for appeals relating to Sicilian laws before their own Constitutional Court. In addition, the Italian Government never had the opportunity as it had with other special and ordinary regions to examine the constitutionality of Sicilian laws before they came into force and to veto their passage through the Regional Parliament (as was the case elsewhere prior to 2001, as mentioned previously). With the entry into force of Title V of the 2001 Constitution, this veto procedure was abolished for all regions[156] and replaced with the option of an appeal to the Constitutional Court. In this case, the Court therefore had to clarify which of the two procedures, that of the Autonomy Statute of Sicily or the new procedure for regions with ordinary statutes, should be applied. It concluded that the two systems were not comparable; therefore, with regard to Sicily, it found that the system provided for in its Statute of Autonomy should be used. This pronouncement did not affect the same issue in other autonomy statutes, as the new process of Constitutional Court review was a noticeable improvement in their relative autonomy.

Various related cases have been brought by other regions as well. For example, following the 2001 constitutional revision, the Region of Valle d'Aosta decided to apply the new procedure for the entry into force of its legislation and did not

[153] Art. 10, Constitutional Law No. 3, 18 October 2001.

[154] Francesco Marcelli and Valeria Giammusso, *La giurisprudenza costituzionale sulla novella del titolo V*, [The jurisprudence of the Constitutional Court on the innovations of Title V of the Constitution] (Roma: Senato della Repubblica, Servizio Studi Nr 44, 2006).

[155] Decision No. 314/2003.

[156] Constitutional Law No. 3, 2001.

request prior government approval, as provided for in its Autonomy Statute. In response, the Italian Government submitted a proposal to the Constitutional Court that all legislation from the Valle d'Aosta Region should be subject to prior review, but the Court rejected it.[157] The Court noted that, due to the 'more favourable' clause mentioned earlier, this procedure should also be applied to the special regions, and thus regional law would not be subject to pre-enactment review by the Italian Government. The Court issued a similar ruling allowing for passage of legislation without prior review by the autonomous Province of Bozen/Bolzano.[158]

As these cases have shown, the Constitutional Court's decisions have often served to endorse and even expand the powers of the provinces and autonomous regions with special Statutes. It is beyond the scope of this chapter to analyse all the judgments the Constitutional Court has handed down dealing with disputes between the regions and the government since the 2001 reforms. However, it is apparent that from that time the Constitutional Court has adopted a more state-centric view, as some examples presented next make clear.

It has been noted that the limits of legislation for the ordinary regions have been eased by the 2001 constitutional reform. However, the statutes of the special regions still contain limitations from the past, such as the 'national interest' restriction and requirement for legislation to comply with 'the principles of social and economic reforms'. The loosened limitations for the legislation of ordinary regions are not, according to the Constitutional Court, fully applicable to the regions with special statutes. The loosened limits apply only to those powers granted by the constitutional reform for all regions. For the 'old' powers of the special statutes, the old restrictions remain in force.[159] This has created an anomaly: in their legislation, the state and the ordinary regions must respect only the new limits of Article 117, paragraph 1, requiring conformity to the Constitution, EU rules and international obligations. The regions with special statute must, however, for their additional competences, respect the narrower limits of the past. Only in the areas of powers that are also accorded to ordinary regions can the regions with special statutes act with fewer limitations.

Another example of a state-oriented interpretation by the Court relates to balancing regional and state responsibilities, such as regional hunting laws against the state competence for environmental protection, or regional labour laws against the state competence relating to immigration. The 'more favourable' clause does not apply if, in balancing the responsibilities of central government and the regions, the state's responsibilities predominate. The criterion of 'prevalence' excludes the more favourable treatment clause.[160] For example, the

[157] Decision No. 377/2002. [158] Decision No. 408/2002.

[159] Decisions No. 103/2003 and No. 274/2003.

[160] Case No. 234/2005. For a discussion, see Marcelli and Giammusso, *La giurisprudenza costituzionale sulla novella del titolo V.*

Constitutional Court rejected challenges brought by the Provinces of Trento and Bolzano to a state law that had set up a Committee on Undeclared Work.[161] The state has exclusive competence in the field of tax legislation, and, according to the Constitutional Court, these can override the powers of the provinces in the area of employment.

Despite the formal equality of municipalities, provinces, cities and the state stipulated in the Constitution,[162] according to the Constitutional Court the state occupies a special role in the Constitutional order and therefore has a higher status.

The experience in the period 2001–6 has confirmed these observations. In this period the regions have challenged a number of state laws that infringed on their competences. In many cases, the Constitutional Court dismissed the claims and confirmed the state laws in question.[163]

The International Court of Justice

Internationally, the decrees in the European Convention for Peaceful Settlement of Disputes[164] are applicable to South Tyrol. Disputes arising from matters covered under the 1946 Paris Agreement should fall within the jurisdiction of the International Court of Justice. Both for Austria and for South Tyrol, 'The Hague was the price to be paid for the Package', recalls Antony Alcock.[165] Italy wanted to ensure that disputes on the implementation of the Paris Agreement would be heard by the International Court of Justice, rather than by the political organs of the United Nations.[166] However, to date no cases have been brought before the Court regarding South Tyrol.

Conclusion

The Autonomy Statute of 1972, which democratic Italy eventually accepted after a long struggle, represents an attempt to ensure that the German and Ladin linguistic minorities can survive as ethnic groups with their own linguistic and

161 Decision No. 234/2005. 162 Art. 114 of the Constitution.

163 Peterlini, Die Föderalismusentwicklung in Italien und ihre Auswirkungen auf die Sonderautonomien, 63.

164 Signed on 29 April 1957 in Strasbourg.

165 Antony E. Alcock, *The History of the South Tyrol Question* (London: Michael Joseph, 1970), 453.

166 Regarding the ratification of the International Court of Justice Agreement, the Italian position is clearly expressed in the report accompanying the draft: Atti Parlamentari, Camera dei Deputati, Roma, No. 3822, sitting of 25 November 1971. This viewpoint also concerns the problem of the international anchoring of the South Tyrol package: see Karl Zeller, *Das Problem der völkerrechtlichen Verankerung des Südtirol-Pakets und die Zuständigkeit des internationalen Gerichtshofes* [The problem of international legal anchoring of the South Tyrol Package and the jurisdiction of the International Court] (Vienna: Ethnos 34, Wilhelm Braumüller, Universitätsverlag, 1989), 85.

cultural identities. The Statute also forms the basis for peaceful co-existence and development of the three linguistic groups in the Province.

It has been said that autonomy is neither a guarantee of survival nor the best solution for South Tyrol. However, it does not mean that South Tyrol has given up its struggle for self-determination; it is an attempt to ensure the preservation of three distinct cultural identities.

The Europe of the future, with the membership of Austria in the European Union since 1995, opens up significant possibilities. For example, the border at the Brenner Pass became less critical. But this new Europe should not be a centralised body; it has to grant the regional population the right to participate in clearly defined areas. Ancient Tyrol, with its freedom, democratic rights and cultural and linguistic diversity, could be revived in a new form to become a modern, transnational European region.[167] The aim is not to move the frontiers but to transcend them. This new European Region could serve as a model for such co-operation across national borders, and thus a beacon for creating justice.

The challenge in South Tyrol does not end here. The challenge is to make all groups feel at home, with none dominating the others, making diversity a value rather than a source of confrontation. We want to be proud of living in this country, of enjoying a degree of autonomy that can better respond to people's needs, which has clearly borne fruit for everyone; we are proud of speaking more languages and knowing more cultures, of living and anticipating tomorrow's Europe and giving young people not only more opportunities to work in Italy and abroad, but also a broader cultural and professional horizon.

To this end, greater consensus should be achieved among the language groups on their future, and a vision of autonomy should be developed with which all linguistic groups can identify. The idea is to work for the advancement of a project for sharing values and common perspectives and against the politics predicated on confrontation and ethnic division that has always been pursued by right-wing forces.

One of the biggest threats to world peace lies in the absence of modalities for co-operation between different nationalities and ethnic minorities. Historically speaking, the territory of states and nationalities has rarely coincided.

Therefore, the solution of minority problems and the nationality question is essential to eliminating potential flashpoints and for ensuring peace. The more a state can develop federally – with a vertical distribution of powers – following the principle of subsidiarity, replacing the obligation of citizenship with free will and federalism, solving minority problems in an autonomous and

[167] Neue Mitte, *Südtirol 2000, Modell für eine Vollautonomie* [South Tyrol 2000, Model for a full autonomy] (Bozen: Umwelt, Kultur- und Sozialverein, 1991). See also the Agreement of 27 January 1993 between the Republic of Austria and the Italian Republic on Cooperation across Frontiers between Local Bodies, which came into force on 1 August 1995, in Peterlini, *Autonomy and the Protection of Ethnic Minorities in Trentino-South Tyrol*, 233.

respectful way, the more its existence will be guaranteed, because it will have greater potential to deal with emerging conflicts thus making any changes of borders unnecessary. Such arrangements give rise to hope that learning from history can ensure peace in the future.[168]

[168] Oskar Peterlini, 'L'autonomia – strumento di pace' [Autonomy, an instrument of peace] in Francesco M. Provenzano, *Federalismo, Devolution, Secessione – La storia continua. Ritorno al futuro* [Federalism, Devolution, Secession – The history continues. Back to the Future] (Cosenza: Editore Pellegrini, 2011).

5

Kashmir
The vanishing autonomy

Jill Cottrell

The Indian State of Jammu and Kashmir,[1] and the 'Kashmir problem', are a great deal more complex than a 'Muslim problem'. The state, now with a population of 12.5 million, about 1 per cent of India's total,[2] comprises Kashmir, largely Muslim,[3] Jammu, largely Hindu, and Ladakh, largely Buddhist. Although Kashmir had been part of the Mogul empire, then was lost to the Afghans, it never formally became a British colony. The Sikhs drove out the Afghans. The Dogra rulers of Jammu allied themselves with the Sikhs, but, at a crucial stage of the struggle with the British, remained neutral. The British/Sikh Treaty of Amritsar in 1846 recognised the Dogra Raja as ruler of combined Kashmir, Jammu, Ladakh and Baltistan; in fact the Kashmir Valley was sold to the Raja for 7.5 million rupees.

By the early twentieth century the British had imposed a constitution on Kashmir, and removed and then replaced the Raja – now under firm control of the British Resident, such Residents being 'how they kept control of the [. . .] princely states'.[4]

The Hindu ruler probably did not want to become part of India, while the Muslim leader, Sheikh Mohammed Abdullah,[5] leader of the main Kashmir party, the National Conference,[6] did – albeit on the basis of autonomy, the disappearance of which this chapter traces.

Kashmir is currently effectively divided between India and Pakistan and some parts are occupied by China. Separatists, who remain active in Indian

[1] 'Kashmir' is used for the whole.

[2] Provisional figures are available for the 2011 census: http://censusindia.gov.in/.

[3] The proportion of Hindus in the Kashmir Valley has remained steady at around 4 per cent. Wikipedia (http://en.wikipedia.org/wiki/Kashmir) citing *Imperial Gazetteer of India*, Volume 15 (Oxford and London: Oxford University Press, 2008), 99–102 for 2001, and Rai, Mridu, *Hindu Ruler, Muslim Subjects: Islam and the History of Kashmir* (Princeton University Press, 2004), 27 for the 1941 census. This is despite the departure of a majority of a particular group of Hindus: the Kashmiri Pandits, see www.panunkashmir.org/ and www.kashmir-information.com.

[4] M. J. Akbar, *Kashmir: Behind the Vale* (New Delhi: Lotus, 2002), 65.

[5] On the 'Lion of Kashmir' see for example, Ajit Bhattacharjea, *Sheikh Mohammad Abdullah – Tragic Hero of Kashmir* (New Delhi: Lotus Collection, Roli Books, 2008). He founded a dynasty: his son is currently in the federal Cabinet and his grandson Chief Minister of Kashmir.

[6] Originally Muslim Conference.

occupied Kashmir, do not necessarily aim for union with Pakistan but receive various types of aid and comfort from the other side of the Line of Control. The insurgency in the state, the strong presence of the Indian army and the international element make it very difficult to treat this autonomy as a purely legal issue. Nor can the fact that Kashmir is not a unity be ignored. One reason the centre would not accept the 2000 autonomy proposals outlined later was the internal divisions, especially the position of the Hindus of Jammu.[7]

Kashmir becomes part of independent India

Though the last Viceroy, Mountbatten, told the Princes that, on the passing of the Indian Independence Act, 'technically and legally [the States] become completely independent',[8] Britain gave little support to ideas of separate existence for the princely states. Mountbatten also told the princes:

> [E]very wise Ruler and wise Government would desire to link up with the great Dominion of India on a basis which leaves you great internal autonomy and which at the same time gets rid of your worries and cares over External Affairs, Defence and Communications [. . .] My scheme leaves you all the practical independence you could possibly use and makes you free of all those subjects which you cannot possibly manage on your own.[9]

Sardar Patel, the Minister for States, cajoled the princely states into joining the Union.[10] They initially acceded to India using Mountbatten's 'scheme', pending further negotiation, and the drawing up of the national constitution.

Kashmir's ruler, Hari Singh, seems to have hoped to remain separate; his son suggests that he was misled by some advisers to believe that he could reclaim extensive lands once ruled by his ancestors.[11] He only signed[12] – 'in a panic' says Akbar – when tribesmen with the support, tacit or at most *sotto voce*, of Pakistan,[13] invaded. Akbar also discusses why Patel had not tried harder to persuade Singh to accede at an earlier stage, and wonders whether he might even have come to accept that it was not realistic to bring 'a Muslim majority border state' into India.[14]

7 Rekha Choudhary, 'Debating autonomy', *Seminar* No. 496 (December 2000).

8 'Lord Mountbatten's Address to Princes, 25 July 1947' in Verinder Grover, *The Story of Kashmir: Yesterday and Today* (New Delhi: Deep & Deep, 1995), Vol. 3, 105.

9 Ibid.

10 The classic account is V. P. Menon, *The Story of the Integration of the Indian States* (Chennai: Orient Longman, 1956, reprinted 1997).

11 Karan Singh, *Autobiography* (New Delhi: Oxford, 1994), 38.

12 See Appendices XIII and XIV in H. S. Gururaj Rao, *Legal Aspects of the Kashmir Problem* (London: Asia Publishing House, 1967) for the instruments of accession signed by Singh and the other princes. On the signing see Prem Shankar Jha, *Kashmir 1947: Rival Versions of History* (Delhi: Oxford University Press, 1996); and Menon, *The Story of the Integration of the Indian States*, 400.

13 Alastair Lamb, *Kashmir: A Disputed Legacy, 1846–1990* (Hertingfordbury, Hertfordshire: Roxford Books, 1991), disputes the Pakistan support story; but see Jha, *Kashmir 1947*.

14 Akbar, *Kashmir: Behind the Vale*, 100–102.

Another view is that Singh wanted to sign earlier but Jawaharlal Nehru, Prime Minister of India, insisted that the democratic forces, namely Sheikh Abdullah and his party, should be joined in this decision,[15] not wanting to alienate Abdullah by accepting accession without involving him.[16] Sathe argues that India had never considered that the deciding factors should be the wishes of the Ruler, as opposed to the people, of a state, and never accepted the 'two nation theory' that led to partition, and therefore could not insist that Muslims must go to Pakistan, or Hindus to India.[17]

Federalism under the Indian Constitution

Kashmir enjoys certain autonomy not accorded to other states in the Indian federation,[18] which is officially 'the Union', reflecting the framers' decision to create a highly centralised federation. Initially, central influence over the states tended to grow rather than weaken, one reason being the dominance of the Congress Party. But more recently, that party has lost its pre-eminence, and central governments tend to be coalitions, usually dependent on parties holding power in the states; this has enormously increased the states' influence.[19]

For other states, there is a 'Union List' of ninety-six items (many themselves complex) on which the central government may legislate (and the states may not), including defence, the military and foreign affairs, major transport topics like railways, commercial questions like banking and stock exchanges and various taxes.[20] The 'State List' of exclusive state topics includes sixty-six items covering prisons, agriculture, most industries and certain taxes.[21] The 'Concurrent List', on which both centre and states may legislate, includes criminal law, marriage, bankruptcy, trade unions, professions and price control.[22] In case of conflict, the state legislation is invalid to the extent of the conflict.[23] The residual power – to make laws on matters not specified – rests with the Union. The centre may declare certain industries, waterways, ports, roads, libraries and so on to be national, or of national importance, shifting responsibility for them from the state list to the Union list, or from the concurrent to the Union list.[24]

Other significant features are the existence of not only a national Supreme Court but a national system of High Courts, and the two-chamber Parliament, with the Rajya Sabha (House of States) representing the interests of the states.

[15] Jha *Kashmir 1947*, 124. [16] Ibid., 126.

[17] S. P. Sathe, 'J and K and Article 370 of the Constitution: guidelines for future federalization of the polity' in Baxi, Jacobs and Singh, *Reconstructing the Republic* (New Delhi: Har-Anand, 1999), 337 at 340 (written some years before).

[18] Various other states (mostly in the North-East) have now some degree of autonomy, and some areas within states have special powers for example, Articles 371A (Nagaland). For 'tribal areas' within the North-Eastern States see Schedule 6.

[19] Professor M. P. Singh, then of National University of Juridical Sciences, Kolkata, at a workshop on federalism in Kathmandu, 2007.

[20] Art. 246 and Schedule 7 List I. [21] Ibid., List II. [22] Ibid., List III. [23] Art. 254.

[24] For example, Union List items 7 (defence industries), 23 (national highways) and 24 (national inland waterways).

The Governor

The Governor, the formal head of a state and link between centre and state, is a key element in the system. Like the President, the Governor normally acts on the advice of some other body (usually the state Council of Ministers):[25] 'a person having a crown on the head and fetters on the feet', commented one Governor.[26]

Governors, who often do not come from the state concerned, are appointed by the President,[27] which means the Union government, and can be dismissed in the same way.[28] There is no procedure for the Governor to be removed by the state legislature. The fact that they can be dismissed readily by the centre means that Governors are likely to use any discretion they have in a way that is sought, or at least favoured, by the centre, which is answerable for this to the national, not the state, legislature. Whether for reasons of politics or moral conviction, some Governors have stood up to the centre; some have acted with what seems to be a genuine concern to uphold the constitutional principles within their states, while others have behaved in ways very destructive of democracy. But Governors have very little to back them up except their moral authority and personality. The Sarkaria Commission proposal that Governors ought to be 'eminent in some walk of life', not belong to the state in question, be detached from the politics of the state and be persons without too much past political involvement, has not been implemented, though endorsed by later Commissions.[29]

The constitutional basis for Kashmir's autonomy

Article 370 of the Constitution of India[30] might give the impression that Kashmir still has a very high degree of autonomy. In reality Kashmir never effectively enjoyed anything like the autonomy that Article 370 seemed to promise, and hardly anyone involved intended, at least in the late 1940s when the Indian Constitution was being drafted, that it should do so, though not everyone had the same expectations of the Article.

Article 370 was a 'holding operation', devised to ensure that Kashmir could have a place in that Constitution. Following an agreement between the National

[25] Art. 163.

[26] Jagmohan, *My Frozen Turbulence in Kashmir* (New Delhi: Allied Publishers, 2006 edn.), 256.

[27] Art. 155. [28] Art. 156.

[29] The Commission was appointed to look at Centre-State Relations and reported in 1987: its report is on the website of the Inter-State Council: see http://interstatecouncil.nic.in/. The *Report of the National Commission to Review the Working of the Constitution* (2002) is at http://lawmin.nic.in/ncrwc/finalreport.htm. The relevant paragraph is 8.14.3. Most recently the Punchhi Commission on Centre-State Relations (2010), report available at http://interstatecouncil.nic.in/ccsr_report.html) ('Punchhi') endorsed the Sarkaria recommendations.

[30] Reference to 'Articles' are to the Constitution of India, and to 'sections' to the Constitution of Jammu and Kashmir.

Conference and national leaders in May 1949, the draft Article provided that the constitutional provisions relating to the territory of India, human rights and directive principles would apply to Kashmir. Other provisions would apply, with exceptions agreed by the national and state governments. It also provided that the Article was transitional, and that it could be changed by the State Constituent Assembly. Even before the draft Article was prepared, the National Conference – marginalising its Hindu and Sikh members – was resiling from the agreement, and it rejected the draft. Gopalaswami Ayyangar, in charge of the negotiations for the Indian side, revised the draft while Nehru was in New York, removing the provisions about human rights and directive principles. However, National Conference leaders rejected this too. Ayyangar again revised the draft, to the form passed by the national Constituent Assembly – pleasing neither Sardar Patel nor Sheikh Abdullah.[31]

There was little debate in the Constituent Assembly. Ayyangar explained that Kashmir's position was special, with internal war, part of the state occupied by rebels and enemies, and UN involvement that India had invited; India had made commitments to a plebiscite by its people on their future, and freedom to make their own constitution. As neither a legislative nor a constituent assembly could function due to the troubled situation, the only solution was an interim arrangement, negotiated with the government of Kashmir.[32]

No one involved intended that Article 370 should enshrine Kashmir's relationship with India forever. Nehru was determined that Kashmir should be part of India and essentially like any other state, though hoping that there would be a willing acceptance by Kashmir. Mountbatten, who had earlier assured Sheikh Abdullah that Kashmir could become independent, but with close relations to both India and Pakistan, now told him that this was not feasible, but, under an expanded Joint Defence Council, Kashmir could be dealt with 'as a state acceding to both dominions rather than to only one'.[33]

No doubt there were Muslims in Kashmir who wanted union with Pakistan, and others who would have been happy with the autonomy reflected in Article 370, but theirs were not the views that counted. While Hindus would have preferred fuller integration, many perhaps would have tolerated autonomy.[34]

[31] See Mohan Krishen Teng, *Kashmir: Article 370* (New Delhi: Anmol Publications, 1990), Chapter 3 on the negotiations.

[32] CA Debates Monday, 17 October 1949 (available http://parliamentofindia.nic.in/ls/debates/v10p10m.htm).

[33] Shashi Joshi, *The Last Durbar: A Dramatic Presentation of the Division of British India* (Karachi: Oxford University Press, 2006).

[34] The people of Kashmir have never had the opportunity to vote on this issue, despite promises of a plebiscite by both Mountbatten and Nehru. See Karan Singh, *Autobiography*, 80, on the former, and also Sumantra Bose, *Contested Lands* (Cambridge, MA, and New Delhi: Harvard University Press and HarperCollins India, 2007), 154, 169. In 2009 a survey was carried out by

The underlying design of Article 370 (see Table 5.1), if not the drafting or the execution, was arguably rather elegant: a State Constituent Assembly would, like the Constituent Assembly of the Union, draft a constitution. In that process it would resolve the question of the relationship of Kashmir to the Union; that done, the State Constituent Assembly would ask the President either to remove Article 370 from the Constitution, which would have meant that Kashmir would no longer have any special status, or amend Article 370 to apply the Indian Constitution to Kashmir with certain exceptions (which would have meant that some special features would remain in the relations between Kashmir and the Union). This would have sensibly avoided the current situation, where Article 370 gives a totally misleading impression, and even a careful perusal of the rest of the Constitution does not show how much of it applies to Kashmir.[35] Had further changes been needed to Article 370 – perhaps because Kashmir would have come closer to the Union – it would have been amended again, following the normal procedures.

The requirement that any abrogation or modification of Article 370 was to be done only on the recommendation of the State Constituent Assembly strongly suggests an assumption that everything would be completed by the time it wound up its business (a position reiterated by Ayyangar).[36]

After the Constitution of India

Soon after the Constitution of India came into force in 1950 the first Presidential Order was issued, based upon agreement between Srinagar and Delhi, and went before the State Constituent Assembly when the latter was established in 1951.

Chatham House, UK, with other agencies, on both sides of the Line of Control. The report comments,

> [T]here is no evidence that either joining India or joining Pakistan would come close to obtaining more than a quarter of the total vote. Moreover [. . .] such intention as there is to vote for either option is heavily polarised. 1% in AJK [Azad Kashmir – under Pakistan control] say they would vote to join India. Only 28% in J&K indicated an intention to vote to join India. But that 28% is itself polarized. [. . .] There is even less support across the whole of Kashmir for joining Pakistan. [. . .] it is difficult to see how the plebiscite proposed in the UN resolutions of 1948/49 could play any part today in the resolution of the dispute. However, there is no clear majority in prospect for independence either. In J&K there is a majority in favour of outright independence for the whole of Kashmir in only four districts, all in Kashmir Valley Division.

Robert W. Bradnock, *Kashmir: Paths to Peace* (London: Chatham House, 2010), 17–18, available at www.chathamhouse.org.uk/. Unfortunately the questionnaire did not include 'autonomy' as an element in the mix in joining India or Pakistan, except as an element in a possibility of joint sovereignty, which was most unpopular.

35 See the biting article by Arvind Lavakare, 'The indeterminate life of Article 370' (in two parts), June 2002, available at www.rediff.com/news/2002/may/29arvind.htm, and www.rediff.com/news/2002/jun/05arvind.htm.

36 Ayyangar's statement is clear that the recommendation must be accepted. The Delhi Agreement used the more common 'on the recommendation', which means that it must exist and must be followed.

Table 5.1 Constitution of India, Article 370

Provision	Comment
370. Temporary provisions with respect to the State of Jammu and Kashmir	
(1) Notwithstanding anything in this Constitution, –	
(*a*) [now repealed];	(a) refers to repealed Article 238 that concerned princely states generally.
(*b*) the power of Parliament to make laws for the said State shall be limited to –	
(*i*) those matters in the Union List and the Concurrent List which, *in consultation with the Government of the State*,[37] are declared by the President to correspond to matters specified in the Instrument of Accession governing the accession of the State to the Dominion of India as the matters with respect to which the Dominion Legislature may make laws for that State; and	(*i*) deals with the making of laws by the national Parliament only on matters that are within the initial agreed scope of Kashmir's accession to India. The only complexity relates to ensuring that the scope of the topics is not exceeded. 'The President' means the national government.[38]
(*ii*) such other matters in the said Lists as, *with the concurrence* of the Government of the State, the President may by order specify.	(*ii*) This deals with the possibility of extending the scope of topics through a Presidential Order. As well as a prerequisite of 'the concurrence of the Government of the State', we shall see there is a further, subsequent, required formality.
Explanation. For the purposes of this article, the Government of the State means the person for the time being recognised by the President as the Maharaja of Jammu and Kashmir acting on the advice of the Council of Ministers for the time being in office under the Maharaja's Proclamation dated the fifth day of March, 1948;	See footnote on the history of this.[39] It now reads 'the person for the time being recognised by the President on the recommendation of the Legislative Assembly of the State as the Sardar-i-Riyasat [Governor] of Jammu and Kashmir, acting on the advice of the Council of Ministers for the time being in office'.
(*c*) the provisions of Article 1 and of this article shall apply in relation to that State;	(*c*) This takes the matter beyond the legislative Lists; Article 1, defines the name and territory of the country.
(*d*) such of the other provisions of this Constitution shall apply in relation to that State subject to such exceptions and modifications as the President may by order specify:	(*d*) The drafting is weak: it is clearly intended that the President should prescribe which other provisions are to apply, *and* may also prescribe appropriate 'exceptions and modifications'.

(*cont.*)

[37] Emphasis added, here and throughout this table.

[38] This is now explicit – Article 74(1) – but was originally assumed.

[39] As originally drafted, 'Government of Kashmir' meant the government appointed under the Maharaja's Proclamation of 5 March 1948 – again indicating an expectation that the whole Article 370 process would soon be completed. Apparently some Constituent Assembly members objected to this, and it was changed to the rather odd formulation that would embrace any other government – though still not seeming to contemplate its being relevant far into the future, for when it was drafted everyone realised that the State Constituent Assembly was to decide on the future of the monarchy, that the Maharaja was already in exile, and the monarchy probably doomed. In 1952 the text was changed; see Table, and later.

Table 5.1 (*cont.*)

Provision	Comment
Provided that no such order which relates to the matters specified in the Instrument of Accession of the State referred to in paragraph (*i*) of sub-clause (*b*) shall be issued except *in consultation* with the Government of the State:	Again this relates only to the operationalising of the agreed terms of accession.
Provided further that no such order which relates to matters other than those referred to in the last preceding proviso shall be issued except *with the concurrence* of that Government.	This would involve expansion beyond those original terms, and is subject to the important additional requirement which follows.
(2) If the concurrence of the Government of the State referred to in paragraph (*ii*) of sub-clause (*b*) of clause (1) or in the second proviso to sub-clause (*d*) of that clause be given before the Constituent Assembly for the purpose of framing the Constitution of the State is convened, it shall be placed before such Assembly for such *decision* as it may take thereon.	It seems that clause (1)(b)(ii) or (d) orders could be made either before or after the State Constituent Assembly came into being; yet in either case the concurrence required was to be that of the Government not of the State Constituent Assembly, though in the former case subject to 'a decision' of the State Constituent Assembly (Presumably they could endorse or reject it, or the substance of it would be subsumed into the overall decision on the Constitution). These, therefore, would initially be provisional orders. Clause (1)(d) orders were assumed to be essentially those of the State Constituent Assembly. Gopalaswami Ayyangar said in relation to clause (1)(d), [. . .] it is one of our commitments to the people and Government of Kashmir that no such additions should be made except with the consent of the Constituent Assembly which may be called in the State for the purpose of framing its Constitution.
(3) Notwithstanding anything in the foregoing provisions of this article, the President may, by public notification, declare that this article shall cease to be operative or shall be operative only with such exceptions and modifications and from such date as he may specify: Provided that *the recommendation of the Constituent Assembly* of the State referred to in clause (2) shall be necessary before the President issues such a notification.	This is the only clause of Article 370 that envisages change to that Article itself. It requires the prior recommendation of the State Constituent Assembly.[40]

[40] Of course Article 370 implicitly recognises the application of a good deal more of the Constitution of India, including those articles setting up the Indian Parliament, the President and government.

That Constituent Assembly was hardly the sort of body envisaged when Article 370 was passed: the opposition boycotted it and almost all its members were National Conference members elected unopposed.

In March 1952 the Chair of the Basic Principles Committee of the State Constituent Assembly outlined its initial thinking: the state would be 'an autonomous republic within the Indian Union, with a separate President, National Assembly, Judiciary, Regional Autonomy and separate citizenship'.[41] Hard negotiations followed between Delhi and Kashmir, and in August a further agreement was reached between the Governments of India and Kashmir about which provisions of the Constitution of India would apply (Delhi Agreement).

When the draft Kashmir Constitution was produced, Bakshi Gulam Mohammad reacted: '[T]he drafts would set India ablaze, because the Indian people would clearly see that Kashmir wanted to leave India'.[42] Relations between Srinagar and Delhi, between Sheikh Abdullah and Nehru, deteriorated rapidly; the Sheikh, Prime Minister of Kashmir, was removed from office in 1953 and arrested[43] and Bakshi Gulam Mohammad appointed in his stead. Recent work has examined Abdullah's attitudes at the time and reasons for his arrest.[44] He is reported as saying that he was betrayed by India, that it would have been better if Kashmir had joined Pakistan and Kashmiri youth would be willing to fight for liberation, as had the youth in Algeria.[45]

The Delhi Agreement was now more positively accepted by the National Conference and the State Constituent Assembly. The final report of the Assembly's Basic Principles Committee (1954) clearly envisaged that the adoption of the constitution would finally resolve the relationship between Kashmir and the Centre:

> While preserving the internal autonomy of the State, all the obligations which flow from the fact of accession and also its elaborations as contained in the Delhi Agreement should find an appropriate place in the Constitution. The Committee is of the opinion that it is high time that finality in this respect should be reached and the relationship of the State with the Union should be expressed in clear and precise terms.[46]

Additionally, it proposed that the Drafting Committee for the Constitution should propose the changes needed in the 1950 Presidential Order

41 Teng, *Kashmir: Article 370*, Chapter 4.

42 Ibid., quoting Mir Qasim, Secretary of the Basic Principles Committee of the State Constituent Assembly.

43 By Karan Singh, son of the Maharaja, who had acted as regent and then became first head of the state, or Sadar-i-Riyasat.

44 See Sandeep Bamzai, *Bonfire of Kashmiriyat: Deconstructing the Accession* (New Delhi: Rupa, 2006), 187, 194ff.

45 Apparently contained in 'A report released on April 20 [2011] ... by noted historian, Shabnam Qayoom' See 'Yes, Sher-e-Kashmir favoured liberation of JK in 1953; Goni's interview corroborates Qayoom's report', www.earlytimes.in/newsdet.aspx?q=71881.

46 Available at: www.kashmir-information.com/historicaldocuments/136.html.

to bring this about. A new Jammu and Kashmir Order[47] replaced that of 1950, though arguably going further in some respects than the Delhi agreement.[48]

Article 370 now

No culminating Presidential Order under Article 370(3) was ever made. In 1952, Nehru wrote, 'It is not a perfectly clear matter from the legal point of view how far the President can issue notifications under Article 370 several times'.[49] Rajendra Prasad, first President of India, wrote:

> The conclusion [. . .] seems to me to be irresistible that Clause (3) of Article 370 was not intended to be used from time to time as occasion required [. . .] The correct view appears to be that recourse is to be had to this clause only when the Constituent Assembly of the State has been fully framed.[50]

In *Sampat Prakash v. State of Jammu and Kashmir* the Supreme Court held that the power to make Presidential Orders continued.[51] Their reasoning was firstly that the circumstances that gave rise to Article 370 had not ceased to be valid (a somewhat weak reason, being based on events after the adoption of the Article); secondly, Article 370 was to continue in effect unless and until the powers of the President were exercised under clause (3). That had not happened, and indeed, the State Constituent Assembly's request that the 'Explanation' to the article be changed indicated that the Assembly wished the article to remain in effect. The amendment article of the Constitution (368) had itself been changed to provide that in respect of Kashmir the Constitution could be amended only by the Article 370 process – therefore that process must still be a possibility (again this reasoning, based on post-enactment events, is questionable).

The Court did not cite its own decision in *Prem Nath Kaul v. State of Jammu and Kashmir*, where it had said, 'The continuance of the exercise of powers

47 Constitution (Application to Jammu and Kashmir) Order, 1954.

48 See A. G. Noorani, 'Article 370: Law and politics' *Frontline* 17, 16–29 September (2000), 19, available at www.hindu.com/fline/fl1719/17190890.htm. Also in Noorani, *Constitutional Questions and Citizens' Rights: An Omnibus Comprising Constitutional Questions in India: the President, Parliament and the States and Citizens' Rights, Judges and State Accountability* (New Delhi: Oxford University Press, 2006).

49 The letter, to Sheikh Abdullah, is reproduced in the State Autonomy Committee *Report* (adopted by the legislature of the State 2000), 50, available at the Jammu and Kashmir National Conference website: www.jknc.in/UploadFiles/1aac23c2-365a-42b1-b0cb-0fea56d5aa42_Autonomy.pdf, 34.

50 Reproduced as Appendix VII in the State Autonomy Committee Report. He specified clause 3 because he was asked to sign an order amending Article 370, changing the 'explanation': see previous.

51 [1969] 2 SCR 365.

conferred on the Parliament and the President by the relevant temporary provisions of Article 370(1) is made conditional upon the final approval by the said Constituent Assembly in the said matters'.[52] Its view of clause (3) had been similar.

Can Article 370 now be amended or repealed?

Hindu parties and groups have been pressing for repeal of Article 370, to place Kashmir on the same basis as other states. Article 368 (2), on amendment generally, now reads 'Provided further that no such amendment shall have effect in relation to the State of Jammu and Kashmir unless applied by order of the President under clause (1) of article 370'.[53] As we have seen, the Supreme Court has assumed that only the Article 370 procedure could be used. But Noorani maintains that the Article 370 procedure can no longer be used, so no amendments affecting Kashmir can be made at all.[54] Some have argued that the proviso must now be ignored, and that Article 370 may be amended by the Article 368 procedure like any other article. On one view, Article 370 cannot be removed because it (or the Kashmir autonomy that it represents) is part of the basic structure of the Constitution of India.[55] Sathe argues that the only mechanism for change would be to pass legislation under Article 368 abrogating Article 370, and then, with the concurrence of the state government, for the President to apply that to Kashmir.[56]

The amendment introducing the proviso to Article 368 was presumably intended to reinforce Kashmir's autonomy. As we shall see, it has actually enabled erosion of that autonomy.

One way traffic?

Once a provision of the Constitution of India was applied, could a later President's Order disapply it? Normal principles would suggest a positive answer. But a 1974 agreement between Sheikh Abdullah and Indira Gandhi included the provision that no such backtracking was possible: 'provisions of the Constitution of India already applied to the State of Jammu and Kashmir without

52 [1959] Supp. 2 SCR 270, para. 294. Hidayatullah J sat in both cases.

53 See The Constitution (Application to Jammu and Kashmir) Order, 1954 C.O. 48.

54 A. G. Noorani, 'Article 370: Victim of Deceitful Conduct', 5 March 1998, see www.oocities.org/jklf_uk_europe/features.html#articl370.

55 Rajindar Sachar, 'Kashmir: Need of the Hour' *Mainstream* 44:6, 15 July 2006.
The Supreme Court's 'basic structure' concept means even a constitutional amendment could not change certain issues radically. The leading case is *Kesavananda Bharati v. the State of Kerala* (1973) Supp. S.C.R. 1.

56 Sathe, 'J and K and Article 370 of the Constitution: guidelines for future federalization of the polity', 343.

adaptation or modification are unalterable'.[57] Noorani maintains that this was 'based on gross error'.[58]

The erosion of autonomy

The state Constitution came into force in 1957, with Abdullah already in detention. Thereafter, successive governments of India, in collaboration with governments of Kashmir, have applied elements of the Constitution of India by means of forty-three Presidential Orders under Article 370 (1)(b)(ii) and (d), the latest in 1994. Article 370 has proved less a bulwark for autonomy than 'a tunnel in the wall'.[59]

Most extensions of the Constitution of India to the state took place while Sheikh Abdullah was in detention. And once the Constituent Assembly had ceased to sit, the subsequent approvals were given by the Government. But:

> From 1953 to 1975, Chief Ministers of that State had been nominees of Delhi. Their appointment to that post was legitimised by the holding of farcical and totally rigged elections in which the Congress party led by Delhi's nominee was elected by huge majorities.[60]

A number of the Presidential Orders were made when President's Rule – rule from Delhi – was in effect: with no Kashmir Government at all to give the necessary approval. Noorani comments:

> On July 30, 1986, the President made an order under Article 370, extending to Kashmir Article 249 of the Constitution in order to empower Parliament to legislate even on a matter in the State List on the strength of a Rajya Sabha resolution. 'Concurrence' to this was given by the Centre's own appointee, Governor Jagmohan. G. A. Lone, a former Secretary, Law and Parliamentary Affairs, to the State Government described in *Kashmir Times* (April 20, 1995) how the 'manipulation' was done 'in a single day' against the Law Secretary's advice and 'in the absence of a Council of Ministers'.[61]

Presidential Orders have amended rather than replaced the 1954 Order, possibly in recognition of the doubts over the constitutionality of repeated Article 370 Orders, but this style of amendment has made it hard to be confident about what parts of the Constitution of India apply to Kashmir.

Immediately following the 1950 Presidential Order, none of the parts of the Indian Constitution on citizenship, fundamental rights, directive principles,

57 See www.jammu-kashmir.com/documents/kashmiraccord.html.

58 Because M. A. Beg (negotiator for the Kashmir side) was very ill, and relied on advice from an advisor to the Indian side on the negotiations, see Noorani, 'Article 370: Law and politics'.

59 Home Minister G. L. Nanda, 4 December 1964; quoted in for example, the State Autonomy Committee *Report*, 88.

60 B. K. Nehru, *Nice Guys Finish Second* (Delhi: Viking Penguin India, 1997), quoted by Noorani, in 'Article 370: Law and politics'.

61 Ibid.

trade and so on, within India, Services, Emergency Provisions, nor the provisions on the governmental structures for the states (the constitution for the states) applied to Kashmir. Of the articles of the Constitution, 235 did not apply at all, nine applied partially and twenty-nine applied with modifications.[62] In the Union Legislative List thirty-eight of the ninety-six items applied, relating to external affairs, communications, the national governmental machinery and incidental matters.[63] The 1952 Delhi Agreement was summarised, by the State Autonomy Committee:

> It was agreed that residuary powers would continue to vest in the State as provided in Article 370; within the ambit of Indian citizenship, the State legislature would have the power to regulate the rights and privileges of permanent residents or 'State Subjects' as defined in a 1927 State Order, the Fundamental Rights chapter of the Indian Constitution be applied to the State with modifications and exceptions such as enabling transfer of land to the tiller without payment of compensation;[64] the jurisdiction of the Supreme Court would extend to the State; the State flag would not be a rival to the national tricolour which would occupy a supremely distinctive place in the State, the power to grant reprieve and commute sentences would vest in the President of India; with the abolition of hereditary rulership, the Head of the State of Jammu and Kashmir shall be recognized by the President on the recommendations of the Legislative Assembly of the State; a financial arrangement between the State and the Union be evolved; with regard to emergency powers, Article 352 be modified to provide for its promulgation in case of external aggression but in case of internal disturbance only at the request of or with the concurrence of the State Government; and the election Commission will conduct elections to Parliament and to the offices of President and Vice-President.[65]

The report also said:

> What followed 1954 is a series of Constitution (Application to J&K) Orders which were not conceived at any point of time either in 1950 or in 1952 or even later in May 1954. Among the changes brought about the most important were in restricting the powers of legislature of the State, extension of powers of the Union Parliament, application to the State of financial provisions of the

[62] Bodh Raj Sharma, 'The special position of Jammu and Kashmir in the Indian Constitution', in Grover, *Story of Kashmir*, Vol. 2, 173, 177.

[63] For text of the 1950 Order, see ibid., Vol. 3, 194–8.

[64] The relevance was to Abdullah's land reform plans; see later.

[65] *Report* (adopted by the legislature of the State 2000), 50, available at the Jammu and Kashmir National Conference website: www.jknc.in/. Sunita Mandla, *The Politics of State Autonomy and Regional Identity: Jammu and Kashmir* (Delhi: Gyan Books, 2006) Appendix 4, and www.satp.org/satporgtp/countries/india/states/jandk/documents/papers/delhi_agreement_1952.htm. See also Sheikh Mohammad Abdullah's Statement to the Constituent Assembly on Delhi Agreement, 11 August 1952, available at: www.kashmir-information.com/LegalDocs/130.html. According to Teng, *Kashmir: Article 370*, the Sheikh's speech was not an entirely accurate reflection of the agreement.

> Constitution of India, provisions relating to emergency, All India Services, superintendence, direction and control of elections of the state legislature and several other matters.[66]

Overall, Sathe comments, 'all important provisions [of the Constitution of India] have been made applicable'.[67] Various Jammu and Kashmir (Extension of Laws) Acts applied to the state Union Acts now within the legislative power of the centre, and repealed any 'corresponding law' on the Kashmir statute book.[68]

The institutions and processes of autonomy now

We turn to the legal structures and rules that are relevant today to the maintenance, or even to the subversion, of Kashmir's autonomy. There is some unreality in this, because, just as the functioning of Indian federalism generally depends on non-legal factors as much as legal, the same is true of Kashmir. In 2000 an expert on Kashmir wrote, surprisingly perhaps, in view of what has gone before:

> with a two-thirds majority in the Legislative Council, and with no effective opposition in the Valley, no inner-party democracy and no opposition from any party at the national level, Farooq Abdullah enjoys far more power than ever enjoyed by any Chief Minister in any other State of India.[69]

The Constitution of Kashmir

The Hindu right-wing slogan was: 'In one country two constitutions, in one country two flags, in one country two heads of state: will not, will not be accepted'. Kashmir still has its own constitution and flag.

Kashmir's 1939 Constitution placed all effective power in the hands of the Maharaja. It was amended incrementally, until the State Constituent Assembly passed the new document, much of which draws heavily on the Constitution of India. Article 1 reads, 'The State of Jammu and Kashmir is and shall be an integral part of the Union of India'. Without its own bill of rights, it does have directive principles of state policy, generally more socialist and aspirational in tone than the Constitution of India, including, for example,

> the prime object of the State consistent with the ideals and objectives of the freedom movement envisaged in 'New Kashmir' shall be the promotion of the

66 Para. 84. See also Grover, *The Story of Kashmir*, Vol. 3, 331–2.

67 Sathe, 'J and K and Article 370 of the Constitution', 353.

68 For example, Act. No. 52 of 1956, which applies to the state some 30 statutes ranging from the Opium Act 1857 to the Companies Act 1956. Earlier Act No. 41 of 1954 The Taxation Laws (Extension to Jammu and Kashmir) Act had applied various tax statutes.

69 Balraj Puri, 'The autonomy debate', *Frontline* 17:6, 18–31 March (2000), reprinted in Sabyasachi Basu Ray Chaudhury et al., *Indian Autonomies: Keywords and Key Texts* (Calcutta: Sampark, 2005), 303.

welfare of the mass of the people by establishing and preserving a socialist order of society wherein all exploitation of man has been abolished.[70]

The Kashmir Constitution sets up a parliamentary system with a largely ceremonial head (now the 'Governor'), a Chief Minister and two legislative houses: the Legislative Assembly and the Legislative Council (an option open to other states also).[71] Unlike the Constitution of India, Part IX, introduced by the Seventy-third Amendment, but not made applicable to Kashmir, the Kashmir Constitution does not provide for panchayats (local councils) or municipal bodies, although the state does have its own legislation about these. Full implementation of the principles of the Seventy-third Amendment is a matter of current contention in the state legislature, even within the National Conference-Congress alliance, with the former arguing both that it has adequately empowered the elected representatives, and that implementing the Seventy-third amendment as such would be an infringement of the state's autonomy.[72]

The state legislature and its powers

The Assembly comprises 111 members, plus possibly two nominated women members, but twenty-four of the seats remain vacant for 'the area of the State under the occupation of Pakistan';[73] otherwise, the structure is similar to that in other states. The main difference is that only 'permanent residents' are entitled to vote or to stand (see later). However, the upper house is constituted slightly differently from that of the Constitution of India design: eleven of the thirty-six members are elected from among Kashmir residents by the Legislative Assembly and eleven similarly from Jammu residents; there is no equivalent distribution provision for other states in the Constitution of India.

Turning to legislative powers, the State Autonomy Committee[74] said that ninety-four of the ninety-seven items in the Union legislative list now apply to Kashmir;[75] the provisions on the Central Bureau of Intelligence and Investigation (item 8) and preventive detention (item 9) still do not apply. Twenty-six of the forty-seven concurrent items now apply; omissions (therefore within Kashmir's exclusive jurisdiction) include marriage and divorce, infants and minors, transfer of property other than agricultural land, contracts[76] and torts, bankruptcy, trusts, courts, family planning, and charities.[77] States generally may

70 Constitution of Jammu and Kashmir, s.13. 71 Constitution of India Art. 168.

72 One of the many news items is 'Panchayat crisis could trigger Omar collapse', *Sunday Guardian*, 30 September 2012; www.sunday-guardian.com.

73 Constitution of Jammu and Kashmir, Art. 48.

74 *Report*, 86. 75 The revised item 97 is omitted.

76 The Law Commission in its 147th Report (1993) on the *Specific Relief Act*, 3, proposed that it be extended to Kashmir, following the necessary Order under Article 370. The Commission also proposed that the law on topics such as contract generally and partnership should be uniform in the country.

77 See Appendix II, 'A restatement of the exceptions and modifications', as published in P. M. Bakshi, *The Constitution of India* (New Delhi: Universal Book Publishing Co., 11th edn., 2011).

legislate on some aspects of elections to state bodies, but only to the extent that there is no central legislation (Article 328); this does not apply to Kashmir, which presumably has full powers to legislate on this.[78]

Residual legislative power still rests, in the case of Kashmir alone, with the state. It is not easy to assess the full implications of this as new issues may appear years after a legislative list is drafted. Certain other residual items are specially included in the Union list for Kashmir only, especially prevention of activities involving terrorist acts or which are 'directed towards disclaiming, questioning or disrupting the sovereignty and territorial integrity of India or bringing about cession of a part of the territory of India' or 'causing insult to the Indian National Flag, the Indian National Anthem and this Constitution'.[79]

Since 1975 the state has been unable without the assent of 'the President' to change the Kashmir Constitution to affect the appointment, powers and functions, emoluments or immunities of the Governor or alter the provisions about elections to the Legislative Assembly being regulated by the Election Commission of India, also matters related to non-discrimination in the electoral rolls and eligibility to vote. The State Autonomy Committee asserted: 'This uncalled for clog on the constituent powers of State Legislature needs to be removed lock, stock and barrel'.[80]

Constraints on legislative power

In all states, including Kashmir, Governors may send a bill passed by the state legislature to the President, usually in the discretion of the Governor.[81] They *must* reserve a bill derogating from the powers of the High Court (which is given a particular role by the Constitution in ensuring the legality of public actions, and in supervising lower courts).[82] And, if a state plans (because it considers it in the public interest) to introduce reasonable restrictions on trade, approval of the centre is required before a Bill is even introduced into the state legislature.[83]

The 1952 Delhi Agreement said, 'In view of the peculiar position in which the State was placed, in particular Sheikh Abdullah's land reforms programme, the Fundamental Rights enshrined in the Constitution [of India] could not be made applicable to the State'.[84] However, in 1954 the human rights provisions

I have drawn on A. G. Anand, *The Constitution of Jammu and Kashmir* (Delhi: Universal Law Publishers, 3rd edn., 1998), 140, and 436–51.

78 Jammu and Kashmir Representation of the People Act, 1957, website of the State Election Commissioner at http://ceojk.nic.in/emanuals_rpa1957.pdf.

79 List I item 97 as applied to Kashmir.

80 *Report*.

81 See central government circular from 1972 on the procedure to be followed addressed to all states (except Kashmir): available at: http://himachal.nic.in/law/annex-a.htm. On discretion see M. P. Singh, *V N Shukla's Constitution of India* (Lucknow: Eastern Book Co., 9th edn., 1994), 524.

82 Art. 200, second proviso.

83 Art. 304(b) proviso.

84 Available on the South Asian Terrorism Portal website at www.satp.org/. Others have different explanations: 'The parties shared the concern that fundamental rights might have the effect of impeding the government's ability to deal "swiftly and effectively" with "people infiltrating for espionage, sabotage, or to create trouble otherwise", and that robust fundamental rights may

were made applicable to Kashmir, though with a few differences. The right to property provision[85] caused enormous problems for the Government of India and its own land reforms. Eventually the right was taken out of the fundamental rights provisions (see Article 300-A); constitutional protection was given in Schedule 9 (1951) to a list of central and state laws (including some Kashmir laws), many of which relate to land reform. Article 300-A still does not apply in Kashmir where earlier, amended, versions of Article 31 still apply.[86] Articles 31A and 31C protect certain legislation against challenge under Article 14 (equality before the law) or Article 19 (freedom of movement). The former applies to Kashmir in modified form.[87] Article 31C, protecting legislation intended to implement one or more of the Directive Principles, *if* the law was reserved for the assent of the President, does not apply to Kashmir.

For twenty-five years (progressively extended) certain basic human rights provisions were modified in their application to Kashmir. '[R]easonable restrictions' on freedom of assembly or association which were generally permissible only 'in the interests of the sovereignty and integrity of India or public order' (or morality in the case of freedom of association) became, in the case of Kashmir, what the *legislature* thought reasonable, and 'the security of the State' was added.[88] Additionally, preventive detention laws made by the state were protected against human rights challenges for twenty-five years.[89]

Taxation and revenue

Kashmir's fiscal situation is somewhat different from that of other states. It is a 'special category state' given special treatment because of its difficulty in raising revenue, not as a reflection of its autonomy.[90] Such states are guaranteed a larger share of Union taxes; the ratio of grant to loan is different for them, while the Planning Commission earmarks for them 30 per cent of the money it distributes.[91] Kashmir has also benefitted from other special rules, again not due to Article 370, particularly relating to encouragement of investment, such as

cause the situation to "deteriorate and go out of hand"', Sehla Ashai 'The Jammu and Kashmir state subjects controversy of 2004' *Drexel Law Review* 2(2010), 542, citing Ghulam Shah, *State Subjectship in Jammu and Kashmir* (Srinagar: Jupitor Publishers, 1988), 24.

85 Constitution of India, Art. 31.

86 Applied by the Supreme Court in *Bhuri Nath & ors; The Sewa Committee Baridaran & ors. v. State of Jammu & Kashmir* 1997 AIR 1711, 1997 (1) SCR 138.

87 Among the laws protected are those relating to compulsory acquisition of land. As applied to Kashmir, it covers broadly agricultural or pastoral land only; in the rest of the country it covers any land. For a case applying it see *Prem Nath Raina v. Jammu and Kashmir* (Supreme Court) 1983 AIR 920, 1983 SCR (3) 536, 1983 SCC (4) 616.

88 Art. 19 Constitution of India as applied to Kashmir.

89 Art. 35 (c). Applied in *Lakhanpal v. State of J&K* 1956 AIR 197.

90 Thus the Supreme Court gave Kashmir a grace period when holding that it was wrong to tax imported vegetable oil more than locally produced oil, because of its being economically and industrially undeveloped, and disturbed: *Shree Mahavir Oil Mills v. State of J&K* (1996) 11 SCC 39.

91 For a slightly outdated account of the system of fiscal transfers see D. K. Srivastava, 'India' in Yun-Hwan Kim and Paul Smoke (eds.), *Intergovernmental Fiscal Transfers in Asia: Current*

exemption from certain taxation,[92] allocation of certain grants and the creation of the Jammu and Kashmir Development Finance Corporation by the Union government.[93] Like the North-Eastern States, it received 100 per cent central contribution to the 'Modernisation of State Police Forces' programme of the Union Home Ministry, as opposed to the 75 per cent received by other states.[94]

The main tax raising difference is that only Kashmir can raise service taxes, which were originally a residual legislative item. The Eighty-eighth constitutional amendment (2004) added them explicitly to the Union list, but does not apply to Kashmir. A few other taxes – on foreign and inland air or sea travel, on inland air travel and on postal articles – were transferred to the Union residual list, as applied to Kashmir.[95]

Following the 2000 Eightieth Amendment to the Constitution of India, almost all centrally raised taxes are distributed between the centre and states. Union sales tax is collected by the Union but assigned to the states,[96] but not Kashmir, while some Union stamp duties are actually raised and retained by the states.

Many of the states, including Kashmir, have recently introduced Value Added Tax, and Kashmir has been involved in the major co-ordination effort in recent years to develop a uniform and integrated government sales tax (GST).[97] In March 2011 the Union government introduced a constitution amendment bill to provide for GST, to be levied by the centre and the states, while a GST Council would advise both levels.[98] Many states are wary,[99] but reports suggest that the Kashmir government has no objections.[100]

Apart from constitutional allocations, revenue raised centrally reaches the states in several ways. The expert Finance Commission, which is not a representative body, being appointed afresh every five years by the Union government, makes proposals – which are always accepted – for the devolution of

Practice and Challenges for the Future (Manila: Asian Development Bank, 2003), available at www.adb.org/Documents/Books/Intergovernmental_Fiscal_Transfers/.

92 See Report of the Task Force on Goods and Services Tax, 13th Finance Commission (2009) at http://fincomindia.nic.in/, on Central VAT and see 'Jammu & Kashmir Industrial Policy – 2002–2015' http://jammu.gov.in/.

93 Ibid.

94 Ministry of Home Affairs, Annual Report 2008–9, Ch. 11 at www.satp.org/satporgtp/countries/india/document/papers/annualreport_2008-09.htm (accessed 27 March 2013).

95 As with the security items discussed in the previous section.

96 Constitution of India, revised Art. 269.

97 See 'A White Paper On State-Level Value Added Tax' on the Press Information Bureau website: http://pib.nic.in/, and Report of the Task Force on Goods and Services Tax, 13th FC (2009) at http://fincomindia.nic.in/.

98 At the time of writing the text of the Bill was available at www.prsindia.org/. For a discussion see Anil Agrawal, 'India's Goods and Services Tax – A Primer' www.stcipd.com/research.aspx.

99 Mukul Gupta, 'Discussion on 'The 115th Constitutional Amendment Bill 2011', http://ntnonline.net/Uttar_Pradesh/Articles/GST_Article_MukulGupta.pdf (accessed 27 March 2013).

100 'JK has no serious objection to Goods and Services Tax' at www.greaterkashmir.com/, 18 April 2011.

revenue to the states and its distribution between states on the basis of formulae that it devises.[101] Then there are grants-in-aid under Finance Commission recommendations; grants to achieve national plans, decided by the Planning Commission or national ministries and smaller discretionary grants given by the central ministries not for 'plan' purposes.[102] Under the Thirteenth Finance Commission recommendations, Kashmir would receive the highest grant of all special category states to compensate for anticipated 'non-plan' revenue deficits over 2010–15.[103] Over the years Finance Commission allocations to individual states of devolved funds plus grants have remained fairly steady, with the mean share given to Kashmir at 2.66 per cent since the mid 1950s.[104]

The Head of the Kashmir State

Under the 1952 Delhi agreement the Sardar-i-Riyasat was appointed by the state legislature, then had to be recognised by the President. But, following a further agreement between the state and the centre, the name and system of appointment was changed to 'Governor', appointed to the post as in other states. This change has rankled with Kashmir, but the 1975 Indira Gandhi/Abdullah agreement left it unresolved: '6. No agreement was possible on the question of nomenclature of the Governor and the Chief Minister'.[105]

Currently, the Governor is like that in any other state and is required to act only on the advice of the state Council of Ministers,[106] but with explicit exceptions for appointment of Chief Minister, Ministers, Deputies and assumption of Governor's rule (see later). This provision is more clearly expressed, with fewer grey areas, than Article 163(1) Constitution of India on other Governors.

Appointment and dismissal of government

Neither the Constitution of India[107] nor the Constitution of Jammu and Kashmir[108] indicates who should be invited by the Governor to become Chief Minister. To appoint anyone other than the leader of the majority party would precipitate a crisis, but if there is no clear candidate, because of the existence of various coalitions for example, the Governor has a discretion.

It is now generally accepted that the Governor should be guided by the conventions of the parliamentary system, and should not dismiss the Chief

[101] See 13th FC Report para. 8.1. [102] 12th FC report Para. 10.2.

[103] See http://fincomindia.nic.in 13th Report, Table 12.4. Specific grants in aid to Kashmir recommended by the 13th FC included 'a revenue gap grant' of Rs. 2300 crore [UD$469mn] to liquidate its overdraft and another grant of $204mn, tied to a mechanism for operationalisation of a proposed fiscal reform path, and grants for a modern government secretariat complex in Jammu and others mostly related to water, heritage and tourism as well as for a number of improvements in Ladakh (see Report, Ch. 12).

[104] 13th FC Report Table 3.1. [105] Originally the state head of government was 'Prime Minister'.

[106] Constitution of Jammu and Kashmir s.35(2). [107] Art. 164. [108] S.36.

Minister so long as the latter has the support of the Legislative Assembly. In the case of *Bommai v. Union of India*,[109] the Supreme Court emphasised that the place to test support for the Government was in the Legislative Assembly itself, the 'floor test'.

In the case of Kashmir it seems that the Governor has no power simply to dismiss the Chief Minister, other than by invoking Governor's Rule.[110] However, in 1984 the Governor did dismiss the Chief Minister. Dr Farooq Abdullah had been sworn in within minutes of the death of his father, Sheikh Abdullah, at the request of various senior ministers – whom Dr Abdullah did not re-appoint. Before long, the National Conference split, and eventually a sufficient number of its members joined with other parties to form a majority. Dr Abdullah asked the Governor, Jag Mohan Malhotra (generally called 'Jagmohan'), to declare Governor's Rule, and then to call for a confidence vote or dissolve the assembly. Instead the Governor dismissed Abdullah.[111] Akbar alleges that Jagmohan had been appointed precisely because Delhi planned to topple Abdullah junior.[112] Today, what happened in Srinagar in 1984 would fall foul of the 'floor test' requirement.

Kashmir and national institutions

The national government

Kashmir now sends six MPs to the 550 strong House of the People (Lok Sabha), and four members to the Council of States (Rajya Sabha) where, unlike in some federations, representation of states is not equal but on the basis of population.[113] The role of Parliament in relation to Kashmir, as opposed to other states, is different only to the extent that it has less power to legislate for it on certain topics.

There are no power-sharing arrangements for the executive; the choice of Ministers by the ruling party or coalition is dictated by considerations of party alliances and national inclusion. Normally the National Conference has been allied with the Congress Party; in 2012 one Cabinet Minister (Farooq Abdullah) of thirty-three was from that party (another from Kashmir is a Congress member). Again, the powers of the national executive vis-à-vis Kashmir differ little from its general powers, though slightly reduced because of Kashmir's autonomy, and sometimes enhanced because of special emergency and security powers.

109 AIR 1994 SC 1918. 110 Constitution of Jammu and Kashmir, s.35(2).

111 Dev Batrohi, 'July '84 events in Kashmir: constitutional and political aspects' in Grover, *The Story of Kashmir*, Vol. 2, 519, defending Jagmohan, who defends himself in *My Frozen Turbulence*, 255.

112 Akbar, *Kashmir*, 204ff.

113 The Punchhi Commission recommended equal representation for states; see *Constitutional Governance and the Management of Centre-State Relations*, Vol. II para. 7.3.16.

National institutions with a role within Kashmir

In 1950 many important national government institutions had no presence in Kashmir, including the Auditor General, the Central Bureau of Investigation, the Election Commission, the civil service (Indian Administrative Service) and the High Court. The power of the Supreme Court was limited in comparison with its role in other states. Gradually this has radically changed.

State as well as national audit is carried out by the national Comptroller and Auditor General,[114] whose reports are submitted to the Governor, who lays them before the State Legislature.[115]

Item 8 of the Union legislative list, on the Central Bureau of Intelligence and Investigation, still does not apply to Kashmir. A commentator complained that, 'Sheikh Abdullah and his accomplices were let loose to collude with Pakistani conspirators and infiltrators. The reports of his collusions and conspiracies with Pakistani agents and spies could not reach the ears of the ruling leaders of Hindusthan'.[116] However, it is not clear how much practical difference this makes. The Bureau 'can only investigate a case if specifically requested by the state government concerned or directed by the High Court or the Supreme Court, except if it is a matter that pertains to the central government'.[117] And the Bureau does carry out investigations in Kashmir – including, at the request of the High Court, into the deaths of two young women in 2009, widely believed to have been caused by state police. The outcome seems to have been disastrous: public opinion, and some organisations that carried out their own investigations, rejected the Central Bureau of Investigation findings, resulting in riots in the streets.[118]

Elections for state legislatures are run by the national Election Commission,[119] though it may have regional members for this purpose. The Chief Electoral Officer for each state is appointed and supervised by the national Commission, though proposed by the state government. The statutory national Delimitation Commission[120] fixes the boundaries for Parliamentary and Legislative Assembly elections. For boundaries within a state, the Commission includes the State Election Commissioner and is assisted by some or all of that state's Members of the Lok Sabha and five members of the State Legislative Assembly. Kashmir's separate state legislation provides for the commission to be similar in composition to that for other states.

[114] Constitution of India, Art. 149, extended to Kashmir in 1958. [115] Ibid., Art. 151.

[116] Kanayalal M. Taireja, 'Horrendous consequences of Article 370 in India's Constitution'; see www.partitionofindia.com/_disk1/000005d6.htm.

[117] Manish Tewari, 'Legally empowering the sentinels of the nation', Observer Research Foundation Issue Brief No. 20, August 2009, 2, available at www.observerindia.com/.

[118] See for example, 'Kashmir: Manufacturing a suitable story', *Mainstream*, XLVIII:1, 26 December, 2009 – Annual Number 2009.

[119] Constitution of India, Art. 324, and Constitution of Jammu and Kashmir, s.138.

[120] Now Delimitation Act 2002 available on the Commission's website at www.delimitation-india.com/Acts/act_2002.pdf (accessed 27 March 2013).

A state has a public service commission, unless it decides to ask the Union Commission to carry out this function for the state.[121] Various employees of the national government will also be posted in the state, as part of the various all India services, which include the Indian Administrative Service, the Indian Police Service and the Forestry Service.[122] Among the senior posts in Kashmir currently the Chief Secretary is from Delhi, as is the Chief Elections Officer, for example.[123] Regulations about terms of service are made by the central government 'after consultation with the governments of the states concerned [including the State of Jammu and Kashmir]'.[124] Indian Administrative Service officers in the service of a state are subject to the disciplinary procedures of that state, with an appeal to the central government (and the penalty of dismissal, removal or compulsory retirement is only to be imposed by the centre).[125] The public service examinations in Kashmir include competence in Urdu, oral Kashmiri and Dogri (only required of civil service officers who are not permanent residents of the state).[126]

State control over central bodies

The Kashmir Information Commission, administering the State Right to Information Act, recently, and controversially, insisted that central government organs in the state were bound to comply with the state Act (other states have only the central Act).[127] At the same time, the generally rather ineffective State Human Rights Commission investigated allegations that the Border Security Force (a central government body) had abducted a civilian and recommended that the government order the police take action against the Force.[128]

Courts

There is neither formal provision, nor convention, for the Supreme Court to reflect the national make-up. Appointment is virtually always by promotion from the High Courts, which are also national institutions, though sitting in the states. Of the twenty-eight members of the Supreme Court in 2011, one

121 Constitution of India, Art. 315. 122 Ibid., Art. 312.

123 See http://jkgad.nic.in/ias/IAS-Officers.pdf (accessed 27 March 2013). The same list shows that the Secretaries Ministry of Tourism, and Department of Social Justice and Empowerment, Government of India, (same salary scale as State Chief Secretary) are from Kashmir.

124 The All India Services Act, 1951; the reference to Kashmir was added in 1975.

125 The All India Services (Discipline and Appeal) Rules, 1969 available http://persmin.nic.in/.

126 The Jammu and Kashmir Public Departmental Examination (IAS, KAS and Other Officers) Rules, 1968, www.jkpsc.org/Departmental.asp?PageID=10 (accessed 27 March 2013).

127 Faheem Asla, 'J & K RTI Act applicable to central offices: State Information Commission missive triggers Debate', www.greaterkashmir.com/ (28 April 2011).

128 Arif Shafi Wani, 'SHRC indicts BSF for civilian's custodial disappearance: asks govt to initiate legal action against accused', www.greaterkashmir.com/ (28 April 2011).

had been acting Chief Justice of the High Court of Jammu and Kashmir, and another the Chief Justice, neither originally from Kashmir.[129]

There remain some differences between the jurisdiction of the Supreme Court in relation to Kashmir and to the rest of the country. Though the national Parliament may extend its jurisdiction over criminal appeals from the High Courts and its writ jurisdiction beyond that under Article 32 (which confers this jurisdiction only in human rights cases), in the case of Kashmir, the former requires the approval of the state,[130] while the latter possibility does not apply at all.[131] The Supreme Court may not take over a case from the High Court of Kashmir, on the basis that the same issue is arising in a case before the Supreme Court itself or another High Court.[132] On the other hand, the Supreme Court has transferred a criminal case from trial in Kashmir to another state because the court in Kashmir could not guarantee a fair trial.[133]

The Kashmir High Court, a creature of the Kashmir Constitution, is very like other High Courts, with which it shares, to some extent, its judges. Of its nine judges, all but two currently appear to have been born or have graduated or practised in the state, though the Chief Justice is from Delhi.[134] Judges may be transferred to or from the Kashmir Court only after consultation with the 'Governor' (meaning the state government), whereas no such consultation is required for transfers to or from other High Courts. Judges of state High Courts are removable by parliamentary impeachment, a provision extended to Kashmir in 1959. The Kashmir High Court acquired writ jurisdiction for the purpose of enforcement of human rights in 1954, and for other purposes in 1957,[135] and under Article 226 of the Indian Constitution in 1971.

Lower courts and judges are a matter for the states. For many years there has been discussion of establishing an 'All India Judicial Service'. The Law Commission recommended it, though observing that Jammu and Kashmir had opposed it (on the grounds that they had provision in their separate Constitution, that Kashmir had a separate language and because of local conditions).[136]

There are no special arrangements for disputes over the autonomy of Kashmir. The Supreme Court (always sitting in Delhi) has exclusive jurisdiction over disputes between states or between a state and the Union,[137] but this has never been invoked over Kashmir. Disputes over the powers of different governments may be decided for Kashmir, as for other states, in 'ordinary' cases, in both High

[129] See http://supremecourtofindia.nic.in/judges/judges.htm (accessed 27 March 2013).

[130] Constitution of India, Art. 134, as applied to Kashmir.

[131] Ibid., Art. 139. [132] Ibid., Art. 139(A).

[133] R. Venkataraman and G. Ananthakrishnan, *Indian Express*, 16 December 2012: www.indianexpress.com/news/sc-moves-j&k-sex-case-to-chandigarh-slams-the-bar/12031/ (accessed 27 March 2013).

[134] http://jkhighcourt.nic.in/judges.html (accessed 27 March 2013).

[135] Constitution of Jammu and Kashmir s.103. See Anand, *The Constitution of Jammu and Kashmir*, 147.

[136] 116th Report on *Formation of an All India Judicial Service*, 1986.

[137] Constitution of India, Art. 131.

Court and Supreme Court. For example, in 2006 the Supreme Court held that the central Wealth Tax Act applied in Kashmir.[138]

The *Sampat Prakash* case, discussed earlier, was very important for centre-state relations. The Supreme Court has decided other significant cases for the working of Article 370. It rejected a challenge to a detention order[139] because it was signed by the 'Governor' not the 'Sardar-i-Riyasat',[140] including in its reasoning that the 'Explanation' in Article 370 (see earlier) placed no obstacle in the way of amendment to the Kashmir Constitution.[141] The role of the Court, sometimes upholding acts of the state,[142] sometimes declaring them invalid, sometimes dealing with politically sensitive issues,[143] is similar to that relative to other states. It does not seem that the Supreme Court is a source of significant 'interference' with the state High Court, which on average is affirmed in 73 per cent of appeals.[144] But the High Court itself may decide, on the basis of the Constitution of India, that the state has exceeded its powers; it does not noticeably favour the state government.[145]

Human Rights

A later section demonstrates how autonomy makes it possible for Kashmir to have rather lower standards of human rights protection, by virtue of the non-application of Union statutes, though many Union Acts have their state counterparts.

Balraj Puri commented on the weakness of local human rights protection:

> The people of Kashmir [. . .] would not like, for instance, to be deprived of the fundamental rights guaranteed in the Constitution of India and the safeguards

138 Item 86 of the exclusive Union legislative list, 'Taxes on the capital value of the assets, exclusive of agricultural land, of individuals and companies; taxes on the capital of companies'; see *CWT v. Dr Karan Singh & CWT v. P.C. Oswal* (1993) 200 ITR 614 (www.indiankanoon.com/doc/1230468/), reversing the state High Court.

139 There are many such as, for example *Lakhanpal v. J & K* 1956 AIR 197 1955 SCR (2)1101: the validity of the Jammu and Kashmir Preventive Detention Act was upheld by reason of the additional provision to Art. 35 of the Constitution of India (specific to J&K) protecting detention laws.

140 On the significance of which see previously.

141 *Maqbool Damnoo v. State of Jammu and Kashmir* 1972 AIR 963, 1972 SCR (2)1014, 1972 SCC (1) 536.

142 In *Rehman Shagoo and Others v. State of Jammu and Kashmir* 1960 AIR, 1 1960 SCR (1) 680 the Supreme Court held that the Enemy Agents Ordinance passed by the Ruler in January 1948 was not about defence (and therefore a matter for the centre under the Instrument of Accession) but essentially about criminal law.

143 For example, *State of Jammu and Kashmir v. Bakshi Ghulam Mohammad* 1967 AIR 122, 1966 SCR (4) 1 dealt with whether alleged conduct of a former Prime Minister of the State was of sufficient public importance to warrant setting up a Commission of Inquiry; it held it was – reversing the State High Court.

144 Nick Robinson et al., 'Interpreting the Constitution: Supreme Court constitution benches since Independence', *Economic & Political Weekly*, 46: 9, 26 February 2011, 27.

145 For example, several cases on detention orders in 2010, including *Nazir Ahmad v. State*, HCP No. 28 of 2009 and *Abdul Rashid v. State*, HCP No. 42 of 2009.

> that autonomous federal institutions like the Supreme Court, Election Commission and Auditor and Comptroller General provide against interference by the Centre. Even today the State has more autonomy than other States of India. But it has been used in a manner that its people have less rights than those in other States.[146]

And the NGO Asian Human Rights Commission wrote:

> The Annual Report 2004–2005 [of the State Human Rights Commission] revealed that in the absence of an independent investigating agency, the SHRC had to be dependent on the State Police to conduct investigations even if the cases were against the police personnel. The [Report] stated that the SHRC was financially 'left totally dependent and at the mercy of the government' which endangered the independence of the Commission.[147]

In these circumstances the possibility of an appeal to a strong court like the Supreme Court of India is a potential protection against abuse not only of state law or by state institutions, but of national law by national institutions, as, for example, where it reversed the state High Court's refusal to uphold the rights of a teacher with a disability.[148]

The National Human Rights Commission has jurisdiction in relation to Kashmir but only in relation to Union or concurrent legislative list matters.[149] Recently it refused to accept that it had no power to investigate and issue orders to the Kashmir government, saying,

> It is a clear case where the police tortured a person and killed him. Therefore, it does not come under any of the powers of legislation of the State Legislature in respect of any of the entries mentioned in List II of the State List.[150]

In other words, the Article 370 shield did not protect the state government. The Asian Human Rights Commission implies this shows a new determination by the NHRC.

However, the contribution of the Supreme Court and the Commission seems to be limited. An example of weak state protection of rights is the State Public Safety Act, more severe in some ways than the Union Public Security Act. It provides for detention without trial, and is liberally used; the ratio of detainees to regular prisoners has been at a minimum 11.4 per cent of the prison

[146] 'Azadi, Autonomy and Self-Rule vs Freedom' *Mainstream*, 47:52, 12 December 2009, available at www.mainstreamweekly.net/article1835.html (accessed 27 March 2013).

[147] 'J & K SHRC: In shambles' in India Human Rights Report Oct-Dec. 2010 at www.achrweb.org/ihrrq/issue2/J&K_SHRC.html (accessed 27 March 2013). See also the summary of the Annual Report of the SFRC for 2009–10 'SHRC censures Babus for "undue interference"' at www.greaterkashmir.com/; also in *India Human Rights Quarterly* (previously), 6ff.

[148] *Syed Bashir-ud-din Qadri v. Nazir Ahmed Shah & Ors.* Civil Appeal Nos. 2281–2 of 2010, decided 10 Dec. 2010.

[149] The Protection of Human Rights Act, 1993 s.1. The same is true for Union commissions of inquiry: Commissions of Inquiry Act, 1952, s.1(2).

[150] See www.achrweb.org/ihrrq/issue2/order_extraordinaire.html and 'NHRC disagrees with J&K Government's contention over its jurisdiction in the State (Case No.55/9/2003–2004-AD)', www.nhrc.nic.in/disparchive.asp?fno=2263 (both accessed 27 March 2013).

population of the state, fourteen times the rate nationally.[151] Amnesty International comments that the Supreme Court has had little impact on the abuse of this legislation, hypothesising that 'Possible reasons may include reluctance of J&K lawyers and residents to file petitions in the Supreme Court or reluctance of the Supreme Court to admit such petitions from J&K'.[152] The National Human Rights Commission had been largely silent on the issue.

The potential of the Constitution of India for protecting human rights within Kashmir is perhaps hamstrung by the political context. Ashai comments, in connection with the permanent resident issue outlined next,

> The application of such rights to shape state subjects law was not perceived as a constitutional protection for a marginalized group (women), but rather as a tactic for perpetuating central government domination and the further disenfranchisement of Kashmiris, because the source of these fundamental rights (the Indian Constitution) is viewed as suspect. The Indian Constitution is largely understood by many Kashmiris to be a legal instrument of oppression, its protective guarantees failing when they were most needed. The distrust for protection under Indian law is so profound that the same PDP leaders who opposed the practice of disqualifying permanent resident women reversed their position entirely when they introduced the Disqualification Bill, simply because the authority being used to oppose disqualification had its genesis in the fundamental rights of the Indian Constitution.[153]

Other adjudicating institutions

The Tribunal on inter-state river water disputes was set up under Article 262.[154] The recent Centre-State Relations Commission said of the Ravi Beas dispute between Kashmir and Punjab, before that tribunal:

> The matter was referred to the Tribunal in 1986. A report was given in January 1987. Political differences led to further references being made to the Tribunal and the matter is still before it. Meanwhile Punjab has through legislative enactment terminated all agreements. The legality of this action is the subject matter of a Presidential reference to the Supreme Court made in 2005 under Article 143. The matter is still awaiting the Court's opinion.[155]

The case reflects, as the Commission comments, various problems with the process and the legal system, and it proposed various improvements.[156] Other proposals included strengthening of the Inter-State Council (see later), which,

151 Amnesty International, A 'Lawless Law': Detentions under the Jammu and Kashmir Public Safety Act (London: AI, 2011), 12.

152 Ibid., 65. 153 Ashai, 'State Subjects Controversy', 552.

154 Inter-State Water Disputes Act 1956, applied to Kashmir.

155 Report, *Environment, Natural Resources and Infrastructure*, Vol. 6, para. 2.7.05.01.

156 Ibid., para. 2.17.3(a).

can play a decisive role in infrastructure development. It can be the forum to resolve contentious issues affecting all States like clearances by Central Authorities, land acquisition, rehabilitation and can also act at the national level as a clearing house for good practices.[157]

Institutions of co-operation

The Punchhi Commission, observing that the Constitution provided for 'only limited institutional arrangements' for co-ordination, which were 'inadequately utilized', saw the necessity for more 'consensus building bodies involving the Centre and the States', due to a widespread perception of that states were losing their autonomy in areas assigned to them.[158]

Article 263 provides for an Inter-State Council, with functions to inquire into and advise upon any dispute between states, to investigate and discuss subjects in which all or some states, or the Union and states, have a common interest, and to make recommendations on 'any subject', particularly for better co-ordination. The Council was set up in 1990, and comprises the Prime Minister, the Chief Minister of every state (and Union territory) and six Union Ministers. It meets at least three times a year, in camera, and all decisions are taken by consensus.[159]

Various other bodies have been set up under the same Article,[160] or by executive order.[161] Chief Ministers' conferences are held regularly on specific topics.[162] State Ministers with similar responsibilities also meet periodically. The non-statutory National Development Council also unites the Chief Ministers; it works closely with the Planning Commission and is the voice of the states in the planning process.

Zonal Councils (for which there is no provision in the Constitution), intended 'to develop the habit of cooperative working', to quote Nehru whose idea they were,[163] were established under the States Re-organisation Act, 1956; each Council is chaired by the Union Home Minister and comprises the Chief Minister of each state plus two other ministers. The Northern Zonal Council

157 Ibid., para. 5.10.02. Other mechanisms include a possible authority for the trade and commerce provisions (see Art. 307), while the anticipated amendment to the Constitution of India will include a dispute resolution body on the GST. No Art. 307 authority has been constituted.

158 *Constitutional Governance and the Management of Centre-State Relations*, Vol. 2, paras. 11.13.02. and 6.8.03.

159 It laid down its own guidelines for identifying appropriate topics – see http://interstatecouncil.nic.in/.

160 For example, the Central Council of Health, Central Council of Local Self Government, Council for Sales Tax and State Excise Duties – for each of Northern, Eastern, Western and Southern Zones, Transport Development Council.

161 For example, National Development Council, National Water Resources Council, Indian Labour Conference, Advisory Council on Foodgrains Management and Public Distribution System, Mineral Advisory Council, Central Advisory Board of Education.

162 Affordable housing in 2006, Pension reform in 2007, and so on.

163 See Ministry of Home Affairs website at www.mha.nic.in/uniquepage.asp?ID_PK=470 (accessed 27 March 2013).

comprises Kashmir, Haryana, Himachal Pradesh, Punjab, Rajasthan, National Capital Territory of Delhi and Union Territory of Chandigarh. It met in 2005 after a break of about six years, with water resources prominent on the agenda,[164] and in 2008. One source observes, 'Some of the items have been on the agenda for over two decades without any movement in the direction of meaningful resolution'.[165]

The reversal of the application of Articles 262 and 263 was one of the demands of the State Autonomy Committee in 2000.

Exceptional procedures

President's Rule

President's Rule can be declared if the 'Government of the State cannot be carried on in accordance with the Constitution',[166] and the Governor may advise at his or her discretion that this be done, or the centre may decide to act on its own initiative.[167] If not approved by Parliament, the proclamation automatically expires after two months; if it is approved it lasts for a maximum of six months and can be renewed for six months at a time up to one year, or for up to three years if an Article 352 state of emergency is in force, or there are problems about holding an election in the state. The constitutional provisions on this 'giant instrument of constitutional control of one tier of the constitutional structure over the other',[168] were not applicable to Kashmir until 1965.

Formally the President takes over any or all of the functions of government in the state and of the state Governor. If the Assembly is suspended or dissolved, which is not inevitable, the state legislative powers are exercised by Parliament, which can confer those powers on 'the President' (who can in turn delegate them to any other authority).[169] The President will make law for that state, if needed, in consultation with members of the national Parliament from the state. In 1992 the union Parliament passed the J&K State Legislature (Delegation of Powers) Act, delegating the legislative powers of the state to the President.[170] A member of the Lok Sabha observed,

[164] See 'Water sharing divides northern zonal council', *Tribune*, 26 October 2005 www.tribuneindia.com/2005/20051026/himachal.htm#2 (accessed 27 March 2013).

[165] D. K. Sharma, 'Cooperation among the North Indian States: lessons so far and road ahead', 25 January 2009, on My Himachal website http://himachal.us/2009/01/25/cooperation-among-the-north-indian-states-lessons-so-far-and-road-ahead/10051/activism/dksharma (accessed 27 March 2013).

[166] Art. 356.

[167] According to Art. 365, if a state has not complied with a direction from the centre under the Constitution, the President may decide that this indicates that the Art. 356 situation has arisen; but this does not apply to Jammu and Kashmir.

[168] Commission to Review the Working of the Constitution, para. 8.16.

[169] Art. 357.

[170] Under Constitution of India, Art. 357(1)(a).

> [T]he signal that we are sending is, having taken over the Executive power, exercising it through the Governor, whom we have appointed, about whose appointment the Kashmiris have nothing to say, on whose conduct the Kashmiris have no control whatsoever, who is like an emperor, who is like a Viceroy, then you are taking away the legislative power, also in the hands of the Executive.[171]

The Supreme Court drew on the Sakaria Commission's recommendations in laying down, in the *Bommai* case,[172] important principles, among which are that interference by a state government with any of the elements of the 'basic structure' of the Constitution would be grounds for action under Article 356. Secularism is one such basic element. Since the *Bommai* case, Article 356 has been used much more rarely, and the President has at least twice returned requests to impose President's Rule to the Cabinet.

If states with a 'normal' relationship with the centre resent the use of President's Rule, its use in Kashmir has been especially intrusive, having been imposed there several times, including for seven years in the 1990s, when the Constitution of India was progressively amended to validate such intervention.[173] Calls from the Hindu right wing for its imposition in Kashmir are quite frequent, including in 2006 when twenty-two Hindus were killed by militants.[174]

Governor's Rule

Under a provision unique to Kashmir, the Governor may assume 'all or any of the functions of the Government of the State and all or any of the powers vested in or exercisable by any body or authority in this State', other than the High Court, for up to six months.[175] The preconditions are that the Governor must be satisfied that the 'Government of the State cannot be carried on in accordance with the provisions of this Constitution' and the President concurs.[176] No advice of the state government need be received before Governor's Rule is introduced.[177]

Governor's Rule was declared in 1977, 1986 and 1990, and also in 2002 when the outgoing Chief Minister refused to stay on in a caretaker capacity. Before elections in 2002 a journalist was reported as saying, 'Delhi seems to have accepted that Governor's rule is indispensable to make the poll inclusive and

171 Sri Syed Shahabuddin in debate on Bill 14 July 1992. http://parliamentofindia.nic.in/lsdeb/ls10/ses4/2814079207.htm (accessed 27 March 2013).

172 See *Bommai v. Union of India* AIR 1994 SC 1918.

173 Art. 356(4) second proviso. A Wikipedia table at http://en.wikipedia.org/wiki/List_of_Prime_and_Chief_Ministers_of_Jammu_and_Kashmir (accessed 27 March 2013) shows PR as having been in force in Kashmir at the following times: March–July 1977, March–November 1986, January 1990–October 1996, fifteen days in October–November 2002 and July 2008–January 2009. In fact at least the early part of each of these Governor's Rule was in force – see later.

174 'BJP demands imposition of President's rule in J&K', *Outlook*, 2 May 2006, http://news.outlookindia.com/items.aspx?artid=381955 (accessed 27 March 2013).

175 Constitution of Jammu and Kashmir, s.92. 176 Ibid., s.92(5). 177 Ibid., s.35(2).

credible', and indeed, the incumbent party was defeated.[178] But in 2006 the Governor refused to take over in the wake of killings of Hindus in the state, insisting that the state government could cope. Following the collapse of the ruling coalition in 2008 it was imposed again when a spokesman for the Governor said he,

> initiated a consultative process and met leaders of various political parties and groups in the assembly with a view to arriving at a firm assessment whether any of the parties/groups were inclined and could join hands to form a stable government of the state,

but reached a negative conclusion.[179]

Article 249

The Rajya Sabha may, by a two-thirds majority, confer on the centre the power to make laws on a matter that would otherwise be for the states alone. This must be done 'in the national interest', with the resolution remaining in effect for one year at the most. The Article was made applicable to Kashmir in 1986, in irregular circumstances, as mentioned previously. As Noorani points out, this meant that 'The Union thus acquired the power to legislate not only on all matters in the State List, but others not mentioned in the Union List or the Concurrent List – the residuary power'.[180]

In fact, the limitations on its use, and the fact that it has never been used, make it less significant in practice than Noorani implies. However, the Rajya Sabha did pass a resolution in 1986 to authorise Parliament to legislate against infiltration from Pakistan, which 'was not pursued further'.[181] And Noorani is right that, 'In relation to other States, an amendment to the Constitution would require a two-thirds vote by both Houses of Parliament plus ratification by the States (Article 368)'.[182]

'Security'

Generally a state of emergency in any part of India may not be declared other than on the basis of 'war or external aggression or armed rebellion', but for Kashmir 'armed rebellion' is replaced by the weaker 'internal disturbance'.[183] However, a declaration may not be made on this ground without the request or concurrence of the state government. Article 355 requiring the Union to protect every State against external aggression and internal disturbance and

178 Sudha Ramachandram, 'Kashmir's vote of no confidence', *Asiatimes*, 8 August 2002, available at: www.atimes.com/atimes/South_Asia/DH08Df07.html (accessed 27 March 2013).

179 Mukhtar Ahmad, 'Governor's rule imposed in J&K', 10 July 2008, available at: www.rediff.com/news/2008/jul/10jk1.htm (accessed 27 March 2013).

180 Noorani, 'Article 370: Law and politics', n.p.

181 Singh, *V. N. Shukla's Constitution of India*, 670.

182 Noorani, 'Article 370: Law and politics', n.p.

183 Art. 352 as applied to Kashmir.

ensure that the state government carried on in accordance with the provisions of this Constitution does not apply to Kashmir.[184]

The constitutional relationship between the centre and Kashmir has been changed to deal with the security situation, as we have seen earlier when discussing the 'residual' legislative power.[185]

The state Armed Forces (Special Powers) Act (1990) was passed as an Ordinance (a sort of Presidential decree) and then by the Union Parliament because the state was under rule from the centre. It authorises declaration of any part of the state as a 'disturbed area' if 'the use of the armed forces in aid of the civil power' is necessary to prevent secessionist or terrorist acts. The Act empowers officers to

> fire upon or otherwise use force, even to the causing of death, against any person who is acting in contravention of any law or order for the time being in force in the disturbed area prohibiting the assembly of five or more persons or the carrying of weapons or of things capable as being used as weapons or of firearms, ammunition or explosive substances.[186]

The legislation, and its central counterpart, is the subject of constant controversy.[187] Recently the Union Home Minister has favoured reform and there is talk at least of areas affected by it being reduced. The military are less enthusiastic.[188] The Chief Minister, Omar Abdullah, has promised the repeal of these laws,[189] but in reality they cannot be repealed without the co-operation of the central government.

Union criminal and criminal procedure laws apply to the Union forces in Kashmir and s.45 of the Criminal Procedure Code says that no member of the armed forces may be arrested by civilian authorities for 'anything done or purported to be done by him in the discharge of his official duties except after obtaining the consent of the Central government', and s.197(2) protects them from prosecution; permission is said to be virtually never granted, at least in relation to acts in Kashmir.[190]

[184] So the Supreme Court reasoning in *Naga People's Movement of Human Rights v. Union of India* AIR 1998 SC 431 to the effect that Art. 355 justifies the Union Armed Forces (Special Powers) Act, although law and order is a matter for the states, could not be applied to Kashmir.

[185] List I item 97 as applied to Kashmir.

[186] In 1997 the Supreme Court laid down a series of conditions to be applied in declared disturbed areas. See Amnesty International, *India, Briefing on the Armed Forces (Special Powers) Act, 1958* (2005), Appendix 2, 29.

[187] See for example *Report of the Committee, headed by Justice (Retd) B.P. Jeevan Reddy, to Review the Armed Forces (Special Powers) Act 1958*, www.hinduonnet.com/nic/afa/, Amnesty International, Ibid.

[188] Nitin Gokhale, 'Areas in Kashmir under Armed Forces Special Powers Act could be reduced', 8 September 2010, www.ndtv.com/.

[189] See 'Omar promises revocation of draconian laws during his tenure', 22 July 2011. www.kashmirdispatch.com/,

[190] According to Human Rights Watch, *'Everyone Lives in Fear – Patterns of Impunity in Jammu and Kashmir* September 2006, 31. The Supreme Court has held that the refusal of the central government to give permission is subject to judicial review, *Naga People's Movement of Human Rights v. Union of India.*

Uses of autonomy

Kashmir's eroded, but still significant, autonomy has to some extent been used to protect specifically Kashmiri interests and achieve the programmes of land reform, but also appears to have weakened the human rights protection available to the state's residents (see previously).

Citizenship and residency

Under Kashmir law before the Constitution of India, special rights were given to 'state subjects'. Initially even the citizenship provisions of that Constitution did not apply to Kashmir. But the 1952 Delhi Agreement provided for Indian citizenship for those domiciled in Kashmir, while empowering the State legislature to confer special rights and privileges on state subjects. Article 35A, applicable only to Kashmir, was inserted, preserving the existing and any future law on 'state subjects' (renamed 'permanent residents'), under which non-permanent residents cannot register on the electoral roll, nor can lands be transferred to them. Public service appointments by direct recruitment are restricted to permanent residents.[191]

Previously, a Kashmiri woman's 'Permanent Resident Certificate' was valid only until marriage and would be renewed only if she married an 'in-state' man.[192] When the State High Court held that the legislation did not mean that a woman who was born a permanent resident lost that status on marriage,[193] the State government prepared the Permanent Residents (Disqualification) Bill, providing that regardless of any court order such a woman would lose her status on such a marriage. After it was passed in the lower house of the legislature, the upper house adjourned with no vote taken – amid allegations that the Chair had been bribed by Congress in Delhi.[194] The distinguished lawyer, Rajeev Dhavan, though believing the Bill to be unjust, commented, 'Kashmir cannot be opened up to enable anyone and everyone to claim property-based resident rights in the State. Such resident status should be defined fairly, justly and firmly'.[195]

The draft legislation resurfaced in 2010 to ignite similar controversy,[196] Balraj Puri commented that such bills have 'no sanction in the legal and constitutional

[191] Arvind P. Datar, 'J&K: legalised discrimination ', *The Hindu*, 26 March 2004, www.thehindu.com/.

[192] Ashai, 'State subjects controversy', discusses the background and outlines the events of 2004.

[193] *State of Jammu and Kashmir v. Dr Susheela Sawhney* AIR 2003 J&K 83. The decision of the court did not depend on constitutional guarantees of equality, but on the plain wording of the law.

[194] '"Secret Deal" kills bill', *Asian Age*, 11 March 2004.

[195] 'The J & K Bill 2004', *The Hindu*, 19 March 2004.

[196] Ravi Krishnan, 'Permanent Resident Disqualification Bill; Women see politics, call it discriminatory', 11 March 2010, available at: www.tribuneindia.com/2010/20100312/J&K.htm#3 (accessed 27 March 2013).

history of the state' or in Article 370.[197] In 2012 the government was reported to have abandoned it.[198]

Economic reform

Land reform had been on Sheikh Abdullah's agenda since the 1930s, being one of the reasons for his preference for acceding to India rather than Pakistan, of which he wrote,

> The claim of being a Muslim state is of course only a camouflage. It is a screen to dupe the common man, so that he may not see clearly that Pakistan is a feudal state in which a clique is trying [. . .] to maintain itself in power.[199]

Abdullah's Abolition of Big Landed Estates Act, 1950, said that 'Land shall be transferred to the tillers of such land to the extent of their actual possession',[200] placing a ceiling on large land holdings, and providing for confiscation of the 'surplus'. Strikingly, no compensation was provided, a decision ratified by the State Constituent Assembly.

Between 1949–50 and 1962 the number of land owners in Kashmir increased by 25.47 per cent and the average size of holdings decreased by 25.92 per cent.[201] This study referred to 'exemplary land reform', though also suggesting that reforms could have been carried further.[202] Again, the Distressed Debtors Relief Act wiped out debts if the peasant debtor had paid 150 per cent of the original loan.[203] The beneficiaries of these measures were ordinary citizens, those disadvantaged mainly Hindu land owning classes.

Other issues

Generally, it seems that Kashmir copies much Union legislation that does not apply to it, and co-operates in Union initiatives that it cannot be forced into,

197 Datar, 'J&K: legalised discrimination'.

198 Maqbool, 'Govt dumps Permanent Resident Women Disqualification Bill', 17 June 2012, www.greaterkashmir.com/.

199 Quoted in Bamzai, *Bonfire of Kashmiriyat*, 172 (date of quotation is 1953 or earlier).

200 See Daniel Thomas, *The Agrarian Prospect in India* (2nd edn., Bombay: Allied Publishers, 1976) 49. The legislation was challenged in, for example *Magher Sing v. Chief Secretary, Jammu and Kashmir Government* AIR 1953 K & K 25, holding that the Regent had the power to legislate on this topic; that any article of the Constitution of India that might have affected this power did not apply in Kashmir (particularly human rights, or Art. 254 so far as it deals with resolving conflicts between concurrent list matters).

201 M. S. Bhatt, 'Land distribution in rural Jammu and Kashmir: an inter-temporal analysis' in B. K. Sinha Pushpendra, *Land Reforms in India: An Unfinished Agenda* Vol. 5 (New Delhi: Sage Publications, 2000), 139, 149–50.

202 Ibid., 167.

203 Iffat Malik, *Kashmir: Ethnic Conflict, International Dispute* (Karachi: Oxford University Press, 2002), 93–4.

such as the Government Sales Tax. The Thirteenth Finance Commission proposed establishment of a Water Regulatory Authority in each state, an issue picked up by the Union government.[204] Kashmir passed necessary legislation[205] promptly – no doubt encouraged by the Union grant available to the state.

Much national legislation intended to protect citizens does not automatically apply to the state. In a recent ten-year period, about fifty new central Acts[206] were passed that would generally apply to the states. Twelve were not applied to Jammu and Kashmir including the Pre-natal Diagnostic Techniques (Regulation and Prevention of Misuse) Act, 1994; Persons with Disabilities (Equal Opportunities, Protection of Rights and Full Participation) Act, 1995; the Right to Information Act; and the Protection of Women from Domestic Violence Act, 2005. A recent report commented,

> Successive governments at the Centre, whether it be Congress, Bharatiya Janata Party or other coalition governments, have refused to put pressure on J&K to enact progressive laws based on universal human rights values. Conversely they have expended considerable energy to press for the enactment of India's more repressive legislations.[207]

Other non-applicable Union acts have related to competition, electricity regulation and energy conservation, and even the Evidence and Contracts Acts do not apply, though most have their state equivalent. Another area is forestry, with the consequence that forestry, autonomy and communal tension became entangled: the issue being whether a Supreme Court Order intended to strengthen Union control over use of forest land applied to Kashmir, in the context of a bitter dispute over the allocation of land for pilgrims to a Hindu shrine in the Kashmir Valley.[208]

Some of the recent Union acts also have Kashmir counterparts, including, for example, the Right to Information Act (2009), Persons with Disability . . . Act (2009) and a Domestic Violence Act (2010). A meeting on the need for domestic violence legislation found in 2008 that there would be a necessity for 'some

[204] See memo to all state governments, http://finmin.nic.in/TFC/Guidelines_Water_Sector_Management.pdf.

[205] Water Resources (Regulation and Management) Act 2010 available at: www.indiaenvironmentportal.org.in/files/Water_Resources.pdf (accessed 28 March, 2013).

[206] Ignoring appropriation or finance acts, repealing or amendment acts, and those of no interest to Kashmir.

[207] Suhas Chakma, 'Abuse of Article 370', *India Human Rights Quarterly*, October–December 2010, No. 2 www.achrweb.org.

[208] The case was *T.N. Godavarman Thirumulkpad v. Union of India and Environmental Awareness Forum*, which has been before the court, and elicited many rulings, since 1996. See www.forestcaseindia.org//f2/ (accessed 28 March 2013). For an account of the controversy in Kashmir, which involved major rioting, litigation and much debate, see the issue of *Epilogue* magazine for July 2008 available at www.scribd.com/EpilogueMagazine/d/48151266-Epilogue-Magazine-July-2008 (accessed 28 March 2013). The conclusion of the state's lawyers was that the court's rulings that any declassification of forest land or use of forest land for non-forest purposes did not apply to the state.

amendments which are made keeping in view the social, political, cultural and religious set-up of the state'.[209] While a member of the State Commission for Women seemed to take a similar view,[210] in the event the state Act[211] is identical to the central Act.[212] The state government passed up the opportunity to improve its Right to Information Act, based on its experience of operating the central Act. The Commonwealth Human Rights Initiative comments, 'Government has ignored almost all the important recommendations made by civil society organisations for strengthening the Bill further'.[213]

Conclusion

Kashmir's entire history of autonomy can be understood only in the context of the violence and the tensions that have been so prevalent. Kashmir is a place of frequent violence, where emergency provisions of some sort are virtually always in force, under what Arundhati Roy described as 'one of the most brutal military occupations in the world',[214] and where insurgent groups carry out atrocities against civilians. Human rights have been trampled on by both state and Union governments. Corrupt and ineffective governments, rigged elections and political interference from Delhi (especially depending on the relationship between the parties ruling in each capital) have marked the last sixty years of Kashmir governance.

It might not have become part of India at all had it not been for the Pakistan sponsored invasion. The circumstances of invasion and UN intervention made it impractical to make a final resolution of its status as the Constitution of India was drafted. Most decisions adjusting centre-state relations in relation to Kashmir seem to have been made at times of confrontation, or at least tension, with Sheikh Abdullah in jail, or President's Rule in effect. The imperatives of militarisation around Kashmir dominated, and diminished, its autonomy. The external and internal military threat – compounded by Kashmir's contiguity to Pakistan – invited greater intervention (some said 'occupation') of a powerful centre in Delhi than would have been the case in more settled circumstances.

The tensions within India between Hindus and Muslims, particularly bitter at the time of independence and partition, were reflected in Indian policy towards Kashmir, with many elements among the majority Hindu community intolerant of what they perceived as 'Muslim' autonomy in Kashmir, as they

209 'There is need for domestic violence act say experts in Kashmir', 13 March 2008, womensphere.wordpress.com/.

210 At the 'National Consultation on the Protection of Women from Domestic Violence Act, 2005' of which the report is available at www.hrln.org/, see 45.

211 No. XI of 2010. 212 No. 43 of 2005.

213 'The Jammu and Kashmir Right to Information Bill, 2009 In Perspective' (March 2009) 2, www.humanrightsinitiative.org/programs/ai/rti/india/states/jk/jk_rti_bill_2009_chri_analysis.pdf (accessed 28 March 2013).

214 See Mehdi Hasan, 'In praise of Arundhati Roy', *New Statesman* blog 28 October 2010, at www.newstatesman.com/.

still are. Yet the reality of religion and ethnicity in Kashmir was more complex than this simplistic approach suggested. Unlike many areas that demand and exercise autonomy, Kashmir did not have a predominant majority of one ethnic group. Not all groups in Kashmir wanted 'separation' from India, and those who did not had powerful supporters in Delhi in what is a democratic but ethnicised system of politics of India. These factors plus the continuing threat from Pakistan all but ruled out the solution of a plebiscite. Even without the external factor, this approach might not have worked. Another alternative, the breakup of Kashmir into three autonomous areas based on religion (Muslim, Hindu and Buddhist) – a policy not ruled out in the North East – seemed too risky with hostile neighbours (Pakistan and China), though at the same time as the State Autonomy Committee report was produced, the state government also produced a report on autonomy *within* Kashmir for eight of its constituent regions.[215]

Due particularly to Hindu resistance, and Pakistan's claims, accompanied as they have been by what India views as armed aggression, Kashmir, unlike Spain – or Papua New Guinea at its earlier stage of decentralisation – was not seen in the rest of India as a model, but as something to be rejected, which gradually weakened Kashmir's claim for special treatment.

A full understanding of Kashmir today would require an analysis of these factors, and others that cannot be explored in this chapter, which is essentially concerned with the theme of the book – the legal institutions and processes of autonomy.

One other major factor is the international context. The dispute between Pakistan and India was internationalised by Nehru as early as 1947 when he appealed to the UN Security Council.[216] Various UN sponsored efforts involving distinguished mediators, direct talks between India and several Indo-Pakistan wars have failed to achieve a resolution.[217]

Nobody wants the system they have now, so nobody is really trying to make it work. What we have seen is that Kashmir does not make full use of the diminished possibilities for autonomy that already exist. Nonetheless, the ruling party in Kashmir, the National Conference, insists it will 'continue to strive for the complete restoration of the special status that formed the basis of Srinagar-Delhi relationship'.[218] It relies upon the Report of the State Autonomy Committee it set up in 1999.[219] Confusingly, the opposition People's Democratic

215 A few extracts from the Report are at www.satp.org/satporgtp/countries/india/states/jandk/documents/index.html (accessed 28 March 2013). For a strong critique of the Report's tendencies to harden cleavages, and of the motivation for the Report see Praveen Swami, 'A communal divide', *Frontline*, 17–30, 16 July 1999, www.frontlineonnet.com/.

216 See for example, Malik *Kashmir: Ethnic Conflict*, 118.

217 Ibid. and following pages.

218 Party Manifesto, www.jknc.in.

219 The report of this committee is available at the Jammu and Kashmir National Conference website: www.jknc.in/. There were various summaries including in *Frontline*, 17: 14, 8–21 July 2000, available at www.hindu.com/fline/fl1714/17140120.htm. It also set up the Regional Autonomy Committee to look at the question of autonomy within the state.

Party presses for 'self-rule'.[220] In concrete terms, it asks for amendments to the constitutional framework, including removal of the President's Rule provision in relation to Kashmir; allowing the state as well as the Union to legislate on terrorist activities; restoring the appointment of the Head of the State by the State Assembly; Article 370 to be described as 'special' rather than 'temporary'; disapplying provisions on the All India Services Act to Kashmir; and providing for special representation of the Kashmiri Pandits in the State Assembly.[221]

Nor can we examine the discussions over the years within India and between India and Pakistan. In 1995 Indian Prime Minister Narasimha Rao said that 'the sky was the limit' for autonomy for Kashmir.[222] In 2010 Manmohan Singh said, 'If there is consensus among political parties on autonomy for the state, then it can be considered within the ambit of the Constitution'.[223] But immediately the *Times of India* reported, 'Barring the ruling National Conference, all political outfits, separatists, people's groups and intellectuals in Jammu and Kashmir rejected Prime Minister Manmohan Singh's proposal to discuss autonomy within the constitution for the state'.[224]

The variety of views and the politics of quiet dialogue,[225] boycott and megaphone argument that continue to surround the whole future of Kashmir are too complex to be discussed here. Agreement has seemed so possible, and alternately so impossible, for so long, that it is foolhardy to attempt any prediction as to what the future may hold.

220 See the PDP website at www.jkpdp.org/self-rule/autonomy.

221 This last is a Muslim-led party. These are the main points from *Jammu & Kashmir: The Self-Rule Framework for Resolution* (Srinagar: PDP, 2008), available at: www.jkpdp.org/self-rule-framework.

222 Praveen Swami, 'The autonomy demand', *Frontline* 17: 14, 8–21 July 2000.

223 'Can consider autonomy for J&K within ambit of Constitution: PM' reported by NDTV see www.ndtv.com/. The main opposition in Kashmir, the People's Democratic Party, had boycotted the meeting.

224 'PM's plan for J&K autonomy has few takers', 12 August 2010, http://articles.timesofindia.indiatimes.com/.

225 For example, the 'citizen initiative' Kashmir Committee that comprises Shanti Bhushan (former Union Law Minister), V. K. Grover (Former Secretary, Ministry of External Affairs), M. J. Akbar (Author of *Kashmir: Behind the Vale*, earlier), Wahid Ur Rehman (journalist from Kashmir), convened by Madhu Kishwar (lawyer) and chaired by Ram Jethmalani (former Law Minister) – see www.manushi.in/.

6

Autonomies of scale

Precarious self-government on Norfolk Island

Helen Irving

Autonomy has been the goal of many peoples who constitute a distinct regional minority within a larger nation-state, yet are bound to that state by shared history and constitutional ties. But autonomy is not always without drawbacks. It may, for example, mask an abdication of responsibility or neglect on the part of the national government. It may deprive the members of the autonomous region of the benefits and entitlements associated with full citizenship of the nation-state. Within the autonomy itself, it may permit practices that would not be permitted under the laws and values of the rest of the state.

Even with good will and equitable policies on both sides, autonomy may also, in some cases, be simply unmanageable. Variables relating to population size, demographic mix, cultural practises, economic viability and geographic accessibility will critically affect the suitability of a region for constitutional autonomy. Such variables need to be balanced against a strong desire for autonomy on the part of a particular people.

Might a region, for example, be simply too remote, under-populated and economically vulnerable for autonomy to be both practical and beneficial? Is autonomy desirable when cultural practises and local governance arrangements clash with principles of democracy and the enjoyment of the rights enjoyed by other members of the nation-state? What weight should be given to the desire for autonomy, when the sustainability of the autonomy arrangements is in doubt?

Norfolk Island, one of the self-governing territories of the Commonwealth of Australia ('the Commonwealth'), is a semi-autonomous region in respect of which such questions have long been asked, and where the dilemmas of autonomy are strikingly illustrated.

Originally settled in 1856 by the inhabitants of Pitcairn Island, themselves of mixed English and Tahitian origin, Norfolk Islanders represent their life as ethnically and culturally distinct. This view is reflected in Australia's Norfolk Island Act 1979, which conferred self-government on the Island and which acknowledges the distinctive character of the Islanders and 'their desire to preserve their traditions and culture'.

The Act followed a Royal Commission study of the Island which, in 1976, found a community that was deeply divided between Pitcairn descendants and non-Pitcairners, but which nevertheless remained united around a number of collective interests and wishes: these included the preservation of the Norfolk language and Pitcairn cultural values, way of life and 'historic rights'; and protection of the historical heritage of the natural environment of the Island. The community also shared a desire for improvements in transport and communication services, and for the provision of some services by the Commonwealth of Australia, as well as increased employment opportunities. Central to the community's wishes was 'as large a degree of self-government for the Island as possible', along with 'retention of the present close ties with the [British] Crown'.[1]

A year earlier, however, a Report of the Commonwealth Senate's Standing Committee on Foreign Affairs and Defence had concluded that the Norfolk population 'is ethnically and culturally akin to that of the [Australian] mainland, [and] its economic and social links are with Australia'.[2] Such views are deeply contested on Norfolk, and the divergence between Australia's shifting perceptions of the Island and Norfolk's consistent claims of a unique identity have set the stage for a long and uneasy constitutional history.

Historical background

A small, volcanic island (of 34.5 square kilometres), Norfolk lies in the Pacific Ocean, between New Caledonia and New Zealand,[3] approximately 1,600 kilometres north-east of Sydney, and 1,900 kilometres from Australia's federal capital, Canberra. Its resident population, at the 2006 census, amounted to 2,523, of which 1,576 were permanent residents (constituting less than 0.001 per cent of Australia's total population of approximately 22.5 million people). Around 82 per cent are Australian citizens; 15 per cent are citizens of New Zealand. Descendants of the Pitcairn Islanders – 'natives' of Norfolk – constitute 47.6 per cent of the permanent population.

The Island's strange history – part of its attraction for today's tourists – has particular significance in the history of Australia. Before 1788, Norfolk Island was completely uninhabited.[4] It had been identified in 1774 by the explorer, James Cook, who reported to the British government on its abundance of flax and pine trees, with a recommendation that it be settled for commercial and naval purposes. Norfolk was incorporated into New South Wales in 1788, at the

[1] *Report of the Royal Commission into Matters Relating to Norfolk Island* (Canberra, AGPS, 1976), 51–2.

[2] Senate Standing Committee on Foreign Affairs and Defence, *Report on United Nations Involvement with Australia's Territories* (Australian Parliament, 1975), 112.

[3] New Caledonia is 770 km to the north; New Zealand is 1,100 km to the south.

[4] Archaeological evidence shows that Norfolk was inhabited between 400 and 800 years ago by the same east Polynesian people who occupied New Zealand, Tahiti and other South Pacific Islands: Leigh Dayton, 'Now we know who beat Cook to Norfolk', *Sydney Morning Herald*, 3 April 1997.

time of British settlement, under the first Governor's Instructions.[5] It failed to develop economically, however, and after a short period as a penal colony, was left uninhabited. In 1789, Captain William Bligh (later a highly controversial Governor of New South Wales) was returning from a voyage to Tahiti in command of HMS *Bounty*; in an enduringly notorious (and romanticised) event, the crew mutinied. Bligh and eighteen loyal men were cast adrift in a small boat in the middle of the Pacific, from where they made their way to Timor, and subsequently to England to report the mutiny. The mutineers returned to Tahiti; soon after, a small group fled to the more remote island, Pitcairn, taking with them a number of Tahitians.[6] Some eighteen years passed before the Admiralty finally identified Pitcairn as the mutineers' hideaway and by then, only one of the original men was still alive. The mutineers' descendants were now living as devout, puritan Christians, but their subsistence economy was precarious; doubts about its sustainability were quickly raised by the British. Following a devastating storm in 1845 that washed away large parts of the Island's soil, the decision was taken to abandon Pitcairn. Norfolk Island (some 5,300 kilometres away) with its relatively accommodating terrain, its system of roads and vacant stone buildings, was identified as a suitable site. In 1856, the entire population of 194 was relocated from Pitcairn to Norfolk.[7]

The modern history of Norfolk, thus, began 150 years ago with a population descended from a handful of English men and Polynesian women. Their subsequent descendants now claim a distinct ethnicity, including a discrete 'genetic profile'. English is the principal language, but some also speak a local language – 'Norfolk' – which has been described as a 'patois', developed from Old English, Platt Deutsch and Tahitian.[8] Norfolk has its own special festive and religious days, its own flag and emblem, and Britain's 'God Save the Queen' (discontinued as Australia's national anthem in 1984) is retained as its anthem. The historical rights claimed to derive from Pitcairn Island include: the right to self-government; the right to live as British subjects and in accordance with British law; the right of families to own subsistence land; and the right to graze cattle on commons. There are cultural obligations to provide labour for public works, including communal grave digging and free burials.[9] The right to live free from taxes (especially externally imposed) is said to derive from the original Pitcairn ethos of self-help, simplicity of lifestyle and financial autonomy. Thus, payment of income tax has always been 'prohibited' for cultural reasons.

[5] Letter of Instruction, 25 April 1787, *Historical Records of Australia*, Vol. 1, part 2, 1892.

[6] The fourteen mutineers who remained on Tahiti were tracked down in 1791. They were taken back to England (three drowned *en route*); the remaining eleven were court-martialled, and three were hanged.

[7] Several left Norfolk and returned to Pitcairn in 1858 and in 1863. Their descendants, with some others, make up the current Pitcairn population of just under fifty persons.

[8] Bronwyn Paddick, *Review of Immigration System on Norfolk Island* (Govt of Norfolk Island, 2000), 23. In recent years, 'Norf'k' language classes have been provided in the Island school.

[9] Ibid., 54–5.

In an assessment of the Island's common heritage, a Norfolk-commissioned report identified other cultural practises and traditions:

> The harmonic rather than *polyphonic* style of church music, the availability of voter-initiated intervention in the legislature, the barter economy, the rejection of development for its own sake and the relaxed, relatively low technology lifestyle of the Island are each examples that reflect the Island's past and distinguish it from mainland [Australian] norms that together contribute to the distinctive identity of Norfolk Island.[10]

Status under international law

Norfolk is treated as falling outside the class of territories defined by the United Nations in 1960 as 'geographically separate and [. . .] distinct ethnically and/or culturally from the country administering it'.[11] While such conclusions have always been disputed on Norfolk, the Island enjoys no special status under Australia's international obligations. It is not included among the 'dependent territories' listed by the United Nations, or subject to the United Nations Declaration on the Granting of Independence to Colonial Countries and Peoples (1960). A significant number of Norfolk Islanders, however, claim that Australia is in breach of international law in attempting to 'grotesquely, stealthily and gradually incorporate [Norfolk] into the Australian body politic without the consent of' the Islander people.[12]

Provision VI of the UN General Assembly's Resolution 1541 states that 'a Non-Self-Governing Territory can be said to have reached a measure of self-government by' among other things, 'Emergence as a sovereign independent State', or 'Free association with an independent State'. While Norfolk is far from fully independent and the level of self-government fails to satisfy many of its people, it nevertheless has enjoyed a degree of autonomy that is remarkable for such a small population, and is significantly greater than in other sub-national regions of Australia. The 1979 Act not only granted self-government to the Norfolk people, but also recognised their separate cultural identity as well as their potential for future statehood.

Over the years, the Commonwealth has attracted much criticism for neglect or poor administration of Norfolk, but concerns specifically regarding international obligations have tended to target Norfolk's own laws. Commonwealth proposals for reform of Norfolk law (and in the case of electoral law, Commonwealth intervention) have been justified on several occasions on grounds of Australia's international obligations towards all of its citizens (specifically as

[10] Ibid., 43. [11] General Assembly Resolution 1542 (XV) 15 December 1960.

[12] Human Rights and Equal Opportunities Commission (HREOC), *Territorial Limits: Norfolk Island's Immigration Act* (1999), 24. Peter Hanks et al., *Australian Constitutional Law* (Sydney: Butterworths, 2004), 1062. An interesting comparison can be made with the referendum vote in 1984 of the 600 inhabitants of the Cocos (Keeling) Islands – acquired from Singapore in 1955 – in favour of integration into Australia.

a signatory to the ICCPR and the ICESCR). Norfolk, rather than the Commonwealth, has been resistant to this perspective.

One of the principal concerns has been the immigration regime in operation on the Island. Norfolk's law prevents persons, including other Australian citizens, from living on the Island without a visa, and residency is granted only at the discretion of the responsible Norfolk Minister. Australian citizens travelling to the Island must present their passport (the reverse does not apply); non-Australians must hold a visa. An Australian Government Fact Sheet describes this arrangement thus: 'For immigration purposes only, Norfolk Island is [...] treated as if it were another country despite it being part of Australia'.[13]

Among other things, the Norfolk practice is to treat persons of Pitcairn origin as presumptively entitled to residency. In 1984, an individual who had been declared an 'illegal immigrant' on Norfolk brought a challenge to Norfolk's immigration law in the Federal Court of Australia, on the ground that it made 'race' a criterion of residence and was thus invalid for inconsistency with the Commonwealth's Racial Discrimination Act 1975 (Cth), which gives effect to the International Convention on the Elimination of All Forms of Racial Discrimination (1966). The Court dismissed the claim. The Norfolk law, the Court held, did not demonstrate a nexus with race, colour, descent or national or ethnic origin, and nor did it unreasonably restrict the free movement of Australian citizens.[14]

In 1999, however, in a further investigation into claims that Norfolk's property and immigration laws breached international law (specifically a person's right to dispose of property and freely leave a territory)[15] the Australian Human Rights and Equal Opportunity Commission[16] concluded that

> the implementation of the immigration regime on Norfolk Island violates the rights of all Australians to liberty of movement and freedom of choice of residence without discrimination and free from arbitrary decision making under Article 12 of the International Covenant on Civil and Political Rights.[17]

Recently the Commonwealth Parliament has acknowledged the need for intervention in cases where Norfolk law is contrary to international standards, as well as in conflict with principles of common citizenship. Prior to 2004, for example, Norfolk electoral law demanded both an unusually long period of

[13] Australian Government, Department of Immigration and Citizenship, Fact Sheet 59, 'Immigration Arrangements for Norfolk Island', 2009 (reviewed January 2011).

[14] *Lewis v. Trebilco* (1984) 53 ALR 581.

[15] Norfolk law does not permit a person, even a property owner, to move to Norfolk until a 'vacancy' occurs among the resident population.

[16] Established in 1986, to give effect to the ICCPR, providing a mechanism to monitor breaches of the Convention, and to investigate claims of discrimination. Its powers extend to the Australian territories. Its determinations are, however, not judicial, and remain inferior to decisions of Courts.

[17] 'Everyone lawfully within the territory of a State shall, within that territory, have the right to liberty of movement and freedom to choose his residence.' HREOC, *Territorial Limits*.

residency before an individual was eligible to enrol as an elector on the Island, and it permitted non-citizens to sit in the Norfolk Legislative Assembly. The Commonwealth argued that Australia had 'an obligation to ensure the consistency of local law with Australia's treaty and customary law obligations that applies to Norfolk Island to the same extent that it does to other State and Territory Governments'.[18] In 2004, against the wishes of the Islanders, the Commonwealth Parliament passed legislation amending the Norfolk law, and establishing Australian citizenship as a criterion of eligibility. Norfolk's exclusionary immigration law, however, remains intact.

Constitutional status of Norfolk Island

Norfolk's constitutional status has been altered several times since 1856, and responsibilities for the Island have been concomitantly passed around. It would not be unreasonable to say that Norfolk has been regarded as something of an incubus by each of its governing authorities.[19]

Norfolk remained under British law and (indirect) British control from 1788 until its transfer to the Commonwealth of Australia in 1914. It was first annexed, under Order in Council in 1844, to Van Dieman's Land (now Tasmania) until its separation from that colony in 1855.[20] In 1856, it was proclaimed as a 'distinct and separate Settlement'[21] to be administered by the Governor of New South Wales, as Governor of Norfolk. The colony's government did not welcome it. In 1888, the New South Wales Premier, Sir Henry Parkes, stated that they 'would hardly know what to do with [Norfolk] [. . .] as it would appear to be something like a white elephant'.[22] Constitutional doubts were also raised over whether it was possible for a colony – as New South Wales was then – to have its own dependency, and it was finally agreed that Norfolk would not be fully annexed, but would be under the authority of the Governor of New South Wales, with services provided by the colony's government, assisted financially by Britain. In 1897, after years of negotiation, Norfolk became a 'quasi-dependency' of New South Wales.

18 Joint Standing Committee on the National Capital and External Territories, *Quis custodiet ipsos custodes?: Inquiry into Governance on Norfolk Island* (Canberra, 2003), 40. The Committee also noted Article 27 of the Vienna Convention on the Law of Treaties, providing that a state party to a treaty may not invoke a deficiency in its internal law as a justification for a failure to perform its treaty obligations.

19 In the *Report of the Royal Commission* (1976) are set out extracts from British colonial authorities in which the desire of Her Majesty's Government to rid itself of responsibility for the Island is made abundantly clear. There is one historical counter-example, however; in the late nineteenth century, New Zealand actively sought annexation of the Island, for strategic reasons related to the Pacific cable link, but Britain declined its offer.

20 Tellingly, the transfer of Norfolk was included in an Act called the *Australian Waste Lands Act*, 1855.

21 Preamble to *Norfolk Island Act* 1979 (Cth).

22 8 July 1888. Quoted in Maev O'Collins, *An Uneasy Relationship: Norfolk Island and the Commonwealth of Australia* (ANU, Canberra: Pandanus Books, 2002), 11.

In 1914 the administration of Norfolk was transferred to the Commonwealth of Australia. The Island thus came under the exclusive jurisdiction of the Commonwealth authorities, and subject to the so-called 'Territories Power' (section 122 of the Australian Constitution). Under the Constitution, the six original Australian states have their own parliaments and constitutions, the continuing existence of which is guaranteed by the Commonwealth Constitution.[23] Australia's territories, however, attract few constitutional guarantees. Of Australia's many islands and territories, only three are self-governing. Two of these – the Northern Territory and the Australian Capital Territory (ACT)[24] – are internal territories, situated on the mainland. Norfolk (the second to gain self-government) is external.

The constitutional status of the Island has remained controversial. Against the waxing and waning of autonomy, Norfolk's legal and political status as 'part of the Commonwealth' still remains disputed. One recent report, prepared for and on behalf of the Norfolk government, states,

> Even if it must be accepted that, as a matter of international law, Norfolk Island is deemed to be 'part' of Australia, it is submitted that the question of whether, for constitutional purposes, it has been integrated with Australia is still open.[25]

Many Islanders continue to believe that they have sovereignty over the Island by virtue of an original 'cession' of the land from Britain to the Pitcairners in 1856. At the time of their settlement on Norfolk, each family was given a grant of land (200 acres cleared, and 500 acres un-cleared). This appears to have been understood as a gift from Queen Victoria,[26] although the Governor's instructions made it clear that the grant was 'subject to be revised and amended if necessary by the Governor of New South Wales'.[27]

The view that the original grant amounted to 'cession' was described in a 2003 report of the Commonwealth Parliament Joint Standing Committee on the National Capital and External Territories, as a 'myth perpetuated by a minority of Pitcairn descendants and other more recent, often wealthy, arrivals motivated by self-interest to resist the imposition of [Commonwealth] income tax'.[28] Nevertheless, it remains in circulation and has often been repeated, including in the Commonwealth Parliament. As recently as 2004, during debate on Norfolk Island's electoral law, one Member of the Commonwealth House of Representatives described Norfolk as having been 'gifted' by the Queen to the Pitcairners. He added, controversially,

23 Section 106 of the Constitution of the Commonwealth of Australia.
24 They gained self-government in 1978 and 1988 respectively.
25 Paddick, *Review of Immigration System on Norfolk Island*, 113.
26 One of the reasons, it is sometimes claimed, for the Island's continued attachment to the Monarchy and opposition to proposals for Australia to become a republic.
27 Quoted in Paddick, *Review of Immigration System on Norfolk Island*, 98.
28 Joint Standing Committee on the National Capital and External Territories, *Inquiry into Governance on Norfolk Island.*

> There is a great deal of dispute about what form that gifting took, but I think it is generally recognised by British and Australian officials that, even though it is now part of the Commonwealth of Australia, there is an implied right to independence in that history.[29]

Norfolk's legal status was finally (if arguably, in Norfolk eyes) settled in a case before the High Court of Australia in 1976,[30] following a challenge to the Commonwealth's constitutional power to make a taxation law that applied to Norfolk residents, in respect of income earned on the Australian mainland. Against claims that Norfolk was not subject to Australian jurisdiction, the Court observed, *inter alia*, that there were 'powerful reasons', including the historical records, 'for regarding Norfolk Island as part of the Commonwealth'.[31] The Commonwealth Parliament, it concluded, had the constitutional power to regulate Norfolk closely. In the same year, the Royal Commission Report added that it is 'equally open to the Commonwealth, if it so chooses, to shed all responsibility for the Island by granting it complete independence'.[32]

The level of self-government granted in 1979 (see later) was initially limited, but the Norfolk Island Act also provided for a progressive increase; its Preamble states, among other things, that 'the [Commonwealth] Parliament considers it to be desirable and to be the wish of the people of Norfolk Island that Norfolk Island achieve, over a period of time, internal self-government as a Territory under the authority of the Commonwealth'.

As anticipated, self-government has grown considerably over the years; indeed, measured against the Island's limited capacities, it is now considered by many on the mainland to be over-extended. Indeed, a 2005 Commonwealth report went as far as to describe Norfolk as being 'endowed with greater powers than any other Australian State', but having 'less administrative capacity than most Australian local councils or shires', and with responsibilities 'above and beyond its capacity to administer'.[33]

Recently, albeit with great reluctance and in the face of much internal dissent, the Norfolk government conceded that its powers of self-government needed to be amended. Earlier, the government's submission to the Commonwealth's Joint Standing Committee in 2003 had stated a preference for Norfolk to be designated a 'dependency' of Australia, providing (it was thought) for greater limitations on the exercise of Commonwealth power over the Island, while retaining access to some Australian services and financial support.[34] One year later, in a 'Priorities Plan' for 2004–7, the Norfolk government stated its

[29] Commonwealth of Australia, House of Representatives, 4 March 2004, 25, 970. Member for the electorate of Hinkler.

[30] *Berwick Ltd v. Gray* (1976) 133 CLR 603. [31] Ibid., at 609.

[32] *Report of the Royal Commission*, 1976, 200.

[33] Joint Standing Committee, Report, *Norfolk Island: Financial Sustainability. The Challenge – Sink or Swim*, November, 2005, 87.

[34] Joint Standing Committee, *Inquiry into Governance on Norfolk Island*, 2003, 28.

commitment to 'strengthening of our self government position'.[35] However, by August 2006, following negotiations with the Commonwealth, it appeared willing to accept constitutional arrangements similar to those in place in the other self-governing territories.[36] In 2010, the Commonwealth passed the Territories Law Reform Act (Cth), which implemented reforms to Norfolk's governance arrangements: regularising Norfolk elections; increasing executive responsibility; creating a framework for financial auditing and accountability and introducing mechanisms for administrative law review, all subject to Commonwealth oversight. These initiatives, the relevant Commonwealth Minister said in the parliamentary second reading speech on the Bill, 'will better empower the local community of Norfolk Island and give them a say in how their community is being governed'.[37]

Financial autonomy – an essential cultural attribute in the Islanders' eyes – had emerged as both the source of Norfolk's long-standing difficulties and the instrument for wider, externally imposed reforms. In November 2010, following the passage of the Territories Law Reform Act, a Memorandum of Understanding between the Commonwealth and Norfolk recorded the Commonwealth's agreement to consider requests for financial assistance for essential services on the Island, subject to full financial disclosure and acquittals, and – at the time of writing, unspecified – conditions. Most significantly, it is likely that Islanders will be asked to pay tax on a similar footing to other Australians. The Island's ethos of self-help, the tradition of self-reliance and the interests of the wealthy residents who have long enjoyed the Island's tax-haven status, will all be implicated.

History of governance

A limited form of local government existed on Norfolk, even at the time of re-settlement from Pitcairn. For a time, a Chief Magistrate and a 'House' – a meeting of all adult community members, men and women – exercised delegated powers to amend or alter local laws by majority vote, subject to the approval of the British-appointed Governor of New South Wales, and ultimately the British authorities. By the 1890s the authorities had grown disillusioned with the Norfolk 'experiment', as industry failed to develop and the capacities of the Islanders also failed to live up to earlier assessments. New laws and regulations were proclaimed in 1896, modifying governance and formalising laws relating to property.

35 Government of Norfolk Island, 14 March 2005.

36 'Norfolk Island seeks new political status', ABC News Online, 21 August 2006.

37 Simon Crean, MP, Minister for Regional Australia, Regional Development and Local Government. Commonwealth of Australia, 29 September 2010, House of Representatives Debates, 86.

An Order in Council of 1897 brought Norfolk under the authority of the Governor of New South Wales.[38] A new Council was created, consisting of twelve members elected annually by men aged twenty-five years and over. The Council enjoyed some limited law-making powers, subject to approval of the Chief Magistrate who was now appointed by the New South Wales Governor. In 1903 this arrangement was altered again, with the establishment of an Executive Council, two members of which were elected and four appointed by the Governor.

In 1901, the six Australian colonies were federated under a national Constitution, forming the modern state of the Commonwealth of Australia. In 1914, after many delays and with some ambivalence (but without consultation with the people of the Island), Norfolk became a territory of the Commonwealth. The new Norfolk Executive Council (elected by all adult men and women, in conformity with Commonwealth law) was now a purely advisory body, advising a Chief Executive Officer; the Commonwealth Governor-General was empowered to make ordinances on its advice. The Norfolk Island Act 1913 (Cth) stated that the Island was to be routinely subject to Commonwealth laws; its revenue was to be used only to defray its own expenditure; Australian customs duties would not apply to locally produced goods, and liquor production on the Island would be restricted.[39]

In 1935, the Council was replaced by an eight-member elected Advisory Council. This, in its turn, was abolished in 1957 and under the Norfolk Island Ordinance an elected Norfolk Island Council took its place. An 'Administrator' (representative of 'the Crown'; meaning, in the modern sense, the Executive Government of Australia) was appointed. Much Islander dissatisfaction surrounded these arrangements and, in 1960, the Council voted, albeit ineffectually, to reject the Ordinance 'whilst it contains the Power of Veto [of Norfolk laws] by the Administrator and involves pressure on the Council to raise more taxes'.[40] Further amendments in 1963 saw the Administrator gain greater powers. However, as we have seen, in a reversal of direction in 1979, the Island achieved self-government.

These repeated shifts in governance are symptomatic of the long-standing uncertainty surrounding the Island's status and the Commonwealth's inability to determine its own constitutional responsibilities. In 1975, in response to long-running disputes about such matters and concerns about Commonwealth administration, as we have seen, a Royal Commission on Norfolk Island was established to inquire into 'the future status of Norfolk Island and its constitutional relationship to Australia'; it was tasked to consider the 'most appropriate form of administration for Norfolk Island if its constitutional position were

38 Paddick, *Review of Immigration System on Norfolk Island*, 51.

39 Hanks et al., *Australian Constitutional Law*, 111.

40 Paddick, *Review of Immigration System on Norfolk Island*, 62.

changed'.[41] Its report in 1976 concluded, among other things, that most of the Island's problems

> have had their genesis and perpetuation in slothful and inept mainland administration, which has proved itself unable to activate the seemingly clogged processes of government [. . .] Australia's administration of Norfolk Island has been singularly unimpressive at the policy level.[42]

The Commission recommended integration of Norfolk into the rest of Australia, including by giving full Commonwealth voting rights to Norfolk residents, extending mainland services and applying almost all Commonwealth legislation to Norfolk. It also recommended that 'citizens in Norfolk Island be made liable to the same levels of taxations and other imposts as apply' in the Australian Capital Territory.[43] While none of these specific recommendations was adopted, the last remained a matter of ongoing concern, and is closely implicated in current issues surrounding Norfolk autonomy. In the event, a significantly greater level of self-government than recommended by the Royal Commission was conferred on the Islanders under the Norfolk Island Act in 1979.

The Norfolk Island Act 1979

The Norfolk Island Act 1979 repealed earlier Acts, and has operated (with a number of amendments) since that year. It provides for an Administrator, an Executive Council and a nine-member (part-time) Legislative Assembly, elected every three years. The Assembly is required to meet at least once every two months. The Island's constitutional responsibilities and powers have a mixed local, regional and 'national' character. It is empowered 'to make laws for the peace, order and good government of the Territory'. As these words indicate, this is a plenary power, albeit subject to a few express exclusions and limitations: Norfolk may not make laws for defence forces, the coining of money, the acquisition of property other than on 'just terms', or for legalising euthanasia or assisted suicide. Otherwise, the powers are broad. They are listed in two Schedules to the Act, in respect of which different mechanisms for disallowance apply.

Laws passed under Schedule 2 powers are required to be presented to the Administrator for assent, and the Administrator has a (limited) power to withhold assent or suggest amendments, but unless the exercise of power is, in his or her opinion, *ultra vires*, the Administrator is ultimately required to act 'in accordance with the advice of the Executive Council'.[44] Prior consultation with Commonwealth authorities is not required. Schedule 2 powers are extensive and broad, ranging from subjects normally associated with local government (roads, street lighting, garbage, fences, public pounds, among others) to large

[41] *Report of the Royal Commission*, 1976, 9. [42] *Report of the Royal Commission*, 1976, 88.
[43] Ibid., Recommendation 71. [44] Section 21 (5).

'national' subjects (postal services, corporate affairs, civil defence and emergencies). A range of powers normally exercised by the Australian states also lie in the Schedule: housing, environmental protection, criminal law, public works and many others. This list has been expanded significantly since 1979, enlarging the Assembly's heads of power from forty-two to ninety-three, consistent with the Act's anticipation of progressive self-government.

Laws made in the exercise of Schedule 3 powers must first be referred by the Administrator to the Commonwealth Minister for Territories, but unless the Minister's instructions are to the contrary, the Administrator is obliged to follow Norfolk Executive Council advice and give assent. The Schedule 3 list reflects matters in respect of which the Commonwealth has 'national' interest: fishing, customs, immigration, education, quarantine, labour and industrial relations, moveable cultural heritage objects and social security. Despite Commonwealth oversight, these matters are currently subject to distinct and separate Norfolk legislation. Matters not on either schedule are referred by the Administrator to the Commonwealth for the Governor-General's 'pleasure' (meaning, referred to the Commonwealth government for approval).

The Norfolk Executive Council (the Ministry) advises the Administrator. The number of Council members is not fixed, but the practice is for four of the nine MLAs to hold a ministerial portfolio (but for the portfolios effectively to be open to the exercise of responsibility by any Executive Member). The Council meets, as convened by the Administrator, who presides over meetings when present (although meetings may take place in his absence). Any member of the Legislative Assembly may attend meetings. Public servants are not disqualified from standing for the Legislature,[45] but may not become Executive Members.[46] A Chief Administrative Officer serves as the link between government and administration; since 1997, at the Islanders' insistence, only Norfolk Island residents (or persons with General Entry permits) are entitled to apply for this position.

The Administrator is appointed by the Governor-General of the Commonwealth (on Commonwealth Government advice), and holds office during the Governor-General's 'pleasure'. The position brings with it substantial entitlements, and it has been 'much sought after in political circles'[47] (especially among retiring politicians and public servants). Like other comparable officers (State Governors, for example), the Administrator has both ceremonial duties and executive powers, although the latter are rarely exercised independently. His or her assent is required for a bill to become law; assent may be given or withheld, or the bill may either be returned to the Assembly with suggested amendments, or withheld for the 'pleasure' of the Commonwealth Governor-General.

[45] A contrast with the Commonwealth Constitution, which prohibits a person who holds 'office of profit under the Crown' from standing for the Commonwealth Parliament: Section 44(iv).

[46] Section 13(3).

[47] Michael Millett, 'Liberal moves to find seat for Robb', *Sydney Morning Herald*, 11 June 1997.

The Administrator is obliged to follow Norfolk Executive Council advice with respect to Schedule 2 laws, but the Commonwealth Minister for Territories retains a veto over Schedule 3 legislation. For matters outside the Schedules, the Administrator must follow instructions of the Minister. An Executive Council appointment may be terminated by the Administrator if, in his or her opinion, there are exceptional circumstances that justify it.[48] This power, however, has never been exercised.

The Commonwealth government may introduce proposed laws into the Norfolk Legislative Assembly (constitutionally this is done through the Governor-General), and has the power to make ordinances for the Island. In most cases these must first be introduced into and approved by the Norfolk Legislative Assembly, although there is a Commonwealth emergency power to make ordinances without approval. This has not yet been invoked.

Many Islanders regard direct democracy as part of the Norfolk tradition. Citizen-initiated referendums are promoted as a modern counterpart to the traditional community, or 'House' meeting. Although the 1979 Act itself does not provide for referendums, these are a familiar part of Norfolk politics, with a referendum on average every two years since 1979.[49] Under Norfolk's Referendum Act 1964 (NI), three bodies are empowered to initiate a referendum: the Legislative Assembly; a petition of one third of the voters on the electoral roll; or the Commonwealth Minister, via the Administrator, regarding proposed Commonwealth legislation. To be successful, the number of affirmative votes must exceed negative votes by at least 10 per cent of the total. Voting in a referendum is compulsory, but the result is not binding and has no legal force;[50] it is, however, regarded by the Legislative Assembly as authoritative. The subject matter of referendums is at large, with the exception that citizen-initiated referendums concerning the constitution of the Legislative Assembly are not permitted. A further restriction prohibits referendums on the same or substantially similar question being held more than once in a two-year period.

Norfolk's relations with the Commonwealth of Australia

Citizenship and immigration

The Australian Citizenship Act is among the laws of the Commonwealth extending to Norfolk Island. Citizenship is acquired by birth in Australian territory where one parent (or both) is an Australian citizen or a permanent resident of Australia. Children born in Australia of other parents become citizens if they

48 Section 12(2).

49 A referendum, for example, rejected the extension of a mobile phone signal reaching beyond the Island, despite Commonwealth promises of a grant for this purpose.

50 The 2003 Joint Standing Committee report suggested that these features made the referendum on Norfolk 'more accurately described as a form of compulsory opinion polling'. *Inquiry into Governance on Norfolk Island*, 110.

reside in Australia for a minimum of ten years from the date of their birth.[51] The children born to citizens or permanent residents on Norfolk are, thus, Australian citizens. However, not all the legal obligations or entitlements enjoyed by citizens elsewhere in the Australian Commonwealth apply to these particular citizens. There is no Commonwealth parliament electorate for Norfolk; citizens may enrol in a mainland electorate where they have a connection (as can itinerants in the rest of Australia), but they are not obliged to enrol (unlike in the rest of Australia). Alternatively, Islanders may enrol to vote in an electorate of the Australian Capital Territory. Enrolment is not popular, however; indeed, it appears to be resisted for reasons relating to Norfolk's own claims to self-government.

Until 2004, eligibility to vote for Norfolk's Legislative Assembly was based not on citizenship, but on residence. The residency requirement was set at 900 days out of the four years immediately preceding the application for enrolment. Eligibility to stand for election to the Legislative Assembly was based upon eligibility to vote. These requirements reflected the Islanders' strongly held view that genuine adoption of the 'Pitcairn lifestyle' and its values should be linked to the exercise of power.[52] The disenfranchisement of Australian citizens, the unusually long residency period, and the reality of non-citizens being elected to the Assembly (and thus being empowered to make laws for citizens resident on the Island but not entitled to vote), had attracted much criticism on the mainland, both for the incompatibility with Australian law and the violation of the rights recognised in international instruments. Following a resounding condemnation by the Commonwealth Joint Standing Committee inquiry into Norfolk governance in 2003, the Norfolk Legislative Assembly introduced an amendment bill, seeking to lower the period of residency before qualifying, and attaching a citizenship qualification to the right to enrol to vote. Rather than confining this to Australian citizens, however, it proposed that citizens of New Zealand and the United Kingdom should also have the right to vote.[53] Such eligibility, it was said, reflected Norfolk's self-identification as 'British'. The Commonwealth Minister, however, declined to submit the bill for the Governor-General's assent. A Commonwealth Act subsequently replaced it, setting Australian citizenship, plus a six-month residency period as the qualifying criteria.[54] It did not, however, seek to disenfranchise non-citizens

51 Australian Citizenship Act 1948 (Cth), Section 10.

52 *Report of the Royal Commission*, 1976, 77.

53 The Norfolk Bill had attempted, among other things, to acknowledge the Island's close historical ties with Pitcairn Island, the inhabitants of which are UK citizens.

54 The reduced qualifying period is said to have addressed some concerns about failure to meet Australia's obligations under Art. 25 of the ICCPR, providing that all citizens must have reasonable access to vote and be elected and take part in public affairs. Although the six months' residence qualifying period is considerably higher than in any other part of Australia (with the exception of Tasmania) it was adopted by the Commonwealth as a concession to the Norfolk view that electors should have a real understanding of Norfolk culture and way of life. There was also historical precedent, as a six months' qualifying period applied on the Island

already on the electoral roll; thus a number of non-citizens will continue to vote on Norfolk for some time to come, subject only to departure or natural attrition.[55]

If the common entitlements of Australian citizenship are not available to all citizens resident on Norfolk, the reverse is also true: not all Australian citizens enjoy the entitlements available to Norfolk-Australian citizens. While the residency requirements for voting have been eased, residence on the Island remains difficult to achieve. Immigration is among the Island's Schedule 3 powers in the Norfolk Island Act 1979, but despite the Act's provision for some level of Commonwealth oversight over the exercise of these powers, Norfolk Island maintains its own immigration policy and operates as a separate migration zone. The policy is restrictive. While Norfolk is part of Australia and persons born on Norfolk are Australian citizens, residency, as we have seen, is unrelated to citizenship. Under Norfolk's Immigration Act 1985, persons born on Norfolk, or with a parent who is a resident of Norfolk at the time of his or her birth, are permitted to live on the Island. Residency status may be granted to others at the discretion of the responsible Executive Council member. Relevant considerations include the capacity for assimilation into the Norfolk community, good character and good health. Although Pitcairn descent is said not to confer automatic residency rights, it is well understood that it favours applications for residency, serving as a positive indicator of likely assimilation. Indeed, there is a widely held belief both outside and inside the community that an 'open invitation' exists for Pitcairners to live on the Island.[56]

An immigration quota is fixed by the relevant Executive Member on the advice of the Legislative Assembly, and persons newly applying for residency must wait for a 'vacancy' on the Island. Residency permits specify a limited period of time and are subject to conditions, for example, to conduct a business, or engage in research. Other conditions may be imposed by the responsible Executive Member, who may also cancel the visa and issue a declaration of 'illegal immigrant' status. Property owners, whether Australian or not, do not have automatic right to a residency permit.

Norfolk defends these restrictions on environmental and public health grounds, as well as on grounds of traditional cultural integrity.[57] In 1999,

from 1857 to 1968: Parliament of Australia, Parliamentary Library, *Bills Digest* No. 89, 2003–2004, Norfolk Island Amendment Bill 2003, 6.

55 This is consistent with the Commonwealth's own electoral law, which permits non-citizens who were on the electoral roll in 1984 (the year citizenship became a necessary criterion of eligibility) to remain enrolled and continue to vote.

56 Dea Birkett, 'A private mutiny', *Sydney Morning Herald*, 3 October 1998.

57 Applications from intending immigrants have been processed on Norfolk since 2001 (they were previously processed in Canberra). In the first legal case since 2001 regarding an off-shore business applicant, a woman of Chinese origin who had purchased the local café was denied a general entry (residency) permit. The conditions attached to her application included that she (and her family) 'undertake study of the English language'. Although she passed a written test, her oral English was not deemed adequate. She applied for a writ of mandamus against the

the Commonwealth Human Rights and Equal Opportunities Commission concluded, as we saw, that such restrictions were a breach of human rights and could not be justified as a necessary or appropriate measure for population control.[58]

Representation at the national level

Representation of the territories in the Commonwealth Parliament is limited – only the Northern Territory and the ACT currently have seats in the Parliament.[59] Norfolk is 'represented' by the responsible Commonwealth Minister for Territories, but has no member of the House of Representatives or Senator of its own.

Following the Norfolk Island (Electoral and Judicial) Amendment Act 1992 (Cth) provision was made for Islanders to enrol in a mainland electorate, either in one with which the individual has some connection (or in which he or she was previously enrolled), or alternatively in one of the Commonwealth electorates for the ACT. Exceptionally, as we have seen, enrolment for Norfolk Islanders is optional, while it is compulsory in the rest of Australia.

Again, these arrangements have been a source of grievance on the Island, not so much (as might be thought) because they underscore a lack of representation, but because of what some Islanders regard as inappropriate 'integration' into the Commonwealth. Even the minimal inclusion in Commonwealth electoral law was originally opposed by the Islanders, with 80 per cent voting against it in a local (non-binding) referendum. Ten years later only 149 Islanders had enrolled.

Notwithstanding these expressions of resistance, the powers of the Islanders to change their fundamental constitutional relations with the Commonwealth are limited. Under Section 128 of the Commonwealth Constitution, constitutional alteration requires a proposal passed by the Parliament to be supported by a referendum of the Australian people. The people of Australia's territories were unable to vote in such referendums until 1977. Only those with representation in the House of Representatives, however, are now permitted to vote in such referendums. Citizens in territories without representation, or those who are not enrolled to vote for the Commonwealth Parliament, are excluded from voting on proposals to change the Constitution under which their own self-government is framed. Norfolk Islanders may vote as electors of another Australian electorate, but not as Islanders.

local Minister for Immigration in the Norfolk Island Supreme Court in February 2005. Michael Pelly, 'Island minds its own business', *Sydney Morning Herald*, 17 February 2005.

58 HREOC, *Territorial Limits*.

59 The Northern Territory initially gained only a non-voting presence in 1922 and the ACT in 1948. Voting rights in the Parliament were granted in 1968 and 1973, respectively. The decision to create Senate positions for these Territories was controversial, although Section 122 of the Commonwealth Constitution expressly permits it. In the first *Territory Senators Case* (1975) 134 CLR 201, the creation of Territory Senators was unsuccessfully challenged. Both mainland Territories currently have two members of the House of Representatives and two Senators each.

Law and judicial powers

The general law applicable on the Island has alternated. New South Wales laws in force were repealed in 1913 prior to the transfer to the Commonwealth, and Imperial law as in force in 1828[60] was then applied. The Norfolk Judiciary Ordinance of 1936 reinstated New South Wales laws until 1960, when English statutes in force in 1828 were again applied. Subsequent Norfolk Island Acts, including the 1979 Act, preserved pre-existing English laws, allowing the new Legislative Assembly to repeal or amend them. Commonwealth law now applies only if intended. Under Section 18(1) of the 1979 Act, Commonwealth legislation, whether passed before or after 1979, 'is not, except as otherwise provided [. . .] in force as such in the Territory, unless expressed to extend to the Territory'.

The Norfolk Island Act 1979 also provides for the resolution of inconsistency between Norfolk laws and Commonwealth ordinances: the latter prevail to the extent of the inconsistency, 'but an enactment and an Ordinance shall not be taken [. . .] to be inconsistent to the extent that they are capable of operating concurrently'.[61]

Norfolk has a Court of Petty Sessions that can hear summary criminal offences and civil claims up to a limited sum. Matters are usually heard by three local magistrates appointed from within the Island community. The Chief Magistrate of the ACT sits as Norfolk's Chief Magistrate on this Court. Norfolk also has a Supreme Court, established under the Norfolk Island Act of 1957 (and renewed under the 1979 Act), with powers over higher civil claims, and over the criminal laws of Norfolk.[62] The Supreme Court Ordinance of 1960 sets out the Court's jurisdiction, practice and procedure. The Court consists entirely of judges of the Federal Court of Australia (a single judge normally sits), but appointment is not outside Norfolk control. Under Section 53(2) of the 1979 Act, the Commonwealth Minster is obliged to give the Norfolk Executive Council 'the opportunity of furnishing comments to him and shall consider any comments so furnished' on a proposed appointment to the Supreme Court.

The Court may sit on the mainland when this is required in the interest of justice (but not when a Norfolk criminal matter is concerned). Appeals may be taken to the full Federal Court and from there to the High Court of Australia. As both the highest appellate court and constitutional court, the High Court may overrule the judgments of Norfolk's Court or invalidate Norfolk laws where there is a constitutional breach or an inconsistency with Commonwealth law, just as it may do for all other constituent parts of Australia.

[60] The year in which Imperial law was received in all the Australasian colonies.

[61] Section 29(1).

[62] The jurisdiction of the Supreme Court of Norfolk Island also extends to Australia's Coral Sea Islands Territory to the east of Queensland, inhabited by a tiny handful of meteorologists.

Fiscal relations with the Commonwealth of Australia

The 1976 Royal Commission identified Norfolk's value to Australia as: a source of weather information (for defence purposes); as having historical significance and tourist appeal; and as a potential source of undersea mineral wealth. The Australian defence forces have also identified the Norfolk airport as having strategic value in the Pacific. The Island, it is fair to say, has negative fiscal value for the Commonwealth.

For individuals, apart from tourism, one of Norfolk's greatest attractions is its status as a 'tax haven' (albeit open only to those few who can meet the stringent residency requirements). Income tax in Australia is only levied at the national level (there is no state income tax); Commonwealth residents pay income tax in every part of Australia except (in respect of income earned on the Island) on Norfolk. There is no Norfolk company tax, and wealth taxes are non-existent. Land taxes do apply, but only to 'absentee landlords' – that is, persons who own property on the Island without residing there. For many years, a large proportion of all Norfolk revenue has been raised through levies associated, either directly or indirectly, with the tourist industry: landing and departure fees, and accommodation levies. Norfolk is not subject to the constitutional guarantee of 'absolutely free' trade and commerce[63] that prevents Australia's states from imposing tariffs or other fiscal burdens of a discriminatory nature upon goods imported from within the Commonwealth. Customs duties, therefore, remain a major source of revenue. Revenue from financial institutions and Government Business Enterprises (such as the post-office and the 'Liquor Bond Store') and stamp duties are also a significant (albeit lesser) source. In addition to raising the cost of consumer goods, these duties act regressively, falling more heavily on the poor than the wealthy.

All of these fiscal arrangements have come under close and critical Commonwealth scrutiny, and many, if not most, are likely to be reformed following the passage of the 2010 Territories Law Reform Act. The reliance on revenue from tourism appears to be unsustainable, and the regime of customs duties is problematic, given the Island's dependence on imported goods. The cost of living is higher on Norfolk than on the mainland, while most salaries and the average income are lower. There are, however, extremes of wealth: an estimated forty to eighty millionaires, and several multi-millionaires, are to be found among the population.

Regular Commonwealth grants amount to only around 5 per cent of total revenue.[64] The bulk of the Island's revenue is raised on Norfolk itself, principally through tourism.[65] Unlike the other Australian territories, or indeed Australia's

[63] Commonwealth Constitution, Section 92.

[64] The Commonwealth does, however, give substantial special purpose grants for particular projects.

[65] Joint Standing Committee on the National Capital and External Territories, *Norfolk Island: Financial Sustainability*.

states, Norfolk receives a relatively low percentage of its total revenue in grants from Australia's Commonwealth Parliament.[66] Norfolk has the constitutional capacity to borrow, subject to approval by the Commonwealth Treasurer, but its government is said to prefer paying for public infrastructure 'in cash', out of savings. Two large (interest free, or 'soft') Commonwealth loans have been made in recent years, however – including one for re-surfacing the airport runway – but the infrastructure projects for which they were dedicated have not been completed in time, and the Island's capacity to re-pay is now in doubt.

Since Commonwealth taxes are not collected on Norfolk, Commonwealth programs are limited or unavailable. Neither the Commonwealth's public medical insurance scheme ('Medicare') nor its social welfare pensions are available to the Islanders. Norfolk has a single welfare scheme for all types of incapacity and distress, available upon demonstration of need.[67] It imposes its own compulsory health levy on residents, and a workers' compensation levy on employers. One of the grounds on which residency status can be denied – poor health – is said to be related to the Island's relatively poor capacity to finance the local hospital.

The 1979 Act, as we have seen, confers very wide responsibilities for government administration, provision of services and other public functions on the Island. Norfolk is required, effectively, to govern itself as if it were a local, state and national government rolled into one. The powers of the Legislative Assembly have been significantly expanded in the last twenty-five years, creating increased demands upon government spending, without an accompanying expansion of the revenue base.

There are no constitutional limitations on Norfolk's power to pass laws imposing the same range of taxes as apply on the mainland. Provided the laws comply with the conditions set out in the Norfolk Island Act 1979, and are not either inconsistent with a Commonwealth Act, or purport to bind the Commonwealth, the Legislative Assembly's powers are not otherwise limited. The principal (and, it must be said, obvious) reason for Norfolk's particular choice of revenue base lies in the 'culture' of resisting mainland taxes. The absence of income and company tax is a significant reason, at least for some, for choosing to reside on Norfolk. In the words of the 1976 Royal Commission, '[i]t is fair to say that residents of non-Pitcairn lineage (with a few notable exceptions . . .) are there predominantly for the monetary advantages which the business opportunities and taxation status of the Island afford them'.[68] There is no evidence that this pattern has substantially altered since that time.

66 Commonwealth Grants Commission, *Report on Norfolk Island* (Canberra: Australian Government Publishing Service [AGPS], 1997).

67 The absence of unemployment benefits draws attention to Norfolk's relatively low level of unemployment, which is partly explained by the fact that holders of temporary working visas are required to leave the Island when work is no longer available.

68 *Report of the Royal Commission*, 1976, 46. Tax evasion also occurs on Norfolk itself, as noted in a Commonwealth Grants Commission Report on Norfolk Island, note 67.

While some social security needs are met by through family assistance and charity, and others are pre-empted by the restrictive immigration policy, the aging of the Islanders, and the declining numbers of children under 15 among the population, have raised significant concerns. A 2005 report noted that these demographic trends have been more 'dramatic' on Norfolk than in other parts of Australia, while public health infrastructure, including aged care facilities, were in a 'sad state'.[69] The capacity to meet current needs, let alone provide for increased future demands, is poor. At the same time, the already-limited sources of revenue are under threat; tourism is declining, and revenue raised by the financial institutions levy has dropped in recent years, due to businesses choosing to bank 'offshore' and other tax mobility strategies.

Several reports[70] have drawn attention to the parlous financial situation on Norfolk and the unsustainability of current fiscal strategies. Even factoring in the uniqueness of the Island 'and taking into account [its] special circumstances', one report stated, the conclusion was inevitable that Norfolk residents were unable to enjoy services and support comparable to the community standard in other parts of Australia.[71] Norfolk, however, has frequently resisted this view. In 2009, in response to a further inquiry conducted by the Joint Standing Committee on the National Capital and External Territories, the Norfolk Government reaffirmed the Island's history of self-reliance and highlighted the achievements in self-government since 1979, as compared both to its previous condition under direct Commonwealth governance, and the Commonwealth-governed Indian Ocean Territories. The Commonwealth's plans for reform on Norfolk, the paper asserted, were 'ideological' and 'unlikely to achieve the kind of results which history has shown can readily be achieved by co-operative partnership' between the Island and the Australian authorities.[72] Norfolk's unique 'sustainable and self-supporting' practices and structures, and 'its sound economic performance and [. . .] flexible immigration regime [. . .] allow for effective movement of temporary workers to and from the Island'.[73] Education, social services and medical facilities, it claimed, were superior to those offered in comparable Australian communities, and in many areas, services were of a much higher standard.

The Commonwealth was not convinced. The 2005 parliamentary Joint Standing Committee concluded that Norfolk had virtually no internal capacity to raise more revenue; it recommended both a reform in governance (albeit without revoking self-government) and bringing Norfolk under the Commonwealth

[69] Joint Standing Committee, *Norfolk Island: Financial Sustainability*, 26.

[70] Ibid.; Commonwealth Grants Commission, 'Review of the Financial Capacity of Norfolk Island', Issues Paper, Canberra, March 2006. Acumen Alliance, *Norfolk Island Government Financial Advisory Report* (November 2005).

[71] Ibid., 7.

[72] Government of Norfolk Island, Submission 16, Joint Standing Committee on the National Capital and External Territories inquiry into the changing economic environment in the Indian Ocean Territories, 5 June 2009, 2.

[73] Ibid., 3.

taxation system, with the Commonwealth resuming responsibility for social security, health and aged care, census, immigration, customs and quarantine.[74] The Committee observed that it 'is concerned that an argument of "difference" on Norfolk Island has underlined an acceptance of below-standard service provision and infrastructure'.[75]

Not surprisingly, Norfolk Islanders disagreed. While accepting the challenges inherent in (among others) an aging population, many continue to believe that the community's preference for a simple lifestyle and the culture of voluntary service, mutual aid and philanthropy have not been adequately appreciated; they challenge the implication that that they are 'second class citizens' as a consequence of their culture.[76]

The Commonwealth Committee report noted that,

> Island responses to the question of financial sustainability have been intrinsically linked to the question of self-government and independence. Proponents of what could be termed 'Norfolk independence' have vehemently pursued policies which call for greater economic self-sufficiency for Norfolk Island.

Among these policies, granting rights to fishing and oil exploration, allowing the (re-) development of a private university and establishing Norfolk Island 'as an offshore financial centre' have been proposed by Norfolk. The Commonwealth Treasury has not responded favourably. As the Committee noted, it was concerned 'about the potential impact such ventures would have on Australia's revenue base, especially in relation to any opportunities for other Australian tax payers to use the Island to reduce their tax obligations'.[77]

In mid 2005 the Norfolk government announced that it would impose a broad-based consumption tax (the 'Norfolk Sustainability Levy'), to replace the various customs, airport, accommodation and banking levies presently collected. The tax was to be on trial for six months on a revenue-neutral basis, ultimately to be used for funding services. However, there was considerable opposition to the proposal, both on the Island and the mainland; among other things, it was thought liable to discourage tourism. The proposal was dropped.

In 2006, the Australian Bureau of Statistics surveyed the Island's private sector businesses, finding, among other things, that tourism – a faltering concern – represented 71 per cent of business income and 68 per cent of private sector employment.[78] While the Commonwealth Grants Commission concluded in the same year that Norfolk had the capacity to meet its service and infra structure needs through internal financial restructuring, in February 2006, at a

[74] Joint Standing Committee, *Norfolk Island: Financial Sustainability.*

[75] Ibid., 27. [76] Ibid., 45. [77] Ibid.

[78] Australian Bureau of Statistics 2006, *Norfolk Island Business Statistics 2004–05*, Cat. No. 8139.0, ABS, Canberra. The recent decline is recorded in a comparison with the estimated contribution of tourism to around 90 per cent of the economy by the Joint Standing Committee on the National Capital and External Territories, *Norfolk Island: Financial Sustainability.*

meeting with the Commonwealth Minister for Territories, the Norfolk Legislative Assembly was told that Norfolk's current governance was unsustainable, and that two alternatives faced the Island: either modified self-government with increased Commonwealth powers, or a local government type arrangement, with the Commonwealth assuming many responsibilities for services.

In response, Norfolk proposed a referendum on the Island's future. The Commonwealth rejected the proposal, and the Chief Minister, Geoff Gardner, in return released a statement condemning the Commonwealth. The 'Canberra bureaucracy', Gardner said, was resentful of 'the Norfolk Island approach [that had] created an independent and sustainable community on different lines to those followed in mainland Australia'.[79] In early April 2006, he commenced proceedings in the High Court of Australia seeking a determination on the Island's constitutional status and a declaration of invalidity of the 2004 amendments to the 1979 Act with respect to electoral law. It was, Gardner said, '[i]n the interests of good governance, [that] we seek to rectify this denial of democratic rights'.[80] The Commonwealth proceeded, however, and in 2010, as we have seen, began the process of constitutional reform on the Island.

Non-fiscal relations with the Commonwealth

Norfolk's main exchanges with the Commonwealth are with the Commonwealth Minister for Territories via the Administrator. Norfolk is unrepresented on Australia's peak inter-governmental forum at which major national issues are discussed – the Council of Australian Governments.[81] The Norfolk government does have some limited representation on other inter-governmental bodies: of Australia's forty or so Ministerial Councils, Norfolk is represented (with observer status) on the Education, Employment, Training and Youth Affairs Ministerial Council; the Immigration and Multicultural Affairs Ministerial Council; and the Tourism Ministerial Council. It has full membership (through the Norfolk Minister for Health and Environment) on the Ministerial Council on Gambling.

Norfolk holds certain Memoranda of Understanding with mainland governments; for example, with the government of New South Wales regarding the provision of educational services (trained teachers are supplied, the NSW schools curriculum is followed on the Island and upper-level school examinations are conducted by NSW). Temporary MOUs are struck from time to time; for example, in 1995, prior to the coming into force of a legislative amendment designed to circumvent a 'potential loophole'[82] in Norfolk law, whereby

[79] Denis Peters, 'Norfolk Island way "to be lost",' AAP report, 21 February 2006.
[80] Australian Associated Press, news, 12 April 2006.
[81] Consisting of the Prime Minister, State Premiers, the Chief Ministers of the Northern Territory and the ACT, as well as a representative of the Australian Local Government Association.
[82] HREOC, *Territorial Limits*, 30.

a prohibited migrant on Norfolk might validly apply for refugee status on the mainland.

Without a Member for Norfolk in the House of Representatives, or a Norfolk Senator, there is no Commonwealth political representative for the Islanders. The Administrator does not play this role; he or she is appointed by the Commonwealth, and sits between the Norfolk government and the Commonwealth Minister for Territories. This lack of representation is incompatible with the Commonwealth's view that citizens on Norfolk should enjoy comparable conditions to those in the rest of Australia. At the same time, the paradox for Norfolk lies in the fact that the Island's resistance to 'integration', including the reluctance of its population to vote in Commonwealth elections, deprives the Island of avenues for representing its own interests and asserting its autonomy. Its preference for isolation and its repeated assertions of exceptionalism have the potential to undermine, rather than strengthen, long-standing autonomy arrangements.

Self-government and independence

Reports into aspects of Norfolk's life have repeatedly drawn attention to the problems associated with self-government in such a small community. These problems lie along several lines – in the difficulties of managing numerous, quasi-national legislative responsibilities, and in local resistance to recognised principles of good government. The Island, it has been noted, has had few modern mechanisms of accountability and transparency: there are almost no codes of conduct, registers of pecuniary and non-pecuniary interests,[83] or offices of Auditor-General or Ombudsman.[84] The Australian Bureau of Statistics does not normally collect statistics on Norfolk, and the Island's statistical records and data collection are manifestly inadequate.

Maintaining a meaningful separation of powers is almost impossible, not merely because of the small pool of willing candidates for office, but because of the difficulty of separating political from daily life. Positions on the Legislative Assembly are part-time. The fact that members live and work in the general community raises concerns not merely about time commitment, but also about

[83] The only exception is Section 39(3) of the 1979 Act which disqualifies a Norfolk MLA who is party to or has direct interest in a Commonwealth contract for goods or services from taking part in a discussion of the matter, or voting on a question that relates directly or indirectly to that contract.

[84] Joint Standing Committee, *Inquiry into Governance on Norfolk Island*, 48. An Administrative Review Tribunal has been established, however, to allow review of certain administrative decisions made by Island officials. Its President is the Chief Magistrate of the ACT. The 1979 Norfolk Island Act also establishes a Public Account of Norfolk Island, and requires the appointment of a registered auditor to conduct annual Audits, reporting to the Norfolk Administrator and the Legislative Assembly. This requirement, however, appears not to have been followed, and until 2010, Norfolk was largely permitted to set its own auditing standards. See Hanks, *Australian Constitutional Law*, 1121.

the potential for conflict of interest. Evidence to the 2003 Joint Standing Committee given by one Islander demonstrates the lack of understanding of this problem. The Committee was told that,

> in many ways, [Norfolk has] checks and balances in play. The electorate here is pretty close [. . .] [I]f you are out shopping and the Chief Minister goes by you can grab him by the collar. You can walk straight into his office. You have accessibility that is unheard of elsewhere.[85]

The small size of the community encourages much co-operation and communal activity. It also discourages the cleavages and diversity of views that are important in modern systems of government in generating criticism, proposals for reform and, ultimately, change. Despite its Westminster-style government, Norfolk has no political parties. All members are elected as Independents, and there is no official Opposition in the Legislative Assembly. It is said that this arrangement reflects a culture of unity and common purpose, but pressure not only against change, but also against promoting change, is an underlying and repeated theme in official reports and visitors' accounts. The 2003 Joint Standing Committee inquiry into governance was uncompromising in its condemnation of the atmosphere of intimidation and the fear of reprisals that, it concluded, made many in the community reluctant to give evidence critical of current practices, or willing only to give evidence in confidence.[86] The Committee went so far as to observe that suppression of ideas and discouragement of participation in Island life undermined Norfolk's capacity for self-government.[87]

In August 2006, members of the Commonwealth Parliament's Joint Standing Committee on the National Capital and External Territories visited Norfolk 'to engage in discussions with the Norfolk Island community on matters of concern, particularly in light of foreshadowed changes to the Island's governance arrangements'.[88] The Committee noted that there had been 'strained relations in the recent past', alongside a willingness to 'move forward in [a] productive fashion'.[89] The Norfolk government, it recognised, 'did not share the Commonwealth's views on the need for change' and the Islanders 'wished to maintain control of their own affairs'. It also acknowledged that the Norfolk government disputed the accuracy of the 2005 findings on the parlous state of the Island's finances, claiming, among other things, that the report's costings were 'predicated on assumptions that did not apply to Norfolk', and that any existing shortfalls could be rectified over time without intervention from

85 Joint Standing Committee, *Inquiry into Governance on Norfolk Island*, 50.

86 The closed and close-knit nature of the community was tragically illustrated by the Norfolk response to the brutal murder of a young woman who was working on the Island on a temporary visa, in 2003. Although the identity of all suspects was well known, an arrest was not made until 2006.

87 Joint Standing Committee, *Inquiry into Governance on Norfolk Island*, 15.

88 Foreword, Parliament of the Commonwealth of Australia, *Report on the visit to Norfolk Island*, September 2006.

89 Ibid., 6.

the mainland. The idea of adopting Commonwealth taxation, the Committee noted, received little support. In addition, 'freedom from Australian customs duties was highlighted as one of the attractions' of Norfolk. Norfolk's duty free status, it was claimed on the Island, 'was essential to the economic viability of the [. . .] community'.[90]

The Commonwealth Committee observed that much of the Island's infra structure was inadequate or old and in need of repair. They noted disagreement in the community about the adequacy of social services, at the same time as,

> widespread hostility to the introduction of mainland-style unemployment benefits, which it was believed would undermine the work ethic of the community; and positive abhorrence at the prospect of Norfolk Island becoming a destination for unemployed mainlanders looking for somewhere to 'drop out'.[91]

The Committee's Report, however, confirmed the Commonwealth's view both that the people of Norfolk should enjoy the benefits offered to other Australians and that they should share the same responsibilities, albeit implemented 'in a way that is sensitive to the unique circumstances of Norfolk Island'. The Committee also rejected the Island's claim that its control over immigration (and, thus, exclusion of Australian migration laws) was 'essential to protect their unique identity'.[92] At the time of writing, however, reform of immigration laws has not been implemented.

Degree of autonomy

If the test of autonomy lies in the power of a region to amend or otherwise control its own constitution – and if the test of the latter lies in immunity from outside interference in law-making – then Norfolk fails. However, this is a formalist test, which ignores the political and historical process through which many of Britain's former colonies (including those that joined together to form the Commonwealth of Australia in 1901) acquired self-government in the nineteenth century, evolving into Dominions in the early twentieth century, and ultimately gaining full independence. Along the way, notwithstanding formal powers suggesting the contrary, they arrived at a position where it would have been politically inconceivable for Britain to have exercised its powers of interference in their law-making. Constitutional change, at a number of points, *followed* rather than preceded the assumption of independence. For many decades Australia itself was, technically, not free from British paramountcy,[93] and yet it acted as if it were.

[90] Ibid., 12. [91] Ibid., 14. [92] Ibid., 16.

[93] The Commonwealth Constitution still contains provisions – ss. 58 to 60 – through which the Governor-General, acting as the Queen's representative, or the Queen herself, is empowered to disallow Australian laws. These are regarded as 'dead letters' now, due to the effect of the Statute of Westminster, 1931.

The question whether the Australian government could repeal the Norfolk Act, withdrawing self-government and re-instating direct rule, cannot be answered merely from a formal legal perspective. Legally, the answer is yes, but politically it is far from clear. Since 1979, the many Commonwealth inquiries conducted into the Island have almost all concluded unfavourably about one or more aspects of Norfolk's law or system of governance. With the exception of the 2004 amendment to the electoral law, however, almost none of the recommendations for reform have been activated. The Commonwealth Executive's powers to disallow a Norfolk law within six months of its enactment (under Section 23 of the Norfolk Island Act) have not been invoked. The Commonwealth has been extremely reluctant to appear to interfere in Norfolk business. The most recent initiative, the 2010 Territories Reform Act, may represent a break from this pattern. At the same time, the Act offers 'inducements' to internal reform and enhancement of self-government, rather than its diminution. It neither threatens a takeover nor even targeted micromanagement, and under it, the conditions attached to financial aid will remain subject to Commonwealth negotiation with Norfolk.

The size of Norfolk's population has created many fiscal and administrative difficulties. The 2003 report of the Commonwealth's Joint Standing Committee on the National Capital and External Territories concluded, as we saw, that the Island's responsibilities of government and administration were too great for its small population: 'Norfolk Island is in deep and growing trouble and needs help'.[94] It recommended major reforms in the institutions of elections and governance, as well as in health, social welfare and immigration policy. It did not, however, recommend re-integration into the Commonwealth. The 'trouble' that it forecast has now arrived but, Norfolk fears notwithstanding, direct rule from Canberra is still highly unlikely.

Paradoxically, the Island's tiny size has also been advantageous for the defenders of self-government. For most of its history, Norfolk has been treated by the rest of Australia as simply too small, too poor and too undemanding to be of great significance. In addition, a long line of fierce and persistent individuals has created a reputation for obstreperousness among the Islanders. Several influential and wealthy residents – notably the internationally popular novelist, Colleen McCulloch – have been powerful voices in promoting what they consider to be its interests.

At the same time, there is sufficient interest on the part of the Commonwealth in the Island's historical ties with Australia, as well as in its potential usefulness, for the Commonwealth to be unwilling to let it go. So long as Norfolk does not resist or obstruct Australia's foreign policy and external relations, the Commonwealth has little incentive to interfere in a dramatic way, with every likelihood of adverse publicity if it attempted to do so. With the 2010 Act, the Commonwealth has come closest to forcing its hand. However, the Commonwealth's current

[94] *Inquiry into Governance on Norfolk Island*, vi.

reforms appear more attuned to maximising Norfolk community control over its own government, than standardising Norfolk practices with the rest of Australia. The message to Norfolk appears to be that a demonstration of sound (or at least, better) financial management and executive responsibility will be sufficient to keep the Commonwealth's hands off the Island's non-fiscal cultural practises.

Conclusion

The Commonwealth has recognised that erosion of services and infrastructure on Norfolk will continue to deepen without reform, and Norfolk seems finally to have accepted this conclusion. The majority of Australians are also likely to accept the Commonwealth's reforms. They may bristle, however, at Commonwealth spending on a community that makes virtually no contribution to Commonwealth revenue, and will find it hard to accept that a prohibition on paying income tax is genuinely 'cultural'. However, so long as Norfolk's culture appears otherwise benign,[95] the Island's insistence on its historical right to self-government will offend few members of the wider public and may win some admiration. Indeed, the Island's plight has already attracted sympathy in the Australian media. A 2011 Australian Broadcasting Corporation television report on the recent reforms – entitled 'Paradise Lost' – opened with the reporter describing Norfolk as:

> a carefree and unique location, with its own laws and customs. It flies its own flag and wearing seatbelts is optional, but waving 'G'day' at your neighbour is not. It's [. . .] a place where paying income tax and rates is unheard of and livestock have right of way on the road.

The programme quoted the current Chief Minister and some local business people in support of fiscal reforms, but highlighted the 'betrayal' many Islanders felt. Ric Robinson, from the Society of Pitcairn Descendants, for example, claimed,

> You want the money, here's the trade-off, and that's our self-government gone down the gurgler [. . .] All one hundred and ninety-three [sic] people came here to live from Pitcairn. Since then, we've been recognised by the UN as the Indigenous people of Norfolk. It's our homeland [. . .] We're gonna lose our

[95] A comparison with modern day Pitcairn Island is difficult to avoid here. In 2004, after decades of neglect, British authorities took action against a dozen men – around half the adult population, including many leaders in the Pitcairn community – for sexual offences against under-age girls committed over decades on the Island. The Pitcairners claimed, among other things, that their activities were part of the Island's culture, and that they were not subject to British laws. Their challenge to British jurisdiction was unsuccessful. Norfolk's own 'scandal' following a murder in 2002 drew attention to unsavory sexual relations on the Island, but these were between consenting adults and cultural practises were not implicated. To the relief of the Island community, when an arrest was finally made in early 2006, the accused, subsequently convicted, was found to be a New Zealander.

> culture, and that's all mixed up with our way of life. And that would be more than just sad, it'd be a calamity.[96]

In return, it may be said that, combined with geographical isolation, the culture and traditional practices themselves have eroded the very capacity for sustainable autonomy that is so central to this way of thinking. This would not, however, be the first time that such things have been said of Norfolk. It cannot be imagined, whatever is resolved regarding Norfolk's status in 2011, that this will be the last word for this strange and troubled place.

[96] ABC, 7.30 Report, 27 May 2011.

7

The autonomy of Catalonia

The unending search for a place within pluralist Spain

Carlos Flores Juberías

With a population of 7.5 million (19.8 per cent born in other regions of Spain; 17.3 per cent originating outside the country), Catalonia is one of Spain's most populous and ethnically diverse territories. Of its 3.8 million strong labour force, 69.7 per cent work in the service industries. GDP was €209.727 million in 2011, while GDP per capita was well above €28,000. An annual growth rate of between 3.2 and 3.7 per cent prior to the recent financial crisis shows that Catalonia has one of Spain's most dynamic and globalised economies. With 93.7 per cent of the population able to understand both Catalan and Spanish, 72 per cent able to speak and read the former, a computer literacy rate of 73 per cent, and 233,000 college-level students, Catalonia is among Spain's most educated, developed and pluralist societies.[1]

For the purpose of this chapter, however, what is most significant is that for several hundred years, including the last thirty-seven years of Spanish democracy, Catalonia has been at the forefront of the struggle for autonomy and a system of territorial organisation that respects the different characters of the territories which make up what Article 2 of the 1978 Constitution refers to as 'the common and indivisible homeland of all Spaniards'. In addition, it has worked to improve the efficiency of the Spanish state and has participated in efforts to make Spain's democratic governance more genuinely participatory. The intensity of Catalonia's involvement in the transition to democracy and in the constitution-making process during the second half of the seventies,[2] as well as in the development of the 'Estado de las Autonomías' over the last three and a half decades, have both reflected the region's demands for greater self-government and also acted as a critical example for less influential Spanish territories engaged in similar processes.

However, in recent years major challenges to the legal order and widespread civil discontent have emerged in Catalonia. The Catalan legislature has engaged

[1] These figures are from the *Generalitat de Catalunya* (online at www.gencat.cat/gencat_dades/, accessed 1 July 2011).

[2] For a broad perspective on the issue, see José Antonio González Casanova, 'Cataluña en la construcción del Estado español' [Catalonia in the building up of the Spanish state], 54/55 *Cuadernos constitucionales de la Cátedra Fadrique Furió Ceriol* (2006), 125–144, who refers to the 1978 Constitution as '*la constitución de los catalanes*'.

in efforts to enact constitutional reform through revision of its Statute of Autonomy and is now proposing a popular referendum on self determination. Calls to disobey Constitutional Court resolutions, and even the questioning of the Court's role as guarantor of the rule of law no longer raise eyebrows; reluctance to fly the national flag has become open resistance to doing so; and while historic lows in voter turnout have been recorded for key legal referendums and elections, senior government officials have been eager to participate in informal polls on independence which have no legal basis or procedural guarantees.

This chapter's analysis of how Catalonia has achieved self-government begins with a brief historical overview of its path to autonomy, outlines the constitutional framework for autonomy and the manner in which it was developed through the 1979 and 2006 Statutes of Autonomy and continues with a description of Catalonia's institutions and their powers. The discussion of key issues, such as the region's relationship to the state, its international position, finance and the use of conflict resolution mechanisms will complete this summary overview of Catalonia's unfinished search for a place within pluralist Spain.[3]

The historical origins of Catalan autonomy

Unlike other autonomous European enclaves created by international treaty, which came into being as a result of external pressure from a neighbouring state, or whose existence has been justified by the presence of a separate ethnic group, Catalonia's autonomy is grounded in a centuries-long tradition of self-government, recognised and protected by the present Spanish Constitution, and supported by the conviction of most Spaniards that self-government is compatible with national unity and is an appropriate way of accommodating the rich diversity of its territories.

As with several other Spanish medieval kingdoms, the origins of Catalonia's institutions of self-government can be traced back to the late fourteenth century and the General Council, or *Deputació del General*. This body was created to provide for the collection of taxes on trade applicable to the entire population, hence the name '*Generalitat*'. Following the extinction of the House of Barcelona in 1410 and the establishment of a new dynasty, the General Council significantly increased its powers, to the detriment of the king, eventually resulting in conflict breaking out. The ensuing war, from 1462 to 1472, exposed the weaknesses and oligarchic nature of the General Council, and resulted in the consolidation of royal primacy in the person of Ferdinand II – probably the first absolute monarch in European history – who introduced new governmental institutions

[3] For a broader perspective on the regulation of autonomy in Spain, putting the Catalan case in its proper context, see Carlos Flores Juberías, 'Regionalization and autonomy in Spain: the making of the "Estado de las Autonomías",' in Markku Suksi, (ed.), *Autonomy: Applications and Implications* (Doordrecht: Kluwer Law International, 1998), 195–221.

that he controlled more directly, and reformed older ones, such as Barcelona's local self-government assembly – the *Consell de Cent*, originally composed of one hundred citizens – and the *Generalitat*.

Throughout the sixteenth century, the first Habsburg Kings paid little regard to the *Corts*, or Parliament, and convened them more and more rarely. By contrast, the *Generalitat* grew in size and complexity, though its main function continued to be tax collection. Since the imperial ambitions of the monarchs required a permanent source of revenue, which could only be provided by an increasingly voracious tax system, conflict was not long in developing. Pressure on the *Generalitat* from Philip IV intensified, culminating in the peasants' revolt of 1640, the so-called *Corpus de Sang*. The subsequent *Guerra dels Segadors* and the Pact of Ceret separated Catalonia from the Spanish crown and brought it under the protection of France as a republic. The Treaty of the Pyrenees in 1659 returned Catalonia to Spain, but the Catalan territories Roselló, Conflent, Vallespir and a part of the Cerdanya were relinquished and ceded to France. As the power of the *Generalitat* declined it became largely subservient to the King's viceroys and ceased to represent Catalonia's interests.

Following the *Decreto de Nueva Planta*, the Reorganisation Decree, issued by Phillip V on 16 January 1716 in retaliation against Catalonia's support for his opponent Archduke Charles of Austria in the war of succession arising from the dissolution of the Spanish branch of the Habsburg dynasty, Catalonia's self-governing institutions were abolished. The triumphant Bourbon monarchs suppressed the particularities of the Catalan legal system and set in place a political system that excluded representation for the Catalans, abolishing both the *Generalitat* and Barcelona's *Consell de Cent*.

Spain's War of Independence (1808–14), the abolition of the absolute monarchy, and the emergence of liberalism in the first half of the nineteenth century did not immediately lead to self-government or the restoration of Catalonia's institutions. In 1833, in Jacobin fashion, new provinces and Provincial Councils, *Diputaciones provinciales*, were created, dividing Catalonia into the four administrative units of Barcelona, Lleida, Girona and Tarragona that still exist today, continuing the trend towards centralisation and homogenisation. Civil and military governors, directly appointed from Madrid, became the key power holders.

As in the Basque Country, and to a lesser extent in Galicia and Valencia, it was not until late in the nineteenth century that Catalan nationalism began to develop momentum, generating demands not only for changes in the political practices of the constitutional monarchy, but also for self-government.[4] The promulgation of the *Manresa Bases* – a framework for the drafting of a

[4] On this period, see José A. González Casanova, *Federalismo y autonomía: Cataluña y el estado español, 1868–1938* [Federalism and autonomy: Catalonia and the Spanish State, 1868–1938] (Barcelona: Crítica, 1979), and Borja de Riquer i Permanyer and Josep Fontana i Lázaro, *Lliga regionalista: la burguesia catalana i el nacionalisme (1893–1904)* [The Regionalist League: Catalan bourgeoisie and nationalism (1893–1904)] (Barcelona: Edicions 62, 1977).

future Catalan constitution – in 1892; the creation of the *Lliga Regionalista* in 1901; the creation of the Institute of Catalan Studies in 1907; and, finally, the institution of the Commonwealth of Catalonia, *Mancomunitat*, in 1914, were all significant advances in Catalonia's bid for self-government. The latter was created shortly after a Decree dated 12 December 1913 had made it possible for the Provincial Councils of the regions to associate and share administrative responsibilities. This included the creation of an Assembly, a Presidency, which went at first to Enric Prat de la Riba and then to Josep Puig i Cadafalch, and an Executive Council, where each province was represented by two delegates. Though it possessed only limited powers and scarce resources, its uniqueness and its status as the sole representative of the Catalan people, with support from Catalan nationalists and strong leadership from Prat de la Riba, ensured a lasting influence on the development of Catalan autonomy.[5]

The abolition of the Commonwealth by General Primo de Rivera in 1925 encouraged Catalan nationalist parties to strengthen co-operation with Socialists, Republicans and other regionalist groups, who were in favour of the formation of a republic. The proclamation of the Second Republic on 14 April 1931 was matched by the simultaneous declaration of a 'Catalan Republic as a state of the Iberian Federation' by Francesc Macià, leader of the Republican Left of Catalonia, then the leading party in the region. Macià reached an agreement with the provisional government of the Republic by which the new regime would immediately grant and guarantee autonomy to Catalonia, and restore the *Generalitat* within the framework of a Statute of Autonomy.

Consequently, the 1931 republican Constitution established a 'comprehensive state', *Estado integral*, which was declared 'compatible with the autonomy of municipalities and regions', thus laying the foundation for the approval of specific Statutes of Autonomy, with Catalonia being the first of the territories to support this development. The so-called *Estatut de Nuria*, already drafted by mid 1931, was supported by 99.45 per cent of Catalan voters on a 75 per cent election turnout. On 9 September 1932, it was approved by the national legislature, but only after undergoing a substantial reduction in scope, and was finally put into effect without further ratification by the Catalan electorate.[6] Following the October 1934 revolution and the aborted proclamation of the Catalan state by President of the *Generalitat*, Lluís

[5] See Alberto Balcells González, Enric Pujol and Jordi Sabater, *La Mancomunitat de Catalunya i l'autonomia* [The Commonwealth of Catalonia and autonomy] (Barcelona: Proa, 1996) and Jordi Llorens, *La Mancomunitat de Catalunya: 1914–1925*, [The Commonwealth of Catalonia: 1914–1925] (Barcelona: Barcanova, 1994).

[6] On the 1932 Statute, see Manuel Gerpe Landín, *L'Estatut d'Autonomia de Catalunya i l'Estat integral* [The Statute of Autonomy for Catalonia and the integral State] (Barcelona: Edicions 62, 1977), and Rafael Palomero, *República i autonomía: La Generalitat republicana* (1931–1936) [Republic and autonomy: the republican Generalitat (1931–1936)], (Barcelona: Barcanova, 1991). On the preceding constitutional debate, see Francisco Astarloa Villena, *Región y religión en las Constituyentes de 1931* [Region and religion in the constitution-making process of 1931] (Valencia: Universidad de Valencia, 1976).

Companys, the Statute was suspended, but then restored in February 1936 after the Popular Front electoral victory. After Franco's entry into Barcelona in January 1939 it was nullified, though a Catalan government in exile maintained the symbolic existence of Catalan self-government until its effective restoration in 1977.[7]

Constitutional framework: problems of an open-ended model

The need for a new political system followed General Franco's death in November 1975. At that time, the call for autonomy was voiced with the same force, if not with more passion, as claims for party pluralism, free elections, government accountability, political rights and amnesty for political prisoners. Although demands for self-government were widespread in such territories as Catalonia and the Basque Country, and to a lesser extent Galicia, Valencia and Andalusia, the rest of the country was equally caught up in the desire for political change.[8] Autonomy became not only a demand by those who wanted to redress past wrongs and recover their cultural identity, but also a goal for those who saw it as a means to enhance the process of democratisation and draw the government more closely to the people.

A direct consequence of these new political demands was the creation of provisional autonomous institutions across a number of territories. Even before the Constitution was agreed upon, these institutions went to work, despite insufficient resources and the lack of a clear legal framework.[9] Just as the building of a parliamentary democracy and the introduction of political rights began well before the Constitution was passed on 6 December 1978, also the actual formation of the autonomous communities influenced the eventual wording of the Constitution.[10]

During the constitution-making process it became clear that neither the Union of the Democratic Center (UCD) in government, nor the Socialist Party (PSOE) in opposition, and not even the nationalist parties from Catalonia, the Basque Country (PNV) and other regions that had gained parliamentary representation after the June 1977 elections had a clear vision of how the

[7] Literature in English on Catalan nationalism and the desire for self-government is abundant. See, among others, Albert Balcells, *Catalan Nationalism: past and present* (St. Martin's Press, 1996), and Josep R. Llobera, *Foundations of national identity: from Catalonia to Europe* (New York/Oxford: Berghahn Books, 2005).

[8] See Maria Montserrat Guibernau, *Catalan Nationalism: Francoism, Transition and Democracy* (London: Routledge, 2004).

[9] Such institutions were created, in every case by means of a government-issued Royal Decree Law, in Catalonia (29 September 1977), the Basque Country (4 January 1978), Galicia (16 March 1978), Aragon, the Canary Islands and the *País Valencià* (17 March 1978), Andalusia (27 April 1978), the Balearic Islands (13 June 1978), Extremadura and Castile-Leon (13 June 1978), Asturias and Murcia (27 June 1978) and Castile-La Mancha (31 October 1978). See Juan Ferrando Badía, 'Las comunidades preautonómicas' [The pre-autonomic communities], 2 *Revista de Estudios Regionales* (1980), 203–39.

[10] Francisco Rubio Llorente, 'The writing of the Constitution of Spain', in *Constitution Makers on Constitution Making* (Washington, DC: American Enterprise Institute, 1988), 239–65.

territorial structure of the Spanish state ought to be constituted, let alone the power to impose it on the other players. With the need to achieve the widest possible consensus on the issue, the drafting of the constitutional provisions referring to the autonomous communities, which became Title VIII of the Constitution, became one of the most complex challenges of the constitution-making process, and its outcome one of the most ambiguous and disputed parts of the 1978 Constitution.[11]

In essence, the UCD was prepared to recognise some form of self-government for Catalonia, Galicia and the Basque Country, as long as it did not involve a radical transformation of the state organisation as a whole, although some regional leaders made it clear that they would only support this position if avenues for access to autonomy became feasible for their own territories. On the other hand, socialists and communists were in favour of a uniform federal model providing self-government for all, even though at this point the Catalan socialists were more aligned with their nationalist opponents, who, along with Basque nationalists, demanded constitutional recognition of their historical rights and the restoration of the autonomy lost under the Franco regime. Nonetheless, they were ready to support the extension of autonomy to all regions provided the framework ensured adequate recognition of their uniqueness among the other the territories of the country.

The formula finally incorporated into Title VIII of the Constitution was the result of the marginalisation of the conservative right and the Basque nationalists – at some political cost, as the PNV continues to maintain that 'the Basques did not vote for the Constitution' – and a consensus of views between centrists, socialists and Catalan nationalists (always more pragmatic than their Basque counterparts), made possible by the inclusion of elements in the Constitution intended to satisfy all these parties, even at the cost of introducing further ambiguity.

Thus, the Constitution retained the existing provincial structure, as required by the UCD. Additionally, it opened the possibility of autonomy for all the territories and defined the legal basis for establishing a model of territorial self-government that could operate on patterns not so different from those of a federal state, as desired by the parties on the left. Finally, it also allowed a qualified autonomy exclusively to the so-called 'historical nationalities' whose 'historical rights' received explicit constitutional recognition by being granted the right to participate at the maximum level of self-government, as demanded by the nationalists.[12]

[11] See Pedro Cruz Villalón, 'La estructura del estado o la curiosidad del jurista persa' [The state's structure or the curiosity of the Persian lawyer], *Revista de la Facultad de Derecho de la Universidad Complutense* 4 (1982); and Laureano López Rodó, *En torno a la indefinición constitucional del modelo de Estado* [On the constitutional indefinition of the State model] (Madrid: Real Academia de Jurisprudencia y Legislación, 1984).

[12] See on the issue the controversial position of Miguel Herrero y Rodríguez de Miñón, *Derechos históricos y Constitución* [Historical rights and the Constitution] (Madrid: Taurus, 1998). Also, Francisco J. Corcuera Atienza and Miguel Á. García Herrera, *La constitucionalización de los*

The constituent assembly chose not to adopt any of the tested models of territorial self-government, such as a German type of federation, or an Italian type of regional state, thereby avoiding the risk of specifying the territorial form of the state. Instead, the constitution's drafters adopted a more pragmatic stance, declaring in Article 2 that the constitution guaranteed 'the right to self-government of the nationalities and regions of which [Spain] is composed', and that 'the indissoluble unity of the Spanish Nation, the common and indivisible homeland of all Spaniards' was the basis on which autonomy should be grounded. Article 143.1 defined which kind of territories could become autonomous, and in Articles 143.2, 144, and 151 prescribed various mechanisms for their development. They then decided to wait until the exercising of this right by the different territories provided a more precise profile of what the new state would look like.

The consequences of this open-ended constitutional arrangement have been manifold. It has generated a still unfinished debate among scholars on whether the so-called 'Estado de las Autonomías' is 'a politically decentralised unitary state',[13] a 'regional state',[14] a 'multi-regional state',[15] 'a decentralised state not too far in its structure from a federal state',[16] a 'unitary-federal state',[17] or a 'federal-regional state';[18] thus proving, in the words of Lucas Verdú, that it 'escapes any definition and any precise location in the classification of the forms of the state'.[19] More significantly, it has given way to a still ongoing, somewhat sterile and increasingly polarised debate between the two major parliamentary parties, and between successive governments in Madrid and the autonomous governments of Catalonia and the Basque Country. More than three decades after the Constitution was passed, the final formulation of the Spanish system of territorial self-government has still to be agreed upon.[20]

derechos históricos [The constitutionalisation of historical rights] (Madrid: CEPC, 2002); and Francisco J. Laporta San Miguel and Alejandro Sáiz Arnaiz, *Los derechos históricos en la Constitución* [Historical rights in the Constitution] (Madrid: CEPC, 2006).

13 Francisco Fernández Segado, *El sistema constitucional español* [The Spanish constitutional state] (Madrid: Dykinson, 1992), 867.

14 Juan Ferrando Badía, *El Estado unitario, el federal y el Estado autonómico* [The unitary, the federal and the autonomic State] (Madrid: Tecnos, 1986), 151.

15 Fernando Lasuén, *El Estado Multi-Regional* [The multi-regional State] (Madrid: Alianza, 1986).

16 Pablo Pérez Tremps, 'Principios generales de la organización territorial del Estado' [General principles of the State's territorial organization], in Luís López Guerra and others, *Derecho constitucional. Vol. II: Los poderes del Estado. La organización territorial del Estado* [Constitutional Law, Vol. II. The State's powers. The State's territorial organization] (Valencia: Tirant lo Blanch, 1994), 302.

17 José J. González Encinar, *El Estado Unitario-Federal. La Autonomía Como Principio Estructural del Estado* [The unitarian-federal state. Autonomy as a structural principle of the state] (Madrid: Tecnos, 1985).

18 Gumersindo Trujillo, 'Federalismo y regionalismo en la Constitución española de 1978: el Estado federo-regional' [Federalism and regionalism in the Spanish 1978 Constitution: the federal-regional state], in *Federalismo y regionalismo* (Madrid: Centro de Estudios Constitucionales, 1979), 13–51.

19 Pablo Lucas Verdú, 'El Estado autonómico' [The autonomic State], *Vida Nueva* (1981), 459.

20 On this issue, see the opinions of Manuel Jiménez de Parga, Manuel Aragón Reyes, Vicente Garrido Mayol, Lourdes López Nieto and others in 'El Modelo de Estado a debate' [Debating

Catalonia's Autonomy Statutes

Within the framework of the 1978 Constitution, Catalonia has enacted two Statutes of Autonomy.[21] The origins of the first can be traced to the first mobilisations sponsored by the *Assemblea de Catalunya* and the *Consell de Forces Polítiques de Catalunya*, which following General Franco's death demanded the re-establishment of the *Generalitat de Catalunya*, and the 1932 Statute.[22] After the success of nationalist, communist and socialist parties in Catalonia in the first democratic elections, held in June 1977, these demands gained considerable momentum and legitimacy. It was then that Prime Minister Suárez took the politically risky step of summoning to Madrid the President of the *Generalitat* in exile, Josep Tarradellas, and opened negotiations with him – not with the Assembly of Members of Parliament – on the formal re-establishment of the government of Catalonia. After nationalist demands for self-government took the form of massive street demonstrations on the of 11 September 1977 *Diada* national holiday, the Prime Minister issued an historic decree on 29 September provisionally re-establishing the *Generalitat de Catalunya* and naming Tarradellas President, and urged him to form a cabinet comprising members of the most representative parties in parliament. However, he did not go as far as to restore the 1932 Statute.

The Assembly, which included all Catalan deputies and senators, created a commission of experts, the 'Commission of Twenty', and authorized them to begin the drafting of a new Statute of Autonomy. The draft Statute, finalised after a series of meetings at the *Parador* of Vilanova de Sau, and subsequently known as the Sau Statute, was accepted by the parliamentary Assembly on 16 December 1978, approved by the Constitutional Commission of the national legislature on 13 August 1979, and accepted by Catalan voters in a referendum on 25 October.

The 1979 Statute was brief and concise: it was composed of just fifty-seven articles, seven additional and eight transitional provisions. Its Preamble declared Catalonia's wish to exercise 'the right to autonomy recognised in the Constitution and guaranteed to the nationalities and regions making up Spain' and proclaimed itself 'the expression of the collective identity of Catalonia'. It established the political principles on which Catalan autonomy was to be based (Articles 1–8), the powers to be assumed by the *Generalitat* (Articles 29–42),

the model of the state], *Cuadernos Constitucionales de la Cátedra Fadrique Furió Ceriol* 54/55 (2006), 65–230. See also Vicente Garrido Mayol, (ed.), *Modelo de Estado y reforma de los Estatutos* [The model of the state and statute reform] (Valencia: Fundación Broseta, 2007).

21 See Joaquín Tornos Mas, *Los estatutos de autonomía de Cataluña* [Catalonia's statutes of autonomy] (Madrid: Iustel, 2007).

22 On the 1979 Statute, see Jaume Sobrequés i Callicó, *Autonomia i democràcia a Catalunya: crònica política de la transició* [Autonomy and democracy in Catalonia: a political chronicle of transition] (Barcelona: Columna, 1986); Josep Pagès, *La autonomía política de Cataluña: orígenes, competencias y organización de la Generalidad* [The political autonomy of Catalonia: the origins, powers, and organization of the Generalitat] (Barcelona: Departament de la Presidència, 1996); and Josep M. Castellà, *La función constitucional del estatuto de autonomía de Cataluña* [The constitutional role of Catalonia's Statute of Autonomy] (Barcelona: Institut d'Estudis Autonòmics, 2004).

Table 7.1 Referendums on the Catalan Statutes of Autonomy*

Statute	Date	Registered voters (millions)	Turnout	For	Against	Blank	Null
1979	25 Oct.	4.421	2.639 (59.3%)	2.327 (88.15%)	0.204 (7.76%)	0.093 (3.55%)	0.012 (0.5%)
2006	18 June	5.310	2.594 (48.85%)	1.899 (73.90%)	0.533 (20.76%)	0.137 (5.34%)	0.023 (0.90%)

* All population figures are in millions.
Source: Congreso de los Diputados (online at *www.congreso.es/consti/elecciones/referendos/*, retrieved 1 July 2011).

the institutions that would articulate them (Articles 29–42), the financial system to be used (Articles 43–55) and the procedure for Statute reform (Articles 56–7). The 1979 Statute was widely supported by all major parliamentary parties, and was approved in a referendum by almost 90 per cent of the vote on a turnout of nearly 60 per cent (see Table 7.1).

By contrast, when the current Statute of Autonomy for Catalonia was submitted to a referendum, less than half the people voted. The Statute was approved on 18 June 2006 by a majority of 73.9 per cent, following a campaign during which three parliamentary parties – one of them in the government – had called for a 'No' vote. Prior to that, it had been approved in less than triumphant fashion by a 189 to 154 vote in the Congress of Deputies.

The 2006 Statute presents a stark contrast to its predecessor in terms of content, as well: it is extremely lengthy, comprising 223 articles, fifteen additional and four transitional provisions;[23] it is excessively detailed in everything but the regulation of the institutions of self-government; and it addresses issues that were largely, if not entirely, overlooked in the 1979 Statute, such as civil, social, political and linguistic rights, governing principles, judicial power and the institutional relations of the *Generalitat* with other Communities, the state and the European Union. Moreover, it establishes a very complex amendment process that may well transform most of its content into petrified law.[24]

23 By comparison, the Valencian Statute, passed in the same year, comprises just eighty-one articles, with four additional and five transitional provisions; and the Balearic Statute, passed immediately afterwards, has 139 articles, with six additional and eleven transitional provisions.

24 The 2006 Statute foresees two procedures for amendment. The first, regulated by Art. 222, is applicable to the reform of Titles I and II on the grounds that these do not affect the relations between Catalonia and the state. The initiative for reform lies with the Parliament of Catalonia and with the government of the *Generalitat*, and may also be proposed by 300,000 voters. Its approval requires a two-thirds vote in Parliament, the ratification by the *Cortes Generales* by means of an organic law, and approval in a referendum by the Catalan electorate. As for the rest of the Statute, Art. 223 states that reform may be initiated by the *Cortes Generales*, too, but not by the voters themselves; it contemplates the creation of a joint commission in the event of conflict between the Congress of Deputies or the Senate and the Parliament of Catalonia in

The drafting of this new Statute[25] was a direct consequence of the success of the Catalan left in the November 2003 elections, which allowed for the formation of a three-party coalition government led by the Party of the Catalan Socialists (PSC), the Republican Left of Catalonia (ERC) and Initiative for Catalonia-Greens-Alternative Left, sustained by a parliamentary agreement known as the Tinell Pact. The new leftist majority in the Catalan legislature was soon matched by another in the national legislature as a result of the electoral victory of the Socialist Party in the June 2004 parliamentary elections, which elevated José L. Rodríguez Zapatero to the office of Prime Minister. With the Socialists in control of the *Generalitat* and the central government, both the will and the opportunity to enact a new Statute coincided. The drafting of the new Statute was also a significant consequence of the ongoing process of redefinition of the Spanish model of territorial self-government, which had started to develop just as the first statutes entered into force, and which, as yet, has not been concluded.

Law professor and Constitutional Court Justice Manuel Aragón has convincingly argued that the development of the Spanish autonomy system has gone through three different phases.[26] The first, between 1979 and 1983, was characterised by the expansion of the framework of self-government to all the territories that wished to achieve autonomy, but also by differences in the institutional structures and powers of the Basque Country, Catalonia, Galicia, Andalusia and Navarre from communities in the rest of Spain, with Valencia and the Canary Islands comprising a third, intermediate group. The second phase began in 1992, with a new pact between the Socialist and the Popular parties. During this time, communities at the lowest levels of autonomy saw their powers increased up to the level enjoyed by more advanced autonomous communities through reform of their statutes, thus leading gradually to a substantial degree of uniformity in the system of territorial self-government. All statutes were subject to change only by agreement between the state and the communities themselves. The third phase began in 2003, with the failed attempt at the revision of the position of the Basque Country in the Spanish constitutional system by the unconstitutional 'Proposal for a New Political Statute for *Euskadi*' (more often

order 'to formulate a joint proposal by common agreement', and allows the Parliament, by an absolute majority of its members, to withdraw the proposal for reform 'at any time during presentation to the *Cortes Generales* and before this is definitively approved'.

It can be argued that this complex reform procedure not only turns the Statute into a virtually irreversible act, but transforms it into a sort of negotiated arrangement, or pact, between the Spanish and the Catalan legislatures, that cannot be amended without the consent of both, nor against the will of either, and certainly not against the wishes of the people of Catalonia, who in every case have the last word.

25 For details see Joan Vintró i Castells, 'El desarrollo del Estatuto de 1979 y la elaboración del Estatuto de 2006' [The legal development of the 1979 Statute and the making of the 2006 Statute], in Mercé Barceló i Serramalera and Joan Vintró i Castells, (eds.), *Derecho público de Cataluña* [Public Law of Catalonia] (Barcelona: Atelier, 2008), 77–118.

26 Manuel Aragón Reyes, 'La construcción del Estado autonómico' [The making of the autonomic State], *Cuadernos Constitucionales de la Cátedra Fadrique Furió Ceriol* 54/55 (2006), 75–95.

referred to as the 'Ibarretxe Plan'), which was defeated in Congress by the opposition of the Socialists and the Popular Party on 2 February 2005.[27] However, this new attempt at deepening existing autonomy institutions and testing the limits of the Constitution did have collateral effects: new Statutes of Autonomy, or substantial reforms of the existing ones, were passed in the Valencian Community (Organic Law 1/2006, 10 April), Catalonia (Organic Law 6/2006, 19 July), the Balearic Islands (Organic Law 1/2007, 28 February), Andalusia (Organic Law 2/2007, 19 March), Aragon (Organic Law 5/2007, 20 April), Castile-León (Organic Law 14/2007, 30 November), Navarre (Organic Law 7/2010, 27 October) and Extremadura (Organic Law 1/2011, 28 January). Similar attempts failed in several other communities, such as Galicia, the Canary Islands and Castile-La Mancha, due to a lack of political consensus.[28]

On 30 September 2005, the Catalonian Parliament, with the support of the three parties of the governing coalition, plus the coalition Convergence and Union (CiU), then the largest opposition force – joining the consensus only after concessions on education and finance issues – approved the reform proposal in a resounding 120 to 15 vote. However, this initial unity evaporated when the bill began to be debated in the Constitutional Affairs Committee of the national legislature: despite Prime Minister Zapatero's solemn promise to support any draft Statute approved by the Parliament of Catalonia, some sectors of the Socialist Party were reluctant to accept a Statute perceived by many as heavily favouring Catalonia, and there was a perception that the reform proposal contained provisions that were unconstitutional.[29] Internal conflict within the Socialist caucus in Congress fractured the joint strategy of the four Catalan parties that had supported the draft in the *Parlament*. A meeting between Spanish Prime Minister Zapatero and Catalan opposition leader Mas on 26 January 2006 led to a new pact and a significantly amended Statute, approved first by Congress on 30 March, and then by the Senate on 10 May.

[27] On the Ibarretxe Plan, see 'El Plan Ibarretxe a examen' [The Ibarretxe Plan, under review] *Cuadernos de Alzate: revista vasca de la cultura y las ideas* 28 (2003), 5–228, and Mariano Vivancos Comes, *La propuesta de nuevo estatuto político de la Comunidad de Euskadi. Análisis de un nuevo estatuto de segunda generación* [The proposal for a new political statute for the community of the Basque country. Analysis of a new second generation statute] (unpublished Ph.D. Thesis, Valencia, 2011).

[28] See, Carles Viver i Pi-Sunyer, Francisco Balaguer Callejón and Javier Tajadura Tejada, *La Reforma de los Estatutos de Autonomía: Con Especial Referencia al Caso de Cataluña* [The reform of the statutes of autonomy: with a special reference to the case of Catalonia] (Madrid: CEPC, 2005); Angel Luis Sanz Pérez, *La Reforma de los Estatutos de Autonomía: (Con Especial Referencia a los Estatutos de Autonomía de Cataluña y de la Comunidad Valenciana)* [The reform of the statutes of autonomy (with a special reference to the Statutes of Autonomy of Catalonia and the Valencian Community] (Cizur Menor: Thomson-Aranzadi, 2006) and the specific analysis of the Valencian, the Andalusian and the Galician cases contained in Vicente Garrido Mayol (ed.), *Modelo de Estado y reforma de los Estatutos* [The model of the state and statute reform], 131–260 and 305–62.

[29] César Colino, 'Constitutional change without constitutional reform: Spanish federalism and the revision of Catalonia's Statute of Autonomy', *Publius: the Journal of Federalism* 39:2 (2009), 262–88.

The consequence of this realignment of forces and the passing of this new version of the Statute was the abandonment of the tripartite government of Pasqual Maragall by ERC, and its realignment, albeit with radically diverging positions, with the Popular Party, which had been opposed to the Statute from the beginning. In a referendum held on 18 June 2006 the new Statute was approved by the people of Catalonia and came into effect on 9 August that year.

However, this was not the conclusion of the process: immediately after coming into effect, the new Statute was brought before the Constitutional Court. The deputies and senators of the Popular Party unearthed elements of unconstitutionality in no less than 187 articles; the Ombudsman denounced 112 articles and four additional provisions; and the autonomous communities of Murcia, La Rioja, Aragon, Valencia and Balearic Islands, denounced its invasion of their respective competences.

Political pressure on the Court during the nearly four years it took to resolve the complaints[30] went from intense to unbearable, with frequent street demonstrations and calls for civil disobedience in the event of an unfavourable decision by the Court. Due to the intensity of the political climate and a lack of consensus on the issue within the political elite, those members of the Court who had fulfilled their nine-year mandates were unable to have their terms renewed as a result of their decisions in this case. The legitimacy of the Court's role was called into question by the highest-ranking officials of the Catalonian government, who appeared to ignore the fact that since its creation the Spanish Constitutional Court had supported the position of successive Catalan governments in hundreds of cases brought before it, and had proven itself an autonomy-friendly institution.

The eventual decision of the Constitutional Court, 31/2010, adopted by a six-to-four vote on 28 June, declared fourteen provisions unconstitutional. These included Article 6 (favouring the Catalan language over co-official Castilian in public administration, media and education); Article 76 (on the binding nature of the advice of the Council for Statutory Guarantees); Article 78 (on the exclusive jurisdiction of the Catalan ombudsman); Articles 97–101 (on the Council of Justice of Catalonia);[31] Article 111 (on the shared competence between the state and the *Generalitat* of Catalonia); and Article 206.3 (on the calculation of the share of Catalonia in the state taxes and the equalising and solidarity

[30] The resolution, plus all related documents (including the complaints presented, the allegations, other related acts and other affected Statutes) have been made available online by the *Revista Catalana de Dret Públic* at: www10.gencat.net/eapc_revistadret/recursos_interes/ (accessed 1 July 2011).

[31] Along with the symbolic, the language-related and the financial issues, the attempt to establish the so called Council of Justice of Catalonia, defined as 'the body governing judicial power in Catalonia', counted among the most controversial aspects of the new Statute. Despite the fact that Art. 97 of the Statute established that it would perform as a devolved body of the General Council of the Judicial Power, without prejudice to the powers of the latter, many feared, as did the Constitutional Court, that it would be a fatal blow to the unity of Spanish judicial power, enshrined in Chapter VI of the Constitution.

mechanisms). The Court issued a constitutional interpretation on twenty-six other provisions, which would remain compatible within the Constitution as long as they were interpreted in the manner specified by the Court, and pointed out that the controversial Preamble of the Statute, in which Catalonia appeared to be identified as a 'Nation', was devoid of legal and interpretative force.[32] The resolution, received with more relief than enthusiasm by the plaintiffs, was considered by many analysts to be too timid and too late, and was viewed as betrayal of Catalan self-government by the entire nationalist camp. The resolution was greeted with calls for civil disobedience and a massive street demonstration claiming the right of Catalan people to decide on the issues themselves; but its release at least took the pressure off an embattled Constitutional Court.

The *Generalitat de Catalunya*

The organisation of their own self-government institutions is one of the most obvious competences autonomous communities can assume under Article 148 (1) of the Constitution, and its elaboration in a Statute of Autonomy is one of the few requirements it imposes on such arrangements, in Article 147(2).

The Constitution itself provides few details on the structure of these institutions, except for those communities wanting to realise their autonomy via the so-called 'speedy' path, achieving the largest possible degree of autonomy in the shortest possible time. However, as the process of developing autonomous communities advanced, and as a direct consequence of the 1981 Autonomy Pacts, it became evident that a logic of imitation had become widespread, since communities achieving self-government at a later stage replicated the institutional systems adopted by the first autonomous communities, which, in turn, reproduced the most characteristic features of the parliamentary system established at the national level by the 1978 Constitution.

The constitutional framework for institutions at the community level is dealt with in Article 152 (1), as follows:

> a Legislative Assembly elected by universal suffrage under a system of proportional representation which shall also assure the representation of the various areas of the territory; an Executive Council with executive and administrative functions

[32] Among the abundant academic literature generated by this landmark Constitutional Court resolution, see Mercè Barceló, Xavier Bernadí and Joan Vintró (eds.), *Especial Sentència 31/2010 del Tribunal Constitucional, sobre l'Estatut d'Autonomia de Catalunya de 2006* [Special Issue on the Constitutional Court Resolution 31/2010, on the 2006 Catalan Statute of Autonomy] (Barcelona: Revista Catalana de Dret Públic, 2010); 'Especial sobre la Sentència de l'Estatut d'Autonomia de Catalunya' [Special Issue on the Resolution on the Catalan Statute of Autonomy], *Revista d'Estudis Autonòmics i Federals* 12 (2011), 1–501; 'La STC 31/2010 sobre el Estatuto de Cataluña' [Const. Ct. Res. 31/2010, on the Catalan Statute of Autonomy], *Teoría y Realidad Constitucional* 27 (2011), 11–544; and Enrique Álvarez Conde (ed.), *Estudios sobre la Sentencia 31/2010, de 28 de junio, del Tribunal Constitucional sobre el Estatuto de Autonomía de Cataluña* [Essays on the Constitutional Court Resolution 31/2010, of June 28, on the Catalan Statute of Autonomy] (Madrid: Instituto de Derecho Público-Universidad Rey Juan Carlos, 2011).

and a President elected by the Assembly among its members and appointed by the King. The President shall assume leadership of the Executive Council, the supreme representation of the Community and the state's ordinary representation in the latter. The President and the members of the Executive Council shall be politically accountable to the Assembly.

Following these somewhat loose guidelines, the institutions of Catalan self-government were originally enumerated and defined in Title II (Articles 29–42) of the 1979 Statute of Autonomy. The current Statute of 2006 describes them in the same title (now comprising Articles 55–94) in extremely vague terms, thus allowing a wide regulatory margin for existing or future Acts of Parliament. However, a first reference to these institutions is made in Article 2 of the Statute, which introduces the term *Generalitat* as 'the institutional system around which Catalonia's self-government is politically organised', comprising the Parliament, the Presidency, the government, the other institutions established in Chapter V of Title II, the Municipalities, *vegueries*, *comarques* and other local government bodies that may be determined by law, which 'also constitute the institutional system of the *Generalitat*'.[33]

Thus, the institutional system of Catalan self-government is basically constructed on the three pillars required by Article 152 (1) of the Constitution and explicitly mentioned in Article 2 (2) of the Autonomy Statute, on the basis of which several other institutions not required by the Constitution but created by the Statute have been introduced.

Legislature

The Parliament of Catalonia (*Parlament de Catalunya*) represents the people of Catalonia and is 'the seat for the expression of pluralism and political debate', exercising legislative power, approval of the budget of the *Generalitat*, and control and promotion of political and government action.[34]

The legislature is unicameral, consisting of 135 deputies elected for a period of four years by a universal, free, equal, direct and secret ballot, in accordance with the Statute and an Act of Parliament to be approved by a majority of two thirds of its members. However, this Act has not yet been passed, and, consequently, the Catalan electoral system is chaotically regulated by provisions derived from several sources: Article 56 of the 2006 Statute, which limits itself to fixing a maximum and minimum number of deputies, prescribing proportionality in the

[33] It should be noted that doing away with a provincial structure inherited from the nineteenth century, and supposedly devoid of any historical justification, and substituting it with a set of smaller territorial units, called *vegueries*, has been one of the historical demands of Catalan nationalism. A 'comarca' is a territorial subdivision, smaller than a province but larger than a municipality. However, doing away with the provinces exceeds the powers of the *Generalitat*, since provinces are enshrined in the Constitution and function as administrative units of the state; they also serve as electoral districts for the election of the two houses of the national legislature. See Rafael Gómez-Ferrer, *La provincia en el sistema constitucional* [The province in the constitutional system] (Madrid: Civitas, 1991).

[34] Art. 55 Autonomy Statute.

election, requiring adequate representation of all areas of the territory of Catalonia and imposing gender parity in the nomination of electoral candidates; the fourth transitory provision of the 1979 Statute, declared still applicable by the second transitory provision of the 2006 Statute, which proclaims the existing provinces as electoral constituencies, and grants eighty-five seats to Barcelona, eighteen to Tarragona, seventeen to Girona and fifteen to Lleida; and the rules regulating the election of the Congress of Deputies contained in Organic Law 5/1985 of the General Electoral Regime, which remains applicable as long as the Catalan Electoral Law is not passed. The General Electoral Regime administers and regulates the right to vote, the electoral administration, the electoral roll, the requirements for calling elections, the procedures to be followed for candidate nomination, electoral publicity, campaign financing and public subsidies, electoral crimes and election violations. Seats are distributed among closed and blocked lists of candidates presented by parties proportional to their share of the vote by applying the so-called d'Hondt Formula, with a threshold of three per cent of the valid votes in each constituency for any candidates to be elected.[35]

To date, nine elections have been held, the moderate nationalist coalition Convergence and Union being the party with the largest vote share, and the most seats in each of them, and thus leading the government between 1980 and 2003, and from 2010. However, between 2003 and 2010 the Party of the Catalan Socialists was able to muster a broad, though heterogeneous and unstable coalition with the former communists of Initiative for Catalonia-Greens-Alternative Left and the secessionist ERC (Republican Left of Catalonia), and managed to lead a three-party government, the so-called *Tripartit*, which temporarily dislodged CiU from power (see Table 7.2).[36]

The Parliament of Catalonia has its organisational, financial, administrative and disciplinary autonomy granted by the Statute, which allows it to elect its own President and Presiding Board (Article 59 [1]), to create committees of all kinds (Article 59 [6]), to draft and approve its Rules of Procedure and its budget, and to establish the legal status of its staff (Article 52 [2]).[37]

Besides the functions specified in Article 55 of the Statute, the Parliament also has the power to designate senators to represent the *Generalitat* at national

[35] On the Catalan electoral system, see Joan Marcet Morera, 'Los regímenes electorales autonómicos en concreto: Cataluña' [The specific autonomic electoral systems: Catalonia], *Cuadernos de Derecho Público* 22/23 (2004) 327–46. On its possible reform, see Jaime Magré Ferrán, 'Reflexions entorn del sistema electoral del Parlament de Catalunya: efectes, propostes i límits' [Reflections on the electoral system for the Parliament of Catalonia: consequences, proposals and limits], *Revista d'Estudis Autonòmics i Federals* 1 (2005), 163.

[36] On the Catalan party system and elections in Catalonia, see Chapter 3, 'Political Parties in Catalonia', in David L. Hanley, John Loughlin, *Spanish Political Parties* (Cardiff: University of Wales Press, 2006), 74. See also Gabriel Colomé, *The Left Parties in Catalonia: the Case of the PSC and the PSUC* (Madrid: Instituto Juan March de Estudios e Investigaciones, 1996).

[37] See 'Reglament del Parlament de Catalunya of December 15, 22, 2005', *Diari Oficial de la Generalitat de Catalunya* 4553 (18 January 2006).

Table 7.2 Elections to the Catalan Parliament and Presidents of the *Generalitat de Catalunya* (1980–2012)

	Share of the vote (and seats)									
Parties	1980	1984	1988	1992	1995	1999	2003	2006	2010	2012
Cs								3.0	3.3	7.5
								(3)	(3)	(9)
CP > AP > PP		7.7	5.3	5.9	13.8	9.5	11.8	10.6	12.3	12.9
		(11)	(6)	(7)	(17)	(12)	(15)	(14)	(18)	(19)
CC-UCD > CDS	10.6		3.8	0.9		0.0	0.0		0.0	
	(18)		(3)	–		–	–		–	
CiU	27.8	46.8	45.7	46.1	40.9	37.7	30.9	31.5	38.4	30.7
	(43)	(72)	(69)	(70)	(60)	(56)	(46)	(48)	(62)	(50)
PSC-PSOE > PSC-CpC	22.4	30.1	29.7	27.5	24.8	30.3	31.1	26.8	18.3	14.4
	(33)	(41)	(42)	(40)	(34)	(36)	(42)	(37)	(28)	(20)
PSUC > IC > ICV . . .	18.7	5.5	7.7	6.5	9.7	2.5	7.2	9.5	7.3	9.8
	(25)	(6)	(9)	(7)	(11)	(3)	(9)	(12)	(10)	(13)
ERC	8.9	4.4	4.1	7.9	9.4	8.7	16.4	14.0	7.0	13.7
	(14)	(5)	(6)	(11)	(13)	(12)	(23)	(21)	(10)	(21)
Other parties	2.6					7.5			3.2	3.4
	(2)					(16)			(4)	(3)
Abstention (per cent)	38.6	35.6	40.6	45.1	36.3	40.8	37.4	43.9	41.2	32.2
President of the *Generalitat*	Jordi Pujol (CiU)						Pasqual Maragall (PSC)	José Montilla (PSC)	Artur Mas (CiU)	

Abbreviations: C's (Citizens-Party for Citizenship); CP (in 1984, Popular Coalition); AP (in 1988, Popular Alliance); PP (since 1992, Popular Party); CC-UCD (in 1980, Centrists of Catalonia-Union of the Democratic Center); CDS (in 1988, Democratic and Social Center); CiU (Convergence and Union: Catalan Democratic Convergence + Catalan Democratic Union); PSC-PSOE (from 1980 to 1995, Party of the Catalan Socialists-Spanish Socialist Worker's Party); PSC-CpC (from 1999 to 2006, Party of the Catalan Socialists-Citizens for Change); PSC (in 2010 and 2012, Party of the Catalan Socialists); PSUC (in 1980 and 1984, Unified Socialist Party of Catalonia); IC (in 1988 and 1992, Initiative for Catalonia); ICV (in 1995 and 1999, Initiative for Catalonia-Greens); ICV-EA (in 2003, Initiative for Catalonia-Greens-Alternative Left); ICV-EUiA (in 2006, Initiative for Catalonia-Greens-United Left and Alternative); ERC (Republican Left of Catalonia).

Other parties include: In 1980, PSA-PA (Socialist Party of Andalusia-Andalusian Party): 2.6%, 2 seats; in 2010, SCI (Catalan Solidarity for Independence): 3.2%, 4 seats; and in 2012 CUP (Popular Unity List): 3.4%, 3 seats. In 1999 joint lists of PSC-CpC-ICV obtained 7.5% of the vote and 16 seats.

Only parties that obtained parliamentary representation at some point are included.

Source: Departament de Governació i Relacions Institucionals, Generalitat de Catalunya (online at www20.gencat.cat, retrieved 20.12.2012)

level; draft bills for presentation before the Presiding Board of Congress; nominate Members of Parliament charged with defending these bills; request the adoption of government bills by the state government; demand from the state the transfer or delegation of new powers; lodge appeals on the basis of unconstitutionality; and appear before the Constitutional Court in constitutional proceedings (Article 61).[38]

Executive

The President of the Catalan government (*President de la Generalitat*) is defined as 'the highest representative of the *Generalitat*', and directs the actions of the Catalan government. The President 'embodies the ordinary representation of the state in Catalonia'[39] and is elected by Parliament from among its members and appointed by the King.[40] Presently, there are no term limits for the office, although the 2006 Statute anticipated that they may be introduced by Act of Parliament. As is usual in parliamentary systems, the President is subject to the control of the legislature, and the term in office may come to an end either by the convening of a new Parliament, by a motion of censure, or with defeat on a vote of confidence.[41] As counterweight, Parliament may be dissolved under the President's exclusive responsibility after discussion with the government. New elections must be held within forty to sixty days. Additionally, there can be no dissolution when a vote of censure has been tabled, or within one year of the last dissolution.[42] Since the 1979 Statute entered into force, four leaders have held the Presidency of the *Generalitat*.[43] Jordi Pujol, nationalist leader and founder of Catalan Democratic Convergence (CDC), was elected on 24 April 1980 and was subsequently re-elected on five further occasions, holding office uninterruptedly for twenty-three years.[44] Following the Socialist victory in 2003,

[38] On the *Parlament de Catalunya* and its powers, see Pere Sol i Ordis and Fernando Domínguez García, 'Las instituciones de la Generalidad (I): El Parlamento de Cataluña' [The institutions of the Generalitat (I): The Parliament of Catalonia] in Barceló i Serramalera and Vintró i Castells, (eds.), *Derecho público de Cataluña*, 269–334.

[39] Autonomy Statute, Art. 67.1, s.5. His legal status is regulated by Act 13/2008, of 5 November, *de la Presidència de la Generalitat i del Govern.*

[40] Autonomy Statute, Art. 67 (2), s.4. [41] Ibid., Art. 67 (7). [42] Ibid., Art. 75.

[43] The name of Josep Tarradellas (1899–1988), who was elected President of the Catalan government in exile in 1954, should be added to these four. Following his historic return to Spain in 1977, and in recognition of his political significance and symbolic relevance, he was appointed President of the pre-autonomy coalition government by the Suárez government. Tarradellas, who held this office until the election of Jordi Pujol, and then retired from political life, belonged to Esquerra Republicana de Catalunya. Adopting a broader historical perspective, it should also be noted that 125 Presidents of the *Generalitat* held this position prior to Jordi Pujol since the office was first held by Berenguer de Cruïlles in the fourteenth century.

[44] On Pujol's legacy, see Kathryn Crameri, *Catalonia: National Identity and Cultural Policy, 1980–2003* (Cardiff: University of Wales Press, 2008). On his political ideas, see Jordi Pujol and Albert Alay, *Antología Política de Jordi Pujol* [Collected political works of Jordi Pujol] (Barcelona: Pòrtic, 2003) and Jordi Pujol and Josep Faulí, *El Pensament Polític de Jordi Pujol (1980–1987)* [Political thought of Jordi Pujol] (Barcelona: Planeta, 1988). For an assessment of his legacy, see Ignasi Riera, *Jordi Pujol: Luces y Sombras* [Jordi Pujol: lights and shadows] (Barcelona: Angle, 2002); Antoni Plaja i Mateu, *Jordi Pujol: Una Vida Dedicada a Construir Catalunya* [Jordi Pujol: a life dedicated to building Catalonia] (Barcelona: Mediterrània, 2003), and Félix Martínez Zapata and Jordi Oliveres, *Jordi Pujol: En Nom de Catalunya* [Jordi Pujol: in the name of Catalonia] (Barcelona: Plaza and Janés, 2005).

the Presidency went to the former Mayor of Barcelona, Pasqual Maragall (PSC), who, after the second Socialist victory, was replaced by José Montilla (PSC). The return of CiU to power after the 2010 elections saw the investiture of Artur Mas, who had succeeded Pujol at the helm of CDC in 2003.

The President may appoint a First Minister (*Conseller primer*) as a member of the government, to assist in the discharge of presidential functions and responsibilities and provide political leverage for a coalition partner. The First Minister substitutes for the President during times of absence, illness, disability, or death.[45]

The government (*Govern*) 'is the superior collegiate body that directs political action and the Administration of the *Generalitat*', exercising executive functions and regulatory powers in accordance with the Autonomy Statute and the law.[46] Its members are chosen and can be replaced by the President, and although the Autonomy Statute states that, 'Politically, the President and the ministers of the *Generalitat* answer jointly to Parliament, without prejudice to the direct responsibility of each', the latter may not be subject to a motion of censure, nor request a vote of confidence.[47]

Other institutions

The 1979 Statute went beyond the constitutional scheme in providing for three additional institutions, which were further specified in Chapter V of Title II of the 2006 Statute.[48] The first of these, the Council for Statutory Guarantees (*Consell de Garanties Estatutàries*), is defined as 'the institution of the *Generalitat* that ensures that the regulations of the *Generalitat* comply with this Statute and the Constitution'.[49] Its members must be jurists of recognised competence, two thirds of whom are nominated by a three-fifths majority of parliament, with the remaining third appointed by the government.[50] The Council monitors compliance of Statute reform proposals with the Constitution prior to their approval by Parliament, and is also responsible for reviewing bills submitted to Parliament by the government or by MPs and assessing their compatibility

45 On the office of the *President de la Generalitat*, see Carles Viver i Pi-Sunyer, 'La figura jurídica del President de la Generalitat a l'Estatut d'Autonomia de Catalunya' [The legal position of the President of the Catalan Generalitat in the Statute of Autonomy for Catalonia], *Revista Jurídica de Catalunya* 79:1 (1980), 133–78; and Inma Folchi i Bonafonte, 'Las instituciones de la Generalidad (II): El presidente de la Generalidad y el Gobierno' [The institutions of the Generalitat (III): The President of the Generalitat and the Government] in Barceló i Serramalera andVintró i Castells, (eds.), *Derecho público de Cataluña*, 335–70.

46 Autonomy Statute, Art. 68 (1).

47 Ibid., Art. 74 (1).

48 See Joan Vintró i Castells and Antoni Bayona i Rocamora, 'Las instituciones de la Generalidad (III): el Consejo de Garantías Estatutarias, el Síndic de Greuges, la Sindicatura de Cuentas y el Consejo Audiovisual de Cataluña' [The institutions of the Generalitat (III): the Council for Statutory Guarantees, the Ombudsman, the Audit Office and the Catalan Broadcasting Authority] in Barceló i Serramalera and Vintró i Castells, (eds.), *Derecho público de Cataluña*, 371–426.

49 Autonomy Statute, Art. 76 (1).

50 Ibid., Art. 77 (1).

with the Statute and the Constitution. Additionally, it reviews legal decrees requiring validation by Parliament as well as draft legislative decrees approved by the government; it also checks the compliance with local autonomy of bills and draft legislative decrees approved by the government. The original wording of the Statute declared judgments of the Council binding as regards bills that developed or affected statutory rights.[51] However, the Constitutional Court considered that this clause entailed a limitation on the powers of Parliament and the right to voter political participation and declared it unconstitutional.[52]

The second institution, that of the Ombudsman (*Síndic de Greuges*), co-operates with the national Ombudsman to protect the rights and freedoms recognised in the Constitution and the Statute. The Ombudsman may oversee the activities of the *Generalitat* and local administrations in Catalonia, as well as of any public or private bodies, companies and individuals associated with, or answerable to it, who hold a contractual relationship with it, manage public services or carry out activities of general or universal interest. Election to the post requires a majority of three fifths of the deputies in Parliament. The Ombudsman is impartial, independent and enjoys immunity in relation to opinions expressed about the cases dealt with in the course of carrying out the duties of the office.[53]

The third institution is the Audit Office (*Sindicatura de Comptes*), which monitors and reviews the finances, economic management and efficiency of the *Generalitat*, local bodies, and of Catalonia's entire public sector. It is given full organisational, working and budgetary autonomy.[54] Appointment to this Office requires confirmation by three fifths of the deputies in Parliament.

A fourth institution – not mentioned by the 1979 Statute, but introduced at a later stage by an act of Parliament – is the Catalan Broadcasting Authority (*Consell de l'Audiovisual de Catalunya*), an independent regulatory authority operating in the field of public and private audio-visual communication.[55]

The competences of the *Generalitat*

The distribution of competences between the state and the autonomous communities is regulated in general terms by Articles 148–50 of the Constitution, and in the specific case of each autonomous community by its own Statute of Autonomy. The Spanish system of competence distribution is a complex one, as has been shown by the enormous number of conflicts in the three decades since its implementation, many of which have originated in the decisions made by

51 Ibid., Art. 76 (2), s.4.

52 See Joaquín Tornos Mas, 'Les institucions de la Generalitat davant el Tribunal Constitucional. La Sentència 31/2010, el Consell de Garanties Estatutàries i el Síndic de Greuges' [The institutions of the Generalitat before the Constitutional Court: Resolution 31/2010, the Council for Statutory Guarantees, and the Ombudsman], *Revista d'Estudis Autonòmics i Federalistes* 12 (2011), 192–210.

53 Autonomy Statute, Arts. 78.1, s.2 and 79.1, s.2

54 Ibid., Arts. 80 (1), s.2 and 81 (1).

55 Ibid., Art. 82.

Catalonian institutions.[56] This complexity derives, on the one hand, from the fact that when attaining self-government autonomous communities were not given a uniform set of competences but one tailored to their respective needs; this was not intended to be final, since the Constitution itself envisaged at least two mechanisms – statute reform and extra-statutory transfers – for its eventual enlargement.[57] And on the other hand, this results from the fact that it is a system in which *functions*, rather than subject matters, are distributed between the state and the communities, therefore allowing that, in specific areas, such as social security, media regulation or environmental protection, both parties are entitled to take action, with each one performing a particular function, such as legislating, co-ordinating, regulating, executing or controlling. To make their respective competences compatible and functional, the state and the communities require efficient mechanisms for co-operation and conflict resolution to ensure the smooth operation of the system.[58]

Exclusive state competences are enumerated in the thirty-two paragraphs of the Constitution's Article 149 (1), which charges the state with the 'regulation of the basic conditions guaranteeing the equality of all Spaniards in the exercise of their rights and in the fulfilment of their constitutional duties'. It is followed by a list of areas that include nationality and immigration; international relations; defence; justice; commercial, criminal, prison, procedural, labour and civil legislation; customs; the monetary system; credit and insurance; and social security.[59] Paragraphs one and two of Article 148 contain a list of twenty-two

[56] A telling proof of this assertion can be found in the fourteen volumes published under the general heading of *La conflictivitat competencial* [Conflicts of competence] by the Barcelona-based Institut d'Estudis Autonòmics between 1994 and 1995. These works address jurisdictional conflicts in such areas as the environment, energy, media regulation, healthcare, education, public safety, trade, civil law and language policies.

[57] On the difference between transference laws and statute reform, see Eduardo García de Enterría, *La revisión del sistema de autonomías territoriales: reforma de Estatutos, leyes de transferencia y delegación, federalismo* [Revising the system of territorial autonomies: statute reforms, transference and delegation laws, and federalism] (Madrid: Civitas, 1988). On the broader issue of Statute reform, see Antonio Gutiérrez Llamas and Antonio Martínez Marín, *Los procedimientos para la reforma de los estatutos de autonomía de las comunidades autónomas* [Procedures for the reform of the statutes of autonomy of the autonomous communities] (Madrid: Civitas, 1991) and Roberto Viciano Pastor, *Constitución y reforma de los estatutos de autonomía: procedimientos constitucionales de modificación del Estado autonómico* [Constitution and reform of the statutes of autonomy: constitutional procedures for the modification of the autonomic State] (Valencia: Tirant lo Blanch, 2005).

[58] The perspectives of two former Constitutional Court justices on the issue can be found at Francisco Tomás y Valiente, *El Reparto Competencial en la Jurisprudencia del Tribunal Constitucional* [The distribution of competences in the Constitutional Court jurisprudence] (Madrid: Tecnos, 1988) and Carles Viver Pí-Sunyer, *Materias Competenciales y Tribunal Constitucional* [Competences and the Constitutional Court] (Barcelona: Ariel, 1989).

[59] It should be noted that some other articles of the Constitution confer additional competences on the state, such as when an issue has to be addressed by an organic act. And also that if a community does not assume an available competence in its statute – and they are not obliged to do so – the competence shall be assumed by the state, 'whose norms shall prevail in case of conflict over those of the autonomous communities regarding all matters in which exclusive jurisdiction has not been conferred upon the latter' and whose law 'shall in any case be suppletory of that of the autonomous communities' (Art. 149 [3]).

matters over which autonomous communities may assume competence, but it also foresees the progressive expansion of their powers within the framework laid down in Article 149. Therefore, the Statute of Autonomy becomes the frame of reference for defining the scope of a community's powers.

Catalonia, being a 'historical community' that had already experienced self-government, and possessing at the time of the promulgation of the Constitution a set of provisional self-government institutions, was able to benefit from the clause contained in the Second Transitory Provision of the Constitution, and incorporated competences in its 1979 Statute that went far beyond the parameters outlined in Article 148 (1) of the Constitution. This was not enough, however, and based on the experience of more than three decades of self-government, and fuelled by the desire to assume even greater responsibilities, the 2006 Statute established the legal ground for an ambitious expansion of Catalonia's powers.[60] This new set of competences is in most part regulated by Title IV of the Autonomy Statute, which lists no less than fifty-seven matters as being within the competence of the *Generalitat de Catalunya*.[61] These are not restricted – as is usually the case with sub-national units – to topics such as agriculture, hunting, fishing, culture, civil law, education, language policy, housing, environment, radio and television services, territorial and landscape planning, urban planning, territorial organisation, local government, healthcare, social services or tourism, but also include matters usually under the jurisdiction of the state, such as justice, public law corporations, credit and banks, immigration, stock exchanges, intellectual and industrial property, personal data protection, work and labour relations and the prison system. These autonomous powers also include issues closely related to the regulation of basic political rights, such as consultations, gender policies and relations with religious entities.

To appreciate this expansion in the jurisdiction of Catalan institutions of self-government it should be understood that these powers are exercised at three different levels, since the Autonomy Statute specifies the existence of matters in which the *Generalitat* enjoys 'exclusive powers', 'shared powers' and 'executive powers'.[62] In the first instance, legislative power, regulatory power and the executive function reside fully with the *Generalitat*, with Catalan law prevailing over any other; while in matters in which the Statute attributes powers to the *Generalitat* that are shared with the state, legislative power, regulatory power and the executive function are exercised by the *Generalitat* 'within the framework of the basic conditions established by the state as principles or lowest common legislative denominators', with exceptions determined by the Constitution and the Statute. And in matters in which the *Generalitat* has only executive power, it limits itself to the enactment of provisions for the execution of state rules, the

[60] See Mercé Barceló i Serramalera, Jaume Vernet i Llobet and Joan Vintró i Castells, 'Las competencias de la Generalitat' [The competences of the Generalitat] in Barceló i Serramalera and Vintró i Castells (eds.), *Derecho público de Cataluña*, 505–58.

[61] Chapter II (Arts. 116–73). [62] Arts. 110–12.

organisation of its own administration and the exercise of those functions and activities required for public administration.

However, it should be kept in mind that the Constitutional Court revised this specific characterisation of competences in its landmark 31/2010 decision.[63] Article 111 on the shared competences was considered unconstitutional; while the Court determined that Article 110, on the exclusive competences of the *Generalitat*, should apply only to matters within the jurisdiction of Catalan institutions, and should not preclude the exercise of the exclusive powers of the state, as specified in Article 149 of the Constitution, when the latter concur with the powers of the *Generalitat* on the same physical space or legal subject, as in the case of matters of shared competence between the state and the autonomous community.

Catalonia in the politics of Spain and of Europe

Catalonia's influence on Spanish national politics cannot be underestimated. In purely numerical terms, its impact is significant: Catalan voters elect forty-seven of the 350 deputies of Congress, as well as twenty-four of the 264 Senators. Though Catalonia remains underrepresented in the Spanish legislature,[64] due to the fact that the electoral system for the lower house gives larger districts, like Barcelona, the second most underrepresented province after Madrid, less representation, and the distribution of seats in the upper house grants each province the same number of Senators regardless of its population, it still enjoys the second largest parliamentary representation in Congress of any community but Andalusia, which has sixty-one seats. It has the third greatest number of seats in the Senate, after Andalusia, which has forty-one, and Castile-Leon, which has thirty-nine.

However, the decisive influence of Catalonia on Spanish politics in the post-Franco era has not derived so much from the size of its parliamentary representation as from the key political position held by the major Catalonian power player, the centre-right nationalist coalition *Convergència i Unió*. Throughout the time of office of the eleven legislatures since the election of the first

[63] See Mercè Barceló et al., 'Les competències' [The powers], in *Especial Sentència 31/2010 del Tribunal Constitucional*, 249–381; Carles Viver Pi-Sunyer, 'El Tribunal Constitucional'? 'Sempre, Només . . . i indiscutible'? La funció constitucional dels estatuts en l'àmbit de la distribució de competències segons la STC 31/2010' [The Constitutional Court: 'Always, Only . . . and Undisputed'? The constitutional role of statutes regarding competence distribution after the Const. Ct. Res. 31/2010], *Revista d'Estudis Autonòmics i Federals* 12 (2011), 363–402; and Germán Fernández Farreres, 'El futuro de la cuestión competencial tras la sentencia 31/2010 sobre el Estatuto de Autonomía de Cataluña' [The future of competence distribution after Const. Ct. Res. 31/2010, on the Statute of Autonomy for Catalonia], in Álvarez Conde (ed.), *Estudios sobre la Sentencia 31/2010*, 269–96.

[64] María Garrote de Marcos, 'Las elecciones del 9 de marzo de 2008 y la igualdad de voto' [The 9 March, 2008 elections and the equality of voting], *InDret. Revista para el Análisis del Derecho* 2 (2008), 9–10.

democratic parliament on 15 June 1977, on only four occasions – 1982, 1986, 2000 and 2011 – has the party in power enjoyed a majority of seats in Congress; on a fifth occasion, in 1989, the Socialist Party held just half. On the other six occasions, the UCD in 1977 and 1979, the Socialist Party in 1993, 2004 and 2008, and the Popular Party in 1996, each party almost reached the critical number of 176 seats required to rule out the formation of a coalition government, but was still left needing parliamentary partners for the adoption of key legislative measures. In this search, CiU, which has regularly obtained eight to eighteen parliamentary seats, has usually been first in line, therefore providing Catalan nationalism with a central political influence on national affairs, regardless of whether the Socialist or the Popular Party held the reins of power.[65] Not to mention the decisive political weight of the Catalan socialists within the PSOE, to which in the last elections it contributed nearly 14 per cent of its overall number of votes, in addition to fourteen seats in Congress (down from 25 in the previous legislature). Thus the Catalan fraction has become the second largest territorial organisation within the Party, after that of Andalusia.

This pervasive influence of Catalan nationalism on Spanish national politics has been a source of growing conflict. How this power should be used, and to what extent Catalonia's concerns should reach beyond the borders of the Spanish state into the European Union and other global forums relevant to Catalonia's ambitious political and economic goals, has become a key issue.

The position taken by successive Catalan governments, regardless of their political affiliation, has been that Catalonia's relations with the Spanish state should be based on the recognition of Catalonia's identity as a nation and its right to self-government. Consequently, the only restraints on it should be those freely accepted by the Catalonian people; they should be articulated through bilateral mechanisms, and not remain framed within the existing multilateral forums co-ordinating autonomous institutions; and they should acknowledge the distinctiveness of Catalonia, which should therefore be treated differently than the other Spanish territories. With these purposes in mind the 2006 Statute introduced a number of provisions and procedures for the participation of Catalonia in state decision-making institutions.[66] These provisions were intended to regulate the composition and functions of the State-*Generalitat* Bilateral Commission, defined as:

> the general and permanent framework for relations between the government of the *Generalitat* and the government of the state for [. . .] participation and

[65] See Cesáreo R. Aguilera de Prat, 'Convergencia i Unió ante los pactos de gobernabilidad de 1993 y 1996' [Convergence and Union before the governability agreements of 1993 and 1996], *Sistema: Revista de ciencias sociales* 165 (2001), 99–130 and Josep Antoni Durán i Lleida, 'La aportación de Convergència i Unió a la política española' [The contribution of Convergence and Union to Spanish politics], in *Escenarios de España, Vol. 1* (Madrid: Nueva Economía Forum, 2005), 281–92. Durán has been a representative in five legislatures and the CiU spokesman in Congress since 2004.

[66] Arts. 179–82; Art. 183.

> collaboration of the *Generalitat* in the exercise of state powers affecting the autonomy of Catalonia [and for the] exchange of information and establishment, when appropriate, of mechanisms for collaboration in their respective public policies and in matters of common interest.[67]

However, it is a fact that all the provisions contained in the Statute regarding the participation of Catalan institutions in the selection of members of state institutions, such as the Constitutional Court, the General Council of Judicial Power, the Bank of Spain, the National Stock Market Commission, the Telecommunications Market Commission, the Accounts Court, the Economic and Social Council, the Taxation Agency, the National Energy Commission or the Spanish Data Protection Agency, require the introduction of corresponding amendments in the applicable laws in order to become effective. Such reforms could not be made without causing conflict with other territories. Especially problematic is the fact that such bilateralism can only be extended to other autonomous territories by depriving common state institutions of any significant role, and at the cost of proliferating bureaucracy and the risk of making the country ungovernable.

Successive Catalan governments have also lobbied for Catalonia to have an independent presence on the international scene, and for the recognition of Catalan institutions as the representatives of Catalan interests abroad, or, at least, for the participation of Catalan institutions in the making and implementation of Spanish foreign policy. With this purpose in mind, the 2006 Statute made the following provisions: (a) 'The *Generalitat* participates in the formation of state positions before the European Union, especially before the Council of Ministers, in matters concerning the powers or interests of Catalonia, under the terms established by this Statute and the legislation on these matters'. (b) 'The *Generalitat* shall participate bilaterally in forming the state positions in those European affairs which affect it exclusively. In other cases, participation shall be in the framework of multilateral procedures to be established'.[68] (c) 'The *Generalitat* participates in Spanish delegations to the European Union that deal with affairs within the legislative power of the *Generalitat*'.[69] (d) 'The *Generalitat* applies and implements the law of the European Union within its jurisdiction', while this may not modify 'the internal distribution of powers established by the Constitution and this Statute'.[70] (e) 'The *Generalitat* is responsible for the management of European funds in matters within its jurisdiction',[71] and, finally, (f) 'The *Generalitat* may establish a delegation to better defend its interests before the institutions of the European Union'.[72]

[67] See Mercé Barceló i Serramalera, Joan Vintró i Castells and Fernando Domínguez García, 'Las relaciones institucionales de la Generalidad con el Estado y con la Unión Europea. La acción exterior de la Generalidad' [The institutional relationships of the Generalitat with the State and the European Union. The external action of the Generalitat] in Barceló i Serramalera and Vintró i Castells (eds.), *Derecho público de Cataluña*, 559–624.

[68] Art. 186 (1) and (2). [69] Art. 187 (1). [70] Art. 189 (1).

[71] Art. 190. [72] Art. 191.

As far as Catalonia's international activities are concerned, the Statute prescribes that the *Generalitat* (a) 'shall foster the external projection of Catalonia and promote its interests in this area, while respecting the powers of the state in foreign affairs'; (b) may establish offices abroad 'in order to promote the interests of Catalonia'; (c) 'may sign collaboration agreements in areas falling within its powers' and 'request that the government sign international treaties in areas within its jurisdiction'; (d) 'shall promote cooperation and establish appropriate relations with the European regions with which it shares economic, social, environmental and cultural interests' and (e) 'shall participate in the relevant international bodies in matters of important interest for Catalonia'.[73] The legal development and implementation of these provisions has the potential for conflicting with Spanish foreign policy and risks undermining its effectiveness.

Financing Catalonia's self-government

Reflecting the complex balance between the principles of unity, autonomy and solidarity, the Constitution states that '[t]he autonomous Communities shall enjoy financial autonomy for the development and exercise of their powers, in conformity with the principles of co-ordination with the state Treasury and solidarity among all Spaniards'.[74]

The instruments by which financial autonomy may be achieved by the autonomous communities are enumerated in a comprehensive list of possible sources of income, including,

> a)Taxes wholly or partially made over to them by the state; surcharges on state taxes and other shares in state revenue; b) Their own taxes, rates and special levies; c) Transfers from an inter-territorial compensation fund and other allocations to be charged to the state budget; d) Revenues accruing from their property and private law income; e) Interest from loan operations.[75]

[73] These provisions are contained in Arts. 193–200. Currently, the *Generalitat de Catalunya* has six 'government delegations', known informally as the 'Catalan embassies', in Brussels, Paris, London, Berlin, New York and Buenos Aires, in addition to twenty-seven commercial delegations in all five continents. The former are co-ordinated by the *Secretaria d'Afers Exteriors*, belonging to the Department of the Presidency, the latter from the Department of Business and Labor, with a global budget of €32.8mn. See www20.gencat.cat/portal/site/afersexteriors and 'Viaje a las embajadas catalanas del derroche' [A trip to the Catalan waste embassies], *ABC*, 5 December 2011. See also Francesc Xavier Pons Rafols and Eduard Sagarra Trías, *La acción exterior de la Generalitat en el nuevo Estatuto de autonomía de Cataluña* [The external action of the Generalitat in the new Statute of autonomy of Catalonia] (Barcelona: Universitat de Barcelona, 2006); Barceló i Serramalera, Vintró i Castells and Domínguez García, 'Las relaciones institucionales de la Generalidad con el Estado', and Jordi Xifra, 'Catalan public diplomacy, soft power, and noopolitik: a public relations approach to Catalonia's governance', *Catalan Journal of Communication and Cultural Studies* 1:1 (2009), 67–85.

[74] Art. 156 (1). [75] Art. 157 (1).

In turn, the instruments available to the state to enable it to carry out its 'co-ordination' duties and achieve 'solidarity' are grounded on its assumption of exclusive competence to regulate the debt and the treasury [*Hacienda general*].[76] In the words of Ferreiro Lapatza, this comprises not only the state treasury, but also:

> what is fundamental and basic to other public treasuries, including those of the autonomous communities and local entities, whose primary and essential core guarantees its existence and functions as a part of a whole conformed by all public treasuries of the country, which also directly affects the general interest.[77]

The Constitution also mandates that 'The state guarantees the effective implementation of the principle of solidarity [. . .] by endeavouring to establish a fair and adequate economic balance between the different areas of Spanish territory', thus ensuring that differences in the Statutes of the autonomous communities do not generate economic or social privileges for any of them.[78] To give effect to these arrangements, the Constitution authorises the national legislature to regulate by means of an organic act the exercise of the financial competences of the autonomous communities, the norms for the resolution of any disputes that may arise, and the mechanism for financial collaboration between them and the state.[79] And finally, the Constitution mandates the creation of an Inter-territorial Compensation Fund to promote financial solidarity among the communities.[80]

In relation to the financing of autonomous communities, the state has comprehensive powers to (a) regulate all the financial competences of the autonomous communities regarding their income; (b) fix the rules for the resolution of conflicts that may arise and for the articulation of formulas for collaboration between the state and the communities; (c) lay down the necessary principles for harmonising the rule-making provisions of the self-governing communities, even in the case of matters over which jurisdiction has been vested with the latter, where this is necessary in the general interest, in all three cases by means of an organic law; (d) subject the budgets of the autonomous communities to the supervision of the Audit Court; and (e) by means of an act of parliament, plan general economic activity 'in order to meet collective needs, to balance and harmonise regional and sectoral development and to

[76] Art. 149 (1) s.14.

[77] See Organic Act 8/1980, of 22 September, on the Finances of Autonomous Communities, amended by Organic Acts 5/2001, 7/2001 and 3/2009. See José Juan Ferreiro Lapatza, 'El sistema de financiación autonómico de Catalunya: Estatuto y Constitución' [The autonomic finance system of Catalonia: the Statute and the Constitution], *Revista Catalana de Dret Públic* 32 (2006).

[78] Constitution, Arts. 138 (1) and 138 (2).

[79] Constitution, Art. 157 (3). See Ferreiro Lapatza, 'El sistema de financiación autonómico de Catalunya: Estatuto y Constitución', 37–74, 41.

[80] Art. 158 (2).

stimulate the growth of income and wealth and their more equitable distribution'. Far from establishing a closed model for the financing of autonomous communities, this set of functions 'draws an open framework or space where multiple and highly diverse possibilities may fit', as Ferreiro Lapatza puts it.[81]

Within this framework, and at times also choosing to ignore it, Catalonia has traditionally lobbied for a system emphasising asymmetry, bilateralism and what in Spanish political slang is usually referred to as *blindaje competencial* ('shielded powers'), in which inter-territorial compensation mechanisms are counterbalanced with other considerations; hence the continuous usage of *esfuerzo fiscal* ('tax effort'), where, regardless of the final distribution of regulatory competences, the actual management of tax monies ends up under the control of the *Generalitat*. In brief, the desire was for a system in which Catalan finances were regulated in the form best suited to Catalan interests, negotiated bilaterally, not multilaterally, via *ad hoc* rather than institutionalised forums, where Catalan taxpayers deal directly with a Taxation Agency of Catalonia and are protected from future changes from the state's side.[82] Considering this still insufficient, some sectors have even been pressing for the extension to Catalonia of the finance system employed in the Basque Country; the *concierto económico*, a formula derived from historical compromises dating from the nineteenth century, whereby Basque institutions are entitled to collect their own taxes, subsequently transferring a portion of them to the state – the *cupo* ('quota') – as compensation for state expenditure in Basque territory.

Title VI of the 2006 Statute regulates the finances of the *Generalitat*.[83] After articulating the principles of 'financial autonomy, coordination, solidarity and transparency in fiscal and financial relations between the Public Administration bodies [. . .], sufficiency of resources, fiscal responsibility, equity and institutional loyalty',[84] the Statute further states that the development of Catalonia's financial system shall be the responsibility of the *Generalitat*'s Joint Economic and Fiscal Affairs Commission.[85] This anticipates the creation of a Taxation Agency of Catalonia, responsible for the management, collection, settlement and inspection of all *Generalitat* of Catalonia taxes and also, when delegated by the state, of state taxes, which are ceded to the *Generalitat*;[86] the Commission determining also its powers in this area and the resources available to the *Generalitat*.[87] These resources include (a) taxation income, tax rates, special charges and other taxes raised in Catalonia; (b) the income of all ceded state taxes; (c) surcharges on state taxes; (d) revenues from the Inter-territorial

[81] Ferreiro Lapatza, 'El sistema de financiación autonómico de Catalunya', 47.

[82] See Pere Sol i Ordis, 'Las finanzas de la Generalidad' [The finances of the Generalitat] in Barceló i Serramalera and Vintró i Castells (eds.), *Derecho público de Cataluña*, 625–73, and Pere Sol i Ordis, 'El nou model de finançament autonòmic' [The new model of financing autonomies], *Revista Catalana de Dret Públic* 32 (2006), 1–321.

[83] Arts. 201–221. [84] Art. 201 (2). [85] This is provided for in Art. 210.

[86] Art. 204. [87] Art. 203, Art. 202.

Compensation Fund and from other allocations; (e) other possible transfers and allocations coming from the general state budget; (f) revenues from payments for public services; (g) income earned on the assets of the *Generalitat*; (h) private law revenues; (i) income yielded by debt issues and credit operations; (j) revenues arising from fines and sanctions applied in areas falling within its powers; (k) resources originating from the European Union and from community programmes; and (l) any other resource that may be established by virtue of the provisions of the Statute and the Constitution. The powers of the *Generalitat* allow the Catalan government to (a) determine the volume and composition of revenues falling within its financial powers, and to freely apply its resources to expenditure items as it deems fit; (b) participate in the income arising from state taxes totally or partially ceded to Catalonia; (c) within the framework of the powers of the state and of the European Union, participate in the establishment of the tax rate, exemptions, reductions and rebates on the tax base and deductions in the quota; (d) manage, collect, settle and inspect totally ceded state taxes, and do the same regarding partially ceded taxes; and (e) establish, by means of an Act of Parliament, its own taxes, over which it has regulatory power.

A number of these provisions were scrutinised by the Constitutional Court in its 31/2010 resolution, and were declared in contravention of Articles 206 and 218 of the Constitution, while the Court prescribed a specific, somewhat limited interpretation of some of the other provisions in order to preserve their constitutionality.[88] The resolution to create a Joint Economic and Fiscal Affairs Commission was accepted, but it was made clear that it would be a consultative and drafting body, whose decisions were not binding on the state; the specifications contained in the Additional Dispositions seven to ten of the Statute regarding the scope of the cession of some state taxes to the *Generalitat* were accepted, but on the principle of institutional loyalty and not as a compromise; the same approach was taken with the controversial prescription contained in Additional Disposition three, according to which state investment in Catalonia should be proportional to its contribution to the GDP; the creation of the Taxation Agency of Catalonia was accepted, but the Court stated that its powers relating to state taxes would be determined by state law; the requirement that unless all autonomous communities made a similar fiscal effort, Catalonia would cease to put taxpayers' money into state-wide initiatives, and the attribution to the *Generalitat* of power in matters of local financing, were declared unconstitutional.

[88] See Lluís M. Alonso González et al., 'El finançament' [Financial issues], in *Especial Sentència 31/2010 del Tribunal Constitucional*, 417–53; Manuel Medina Guerrero, 'Las haciendas autonómica y local en la STC 31/2010' [The autonomic and local treasuries in Const. Ct. Res. 31/2010], *Revista d'Estudis Autonòmics i Federals* 12 (2011), 471–501; and Alfonso M. García Moncó, 'El sistema de financiación autonómica' [The autonomic financial system], in Álvarez Conde, (ed.), *Estudios sobre la Sentencia 31/2010*, 425–58.

Conclusion

Historically, relations between Catalonia and Spain have not always been marked by cordiality, mutual loyalty and a constructive spirit. Instead, they often have been dominated by a mutual distrust, and sometimes even by a downright hostility. As a result, institutional solutions to the problem of how to integrate Catalonia with Spain have been based mostly on formulas not wholly desirable to either party, but bearable for both. If it is clear that Catalonia did not get everything it pressed for in 1913, 1931, 1979, or in 2006 with the new Statute of Autonomy, the fact remains that the concessions obtained at each of these historical junctures created in Spain either a perception of unfairness, or one that invited emulation by other territories. In any case, these generated the effects derived from the necessary adjustment of Spain's overall political system to the demands of Catalonia.

The singular paradox at this moment is that Catalonia has achieved the highest share of self-government in its modern history, yet its citizens appear to be unhappier in their relationship with Spain than they have ever been. While the former assertion can be verified by comparing the powers of the *Mancomunitat* of Catalonia, or those granted to the *Generalitat* in the Statutes of Nuria and Sau, with those currently provided by the 2006 Statute, the latter is proven by opinion polls, election returns and mass participation in demonstrations and public mobilisations revealing a substantial dissatisfaction with the status quo, which the political class incites and claims to represent.

If this problem were not sufficiently serious, two further closely related issues should also be taken into consideration. On the one hand, there is the apparent political apathy of a substantial section of the Catalan electorate, whose increasing disappearance from the polls calls into question the representativeness of the Catalan political class. And on the other hand, there is increasing polarisation among Spanish citizens regarding their current system of territorial organisation. It is noteworthy that over the last half-decade of Statute reform the number of citizens who have felt comfortable with the existing system of territorial self-government has significantly diminished. The numbers of people who consider the independence of their territory as the only way forward have increased, especially in the Basque Country and Catalonia, but at the other end of the political spectrum are those who believe that the decentralisation process launched in the 1978 Constitution has gone too far, and a step back needs to be taken, re-centralising the system and strengthening the state.[89]

While centralisation and independence are formulas that may be imposed, whether by force of arms or via the polling booth, autonomy is only possible on the basis of broad consensus and mutual willingness to make concessions.

[89] For some conclusive data see, Mireia Grau, 'Self-government reforms and public support for Spain's territorial model: changes and stability (1992–2010)', *Revista d'Estudis Autonòmics i Federals* 13 (2011), 186–215.

The recent history of Spain and its relations with Catalonia presents many examples of consensus, and also provides several examples of the willingness to accommodate the concerns of other parties by making concessions. All these experiences ought to be the basis of future arrangements if the current tensions in the relationship between Catalonia and the rest of Spain are to be overcome.

8

Zanzibar in Tanzania

From sovereignty to autonomy?

Yash Ghai

Autonomy in Tanzania has several interesting features: it is the only surviving autonomy in Africa. There is controversy about its classification: appearance of federation but reality of autonomy. It is also a rare case of autonomy by aggregation, that is when two sovereign entities come together to form one state. It comes closest to old fashioned mergers, by agreements among monarchs. It represents the merger of entities of vastly unequal size, population and resources. Its state structure is also unusual, with three forms of authority and jurisdiction, but two governments. Of all autonomies examined in this study, the role played by political parties is the most dominating.

In 1964 the newly independent states of Tanganyika (1961) and Zanzibar (1963) merged to form what is today known as Tanzania. Tanganyika is in eastern Africa, stretching from Lake Victoria in the west to the Indian Ocean in the east. Zanzibar, consisting principally of two major islands, is a short distance from Tanganyika in the Indian Ocean. The people of Tanganyika are mainly of Bantu origin, but there are also small communities who are descendents of Arab and Indian migrants. The struggle for freedom from British rule was led by the Tanganyika African National Union under Julius Nyerere. Despite the large number of ethnic groups there, Tanganyika was not troubled by ethnic conflicts, and under Nyerere built and sustained a remarkable degree of national unity and political integration. The independence constitutional structure of a unitary state and the dominance of one party resulted in a strong government at the centre, and only a limited decentralisation of administrative powers to provinces.

Zanzibar was at first settled by Bantu people but over centuries traders and administrators from the Middle East and India made their home there. In the late seventeenth century Omanis ousted the then ruling power, Portugal, and established their rule, which lasted until the independence of Zanzibar. But from the late nineteenth century, effective control passed to the British, with increasing British administrative presence. For its size, a considerable mixture of races developed in Zanzibar, at first under the hegemony of Omani Arabs and later of the British. By independence, the Omani Arabs were a minority but the new head of state, the Sultan of Zanzibar, was their hereditary ruler. The constitution provided for a democratic system, based on citizenship, not ethnicity, although it was expected that the dominant political class would remain the Arabs, and the dominant commercial class, Indians. The majority of the people were of African origin, lowly in their economic and social situation.[1]

Just over a month after independence, on 12 January 1964, a coup overthrew the Zanzibar government (the leader was an illiterate person, John Okello, who had little ability to run the administration). A Revolutionary Council was established and Abeid Karume, leader of a political party, the Afro-Sirazi Party, became its chair – and the president of Zanzibar. The new regime consisted primarily of members of the African community, representing the victory of the landless peasantry against a landed aristocracy and political oligarchy.[2] Some left wing members of the Arab community, prominent in the Umma Party, were also deemed to have been involved; certainly, some joined the new government. It was the orientation of this group rather than the 'African' leader of the rebellion and coup, Abeid Karume, that worried both East Africa and the West. The revolution turned violent, the principal victims being Arabs and Indians (estimates of those killed ranged from 5,000 to 15,000 – together with those who fled Zanzibar, this represented 20 per cent of the people).[3]

On 26 April, a few weeks into the new regime, Zanzibar joined Tanganyika in a union, the deal signed and announced by Nyerere and Abeid Karume, the leader of the coup – news that surprised the people of both Zanzibar and Tanganyika, including senior politicians on both sides. Considerable mystery, and much controversy, surrounds the Union – particularly as to the motives and negotiators.[4] There is considerable evidence that the West, particularly the United States, was greatly concerned about what it perceived to be a communist coup – especially after its satellite facilities were closed down (due to the US refusal to recognise the new regime). President Julius Nyerere appeared to be under considerable pressure from the United States to take over Zanzibar, to prevent a radical disruptive regime affecting Eastern Africa (a Cuba, as it were, on its doorstep). Western fears were fuelled by the prompt establishment by the Chinese and East Germans of diplomatic offices, just as the West was getting anxious because of the violence and Marxist rhetoric of some members of the new regime – and domino type army revolts in mainland states of Kenya, Uganda and Tanganyika (one author records that the 'revolt sent the

1 There is some simplification in this account; for a more nuanced class analysis, see Issa Shivji, *Pan-Africanism or Pragmatism? Lessons of Tanganyika-Zanzibar Union* (Dar es Salaam: Mkuki na Nyota, 2008).

2 Shivji, *Pan-Africanism or Pragmatism?*; Fredrick Jjuuko and Godfrey Muriuki (eds.), *Federation Within Federation: The Tanzania Union Experience and the East African Integration Process* (Kampala: Fountain Publishers, 2010).

3 Jjuuko and Muriuki, *Federation Within Federation*, 5.

4 Michael Lofchie, *Zanzibar: Background to Revolution* (Oxford University Press, 1965); Jjuuko and Muriuki, *Federation Within Federation*, 5–9; Shivji, *Pan-Africanism or Pragmatism?*, 72–6.

Western world into a spin').[5] The Western powers considered that a union with Tanganyika, one under its tutelage, would bring sufficient sobriety and restraint in Zanzibar.

Meanwhile the political and administrative situation in Zanzibar deteriorated, with harassment and killings of minorities and divisions within the Revolutionary Council. Karume feared that he would be ousted, and sought Nyerere's military assistance (Tanganyika had backed the Afro-Sirazi Party during the colonial period). It is believed that with the same objective, he asked Nyerere to take over Zanzibar as a province of Tanganyika (Nyerere declined). However, Nyerere sent some police to keep law and order (and presumably to keep Karume in office). But Nyerere was concerned with the troubled and uncertain situation in Zanzibar and its implications for East Africa. He proposed a merger of the two countries under a federal type of arrangement. An explanation for this approach was said to be his frustration at the failure to establish an East African Federation; Nyerere had visions of a pan-African federation, and, it is said, saw this as a beginning. In his brief statement to the Tanganyikan Parliament on the ratification of the agreement, he emphasised the need for unity, as a pan-African objective, and the long historical association between the people of Tanganyika and Zanzibar that made unity natural.[6] However, this explanation may not be entirely convincing – a takeover of a troubled and troubling island is hardly the harbinger of a continent-wide coming together. It is also likely that President Nyerere felt that his philosophy of African socialism would be contaminated by the communist doctrine infiltrating from Zanzibar.[7]

Negotiations for the Union

There were no negotiations. The Union was a matter of convenience, but as mentioned earlier, the convenience was on different terms for the two key figures involved in the merger. Even between them there seems to have been little of what might called negotiations. After the coup, which seemed to have surprised everyone, even those close to Karume, Nyerere sent Tanganyikan police to keep law and order in Zanzibar, and to keep Karume in office. It was the threat of withdrawing the police that compelled Karume, given his vulnerability, to

[5] Don Peterson, *Revolution in Zanzibar: An American Cold War Tale* (Boulder: Westview Press, 2002), 121.

[6] The preamble of the Articles of Union talked of the 'long association of the people of these lands and their ties of kinship and amity' claiming that they were 'desirous of furthering that association and strengthening of these ties and furthering the unity of African peoples'. See also Shivji, *Pan-Africanism or Pragmatism?*, 82–3. This book is an authoritative account of the politics and procedure of the Union.

[7] Nyerere is quoted as saying, 'If I could tow that Island [Zanzibar] out in the middle of the Indian Ocean, I'd do it . . . it is very vulnerable to outside influence. I fear it will be a big headache to me'. This statement is quoted in several publications, but no reference is provided. See for example Shivji, *Pan-Africanism or Pragmatism?*, 76.

agree to the merger. Nyerere's interest in merger was less personal, but it was his personal assessment of risks that drove him to it. And in the end it was merger by threat. Neither Karume nor Nyerere consulted any of their cabinet colleagues. All the paperwork, which included the form of governmental arrangements after merger, was done in secret in Dar es Salaam, by Nyerere's foreign advisors, in extreme haste, and taken by him to Zanzibar. Zanzibar's attorney-general was not around (some say he was banished by the Tanganyika team) to advise Karume on the legal structures (which in any case did not amount to more than a couple of pages). Karume himself, barely literate, was not renowned for his legal or political knowledge or skills, and so it is quite likely that he never read or at least understood the document by which he surrendered the sovereignty of Zanzibar to Tanganyika.[8]

The ratification of the agreement involved some procedures, but these were of little consequence in the chaotic situation prevailing in Zanzibar (there is now much learned disquisition on whether the agreement was ever formally ratified there, but the better view holds that there was no ratification). As for Tanganyika, the autocratic and dominant status of Nyerere in what was essentially a one party system meant there was no real debate, and the ratification was completed in record time (one hour and forty minutes). In retrospect it would appear that the secrecy and speed was to pre-empt opposition to the Union from significant groups in both Zanzibar and Tanganyika.

In neither part of the new Union were the people involved in any way whatsoever in the historic event of the merger. Nyerere's account of the long historical links between the two entities and their wish for unity does not square well with the secrecy surrounding the negotiations and the speed of ratification. The Arab population of Zanzibar would have had little reason for merger with Tanganyika, and many interpreted the merger in terms of their marginalisation. The links between Tanganyika and Zanzibar were based on the migration of a significant number of people from Tanganyika to Zanzibar, to the point that the Africans outnumber the Arabs (or, as two scholars have put it in class terms, 'a landless peasantry against a landed aristocracy and political oligarchy').[9]

Certainly few people understood its significance, and not many were much bothered. The people of either part, used to the politics of one party government (Tanganyika) or autocratic rule (Zanzibar) knew better than to question the merger, much less to protest. The terrible atrocities inflicted on the minorities in Zanzibar who might have had a stake in its lifestyle silenced them (thousands migrated away from the island). So almost uniquely among the case studies in this volume, there were no struggles for secession or freedom (other than the struggle for sovereignty in Tanganyika), or mass movements for cultural or political identity, no appeals to human dignity or group rights, no protracted negotiations – just two signatures on a thin document – drawing on a model

[8] Shivji, *Pan-Africanism or Pragmatism?*, 82–3

[9] Jjuuko and Muriuki, *Federation Within Federation*, 4.

from a far off place not many had heard of: Northern Ireland, yet without its passions, and without great success. Tanganyika and Zanzibar were separate states, so providing self-government for the latter made no sense as a purpose for the autonomy. Nor were the bonds between the peoples so strong or ideologies so similar that their coming together had much inherent logic. This lack of purpose has been the bane of the Union.

The first list of division of powers shows a limited, obvious, but not unimportant role for the central authorities, although not one that suggests much common purpose or broad consensus on critical issues. So consensus on local issues, much less a common vision of the future merged nation, was considered less important than that Tanganyika should control foreign policy and foreign influences. The rigorous exclusion of Zanzibar from foreign organisations or affairs (such as prohibition on joining the Organisation of Islamic States) reinforces that interpretation of the primary reason for the merger.

The consequences were predictable: indifference in Tanganyika and anxiety in Zanzibar. Not really a good start to the difficult journey to co-existence. Nor was there much co-existence, as Zanzibar under both Karume and his successors behaved as if there were no merger – mainlanders, citizens or residents, required visas to enter Zanzibar, not easy to obtain.

Constitutional basis of the Union

As outlined previously, the Union was based on a treaty and implemented through constitutional and other laws in both units. It is unclear whether Karume had the authority to make such a treaty (so confused was the constitutional situation). Since 1964, the importance of the treaty has been minimal, and reference to it has been rare. Meanwhile many terms of the original agreement have been altered, using amendments to the Constitution. The treaty remains unaltered.

The two bases are interconnected, to the extent that the treaty states that 'the Articles shall be subject to (a) ratification by the respective legislatures' (i.e., the Parliament in the case of Tanganyika and the Revolutionary Council in conjunction with the Cabinet in the case of Zanzibar) and (b) enactment of laws 'providing for the Government of the United Republic and Zanzibar in accordance therewith'.[10]

The Tanganyika Parliament ratified the Agreement through an Act that gave effect to the terms of the treaty, by the votes of more than two thirds of the members, as required for constitutional amendment. Doubts persist whether it was ratified by the Zanzibar Revolutionary Council, which also acted as Zanzibar's legislature; but it does seem that despite the absence of a Gazette Notice, on the same day as Tanganyika, the Agreement was ratified. Instruments of ratification were exchanged two days later before the Speaker of the Tanganyika

[10] Art. viii.

Parliament, and five members of the Revolutionary Council were sworn in as ministers of the Union.

In identical language, the Acts of Union (sometimes called Articles of Union) declared, 'The Republic of Tanganyika and the People's Republic of Zanzibar shall, upon Union Day and ever after, be united into one Sovereign Republic by the name of the United Republic of Tanganyika and Zanzibar' (Union Day was fixed as 26 April). The Acts of Union in both entities provided for a permanent constitution to be made within a year by a constituent assembly on the basis of a draft prepared by a constitutional commission. Meanwhile Tanganyika's Republic Constitution of 1964 as modified by the Articles of Union would serve as the interim constitution. But the Interim Constitution was to last for twelve years, to be replaced only in 1977.[11] An opportunity was lost to engage the people in both parts on the merits of the Union and the appropriate constitutional structures for it.

Tanganyika's Republic Constitution of 1964 as modified by the Articles of Union provided for the United Republic Government, under an executive presidency, with responsibility for Union matters (as, at that time, agreed in the Articles of Union) and a government in Zanzibar in accordance with its own constitution, with responsibility there for non-Union matters – also dominated by its president. Links between Tanganyika/Tanzania on the one hand and Zanzibar on the other were to be through membership in the previous Tanganyika parliament (now the Union Parliament) of Zanzibar members (which in the absence of elections, meant nominees of the Zanzibar Revolutionary Council), the appointment of the Zanzibar President *ex officio* as the First Vice President of the Union to assist the Union President in the discharge of Union responsibilities in Zanzibar and the appointment of a small number of Zanzibaris to the Tanzanian (Union) cabinet. The public service and judiciaries of the two parts remained separate.

In 1965, the Tanganyika Constitution of 1964 was replaced by an Interim Constitution (destined to last until 1977, though frequently amended) that established the United Republic as a one party state – ironically, with two parties. In Tanganyika/Tanzania, the Tanganyika African National Union became the sole party and in Zanzibar, the Afro-Sirazi Party. Gradually the role of the single party increased; an amendment in 1975 declared that all state organs had to function under direction from the party.

In 1977 the Permanent Constitution, as it is often called, was enacted. It was in part the consolidation of advances made by the single parties, and partly innovative. Before its enactment, the two parties had merged into one party, Chama Cha Mapinduzi – a further loss of autonomy for Zanzibar.[12]

[11] An Act of the Parliament of the United Republic dated 26 March 1965 postponed the convening of the Constituent Assembly indefinitely ('at such times as shall be opportune').

[12] Shivji, *Pan-Africanism or Pragmatism?* argues that the merger was to strengthen the position of former members of the Afro-Shirazi Party who were rapidly losing support in Zanzibar.

The draft constitution was prepared by a twenty-person committee of Chama Cha Mapinduzi, which was later designated as the constitutional commission envisaged in the Articles of Union, but with little public consultation or debate. The draft was approved by the Chama Cha Mapinduzi executive committee in one day in camera, after which it was sent to a constituent assembly appointed by the United Republic President – in fact Nyerere converted the National Assembly (all Chama Cha Mapinduzi members) into the constituent assembly! The constituent assembly had a week to study the draft and the public four days, but few seemed to have read it. The constituent assembly adopted it in a record three hours, on 16 March 1977.[13]

The 1977 Constitution, for the first time, sets out the framework of the Zanzibar Constitution in a United Republic document. Perhaps the real significance is symbolic, since the essential details are as stated in the 1982 Zanzibar Constitution. The powers and functions of the Zanzibar Government are restricted to non-Union matters. The Constitution provides for the office, elections, tenure and powers of the president of Zanzibar and the relationship of the president with the Revolutionary Council (which is essentially advisory). However, there is a major change from the original rule that the president of Zanzibar was to be the First Vice-President of the Republic, assisting the president of Tanzania in respect of the administration of Union affairs in Zanzibar. That office and role have been removed, providing for the direct administration of Union matters. Instead the Zanzibar president is now a member of the Tanzanian cabinet – thus preserving some link.[14] There is also provision for the post of prime minister; the member of the National Assembly who leads the majority party or has the support of the largest number of MPs is appointed to that post.[15] The prime minister leads the executive under the direction of the president; is the leader of government business in parliament; and the chief assistant to the president. It is likely that a post like this would affect the hierarchy of state officials, with perhaps some downgrading of the Zanzibar president.

The Constitution also establishes Zanzibar's legislature called the House of Representatives, prescribes its composition and gives it a function of accountability to the executive. There is also recognition of the Zanzibar High Court and the jurisdiction of the Tanzania Court of Appeal over Zanzibar. A special court is established to deal with disputes between the governments of the Republic and Zanzibar (more on this later).

[13] The then Prime Minister, Edward Sokoine, left little choice to the parliamentarians, opening the debate thus:

> '[I]n exercising our authority we ought to be conscious of its limitations. The proposals we are about to debate are the outcome of the Party directives. We Tanzanians, in our wisdom, have determined without hesitation that the Party shall be the ultimate authority in the country. Therefore this Constituent Assembly has full powers to reject or amend these Government proposals if it feels that they are contrary to, or in conflict with, the Party directives. On the other hand, if these proposals correctly implement the Party's wishes, I beg the Assembly to accept them without a moment's hesitation (applause).' *Pan-Africanism or Pragmatism?* 169.

[14] Art. 54. [15] Art. 51.

The 1977 Constitution was the high water mark of single party domination, inherently antithetical to autonomy. It was not for several years that the tide turned, and it was set in motion by a United Republic President from Zanzibar, Ali Hassan Mwinyi, who set up a relatively independent commission under a former chief justice to seek public opinion on the question of whether to establish a one- or multi-party system. The recommendation was overwhelmingly for a multi-party system, which is now in place, as described next. The public also demanded a bill of rights – which is now part of the Constitution, for the first time in the country's history.

The Articles of Union and constitutional developments

The Articles of the Union have not been always followed in subsequent constitutional developments. The current constitutional system is significantly different from the 1964 Constitution under which the merger of the two countries took place. The changes were made by amendments to that Constitution, before it itself was replaced in 1977. The Articles/Acts of Union have not been amended to match the changes in the Constitution. There seem to be deliberate attempts on the part of Tanzania to downplay the status and role of the Articles of Union. Those who, like Shivji, regard the Articles as the *grundnorm* of Tanzania's constitutional order see many aspects of the Constitution concerning the relationship of Zanzibar to Tanzania as unconstitutional.[16] Shivji states that the Articles of Union, through the Acts of Union, are part of the Constitution of the Union and that of Zanzibar. Both the Constitution of Zanzibar and the Union Constitution are subordinate to the Acts of Union and, in case of conflict, the Acts of Union should prevail. This view of the Articles has considerable appeal to Zanzibaris, who feel deeply resentful of what they regard as the attrition of their sovereignty and specific powers since the establishment of the Union.[17]

But Shivji acknowledges that this position is not uncontested. In the case of *Mtumwa Saidi Haji and 49 Others v. The Attorney General* the Court of Appeal, while agreeing that the Articles/Acts of Union still had the force of law, decided that they could be amended by the Constitution because they were a schedule to it.

The issue came up indirectly before the High Court of Zanzibar and on appeal to the Tanzania Court of Appeal.[18] At issue was whether there could be an offence of treason against the Zanzibar government. This, the parties agreed, depended on whether Zanzibar was a sovereign state. The accused argued that it was not, having been merged with Tanganyika to create a new state in which sovereignty was then vested. Reference was made to Article 1

[16] Issa Shivji's position is set out in two publications: *Legal Foundations of the Union* (Dar es Salaam: Dar es Salaam University Press, 2009) 2nd edn., and *Pan-Africanism or Pragmatism?* (Dar es Salaam: Mkuki na Nyota Publishers, 2008).

[17] Shivji, *Legal Foundations of the Union*.

[18] *S.M.Z. v. Machano Khamis Ali & 17 Others*, Criminal Application No. 8 of 2000 [2000] TZCA 1.

of the Zanzibar Constitution 1984, which says, 'Zanzibar is an integral part of the United Republic of Tanzania', and Article 1 of the Union Constitution, which states that 'Tanzania is one State and is a sovereign United Republic'. Zanzibar had limited powers (which excluded Union matters) and so could not be sovereign.

The prosecution argued that sovereignty is divisible (giving examples from various federations) and in the case of Tanzania, some of it lies in Zanzibar (the authority of the Tanzania legislature, executive and judiciary being limited). The court accepted the theory of divided loyalty; and ruled that there could be treason against the Government of Zanzibar, as it was performing functions of the state, with executive, legislative and judicial powers.

The accused appealed against this ruling to the Court of Appeal. Although the prosecution entered *nolle prosequi*, the Court of Appeal proceeded with the appeal (although on the whole Tanzania courts avoid dealing with disputes between the two governments). The way the issue was put by the Court of Appeal was whether Zanzibar is a state and is the Revolutionary Government of Zanzibar sovereign? The Court of Appeal relied on the Tanzania Constitution, disregarding the Zanzibar Constitution 1982, except for Article 1, which declares that 'Zanzibar is part of the United Republic' (although as Shivji notes, the Union Constitution itself points to the Zanzibar Constitution when it provides in Article 102(2) that 'the Revolutionary Government of Zanzibar will be constituted and exercise its powers in accordance with this Constitution and the Constitution of Zanzibar').[19]

The Court of Appeal too accepted the theory of divisible sovereignty, but relying on the Swahili translation of the Constitution (Swahili being the ruling language) of Article 1 of the Union Constitution, that 'Tanzania is one country and is a United Republic', concluded that there was no divided sovereignty. The judgments ends emphatically, 'There is absolutely no iota of dispute that the United Republic of Tanzania is indeed one country, one state'. This conclusion was reached through a rather formal approach, without much regard to history or the considerable powers of the Zanzibar Government, which are beyond the reach of the Tanzania Government.

But this ruling is consistent with the general approach of the Tanzania Government, frequently of the Zanzibar Government and of the judiciary. This position was challenged by a president of Zanzibar, Aboud Jumbe, who was anxious to maintain the autonomy of Zanzibar. He was concerned that the fusion of the parties and the influence of the single party would erode the autonomy of state organs and their ability to preserve the sovereignty of Zanzibar in non-Union matters through the two-government structure.[20]

[19] Shivji, *Legal Foundations of the Union*, 88–9.

[20] As quoted in Shivji, *Pan-Africanism or Pragmatism?*, 182. Chapter 6 of his book provides an excellent account of Jumbe's efforts to maintain Zanzibar's autonomy, and the history of constitution making in Zanzibar.

There is no space to discuss further the interesting debate on this issue. But it does raise a question of general interest in countries that established federalism or autonomy as a result of the coming together of separate entities through some form of agreement, binding perhaps under international law and of course pre-dating the new constitutional arrangement (as do many studies in this volume).

The Articles of Union provide for enactments of laws by the two legislatures including 'providing for the Government of the United Republic and of Zanzibar in accordance therewith'.[21] Soon the Tanganyika Constitution was amended to serve as the Interim Union Constitution. Further amendments and laws were made to conform to this new arrangement (with the participation of members from both sides). The Articles as well as Acts of Union assume the development of a fuller constitutional system. Does the constitution not become the basis of future relationships? Has not a new sovereign emerged? Can there be further treaty negotiations between two parts of the same state? Would the situation be different if the relationship was seen as autonomy, so the agreement would have the character of constitutional law, and therefore be amenable to re-negotiation? What happens to an agreement to federate once federation happens? India, Canada, Australia and the United States are examples of union on the basis of agreements or new constitutions. Some may give a veto to constitutional amendment to each unit, previously separate and sovereign, but many will require a particular national majority, a second chamber, or a majority vote in a specified number of states. The new arrangements thus reached would modify or replace the original agreement. Most autonomy systems studied in this volume have undergone changes, some quite fundamental (as for example in the re-organisation of states). Can it be argued that they are invalid if they contradict a provision of the original agreement? Federalism and autonomy are dynamic systems and must adjust to changing circumstances (provided the process follows rules for amendment). Or are there some provisions that are unalterable, whose amendment introduces a system incompatible with fundamental principles or undertakings at the time of formation?

The Articles of Union were drawn in great haste, with one party dominating, without public consultations, much less approval, by lawyers obviously not familiar with federal or autonomy systems, and are skeletal. They have been criticised by the same people and scholars who lament departures from the Articles of Union, and call them unconstitutional. So what is alterable in the Articles and what not?

Federation or autonomy?

Before I turn to the features of the relationship between Zanzibar and Tanzania, I discuss briefly how to categorise the Union. The Court of Appeal, while

[21] Clause viii.

commenting that the constitutional set-up of the United Republic is unique, observed, 'It is a union but with some elements of federalism'. Shivji calls it federal. However, few lists of federal countries prepared by scholars (such as the eminent authority, Ronald Watts) or the international Forum of Federations include Tanzania, nor does the Tanzanian Constitution use the term. But Shivji says emphatically (and in my view correctly) that Tanzania is federal, stating that federations come in many guises. He maintains that neither part was intended to dominate the other. A federation is in part a matter of constitution and laws, and in part political approaches and attitudes. Tanzania satisfies most of the formal criteria of a federation: the relations between its different components are set out in the constitution, which is supreme law, and cannot be altered in its federal elements without the support of a prescribed number of members of the national legislature representing Zanzibar and the Mainland (i.e., the former Tanganyika), voting separately. The constitution is reviewable by the courts. There are two orders of government (national and regional), each with its powers clearly specified. There are federal and regional legislatures and governments, with regional and federal laws applying through the country. However, the institutional arrangements, whereby the Union legislature and executive double up as the Mainland's legislature and executive, obscure, somewhat, the reality of federalism, and might suggest that Zanzibar, with its own institutions for these purposes, is merely 'autonomous', a form of devolution (which it is certainly not in its origins). But on the second count, political attitudes, the case for federal designation may be less convincing, with overwhelming Mainland influence, and the Union Parliament legislating for the whole country, while the jurisdiction of Zanzibar's institutions is confined to Zanzibar. The institutional arrangements suggest that Zanzibar's status may well be defined as 'autonomous'.

Two related comments on the viability of the federation can be made in respect of these institutional arrangements, both tending towards the diminution of the standing of the federal unit, which also has its separate institutions. The first is that the arrangements look similar to those found in autonomy systems, where the powers of the unit with its own institutions come from the centre, through devolution and thus are lesser than those in a federation, even if devolved powers are recognised in the constitution (examples include Puerto Rico, Åland, South Tyrol and Scotland). It is important to emphasise that the status and powers of Zanzibar are not of this kind (and cannot be taken away by the Union legislature except with the consent of its representatives). But the constant references to powers and institutions of the United Republic (in the constitution and elsewhere) do give the impression of a subordinate status for Zanzibar. Secondly, the dominance of Mainland members in the legislature and executive authorities of the Union might make the resources and viability of Zanzibar contingent (or seem to be so) on the Mainland. These arrangements are prone to make people in both parts uncomfortable, even resentful (in circumstances where there is such disparity in their size). The smaller unit fears the power of the other, and the larger unit resents what it feels is unfairly high representation of the other in Union institutions, including the right of the members from that unit to vote on legislative issues that do not concern it.

Institutions

Structure of union: two or three governments?

As noted previously, Tanzania consists of two governments, but has three entities. From the very beginning, what was the Tanganyika Government became the Tanzanian or Union government dealing with Union matters throughout the Republic – in addition to dealing also with non-Union matters in Tanganyika (or the Mainland). The system of two governments has been a source of considerable tension, much resented by Zanzibaris, who see it as a device for the Mainland to dominate the Republic. By virtue of its size and population, the Mainland commands institutions and policies of the Republic, and in the simultaneous exercise of its authority over non-Union matters, it blurs the line between Union and non-Union matters – and thus an essential principle of federalism as well as autonomy. Although most Mainlanders regard the combination of Union and non-Union as unproblematic, there are critics among them who consider that Zanzibar members in Union institutions exercise undue influence on what are internal Tanganyikan affairs – often classified as the 'West Lothian problem' in the UK, where Scottish and Irish members of the UK Parliament vote on issues over which they have autonomy, and so are not subject to the law in whose enactment they participate.

Zanzibaris have long argued that there should be three governments, with the Union Government dealing only with Union matters. Aboud Jumbe argued that this was indeed the original intention behind the Articles of Union in 1964, and which the constitutional process to be set up within a year was to accomplish. The long postponement of the commission and the constituent assembly, decided unilaterally by the Republic institutions without consultation with the Vice-President or the Zanzibar President, consolidated the two-government system.[22] The two-government system might well have made sense for a short interim period. It represented minimum change, and a rather simple structure, when the limited capacity for a complex system was probably lacking. But it failed to address some difficult questions, and produced a system that did not respond to the growing complexity of the situation.

Citizenship: one or more

Citizenship of the Republic was dealt with in the Union Constitution. Citizenship entailed full rights on the Mainland but for the full exercise of citizenship

[22] See Shivji, *Pan-Africanism or Pragmatism?*, 209–10.

rights in Zanzibar (voting electoral rights) a citizen of Tanzania had to be resident for there for five years (later reduced). This rule caused considerable resentment among those who had come from the Mainland. In 1999 this was reduced to three years. And until 1999 Mainlanders needed a passport to be able to enter Zanzibar, which did little to establish a sense of common citizenship. And that Zanzibaris could enter the Mainland, find employment and settle there, gave the impression of unequal citizenship. Not surprisingly, this discrimination was much resented by Mainlanders.

Distribution of powers

Since its inception, Tanzania has had only one list of powers. These powers belong exclusively to the United Republic. All other powers were to remain with Tanganyika and Zanzibar. The Zanzibar government has, in respect of Zanzibar, exclusive powers over all matters not on the one list. But the residual powers belonging to Tanganyika were to be exercised by the Union Government; in other words unlike in Zanzibar, there was to be no separate government for Tanganyika. Thus the United Republic has plenary responsibility for all matters for Tanganyika. So there are three sets of powers or jurisdictions, but only two levels of government. As we shall see, having a centre which has two sets of powers has caused various problems, especially as the same institutions and procedures are deployed by the Union Government for the exercise of both sets of powers.

The original list contained eleven items set out in the Articles of Union: (1) the Constitution and government of the United Republic; (2) external affairs; (3) defence; (4) police; (5) emergency powers; (6) citizenship; (7) immigration; (8) external trade and borrowing; (9) public service of the United Republic; (10) income tax, corporation tax, customs and excise duties; and (11) harbours, civil aviation, posts and telegraph.

Twice as many additional matters were added to the Union list in a short space of time (which now appears in the first Schedule to the Constitution). The first, added by the Interim Constitution in 1965, concerned the financial sector: currency (and bank notes), commercial banks and banking transactions (to strengthen the management of foreign currency and banks in the Union). Another set of provisions were triggered by the creation of the East African Community in 1967, including industrial licenses and statistics, higher education, civil aviation and air transport (which fell within the jurisdiction of the Community).

In 1968 oil products, including crude oil, petroleum products and natural gas were added. The permanent constitution of 1977 introduced in the Union list Tanzania National Examinations Council and matters related to it (to harmonise the system of examinations throughout the country). On the collapse of the East African Community, some items were transferred to the Union Government, including civil aviation, research, statistics and meteorology. In 1979 the Court of Appeal became a Union matter, with the collapse of the East African Court of Appeals. Finally, in 1992, following political reforms, the registration of political parties and other matters related to political parties were added to the list.

Various items are included in individual Union matters, and thus the list is longer than might appear at first glance, for example defence is coupled with security, and currency with banking ('all banking business'). And this list is, however, not exhaustive of Union matters. Courts have acknowledged other ways in which a matter becomes essentially Union. Some issues or institutions specified in the Constitution may apply to both sides of the Republic, and are effectively under Union control.

In *Haji v. Nungu & Anor.*,[23] the Chief Justice Nyalali identified matters in the Constitution that concern both sides of the Union, such as the former Permanent Commission of Enquiry now replaced by the Human Rights Commission[24] and the Constitutional Court.[25] C. J. Nyalali mentioned also legislation under Art. 64(4) of the Constitution, which applies in both parts, and gave as an example the Elections Act, which applies throughout the Republic (and has had a major impact on elections in Zanzibar). There is no foundation for it in the Articles of Union and this in fact violates the Zanzibar Constitution under which 'All legislative power in Zanzibar over all non-Union matters is vested in the House of Representatives' (the Zanzibar legislature).[26]

Nevertheless, many important matters are left to Zanzibar such as agriculture, industry, trade, health, land, primary and secondary education, corporations and co-operatives and social matters like family, marriage and inheritance.

It is not easy to understand the logic of the division of powers.[27] The original list did perhaps have logic: the Union powers were primarily concerned with foreign affairs and defence, understandable in view of the circumstances leading to the Union. Subsequent additions show no particular logic, nor are they all equally precise. One can also question the logic of only one list. It conveys the impression that the intention of the Union was to keep the two parts largely separated, which may not be consistent with Nyerere's commitment to closer unity and co-operation. There is not enough flexibility in this approach; flexibility is often achieved by having additionally a list of concurrent powers available to either part as necessary and as negotiated – and a good basis for co-operation. With a single list, periodic resort to the amendment of the constitution as conditions change is necessary. And it is unfortunate that the initiative for the amendment lies with the bigger partner with more political and administrative clout.[28] The Union Government may also be less aware of

[23] (1987) LRC (Const.) 224. [24] Art. 129. [25] Art. 125. [26] Art. 78(1).

[27] The Constitution unhelpfully and unimaginatively says that for more efficient discharge of public affairs and the effective division of the functions among the designated organs, Article 4(3) categorises affairs into Union Matters and non-Union Matters.

[28] The present rules for amendment of the list require the approval of two thirds of MPs from both Tanzania Mainland (Tanganyika) and Zanzibar (Art. 98(1)(b)). In practice Zanzibar MPs are less engaged or active in Union parliamentary proceedings. And decisions on amendments

the constraints that Zanzibar faces due to the division of powers, as the division makes little difference to it, being in charge of Union and regional powers (and not infrequently a Union ministry would deal with both Union and non-Union matters, further blurring the distinction).

So it is not surprising that Zanzibar feels that the Union government is not sensitive to its needs, and that the additions to the Union matters have gradually limited the scope of its autonomy. Some see in the gradual increase confirmation of their suspicions that Tanganyika intends to absorb Zanzibar, in what will become even more of a unitary system. Zanzibaris (and not only they) consider that the additions are unconstitutional because they violate the division agreed in the Articles of the Union. For all these reasons, the division of powers has become an awkward and difficult issue (although perhaps also reflective of other frustrations on the part of Zanzibaris) – even though the division is not strictly observed. The lack of any effective method to resolve differences in interpretation of what exactly is entailed in a particular item contributes to controversy, and enables both governments to exceed their authority with impunity.

Financial provisions

After nearly fifty years of the Union, there are no proper mechanisms or formulas for the distribution of finances – these were not provided for in the constitutional and legal instruments established at the time of the Union. The original assumption was that each side would keep the revenue that it generates. Eventually agreement was reached on an interim arrangement that Zanzibar would receive 4.5 per cent of the national revenue. Zanzibaris complain that this is too little and seek 10 per cent; the Tanzanian Government says that it would, reluctantly, increase it to 5 per cent. The practice seems to be that the revenue collection authority transfers to each government the revenue collected in its area (regardless of origin).[29]

A Joint Financial Commission with members from both sides, and including the Governor of the Bank of Tanzania and the Chair of the Tanzania Revenue Authority, was established in 2003 to determine rules for collection and distribution of revenue.[30] Its task is complicated by the structure of ministries on the Mainland, which straddle Union and non-Union matters, and others have jurisdiction over only non-Union matters. From which fund should their budget come? The Constitution provides for two funds: a Joint Finance Account (for contributions from the two governments)[31] and a Consolidated Fund for the Union.[32] Differences as to the holding and use of foreign currency have

have always been made by the Union government. However, it is important to note that before a proposal for addition is submitted to the Union parliament, it must have been approved by Union and Zanzibar governments.

[29] Jjuuko and Muriuki, *Federation Within Federation*, 56–8.

[30] Constitution, Art. 134. [31] Art. 133. [32] Art. 135.

remained unresolved, Zanzibar claiming that its funds should not be handled by the national bank. The Joint Financial Commission has an important advisory role in the financial system, but it seems that in practice, its impact is limited. As with some other areas, while Zanzibar is keen on clear rules on implementing policies, as well as specific institutions to carry them out, the Mainland government is reluctant to move away from informal and unregulated procedures.

Inter-governmental and dispute resolution mechanisms

Tanzania started with a sharp separation of territory, governments and powers and functions. There were few institutions for discussions, negotiations or co-operation between the two entities. On the Mainland two jurisdictions were managed by the same government, which may have removed the need for formal institutions there. But the very mixing of the functions of two jurisdictions in this way without a mediating mechanism led essentially to the denial of the distinctiveness of one type of jurisdiction. But there were no formal mechanisms for consultation between the governments in the Mainland and in Zanzibar. A certain number of Zanzibaris were appointed to the Tanzanian legislature and executive, and though overrepresented by population size, were nevertheless a minority (and outside the Mainland ruling party). As we have seen and as I later explore further, the single parties of the two units became the fora for negotiations – and subsequently within the party based on their merger (Chama Cha Mapinduzi). This mechanism was probably worse than the former situation.

Judiciary

As to the judiciary's role as settler of disputes, the Mainland and Zanzibar had completely separate judicial systems, in terms of court structures and philosophies of justice (but appeals to the Tanzanian Court of Appeal from Zanzibar were allowed in due course). The Court of Appeal has judges from both the Mainland and Zanzibar and hears appeals from the High Courts of both parts. However the Zanzibar Constitution denies the Court of Appeal jurisdiction to interpret the Zanzibar Constitution.[33] And the Union Constitution forbids the Court of Appeal from hearing any case that should be dealt with by the Special Constitutional Court of the United Republic.[34] On the whole, courts have avoided issues regarding the relationship of the Mainland and Zanzibar, and on the few occasions when these arose in the context of other cases (such as the prosecution for treason discussed previously), the basis of the decision was rather formal and brief. The exclusions of jurisdiction and the reluctance of judges to enter this territory has meant that there has been no formal

[33] Art. 99(a). [34] Art. 117.

resolution of substantial inconsistencies and contradictions between the Union and Zanzibar constitutions, and as a result, the federal characteristics of the Union have been undercut as the system has become increasingly unitary by nibbling away at Zanzibar's autonomy.

Despite its title, the Special Constitutional Court is not a court in the normal sense. Its members, half from each part of the Republic, are appointed by its government, on an ad hoc basis, to hear a reference (presumably by one of the governments – the matter is left to legislation). The Court must give a 'conciliatory decision' (whatever that means) – less like arbitration and more like mediation (there is no appeal from the decision). Decisions are made by the support of two thirds of judges from each side. The court has not played any role in the resolution of disputes or in constitutional interpretation.

The circumstances of its origin suggest that perhaps it was not expected to play a role – it would have represented a major change from the somewhat informal, secretive, party driven and Mainland dominated procedure, whether in the Union cabinet or the inner sanctum of the Party. It was this procedure that was criticised by Zanzibar's President Jumbe, who made various proposals to safeguard Zanzibar's autonomy and bring openness and democracy to bear upon the relations between the two parts.[35] Although his criticism prompted Nyerere to introduce this Court, Nyerere accused him of seeking a legalistic approach to a political issue and sacked him from his post and the inner sanctum of the Chama Cha Mapinduzi.[36] So far, no reference has been made to the Court – and consequently the Court has never been convened.

Tanzania has also tried commissions and committees to tackle Union issues (including the Joint Financial Commission, discussed earlier). A particularly important body is the high-powered Committee of the Vice-President, composed of ministers, including both the prime minister and Zanzibar chief minister. It generally works through sub-committees, including on customs (especially on transit goods), oil and energy (particularly oil exploration). Under its direction the Commission on Human Rights and Good Governance was established in Zanzibar, and progress has been made on other issues, including deep-sea fishing and merchant shipping. But in some other areas, like national unity and proportional representation, it has failed.[37]

[35] For an account of Jumbe's efforts in this regard, see Shivji, *Pan-Africanism or Pragmatism?*, Chapter 6 ('Constitutional Opening and Closure: Jumbe's Downfall (1979–1985)'). For reasons of space, here I do not discuss fully the attempts of the Mainland to minimise Zanzibar's autonomy and to suppress attempts at open discussion of Union relations and related issues.

[36] Jjuuko and Muruiki, *Federation Within Federation*, 51–2. The authors add, 'The Jumbe experience is said to have dampened any enthusiasm to invoke the court to resolve Union problems'.

[37] Ibid., 58–61.

Political parties

Even more than is the case in most autonomy systems, it is hard to understand the dynamics of the relationship between Tanzania and Zanzibar without paying close attention to the structure and role of political parties.

Tanganyika achieved independence effectively as a one-party state. The independence movement was led by the Tanganyika African National Union under the leadership of Julius Nyerere. The dominance of the party increased as it took over the reins of government, so that the country became a de facto one-party state.[38] The institutions of the party, at least for the purposes of policy making, became much more important than those of the state – and led to the restriction of democracy. The eventual establishment of Tanganyika as a one-party state was justified by Nyerere on the grounds that the recognition of the Tanganyika African National Union as the sole party would enable the democratisation of the state as the differences and debates within the party could then be played out in the open.

After the Union both parts became one-party systems, but with different parties (in Zanzibar the Afro-Shirazi Party became the one party). Eventually the parties were merged as the Chama Cha Mapinduzi so that the whole country became a single one-party system. Consequently, relations between the two parts were mediated increasingly within the party councils, lessening the role of and opportunity for democracy (in an ironic contrast to the Nyerere thesis that a legal one-party system promotes democracy). And it led to the effective diminution of the autonomy of Zanzibar (illustrated by the disciplining and expulsion of Aboud Jumbe), leading Zanzibaris to complain that 'the leadership of Zanzibar is plotted in Dodomo [capital of Tanzania], not Zanzibar; that a special committee on Zanzibar with the president as chair considers the aspirants for Zanzibar leadership'.[39]

Zanzibar was from the beginning marked by greater divergence among political parties. The merger of the Afro-Sirazi Party and Umma Party at the time of the coup generated particular difficulty, resolved in part by Karume by sending Umma leaders away to the cabinet in Dar es Salaam. The emergence of the Chama Cha Mapinduzi as a single national party also exposed divisions among Zanzibar members, as when powerful Zanzibar members opposed Jumbe when he proposed constitutional reform – perhaps, some suspected, provoked by Nyerere himself. With the emergence of a multi-party system in the 1980s, a new party, the Civic United Front, arose to oppose the Zanzibar branch of the Chama Cha Mapinduzi (composed of remnants of the Afro-Sirazi Party). In subsequent elections, there was considerable fighting between the two parties. In one election, there was such massive vote rigging that the elections were

[38] Cranford Pratt, *The Critical Phase in Tanzania 1945–1968: Nyerere and the Emergence of a Socialist Strategy* (Cambridge University Press, 1976), 201–11. Nyerere's own defence of one-party state is expressed best in his paper, *Democracy and the Party System* (1963).

[39] Pratt, *The Critical Phase in Tanzania*, 32.

declared void. The security forces were frequently used in such conflicts, and came to be viewed by many in Zanzibar as foreign oppressive forces. These squabbles not only deepened internal differences, but weakened Zanzibar's position vis-à-vis the Mainland. For these reasons the Zanzibar parties agreed to a power-sharing coalition following the elections (the legal amendments were approved in a referendum) – which produced a more united position as regards the Mainland.

The effect of such a long period of one-party dominance has been to downplay the Constitution and law. In the early years the precise legal arrangements may not have mattered much. Each unit was a one-party system, with near absolute powers held by the head of the unit. Nor was there a tradition of constitutionalism or the rule of law that would have checked departures from or disregard of the legal framework. But more recently there has been a deliberate attempt to put the functioning of the Union and its components on constitutional basis. There is wide perception (and in fact reality) that the Union has been managed purely as a political system rather than as a constitutional one, and that the political system undermines the checks and balances that would have led to a better managed Union.[40]

Parties often play an integrative role in federations or autonomies. On the one hand, the balance between national and regional parties can have a significant or even a major impact on politics and government (with India and Canada being good examples). On the other hand, when a region has a strong identity and wishes to maintain it, a regional party becomes dominant there and manages to insulate it from national influences. The fact that in Tanzania for a considerable period only one party could function in each of the two parts meant that the kind of relations that develop between governments and the people at national and other levels through the mediation of parties, including perhaps greater democracy, did not develop in Tanzania. Given the nature of one-party entities, and the politicisation of the overall system, most differences and agreements were negotiated through parties rather than in an open political process. And when the two parties did merge into the Chama Cha Mapinduzi, the entire political focus shifted to the inner sanctum of that party, dominated by the Mainland. Inter-government issues were turned into party issues. This decreased both the scope of democracy overall and the autonomy of Zanzibar. Relations between the two wings of the Chama Cha Mapinduzi have been tense.

Now Tanzania has come full circle with the introduction of a multi-party system, with more than one party at each level and Chama Cha Mapinduzi with minority support in Zanzibar. This has brought to the surface fissures in society at both levels. It will no longer be possible for Chama Cha Mapinduzi to deal with inter-governmental relations through its internal mechanisms. On some issues Zanzibar parties will disagree, on others they would agree (particularly those dealing with relations with Tanzania – and this may also be the case with Mainland parties). The intention, however, is to promote cross-channel parties,

[40] Jjuuko and Muriuki, *Federation Within Federation*, 27–8.

so the Political Parties Act requires that a party have membership in both entities for registration to be granted. It is doubtful if a multi-party framework can function within the present system and structures of government. Moreover, public attitudes have changed from the time when the Union was initiated and developed, and people want to consider alternative arrangements, in which a third government is an option.

On the whole the record of committees and other devices to solve Union problems has been unimpressive. Perhaps the reason is that the purpose of the merger is still unclear, and its persistence is contested. There are numerous grievances, and not only from Zanzibar. Mainlanders resented that they had to carry passports to enter Zanzibar, and if they move there, they do not enjoy equal rights, while by contrast, Zanzibar residents moving to the Mainland enjoy equal rights there. Some feel, perhaps unjustifiably, that the Mainland is subsidising Zanzibar. Mainlanders have objected to a system that gives them no 'self government', as the government ruling its affairs includes, in disproportionate number, members from Zanzibar. A group (the 55 Group) has been agitating for a third government for the Mainland on non-Union matters. This group had formed an alliance with Jumbe who wanted greater and more secure autonomy for Zanzibar. Both were chastised by Nyerere.[41]

Zanzibar's grievances are more numerous. Many were unhappy with the merger of the two single parties, which effectively diminished their autonomy, though this was less critical after the adoption of a multi-party system, but allegations were made that the authorities favoured Chama Cha Mapinduzi over local parties. The removal of Zanzibar's president from the office of the first vice-president was not popular. Mention has already been made of the addition of Union matters, particularly oil (most of which so far is thought to lie in the sea around Zanzibar), while minerals have not been added to the Union list. Zanzibaris resent the conflation of Union and non-Union matters on the Mainland. Underlying these grievances is bitter resentment that there is no recognition of Zanzibar's sovereignty or of its special status within Tanzania, and Zanzibar is treated as another province of the Mainland, stemming from the disregard of the Articles of Union.

Perhaps in view of the discontent outlined here, and the failure of mechanisms to tackle problems and build consensus, the government announced plans for a constitutional review process, albeit somewhat restricted in scope and procedure. Following criticisms, a new scheme was announced in 2012, which promises to be open and participatory, with a broad agenda.

Conclusion

Several reasons for the failure to stick to the original scheme of the Union can be identified. One is that there was and has been a lack of consensus on ideology and the goals of the Union. Another important element, in part following from

[41] Shivji, *Pan-Africanism or Pragmatism?*, 208–25.

the ideological differences, was the institutional design. The design was rushed, and drafted by people lacking expertise in the constitutional design for autonomy.

Two related general comments on the viability of the federation can be made in respect of these institutional arrangements, both of which highlight the diminution of the standing of the federal unit which has its separate institutions. The first is that the arrangements look similar to those found in autonomy systems, where the powers of the unit with its own institutions come from the centre, resulting from devolution and thus of lesser import than would be the case in a federation, even if devolved powers are recognised in the constitution (examples include Puerto Rico, Åland, South Tyrol and Scotland). It is important to emphasise that the status and powers of Zanzibar are not of this kind (and cannot be taken away by the Union legislature except with the consent of its representatives). But the constant references to powers and institutions of the Union (in the Constitution and elsewhere) do give the impression of a subordinate status for Zanzibar. Secondly, the dominance of Mainland members in the legislature and executive authorities of the Union might make the resources and viability of Zanzibar contingent (or seem to be) on the Mainland. These arrangements are prone to make people in both parts uncomfortable, even resentful (in circumstances where there is such disparity in their size). The smaller unit fears the power of the other, and the larger unit resents what it feels is unfairly high representation of the other in Union institutions, including the right of the members from that unit to vote on legislative issues that do not concern it.

Such mutual resentments in Tanzania would not be surprising. In the UK, there has long been resentment against members of the national parliament from Northern Ireland, who are full voting members, and take part in decisions on laws for Britain that would not apply in Northern Ireland, as their subject matter is within Northern Irish autonomy. Similar complaints are now being made against Scottish members in Westminster for voting on issues which fall within Scottish autonomy (the problem known in the literature as the 'West Lothian' question). Serious proposals have been advanced that such members should only vote on laws that would apply in their regions. In less well-established systems, such arrangements can lead to the collapse of the federation.

Currently such circumstances are apparent in the Caribbean federation of Saint Kitts and Nevis, where the institutional structures are very similar to Tanzania's and where the smaller partner, Nevis, feels neglected by Saint Kitts. Political parties in Nevis have recently been agitating for the dissolution of the federation. The Constitution allows the Nevis legislature to initiate the process for secession, the final decision being that of the people of Nevis in a referendum. The short-lived federation of Ethiopia and Eritrea, which was inaugurated in 1952 under UN auspices, was based on somewhat similar institutional arrangements. But the relationship of Eritrea to Ethiopia, and the internal constitutional arrangements within Eritrea, were defined in Eritrea's Constitution, which was approved by the UN General Assembly. This was at the time of the Ethiopian emperor, who personified the sovereignty of the federation, and consequently Eritrea was subservient to the Emperor (and thus to Ethiopia) in much greater degree than the smaller unit in Tanzania and Saint Kitts and Nevis. The United Nations described the new status of Eritrea as 'an autonomous unit federated with Ethiopia under the sovereignty of the Ethiopian crown'. The dominance of the emperor made it hard to apply adequately federal principles, particularly those of 'self-rule' and 'shared rule'. Despite having this inferior status, the collapse of the federation was not due to the initiative of Eritreans, but of the Emperor, who, one might say, first dominated Eritrean affairs and then swallowed Eritrea, converting the new entity into a unitary state. It was perhaps ominous that the Sudan peace agreement provided for a similar institutional arrangement in respect of Southern Sudan, which failed to persuade it to stay within the federation.

It should be emphasised that forms of asymmetry, as reflected in the Tanzanian institutional arrangements, are not necessarily an indication of the inferiority of the 'asymmetrical' unit. Indeed it may well be recognition of its special needs or status. Asymmetry is also a response to the differing circumstances (historical, ethnic or otherwise) or aspirations of the regions (as in Canada or Spain). But asymmetry is harder to manage, and is liable to offend one or more units. Thus great sensitivity is necessary in these situations – and it seems that the Mainland has not shown that degree of sensitivity.

Another impediment to the flourishing of federal relationships may be the lack of the rule of law. Adherence to agreements and legal texts is essential to sustain a federation or autonomy, with a careful keeping of the boundaries between different internal jurisdictions. The fidelity to the letter and spirit of the agreement on the Union and the constitution is an essential condition. This assumes respect for the rule of law. For various reasons, including long periods of one-party rule, neither the Mainland nor Zanzibar has succeeded in establishing reliable traditions of legality. Key decisions have been made and important differences resolved through political negotiations between leaders of one-party governments. Federalism establishes intricate relationships between institutions at different levels (including a complex and sometimes a divided legal system), which requires for their functioning careful understanding and respect for law.

But equally, unthinking respect for the founding instruments must not be allowed to ossify the federation. Federalism is not merely a state of affairs; it is a dynamic process. Federal or autonomy relations need to be constantly re-negotiated for the vitality of the state. The recognition of this necessity is increasingly reflected in the institutions and procedures for inter-governmental relations. The judiciary is indeed a part of this scheme, but the emphasis is now on political negotiations – the South African Constitution does not allow recourse to courts unless mediation efforts have been tried first. It also sets out the principles and norms of 'co-operative government', placing special emphasis on consultations, negotiation and mediation. The Tanzanian constitution is undoubtedly weak in this respect – perhaps because in its origin it was assumed that Nyerere and Karume would resolve differences informally. Now the need for special institutions and procedures for negotiations and mediation is recognised, but so far the right forms have not emerged.

Finally, the formation of a federation or autonomy, which completely transfigures the structure of the state, expands the political community and may affect rights of citizenship, requires the support of the people – for reasons of sovereignty and legitimacy. If federation is forced upon a people, they will probably reject it. The failure of the Central African Federation, the United Arab Republic and Ethiopia-Eritrea can be attributed in part to the failure to engage the people in the processes and decisions that led to these federal structures. The people of Tanganyika or Zanzibar were not consulted on the Union. It may be that Nyerere and Karume had different reasons for and expectations from the Union, both in different ways connected to security issues. Perhaps there were no great affinities of ideology or national goals either. No referenda were held to canvass public opinion or consent, and no efforts seem to have been made to promote public awareness of the reasons for and the structure of the Union. In the circumstances, the surprise is not that the Union has run into difficulties, but that it has survived at all – and bucked the trend in Africa.

A federation or autonomy survives only where there is consultation and respect for the concerns and identity of smaller units; when a unit is involved in decisions that affect it (regardless of questions of jurisdiction). A federation of the Tanzanian kind, that of the coming together of formerly free and sovereign entities, is a matter of trust and confidence, underpinned by law. Otherwise it degenerates into an imposition of the powerful, and the inevitable attenuation of the autonomy of a formerly free people.

9

Defective democracy in a failed state?

Bridging constitutional design, politics and ethnic division in Bosnia-Herzegovina

Joseph Marko

The General Framework Agreement for Peace, concluded at the US military base in Dayton, Ohio in December 1995 ('Dayton Agreement'), brought an end to the four years of war in the former Yugoslav Republic of Bosnia and Herzegovina marked by ethnic cleansing and other terrible atrocities against the civilian population, including genocide of about 8,000 Muslim men (in Srebrenica in July 1995). The peace settlement established, in the aftermath of the dissolution of the former Socialist Federal Republic of Yugoslavia (SFRY), a legal framework for reconciliation of a severely ethnically divided society and reconstruction of a war-torn economy. The institutional structures followed Arend Lijphart's model of consociational democracy, with mechanisms for power-sharing between the three major ethnic groups, namely Muslims, Serbs and Croats, who had lived together, territorially intermingled, in Bosnia-Herzegovina (or 'BiH') for centuries.[1] Both the international parties, in particular the US and EU representatives, and the local parties representing the warring factions, must have been of the opinion that after such a terrible war only ethnic representation of these major groups and power sharing could preserve the fragile peace and ensure the reconstruction and functioning of democratically legitimised state institutions – necessary preconditions for the reconstruction of the economy and, ultimately, the reconciliation of the former enemies.

Fifteen years after the conclusion of the Dayton Agreement, however, the reports of the High Representative[2] to the UN Secretary General show little success with regard to state-building, reconstruction of the economy and reconciliation. In his report covering the period 1 November 2009 – 30 April 2010 the

[1] See Noel Malcolm, *Bosnia: A Short History* (New York University Press, 1998) and Edith Marko-Stöckl, 'Identity formation, state- and nation-building in Bosnia-Herzegovina and Kosovo: on historical continuities and discontinuities of minority conflicts in South East Europe', in Emma Lantscher, Joseph Marko, Antonija Petričušić (eds.), *European Integration and its Effects on Minority Protection in Europe* (Baden-Baden: Nomos, 2008), 11–51.

[2] The High Representative and his 'Office' (OHR) were created by Annex 10 of the Dayton Agreement as an institution responsible for the international supervision and co-ordination of the civilian implementation of the Dayton Agreement. This legal construction was endorsed by a resolution of the UN Security Council under Chapter VII of the UN Statute. From this follows this reporting responsibility.

High Representative complained about the decisions of the government and National Assembly of Republika Srpska (or 'RS')[3] to hold a referendum by the end of 2009 on his decisions to extend the mandates of international judges and prosecutors in the war crimes division of the BiH State Court and declared the decisions of the RS government 'a serious challenge to Bosnia-Herzegovina's constitutional order'.[4] With the general elections in 2010, the political situation deteriorated further. The legal and political actions of RS challenging the state-level institutions of BiH and the decisions of the High Representative intensified, as did the use of nationalistic and divisive rhetoric substantially within both Entities,[5] 'at times rising to the level of hate speech'.[6] In April 2011, the RS National Assembly again adopted a decision to hold a referendum that would potentially reject the authority of the BiH Court and Prosecutor´s Office within that Entity, as well as the High Representative's authority, in particular all laws that had been enacted by him. In a 'Special Report' of the High Representative to the UN Secretary General in May 2011, the High Representative concluded:

> [T]he authorities of Republika Srpska and in particular its President, have continued openly to question the territorial integrity and sovereignty of Bosnia and Herzegovina, repeatedly questioning the sustainability of the country and advocating its dissolution. The authorities of Republika Srpska have also pursued a policy of obstructing, undermining and questioning the authority of other key-level institutions [. . .] and they have continued to deny that genocide took place in Srebrenica in 1995, notwithstanding the confirmation of this fact by two international tribunals in numerous rulings. It is my firm belief that the recent decisions taken by Republika Srpska authorities represent the most serious violation of the Peace Agreement since it was signed more than fifteen years ago.[7]

However, the political situation had massively deteriorated also in the other, bi-national Muslim-Croat Entity, the 'Federation of Bosnia and Herzegovina' ('FBiH').[8] No government was formed in this Entity until March 2011, and the then newly elected government, endorsed by the High Representative, was immediately accused of being 'illegal' by the Croat parties for not being in conformity with the ethnic representation for government positions foreseen in the Constitution of FBiH. Hence, in April 2011 an 'extra-constitutional' Croat National Assembly was founded and the leaders of the Croat parties

[3] On the creation of 'Republika Srpska' as Serb national state having seceded from the Republic of BiH in 1992 and legally recognised by the Dayton Agreement as one of the two 'Entities' of BiH see the section later on the historical context.

[4] Office of the High Representative (OHR), 37th Report of the High Representative for Implementation of the Peace Agreement on Bosnia and Herzegovina to the Secretary-General of the United Nations, 19 May 2011, at ss.18–19, available at: www.ohr.int.

[5] That is, the Republika Srpska and the Federation of BiH, which had been created by the Washington Agreement 2004. For further details see later.

[6] OHR, 39th Report of the High Representative for Implementation of the Peace Agreement on Bosnia and Herzegovina to the Secretary-General of the United Nations, 6 May 2011, at s.10.

[7] Ibid. [8] For more details see later on the historical context.

claimed the formation of a third, Croat-dominated Entity in the territory of the cantons with Croat majority population within FBiH.[9] Moreover, no delegates to the BiH House of Peoples, the second parliamentary chamber representing Muslims/Bosniacs, Serbs and Croats as ethnic groups at state-level, had been appointed from the House of Peoples of the Federation Parliament, so that no laws were adopted for more than six months after the elections nor was the budget for 2011 approved in time. In short, the Parliament of BiH had not functioned for more than six months.

As studies on the dissolution of former Yugoslavia have demonstrated, the spiral of ethnic conflict into violence has led from the construction of ethnic 'We'/'They' antagonisms and 'enemy-stereotyping' by political and religious leaders and the media, to increasing radicalisation of political claims and behaviour such as the creation of 'extra-constitutional', allegedly 'representative' ethno-national institutions and territories, called 'autonomous regions' and 'republics' – ending finally with the use of violence by para-militaries in order to achieve the goals of secession and ethno-national exclusivity and domination over a given territory.[10] Hence, after fifteen years of implementation of the Dayton Agreement one must pose the question whether the constitutional design and politics in BiH have become the means for continuation of the war by other means, poised for the renewed outbreak of violence. Is BiH not only a 'defective' democracy,[11] but also a failed state, such that only the separation of its parts along ethnic lines can bring a peaceful solution?

The purpose of this chapter is to examine what went wrong with the Dayton Agreement and its implementation through an analysis of the constitutional design of the institutional structures it created and their effects on state- and nation-building efforts by both internal and external actors in order to 'accommodate' or even 'reintegrate' the deeply divided ethnic communities. Moreover, in line with the overall focus of this volume on self-governance and autonomous regions, this chapter will also try to test the hypotheses from comparative research on the sustainability of various forms of autonomy.[12] As will be explained next in detail, the peculiar constitutional and political system of post-Dayton Bosnia and Herzegovina is based on a strict system of 'corporate' power sharing in the institutions at state level, in other words the ethnic

[9] See, Ibid., s.10 and a thorough analysis by International Crisis Group, Bosnia: State Institutions under Attack, Europe Briefing No. 62, 6 May 2011.

[10] See Joseph Marko, 'Processes of ethnic mobilization in the former Yugoslav Republics reconsidered', *Southeastern Europe*, 34:1 (2010) 1–15 and Joseph Marko, 'Human Rights and Ethnopolitics', in Karl Cordell and Stefan Wolff (eds), *Routledge Handbook of Ethnic Conflict*, (New York: Routledge 2011), in particular 241–6.

[11] I will use the concept of 'defective' democracy in the following in the sense developed by Wolfgang Merkel, 'Embedded and defective democracies', *Democratization*, 11: 5 (2004), 33–58.

[12] See Yash Ghai (ed.), *Autonomy and Ethnicity: Negotiating Competing Claims in Multi-ethnic States* (Cambridge University Press, 2000); and Thomas Benedikter, *The World's Working Regional Autonomies: An Introduction and Comparative Analysis* (London; New York; Delhi: Anthem Press, 2007).

representation only of Bosniacs, Serbs and Croats in the collective Presidency and the second parliamentary chamber, the House of Peoples, together with veto powers in decision making. This system of power sharing is in itself based on the constitutionally guaranteed territorial 'autonomy' of the RS and FBiH, having been originally created through secession, war and ethnic cleansing. Hence, this structural context creates several questions for the sustainability of the Dayton system: can the newly established territorial autonomy within a quasi-confederal state structure silence further claims for secession? The new system came into force through the intervention of the international community, not through negotiations involving participatory and democratic engagements, but by a combination of political compromise with and military pressure on the leaders of the warring parties. Can such an approach confer legitimacy on the newly established territorial and institutional arrangements, in particular if there is no regime change in political terms even after the enforced peace settlement? Federalism and territorial autonomies will be more sustainable if links across exclusive areas of sovereignty can be established. This raises the question of the relationship between ethnicity and autonomy. Is it possible to establish ethnically cross-cutting links if, as is the case in BiH, ethnic identity and territory are inseparably linked after horrible atrocities have been committed by ethnic cleansing of territory, not as a consequence, but as political goal of the war? The experience of BiH challenges the hypothesis that autonomy and federalism are more likely to succeed if there are several ethnic groups rather than only two. Finally, comparative research indicates that successful arrangements for autonomy and federalism are likely to have built in flexibility to deal with an evolving situation, in particular through arrangements for independent dispute settlement, such as courts. As will be demonstrated, both elements were in place in post-Dayton BiH, but were doomed to fail by the combination of entrenched and reinforced ethno-politics and the counter-productive institution-building strategies of the international community.

The historical context: from the dissolution of SRFY to the Dayton Peace Agreement

With the dissolution of the former Yugoslavia in 1990–91, Bosnia and Herzegovina was in a particularly difficult position. The federal constitutional system, which had been established by the victorious Yugoslav Communist Party after 1945,[13] was based on the concept of a multi-national state. The federal entities were seen as 'sovereign' republics based on the 'nationality principle' following from the Central- and East-European concept of the 'ethnic' nation-state,[14] that

[13] The texts of the post–World War II Yugoslav constitutions are published in English translation in Jan F. Triska, *Constitutions of the Communist Party States* (Stanford University Press, 1968).

[14] For the distinction between the 'French', 'civic' concept of a state-nation and the 'German', 'ethnic' concept of a nation-state see Joseph Marko, 'The Law and Politics of Diversity

is, with the 'ethnic' majority population in the respective territory conceived as the state-forming nation giving its name to the respective 'Yugoslav' republics, Slovenia, Croatia, Serbia, Macedonia and Montenegro. There were, however, two exceptions from the constitutionally entrenched nationality principle from the very beginning: within the Republic of Serbia, two 'autonomous' regions had been created, namely Vojvodina and Kosovo, in order to protect the interests of the Hungarian and Albanian populations. Secondly, due to the historic legacy and the demographic situation with no ethnic group in an absolute majority position, Bosnia and Herzegovina was never considered to be the state of only one state-forming 'nation', but of three: Muslims,[15] Serbs and Croats. Therefore, in order to preserve a balance of power against centrifugal forces in the nation-building processes of the nineteenth and twentieth centuries, not only the first Austrian Constitution of 1910,[16] but also the communist system, provided for proportional representation and participation of these ethnic groups in the legislature and executive.[17] In the course of the transformation from communism to party pluralism in 1990, this principle was legally entrenched by Amendment LXI[18] to the 1974 Republican Constitution and became the basis for the first multi-party elections in November 1990. However, due to the strong ethnic polarisation with the formation of political parties along ethno-national lines, these elections resembled more a census than elections, as can be seen from Table 9.1.

The cross-cutting of ethnic cleavages thus obviously failed in the first multi-party elections as a more 'liberal' oriented Muslim Party or the multi-ethnic party list 'Alliance of Reform Forces of Yugoslavia' as well as the reform communists' 'League of Communists – Party for Social Change' could not compete with the three ethno-nationalist oriented parties. Obviously SDA, SDS and HDZ represented the huge majority of those three ethnic groups or

Management: A Neo-institutional Approach', in *European Yearbook of Minority Issues*, 6 (2006/7), 256–8.

15 Most authors on the history of nation-building by Muslims in Yugoslavia follow the official communist doctrine and party history that muslims with a lower-case 'm' were merely seen as a religious, but not ethnic, group and were thus legally recognised as an (ethnically conceived) 'nation' only through the Republican Constitution of 1974, henceforth Muslims with a capital 'M.' However, as can be seen from the text of the resolution of the so-called 'Regional Antifascist Council for the People's Liberation of Bosnia and Herzegovina' of 26/27 November 1943, not only Serbs and Croats, but also Muslims were considered a '*narod*' (nation) 'forming, together with the other Yugoslav nations, a new, democratic Yugoslav federation'. The text of this resolution is reprinted in Dženana Čaušević, *Pravno-politički razvitak Bosne i Hercegovine, Dokumenti sa komentarima* [The Legal-political Development of Bosnia-Herzegovina, Documents with Commentaries] (Sarajevo: Editio Juristica, 2005), 422–7.

16 See Edmund Bernatzik, *Die österreichischen Verfassungsgesetze* [The Austrian Constitutional Laws) (Wien: Manz Verlag, 1911, 2nd edn.,), 1050–1.

17 See Mirsad Abazović, *Nationalni aspekti kadrova u BiH 1945–1991* [National Aspects of the Formation of Cadres in Bosnia-Herzegovina 1945–1991] (Sarajevo: Biblioteka Posebna Izdanja, br. 66, 2000).

18 See *Službeni list Socijalističke Republike Bosne i Hercegovine* (Official Gazette, henceforth: Sl. l. SRBiH), br. 21/1990.

Table 9.1 Population figures for BiH from the Yugoslav Census 1991 and results of the first multi-party elections 1990

Groups	Census 1991 in per cent	Party	Chamber of Citizens: per cent of seats	Chamber of Municipalities: per cent of seats
Muslims	43.7	SDA	33.00	39.1
Serbs	31.3	SDS	26.15	34.6
Croats	17.5	HDZ	16.15	20.9
		SKBiH-SDP	11.50	3.6
		SRSJ	8.50	0.9

Source: Arnautović 1996 and 2006.
SDA: Stranka Demokratske Akcije (Party of Democratic Action, later under the leadership of A. Izetbegović).
SDS: Srpska Demokratska Stranka (Serb Democratic Party, founded by R. Karadžić, under strong influence of S. Miloševič).
HDZ: Hrvatska Demokratska Zajednica (Croat Democratic Community, Bosnian branch of the Croatian party founded by F. Tuđman, under the leadership of M. Boban).
SKBiH-SDP: Savez Komunista BiH-Socijalistička Demokratska Partija (League of Communists BiH; reform communists).
SRSJ: Savez Reformske Snage Jugoslavije za BiH (Alliance of Reform Forces of Yugoslavia; founded by then Yugoslav Prime Minister Marković).

'state-forming' nations, which later, under the Washington and Dayton Agreements of 1994 and 1995, became constitutionally recognised as 'constituent peoples'.

Hence, with the final breakdown of the Communist Yugoslav Federation after the declarations of independence of Slovenia and Croatia in June 1991, the ten days war in Slovenia, the Brioni moratorium in summer 1991 and – after the failure of EU mediation – the outbreak of a fully fledged war in Croatia in fall 1991, the tripartite Muslim/Serb/Croat Bosnian government faced a precarious situation: both Muslim and Croat party leaders were in fear of becoming part of a Serb dominated and – due to the autocratic regime established by S. Milošević – by no means democratically oriented 'rump Yugoslavia', whereas the SDS under Radovan Karadžič threatened war in case of a declaration of independence by a majority vote of Muslim and Croat representatives. All efforts to reach a political compromise failed and a fully fledged war broke out in BiH in April 1992. Thus, based on war and ethnic cleansing of occupied territories, two new political 'units' came into being, one of them, Republika Srpska (RS), having seceded from the internationally recognised Republic of Bosnia and Herzegovina in April 1992, held around 70 per cent of the entire territory until 1995. The other entity, called 'Herceg-Bosna', was established in July 1992 by the HDZ leaders in those parts of Herzegovina that were held by the 'Croatian Defence Forces' (HVO). In order to stop the war within the war that had broken out between Muslim and Croat government forces in 1993, under strong American pressure a 'Federation of Bosnia and Herzegovina' (FBiH) was created through the Washington Agreement of April 1994. Whereas the war constitution of RS provided for a strong central state model without any legal reference to the representation of ethnic groups, the constitution of FBiH provided for a bi-national federal state of Muslims, who were renamed Bosniacs, and Croats. This federation was also territorially subdivided into 'cantons' with Bosniac or Croat majority population. At the federal level the constitutional provisions introduced the classic institutional elements of Lijphart's model of consociational democracy: proportional representation and participation of these two 'constituent peoples' and 'Others' in a bicameral parliament and for the judiciary, in particular the Supreme Court and a Constitutional Court with the power of judicial review; the provisions for the President and Vice-president as well as the cabinet foresaw power sharing only between the two constituent peoples. In addition, a 'national vital interest' veto mechanism was foreseen in the legislative process, to be triggered by representatives from the caucuses of the two constituent peoples. In addition, the Washington Agreement provided for a Confederation between the Republic of Croatia and the FBiH.

In conclusion, before the end of the war the territorial and institutional design of political entities on the territory of BiH was characterised by a multiple and high degree of territorial and functional asymmetry. In addition, two neighbouring states, Croatia and Serbia, were parties to the conflict, and there were many efforts of international organisations and the United States to mediate. Eventually, after the genocide in Srebrenica, they were also ready to intervene militarily in order to stop the war.[19]

Institutions and structures according to the Dayton Agreement 1995

'Autonomy': territorial division and division of powers

The institutional design of the General Framework Agreement for Peace,[20] brokered in Dayton under strong American leadership after NATO intervention in fall of 1995, constitutionally entrenches Lijphart's model of consociational

[19] On the dissolution of Yugoslavia and the war in Bosnia-Herzegovina see in particular Charles Ingrao and Thomas A. Emmert (eds.), *Confronting the Yugoslav Controversies – A Scholars' Initiative* (West Lafayette/Indiana: Purdue University Press 2009); Richard Holbrooke, *To End A War* (New York: Random House, 1999); and Marie-Janine Calic, *Der Krieg in Bosnien-Hercegovina: Ursachen – Konfliktstrukturen – Internationale Lösungsversuche* [The War in BiH: Causes – Conflict Structures – International Mediation] (Frankfurt: Suhrkamp, 1995).

[20] See General Framework Agreement for Peace in Bosnia and Herzegovina, 14 December 1995, 35 I.L.M., 75, 89.

democracy in the form of 'corporate power sharing', which had already served as a blueprint for the Washington Agreement.[21]

First of all, as can be seen from Article 1, paragraphs 1 and 3 of Annex 4 of the Dayton Agreement, which is colloquially called the Dayton Constitution, the legal fiction of the continuity of the internationally recognised state 'Republic of Bosnia and Herzegovina', renamed without the indication of the form of government into 'Bosnia and Herzegovina', is balanced with the recognition of the legal status of what are now officially called 'Entities', namely FBiH and RS. Hence, in order to stop the secessionist claims of SDS leaders in their de facto statelet, these constitutional provisions mirror the basic political compromise that RS – unlike the Croat 'Herceg-Bosna' – became legally recognised, not as a sovereign state, but at least as an internationally and constitutionally protected political Entity with the highest degree of territorial and institutional autonomy. The war-time constitution of RS from 1992 did provide for a fully fledged institutional system of a sovereign state with a unicameral parliament, a President and Cabinet as the dual executive, and a Supreme Court as well as a Constitutional Court with the power of judicial review. As described previously, the constitution of FBiH also provided for such a fully fledged institutional system. Since as part of the compromise, the Dayton Constitution itself does not include any provisions on the internal institutional structures of both Entities, their highly asymmetrical territorial and institutional structures were thus incorporated into the entire 'constitutional framework', composed not only of the Dayton Constitution, but also the Entity constitutions and the constitutions of the cantons within FBiH. Moreover, the so-called 'Inter-Entity Boundary Line' between RS and FBiH – again the product of military conflict and the policy of ethnic cleansing during the war – legally recognised the territorial divide of Bosnia-Herzegovina along ethno-national lines.

With regard to the division of powers between the state level and the Entities, Article 3 of the Dayton Constitution contains a general system of allocation of powers with a list of enumerated powers of the 'institutions of Bosnia and Herzegovina' under paragraph 1, whereas, according to paragraph 3, all governmental powers not expressly assigned to what are colloquially called 'common institutions' are declared to belong to the Entities. This provision was immediately interpreted by Serb constitutional lawyers to provide for a system of mutually 'exclusive' powers of either the State or the Entity institutions. More striking from a comparative point of view is, however, that most of the powers

[21] No stenographic records of the drafting and negotiations for Annex 4, the Dayton Constitution, exist or are publicly available. When I was judge rapporteur in the case U5/98 of the Constitutional Court of BiH dealing with the legal status of 'constituent peoples' (see previously) in the period 1998–2000, during the preparations for this judgment I learned from my interviews with the chief-legal advisor of the American administration, Jim O'Brian, that he, but also members of the Bosnian delegations, were aware of Lijphart´s theories, but that the communist tradition of ethnic group representation and the fear of 'being outvoted' by simple parliamentary majority was much more important for them.

that can be seen as 'essential' elements of state sovereignty, namely defence, police or fiscal policy, do not belong to the common institutions of the state, but to the Entities. Mirroring the territorial division along ethnic lines and the claims for an annexation to the neighbouring ethnic kin-states, Article 1, paragraph 7 provides for a system of 'dual-dual' citizenship: in addition to the citizenship of the BiH, this provision provides also for Entity citizenships, as well as the holding of 'the citizenship of another state'. Article 8 of the Dayton Constitution even entrenches an almost total dependence of the state institutions on financing from the revenues of the Entities. Under Article 3, paragraph 2 the Entities were given the power to conclude international treaties with states or international organisations upon consent of the BiH parliament and to establish 'special parallel relationships' with neighbouring states even without this consent with the only limitation of 'consistency' with the sovereignty and territorial integrity of BiH.

This constitutional design makes BiH by far the weakest 'federation' from the perspective of comparative federalism – to the extent that the Entities were not required to dismantle the three different armies or to integrate police forces. The preservation of the territorial and institutional structures of the former warring parties through the Dayton Constitution must be seen thus as part of the basic political compromise in Dayton.

'Accommodation' through power-sharing and veto rights

In order to balance the disintegrating forces stemming from both the high degree of 'autonomy' and asymmetry of the institutional structures of the Entities, the Dayton Constitution provided for 'corporate'[22] power sharing on state level, similar, but nevertheless considerably different from the Constitution of FBiH. This has two main features, outlined later.

Firstly, Article 4 of the Dayton Constitution provides for a bicameral parliament, a House of Representatives composed of forty-two members and a House of Peoples composed of fifteen members. Two thirds of the House of Representative members are directly elected from the territory of FBiH, one third from the RS territory. For the second chamber, the House of Peoples, the Constitution provides for a strict system of representation of the three 'constituent peoples' as a group right. The constitution prescribes that the House of Peoples must be composed of five Bosniacs, five Serbs and five Croats who shall be indirectly elected: Bosniacs and Croats from the respective caucuses

[22] The concept of 'corporate' power sharing refers to the constitutionally entrenched and thereby pre-determined ethnic allegiance of office holders in the system of proportional representation of ethnic groups in governmental institutions. The distinction between coporate and liberal power sharing or consociationalism in scholarly literature goes back to Arend Lijphart, 'Self-determination versus pre-determination of ethnic minorities in power-sharing systems', reprinted in Will Kymlicka (ed.), *The Rights of Minority Cultures* (Oxford University Press, 1995), 275–87.

of the House of Peoples of FBiH and Serbs from the National Assembly of RS. Unlike the FBiH Constitution, these provisions no longer provide for the representation of 'Others' and explicitly link territory with ethnic identity, since Serbs can only be elected from RS territory and Croats and Bosniacs only from FBiH territory. The same system is provided by Article 5 for the elections of the three-member Presidency. The Serb member has to be directly elected from RS territory as electoral unit, whereas the Bosniac and Croat members have to be directly elected from FBiH territory as electoral unit.

These constitutional provisions have a multiple exclusive effect in the logic of 'ethnic' group representation: first, only persons declaring their ethnic affiliation to one of the three constituent peoples can stand as candidates in the election, so that 'Others' who for whatever reason do not want to declare any ethnic affiliation or who see themselves as member of a national minority are excluded from the (passive) right to vote. Second, Serb voters living on the territory of FBiH cannot vote for the Serb candidate for the Presidency, nor can Bosniac or Croat voters living on the territory of RS cast their vote for the respective Bosniac and Croat candidate in the Presidency elections. Thus their right to vote is not totally negated, but diluted insofar as they cannot vote for the 'candidate of their choice' in the meaning of the American Voting Rights Act, that is, a candidate belonging to the same ethnic group; third, with regard to the indirect elections of the members of the House of Peoples, the Serb members of the FBiH House of Peoples are even by constitutional fiat excluded from their right to vote for the five Serb members of the House of Peoples at state level. The same holds true the other way around for Bosniac and Croat voters in RS. However, dissimilar to the total exclusion of Serb representatives in the FBiH House of Peoples, Croat and Bosniac representatives in the RS National Assembly can participate in the (s)election of the five Serb members in the House of Peoples on state level. Again all 'Others', who are by definition not members of these three 'constituent peoples', are totally excluded from the right to stand as candidates in elections for House of Peoples on state level. Their right to vote is diluted as well. Finally, since the Dayton Constitution itself prescribes the ethnic affiliation of these positions, this constitutional system provides for a fully fledged 'corporate' system of power sharing with exclusive mechanisms based on the obvious assumption of internally homogenous and externally, that is, territorially, bounded ethnic groups.

The second feature, again deviating from the FBiH 'model', provides for a double-veto mechanism in Article 4, paragraph 3 and sub-paragraphs (d) and (e) of the Dayton Constitution. Sub-paragraph (d) enables a veto mechanism which is called 'Entity voting' and provides for an absolute veto in any decision-making process in the House of Representatives, if two thirds of the representatives from one of the Entities do not agree with a bill and if the Chair and deputy chairs have not brokered a compromise. In effect, nine representatives from RS and eighteen from the FBiH can block every decision in the House of Representatives. In addition, sub-paragraph (e) provides for the so-called 'vital national interest' veto in the House of Peoples with the effect of a suspensive veto. If a joint commission cannot find a compromise, the case has to be referred to the Constitutional Court for review of 'procedural regularity' in an expedited procedure. Article 5, paragraph 2, sub-paragraph (d) provides also for a vital national interest veto for each of the Presidency members.

As can be seen from these constitutional mechanisms of ethnic representation and double veto power, it is an inherent and great danger to the proper functioning of the Parliament and the Presidency if – based on electoral alignment along ethnic lines – one mono-ethnic party holds all public offices of the respective ethnic group and can therefore 'blackmail' a parliamentary majority with a threat to effectively block any decision.[23]

Mechanisms of co-ordination

The Dayton Constitution provides for both internal and internationally supported mechanisms of co-ordination in order to counterbalance the inherent disintegrating tendencies following from both the territorial delimitation and corporate power sharing.

According to Article 3, paragraph 5, the three-member Presidency is tasked with the role of 'facilitat[ing] inter-Entity coordination on matters not within the responsibilities of Bosnia and Herzegovina', in other words, horizontal inter-Entity co-operation. The weakness of this provision is apparent in language such as: 'the Presidency may decide to facilitate' and 'unless an Entity objects . . . '.

The mechanism to trigger the vertical transfer of competences from Entity level to state level in order to strengthen the functioning of the state as such is laid down in Article 3, paragraph 5 of the Dayton Constitution:

- First, on the basis of negotiations and consensus any power can be transferred to state level;
- Second, the institutions of BiH shall assume the responsibilities which are provided in Annexes 5 through 8. These are arbitration; the responsibilities of the Human Rights Commission under Annex 6, composed of an Ombudsperson and a Human Rights Chamber with a majority of international members as a parallel mechanism for the protection of human rights; a Real Property Claims Commission to foster refugee return under Annex 7 and a Commission to Preserve National Monuments under Annex 8;
- Third, as a sort of 'reserve power', the institutions of BiH are empowered to assume responsibilities 'which are necessary to preserve the sovereignty, territorial integrity, political independence and international personality of BiH'.

23 It is more than an interesting historical note that this was exactly the claim made by Karadžić in October 1991 before the creation and secession of RS.

In all cases additional institutions may be established to carry out such responsibilities.

The most important provision to ensure legal integration in such a system with the highest possible form of territorial and institutional autonomy is the supremacy clause under Article 3, paragraph 3, sub-paragraph (b) which stipulates that the Dayton Constitution supersedes not only inconsistent provisions of the law of BiH, but also of the constitutions and the law of the Entities. In addition, Article 12, paragraph 2 imposes a duty on the Entities to amend their constitutions so as to ensure conformity with the Dayton Constitution. In order to give the supremacy clause effect, the Constitutional Court of BiH – as the only court established at state level from the start – is entrusted with the responsibility of judicial review according to Article 6, paragraph 3. The Constitutional Court was also staffed with international judges, unlike the Human Rights Chamber, though in a minority position.[24]

The most important exogenous mechanism of co-ordination is the Office of the High Representative, entrusted, according to Annex 10, with the 'co-ordination' of the entire civilian implementation of the General Framework of Agreement.

Finally, all of the human rights provisions and the special provisions guaranteeing the return of refugees and internally displaced persons (IDPs) under Article 2 of the Dayton Constitution as well as Annex 6 and 7 of the General Framework of Agreement must be seen as legally entrenched mechanisms to tackle not only the immediate effects of ethnic cleansing during and even after the war, but also to provide for social inclusion in order to overcome the strong ethnic division of society in the long run. The basic rules and principles are the following:

- According to Article 2, paragraph 5 of the Dayton Constitution refugees and IDPs have a constitutionally guaranteed right to freely return to their homes of origin and to have restored to them the property of which they were deprived in the course of hostilities since 1991; and
- According to Article 2 of Annex 7 a constitutional obligation is imposed on all authorities at both state and Entity level 'to create in their territories the political, economic and social conditions conducive to the voluntary return and harmonious reintegration of refugees and displaced persons, without preference for any particular group'.

In terms of constitutional design, the constitutional provisions of the Dayton Agreement provided for a 'creative ambiguity' with regard to its implementation: on the one hand, the separation of the territory along ethnic lines, the

[24] Whereas the Human Rights Chamber was composed of eight international judges and six Bosnian judges, with the President selected from the former, the BiH Constitutional Court was composed of three international judges and six Bosnian judges, to be elected by the parliaments of the Entities!

pre-determined ethnic representation in the common institutions, the dual veto mechanism and the very weak powers of the state institutions mirror the political compromise achieved at Dayton with the leaders of the warring parties, but the power-sharing and ethno-federal mechanisms were also thought to provide the necessary trust for reconstruction of functioning state institutions and a war-torn economy through elite co-operation. On the other hand, all the provisions of Annexes 6 and 7 referring to the protection of human and minority rights, in particular for refugees' return to their homes of origin and the restitution of their property, and the strong international involvement in the quasi-judicial bodies established, particularly the Human Rights Commission and the Real Estate Property Claims Commission, clearly demonstrate the will of the international parties at Dayton to counteract the effects of ethnic cleansing during the war and to provide for 'tolerance through law' by an institutional mechanism for the reconstruction of the multi-ethnic society of Bosnia-Herzegovina that had existed before the war.

However, despite the 'good' intentions of the constitutional design and institutional make-up, obviously unexpected consequences in the implementation have led to a failed state and defective democracy. What went wrong in the last fifteen years will be analysed in the following section from three interrelated perspectives: first, in order to provide the structural context for analysis, the effects of the war and ethnic cleansing on the ground must be analysed in detail. This provides, second, the framework for the analysis of the behaviour of both international and local actors and their interrelatedness in the implementation of the Dayton Agreement. Third, in light of these results, a reconsideration of academic literature on political and conflict-management theories and their assumed prerequisites as well as of the policy strategies of actors will help to explain the problems that have arisen in reconstruction and reconciliation in BiH.

After fifteen years of implementation: failed state and defective democracy?

The effects of ethnic cleansing and division

First, the effects of ethnic cleansing with regard to the demographic distribution of the population after the war can be seen from statistics provided by the Constitutional Court of BiH in case U5/98, which became known as the 'constituent peoples' case (see Table 9.2).[25] Ethnic cleansing, not a consequence, but

[25] Case U5/98 was handed down in four Partial Decisions. Partial Decision III became known as the 'Constituent Peoples' decision. See Službeni glasnik BiH, No. 11/00, Nr. 17/00, No. 23/00 and No. 36/00 and the comments by Carsten Stahn, 'Die verfassungsrechtliche Pflicht zur Gleichstellung der drei ethnischen Volksgruppen in den bosnischen Teilrepubliken – Neue Hoffnung für das Friedensmodell von Dayton?' [The constitutional obligation to guarantee collective equality of the three ethnic groups in the Bosnian Entities – New hope for the peace

Table 9.2 Ethnic breakdown of the population on hypothetical RS and FBiH territory according to the 1991 census in comparison with 1997, estimates by UNHCR

Republika Srpska	1991 (per cent)	1997 (per cent)
Serbs	54.30	96.79
Bosniacs	28.77	2.19
Croats	9.39	1.02
Others	7.53	0.00
Federation BiH		
Bosniacs	52.09	72.61
Croats	22.13	22.27
Serbs	17.62	2.32
Others	8.16	2.38

Source: Constitutional Court of BiH, case U5/98, 3rd partial decision, *Official Gazette*, No. 23/00.

instrument of warfare in order to achieve the political goal of ethno-national domination of a given territory, almost destroyed the intercultural co-existence that had existed for centuries. Muslims, Serbs and Croats had been living together territorially intermingled in all of the municipalities so that the comparison of the map of BiH with a 'leopard's skin' had become synonymous with the 'multicultural society' of Bosnia-Herzegovina. The degree of ethnic cleansing in this respect was, of course, different in various parts of the territory of BiH: whereas two cantons in the Federation BiH remain so-called 'mixed cantons' with neither Bosniac nor Croat majority population, the eastern part of today's RS – where Serbs had nowhere been in the majority except for one municipality – is now settled with 99 per cent Serb population.

Secondly, the ethnic cleansing of territories went hand in hand with the ethno-national homogenisation of institutions, the extent of which was revealed by the Constitutional Court in the same case: despite the fact that there were about one quarter of non-Serb representatives in the unicameral parliament of RS, all twenty-one ministers including the Prime Minister were of Serb origin. Also the President and an 'advisory body' called the 'Senate' with twenty-five members were Serb only. Due to the bi-national character of the FBiH institutions, Serbs

model of Dayton?], in *Zeitschrift für ausländisches öffentliches Recht und Völkerrecht*, 60 (2000), 663–701; International Crisis Group, Implementing Equality: The 'Constituent Peoples' Decision in Bosnia and Herzegovina, Balkans Report No. 128, 16 April 2002; Anna Morawiec Mansfield, 'Ethnic but equal: the quest for a new democractic order in Bosnia and Herzegovina', *Columbia Law Review*, 103 (2003), 2052–93.

Table 9.3 Ethnic breakdown of judiciary and police forces in 1999

Republika Srpska	Serbs (per cent)	Bosniacs (per cent)	Croats (per cent)	Others
Judges and prosecutors	97.6	1.6	0.8	–
Police officers	93.7	5.3	1.0	–
Federation BiH	**Bosniacs (per cent)**	**Croats (per cent)**	**Serbs (per cent)**	**Others (per cent)**
Judges and prosecutors	71.72	23.26	5.00	no figures
Police officers	68.81	29.89	1.22	0.08

(*Source*: International Police Task Force with figures of 17 January 1999 made available to the Court).

were excluded already by constitutional fiat from all these top positions in the executive.

Ethnic homogenisation, however, was not restricted to the 'top ranks' of the executive, but affected also the entire police force and the entire judiciary as can be seen from Table 9.3.

Thirdly, these figures point to why the return of refugees and IDPs to their homes of origin – one of the most important goals spelled out not only by the spirit, but also through the letter of the Dayton Agreement – was not successful at all in the first five years of implementation. Positive measures by the Entity authorities to enable refugee return should have focused in particular on what became called 'minority' returns, despite the fact that all 'majority' areas had been created by ethnic cleansing during the war. However, as figures provided to the Constitutional Court by UNHCR revealed in 1999, only 10 per cent of returnees into RS were Bosniacs and Croats, whereas the figure of Serb returnees to FBiH was even lower, amounting only to 4 per cent of all returnees. As the Constitutional Court factually determined based on numerous reports of the OHR, the Ombudsperson and INGOs in case U 5/98, in both Entities the police stood passively by when returnees entering a village were 'welcomed' by a stone throwing mob or reconstructed houses were blown up during the night, or mayors were not willing to connect reconstructed houses to electricity supply. The Constitutional Court therefore concluded that 'systematic, long-lasting, purposeful discriminatory practice' of the Entity authorities amounted to upholding the effects of past *de jure* discrimination and ethnic cleansing.[26]

[26] A case in point is the attempts at reconstruction of the Ferhadija mosque in Banja Luka where the Human Rights Chamber had found the RS authorities responsible for severe discrimination. During the ceremony for the laying of the foundation stone in 1997, a mob attacked not only the representatives of the Muslim religious community, but also the Human Rights representatives and a number of foreign diplomats present at the ceremony. The reconstruction of the mosque only restarted in summer 2011.

Finally, the entire system of education serves as an illustration of the ongoing ethno-national mobilisation and cementing of ethnic divides. Primary, secondary and tertiary education had been institutionally segregated during the war on the ethnically cleansed territories, in conjunction with language policies. The language of instruction and the scripts used[27] became clear markers for ethnic exclusion, as education and language policy were left by the Dayton Agreement to be the responsibility of the Entities and were even devolved to the level of cantons by the FBiH Constitution. As a matter of fact, no longer were any common curricula or textbooks used. Croat children in Herzegovina read in their textbooks that F. Tudjman is 'their' president and Croatia 'their' home country, whereas Serb children in RS got the same information with regard to S. Milošević and the Republic of Serbia. The map of the Balkan region on the cover of a geography textbook for the eighth grade in RS highlighted in red the existence of two Serb states, a neighbouring state Croatia and a white spot without any indication of the existence of BiH as a state or the existence of FBiH.[28] First efforts to remove ethnically biased paragraphs from textbooks had the reverse effect. Pupils got even more interested in ethno-national propaganda and 'Agreements Regarding Textbook Review and Removal of Objectionable Material' in May 1998 and July 1999 as well as a 'Textbook Review Commission' produced no results. Seen from the perspective of 'de-ethnicisation' of education, at best a moratorium in history teaching was practised by teachers themselves.[29]

The Implementation of the Dayton Agreement

After the breakdown of communism in East and Central Europe in 1989, the transformation from authoritarian, communist regimes to liberal democracies as the fourth wave of 'democratisation' has been theoretically subdivided into three phases: first, the 'liberalisation' of the authoritarian regime preparing for

[27] Before the dissolution of Yugoslavia, Serbo-Croatian was considered one of the three South-Slav languages (besides Slovene and Macedonian) used as official languages in the Yugoslav republics. Following the political separation, languages were likewise separated. Both the newly independent Republics of Serbia and Croatia declared Serbian with the Cyrillic script and Croatian with the Latin script the official languages of their republics. The Washington Agreement of 1994 (re-)created a 'Bosnian' language as official language of FBiH. Hence, three languages and two scripts are in official use in BiH with all their 'narcissisms of minor differences'. As if to prove the iron law of language separation following political break-aways, in 2006 after its declaration of independence from the 'State Union of Serbia and Montenegro' Montenegro declared that the official language is now 'Montenegrin'.

[28] I bought such a textbook in Banja Luka in 2001.

[29] See Edith Marko-Stöckl, 'My truth, your truth – our truth? The role of truth commissions and history teaching for reconciliation', in *European Yearbook of Minority Issues*, 7 (2007/08), 327–52 and Slobodanka Milikić, 'Bosnia and Herzegovina', in Lantschner, Marko and Petričušić (eds.), *European Integration*, in particular 321–3.

political party pluralism; second, the 'refolution',[30] that is, peaceful revolution through toppling the authoritarian regime through free multi-party elections; and finally, in almost all cases legally based on new constitutions adopted, the 'consolidation' of democracy through now representative and accountable legislative and executive institutions and an independent judiciary.

It goes without saying that this pattern of 'democratisation' did not work in the same way in two of the three former communist federations, namely the Soviet Union and Yugoslavia, due to the break down of the entire state structure and subsequent violent conflicts. Nevertheless it is clear that there is an intimate link between the exercise of representative, accountable and effective state powers, in short 'liberal democracy', and the underlying system of political parties, responsible both for the articulation, aggregation and representation of the interests of the electorate vis-à-vis the state powers and for the purpose of post-conflict reconstruction of institutions and reconciliation of society. Following Stepan and Linz´s classification of five 'arenas' of consolidated democracy, political parties, the party system and 'free and inclusive electoral contestation' form the core of what they call 'political society' in distinction from 'civil society' and the 'state apparatus.'[31] The following section analyses elections and the party system in the process of implementation of the Dayton Agreement to explore the extent to which they fulfil these functions of representation, accountability and effectiveness.

Elections and parties

The results of the general elections for both Houses of the BiH Parliamentary Assembly from 1996 until 2010 show the following trends.[32]

In the first general elections after the war in 1996, the three ethno-national parties that had won the 1990 elections, namely the Bosniac SDA, the Serb SDS and the Croat HDZ, were again successful in garnering most of the votes of the electorate in their respective ethnic camps. Hence, not surprisingly, the system of three mono-ethnic parties representing the ethno-national divide in society, established before the war, was maintained with the much deeper ethnic division of society because of the policy of ethnic cleansing during the war.

Since government stability in a parliamentary system should be higher if there are fewer parties necessary for the formation of a coalition government, as this is also the case in every power-sharing system, this electoral result was

[30] Timothy G. Ash, *The Uses of Adversity. Essays on the Fate of Central Europe* (New York: Random House, 1989), in particular 309.

[31] See Juan J. Linz and Alfred Stepan, *Problems of Democratic Transition and Consolidation – Southern Europe, South America, and Post-Communist Europe* (Baltimore; London: Johns Hopkins University Press, 1996), 3–15.

[32] The results of the general elections until 2006 are available in Suad Arnautović, *Ten Years of Democractic Chaos* (Sarajevo: Procult, 2007). Other sources are the home page of the Central Election Commission and interviews with secretaries of the Houses of Parliament.

also in line with Lijphart's assumptions regarding successful 'accommodation'[33] through a power-sharing system, namely to have only a small number of parties in each ethnic camp.

By contrast, Horowitz strongly argues for electoral mechanisms to enforce inter-ethnic voting behaviour in order to bridge the ethnic divide and to trigger centripetal 'integration' through de-ethnification of voting behaviour and of institutions. When the OSCE, responsible for the first free elections according to Annex 3 of the Dayton Agreement, organised subsequent rounds of elections in 1998 and 2000, it followed the strategy of 'liberalisation first'[34] in order to break up the monopoly of the three ethno-nationalist parties and to 'pluralise' and thereby also to 'de-ethnify' the party system. What were the consequences?

First, there has indeed been a 'pluralisation' of the party system. Due to the minimal thresholds in the electoral system for splinter parties and coalitions to gain seats in parliament, the three ethno-nationalist parties, which had dominated their respective ethnic electorates in 1996, lost seats to party leaders who had broken away from these parties and formed new parties, or voters shifted to splinter parties with a tradition dating back to the communist period (various 'Socialist' party formations) or even before World War II (such as the Croat Farmers' Party, HSS). In all of the three ethnic camps, one party emerged to dominate the scene, successfully competing with the traditional ethno-nationalist party from 1990/1996. Hence, there is currently constant 'intra-ethnic' competition between the SDA and the Party for Bosnia and Herzegovina (SBiH) under the leadership of H. Silajdžič in the Bosniac camp; between the HDZ and the New Croat Initiative (NHI) and then HDZ '90 in the Croat camp; and between the SDS and the Party of Independent Social Democrats (SNSD) under the leadership of M. Dodik in the Serb camp. This latter camp was even more pluralised from the very beginning with the Party for Democratic Progress (PDP) as a constant competitor, whereas parties led by former communists faded away. Strongly supported by the OSCE and the entire international community, the only party on state level that put candidates of different ethnic origins on its party list was the Social Democratic Party of BiH (SDPBiH) under the leadership of S. Lagumdžija.

In contrast to what one might expect, however, the only political party that runs in both Entities in the general elections is not the 'multi-ethnic' party SDPBiH, but the traditional and more moderate ethno-national Bosniac party SDA and, since 2000, also its more radical competitor SBiH. This can only be explained by the fact that there are not enough voters who would be ready to

[33] On the Lijphart–Horowitz debate and the conflicting views on 'accommodation' versus 'integration' in scholarly literature see various chapters in Sujit Choudhry (ed.), *Constitutional Design in Divided Societies, Integration or Accommodation?* (Oxford University Press 2008).

[34] See Ulrich Schneckener, *Internationales Statebuilding: Dilemmata, Strategien und Anforderungen an die deutsche Politik* [International State-building: Dilemmas, Strategies, and Demands on German Politics] (Berlin: SWF-Foundation, 2007), 15–20, available at www.swp-berlin.org.

overcome the ethnic polarisation through inter-ethnic voting so that – against the presumptions of Horowitz – the ongoing 'intra-ethnic' pluralisation of the mono-ethnic party system did not translate into inter-ethnic voting behaviour, in particular by voting for a 'multi-ethnic' party or into the transformation of the mono-ethnic parties to multi-ethnic parties, let alone triggering the creation of a 'civic' party based on the representation of interests and ideologies. Quite the contrary! The description of the events since the general elections in 2006 in the introduction has demonstrated that instead of moderation of the party system as predicted by Horowitz, ethno-national 'moderates' such as M. Dodik in the RS simply became 'radicals' after 2006, whereas the former 'radical' Karadžić party SDS became the new 'moderate' Serb party and the 'moderate' Serb PDP tries to balance its image between Serb nationalism when possible, and European integration when unavoidable.[35] The same is true for the relationship of the Croat HDZ and HDZ '90 leadership. Thus intra-ethnic party competition does not automatically translate into moderation of the ethno-national party system, a phenomenon that can also be observed in Macedonia.[36] Even 'worse' for the theoretical approach proposed by Horowitz, the ethno-national parties and former war enemies were already democratically legitimised by the early elections in 1996 so that the ethnic division was cemented by the subsequent biannual elections until 2002.

An analysis modelling Bosnian voting behaviour in terms of game theory has demonstrated that 'it is possible for Bosnian voters to prefer a change from the current context and desire to remove inefficient politicians but still find it in their best interests to vote for incumbent Nationalists because of their belief that the other side will vote Nationalist'.[37] Hence, it is in the rational interest of nationalist politicians to continue to foster an environment of mistrust and animosity and the task facing non-nationalist parties seems to be a mission impossible: they must not only convince voters that politics is not a zero-sum game, as it seems to be at first glance in a power-sharing system, but also convince voters that the other groups would accept their 'multi-ethnic' or even 'civic' conceptions since they otherwise risk being ousted from office by parties that claim to be staunch defenders of the 'vital national interest' of the respective ethnic camp. This indeed happened to the 'Coalition of Change' that had come into power in the general elections in 2000 and lost again

[35] See ICG, Balkans Report No. 132, 24–5.

[36] For an interesting new approach trying to bridge the divide between primordialists and social constructivists/instrumentalists in the study of nationalism see Gordon Bardos, 'Balkan ethnoconfessional nationalism: analysis and management', in *Südosteuropa*, 59 (2011), 192–213, where he strongly argues for an understanding of Balkan ethnoconfessional nationalism as a 'collective phenomenon' with strong historic roots so that the 'understanding of the Balkan political spectrum' based on the Western European experience that 'ideology trumps ethnicity' is, in his view, 'substantially off the mark'. His new conceptualisation of why 'ethnicity trumps ideology' thus finds strong empirical evidence.

[37] Azim Mujkić and John Hulsey, *Explaining the Success of Nationalist Parties in Bosnia and Herzegovina*, unpublished manuscript, on file with the author.

against the opposition of the traditional ethno-national parties in 2002. Hence, the grim outlook: 'With each passing election the problem gets worse instead of better'.[38]

Problems of institution-building

As mentioned earlier, the normative and institutional design of the Dayton Agreement was based on Lijphart´s model of consociational power sharing with ethnic group representation, mutual veto powers and segmented autonomy. Moreover, it also included all the necessary elements for reconstruction and reconciliation or – translated into the theoretical debates between Horowitz and his followers on the one hand, and O`Leary and McGarry on the other – 'accommodation' or 'integration'.[39] Of course the real test of these designs lies in their implementation. Both power-sharing mechanisms and human rights and refugee return provisions and institutions provided significant 'creative ambiguity' and flexibility for implementation, in particular for the strengthening of state-level institutions by transfer of competences from the Entities to the state level. In line with Lijphart´s assumptions, the recognition of ethnic group identities through constitutional designation as 'constituent peoples' and the territorial divide into Entities as territorial forms of segmented 'autonomy' were obviously conceived by the constitutional architects in Dayton as building blocks for the creation of a feeling of 'security' and mutual 'trust' between the political elites of the major parties. The feeling of security and mutual trust should then enable elite co-operation for the reconstruction of functioning state-level institutions. These expectations went also hand in hand with a 'strategy of institutionalisation'[40] under the co-ordination and supervision of the Office of the High Representative according to Annex 10 of the Dayton Agreement. The creation of the new institutions with strong international influence[41] was obviously thought to establish a strong rule of law component for institution-building and thereby bring about a change in the attitude and behaviour of local actors.

However, both the assumptions of Lijphart's model with regard to elite co-operation as well as the 'institutionalisation strategy' were called into question

[38] Ibid.

[39] The original theoretical dispute between Lijphart and Horowitz is reconstructed by Sujit Choudhry, 'Bridging comparative politics and comparative constitutional law: constitutional design in divided societies', in Choudhry (ed.), *Constitutional Design in Divided Societies*, 3–40. See also John McGarry, Brendan O`Leary and Richard Simeon, 'Integration or accommodation? The enduring debate in conflict regulation', in ibid., 41–88.

[40] See Roland Paris, *At War´s End: Building Peace After Civil Conflict* (Cambridge University Press, 2004), 173–4.

[41] Namely the BiH Constitutional Court under Annex 4, the Human Rights Commission under Annex 6, composed of an Ombudsperson as first instance and the Human Rights Chamber as second instance mirroring the European Commission and European Court of Human Rights, as well as the Real Property Claims Commission under Annex 7 for the restitution of immovable property to enable refugee return.

Table 9.4 Legislative (in-)activity 1997–2007 in the Parliament of BiH

	Number of laws adopted	Number of bills rejected by Entity veto			Number of laws imposed by the HR
			FBiH	RS	
1996	1	2			3
1997	11	0			1
1998	4	9		1	4
1999	7	13	1	9	5
2000	8	2			20
2001	23	40		26	4
2002	12	43		26	24
2003	40	16	2	11	14
2004	73	32	2	16	13
2005	39	31	8	10	6
2006	37	36	6	13	6
2007	25	38	1	24	15
Total	279	260	20	136	112

Source: Report by Kasim Trnka.[42]

from the very beginning. Decision making in the BiH Parliament for the adoption of the laws on citizenship, ethnically 'neutral' license plates for cars as the most important instrument to ensure free movement across the Inter-Entity Boundary Line, or laws on the flag and anthem, were obstructed so that the respective High Representatives in their reports to the Peace Implementation Conferences started to complain about the unwillingness of the political party leaders to effectively work and co-operate in the state institutions. In order to stop obstructionism by the political elites, the Bonn Peace Implementation Conference 1997, facilitated by a Security Council Resolution, extended the mandate of the OHR and conferred the power on him to adopt laws instead of the responsible parliamentary institutions as well as to dismiss public officials from their posts if they obstructed the implementation of the General Framework Agreement.[43] Table 9.4 demonstrates in quantitative terms the legislative activities and the use of Bonn powers by the High Representatives.

42 Kasim Trnka, 'Evaluation der Entscheidungsprozesse in der Parlamentarischen Versammlung Bosnien und Herzegowinas 1996–2007' [Evaluation of the Decision-making Processes in the Parliamentary Assembly of BiH 1996–2007)], in Konrad-Adenauer-Stiftung, Fachkolloquium 'Reform der Verfassung von Bosnien-Herzegowina [Konrad Adenauer Foundation, Conference proceedings 'Reform of the Constitution of BiH'], Cadenabbia/Italy, 13–16 November 2008 (unpublished manuscript, on file with the author).

43 See the conclusions from the Bonn Peace Implementation Conference 1997, XI. 2. b. and c. in OHR, Essential Texts, 199. These powers were contested before the Constitutional Court: the power to adopt laws was basically confirmed under the condition that the Court has also the jurisdiction to review these laws, whereas the Court declared complaints against dismissals inadmissible. See Joseph Marko, 'Challenging the authority of the UN High Representative

Table 9.5 Use of Bonn Powers by fields of intervention 1996–2007

Field of intervention	Number of interventions
Judicial Reform Sector (e.g., establishment of the High Judicial and Prosecutorial Council, BiH State Court, BiH Ombudsmen, Criminal Law, Administrative Law, Law on Procedures, Witness Protection, etc.)	59
Citizenship, passports, ID-cards	20
State property and privatisation	18
Electoral system	12
Taxation	11
Telecommunication regulation	10
Public Broadcasting	10

Source: Report by Kasim Trnka.[44]

Table 9.5 provides an overview of the substance of the issues as regards the interventions of the High Representatives in the decision-making processes of the legislative and executive powers and his impositions.

As can be seen from Table 9.5, the respective High Representatives Wolfgang Petritsch and Paddy Ashdown used the Bonn Powers to effect the transfer of power to the state level and thereby the creation of new institutions. Hence, the number of ministries on state level was increased to eight and a State Court including a war crimes chamber was established in 2000 in addition to the BiH Constitutional Court, as the only court on state level provided for in the Dayton Agreement.[45] As a starting point for the future integration of police forces, a State Border Service took over control of the external borders from the Entities in 2001.[46] With the Law on Defence and a common command structure an integrated army was created in 2003.[47] Finally, in order to counterbalance the total dependency of state institutions in fiscal matters, a state-level VAT with financial institutions for tax collection was introduced in 2005.[48]

The figures given in these two tables demonstrate several interesting features of the functioning of the legislative and executive powers in BiH:

before the Constitutional Court of Bosnia and Herzegovina', in Erika de Wett and André Nollkaemper (eds), *Review of the Security Council by Member States* (Antwerp: Intersentia, 2003), 113–17.

44 Ibid.

45 OHR, Decision establishing the BiH State Court, 12 November 2000, at www.ohr.int/decisions/statemattersdec/default.asp?content-id=362.

46 Zakon o državnoj graničnoj službi Bosne i Hercegovine [Law on the State Border Service of BiH], Službeni glasnik BiH, No. 19/01.

47 Zakon o odbrani Bosne i Hercegovine [Law on Defence of BiH], Službeni glasnik BiH, No. 43/03.

48 Zakon o porezu na dodatu vrijednost [Law on the Value Added Tax], Službeni glasnik, BiH, No. 09/05.

- Despite the initial complaints of obstructionism in the legislative process at state level, which had led to the expansion of the powers of the OHR in 1997, the number of bills rejected until 2000 – albeit on a general low level of legislative activities – is much lower in comparison to the following period. In 2000, the impositions by HR Petritsch quadrupled from five to twenty despite the fact that only two bills had been rejected and he had proclaimed a strategy of promoting 'ownership', in other words, non-intervention in domestic affairs, when he had taken office a year earlier.
- With the strong increase of impositions by High Representative Petritsch in 2000 also the number of bills rejected strongly increases from 2001 onwards. Years 2001 and 2002 when the numbers were high are the years when the three ethno-national parties were in opposition after the general elections of 2000. The figures also demonstrate in particular that the representatives from RS made much more use of the Entity veto mechanism in order to block parliamentary decision making after 2000, so that only the High Representatives can overrule this blockade of the legislature. In comparative terms, of the 260 bills rejected altogether in the period 1996–2007, 52.3 per cent were rejected on the basis of an Entity veto from RS and 7.6 per cent from an Entity veto by FBiH.[49]
- As Table 9.5 demonstrates, all the High Representatives' legal impositions concerned necessary reforms for strengthening the functioning of state institutions and preparing BiH for EU integration, after the EU had promised, with the launch of the Stabilisation and Association Process in 2000, to fully integrate all Western Balkan countries.[50]

However, the increasing number of interventions of the High Representatives into legislative business did not stimulate more readiness to compromise or willingness to engage in inter-ethnic co-operation. Quite the contrary, the excessive use of the Entity veto mechanism and electoral results outlined earlier clearly show that party leaders learned very quickly that they need not risk tarnishing their image as staunch defenders of the 'national interests' of their electorate, but could provoke OHR intervention in order to be able to blame the 'internationals' for the adoption of laws that were necessary for the promotion of rule of law, refugee return, or economic reforms. The external interventions

49 An excellent analysis of how the Entity veto mechanism was transformed into an ethnic veto so that every 'political' conflict between government and opposition is transformed into permanent ethnic conflict is given by Birgit Kunrath: 'Od zaštitne mjere do prepreke za dalje djelovanje: Entitetsko glasanje u Bosni i Hercegovini' [From protection measure to barrier to further action: entity voting in BiH], in Abazović and Hammer, *Bosna i Hercegovina petnaest godina nakon Daytona* [BiH fifteen years after Dayton] (Sarajevo: Fakultet političkih nauka 2010), 19–46.

50 For an overview of the history and structure of the Stabilisation and Association Process see Joseph Marko, 'The Stabilisation and Association Process for Western Balkan Countries: successes and failures', in Herbert Kröll (ed.), *Austrian–Greek Encounters* (Innsbruck: Studienverlag, 2007), 22–134.

by the international actors therefore tended to enforce the already existing 'negative' elite consensus of divide and rule instead of creating a positive elite consensus to co-operate across ethnic lines, which would have been required for the reconstruction of the state and war-torn economy.

Constitutional reform efforts

At the beginning of 2005 more and more voices started to raise the concern that any meaningful political, economic and cultural reform had to tackle the entire legal and institutional framework of the Dayton Agreement.

Again it was left to the United States to take the lead and broker a constitutional reform package,[51] with the leaders of the six biggest parties in the BiH Parliament being able to pass the two-thirds majority requirement. Despite its rather cosmetic approach to constitutional reform, this package was two votes short of gaining the necessary two-thirds majority in the BiH Parliament in April 2006. Rumour has it that the SBiH party of H. Silajdžić was successful in mobilising resistance against the reform even within the ranks of the representatives in SDA.

In the elections for both the BiH Parliament and the Presidency in October 2006, the two party leaders with obviously opposing concepts for the future territorial and institutional outlook of the country, namely H. Silajdžić and Milorad Dodik (SNDS), gained the most votes and seats so that the structural preconditions for constitutional reform further worsened.

On a conceptual level, the ideas of Silajdžić and Dodik on how to rearrange the territorial and institutional structures were diametrically opposed. Silajdžić, politically strengthened by the judgment of the International Court of Justice in ruling that the massacres in Srebrenica in 1995 had constituted a genocide in terms of public international law,[52] wanted to abolish the Entities, in particular RS, which he constantly called 'the product of genocide', and to remove the ethnic predetermination of institutions in order to create a 'civic state'. On the other hand, all Serb parties under pressure from then RS Prime Minister Dodik and his party stood for the federalisation or even a confederal model after the example of the Yugoslavian constitution of 1974. With the Entity veto in the House of Representatives as their political trump card, Dodik's party was willing to seriously negotiate on constitutional reform only if there was a clear commitment by all actors that the territory, institutions and competences of RS would remain 'untouchable'. The Croat parties were split and disagreed on whether they should push for a third, ethnic majority Croat Entity, or for the

[51] See Joseph Marko, 'Constitutional reform in Bosnia and Herzegovina', *European Yearbook of Minority Issues*, 5 (2005/06), 207–18.

[52] See ICJ, Bosnia and Herzegovina v. Serbia and Montenegro, Case 91, Judgement of 26 February 2007.

model of regionalisation based on economic criteria combined with the idea of multi-ethnicity.

At the same time, all major political parties remained, in their own perception, strong defenders of the respective 'national interests' of Bosniacs, Croats, and Serbs. None of them advanced an economic, social or cultural program or strategy beyond mere slogans, and have failed to do so to date. Since they had learned by then the democratic mechanisms of change of government and opposition, they were pretty well aware that they can lose elections and thus well-paid public mandates and jobs. Paradoxically, this democratic learning curve was again counter productive to fostering the willingness to compromise for fear of losing the next elections.

In addition, there was also a conflict of interest between the US administration represented by the American ambassador on the ground and the European Commission. Triggered by the former HR Paddy Ashdown, the European Commission declared police reform a conditionality for the Stabilisation and Association Agreement with the EU. However, police reform was stuck for the very same reason as constitutional reform, since RS Prime Minister Dodik was not willing to give up its police power. He constantly defended the position of RS by declaring that this would only be the first step towards the abolition of RS. Moreover, the US ambassador continually spoiled the efforts of then HR Schwarz-Schilling to establish a Constitutional Reform Commission by trying to pressure the political parties to instead repeat the voting procedure on the failed April package. The EU Commission, on the other hand, was afraid that a compromise on the establishment of a Constitutional Reform Commission would spoil its desperate efforts to bring about police reform as soon as possible so as to sign the Stabilisation and Association Agreement. So the Head of Delegation of the EU Commission tried everything to stop negotiations on constitutional reform and urged the HR to disentangle police and constitutional reform. Inevitably the Bosnian parties made use of this conflict between the US and the EU.

Since autumn 2007 and despite the efforts of the two next High Representatives, the Slovak and Austrian career diplomats Miroslav Lajčak and Valentin Inzko, constitutional reform remained deadlocked for the same reasons. In April 2008, HR Lajčak was able to finalise the negotiations on police reform as a face-saving device for the EU to be able to conclude the Stabilisation and Association Agreement with BiH. Moreover, several meetings and agreements between the Bosnian parties, finally with strong pressure from the EU and the US again at the NATO base in Butmir in October 2009, finally ended in a political disaster.[53]

The fact that neither HR Schwarz-Schilling, nor HR Lajčak, were willing to remove RS Prime Minister Dodik from office despite his continued open

[53] On the history and political context of these talks see International Crisis Group, *Bosnia's Dual Crisis*, Europe Briefing No. 57, 12 November 2009.

threats against the territorial sovereignty of BiH since 2006 makes clear that, because of his strong democratic legitimation in the 2006 elections, it was no longer possible to use the Bonn Powers against him without provoking an outright constitutional crisis with new elections as the only peaceful way out thus potentially further strengthening his political power. This must also be seen as the reason why the European Commission was willing to give in to a fake compromise on police reform, since the document signed by party leaders including Prime Minister Dodik declared nothing else but the postponement of police reform until the successful completion of constitutional amendments. That the EU was nevertheless willing to sign the Stabilisation and Association Agreement with the Bosnian authorities must have been strong evidence for the party leaders of RS that the EU was ready to give in to their political 'blackmail' strategy based on the constitutionally protected Entity veto mechanism in parliament. Finally, the failure of constitutional reform in Butmir did have another important side-effect: until the negotiations in Butmir, the active High Representatives Schwarz-Schilling and Lajčak had been equal partners to the US administration in these political processes. In 2009, however, the active HR Inzko was not even invited to Butmir. The EU was represented instead by the first HR Carl Bildt and by former HR Lajčak in these negotiations, so that it must have become clear again to the Bosnian party leaders that the active High Representative was no longer politically supported by the respective EU institutions. Hence, the EU/US conflict of interests and the internal conflict between the European Commission and European Council destroyed the political authority of the High Representative.

Why defective democracy and failed state?

In terms of 'negative' peace, simply as an absence of outright, widespread violence and with a cynical notion of 'accommodation' – which was certainly not the intention of Lijphart, O`Leary or McGarry – the power-sharing system in place in BiH could be called successful. In comparison with the agreed dismemberment of the State-Union of Serbia and Montenegro in 2006; the unilateral secession of Kosovo in 2008, with intense violence in majority Serb populated North-Kosovo that continues to date; and the 'frozen conflicts' in the Caucasus area; the legal fiction of Article 1 of the BiH Constitution with BiH's 'legal existence under international law as a state' was maintained despite the hurdles and roadblocks to political and legal reforms elaborated on previously.

In terms of 'positive' peace, using benchmarks for the 'quality of democracy',[54] the balance sheet is negative. Since all the efforts of international intervention demonstrate that it is impossible to turn a negative elite consensus to divide

[54] See Andrew Roberts, *The Quality of Democracy in Eastern Europe* (Cambridge University Press, 2010), 21–50.

and rule based on corporate power sharing[55] into liberal power sharing and 'normal' federalism, and since both the warring parties and the neighbouring states of Croatia and Serbia more or less openly and continuously question the existence of the state, BiH must be called a 'defective democracy' and a 'failed state'.

Merkel developed the concept of 'defective democracy' from a comparative analysis of the 'new' democracies established in the third wave of democratisation when he discovered that the simple dichotomy autocracy/democracy did not allow a distinction between more or less consolidated liberal democracies. He identified four 'sub-types':[56]

- 'Exclusive' democracy, in which one or more segments of the electorate are excluded from the civil right to universal suffrage;
- 'Domain' democracy, when, for instance, the military, entrepreneurs, or landlords take certain political domains out of the hands of democratically elected representatives;
- 'Illiberal' democracy, when the executive and legislative controls of the state are only weakly limited by the judiciary so that constitutional norms have little binding impact on government actions, and the protection of civil rights is weak; and
- 'Delegative' democracy, when the horizontal separation of powers does not function properly so that 'a balanced political representation' is undermined and the executive can circumvent parliament, influence the judiciary and damage the principle of legality.

The notion of 'defective democracy' and these four sub-types can help in explaining what went wrong in the implementation of the Dayton Agreement, in contrast to both Lijphart's assumptions that power sharing would trigger elite co-operation and to the 'liberalisation first' strategy of the international actors through what I call 'imposed institutionalisation'.

First, the 'negative' elite consensus of divide and rule was and still is based on the absence of loyalty of both Serb and Croat elites to the state of Bosnia and Herzegovina that had been imposed on them in Dayton. It is by now almost completely forgotten that the Annex 4 of the Dayton Constitution has never been ratified by the BiH Parliament. Moreover, until now there is no 'official', because legally recognised, translation of the Dayton Constitution into Bosnian, Serbian, or Croatian! From the very beginning Bosniac intellectuals and the

55 For a discussion of the power-sharing model in the BiH academic and intellectual discourse see Mirjana Kasapović, *Bosna i Hercegovina: Podjeljeno Društvo i Nestabilna Država* [BiH: Divided Society and Weak State] (Zagreb: Politička kultura, 2005); 'Ustavne promjene u BiH i konsocijaciski modeli' [Constitutional reforms in BiH and consociational models], *Status*, 9 (2006); and Asim Mujkić, 'Bosna i Hercegovina i izazovi konsocijacije' [BiH and the challenges of consociationalism], *Odjek*, 1 (2007), 6–12.

56 See Merkel, 'Embedded and defective democracies', in *Democratization*, 11:5 (December 2004), 33–58.

Party for Bosnia-Herzegovina (SBiH) under the leadership of Haris Silajdžić strongly criticised the territorial delimitation and power-sharing instruments and accused 'the international community' of having actually 'rewarded' Serb war crimes by giving in to the 'ethnification' of all institutional structures and society at large. In their opinion, only the model of a strong civic and unitary state could guarantee reconstruction and reconciliation.[57] By contrast, Serb parties and their leaders such as Karadžić's SDS and the SNDS under Milorad Dodik, as well as constitutional lawyers from RS, did not understand the Dayton Agreement as a 'political compromise' and its legal and institutional mechanisms as a 'flexible' tool, but an international and constitutional recognition and guarantee of the sovereignty and 'statehood quality' of RS within BiH, which they saw as basically a confederative structure giving RS representatives veto power on all issues of concern to them.[58]

Hence there was no inclination among the political leaders of RS to amend the text of the war-time RS constitution referring to this Entity as a sovereign state and a right of the Serb people to external self-determination.[59] The same was true for some of the HDZ leaders who refused to give up the idea of a separate 'statelet', 'Herceg-Bosna', ready for an Anschluss to Croatia, and to dismantle the institutional structures that had been established during the war.[60] No less than six years after the conclusion of the Dayton Agreement, the Croat HDZ declared 'self-rule' in 2001 in order to preserve the illegal structures of Herceg-Bosna.[61] Only after the elections in 2002, the Serb parties became strong defenders of the Dayton Agreement since it constitutionally guaranteed the status and name of RS against the strong interventionist strategy of the international actors, demonstrated by the impositions of the High Representative. With the discussions on police reform and constitutional reform from 2005 on, however, the rhetoric of the Serb parties, in particular of M. Dodik, again shifted towards threats to hold a referendum on independence, so that the dispute over the 'essence' of the conflict settlement had been revived when Dodik found out that the Bonn Powers were no longer effective. Hence, the warning by Linz and Stepan that 'without a state' – or at least the willingness to live together in a state – 'no modern democracy is possible'[62] has obviously become reality in BiH.

57 See Edin Sarčević, *Ustav i Politika – Kritika etničkih ustava i postrepubličkog ustavotvorstva u Bosni i Hercegovini* [Constitution and Politics – Critique of the Ethnic Constitutions and Post-Republican Constitution-making in Bosnia and Herzegovina] (Sarajevo: Kult B, 1997).

58 See Snežana Savić, *Konstitutivnost Naroda u Bosni i Hercegovini* [Constituent Peoples in Bosnia and Herzegovina] (Banja Luka: Pravni fakultet, 2000).

59 These provisions of the preamble were later declared unconstitutional by the Constitutinal Court of BiH in case U5/98 in 2000.

60 See the conclusions from the Bonn Peace Implementation Conference 1997, II. 1. f. in OHR, *Bosnia and Herzegovina, Essential Texts*, 3rd edn., 2002, p. 190.

61 This constitutional crisis was 'solved' by the intervention of the HR. The Hercegovačka Banka as the financial backbone of HDZ was closed down in a police raid and the Croat member of the Presidency ousted from office. See International Crisis Group, Bosnia's Alliance for (Smallish) Change, Balkans Report No. 132, 2 August 2002, 6.

62 Linz and Stepan, *Problems of Democratic Transition and Consolidation*, 17.

With regard to democratisation efforts,[63] all the election engineering of the OSCE and general elections every second year until 2002 proved counterproductive as an almost paradigmatic example of what was later termed the 'sequencing fallacy'.[64] The elections had certainly been free, but not fair. There was no lustration of the ethno-national parties, even the indicted war criminal R. Karadžić could influence the day-to-day politics of SDS until 2001.[65] The mass media, the educational system and even civil society with its NGOs[66] were split along ethnic lines and used for further ethno-mobilisation by the political parties. Interventions by OHR and the OSCE – for instance, the SRS was banned from the elections in 2000, but not the SDS and HDZ despite their obstruction in the 2002 elections – were not robust enough to be effective and they were discredited as 'undemocratic', insofar as the international community would preach democracy and rule of law without acting in accord with these standards.

Due to the miserable election engineering of the OSCE, which led to the fragmentation of parliaments,[67] and the amendments of Entity constitutions in 2002 imposing symmetric corporate power sharing on the Entities, there was and is no willingness to give up rigid corporate power sharing with the Entity vote mechanism. The general elections after 2000 confirm the trend towards an intra-ethnic 'pluralisation' of the party system and more intra-ethnic party competition, but this does not automatically translate into ethnically cross-cutting election campaigns or voting behaviours.

In conclusion, the power-sharing system with all the external interventions and endogenous reform efforts did not lead to democratisation in terms of representativeness and responsiveness, accountability and effectiveness as the main functional requirements of the 'quality' of liberal democracy. BiH must be qualified as a 'defective' democracy, with elements of all the four sub-types described previously, as outlined later.

[63] See also the recent critical analysis by Adnan Huskić, 'Democratisation against democracy: assessing the failure of state-building in Bosnia and Herzegovina', in Eldar Sarajlić and Davor Marko (eds.), *State or Nation? The Challenges of Political Transition in Bosnia and Herzegovina* (Sarajevo: Center for Interdisciplinary Postgraduate Studies 2011), 67–92.

[64] See the critical position of ICG already expressed in Bosnia's November Elections: Dayton Stumbles, Balkans Report No. 104, 18 December 2000, and Thomas Carothers, 'How democracies emerge: the sequencing fallacy', in *Journal of Democracy*, 16 (2007), 13–27.

[65] ICG, Balkans Report No. 104, 7.

[66] See the excellent analyses by Miroslav Živanović, 'Civil society in Bosnia and Herzegovina – lost in transition', in Wolfgang Benedek (ed.), *Civil Society and Good Governance in Societies in Transition*, (Belgrade: Neuer Wissenschaftlicher Verlag-Belgrade Centre for Human Rights, 2006), 23–54, and Ivana Howard, 'Building civil society in Bosnia and Herzegovina: challenges and mistakes', in Sarajlić and Marko (eds.), *State or Nation?*, 93–126.

[67] See ICG, Balkans Report No. 132, 1 and 3: the engineering of the election was leading to total fragmentation due to the fact that seats could be gained with less than 0.5 per cent of votes in the elections of 2000. A threshold requirement of three per cent was introduced for the elections in 2002, but not for so-called 'compensatory seats'. The election engineering did not substantively weaken the ethno-nationalist parties, but fragmented parliament so that the 'Alliance for Change' coalition was unable to effectively pursue reforms.

In terms of 'exclusive' and 'domain' democracy, democratic representation and participation, as well as responsiveness of state institutions, does not work properly, because of the 'exclusiveness' of elections and the 'domain' of the ethno-national parties over political as well as civil society.[68] 'Others' are already excluded by constitutional fiat from the right to stand as candidates for the elections to the three-member Presidency of BiH and the House of Peoples of the Parliamentary Assembly by the predetermined ethnic representation for Bosniacs, Serbs and Croats only. Despite the fact that the European Court of Human Rights found these provisions of the Dayton Constitution in the case *Sejdić and Finci v. BiH* in violation of the human rights standards of the European Convention of Human Rights in 2009, nothing has changed, since the political parties cannot agree on how to amend the Dayton Constitution in order to fulfill their international law obligations.[69]

Moreover, against any hopes for the creation of more 'inclusiveness' through democratic elections, the limited 'pluralisation' of the mono-ethnic party system with only 'intra-ethnic' competition and very limited inter-ethnic party campaigns or voting behaviour does not provide for – in the liberal-democratic meaning of this term – bottom-up participation of the electorate in the articulation, aggregation and representation of interests, but general elections resemble much more a plebiscitarian legitimation of the already entrenched 'negative' consensus of the political elites to divide and rule over the ethnically segmented electorates in their respective 'domains'. In addition, due to the corporate power-sharing system, the very same political and ethno-national elites can 'capture' the state institutions thereby forming a 'predatory' cartel of power which – in return for the plebiscetarian legitimation – can and does make use of the gains from privatisation[70] through legislation and from their positions in the executive for appointments into posts in public services and public companies, again 'exclusively' for their own ethnic clientele.[71] In addition, the still-segregated educational system[72] enables the ongoing ethno-mobilisation of children and

68 See also Sead Turčalo, 'External nation-building: an outline for a single politico-strategic concept', in Sarajlić and Marko (eds.), *State or Nation?*, in particular 31.

69 See European Court of Human Rights, Case of Sejdić and Finci versus BiH, Appl. Nos. 27996/06 and 34836/06, 22 December 2009. As a private (!) initiative a comparative and theoretical study for the possible alternatives for implementation of this judgment has recently been presented by Edin Hodžić and Nenad Stojanović, *New and Old Constitutional Engineering? Challenges and Implications of the European Court of Human Rights Decision in the Case of Sejdić and Finci v. BiH*, (Sarajevo: Analitika and Center for Social Research, 2011).

70 So that there is a merger of economic and political elites as Turčalo, 'External nation-building: an outline for a single politico-strategic concept', in particular 31, correctly outlines.

71 Since privatisation, public services such as health care or pension systems and public companies remained in the competence of the Entities respectively the cantons in FBiH according to the Dayton Constitution, the parties dominating government offices can use these domains through their office-holders for the economic patronage system, which is thus the basis for their electoral success. After the elections of 2002, only the SDA openly claimed a 'right' to replace 2000 appointees from the former government coalition in the government services and public companies. See ICG, Balkans Report No. 146, 17.

72 After at least three textbook commissions had failed, a Commission for the Development of Guidelines on Textbook Writing for the Subjects History and Geography was finally established

students, which destroys hopes that generational change might lead to the civic 'normalisation' of society.

Finally, in terms of 'illiberal' and 'delegative' democracy, BiH is no longer ruled by a communist one-party system, but in a similar vein by a nationalist 'state-party' system where the cartel of power, in particular the leaders of the ethno-national parties, articulate and determine the 'vital national interests' on 'behalf' of their supporters and the electorate through their 'domain' over media, education and the segregated civil society, which thus cannot exercise its democratic function as a deliberative forum for alternative ideas, interests and values.[73] Hence, the power-sharing institutional mechanisms in combination with the 'exclusive' and 'domain' nature of Bosnia's 'defective' democracy not only allow for state capture, but also destroy the responsiveness of the state institutions in terms of economic development, social welfare and well-being of the population at large.[74] It is thus no surprise that there is neither a vertical nor horizontal separation of powers, with all the consequences for the lack of accountability and effectiveness of state institutions which make BiH also an 'illiberal' and 'delegative' democracy in permanent political and financial crisis with the need for permanent crisis management by international actors. Against any normative and 'idealist' critique of this result, one must see however from an empirical and 'realist' point of view that this status quo is in the rational interest of both local party leaders as well as most of the staff of international organisations working in BiH![75]

Conclusions

The 'sequencing fallacy' based on the 'liberalisation first' strategy and the story of the failed 'institutionalisation from above', both promoted by international actors, tells us that there can be no democracy or democratisation without a state based on a 'political community' with an overarching identity to be created

in 2004. There are still twenty-five so-called 'schools under one roof' in FBiH, which means in reality outright segregation based on ethnicity. See the evaluation by Mileno Brkić and Marko-Antonio Brkić, 'Dvije Škole Pod Jednim Krovom – Od Segregacije do Koedukacije' [Two schools under one roof – from segregation to co-education], in Ivan Markešić (ed.), *Hrvati u BiH: Ustavni Položaj, Kulturni Razvoj i Nacionalni Identitet* [Croats in BiH: Constitutional Status, Cultural Development and National Identity] (Zagreb: Centar za demokraciju i pravo `Miko Tripalo´ and Pravni fakultet Sveučilišta u Zagrebu, 2010), 83–106.

73 In the framework of a research project on access of minorities to education and the labour market I had the opportunity to interview the SNDS party leader M. Dodik in 2004 and asked him in a two-hour conversation three times what 'social democracy' as part of his party's name and characterisation meant. He repeated three times: the defence of the 'vital national interests' of RS and said he saw no necessity to co-operate with other social democratic parties in FBiH.

74 See Nikolas Tzifikis and Charalambos Tsardanidis, 'Economic reconstruction of Bosnia and Herzegovina: the lost decade', *Ethnopolitics*, 1 (2006), 67–84.

75 The argument of rational behaviour is also made by Turčalo, 'External nation-building: an outline for a single politico-strategic concept', in particular 31. From my observation as advisor to HR Schwarz-Schilling in 2006–7, I estimate that only 10 per cent of the international staff of all the international organisations in BiH were 'idealists', whereas the rest work for the very high salaries and rapid career advancement they would not get in their home countries.

by state- and nation-building from within.[76] Merkel warns us that 'defective' democracies 'are by no means necessarily transitional regimes', in particular with 'clientelistic and patrimonial structures',[77] as is the case with ethnic segmentation in BiH. Hence, 'defective' democracies can function according to their own rational logic very well for a long time in the 'empty nutshell' of what is otherwise called 'failed state' structure. This is indeed a grim outlook for the future of BiH, even with the rather abstract prospect of full integration into the EU.[78]

In order to respond to the questions raised in the introduction with regard to autonomy regimes, the combination of ethno-federalism with 'corporate' power sharing in Bosnia and Herzegovina's territorial and institutional arrangements, with the territorial divide into Entities along ethnic lines as well as the strict ethnic representation in the institutions at state level, have not provided the minimum conditions for security and mutual trust in order to trigger elite co-operation, since at least two of the three ethnic communities still do not support the given structures, but make ongoing claims for secession or the creation of a third 'autonomous' Entity according to the ethno-nationalist principle of territorial domination. BiH also presents a case study of how early elections, regularly repeated, along with election engineering by the OSCE, only legitimised and even reinforced the ethnic divisions, so that the original arrangement, which had been elaborated in Dayton by a combination of compromise with and military pressure on the leaders of the warring parties, did not lead to regime change. Despite the flexibility built into the Dayton Agreement to develop the territorial and institutional arrangements toward 'liberal' power sharing combined with 'normal', that is, territorial federalism, not the least by the various courts as 'unwinders' of ethnic political bargains, the fiction of the identification of territory and ethnic identity created by the Dayton compromise remained the most powerful political instrument of the cartel of power formed by the mono-ethnic parties. Hence, the combination of ethno-federalism and 'corporate' power sharing has served to aggravate ethnic consciousness against any notion or consciousness of 'citizenship'.

Is there no way out? Against the advocates of a 'civic state' model on the one hand, and the advocates of a separation of BiH along ethnic lines on the basis of so-called 'realism' on the other,[79] it must be stressed that only a

[76] This is also considered the heart of the problem by Eldar Sarajlić, 'Between state and nation: Bosnia and Herzegovina and the challenge of political analysis', in Sarajlić and Marko (eds.), *State or Nation?*, in particular 11–13.

[77] Merkel, 'Embedded and Defective Democracies', 55.

[78] See also Vedran Džihić, '"Evropa" u Bosni i Hercegovini – Bosna i Hercegovina u "Evropi": EU-kondicionalitet i Interna Previranja u Bosni i Hercegovini: Gdje i Zašto Smo Stali Odnosno Kako da se Pokrenemo?' [' "Europe" in Bosnia-Herzegovina – Bosnia-Herzegovina in "Europe": EU-conditionality and internal agitation in Bosnia-Herzegovina: where and why we stopped, or how to move again?'], in Dino Abazović and Stefan Hammer (eds.), *Bosna i Hercegovina Petnaest Godina Nakon Daytona*, 231–44.

[79] See Chaim Kaufmann, 'When all else fails: ethnic population transfers and partitions in the twentieth century', *International Security*, 2 (Fall 1998), 120–56 and Jerry Z. Muller, 'Us and

combination of both ethnic and civic elements in constitutional design and institutional structures, hence 'collective' rights of groups and individual rights can circumvent the problems of a war-torn state and economy, as well as a deeply ethnically divided society.[80] It is simply naïve to think that anybody can legally prescribe from above that people on the ground have to forget their ethnic identities, after all the atrocities committed among the civilian population during the war. But secession is no solution either; it creates new problems through ethno-national domination and violent resistance against it, as post-independence Kosovo once again proves.[81]

Against all beliefs of local and international actors claiming the necessity of constitutional reform since 2005, it was not the constitutional design of the Dayton Agreement as such that 'caused' the disaster of a failed state and defective democracy, but the wrong strategies of the international actors that played into the hands of the elite cartel of the mono-ethnic parties and their unwillingness to give up their 'negative' consensus to divide and rule. Hence, all efforts to 'gradually' get from corporate power sharing, based on an ethnically segregated civil and political society as well as territory and institutions (euphemistically called 'segmented autonomy' in political theory), to 'liberal' power sharing on the basis of a co-operative, territorial federalism must dismantle the elite cartel of the mono-ethnic parties.[82] This would, however, require a complex mix of institution-engineering, international intervention and the reform of political culture in the sector of education and the media in combination with economic reforms through a strategic collaboration of external and internal actors. Due to the 'pragmatism' and the national interests of the parties involved as the so-called 'international community' in BiH, the development, let alone implementation of such a complex strategy seems impossible.

On the other hand, opinion polls clearly demonstrate that the ethno-national parties no longer 'represent' the majority of voters. There is a 'silent majority' for change: 90 per cent of the population support a change of the political and constitutional system. Only 20 per cent are in favour of the further division of the country into three Entities or even an Anschluss to Croatia or Serbia. Even a majority of people in the RS is against its independence. About 70 per cent of the population advocate a strong central government and a strong mid-layer of

them: the enduring power of ethnic nationalism', *Foreign Affairs* (March/April 2008), available at www.foreignaffairs.com/articles/63217/jerry-z-muller/us-and-them (accessed 28 March 2013).

80 See also the 'nested grammar of state-nations' developed by Alfred Stepan, 'Comparative theory and political practice: do we need a "state-nation" model as well as a "nation-state" model?' in *Government and Opposition*, 43: 1 (2008), in particular 6 and 7.

81 See Igor Jovanović, Kosovo Serbs split over KFOR Agreement, 10 August 2011, at www.SETimes.com.

82 Florian Bieber, 'After Dayton, Dayton? The evolution of an unpopular peace', *Ethnopolitics*, 1 (2006), 15–31 is too optimistic that 'an informal evolution' can take place based on 'flexibility' and 'creative ambiguity.'

governance.[83] This is not a paradox as political elites in BiH would like people to think, but the 'essence' of a normal federal state. It is thus high time that the EU gave up its 'business-as-usual' approach in terms of enlargement procedures,[84] and took the challenge for its Common Foreign and Security Policy which BiH poses seriously by engaging much more in state- and nation-building through economic and political incentives in order to turn the silent majority into a real majority in voting booths. The 'nation-building' the EU should foster must thus stop the ongoing ethno-mobilisation in the educational system, by media and religious leaders[85] and focus – against all forms of denials of the genocide in Srebrenica – on reconciliation through transitional justice and civil society empowerment to lay the ground for gradual institutional reform from within through the pressure of the 'silent majority' from below.

[83] These figures are from a study by Oxford International Ltd., unpublished manuscript 2007, on file with the author. See also the opinion poll data analysed by Slavo Kukić, 'Bosna i Hercegovina i Ustavne Reforme – Građanski Odgovor' [Bosnia and Herzegovina and constitutional reforms – the civic response], in Abazović and Hammer, *Bosna i Hercegovina Petnaest Godina Nakon Daytona*, 187–214.

[84] See Heather Grabbe, Gerald Knaus, Daniel Korski, *Beyond-Wait-And-See: The Way Forward for EU Balkan Policy*, European Council on Foreign Relations, Policy Brief ECFR 21, May 2010, available at ecfr.eu.

[85] See the excellent analysis by Tatjana Ljubić and Davor Marko, 'Religion, nation and state: the "Holy Trinity" of disunity of post-Dayton Bosnia and Herzegovina', in Sarajlić and Marko (eds.), *State or Nation?*, 151–75.

10

Hong Kong's autonomy

Dialects of powers and institutions

Yash Ghai

Hong Kong was part of China when Britain acquired control over it through three treaties with China between 1842 and 1898.[1] The objective was to force on China the liberalisation of trade and secure territorial concessions from which to conduct it. Britain wanted to sell opium to China to generate income for the purchase of tea. Trade with China could be conducted only in Canton, and then only through a guild of Chinese traders. Opium consumption in China increased rapidly, resulting in wide-scale addiction and the loss of valuable Chinese resources in payment. In 1800 China had banned both the import and local production of opium; however, with the connivance of foreign trading houses illegal trade continued, with increasing quantities of the drug being sold. After the failure of the Chinese authorities' efforts to to suppress the opium trade by invoking national and international law, as well as appealing to the norms of morality, they began enforcing the ban strictly in 1839, confiscating and destroying all known stocks of opium.[2]

Under pressure from British traders, the British government, having occupied Chusan Island and blockaded the coast, demanded compensation for the opium destroyed, as well as a special treaty to safeguard British trade interests. In 1841 an agreement, the Convention of Chuenpi, ceded Hong Kong to the British; however, the agreement was repudiated by both sides. In the meantime the opium trade resumed; British forces occupied the chief ports on the coast, sailed up the Yangtze River, blockaded the Grand Canal and threatened Nanking. The Chinese suffered heavy casualties: the vulnerability of the empire to the superior sea power and weaponry of the West was driven home. The Chinese capitulation was the Treaty of Nanking, signed on the British warship *Cornwallis* in 1842 and ratified the following year.

In addition to Canton, China was forced to open other ports to Britons for mercantile purposes. Most importantly, in retrospect, China ceded in perpetuity the island of Hong Kong, it 'being obviously necessary and desirable that British

[1] Anthony Dicks, 'Treaty, grant, usage or sufferance? Some legal aspects of the status of Hong Kong', *China Quarterly* 95 (1983), 427–55 provides an excellent account.

[2] Frank Welsh, *A History of Hong Kong* (London: Harper Collins, 1993) provides a good account of these events.

subjects should have some port where at they may careen and refit their ships when required, and keep stores for that purpose'. Hong Kong was 'to be governed by such laws and regulations' as were directed by Britain.[3]

The second treaty, the Convention of Peking 1860, ceded the Kowloon peninsula to Britain 'to have and hold as a dependency of the colony of Hong Kong'.[4] Hong Kong was only a few hundred yards from Kowloon, at the southern tip of the Chinese mainland, and with improvements in the range of artillery, it was vulnerable to attacks from there.

The Convention was part of a wider peace settlement between China and Western powers, including Britain, following serious conflicts regarding the implementation of the Treaty of Nanking and the forcing of China to allow the permanent diplomatic representation of Western states in Beijing. The Chinese capitulation was again brought about by massive demonstration of Western armed might, numerous Chinese casualties and the destruction of the Summer Palace outside Beijing.[5] The complementary Treaty of Tientsin 1858 was a watershed in China's relations with the West: foreigners were now allowed 'to travel anywhere in China, to preach Christianity, to establish an embassy in Peking and to trade up to the Yangtze to Hankow, which was, with nine others, designated as a treaty port'.[6]

The third treaty, the Convention of Peking, in 1898, provided for a ninety-nine-year lease of the immediate hinterland of Kowloon, which became known as the New Territories. As with Kowloon, the reasons for Britain wanting this area were a mixture of military – further improvement in weaponry rendered the peninsula insufficiently protected – and commerce. Britain's wish was for outright cession, but that option was problematic since other European powers were content with leases, the longest of which was ninety-nine years. The New Territories included several large islands, including Lantau. There is little doubt that the treaty was forced upon the Chinese, although not under threat of military force.

These treaties were considered by the British as giving them full sovereignty over Hong Kong, Kowloon and the New Territories, albeit for a limited period in relation to the New Territories. Although the 1898 treaty had at best given the right of administration of the New Territories to Britain, reserving various matters to China, Britain ruled the New Territories as part of the colony of Hong Kong and Kowloon 'in like manner and for all intents and purposes as if they had originally formed part of the said Colony'.[7] Land in the New Territories was vested in the Crown, and leasehold interests given to the original occupiers on approval by a land court,[8] in what would seem a violation of land guarantees in the treaty.

[3] Treaty of Nanking, Art. III. [4] Art. VI.

[5] See Welsh, *A History of Hong Kong*, 313–30 for for an account of the general situation and negotiations.

[6] Ibid., 199–210, 223–8. [7] New Territories Order in Council, 1898, Art. 1.

[8] New Territories [Land Court] Ordinance, 1900.

The imminence in the 1980s of the expiry of the ninety-nine-year lease over the New Territories raised the question of Hong Kong's future. Initially Britain took the view that Hong Kong and Kowloon were ceded in perpetuity, but, realising the difficulty of administering them in the face of Chinese hostility, it offered to negotiate the terms of the handover with China. The ending of British rule was thus quite different from that in other colonies, which entailed straightforward negotiations between Britain and the colonised. The UN had placed Hong Kong on its list of colonies destined for independence, but on admission to the UN, the PRC persuaded the General Assembly to take it and Macau off the list, as a matter to be resolved with the colonial powers. In this way the residents of Hong Kong, after nearly a century of colonialism, were deprived of the right to self-determination, which would have included the option to stay with Britain.[9] It is therefore to the negotiations between China and Britain that we have to turn to study the present status of Hong Kong, often described as one of a 'high degree of autonomy', under the concept of 'one country two systems', although the process was dominated by the metaphor of Chinese sovereignty.

Many things changed during the eighty-odd years of British occupation. Differences in economic and administrative systems between China and Hong Kong sharpened greatly, as did educational and cultural differences. Several features of British rule outlined next were to be critical to the arrangements for future administration of Hong Kong. British control over Hong Kong was absolute, with final authority residing with London, despite the increasing powers delegated to the governor and other officials in Hong Kong.[10] Local legislation could be repealed or overridden by London, and some legislation required its prior approval. British authority was exercised on the basis of English law (a mixture of prerogative and statute), rather than the treaties. The local legislature was essentially subordinated to the governor. English law – the common law as well as statutes – was introduced, with limited recognition of Chinese customary law. Appeals from the final court in Hong Kong went to the Privy Council sitting in London.

The basic form of the colonial constitution remained remarkably unchanged from 1840 until the 1980s. Subsequent amendments gave greater independence to the legislature vis-à-vis the governor, with some non-officials being appointed to its membership. The principle of the appointment of officials, and subsequently of the representatives of privileged commercial interests – 'functional constituencies' – to the legislature was established early, restricted

9 Contrary to a promise made by China's then leader, Deng Xiaoping, the negotiations between China and Britain were kept highly confidential and the people of Hong Kong had no say in them. Deng also stated that these principles and policies should be acceptable not only to Hong Kong people but also to foreign visitors, and most of all to Britain. Deng Xiaoping, *On the Question of Hong Kong* (Hong Kong: New Horizon Press, 1993), 3.

10 See Peter Wesley-Smith, *Constitutional and Administrative Law in Hong Kong* (2nd edn.) (Hong Kong: Longman Asia, 1994) for an authoritative account of the system of administration.

to a few British companies. Functional representation was not to flower into full bloom until the reforms of the 1980s, when it became the only form of representation.

An open-ended constitution operating under gubernatorial hegemony was still considered necessary because of the way the economy had developed, which was a laissez-faire market dominated by expatriate business houses. The greater formalisation and specification of institutional arrangements that excluded the dominance of the business houses would be seen to undermine the market basis of the economy, while their formal incorporation would be regarded as the abdication of imperial responsibilities and the placing of the Chinese population at the mercy of a handful of transient expatriate businessmen. The continuity of these formal constitutional arrangements was possible due to their flexibility. Resting in part upon the extensive patronage powers of the governor and the provisions for the accommodation of non-official interests and groups into the establishment, they enabled the government to progressively co-opt fresh groups into a partnership, including the growing Chinese bourgeoisie.

The administration was characterised by the dominance and imperatives of the market. A remarkable degree of social consensus centring on a belief in the superiority and efficacy of the laissez-faire market (with low taxes)[11] led to a sharper distinction between the public and the private than in most British colonies. Because the role of the state was narrow and did not enter many controversial areas of social policy, it did not itself become an object of controversy and competition.[12] In order to provide a privileged position for the business community, who were small in numbers, the notion of electoral representation was abandoned. The system of nomination may also have helped to dampen the mobilisation of social demands on the government, thus facilitating the laissez-faire system, as well as political mobilisation.

Because the system lacked normative rules or procedures, profound questions of community morality, public interest and the permissible use of state power could not be raised. The broad framework established by the constitutional arrangements, and within it the dominance of the executive, meant that it became the instrument of demand management; instrumental in generating, as well as facilitated by, the low level of political consciousness and mobilisation. It bred a powerful and paternalistic bureaucracy, a weak legislature and little accountability. It negated the separation of powers. Policy making remained the prerogative of the government.

[11] See Michael Littlewood, *Taxation Without Representation: The History of Hong Kong's Troublingly Successful Tax System* (Hong Kong University Press, 2010) who notes, 'The Hong Kong government is famous for the lightness of its touch, and not least, for the lightness of its taxes', ix.

[12] Lau Siu-kai, *Society and Politics in Hong Kong* (Hong Kong: Chinese University Press, 1982). In practice the economic system, camouflaged by the close collusion between government and the business community, was not as laissez-faire as its reputation suggested. The government, for example, was the principal owner of land, and later a player in the housing market.

By the time of negotiations with China on the handover, the social structure was very different from the earlier period of colonisation, when there was regular migration from China, most often of people escaping from the mainland regime who worked hard to eke out a living. The Hong Kong system enabled some of them to achieve considerable affluence, which emphasised the virtues of hard work. But well before the 1990s, society had become highly stratified, with great disparities of wealth and opportunity; it was no longer the place where hard work alone guaranteed prosperity. As class differentiation developed, wealth became a marker; economic disparities emerged in which class considerations dominated the structures and functioning of Hong Kong. But for various reasons, including the overall prosperity and then the concerns about the handover, class differences became muted.

Since the time it lost Hong Kong, China had changed fundamentally, having passed through a period of tumultuous transformation. Long feared by former refugees from Hong Kong for its socialism and authoritarianism, under the leadership of Deng Xiaoping, China made a decisive shift to the market economy in the 1980s, pronouncing that 'To get rich is glorious'.[13] Deng's vision did not include democratisation, but depended instead on the supremacy of the Communist Party. In the emphasis on profit for privileged groups and no democracy, the Chinese found not only allies among Hong Kong's rich, and the beginnings of a partnership with Chinese communist regime, but also in Margaret Thatcher, the monetarist leader of the British Conservative Party. Mrs. Thatcher's government negotiated the terms of the transfer of the exercise of sovereignty with economic reformer Deng, bringing to the negotiating table a Hong Kong well-versed in the techniques of the market economy – which China was keen to learn – and an efficient administration without democracy, which suited China's agenda.[14] It was in these circumstances that the future of Hong Kong was settled.

International foundations of autonomy

The genesis of the present autonomy of Hong Kong lies in colonialism. Both its acquisition from and return to China by Britain provides the international context. There have been fundamental changes in the nature and substance of international law since the British acquisition of Hong Kong, but in neither case did international law as such play a major role. China has from the very beginning objected to the acquisition as a manifestation of unequal treaties and

[13] This statement is attributed to Deng but it has been suggested that what he meant was 'Wealth is glorious', *Deng Xiaoping: Wikiquote.* But there is little doubt of his enthusiasm about becoming rich.

[14] Deng said to Thatcher that the main concern of the Chinese people was 'that if prosperity is not maintained in Hong Kong, it might retard China's drive for modernisation'. Deng, *On the Question of Hong Kong*, 3.

imperialism.[15] Britain recognised few if any of the rights of the people of Hong Kong when it took it over (with the exception of some vaguely defined rights of 'indigenous inhabitants' of the New Territories). The acquisition and return of Hong Kong was treated largely as a matter between two 'sovereign' states, with almost no participation of the people themselves. Although this may have been understandable in the nineteenth century, by the time of the return of Hong Kong in the late twentieth century, international law had increasingly recognised the rights of peoples and minorities and developed rules to encourage and regulate decolonisation. Central to these norms was the right to self-determination, whereby the views of the colonised and occupied people on their future were paramount.

Hong Kong people did not benefit from these norms. China succeeded in persuading the United Nations to remove Hong Kong and Macao from its list of colonies soon after its re-admission to the UN.[16] In the actual negotiations between China and Britain, neither side paid much attention to the concerns of Hong Kong people or their possible rights under international norms. The Chinese position was that the future of Hong Kong was entirely a matter within its sovereign jurisdiction, consequently the international foundations of Hong Kong's autonomy, such as they are, lie entirely in the Sino-British Joint Declaration of 1984.

Negotiations between China and Britain on Hong Kong's future were conducted on the premise of a high degree of autonomy, as announced by China. The settlement of the Hong Kong question was negotiated within a framework originally formulated for the reunification of Taiwan. China, realising that Taiwan, with its considerable resources and defence capability, would not be an easy prize, offered it what it believed was a generous package. Deng said that China has not only the Hong Kong problem to tackle, but the Taiwan problem; China could neither impose socialism on Taiwan, nor Taiwan its ideology on China. This remarkable realism and flexibility, grounded in Article 31 of the then newly enacted Chinese Constitution, certainly gave reason for optimism about Hong Kong's autonomy as a show case for 'one country, two systems'.[17]

15 Peter Wesley-Smith, *Unequal Treaty 1897–1977: China, Great Britain and Hong Kong* (Hong Kong: Oxford University Press, 1980).

16 Nihal Jayawickrema, 'The Right to Self-Determination' in Peter Wesley-Smith (ed.), *Hong Kong's Basic Law: Problems and Prospects* (Hong Kong: Faculty of Law, 1990).

17 Constitution of the People's Republic of China, 1982, Art. 31 ('The state may establish special administrative regions where necessary. The systems to be instituted in special administrative regions shall be prescribed by law enacted by the National People's Congress in the light of specific conditions'). The Article was established as the basis for negotiations with Taiwan for return to the 'motherland', but failed in that regard. Its language allows flexibility and a diversity of arrangements to suit the circumstances of different territories – and the agenda of the Chinese government. Art. 31 autonomy is different from other and lesser forms of autonomy (restricted to minority 'nationalities', Art. 4 and Chapter 3.VI).

The Joint Declaration was to be implemented by a Chinese law, the Basic Law of the Hong Kong Special Administrative Region of the People's Republic of China under this Article, for a period of fifty years.[18]

China's preference was for a very brief agreement with Britain. It also expressed reservations about the status of the agreement, preferring that it not be a binding treaty. Britain disagreed on both these points. It preferred a detailed document, both to impress upon the world that it was discharging its final colonial obligations honourably, and as a blueprint for the administration of Hong Kong, fearing that China did not really understand how Hong Kong worked. The principles of the Joint Declaration are Chinese, the details British. As a result, the Joint Declaration, with its annexes, became a lengthy document and was registered as a treaty with the UN, putting its status beyond doubt.

The Joint Declaration set out the economic, political, legal and social system that would be applied in Hong Kong, drawing extensively on the law, conventions and practices under British rule. Effectively, Hong Kong would have legislative and executive authority over all matters except foreign affairs and defence, but in foreign affairs it would enjoy important powers to be exercised under China's authorisation. However, provisions on governmental institutions were sparse. Hong Kong's government would consist of 'local inhabitants'.[19] The head of government would be a Chief Executive appointed by the Central People's Government on the basis of local elections or consultations. Principal officials would be nominated by the Chief Executive for appointment by the Central People's Government. All that the Joint Declaration said about the legislature was that it would be 'constituted by elections'.[20] It said a little more about the legal system, promising an independent judiciary and the common law, and maintaining in force all existing laws unless they were inconsistent with the Basic Law. The institutional relationship between Hong Kong and China also received sparse consideration, beyond the appointment of the Chief Executive and principal officials. Laws passed by Hong Kong's legislature had to be reported to the National People's Congress Standing Committee 'for the record', and would be 'regarded as valid' if they were in accordance with the Basic Law and legal procedures.[21] The judiciary was to be the most independent of all Hong Kong institutions, with the 'power of final judgment' vested in Hong Kong's Court of Final Appeal, 'which may as required invite judges from other common law jurisdictions to sit' on it.[22]

The paucity of provisions on institutions and on their relationship to each other was deliberate. China wanted a free hand in designing these, and it would have been difficult to agree with Britain on this matter. For its part, Britain was less interested in institutions than in the substantive protection of its investments and continuing opportunities for trade and other economic activities. The Joint Declaration provides few guarantees on institutions and the relationships both

[18] Art. 3(12). [19] Art. 3(4). [20] Annex I, Part I.
[21] Annex I, Part II. [22] Annex I, Part III.

inter se and with those on the Mainland. That matter would have to be dealt with by the Basic Law.

The Joint Declaration, although binding the two sovereign powers, has no mechanisms of enforcement. China's refusal to sign the optional protocol on the general jurisdiction of the International Court of Justice means that no formal procedures exist to test violations of the Joint Declaration. Either party may initiate diplomatic moves to raise the question of violations, but it is extremely unlikely that Britain would take any such initiative.[23] Under the common law which applies in Hong Kong, a treaty is not binding until it is incorporated into domestic law. This rule forecloses the possibility that a Hong Kong resident might use judicial proceedings in Hong Kong to resolve an issue arising out of the Joint Declaration[24] (although the situation under Mainland law might be different, but the probability of litigation there is remote).

Some autonomies have thrived in the shadow of international guarantees. The most outstanding example of extant autonomies is Åland, which was guaranteed by the League of Nations and underwritten by an agreement between Sweden and Finland (see Chapter 2 by Suksi). Another is South Tyrol's autonomy, which is the result of an agreement between Italy and Austria (see Chapter 4 by Peterlini). Autonomy systems in the former Yugoslavia have been maintained not only through international and regional guarantees but also actual intervention with troops and administrative support (see Chapter 9 by Marko). Some in Hong Kong had hoped that the Joint Declaration would serve a similar purpose, even though it did not provide for any complaints or dispute settlement mechanism. Britain, although a signatory, with moral but not legal obligations to Hong Kong's people, has been more anxious to exploit economic opportunities in China than to hold the Chinese to their promises. The United States has legislation under which it would withdraw special status and treatment accorded to Hong Kong on Chinese assurances of autonomy under the Joint Declaration if that autonomy were seen to be negatively affected in some way.[25] While under the legislation the US State Department has periodically reported to Congress on the situation in Hong Kong, no sanctions against China have ever been imposed as a result of these reports or discussions. There may have been no occasion for sanctions, but few now expect that the United States would put its relations with China at risk over Hong Kong. China has given assurances of Hong Kong's autonomy to multi lateral institutions and foreign

[23] The Joint Declaration set up a Sino-British Joint Liaison Group for 'liaison, consultation and exchange of information' on the implementation of the Declaration. It performed a useful function in setting the basis for the implementation of the Declaration, especially as the transitional period became highly politically charged. But the Joint Declaration provided for its existence only until 2000. (Annex II).

[24] Early attempts to base legal rights on the Joint Declaration failed for this reason (*The Home Restaurant Ltd. and Attorney General* [1987] HKLR 237 and *Tang Ping-hoi and Attorney General* [1987] HKLR 324).

[25] The United States-Hong Kong Policy Act 1992.

states to enable the continuation of Hong Kong's wide and varied treaty rights and obligations, as well as its the membership of international organisations. These could be the basis for political pressure on China, but even this seems unlikely now.[26] The position is more promising as regards human rights where treaty bodies under international agreements have often exercised a supervisory role in Hong Kong and demanded reforms.

The purpose and structure of autonomy

The first general principle of the Basic Law proclaims the Hong Kong Special Administrative Region (HKSAR) as an 'inalienable' part of the People's Republic of China; then promises it a 'high degree of autonomy', to be exercised through its own executive, legislature and judiciary, including the power of final adjudication, fulfilling assurances that 'Hong Kong people rule in Hong Kong'.

Autonomy is explicit in the very concept of 'one country, two systems', however the two systems are fundamentally different, each with its own unique complexities. Capitalism, depending on private initiative, confidence and an intricate set of balances, is harder to manage than socialism, which is largely administered by state organs. The assumption was that, having no experience of capitalism, the Chinese government would leave Hong Kong to manage its own affairs. Thus the Basic Law specifies that the executive and legislative authorities of the HKSAR would be composed of its permanent residents.[27]

By affecting a degree of separation between Hong Kong and the Mainland, autonomy served different purposes. It maintained the capitalist economic system of Hong Kong in the face of a state-planned economy on the Mainland and it preserved Hong Kong's common law system, essential to the market economy. The common law also had a political significance: it was considered essential for the rule of law. Britain would have found it hard to justify handing over Hong Kong to China without, at least, the semblance of democracy. Assurances of democracy and a considerable measure of self-government were also essential to persuade the people of Hong Kong, deeply suspicious of communist China, to stay on.[28]

At the time of the negotiations between China and Britain, China had a command economy, while Hong Kong was regarded – not always justifiably – as an outstanding example of a laissez-faire economy. Until 1978, China had been isolated from the world economy; Hong Kong, on the other hand, was very

[26] Chapter 11 on foreign affairs in Yash Ghai, *Hong Kong's New Constitutional Order: The Resumption of Chinese Sovereignty and the Basic Law* (Hong Kong: Hong Kong University Press, 1997) (2nd edn., 1999); Roda Mushkat, *One Country, Two International Legal Personalities: The Case of Hong Kong* (Hong Kong University Press, 1997).

[27] Basic Law, Art. 3.

[28] In fact China was able to keep democracy out of the Sino-British Joint Declaration (1984) leaving it essentially to China to devise Hong Kong's political system. See Ghai, *Hong Kong's New Constitutional Order*, Chapter 1.

highly integrated into the global economy and international economic institutions. This degree of integration could not be maintained without assurances of autonomy by China to other countries and international organisations, so that they would continue to recognise Hong Kong's separate status as a trading entity, its participation in a myriad of bilateral and multilateral treaties and organisations, extradition arrangements, and so on, all of which are critical to its separate, market economic system. In both China and Hong Kong, politics and economy were intertwined. The economic system in Hong Kong provided a private base of social power; in China, it was membership in the Party and the government that became the means to achieve economic power.

The political systems also reflected great differences. China was still run on Leninist principles of a one-party state: no genuine elections, no separation of powers, no accountability to the people, or protection of rights. The omnipotence of the Communist Party's Politburo was formally reflected in the powers of the National People's Congress (NPC), which had little autonomy of its own. The monopoly of power by a handful of Party leaders left little space for civil society organisations. By contrast, Hong Kong was open, but not democratic: people's rights were reasonably well established and there was a rudimentary separation of powers, albeit under the overarching power of a governor appointed by and accountable to London. There was executive control over the legislature, while ultimate control over Hong Kong was vested in the British government and its parliament. These features were moderated by some 'conventions', principally in the form of consultations and the influence of the business community in government, but also the relatively limited role of government (at least so it was claimed) and an active civil society.[29] Throughout, the Hong Kong administration was dominated by bureaucracy, with a fair dose of paternalism.

Contrasts in the law and legal systems were equally striking. China was just emerging from the Cultural Revolution; there was little law, no legal profession, no notion of legality, no independent judiciary, with what there was of it enjoying little prestige. 'Democratic centralism' was the overriding principle, as it was inscribed even in the 1982 Constitution, a document that was heralded as marking a great leap into legality. On the other hand, Hong Kong had a well-established, even sophisticated system of law; a large and influential legal profession; and an independent judiciary, with appeals to the Privy Council, supposedly above the fray of local politics and policies. Law acted as a discipline on government and public authorities and to a significant extent it acted to empower people. Since, given colonial rule, democracy was not the system of rule, the principal ideology of Hong Kong was the Rule of Law, which was also deemed more suited to capitalism than democracy.

[29] My own view is that claims for the autonomy and vigour of civil society (especially in the political domain) were overdone. See Yash Ghai, 'Citizenship and politics in the HKSAR: the constitutional framework', *Citizenship Studies* 5:2 (2001). See section later on civil society.

There were contrasts not only between Hong Kong and China, but also between China and Britain as sovereign powers. Britain for the most part was not seen as a wicked and exploitative colonial power, as in many of its other colonies; instead it was welcomed as a source of new ideas about democracy, rights and the rule of law, as well as providing the framework for a market economy and space for civil society. Britain was seen as democratic and pluralistic; its parliamentary and civil institutions were regarded as protecting Hong Kong against abuse of power. From the 1950s onwards, Hong Kong was able to exercise considerable autonomy, and Britain's great distance from the territory discouraged its intervention in matters of detail. Its economic system was similar to that of Hong Kong, assuring its people that the 'sovereign' understood the value of limits on governmental powers. Thus China, wedded to fundamentally different political and economic practices, could not simply replace British rule with structures and relationships similar to those that existed under British colonialism.

It is clear that the purpose and system of autonomy poses certain problems. In order to recognise fundamental differences in the economic, social and political systems of China and Hong Kong, it was necessary to confer an extensive degree of autonomy, as reflected in the matters over which Hong Kong had law-making powers. But because of China's suspicion of democracy and fear of losing control over Hong Kong, the concomitant democratisation was not on the agenda. The first problem therefore was a huge disjunction between autonomy in economic and political spheres. As has become obvious, without political autonomy, there cannot be real autonomy in other spheres.

The disjunction was reinforced by the different interpretations in China and Hong Kong of the concept of 'autonomy', with the Mainland being Leninist and in overarching control of the Communist party, and Hong Kong being liberal, with its emphasis on rights and democracy. These competing visions have been a persistent source of tension between China and the people of Hong Kong. Unfortunately Britain, in a weak moral position for its failure to establish foundations of democracy, did not push the democratic vision. Other than a Chief Executive appointed by China after 'elections or consultation to be held locally', a legislature to be 'constituted by elections' and the accountability of the executive to the legislature, the relevant articles in the Joint Declaration were vague as to the system of government. The nature of elections, consultations or the accountability of the executive were not specified, but in no way did they suggest a democratic system. China's restrictive understanding of these provisions became evident in the Basic Law (see later), which emanated from, and was linked to, the weak Chinese constitutional and legal system; thus as an instrument of autonomy, the Basic Law was destined to be an inadequate source of support.

The grant of autonomy was driven by pragmatic, rather than moral or nationalistic, considerations. The economy is undoubtedly a critical factor in the level of contentment and prosperity in every society, while the organisation and distribution of resources and production are also central aspects of democracy and autonomy. Despite this importance to the everyday life of the people, as a motive for establishing autonomy the economy does not evoke the same degree of emotions as the circumstances that have led to the establishment of such arrangements in many other parts of the world, such as the preservation of 'historical homelands', safeguarding traditions of ancient lineage, fulfilling the right to enjoy and practise one's culture, through for example, the use of one's language or observance of one's religion. A threat to these features excites stronger emotions and calls forth a stronger defence of autonomy (including international concern) than the pragmatic discourse of 'stability and prosperity'. The impact of this difference is all the more serious in Hong Kong where it has proved extraordinarily difficult to generate debate around the great themes of the morality of markets and democracy, and thus the Chinese government has sometimes been able to dismiss the struggles for democracy in Hong Kong as merely an expression of discontent with a falling stock market!

Moreover, when autonomy is based on economic considerations it is susceptible to redefinition. Differences in economic organisation were central to the formation of the autonomy; but now with the rapid progress of economic reform in China these differences are rapidly disappearing, and the two economies are becoming increasingly integrated, for example through the Closer Economic Partnership Arrangement concluded between the Mainland and Hong Kong in 2003.[30] Chinese companies are investing in Hong Kong or operating out of Hong Kong, and major investments in China are made by Hong Kong 'tycoons', who are currently Hong Kong's dominant political force; but they have greater economic interests in the Mainland than they do in Hong Kong, and for that and other reasons have sought to please the Mainland authorities. Some people felt secure about the autonomy because they could see a special role for Hong Kong in China's economic development, but little of that now remains as China has forged ahead with its contacts with global economic actors.

Historically, autonomy has generally been secured through struggle. Paradoxically, in Hong Kong, it was more of an imposition, or at best a concession, neither negotiated nor endorsed by its residents. From the very beginning, as China set about negotiations with Britain, drafted the Basic Law and made preparations for the transition to sovereignty, Hong Kong people were mostly treated as objects rather than subjects of autonomy.[31] Another irony of the autonomy was that, by being time specific – fifty years is all that the Joint Declaration promised – it became the device for the full integration of Hong

[30] The Mainland and Hong Kong Closer Economic Partnership Arrangement 2003 as supplemented in 2011.

[31] Unlike the negotiations on the Joint Declaration, there was some participation of, and consultation, with the Hong Kong people on the drafting of the Basic Law, but under tight control. Mainland members were in the majority and able to ensure that Mainland views prevailed. Steve Tsang, *A Modern History of Hong Kong* (Hong Kong Press, 2004), 238–44.

Kong into China.[32] The tension between the reformers and the conservators in the area of political structures and reform lie precisely in this factor, that the preservation of the old system is better suited to ultimate integration.

Finally, it is necessary to raise the question whether what the Basic Law gives Hong Kong is autonomy – distancing Hong Kong from China – or merely entrenches a rather odd version of nineteenth-century capitalism, devoid of democracy and social justice, the legacy of colonialism. The Basic Law is enormously detailed on Hong Kong's economic system (courtesy of the British negotiators) with many restrictions on policy options, including on the issue of democratisation. Ironically, entrenchment has become a means of restricting autonomy – and a cause of extreme frustration.[33]

Thus the principal purpose of the Basic Law is to separate off the economic systems of the Mainland and the HKSAR. Following this logic, the Law specified institutions to support Hong Kong capitalism as understood by Beijing (with some instruction from Britain). When presenting the Basic Law to the National People's Congress for its approval, Ji Pengfei, Chairman of the Basic Law Drafting Committee, explained that the structure of government in Hong Kong 'must facilitate the development of the capitalist economy in the Region'.[34] Moreover, the HKSAR does not have the authority to alter the 'systems'. Consequently, Hong Kong people have to make laws and policies within the confines of the 'systems'. In some respects there is considerable scope for this, but the essential framework, and often the details, cannot be changed. The HKSAR cannot change institutions of its government on its own, nor the electoral laws, nor, significantly, a rather laissez-faire economic system. Another aspect of the institutional arrangements, centring on the office and powers of the Chief Executive, was Beijing's plan to acquire ultimate control over Hong Kong affairs.

Language

Language and religion play an important role in autonomy arrangements, sometimes triggering demands for self-government, as does language as the medium of communication between central and autonomous units. If these two do not share the same language, the language they communicate in varies:

32 It is not foreordained (nor feasible) that Hong Kong's 'systems' will collapse on 30 June 2047. Deng's own view was that the Mainland systems would by then have approximated to Hong Kong's so that it would not be an issue (Deng, *On the Question of Hong Kong*). But things are not that simple, and the political leverage that the 'expiry' date gives the Chinese authorities should not be underestimated. See also Danny Gittings, 'What will happen to Hong Kong after 2047?' *Cal. W. Int'l L.J* 42:37 (2011).

33 I have explored this dichotomy and the resulting tensions in 'The intersection of Chinese law and the common law in the Special Administrative Region of Hong Kong: question of technique or politics?', *Hong Kong Law Journal* 37:2 (2007), 363–7.

34 Ji Pengfei, 'Explanations on the Basic Law of the HKSAR and its related documents', address to the National People's Congress, 28 March 1990. Available at: www.law.hku.hk/conlawhk/sourcebook/10018.htm (accessed 28 March 2013).

in Åland, communication is conducted in the language of the autonomous unit, while in most other areas it is the 'national language'. Chinese legislation on nationality autonomous areas specifies that the central government officials posted to those areas should learn the local language to help them communicate with the residents, but it is in Putonghua that all communications, including education, take place. The Joint Declaration made the English and 'Chinese' (presumably Putonghua) texts equally authoritative and recognised the two languages as the official languages of the HKSAR. The Basic Law provides that English may be used in addition to Chinese by 'executive authorities, the legislature and the judiciary'.[35] But the assumption that there is one Chinese language is incorrect: the Chinese government uses Putonghua (Mandarin) while the vast majority of Hong Kong people speak Cantonese, which is widely used in its legislature and executive. However, communications between Beijing and Hong Kong take place in Putonghua. English is still the language of the Court of Appeal and the Court of Final Appeal and all laws are published in both languages, with the Chinese text as final in the event of conflict.

Identity and the right of abode: permanent residents of Hong Kong

Another important aspect of Hong Kong's autonomy is the freedom to determine its immigration policy and the concept of permanent residency, in other words the right of abode, the right of an individual to vote and, the more limited right, to stand in elections. Such a person would not have to be a Chinese national; indeed Chinese nationals, particularly those on the Mainland, face considerable difficulties in securing this status as they need the permission of the Chinese government to move to Hong Kong. Some rights are tied to residency, rather than nationality, though for a small number of key posts, one has to be both a permanent resident and a Chinese national[36] (and only Chinese nationals can vote in the elections for members of the National People's Congress representing Hong Kong). Hong Kong has its own passports and negotiates independently for visa free entry to other countries, having secured it in many more states than grant this for holders of PRC passports.

These rules acknowledge and facilitate Hong Kong's cosmopolitan character, independent relations with other states, prevent mass migration from the Mainland and emphasise a degree of self-government. And insofar as these rules enable Hong Kong people (without denying their Chineseness) to see themselves as distinct from the Mainland, they reinforce the dominant theme of the Basic Law: continuity. Hong Kong residents' sense of identity is also reinforced by having its own flag, currency and stamps. Despite being endorsed by Deng, the territory's distinct identity has increasingly become something of an irritant to the Chinese government, which emphasises 'patriotism' as a key political virtue.

[35] Art. 9. [36] Basic Law, Art. 36.

Civil society

In order to understand the nature of the HKSAR, it is necessary to look outside formal state structures. During the British period, the role of the government, important though it was, was limited and many initiatives and activities took place within civil society. It is therefore necessary to look at the structure and role of civil society and the regime of human rights to grasp the logic and dynamics of Hong Kong. The exclusion of the Chinese from the colonial administration and the general preoccupation with the concerns of the European merchants and administrators meant that Chinese people developed their own means to manage their social and economic life. Chinese society itself was differentiated between some enterprising merchants, a smaller number of manufacturers, a professional and administrative class and, predominating, workers and labourers, although with considerable prospects of mobility.[37] Philanthropy among the better-off Chinese enabled the provision of social services, security and protection of the vulnerable. This autonomy of civil society also produced social cohesion among the community, hierarchy notwithstanding. The eminence of the Chinese elite among their own group gave them considerable leverage over the administration, and led, slowly, to their incorporation into the administration and gradual social acceptance, especially under the pressure of the transfer of sovereignty.

The importance of the social base for political and, subsequently, economic advance, the self-reliance of the Chinese community and the growth of class-based and therefore social interests and organisations among its members all served to emphasise the role of civil society. The autonomy of individuals and organisations in Hong Kong is no less crucial than the autonomy of HKSAR institutions; even if the latter fall under Mainland influence, there would remain an element of civil society autonomy critical for politics and economy.

In several ways the Basic Law recognises and entrenches the values, roles and organisations of civil society in Hong Kong. Very briefly, community organisations (including religious organisations) and individuals may run educational undertakings of 'various kinds',[38] while educational institutions may 'retain their autonomy and enjoy academic freedom'.[39] A similar role in the provision of health services is guaranteed.[40] Professions may continue to issue their qualifications, and maintain their organisations and independence.[41] Religious groups may continue to own and inherit property and may maintain 'seminaries and other schools, hospitals and welfare institutions and to provide other social services' and maintain relations with similar institutions abroad.[42] Non-governmental organisations are not only allowed to provide services in education, medicine, social recreation, sports and welfare, but are also entitled

[37] W. K. Chan, *The Making of Hong Kong Society* (Oxford: Clarendon Press, 1991), see especially Chapter 3.

[38] Basic Law, Art. 136. [39] Ibid., Art. 137. [40] Ibid., Art. 138.

[41] Ibid., Art. 14. [42] Ibid., Art. 141.

to subventions from the government and to maintain relationships with similar organisations abroad.[43]

The importance of these assurances is not obvious unless one notes the Chinese government's distrust of independent organisations working in close collaboration with the people and its efforts to control every sector of Mainland society. Hong Kong civil society and people are allowed roles and freedoms which are unimaginable on the Mainland, particularly the constitutional recognition of religion by an avowedly atheistic government and ruling party.

The Chinese authorities realise of course the vigour of Hong Kong's civil society and its general orientation towards rights, freedoms, social justice and the rule of law.[44] The protective provisions and the human rights provisions of the Basic Law (discussed later) provide a bulwark against state interference. Even if they were able to capture the official institutions of the HKSAR, the Chinese authorities would have to penetrate civil society institutions and processes. It is not as if all Hong Kong people are averse to Chinese policies or intervention – the number of China's supporters certainly has been increasing, but the majority of people remain suspicious. Chinese penetration of Hong Kong society started during the British period, and has intensified since the handover. The chief targets are political parties – especially for elections to the post of Chief Executive, made possible by the nature and size of the electorate – trade unions, business tycoons and senior civil servants.[45]

Human rights

Another major difference between the Mainland and Hong Kong is in respect of human rights. As is well known, China does not have any regime of human rights as these are universally understood. China without doubt is among the two or three of the world's most authoritarian regimes; human rights are violated daily and human rights defenders suffer great persecution and prosecution. On

43 Ibid., Art. 144.

44 Every year on the anniversary of the Tiananmen massacre of 1989, thousands of Hong Kong people gather to commemorate the victims. The most striking strength of civil society was manifested when hundreds of thousands marched to protest against attempts to restrict various political activities following the government's tabling of proposed legislation to protect 'national security' in Hong Kong. See Carole Peterson, 'Hong Kong spring of discontent: the rise and fall of the national security bill in 2003' in Hualing Fu, Carole Peterson and Simon Young (eds.), *National Security and Fundamental Freedoms: Hong Kong's Article 23 Under Scrutiny* (Hong Kong University Press, 2005). This demonstration was interpreted as a sign of the people's general dissatisfaction with their government and led effectively to the dismissal of Hong Kong's Chief Executive by Beijing.

45 For an account of techniques and institutions for China's pursuit of Hong Kong's civil society, see Christine Loh, *Underground Front: The Chinese Communist Party in Hong Kong* (Hong Kong University Press, 2010). Deng Xiaoping said as early as 1984, 'We should have faith in the Chinese of Hong Kong, who are quite capable of administering their own affairs' (Deng, *On the Question of Hong Kong*, 9).

the other hand, many Hong Kong people regard respect for and observance of human rights as the defining characteristic of Hong Kong, and in practice infinitely more important than democracy. The constitutional framework for human rights is exceptionally strong: human rights, political as well socio-economic, are recognised in the Joint Declaration and made binding in the Basic Law, which also incorporates the two principal international covenants. All major human rights treaties are binding and regular reports are submitted to treaty bodies. On the whole Hong Kong courts have been very protective of human rights, and the Court of Final Appeal has established expansive and learned jurisprudence on human rights. For example, C. J. Li said in *Ng Ka Ling*, discussed later, that the freedoms guaranteed by the Basic Law 'lie at the heart of Hong Kong's separate system'.[46] Both the executive and the legislature are aware of the concern about and respect for human rights. Chinese attempts to downgrade human rights by an interpretation on what laws survive into the new regime have had little effect.[47]

The remarkably extensive range of fundamental rights granted to Hong Kong residents and the strong methods for their enforcement, including supervision by international bodies, are all premised on autonomy. Hong Kong people can enjoy these rights only if Hong Kong has substantial autonomy since they are very different from rights in the PRC, in concept, scope and enforcement. The regime of rights likewise implies a corresponding limitation on the powers of state organs, thus ensuring people are free from interference not only by Hong Kong but also Chinese authorities.

Constitutional and legal foundations

International experience demonstrates that autonomy comes under severe strain if it lacks a secure national legal foundation. This is so even in countries which claim to have a tradition of the rule of law (Puerto Ricans frequently complain about the approach of the US Government and the Supreme Court based on the view that US sovereignty applies in its plenitude to Puerto Rico).[48] In the experience of autonomies in the Soviet Union and the former Yugoslavia, legal forms always gave way to the diktat of the communist party, which was also a great centralising force. Strong constitutional guarantees and effective traditions of the rule of law are an indispensable requirement for autonomy, especially when the autonomous area is but a small part of the state and has little influence over the national system. Some systems (as in Åland and Bougainville) require the consent of the legislature of the autonomous area before constitutional arrangements regarding autonomy can be amended.

[46] *Ng Ka Ling v. Director of Immigration* [1999] 1 HKLRD 326. [47] Basic Law, Art. 160.

[48] See Rivera Ramos, in this volume, and Jose Trias Monge, *Puerto Rico: The Trials of the Oldest Colony in the World* (New Haven: Yale University Press, 1997).

It is often assumed that when examining the constitutional status and arrangements for the HKSAR, the primary source should be not the PRC Constitution but the Basic Law. Support for this approach is to be found in the Basic Law itself, with its frequent statements that the institutions and powers of Hong Kong, and its relationship with the Central Authorities, are to be 'in accordance with the provisions of this Law'.[49] Additional support is to be found in Article 11 of the Basic Law, which in its last paragraph prescribes, 'No law enacted by the legislature of the Hong Kong Special Administrative Region shall contravene' the Basic Law. Nor could the National People's Congress contravene the Basic Law, for the only Mainland laws that can be extended to Hong Kong are 'confined to those matters relating to defence and foreign affairs as well as other matters outside the autonomy of the Region as specified by this law'.[50] Even this may only be done after consulting the Committee for the Basic Law and the Hong Kong government.

Even more dramatically, the proviso in Article 159 of the Basic Law, dealing with the National People's Congress's power to amend it, says that 'No amendment to this Law shall contravene the established policies of the People's Republic of China regarding Hong Kong' (which were set out in the Sino-British Joint Declaration). The Chinese Constitution itself imposes no restrictions on the power of the NPC to amend the Constitution. The Basic Laws for Hong Kong and Macau are the only Chinese laws that provide for their own mode of amendment. It should also, however, be noted that Hong Kong did not establish, and cannot amend, its constitution; this is the responsibility of the National People's Congress. Hong Kong, if key institutions there concur, can suggest amendments, but the final decision rests with the Congress.

Article 31 of the PRC Constitution has therefore to be read as providing a mechanism for opting out of portions of it in relation to special administrative regions and thus enabling great flexibility in the design of their philosophies, powers and institutions. A Decision of the National People's Congress at the time of the adoption of the Basic Law expressly affirms that law's constitutionality, quoting Article 31 as support. Confirming the validity of a law that it has passed may seem odd, but the National People's Congress must have realised that many sections of the Basic Law were incompatible with the Chinese Constitution and wanted to put beyond doubt the integrity and validity of the Basic Law. It said that 'The systems, policies and laws to be instituted after the establishment of the Hong Kong Special Administrative Region shall be based on the Basic Law of the Hong Kong Special Administrative Region'. This injunction is not restricted to the acts of the HKSAR, thus it can only be read as giving an especially high status to the Basic Law, and implying that when there is a conflict between the Basic Law and the PRC Constitution, the former is to prevail. Instead of reading the Constitution into the Basic Law, the Basic Law has to be read into the Constitution for the latter's application to Hong Kong. This is also

[49] Basic Law, Arts. 2, 3, 6, 11, 12, etc. [50] Ibid., Art. 18(3).

a better approach as regards the style of drafting, for it obviates the necessity of going through the entire Constitution and expressly dis-applying its parts.

'One country, two systems' rests therefore on a remarkable sharing and diffusing of the internal sovereignty of the PRC. Ji Pengfei's speech to the NPC when introducing the draft Basic Law explicated clearly that the reach of the sovereignty of the Central Authorities over Hong Kong is only to the extent necessary to maintain the 'one country', which leaves ample room for genuine and effective autonomy.[51] However, this form of high-level guarantee is problematic, as it is stated in the Basic Law, not the Constitution, which stands at the top of the hierarchy of laws. Beijing was not persuaded by those who wanted the guarantee to be also stated in the Constitution, perhaps even with a separate chapter on Hong Kong. Moreover, the scheme for the enforcement of the Basic Law poses various difficulties, particularly those provisions that deal with the relationship between Beijing and the HKSAR, where the final word is with the National People's Congress. And most fundamentally, this kind of constitutional pluralism is antithetical to the Chinese communist mode of government and administration, which brooks no limit to the power of the Chinese Communist Party and the principal expression of state power, the National People's Congress. Curiously, Britain itself did not understand the nature of constitutional autonomy, as the fundamental principle of state organisation is the sovereignty of parliament, from which no derogation is allowed (for recent developments, see Chapter 11 by Himsworth).

Demise of Article 31

It is not therefore surprising that the understanding of Article 31 that I have described did not survive for long. Beijing has armed itself with various points of intervention in Hong Kong under the Basic Law itself that undermine autonomous decision making in Hong Kong. The Basic Law is complex because it deals with several transitions: from colonialism to autonomy; from autonomy to Chinese rule; from semi-authoritarianism to democracy. Hong Kong people see it as the basis of autonomy; China sees it as effecting the transfer of Hong Kong to China, and eventually its complete incorporation into the PRC.

Moreover, the very specific concept of sovereignty employed by the Chinese Central Authorities is inhospitable to autonomy, as can be seen in its denial of residual powers to Hong Kong. There is a conflation of the internal and

[51] In his explanation to the NPC of the Basic Law, on the occasion of its enactment, Ji Pengfei, chair of the Basic Law Drafting Committee, stated that the relationship between the Central Authorities and the HKSAR was defined by the Basic Law. In his lengthy explanation he analysed many provisions of the Basic Law but made no reference to the Constitution. He said, 'Therefore, the draft Basic Law contains both provisions embodying the unity and sovereignty of the country and provisions empowering the Special Administrative Region with a high degree of autonomy in the light of Hong Kong's special circumstances'. Ji, 'Explanations on the Basic Law of the HKSAR and its related documents'.

external aspects of sovereignty, and in both these aspects, the concept allows the centre extensive powers and vast jurisdiction. Yet the reach of the Chinese conception of sovereignty is unclear; at one level it potentially negates the whole of the Basic Law; indeed opinion in high political and academic circles leans towards the proposition that the National People's Congress can make any law for Hong Kong, even if it violates the Basic Law,[52] a view upheld by the Hong Kong Court of Appeal in *HKSAR v. Ma*[53] shortly after July 1997. Soon afterwards judges began to question this proposition in a series of cases on the right of abode in Hong Kong of children of Hong Kong permanent residents born in the Mainland, given under Article 24(3) of the Basic Law.[54] A key issue was whether the right of abode in the Basic Law could be overridden by Mainland legislation. In a magisterial, unanimous decision, the Court of Final Appeal held that no approval under that legislation was necessary.[55] The judgment set out the fundamental principles for the interpretation of the Basic Law as a constitution, the centre piece of which was a 'purposive approach' and particularly with regard to the protection of rights, a 'generous' approach'.[56] The Court of Final Appeal asserted the jurisdiction, indeed the duty, of the Hong Kong courts to review any legislative acts of the National People's Congress or its Standing Committee for consistency with the Basic Law and to declare them invalid if inconsistent with it. The Court was careful to ground its jurisdiction by reference to the Basic Law enacted by the National People's Congress, the 'sovereign'. The Court relied on Article 31, which had allowed for the enactment of the Basic Law, through this instrument distributing and limiting the future power of the Congress. Thus the courts in Hong Kong were given jurisdiction to enforce and interpret the Basic Law, which necessarily entailed jurisdiction over acts of the Congress itself.

The judgment was criticised by Hong Kong deputies to the National People's Congress and both the mainland and Hong Kong members of the Basic Law Committee; Beijing was extremely upset. In a most unusual procedure, the Hong Kong government requested, and the Court agreed, to 'clarify' the parts of its judgment that related to the National People's Congress and its Standing Committee. The Court said that it accepted that it could not question the authority of either body to 'do any act which is in accordance with the provisions of the Basic Law and the procedure therein'.[57] Put in this form, the clarification did not detract from its earlier judgment, as was widely acknowledged in Hong

52 See, for example, Albert Chen, 'The Provisional Legislative Council of the SAR', *Hong Kong Law Journal*, 27 (1997) 1. Drawing upon Kelsen's legal theory, Chen argues that with the transfer of sovereignty, Hong Kong is under a new political order whose *grundnorm* is the supremacy of the National People's Congress, with untrammelled powers over all of China.

53 (1997) 2 HKC 315.

54 For the controversy and documentation on the right of abode case, see Johannes Chan, H. L. Fu and Yash Ghai (eds.), *Hong Kong's Constitutional Debate: Conflict Over Interpretation* (Hong Kong University Press, 2000).

55 *Ng Ka Ling v. Director of Immigration* (1 HKLRD 315). 56 Ibid.

57 *Ng Ka Ling v. Director of Immigration [No.2]*[1999] (2 HKCFA 141), 142.

Kong. The 'clarification' was seen purely as an act to placate the Mainland authorities; and it was seen to have served its purpose.

But that was by no means the end of the story. The ruling in the original *Ng Ka Ling* case still stood, but the HKSAR government did not like it, as it feared large numbers of children in the Mainland, at least 1.7 million, would seek to enter and settle in Hong Kong, causing acute social problems.[58] It issued a request to the State Council for an interpretation of the Basic Law, which amounted to an appeal to the National People's Congress Standing Committee against the decision of the Court of Final Appeal.[59] It rejected the possibility of seeking an amendment of the Basic Law as this would take too long, since the National People's Congress meets once a year for a short period, and a preliminary process under Article 159 would have to be followed. In justifying a re-interpretation of the Basic Law, the Hong Kong government was at pains to state that an interpretation was not an amendment,[60] as it was customarily understood on the Mainland. From the rather tortuous reasoning of the government, it was obvious that an interpretation was seen as a way out of what it regarded as a difficult situation, quite regardless of the legal niceties. The whole tone of its statements implied that the interpretation would deliver what the government sought.

Beijing duly obliged. The Standing Committee overruled the Court of Final Appeal and chastised the Court for not having referred the first matter to the National People's Congress Standing Committee for a ruling before its decision, in accordance with Article 158 of the Basic Law (discussed later). The interpretation and the 'clarification' by the Court of Final Appeal effectively killed Article 31 as authority for the self-contained nature of the Basic Law. It was no longer politically correct to argue that the Chinese Constitution was circumscribed in its application to the HKSAR. The concept of Chinese sovereignty revived again (it appears in many HKSAR statements about law and politics) and marked the total subjugation of Hong Kong to Beijing. The entire constitutional foundation for autonomy disappeared – at the instigation of the government of the HKSAR.

Provisions for autonomy and the method for the division of powers

Constitutional doubts notwithstanding, the Basic Law does indeed confer upon Hong Kong many indicia of semi-sovereignty. It allows Hong Kong the right to

[58] Chan, Fu and Ghai (eds.), *Hong Kong's Constitutional Debate*, 476.

[59] Neither the Basic Law (nor other Mainland laws) gives the Chief Executive of the HKSAR the right to refer a matter to the Standing Committee for interpretation in this way. The provisions of the Basic Law, which were invoked by the Chief Executive to refer the matter to Beijing and seek its assistance, did not really bear the interpretation placed on them by him.

[60] In a paper tabled at the Legislative Council House Committee (18 May 1999), entitled 'Right of Abode: The Solution' (reprinted in Chan, Fu and Ghai (eds.), *Hong Kong's Constitutional Debate*, 310–19).

determine its own immigration policies and to issue its own passports. Hong Kong has its own flag, currency and stamps. It also has its own semi-citizenship in the form of 'the permanent resident of Hong Kong', holders of which are entitled to important rights denied to other Chinese citizens. Its availability to non-Chinese, in recognition of Hong Kong's cosmopolitan nature, is a remarkable acknowledgment of Hong Kong's identity and distinctiveness. It is granted the common law, the use of the English language and a comprehensive set of rights and freedoms. It is also given considerable powers over its external affairs.

These provisions support an extraordinary range of substantive powers. They include almost total control of the economy, monetary and tax affairs, transport (including aviation and shipping), social policies, education, health, sports and so on. Remarkably, the Hong Kong government retains all the revenue it raises and the territory is not required to remit any funds to the centre. Only authority over foreign affairs and defence have been retained by the Central Authorities. The Basic Law gives Hong Kong extensive law-making powers in assigned areas. Although the National People's Congress Standing Committee has the power to veto Hong Kong laws that it considers incompatible with the Basic Law, this same provision emphasises the autonomy of Hong Kong in law making as it states that the Standing Committee may not amend such laws but merely refer them back to Hong Kong.[61] The Basic Law occasionally specifies that the powers of Hong Kong shall be exercised on 'its own', thus further stressing the region's autonomy in law making.[62]

The powers that belong to Hong Kong are not specified clearly or comprehensively. The usual way in which powers are divided is to provide lists of powers of the state or the autonomous area, or just of the state or the area, leaving the residual matters to the one for which powers are not specified in the latter case. Chinese legal experts resisted leaving residual matters to Hong Kong, on the somewhat questionable basis this was possible only when separate political entities join together in a federation.[63] The first draft of the Basic Law in 1988 did contain a list of executive powers for Hong Kong, but this section was dropped in the 1989 draft and never resurrected as the task proved difficult. Such a list would have been exceedingly long, which suggests that specifying the much more limited powers of the Central Authorities and leaving all others to Hong Kong would have been a sensible procedure. In order to piece together Hong Kong's executive and legislative authority it is now necessary to plough through all the provisions of the Basic Law with references to a specific power, Few of these powers are given in an unqualified form as the Basic Law is replete with restrictions on the way powers may be exercised.

[61] Art. 17(3). [62] See Art. 110 'Monetary Policies' and Art. 136 'Educational Policies'.

[63] Wu Jianfan, 'Several issues concerning the relationship between the Centre of the People's Republic of China and the Hong Kong Special Administrative Region', *Journal of Chinese Law* 2 (1988), 95–113.

This mode of granting powers is unsatisfactory. There is no easy way to work out what powers belong to Hong Kong and how they are hedged around with restrictions, some of which are mandatory and others more in the nature of guidelines or exhortation. Hong Kong has for decades exercised some powers that are nowhere stated as belonging to Hong Kong, and the result therefore is a kind of residual list. The restrictions that are imposed can promote arguments that the exercise of powers has to be supervised by Central Authorities. If this line were adopted, there would be a serious diminution of autonomy. The method of allocating powers to Hong Kong may seem to some as demeaning in places as it has the style of local government legislation!

Institutional structure and relationships

Some autonomous areas acquire influence at the national level through participation in national institutions, for autonomy is really an instance of 'self-rule' and 'shared rule'. The Basic Law guarantees Chinese citizens in Hong Kong their rightful place in state institutions.[64] But Hong Kong is only a very, very tiny part of China and unsurprisingly, its delegates cannot be expected to exercise much influence in national institutions. Here the Canadian experience is instructive, for despite their frustrations, the Francophones in Québec wield considerable authority in federal institutions. In China, the Communist Party in any case tends to use membership in state institutions as a device for co-optation, and as a basis for its 'united front' politics. It is no accident that Hong Kong members of PRC organs tend to be the most ardent supporters of the central government and critics of those more autonomy-inclined in Hong Kong.

Most autonomies provide for fully representative institutions for the exercise of autonomy, even when the powers devolved are not hugely substantial.[65] Such institutions reinforce the sense of identity and togetherness of the people of the autonomous area and put pressure on the centre to listen to and negotiate with them. Denied full and universal franchise and a strong legislative body, the people of Hong Kong have lacked a champion to defend the territory's autonomy.[66]

The political structure consists of two components: Hong Kong's internal institutions and their relationship to the Central Authorities. China's primary preoccupations for Hong Kong's internal institutions were to ensure there was an executive-dominated system (in Hong Kong parlance: 'executive-led'), which implied a weak legislature, and to ensure that the chosen form of parliamentary representation would privilege business and professional groups and minimise the role of political parties. The foundation for such a system was well and truly

64 Art. 21.

65 See for example Hurst Hannum, *Autonomy, Sovereignty, and Self-Determination: The Accommodation of Conflicting Rights* (Philadelphia: University of Pennsylvania Press, 1990) and Yoram Dinstein (ed.), *Models of Autonomy* (New Brunswick, NJ: Transaction Press, 1981).

66 Yash Ghai, 'Who will defend our autonomy?' *South China Morning Post*, 19 April 2004.

laid by Britain; China built upon this to create Hong Kong's present political edifice. Rules regarding the Chief Executive draw their inspiration from those for the office of the colonial governor. He or she is appointed by the central government after a process of consultation or nomination in Hong Kong; the prevalent view is that China is free to veto a nomination that emerges from the local process, although no provision is made for fresh nominations.[67] The process is designed to minimise the role of political parties, and indeed to some extent to favour 'independents'. The powers of the government are vested in the Chief Executive, who is assisted by senior officials, subject to the approval of the central government, and an executive council that the Chief Executive appoints and which has a largely advisory role. The Chief Executive has no power to appoint the members of the legislature, nor are senior officials any longer ex-officio members, as they were during the colonial era. Nevertheless, the provisions for parliamentary representation are intended to secure a legislature that is supportive of, and friendly to, the Chief Executive.

The Chief Executive cannot be removed by the legislature on a vote of no confidence, although he or she can be impeached through a complicated procedure weighted in favour of the Chief Executive. Even then, the decision whether or not to accept the impeachment lies with the central government.[68] On the other hand, the Chief Executive may dismiss a recalcitrant legislature, although only once in a term of office. It is clear that the goal of having an 'executive-led' system is secured in part by the weakening of the legislature. There are several additional ways in which this result is achieved. First, the principles and rules for election to the legislature are designed to ensure that the majority of members will be drawn from groups sympathetic to the Chief Executive, assuming that the post holder will in effect be a representative of the business community. China has built on the system of functional constituencies, from which half of the members of the legislature are returned, under which, in general, candidates and electors are restricted to a particular industry or profession. In some cases, voting is corporate, which means that effectively one or more individuals with majority equity in a number of companies can control the outcome of the vote. Secondly, the influence of popularly elected members, who have constituted half the membership since September 2004, is diminished by voting rules that require all bills, motions and amendments by members to be submitted to separate voting by functional constituency members and other categories of members.[69] Thirdly, there are severe restrictions on the power of members to introduce legislative bills, rendering their role in law making subsidiary to that of the executive.[70] All these provisions detract from the legislature's legitimacy.

[67] Basic Law, Art. 45. [68] Ibid., Art. 73.

[69] Ibid., Annex II. For a detailed study of the origins, operation and consequences of functional constituencies, see Simon N. M. Young and A. O. K. Law, *A Critical Introduction to Hong Kong's Functional Constituencies*, Functional Constituency Research Project 2004; a research project commissioned by Civic Exchange (Hong Kong: Civic Exchange, 2004).

[70] Basic Law, Art. 74.

A political system that is dominated by the executive and representatives of the business community lends itself to influence, if not control, by the central government.

This brings me to the second aspect of the political structure, the relationship of the Central Authorities to Hong Kong's institutions. By controlling the appointment of the Chief Executive, and to some extent his or her tenure, the central government can influence the policies and conduct of the Hong Kong government. The central government is also authorised to give directions to the Chief Executive on matters for which it retains responsibility,[71] and since this concept is not free from ambiguity the Chief Executive could find himself or herself caught between his responsibility to the centre and the Legislative Council (LegCo). It is clear that in such a system, the Chief Executive would show greater deference to the former.

The method of election for legislative councillors also gives the central government considerable leverage over the work of the legislature. More formally, the National People's Congress Standing Committee is authorised to scrutinise legislation passed in Hong Kong for compatibility with those provisions of the Basic Law that concern the responsibilities of the Central Authorities or the relationship between them and Hong Kong. In addition, China exercises considerable control over the 'elections' of Hong Kong's representatives to the National People's Congress, retaining the right to make the law for these elections, and can use this control to influence Hong Kong politics with the substance and style of national politics, giving eminence to its supporters. Thus while the Basic Law gives considerable responsibilities to Hong Kong's institutions for policy and administration over Hong Kong, the weak institutional autonomy means that Hong Kong people may not be the primary influence on the discharge of these responsibilities. At the least, no policy the central government opposes is likely to be adopted in Hong Kong. In that sense, one can regard the constitutional arrangements in Hong Kong more as a shell to pursue a different system from that on the Mainland than as a site for a separate, much less an alternative, source of power. The weakness of political institutions has led to street protests and marches, and resort to the courts – all of which has led to pressure on the Hong Kong government and indirectly on China, and resulted in some changes.

Dispute settlement and the interpretation of the Basic Law

Disputes about the respective jurisdictions of national and autonomous governments and differences on the scope of constitutional or legal provisions are endemic to systems of divided authority. In Hong Kong there is often great anxiety when differences with the central government are aired in public, or a case is made for the rights of Hong Kong. This anxiety may be rooted in the

[71] Ibid., Art. 43.

Confucian value of harmony, or it may stem from fear of offending the all powerful centre. In most systems the response is not to hide one's head in the sand but to argue the case for one's interpretation of the law or the merits of policies and search for the resolution of differences. A fair and successful resolution of disputes generally contributes more to the strengthening of national unity and the legitimacy of autonomous arrangements than dispute avoidance. Almost all autonomous and federal systems have provisions for the resolution of disputes. Most provide, either formally or informally, a mechanism for negotiations, with mediation or conciliation as a first step. Only if these mechanisms fail is the dispute turned over to the judiciary, which then makes authoritative rulings of law and hopefully brings the matter to a close.[72] What is crucial is that the body that makes the final determination should have both legal competence and legitimacy. The latter is derived from the independence and impartiality of the court and its status as a neutral umpire between the national and autonomous governments. In general the final court is the national supreme or constitutional court. Some may see it as allied to the national government, but in most democratic countries operating on the principle of separation of powers, national courts are accepted as independent. No threat to autonomy is perceived in vesting them with the final authority to adjudicate and interpret.

The problem in Hong Kong is that there are no formal or informal intergovernmental institutions to deal with differences between China and Hong Kong. Although the Chief Executive is indirectly cast in that role, being accountable to both the central government and the LegCo, he or she is grossly incapacitated from performing this function for the reasons already explored earlier. Nor are there competent bodies with legitimacy that can serve as neutral adjudicators and interpreters between Hong Kong and China. China has a major office in Hong Kong and Hong Kong has a smaller one in Beijing, where, no doubt, policies are cleared and agreements made (these are established under Article 22 of the Basic Law, where functions are not specified). And there are requirements that Hong Kong must provide information on certain matters, such as laws passed in Hong Kong that the National People's Congress Standing Committee may disallow if unconstitutional,[73] or seek approval of China. Likewise, there are certain acts that China cannot do without consultation with Hong Kong, such as extending Mainland laws to Hong Kong.[74] These involve the Chief Executive and not other Hong Kong institutions. The final powers of interpretation are vested in the National People's Congress Standing Committee, which takes its instructions from the central government and ultimately the Chinese Communist Party. As the latter two institutions are frequently protagonists in differences and disputes, there is no independent authority to resolve

[72] South Africa and some other systems require the exhaustion of mediation procedures before resort to the courts. South African Constitution, Sections 41(3) and 41(4).

[73] Basic Law, Art. 17. [74] Ibid., Art. 18.

them, and Hong Kong has no choice but to follow what are widely perceived as biased interpretations. These problems are rooted in the political system of the PRC, particularly its Leninist lineage and conception of sovereignty. Proposals for institutional solutions are generally condemned as denying or challenging the authority of the PRC and thus discussion is stifled.

The arenas of the law

A particular difficulty in the accommodation of Hong Kong's autonomy to Chinese sovereignty lies in the differing systems of law. Hong Kong's common law tradition suggests that the foundation of its public policy and jurisdiction must be the law. Indeed it is hard to think of any effective or meaningful system of autonomy that is not founded on fundamental laws, reinforced by a regime of legality. China, despite its commendable, and in some instances far-reaching legal reforms since 1979, operates with a very different concept of legality, subordinated as it still is to policy or administrative convenience. In Hong Kong in recent years, both pre- and post-transfer of sovereignty, there has been a tendency to turn political issues into legal issues, principally because Hong Kong does not have an effective democratic system but does have a good legal regime of rights. But the practice in China is to turn legal questions into political questions under the guise of legal questions. It is significant that the National People's Congress Standing Committee has made several interpretations of the Basic Law in the short time since it was adopted, while fewer interpretations have been made of the Constitution or other laws for the larger and more complex Mainland.

Nothing better illustrates the differences between the two legal traditions than the system for the interpretation of laws, in this case the Basic Law. The key to the autonomy of Hong Kong lies in this system of interpretation: it hangs precariously on the structure and exigencies of the interpretation of the Basic Law. The Basic Law provides many points at which an act of interpretation by the National People's Congress Standing Committee is required[75] or permitted.[76] Its formulations are frequently vague, there are different understandings of various provisions and the relationship of the Basic Law to the PRC Constitution and laws is unclear. The power to interpret the Basic Law thus becomes critical to Hong Kong's relationship to the Central Authorities and to its autonomy. Here is the Achilles heel of autonomy: the ultimate responsibility for the interpretation of the Basic Law lies with the Standing Committee.[77] The assumption underlying the Basic Law is that the responsibility for policing the boundaries between Hong Kong's institutions lies with the HKSAR courts, while the policing of boundaries between them and the Central Authorities is with the

[75] Arts. 17, 18, 158, 159 and 160. [76] Art. 158. [77] Ibid.

Standing Committee.[78] In doctrine and practice, however as we have seen, there is no restriction on the Standing Committee's powers of interpretation.

In the common law, the function of interpretation is to bring coherence to the constitution, to explicate its underlying principles and to harmonise other laws with it. The very rules for interpretation are designed to increase the predictability of the outcome of legal disputes.[79] In China on the other hand, the rules for interpretation allow the National People's Congress Standing Committee to extend the reach of pre-existing law, and to add to the law. However, the 2000 Legislative Law did serve to limit the scope of such interpretations somewhat, stating that interpretation was not to be used to amend the law.[80] There are no rules that facilitate predictability, especially as no reasons are given for decisions reached by the Standing Committee. Interpretations of law are influenced more by policy changes than by the letter of the law.[81]

The interpretation powers of the Standing Committee were a matter of considerable controversy during the drafting of the Basic Law.[82] Sensing the weakness of the concept and institutions of legality, some Hong Kong members lobbied, unsuccessfully, to vest final powers of interpretation in Hong Kong's judiciary. A small concession was made: the establishment of the Committee for the Basic Law under the Standing Committee, consisting of an equal number of Mainland and Hong Kong members, which the Standing Committee would consult before deciding on points of interpretation. The Basic Law Committee consists of six Mainlanders and six Hong Kong residents. Its precise role is not specified, for example, whether it is to advise on questions of law or broader issues. Nor are any procedures provided for the internal deliberations of the Committee or the mode of consultations with the Standing Committee. In practice, as with other PRC institutions, it has been largely used to co-opt Hong Kong members, who (with one or two honourable exceptions) have become ardent supporters of all central government positions and have no reservations about publicly stating their views on difficult legal questions referred to the Committee. The expectation that the committee would act independently and serve to harmonise the PRC legal system with Hong Kong's common law traditions and techniques has not been borne out.

[78] Many provisions are based on it, for example, the powers of law making in Basic Law Art. 17 and the formulation in Art. 11.

[79] Although it does not always work like that. Judges are, especially in the common law, often a law unto themselves.

[80] The Legislative Law only allows for interpretation in two situations: when the specific meaning of a provision of a law requires clarification (Art. 42[i]) and when new circumstances have arisen since the passage of a law and clarification is needed on the grounds for application of the law (Art. 42[ii]). Thus it excludes a function of interpretation that some scholars previously asserted was within the powers of the NPCSC: amendment of a law through interpretation.

[81] Kong Xiaohong, 'Legal interpretation in China', *Connecticut Journal of International Law* 6:2 (1991).

[82] Martin Lee, 'A tale of two articles', in Peter Wesley-Smith and Albert Chen (eds.), *The Basic Law and Hong Kong's Future* (Hong Kong: Butterworths, 1988).

Perhaps China thought that that the version of the rule of law based on the common law was essential to capitalism, and was prepared to accept a very considerable entrenchment of the common law. The Basic Law makes the common law a principal source of laws. Several provisions expressly provide for the application of the common law and the continuation of the previous legal and judicial systems.[83] There is provision for judges from other common law countries to sit on the Court of Final Appeal and in practice there is always one such judge, chosen from a list of some of the most distinguished common law judges (all from 'white' jurisdictions!).[84] Permanent judges at all levels of court may be recruited from other common law jurisdictions[85] – a broader authorisation to recruit foreigners than is permitted in respect of other officials. The HKSAR may make provision for lawyers from outside Hong Kong to practice ('on the basis of the previous system') – presumably from prescribed common law countries.[86] Courts are free to refer to precedents of other common law jurisdictions.[87] The jury system has been preserved although the jury does not play an important role.[88]

The scope of the jurisdiction of Hong Kong courts is very wide, and includes the interpretation and enforcement of the Basic Law itself, including an impressive range of human rights. Importantly, the judiciary enjoys a high degree of independence, 'free from any interference'.[89] Judges are appointed on the recommendation of an 'independent commission composed of local judges, persons from the legal profession and eminent persons from other sectors'.[90] They must be appointed on the basis of their judicial and professional qualities.[91] Judges cannot be dismissed except for inability to discharge duties or for misconduct as determined by a judicial tribunal set up by the Chief Justice; and in the case of the Chief Justice the tribunal is to be appointed by the Chief Executive.[92] Additionally, the Chief Justice and other judges of the Court of Final Appeal and the Chief Judge of the High Court need the approval of the LegCo for both appointment and dismissal.[93] Hong Kong's legal and judicial system is completely insulated from the Mainland courts. Hong Kong courts have the power of 'final adjudication' and no appeals are possible to any Mainland court.[94]

With the exclusion of most Mainland law from Hong Kong, all these provisions add up to a formidable legal and judicial system. However, despite the Hong Kong courts' comprehensive jurisdiction over Basic Law questions, their ability to protect autonomy is severely restricted by the powers of the National People's Congress Standing Committee, which maintains final authority over interpretation of the Basic Law itself. The competences of the Hong Kong courts and the Standing Committee are dealt with in Article 158 – a most contentious provision. Within the framework of the overarching interpretation

[83] Basic Law, Arts. 8, 18, 19, 80–96 and 160. [84] Ibid., Art. 82. [85] Ibid., Art. 92.
[86] Ibid., Art. 94. [87] Ibid., Art. 84. [88] Ibid., Art. 86. [89] Ibid., Art. 85.
[90] Ibid., Art. 88. [91] Ibid., Art. 92. [92] Ibid., Art. 89. [93] Ibid., Art. 90.
[94] Ibid., Arts. 2 and 158.

powers of the Standing Committee, this article authorises the Hong Kong courts to interpret any Basic Law provision during adjudication. However, the court from which no further appeal is possible cannot interpret provisions dealing with the responsibilities of the Central Authorities or the relationship between them and the HKSAR. If the interpretation of any such provision will 'affect' the judgment, then that court must ask the Standing Committee to provide an interpretation of the provision and then apply it. This procedure only applies to a court from which there can be no further appeal, which in most cases would be the Court of Final Appeal.

Although much of the discussion on interpretation has focused on Article 158, it is necessary to note that other parts of the Basic Law also provide for an interpretative role by Beijing authorities. The Standing Committee had to decide at the birth of the HKSAR which colonial laws would be repealed because of their inconsistency with the Basic Law.[95] When a Mainland law is extended to Hong Kong, there must be a determination that the law relates to defence or foreign affairs, or other matters outside Hong Kong's autonomy.[96] Law passed by Hong Kong's legislature may be reviewed by the Standing Committee for consistency with the Basic Law and declared invalid.[97] Questions of interpretation may also arise in relation to amending the Basic Law, for no such change may contravene the 'established basic policies of the People's Republic of China'.[98] In this case the final power of interpretation would rest with the National People's Congress itself.

Thus the power of interpretation is deeply intertwined in the relationship between Beijing and Hong Kong; it is not simply about the meaning of laws but about power relationships. The Basic Law is primarily about control and not autonomy, as is obvious in the provisions about Beijing's control over the Chief Executive, senior public servants and the LegCo. But the independence of the judiciary and the total unacceptability of a role for the Mainland courts means that the Hong Kong courts cannot be so easily subordinated. The power of interpretation plugs this gap, in addition to performing other functions.

The National People's Congress Standing Committee has to consult the Committee on the Basic Law before rejecting an ordinance of the LegCo,[99] adding or deleting a national law applicable to Hong Kong under Annex III,[100] interpreting the Basic Law, or amending it.[101] In that regard the role of the Basic Law Committee might be regarded as quasi-judicial; according to Ji Pengfei, it was meant to be more representative than it turns out to be: it was supposed 'to heed fully the opinions from all walks of life in Hong Kong'.[102] In practice the Basic Law Committee has become another institution that the Standing Committee uses to achieve its own objectives.

[95] Ibid., Art. 160. [96] Ibid., Art. 18. [97] Ibid., Art. 17. [98] Ibid., Art. 159.
[99] Ibid., Art. 17. [100] Ibid., Art. 18. [101] Ibid., Arts. 158 and 159.
[102] Ji, 'Explanations on the Basic Law of the HKSAR and its related documents'.

The fact that the National People's Congress Standing Committee can decide on the validity of any Hong Kong law by reference to the Basic Law and Mainland authorities means that China can determine what the law in HKSAR will be and secure the total subordination of Hong Kong to China. If China were to make full use of these possibilities, then the autonomous application of the common law in Hong Kong would be impossible, and the common law as we know it would cease to exist. In practice China has desisted from interpretations of the Basic Law provisions closely connected to the common law (largely in the area of private law), and seems not to have exercised its power to review Hong Kong laws after they have been enacted.

However, the various Standing Committee interpretations have been highly politically motivated, whether those relating to the adoption of previous laws, the Chinese Nationality Law as it affects the right of abode of children of permanent residents of Hong Kong, or the scope of constitutional reform under Annexes I and II of the Basic Law.[103] There has been no public consultation on the possible interpretations. The role of the Basic Law Committee seems to have been to rubber stamp decisions made even before Hong Kong members reach Beijing for their deliberations. There are suspicions of collusion between the Hong Kong administration and the central government. The Standing Committee has in no case undertaken a detailed and careful analysis of the nature of Hong Kong's autonomy or the specific provisions interpreted (the closely reasoned *Ng Ka Ling* decision of the Court of Final Appeal running to a typescript of nearly 100 pages was overturned in a couple of paragraphs). No reasons are given that might guide individuals and institutions in future understanding of the Standing Committee's decision, or interpretations of the Basic Law, or Hong Kong's relationship with the Central Authorities. On the contrary, the waters are often muddied, as reports of other bodies endorsed by the Standing Committee become in themselves sources of the Basic Law.[104] This further aggravates the lack of discipline in interpretation when the precise provisions of the Basic Law are glossed over or disregarded by vague formulations that have no place in the text of the Basic Law, such as 'executive led' system, 'stability and prosperity', or 'the sovereign', interpreted to mean what suits the Mainland authorities or their supporters in Hong Kong.[105]

As the indirect method of control and influence via the Hong Kong administration has faltered, the power to interpret has been used as a 'hands-on' device for the central government to intervene in Hong Kong affairs. Future

[103] Yash Ghai, 'The intersection of Chinese law and common law in the Hong Kong Special Administrative Region: question of technique or politics', *Hong Kong Law Journal* 37:II (2007), 363–7 for an analysis of Standing Committee interpretations under 158(1).

[104] For example, the reports of the Preparatory Committee in the run up to the transition of sovereignty, and the reports of the Chief Executive and the Task Force on Constitutional Reform have the potential to become such 'sources'.

[105] Examples are the reports of the Task Force on Constitutional Reform and Chief Executive Tung Chee-hwa's famous 'nine points' in support of the government's approach to political reform.

use of interpretation in this way would also effectively bring about further amendments to the Basic Law, bypassing the formal procedures of Article 159 – which are directed to the preservation of the autonomy of Hong Kong – thereby threatening considerable confusion in its legal system.[106] Do these interpretations affect other provisions where these concepts and procedures apply, such as Article 17, which deals with fundamental questions of the legislative authority of the LegCo, and the role of the Standing Committee? Questions like this point to the ad hoc nature of the PRC approach to law.

As far as references from it were concerned, the Court of Final Appeal managed for a considerable period to hold the Standing Committee at bay by finding, in *Ng Ka Ling*, that a reference was required only if the Basic Law article in question was outside the autonomy of Hong Kong and a Standing Committee interpretation was necessary to resolve the case. If two or more provisions were involved, the court refers only if the predominant article was outside autonomy. When the Standing Committee overruled the Court's interpretation in that case, it relied on Article 158(1), not Article 158(3). Despite considerable pressure, the Court held the line, while the Standing Committee made considerable use of 158(1) to issue 'interpretations' that governed (or more accurately, hindered) the path of 'political reform' and resolved critical questions. But in 2011 the Court capitulated (by three to two) to enormous pressure from the Chinese government, in *DRC v. FG Hemisphere.*[107]

The action was to enforce arbitration awards granted in France and Switzerland against a corporation of the Democratic Republic of Congo based in Hong Kong. The corporation had entered into a contract with a number of Chinese state corporations, under which considerable sums had become payable to the Congolese corporations, payments that the plaintiffs were seeking to obtain. Two important issues were engaged: (a) whether China's authority over foreign affairs meant that the Chinese rule of sovereign immunity applied in Hong Kong, despite the common law rule of restricted immunity and the fact that Chinese rule was not extended to Hong Kong in accordance with Basic Law Article 18, and (b) whether the Court of Final Appeal was obliged to refer this question to the Standing Committee. China had expressed keen interest in the case and issued two notes to the courts stating that the issue must be resolved by Chinese law, a procedure and position supported by the Hong Kong government. In the face of two powerful dissents, the Chinese argument was upheld by a majority of three judges. The same majority also decided that it was obliged to refer the issue to the Standing Committee as the matter depended on articles outside Hong Kong's autonomy. Not surprisingly, the Standing Committee ruled that

106 For example, the NPCSC has decided that there is no difference in law between a matter being referred to the Central People's Government for 'approval', in Annex I and 'for record' in Annex II – both require the consent of the centre – nor between procedures requiring the initial engagement of the Central Authorities. As in these two Annexes, or at a later stage, the Central Authorities can intervene as and when they wish.

107 2011 HKCFA 4.

Chinese law applied. The Court of Final Appeal's majority's position was that Hong Kong courts were obliged to apply whatever rules the Chinese executive (not necessarily only the National People's Congress) told them to in the field of foreign affairs. The judgment has come under severe criticism as it removes the barriers against application of Chinese laws (outside the strict limits of the Basic Law), thereby weakening the basis of the application of the common law and giving wide jurisdiction to the Standing Committee regarding Hong Kong cases, as well as weakening the rule of law by succumbing to pressures from the Chinese authorities.[108]

Conclusion

The functions of autonomy in Hong Kong (and Macau) are unusual, constituting separation of parts of the state in order to acknowledge the differences in their economy, social systems and values – and history. Achieving such aims requires a more extensive autonomy than is usually the case. At the same time Hong Kong's (and Macau's) autonomy is a transitional arrangement to prepare them for full incorporation into the state, an eventuality which militates against the strengthening of autonomy. Another feature of the arrangement is that the Joint Declaration and Basic Law did not, in a sense, create the system in Hong Kong, but merely acknowledged it. The difficult and complex task of establishing a new, separate legal entity for autonomy was not necessary. Hong Kong essentially retained its social and economic system, as well as a whole body of law (statutory and common law), property relations and so on. Where changes or reforms had to be made, especially political and constitutional, there have been enormous obstacles. But Hong Kong's big advantage was that it had a well developed economy, an astute and influential business class and highly sophisticated professional groups, linked to regional and global organisations and networks.

Its major handicap has been the weakness of its institutions and this has prevented a fuller development of democratic practices. This weakness is tied to the 'motherland', which is actively fighting incipient movements for democracy at home and in Hong Kong, thus further weakening social democracy. Institutional arrangements both within Hong Kong and with China mean that key decisions about Hong Kong, including its future, are made by China. Despite this, a significant number of Hong Kong people have sought to democratise Hong Kong and have achieved some success within a fairly participatory and accountable system. Such efforts have sometimes cautioned China against proceeding in opposition to the people. But the nature of this kind of resistance to further erosion of Hong Kong's freedoms is sporadic and is possible only on issues regarded as critical by the people. Nevertheless China's ability to manipulate public opinion or to impose overtly political decisions on Hong Kong

108 See the symposium on the case in *HKLJ* 41:2 (2011).

does have its limits. When it has deemed it necessary it has turned to legal strategy, invoking the interpretation powers of the National People's Congress Standing Committee. Although the Mainland evinces scant respect for law, the Central Authorities have ironically used legal interpretations to control political developments in Hong Kong, despite these being granted under the Joint Declaration. But all things considered, a small Chinese community has done well to preserve its moral values and identity against the populous superpower on its doorstep.

11

The autonomy of devolved Scotland

Chris Himsworth

This is a chapter about devolved government in Scotland but, because it is also a chapter written with comparative purposes in mind, its subject matter, though wholly based on Scotland and the United Kingdom, has been selected with a view to its comparative utility. There are, however, limits to comparative understanding in constitutional law. All analysis will depend on the context; and differences will always tend to outweigh similarities. This is especially true in situations where the use of law to secure constitutional autonomy is under scrutiny. Not only have the conditions of autonomy (operational or proposed) to be considered – and these will vary widely – but also the potential and actual contribution of the institutions and procedures of the law to creating and then sustaining autonomous government within a state. How far can the law make an autonomous contribution to autonomy?

When that question is posed, whether in relation to a single state or more generally and comparatively, a distinction will be drawn between those situations in which the political autonomy derives from the 'settled will' of both the people to whom autonomy is accorded and the people in the remainder of the state and, on the other hand, where the claim to autonomy remains contested. While a checklist of rules for autonomy in conditions of consensus is, all other things being equal, relatively easy to achieve and relatively transferable to similar situations elsewhere, the role of law and the scope for its autonomous contribution is much more fraught where the politics of autonomy are contested. Equally, however, most political situations will, to a degree, combine consensus and contestation and, on a 'consensus-contestation' continuum, Scotland probably takes its place at a mid-point on the scale. Devolution, as a continuing process, poses stark questions about Scotland's constitutional future.

The contested nature of Scotland's autonomy is reflected in what have been regarded as the diametrically opposed ambitions of those who have supported devolution. Some have been supporters because it appears to provide a step on the road to ultimate secession and independence. Such ambitions have been reflected in the policies of the Scottish National Party ('SNP') governments in Scotland since 2007 and their proposal for a referendum on independence. On the other side are those who have seen devolution, through its potential for the accommodation and suppression of separatist tendencies, as a means of strengthening the United Kingdom. This was the intention of those who promoted the Scotland Act 1998; set up a body to review devolution in 2008 (the Calman Commission)[1] and work for the enactment of the Scotland Act 2012 by the UK Parliament.[2]

Scotland stands poised to make significant new decisions. In the longer term, however, the extent to which the opposing views on devolution may be destined eventually to converge on the common ground of a differently defined and much stronger autonomy for Scotland is a matter of some speculation. Scotland may be the future site for intriguing new institutional developments for autonomy within the United Kingdom and the European Union. And they may be of even wider relevance and application.

International foundations of autonomy

As will be explained here, the foundations of Scotland's autonomy lie almost exclusively within the United Kingdom itself. There are, it is true, international influences on the current working of autonomy in Scotland and in other parts[3] of the United Kingdom such as the relationships forged between the Scottish Government[4] (and Parliament) and other regional institutions within the European Union ('EU') and the impact of UK membership of the EU on the distribution of functions between the state and the regions. Scotland's membership of the civilian family of legal systems (as opposed to the common law family) also adds an international aspect.[5] Nor were these influences wholly irrelevant to the emergence of Scotland-based institutions. In particular, the United Kingdom's division into economic planning regions (including Scotland, Wales, Northern Ireland and eight English regions) drew in part upon EU imperatives. European Parliament elections have been held on the basis of twelve UK regions, including Scotland (until 1999 with eight Scottish constituencies and then a single eight, and now only six, member Scottish constituency). Membership of

[1] The Report of the Calman Commission ('Serving Scotland Better: Scotland and the United Kingdom in the 21st Century', 2009) provides a wealth of information and analysis on the current state of devolution in Scotland.

[2] The Act contains a number of modest amendments to the 1998 Act, including the reform of the funding of devolution.

[3] The division of the UK into geographically defined areas gives rise to problems of terminology. Sometimes legislation simply refers to 'parts'. Elsewhere the language of 'territories' (especially 'devolved territories') is used. 'Regions' often serves as a generic term but there is sensitivity in Wales and Scotland where 'region' is often thought to be demeaning and 'nation' preferred. But, of course, the use of 'nation' (or indeed 'country') can create ambiguities where confusion with the UK as a whole arises, unless 'state' (not a term used in the UK for a 'sub-state' entity) is adopted. Northern Ireland is sometimes referred to as a 'province' (and Wales as a 'principality').

[4] The Scotland Act 1998 refers to the 'Scottish Executive' but for a long time now, and especially since the SNP came into power in 2007, the Scottish Executive has been informally known as the 'Scottish Government'. The Scotland Act 2012 has made the official term. Throughout this chapter, 'Scottish Government' is used.

[5] These issues are explored in more detail later.

the EU Committee of the Regions, although adjusted at the time of devolution in 1999, recognised Scotland as the 'region' from the start. The text of the new Treaty on the Functioning of the European Union contains a second Protocol on the principles of subsidiarity and proportionality that includes a limited obligation to consult 'regional parliaments with legislative powers'.

Two other influences, of perhaps greater foundational character, should be mentioned. Weakly influential has been the treaty regime of the Council of Europe. Distinct from the European Union, this Strasbourg-based forty-seven member body has, especially through its Congress of Local and Regional Authorities of Europe, maintained a high profile in the creation of local and regional democracy. Since 1985 the European Charter of Local Self-Government has articulated standards of local autonomy monitored by the Congress. There has not been an equivalent charter of regional autonomy, although the Council of Europe did adopt an advisory Reference Framework on Regional Democracy in 2009.

Completely different in its age and form of internationalism, there should also be mentioned the Treaty of Union between Scotland and England (and Wales) of 1707 under which was founded the United Kingdom of Great Britain.[6] From 1603 the independent countries of Scotland and England shared a single monarchy but it was the union not only of the crowns but also of the two countries themselves and the creation of a single Parliament from 1707, which not only created the new state but also contributed very substantially to establishing Scotland's special status within it.

Local foundations of autonomy[7]

The prospect of an autonomous status for Scotland within the United Kingdom was constructed from the launch of the state itself in 1707. The Treaty of Union, whilst creating a single UK Parliament and the basis for a single UK government that became the institutions at the heart of a highly centralised state, sought to secure the independence of a separate system in Scotland of courts and private law,[8] and of local government.[9] In due course, this produced a framework within which Scotland's domestic governance was conducted by a separate department of government – the Scottish Office, established in 1885[10] – with a separate minister in the UK cabinet – a Secretary for Scotland from

[6] The United Kingdom of Great Britain and Ireland (subsequently Northern Ireland) was later established in 1801.

[7] For fuller accounts, see T. B. Smith, *A Short Commentary on the Law of Scotland* (Edinburgh: Green, 1962); J. D. B. Mitchell, *Constitutional Law* 2nd edn. (Edinburgh: Green, 1968); N. MacCormick (ed.), *The Scottish Debate* (London: Oxford University Press, 1970). See also C. M. G. Himsworth and C. M. O'Neill, *Scotland's Constitution: Law & Practice* 2nd edn. (Haywards Heath: Bloomsbury Professional, 2009).

[8] Arts XVIII and XIX. [9] Art XXI (Royal Burghs).

[10] Prior to that, Scottish arrangements had diverged strongly, in their use (for example) of the Lord Advocate and sheriffs in central and local administration.

1885 and a (higher-status) Secretary of State from 1925 – and special Scottish procedures in the Westminster Parliament that led to a separate body of primary legislation covering most domestic Scottish affairs. From the late nineteenth century there was pressure to establish a parliament in Scotland and, by the time this ambition was achieved at the end of the twentieth century, the foundations of autonomy were very strong. Nor was this an autonomy confined to the institutions of government. As Professor Lindsay Paterson has shown in *The Autonomy of Modern Scotland*,[11] the development of Scotland's autonomy in the eighteenth and nineteenth centuries drew on characteristics of its political management, organisation of local society with its distinctive sheriffs, parishes and burghs, patterns of economic development, the presbyterian church and the 'moderate rationalism' of the enlightenment, the education system (both in schools and universities) and the legal system. These provided the basis for a distinctiveness of governmental organisation (especially the Scottish Office) and policy making in the welfare state of the twentieth century. Voluntary (non-governmental) organisations in Scotland (including charities, political parties and arts organisations) tend to have a separate Scottish identity either as independent bodies or with an autonomous status within UK or GB organisations. Scotland's separate representation in international sport (in particular, rugby and football) is well known.

Although some of Scotland's governmental and social differences have parallels in Wales and Northern Ireland, the distinctiveness of Scotland's legal system is more profound. Scotland joins Northern Ireland in being a separate 'jurisdiction' within the United Kingdom (the third being England and Wales), with a separate court structure (subject to civil appeals going to the UK Supreme Court, formerly the House of Lords), separate legal professions and separate forms of legal education. Scotland is unique in the United Kingdom in its civilian origins and thus its modern hybrid or 'mixed' system combining civilian and Anglo-American 'common law' rules. Particularly distinctive is the robust (but much reformed) system of property law.

While the principal focus of this chapter is on the recently established system of devolved government under the Scotland Act 1998, the pre-existing autonomy which has developed over the 300 years since 1707 is an essential backdrop. The Act of 1998 was in no sense written on a blank sheet of paper, but has to be seen as a new chapter in a much longer story. The new institutions may or may not endure. As we shall see, the degree of autonomy that they secure has yet to be fully revealed. The longer-term autonomy of Scotland within the 'union state' of the United Kingdom has, however, been an enduring phenomenon.

The co-existence of these two Scottish autonomies makes the concept of the 'purpose' of autonomy problematic. It is, in particular, difficult to speak now of the 'purpose' of the autonomy established since 1707. That autonomy has

[11] Edinburgh University Press, 1994.

no strong ethnic, linguistic,[12] or economic base but is nevertheless undoubtedly strongly represented in the governmental, social and legal characteristics already mentioned. It has provided the basis for the national identity of Scotland and, therefore, for the form of Scottish nationalism espoused by the SNP since its foundation in 1934. And the autonomy of devolution since 1998 builds on and develops the earlier forms by providing a new directly elected Scottish Parliament with broad legislative competences exercisable in Scotland and with the capacity to exert new forms of supervision and control over Scottish government. New competences and new accountabilities are provided by the new institutions.

As to the desirability of this new constitutional development from 1998, there are widely differing views that derive from different visions of the future of Scotland and different perceptions of the probable contribution of devolution. The different visions, as explained earlier, are distributed across those who see Scotland's future as an independent state, albeit within the European Union – broadly the view of the more fundamentalist wing of the SNP – and, on the other hand, those whose loyalty is to a continuing United Kingdom. That latter group includes, however, those of a federalist persuasion whose aim would be a stronger and constitutionally entrenched autonomy for Scotland and, on the other hand, those UK unionists who are apprehensive of any such division of the state. Fundamentalist separatists resisted devolution as a distraction. Strong unionists resisted it as a threat. In the middle ground are the more pragmatically inclined nationalists who see devolution as a staging-post to much stronger autonomy or even to independence, federalists who also see devolution as progress towards their ultimate objective and the more pragmatic unionists whose perception of devolution is as a concession to democratic pressures that is necessary to save the union itself rather than, in the memorable words of a high-profile Labour Party opponent of devolution, a 'motorway without exit to a destination that may not have been intended but is indistinguishable from a separate state'.[13] The different political goals of the members of the broad coalition in favour of devolution[14] and the different perceptions of the probable future effects of devolution contribute to the dynamic of devolution itself. There is, in any event, an acceptance that it is not in Wales alone that 'devolution is a process not an event'.[15]

[12] Although the Gaelic and (southern) Scots languages are certainly both distinctive features. On the distinction between ethnicity and civic nationalism as the basis of separate identity, see for example, S. Tierney, *Constitutional Law and National Pluralism* (Oxford University Press, 2004), 36–7.

[13] Tam Dalyell MP, HC Debs 31 July 1997 col. 486.

[14] Including those members of the Conservative and Unionist Party whose natural predisposition might have been to resist devolution but who have benefitted from the higher political profile in Scotland produced by the proportional representation electoral system adopted for the Scottish Parliament.

[15] See Ron Davies MP (former Secretary of State for Wales), *Devolution: A Process Not an Event* (Cardiff: Institute of Welsh Affairs, 1999).

A more detailed discussion of the institutions of devolution follows in the next section of the chapter but it is useful at this stage to provide a brief introduction to the UK constitutional context within which they have emerged. Four principal features should be mentioned.

The absence of a written constitution and the endurance of parliamentary sovereignty

The lack of a written constitution is not a merely trivial feature that distinguishes the United Kingdom from practically all other states worldwide. The absence of entrenched rules, with courts to enforce them, establishing and controlling all organs of state means that we cannot talk of a 'constitution' for the United Kingdom or indeed for its constituent parts in the same way that the term is used elsewhere. It may be that the European Communities Act 1972, which preceded UK accession to the European Community and, less strongly, the Human Rights Act 1998, has dented and, in some measure, contradicted Diceyan certainties. It is true that, in a recent English case,[16] the court (Laws, LJ) wrote of a category of 'constitutional statutes' of higher status than ordinary Acts of Parliament. And, most importantly in a Scottish context, there has been a much longer-standing case for regarding the Treaty of 1707[17] as a partial written constitution for the United Kingdom,[18] arguably with consequences for the Westminster Parliament when making laws that contradict the terms of the Treaty, and for the courts in reaction to such laws.[19] Such considerations apart, however, the general principles of parliamentary sovereignty continue to have very important effects on the UK constitutional order and especially for constitutional reforms that are made, but can also be modified, overridden or undone, by the Westminster Parliament. As we shall see, this has important consequences for the devolution settlement itself.

The Blair government's constitutional reform project

Whatever the consequences of parliamentary sovereignty for constitutional reform, they did not stand in the way of the Blair government, elected in 1997, producing a reform agenda that, on paper at least, was extraordinarily wide-ranging. Probably most significant has been the devolution programme discussed later. This was, however, joined by the project to 'incorporate' or 'bring home' the European Convention on Human Rights by the Human Rights Act 1998; the reform of the House of Lords, which, though still far from complete,

16 *Thoburn v. Sunderland City Council* [2003] QB 151.

17 One of Laws, LJ's 'constitutional statutes', along with *inter alia* the Scotland Act 1998.

18 *MacCormick v. Lord Advocate* 1953 SC 396 and see D. N. MacCormick, 'Does the United Kingdom have a Constitution?' NILQ 29 (1978), 1.

19 See, for instance, N. Walker and C. M. G. Himsworth, 'The Poll Tax and Fundamental Law', *Juridical Review*, 45 (1991).

was started with the removal of most of the hereditary peers by the House of Lords Act 1999; the reform of official secrecy and access to official information by the Freedom of Information Act 2000;[20] and the creation of a new UK Supreme Court from 2009.[21] It is evident that the devolution proposals have to be understood against this wider background of constitutional reform. Indeed, devolution interlocks at many points with the other reforms.

Asymmetric devolution in the United Kingdom

The devolution programme has to be considered in the context of that general programme of constitutional reform; it is important to recognise that Scotland is only one project among many. Historically, this has not been unusual. In the nineteenth century, a primary emphasis on home rule for Ireland was replaced by pressure for home rule for Scotland, Wales and Northern Ireland, as well as for (the regions of) England. In 1973, the report of the (Kilbrandon) Royal Commission on the Constitution provided a substantial and comprehensive analysis of the then state of regional government across the United Kingdom, a survey of possible future frameworks including a federalist solution, and recommendations for different degrees of legislative and executive devolution. In 1978 Acts of Parliament were passed under which there would have been devolution to both Wales and Scotland[22] but these were aborted because insufficient popular support was demonstrated in referendums held in 1979.

By 1997–8 the devolution project had extended more widely and the Blair government introduced Bills leading to the Scotland Act 1998, the Government of Wales Act 1998, the Northern Ireland Act 1998 and the Greater London Authority Act 1999 together with proposals for the introduction of elected regional assemblies across the rest of England. Because of continuing difficulties in the Province, the Northern Ireland Act has only rather haltingly been implemented, and initial steps to introduce a prototype regional assembly in the north-east of England were derailed by an adverse referendum in November 2004. Thus the current asymmetric pattern of devolution across the United Kingdom is represented by the strong model of legislative devolution in Scotland, the initially weaker model of 'executive' devolution in Wales but, from May 2011, expanded to legislative devolution,[23] an even narrower model of regional government for

[20] With the complementary Freedom of Information (Scotland) Act 2002 passed by the Scottish Parliament.

[21] Under the Constitutional Reform Act 2005.

[22] In Northern Ireland this was a period in which there were successive attempts to relaunch devolved government following the breakdown of the Stormont system and the introduction of direct rule from 1972.

[23] Proposals for the strengthening of devolution in Wales were made by the (Richard) Commission on the Powers and Electoral Arrangements of the National Assembly for Wales (March 2004). The UK Government published its own proposals as *Better Governance for Wales* Cm 6582 (2005) and this was followed by the Government of Wales Act 2006, which produced a two-stage transition to legislative devolution.

Greater London, a delayed legislative model in Northern Ireland and a lack of any form of devolution to elected assemblies across England. Scotland's top place in this hierarchy derives from its historically stronger autonomous form of government, the electoral strength of the SNP and, in the period between 1979 and 1987, the well-organised preparatory work of the Campaign for a Scottish Parliament and the Scottish Constitutional Convention[24] producing a manifesto commitment to legislative devolution by the Labour Party in 1997. A convincing referendum result in Scotland in September 1997 in favour of both a Scottish Parliament and its tax-raising powers demolished lingering opposition in the Westminster Parliament and has been a continuing element in maintaining the Scottish Parliament's legitimacy.

Lack of constitutional review

As already indicated, the concept of parliamentary sovereignty continues to dominate British constitutional discourse and no more strongly than in its denial of a role for a constitutional or supreme court capable of invalidating or disallowing an Act of the Westminster Parliament, save in relation to EU law. This did not prevent, however, the creation of new devolution-related powers for the Judicial Committee of the Privy Council (JCPC)[25] or the implementation in 2009 of proposals for a new UK Supreme Court to replace the appellate committee of the House of Lords.[26]

The institutions of autonomy

The Scotland Act 1998 created two principal institutions – the Scottish Parliament and the Scottish Executive – whose composition and relationship to each other broadly replicate the 'Westminster model' of parliamentary government, but which were designed to depart in some measure from the institutions and relationships of the UK Parliament and government.[27] The Scottish judicial system has been left substantially in place,[28] but with modifications to reflect

[24] An organisation broadly representative of political parties (though not the Conservatives or the SNP), trade unions and churches.

[25] Discussed further later. Those powers were subsequently transferred to the UK Supreme Court in 2009.

[26] See later.

[27] In this chapter, a distinction is drawn between this section whose focus is 'institutions' and the next section on 'methods'. Such a distinction probably comes under pressure in the analysis of any constitutional order but it is especially problematic in a UK context. The lack of a written constitution and the prevalence instead of a tradition of a 'political constitution' (see e.g., J. A. G. Griffith. 'The Political Constitution', MLR, 42 (1979), 1) means that distinctions between the constitutional or legal and political, between formal and informal are difficult to sustain.

[28] The Judiciary and Courts (Scotland) Act 2008, enacted by the Scottish Parliament contains many important provisions relating to judicial appointments and removals as well as court administration.

the transfer of responsibilities under the devolution settlement to the Parliament and government and to provide (through new powers first for the Judicial Committee of the Privy Council and subsequently for the UK Supreme Court) for the resolution of 'devolution issues'. Local government was not reorganised in consequence of devolution[29] and nor were all the bodies that constitute 'intermediate' government in Scotland.[30]

Turning briefly to the principal new institutions, the Parliament is a directly elected, 129-member single-chambered body with a fixed four-year term.[31] Seventy-three Members of the Scottish Parliament (MSPs) are elected by single-member constituencies on the 'first past the post' system, with the other fifty-six elected on the (proportional) additional member system from eight regions. Already these rules provide for a Parliament very different from the Westminster model, and with different consequences for executive-formation and parliament-executive relations. There is no doubt that the system of proportional representation was intended to deny any single political party an overall majority in the Parliament and indeed coalition governments (Labour with Liberal Democrat) were produced in 1999 and 2003 and these were followed in 2007 by a minority SNP government. The general election of 2011, however, produced an overall majority for the SNP. The fixed term denies any equivalent of the existing UK prime ministerial power to call a general election at a time of his or her choosing.[32]

Following a general election (or vacancy in the office), a First Minister is appointed by the Queen on the recommendation of the Parliament's Presiding Officer following a vote in the Parliament. Other ministers in the Scottish Government (known collectively as 'Scottish Ministers' for the purposes of the vesting of powers) are appointed by the Queen on the recommendation of the First Minister and the approval of the Parliament. These procedures broadly track those at the UK level, save that some rules which are merely 'conventional' in London are made explicit in the Scotland Act and are joined by the express rules for parliamentary approval of nominations. Also made explicit are rules requiring the resignation of the Scottish Government if there is a vote of no confidence in the Parliament.

These formal differences in the rules between Westminster and Holyrood (Edinburgh) derive from assumptions made by the Scottish Constitutional Convention that whilst, in the words of the UK Government's White Paper,

29 The thirty-two councils created with effect from 1996 were retained. Since the Local Governance (Scotland) Act 2004, elections to authorities have used the Single Transferable Vote system.

30 But see discussion later on cross-border public authorities.

31 Subject to the exceptional possibility of an early dissolution if supported by a two-thirds majority of MSPs. It has been declared (Fixed-term Parliaments Act 2011 s.4(2)) that the current Scottish Parliament elected in May 2011 should run though to 2016 to avoid Scottish and UK parliamentary elections coinciding in 2015.

32 Although that UK prime ministerial power has ended, temporarily at least, under the Fixed-term Parliaments Act 2011.

the 'relationship between the Scottish Executive and the Scottish Parliament will be similar to the relationship between the UK Government and the UK Parliament',[33] there should nevertheless be a different relationship between Government and Parliament representing a 'new politics' further articulated in the report and recommendations of a broadly based Consultative Steering Group (1998). That group's work was influential in the framing of the Parliament's Standing Orders and has continued to provide benchmark criteria on power sharing, accountability, accessibility and equality of opportunity, which were points of reference for the Parliament in its early years.[34] Whether the aspiration of a less executively dominated Parliament has been achieved will need to be assessed over a longer term, but it is clear that the Government-Parliament relationship is one that affects not only the dynamic of Scottish democracy but also the Edinburgh-London relationship. A Scottish Government under pressure from London to conform with centralising measures has its room for manoeuvre restricted (or, alternatively, is better protected) by a strong Parliament with less inclination to conform.

The starting point of any analysis of the overall relationship between the UK and Scottish institutions of government must be the essential formal vulnerability of the Scottish Parliament and Government that derives from the continuing legislative supremacy of the Westminster Parliament. The lack of a written constitution for the United Kingdom leaves that Parliament formally unconstrained in its power to adjust governmental relationships. Membership of the European Union may have created exceptional restrictions on Parliament's powers in those areas which the Union regulates but those do not include the governmental structure of member states. UK governments can use the legislative power of Parliament for constitutional restructuring, but government and Parliament retain the freedom to modify or to undo the new arrangements. Parliament has the power to provide devolutionary structures but also the power to take them away. Devolution in Northern Ireland could be created in 1922 under the Government of Ireland Act 1920 but suspended by the Northern Ireland (Temporary Provisions) Act 1972. The arrangements now created by the Scotland Act 1998 could formally be modified or removed by a subsequent Act of Parliament.[35] Westminster can modify the powers of the Scottish Parliament or the Scottish Government by subsequent Act of Parliament[36] – in addition to which there are powers to make adjustments by ministerial

[33] *Scotland's Parliament* (Cm 3658, 1997) para. 2.6.

[34] See, in particular, the report of the Parliament's Procedures Committee, *The Founding Principles of the Scottish Parliament* SP Paper 818 (2003).

[35] The Scotland Act has indeed already been amended in (mainly) small ways. Perhaps the most significant has been the amendment made by the Scottish Parliament (Constituencies) Act 2004 to retain the size of the Parliament at 129 MSPs rather than have that number reduced in line with the reduction (with effect from the UK general election of 2005) of the number of Scottish MPs at Westminster.

[36] This has been done quite frequently. The Scotland Act 2012 contains several new competences for the Scottish Parliament and removes others.

order, provided that both the Westminster and Scottish Parliaments consent.[37] Furthermore, the Westminster Parliament retains, by virtue of its continuing legislative supremacy, complete constitutional power to legislate for Scotland not only in respect of reserved matters but also in respect of the matters formally devolved to the Scottish Parliament. This is a position expressly confirmed, perhaps only for the avoidance of doubt, in s.28(7) of the Scotland Act itself.

The flip side of these powers retained by the Westminster Parliament is a corresponding vulnerability of the Scottish Parliament. Just as the Government of Ireland Act 1920 was often referred to, during the Stormont years, as the 'Constitution' of Northern Ireland, so the Scotland Act 1998 can, reasonably and with meaning, be referred to as Scotland's 'Constitution'. In formal terms, however, it is a 'Constitution' whose provisions are expressly protected almost entirely[38] from adjustment by the Scottish Parliament itself. This affects not only the powers of the Parliament but also its procedures. Although the Scottish Parliament makes its own Standing Orders, much of the framework for the Parliament's operations is handed down in the Scotland Act itself – a feature of the devolution arrangements that has attracted quite severe criticism within the Parliament.[39] This was also criticised by the Calman Commission and the Scotland Act 2012 contains provisions giving the Parliament greater discretion as to the appointment of Deputy Presiding Officers.

There is need for one other prefatory observation before the rules of intergovernmental relationships are explored. There is a potential complication, familiar in the exported federal versions of the Westminster model of government and also in the Stormont model in Northern Ireland, in the overlapping role of the monarch. The Queen is not directly described as the head of government in Scotland but, as with the UK government, it is she who formally appoints ministers and it is in her name that their powers are exercised. It is, however, to be assumed that convention demands that the Queen's powers in relation to the devolved government of Scotland be exercised on the advice of her Scottish ministers and not her UK ministers. Specific provision is also made by the Scotland Act to enable, for the purposes of their several legal rights and liabilities and the freedom to conduct legal proceedings, the Crown to act in different capacities, whether 'in right of Her Majesty's Government in the United Kingdom' or 'in right of the Scottish Administration'.[40]

Within that framework, there are a number of ways in which the UK government can intervene in the law-making and decision-making processes of the Scottish Parliament and Executive. These are formally designated in the

[37] Scotland Act 1998 ss.30(2), 63.

[38] Schedule 4 to the Scotland Act 1998 permits the Scottish Parliament to make very limited amendments to the Act.

[39] See for example Procedures Committee, *Founding Principles of the Scottish Parliament.*

[40] S.99. This is a position reflected in subsequent 'Crown application' provisions. See for example, the (UK) Equality Act 2006 s.92; Reservoirs (Scotland) Act 2011 s.110.

Scotland Act and their limits defined. There are no overarching powers of veto exercisable by the UK government in relation to the devolved institutions. As to the Scottish Parliament's law-making powers, however, there are two principal forms of intervention prescribed. The first is the power of the UK Attorney General[41] to refer the question of whether a Bill (which has been passed by the Parliament but before its submission by the Presiding Officer for Royal Assent) would be within the Parliament's competence to the UK Supreme Court. Separately, however, there is a more political form of pre-Assent control[42] vested directly in the Secretary of State. It is described as a 'power to intervene in certain cases'.[43] If a Bill contains provisions '(a) which the Secretary of State has reasonable grounds to believe would be incompatible with any international obligations[44] or the interests of defence or national security, or (b) which make modifications of the law, as it applies to reserved matters which the Secretary of State has reasonable grounds to believe would have an adverse effect on the operation of the law as it applies to reserved matters',[45] the Secretary of State may make an order prohibiting the Presiding Officer from submitting the Bill for Royal Assent. This power (presumably judicially reviewable if it were abused) has also not yet been deployed by the UK government. Nor has a similar power available to the Secretary of State[46] to 'prevent or require' action by the Scottish Government (including the revocation of delegated legislation). On the other hand, certain less intrusive and more technical interventions have been made under powers available to the UK government to make provision considered to be 'necessary or expedient' in consequence of a provision made by or under an Act of the Scottish Parliament.[47]

There are other ways too in which the powers of the Scottish Government and their use can be affected by UK ministerial intervention. One is in relation to European Union law. Not only does UK membership of the EU affect the devolution settlements by enabling UK ministers to control the content of UK (including Scots) law in the areas of strong EU competence such as fisheries through their membership of the Council of Ministers but, as mentioned earlier, the power of UK Ministers as well as the Scottish Ministers to exercise powers of implementation under s.57(1) of the Scotland Act provides the opportunity for important UK-level interventions.

[41] Or the Advocate General for Scotland, another UK law officer.

[42] To enable consideration to be given to the possible exercise of these controls, the Parliament's Presiding Officer is required not to submit Bills for Royal Assent within four weeks of their passing.

[43] Scotland Act 1998 s.35.

[44] Defined by s.126(10) to exclude obligations to observe European Union Law or Convention (ECHR) rights which, in part, define the limits of the Parliament's competence in the first place.

[45] This power is to be understood with reference to the provisions of the Act that define the Parliament's legislative competence. The Parliament is restrained from legislating in relation to 'reserved matters' but this might not prevent an 'adverse effect' on the law applicable to reserved matters.

[46] Under s.58 of the Scotland Act 1998.

[47] Ibid. s.104.

Quite separately, the Scotland Act arrangements for shared control of 'cross-border public authorities', even though not formally encroaching on the power of the Scottish Parliament to arrange things differently in the longer term, provide for a substantial level of central intrusion and an adjustment of the general model of devolved powers.[48]

Essential ingredients of any system of autonomous government are the extent of the powers conferred, and the degree to which these powers are placed within the exclusive competence of the autonomous authorities. Also important may be the manner of the definition of these powers and thus, in the case of dispute, the way in which the limits of powers will be interpreted. The Scotland Act confers broad legislative powers on the Scottish Parliament that may, within the same range of competence, confer executive powers on the Scottish Government. In addition, executive powers previously exercised by UK government ministers within the same range[49] were transferred at the time of devolution to the Scottish Government.

The legislative competence of the Parliament is conferred as a general power to make laws subject to the exception of matters reserved to the Westminster Parliament.[50] The list of reserved matters is contained in Schedule 5 to the Act and includes a series of 'General Reservations' in respect of the constitution, foreign affairs, defence, the civil service and some others, and then a much longer list of 'Specific Reservations' that cover very broad ranges of financial matters (including fiscal and monetary policy), home affairs (including powers on drugs, elections, immigration, nationality and national security), trade and industry, energy, much of transport policy, social security, employment and others. These leave the Scottish Parliament free to legislate in a wide range of domestic policy areas relevant to Scotland such as education (including universities), the health service, local government, police, prisons and (in most aspects) the judiciary and legal system. An important feature of the powers of the Scottish Parliament, however, is that they are formally unentrenched and, therefore, subject to modification by the Westminster Parliament.[51] The Scotland Act itself can be amended. In addition, however, the principle of the legislative supremacy of the Westminster Parliament ensures that the devolution of certain powers to the Scottish Parliament leaves Westminster formally free to legislate in those devolved areas as well. The way in which this formal vulnerability of the Scottish Parliament works in practice is considered next.

As mentioned, the devolution of powers to the Scottish Government broadly tracks the powers of the Parliament but with some extensions into areas not

[48] Ibid. ss.88–90.

[49] Together with some others beyond the range of devolved competence, transferred by Order in Council (ministerial order) under s.63 of the Act.

[50] Ss.28–29.

[51] The Scotland Act 1998 itself makes provision for modification by Order in Council of the list of reserved matter with the consent of both Parliaments. See s.30(2).

legislatively devolved. An important distinction between the two sets of powers, however, is that, in contrast with the Scottish Parliament's powers, which inevitably remain 'shared' with those of the Westminster Parliament, the Scottish Government's powers are, save where there is specific provision to the contrary, exclusively conferred.

An overarching feature of the devolution of competences under the Scotland Act is the UK's membership of the European Union. This has two principal effects. The first is that, within their devolved areas, the *implementation* of EU law is a matter within the competence of the Scottish Parliament and, under powers conferred by the European Communities Act 1972 (as amended), the Scottish Government – in the latter case, a competence expressly shared with UK ministers.[52] The second effect, however, derives from the reservation of international (including EU) relations to the UK Parliament and thus the negotiation of the content of new EU law, *including* law in areas devolved to the Scottish Parliament. Thus, subject to processes of consultation more informally established,[53] this has the consequence of 'hollowing out' the Parliament's devolved powers in fields such as sea fishing, agriculture and the environment, which are strongly regulated by Europe.

Participation in UK-level government

Aspects of the ways in which the Scottish institutions share in processes of government conducted at UK level have already been considered and there is further treatment (on e.g., 'devolved' legislation at Westminster and shared public bodies) in the next section. One feature that has been particularly contentious in the asymmetric pattern of British devolution is the issue neatly captured by the question posed originally by Tam Dalyell MP (formerly member for the Scottish West Lothian constituency) at the time of the debate leading to the Scotland Act 1978,[54] but which has a continuing relevance. As he put it, it was a question about why he, as a Westminster MP for a Scottish constituency, could legitimately be expected to participate in, or vote on, business in relation to Blackburn in Lancashire (England) but not in relation to Blackburn in West Lothian because that business would, for Scotland, be devolved (and has now been devolved by the Scotland Act 1998) to the Scottish Parliament. Dalyell viewed this as a fatal flaw in any system of devolution constructed on an asymmetrical basis. Forcing the Westminster Parliament to be both a United Kingdom Parliament dealing with 'reserved' matters across the whole country and also an English (and Welsh) Parliament in relation to the matters devolved to Scotland (and Northern Ireland) created inevitable and unacceptable tensions – in particular the possible use by a United Kingdom government to secure legislation for England of a Commons majority dependent upon Scottish MPs.

[52] Scotland Act 1998, s.57(1). [53] Outlined later.
[54] T. Dalyell, *Devolution: The End of Britain?* (London: Jonathan Cape, 1977), 245–51.

That was a position exacerbated by the 'overrepresentation' of Scotland in the House of Commons, a matter since addressed by legislation to reduce the number of Scottish constituencies from seventy-two to fifty-eight. Other 'answers' to the West Lothian Question have been proposed in terms of the adoption by Scottish MPs of a self-denying ordinance disabling them from voting on English matters, or a more structured creation of a sort of 'English Parliament' within the Commons as a device to exclude Scottish MPs. Both would have been fraught with difficulties in the removal from UK Labour governments prior to 2010 (a completely separate 'English Government' would be unthinkable within the overall Westminster model) of the Commons majority upon which their power and authority depended. Different considerations arise for the current Coalition Government but, more credibly, an 'answer' can be sought by regarding the 'question' as one that is a transient inconvenience on the road to a more fully developed, and perhaps less asymmetrical, system of devolution in which English regions play a much fuller part. In the meantime, any distress caused to Scottish MPs and any annoyance of English MPs can be assuaged by the recognition that an answer in terms of English regionalism could be made available to those who wish to take it up.[55]

The methods of autonomy

The formal rules of the Scotland Act 1998, which create the institutions of devolution and confer their powers, clearly tell only a part of the story of Scotland's new autonomy.[56] For a fuller understanding, we have to take account of some further rules provided by or under the Scotland Act itself, together with the emerging practices of co-operation between the UK and Scottish institutions. In considering these, we have to keep in mind the longer-standing tradition of Scottish autonomy since 1707 within what has been a highly centralised UK state that has only recently launched its new programme of asymmetric devolution. UK-Scotland relations are accommodated within a pattern of other central/regional relationships, in which the continuing domination of the UK (and, within that, England whose population of 60 million far exceeds that of Scotland (5m), Wales (2.9m) and Northern Ireland (1.7m) combined) looms large. And of the highest importance so far have been the patterns of political organisation and control across the United Kingdom. With the exception of Northern Ireland, the nationally organised parties (Labour, Conservative

[55] In January 2012, the UK Government appointed a commission to study the consequences of devolution, including the West Lothian Question. The (Mackay) commission reported in March 2013.

[56] For an early review of intergovernmental relationships, see 'Devolution: Inter-Institutional Relations in the United Kingdom', *Report of the House of Lords Select Committee on the Constitution*, HL Paper 28 (2002–3). The Calman Report contained an important further review. See also the fourth Report of the (House of Commons) Scottish Affairs Committee HC 256 (2010-11).

and Liberal Democrat) dominate politics in all parts of the country, with supplementation in Scotland and Wales by nationalist parties – the Scottish National Party and Plaid Cymru respectively. Furthermore, for the early years (up to 2007) of the devolution experiment, the Labour Party held power at the UK level and also in the devolved administrations through coalition (in Scotland in coalition with the Liberal Democrats and in Wales in coalition for much of the time). In the emergence of inter-governmental relationships characterised as 'partnerships', these party political cohesions were of undoubted significance and much speculation in the early years of devolution revolved around what would become of devolution if at some point the political consensus broke down and the possibility of more contentious relationships arose. In the event, when the SNP government was installed in Edinburgh from 2007, its own minority status combined with a wish to appear diplomatic and effective meant that apparently civil working relations endured. The period of majority SNP government from elections in May 2011 has brought more turbulent conditions.

The following aspects of the working of autonomy will be considered:

1. The financing of Scottish devolution
2. A shared civil service
3. Shared public bodies
4. Dispute resolution
5. Relations between Parliaments and Governments: The Memorandum of Understanding and Concordats
6. Legislation at Westminster on devolved matters and the Sewel Convention
7. Devolution and the autonomy of Scotland's legal system
8. Relations between Scottish devolved institutions and others in the United Kingdom and the European Union
9. Outcomes: Has devolution made a difference?

The financing of Scottish devolution

In the analysis of all systems of decentralised government, great weight is unavoidably attached to financial relationships and the near-complete financial dependence of the Scottish Government on the UK Government is central to understanding the practice of devolved government in Scotland. There is a potential for limited flexibility deriving from the Scottish Parliament's (and Government's) control over the *local* taxation system[57] producing the possibility of shifting some of the Government's financial burden on to the local taxpayer. There is also the limited opportunity for charging for services provided. But, otherwise, the Scottish Government has been almost entirely dependent upon grants from the UK government. The Secretary of State is empowered by the Scotland Act to make such payments into the Scottish Consolidated Fund as he

[57] Scotland Act 1998 Sched. 5, Part II, S.AI .

may determine.[58] In the absence of any general power of taxation (because all legislative power in relation to taxation, with the exception of legislation as to local taxation just mentioned, is reserved to Westminster) the Scottish Parliament has enjoyed virtually no financial autonomy. The reservation of energy resources means that Scotland is not the exclusive beneficiary of the undersea oil which (for a while at least) lies under Scottish waters off the United Kingdom. Another constraint has been that the Scottish Government has no general power to borrow.

The Parliament has a 'tax-varying power' that enables it to vary – up or down – the basic rate of income tax payable by Scottish taxpayers by as much as 3p and which, as an accountability safety valve, is of some constitutional significance. It has been, however, of no practical significance because successive governments in Scotland have committed themselves to refraining from its use. This the Coalition Governments did in their partnership agreements of 1999 and 2003 and, after 2007, the SNP Government also wished to avoid imposing higher taxes and maintained the same stance.[59]

The effects of the resulting dependence on UK government grants have been moderated by the system of distribution based on the 'Barnett formula', which regulated the funding of Scotland, Wales and Northern Ireland by reference to spending levels in England since the late 1970s. The formula has been important both for the relative stability that it provided and also the relative generosity with which Scotland was treated.[60] It has also to be noted that, in contrast with some devolved governments elsewhere, the Scottish Government receives a 'block' grant, without specification of particular levels of expenditure on the different services it provides. The lack of transparency and impartiality in the determination of amounts of grant payable to Scotland and the other territories has, however, been questioned. One change that might have been introduced at the time of devolution was some form of independent board or commission to oversee the process of grant distribution.[61] In a constitutional environment that has become similar to that in federal countries, there would be an advantage in having such an independent body to make recommendations for grant distribution according to relatively objective economic criteria rather than leaving distribution to the hidden judgment of politicians. Disputes between different parts of the United Kingdom might be lessened as a result.

58 S.64(2).

59 There was an interesting squabble in November 2010 over whether the Scottish Government had, in fact, allowed the opportunity ever to impose the marginally higher level of tax in Scotland to lapse because of a failure to fund the Treasury mechanism to enable its imposition. Following criticism from the Scottish Parliament's Finance Committee, the Treasury was asked to revive the mechanism in February 2011.

60 See Himsworth and O'Neill, *Scotland's Constitution*, Chapter 10.

61 See Constitution Unit, *Scotland's Parliament: Fundamentals for a New Scotland Act* (1996), Chapter 5; and HL, 'Devolution: Inter-Institutional Relations in the United Kingdom', paras. 102 and 107.

Such disputes have inevitably arisen.[62] On the one hand, it is argued by some in Scotland that the distribution formula that once favoured Scotland because it deliberately recognised its greater funding needs now discriminates against Scotland because the formula for *amending* levels of expenditure operates, as was intended (or was, at least, wholly predictable), to reduce differentials between territories and thus to leave Scotland without the advantage it once had. There is a 'Barnett squeeze' on Scottish expenditure that arguably should be remedied by a new needs assessment, which would find in favour of a greater allocation to Scotland in future. There has been, on the other hand, an argument mainly associated with London and the north-east of England to the effect that some at least of the English regions are already being *underfunded* in comparison with Scotland. Poignant comparisons have been drawn between the funding of schools in Northumbria and the Scottish Borders.[63] There have similar complaints from Wales about the unfair ways in which the Barnett formula can work.[64]

In the light of both the complaints about the current system of funding and the core relevance of funding generally to the operation of devolution, it is not surprising that these issues have recently loomed large in the discussion and report of the Calman Commission and were at the heart of the debate about the Scotland Act 2012. In brief, Calman (with the help of an independent expert group) articulated a group of principles that should inform the funding of devolved government (identifying these as equity, autonomy, accountability, stability/predictability, simplicity/transparency and efficiency) and then, having considered various available options including a review of overseas models, made a number of recommendations. The principal proposal was to replace the Scottish Parliament's power to make marginal variations in the rate of income tax with a new power to determine a Scottish rate of income tax. To enable that to happen, the general (UK determined) rate of income tax should be reduced by 10 pence in the pound and the block grant would be reduced by an equivalent amount. In addition to transferring that enhanced tax-raising decision making to the Scottish Government and Parliament, a number of other taxes should be transferred, including stamp duty land tax, the aggregates levy and the landfill tax. A strengthening of inter-governmental arrangements for dealing with finance and additional borrowing powers was also proposed.

In very large measure, the Calman recommendations were adopted by the UK Government and were incorporated into the Scotland Act 2012. The financial provisions in the Bill were, however, a principal focus for the

[62] Nicely documented in the memorandum by I. MacLean published as evidence to the HL Committee on the Constitution, in HL, 'Devolution: Inter-Institutional Relations in the United Kingdom'.

[63] HL, 'Devolution: Inter-Institutional Relations in the United Kingdom', para. 3.2.

[64] See the report of the Independent Commission on Funding and Finance for Wales (Holtham) 2010. See also the report of the (Silk) Commission on Devolution in Wales, 2012.

Committee of the Scottish Parliament that scrutinised the Bill[65] and it provided a forum for a bitter dispute between the SNP Government seeking much greater fiscal autonomy and the unionist majority on the Committee. But since the Scottish general election of May 2011, the financial debate has taken on a different tone. The new majority SNP Government increased its demands for greater financial powers and has been seeking, in particular, a power to determine the rate of corporation tax in Scotland and increased borrowing powers.[66]

A shared civil service

The report of the (Kilbrandon) Royal Commission on the Constitution in 1973 expressed the view that the only way in which Scottish devolved government could operate autonomously would be, as had happened during the period of the devolved Northern Ireland Parliament at Stormont (1922–72),[67] with its own, separate civil service.[68] This might indeed appear to be a desirable feature of a devolved government where the loyalty of its own civil service to its own ministers and confidentiality of operation within that service would be necessary to protect its interests, especially in circumstances of antagonistic relations with the London Government. At all events, a separate civil service was denied by the Scotland Act, which provides that the civil service is a reserved matter and that civil servants in the Scottish Administration are members of the general UK home civil service.[69] The general rules of the UK civil service,[70] including the *Civil Service Management Code* and the *Civil Service Code*,[71] therefore extend to the staff of the Scottish Administration, but the appointment function is delegated to the Scottish Ministers, and they also exercise many management functions, as UK departments do.[72] It was the view of the House of Lords Select Committee on the Constitution that, despite the single framework for the civil service, the Scottish Government had 'considerable room for manoeuvre in developing staffing policies and arrangements that are appropriate to their local needs'.[73] This was a position broadly confirmed by John Elvidge, then Permanent Secretary in the Scottish Government, in written evidence to the

65 See later for the Sewel Convention. See also the report on the Bill by the Scottish Affairs Committee of the House of Commons – fourth Report (HC 775, 2010-12).

66 See the First Minister's speech to the Scottish Parliament on 26 May 2011.

67 There has indeed continued to be a separate civil service in Northern Ireland (a successor to the pre-1922 Irish civil service) since 1972.

68 Cmnd 5460 (1973) paras. 807 and 1146.

69 Scotland Act 1998, Sched. 5, Part I, para. 8 and s.51.

70 Until recently, these were largely non-statutory but Chapter 1 of the Constitutional Reform and Governance Act 2010 has placed the government of the civil service on a statutory basis.

71 Both reissued in November 2010 to reflect their new statutory status and, as before, in slightly different Scottish editions.

72 Scotland Act 1998, s.51(1) and (5), extending powers under the Civil Service (Management Functions) Act 1992.

73 HL, 'Devolution: Inter-Institutional Relations in the United Kingdom', para. 151.

Finance Committee of the Scottish Parliament where he wrote of the Scottish Government having 'considerable autonomy within a broad framework of values and systems covering the UK civil service as a whole. This autonomy is formally vested in the First Minister in accordance with the Civil Service (Management Functions) Act 1992 as extended by S.51(4) of the Scotland Act 1998. This enables me and my senior colleagues, working with the First Minister and his Ministerial colleagues, to shape a distinctive civil service culture and set of behaviours which match the ethos of devolution'.[74]

While the autonomy of the Scottish Government (both ministers and officials) to mould its own 'distinctive civil service culture' is doubtless of importance, another civil service consideration is the impact of the retained combined civil service across Great Britain on intergovernmental relations. This arrangement may itself contribute *inter alia* to the maintenance of a guarantee of civil service impartiality, recruitment from a broader internal pool, opportunities for staff exchanges and linkages and a common 'brand' recognised within and beyond the services. These were all benefits recognised by the House of Lords Constitution Committee and they were seen to contribute to the possibility of close working and flows of information between civil servants at the devolved and UK levels. All of this suits the 'partnership' and 'joint working' models of inter-governmental relations under the devolution settlement and it is unsurprising that the Calman Commission favoured this approach and recommended the continued operation of a combined civil service, with limited additional autonomy for the Scottish civil service and improved training in the working of devolution for UK civil servants.[75] It appears that the combined service has accommodated the arrival of the SNP Government in 2007 but there must now be a question about how well it will perform as a higher degree of Scottish Government autonomy comes to be asserted by the majority SNP administration and as conditions of political antagonism between the two levels of government develop.

Shared public bodies

As in many other states, it has for many years been a characteristic of governmental arrangements in the United Kingdom that much executive authority (and also many advisory functions) have not been exercised directly by the ministers and civil servants of the central departments but have been in the hands of arms-length non-departmental public bodies (NDPBs) or quangos, and the handling of these NDPBs under the devolution settlement created, from the start, some of the more acute borderline issues. And these have continued.

[74] Evidence to the Finance Committee meeting of 25 January 2005. Examples of the autonomy claimed by the Government included differential pay grading structures, promotion arrangements, tackling low pay and external recruitment.

[75] 'Serving Scotland Better', paras. 4.38–4.41; recommendations 4.201–203.

The questions involved do not necessarily have the high political profile of those affecting ministerial powers, but are nevertheless illustrative of the impact of devolution on the rich texture of public administration as a whole.

As one would expect, the broad policy aim of the Scotland Act was to distinguish between public authorities that had, at the time of devolution, any responsibilities for Scottish matters along the same general lines adopted by the Act for distinguishing devolved from reserved matters. Some bodies required no special attention under the Act because they fell entirely on the devolved side of the line. The legislation under which they had been created[76] would be entirely at the disposal of the Scottish Parliament to amend or repeal. Similarly, any administrative powers formerly exercised by the Secretary of State in relation to such bodies were transferred to the Scottish Ministers. Since 1999, the Scottish Parliament has created new bodies (such as national park authorities[77] and the Scottish Commission for the Regulation of Care)[78] and terminated others (such as Scottish Homes)[79] within this completely devolved domain.[80] At the other end of the scale, it was clear that the reservations under Schedule 5 to the Act left some public bodies with Scottish responsibilities entirely beyond the legislative competence of the Scottish Parliament. One example here is the Commission for Equality and Human Rights, which has replaced[81] the Equal Opportunities Commission and the Commission for Racial Equality.[82]

This apparently simple dichotomy could not, however, be maintained. It had to be qualified in three principal ways:

> In the first place, there was the need for a category of authorities whose responsibilities were confined to Scotland but which had 'mixed functions'. These were bodies that one might have supposed to be within the devolved sector but which included among their portfolios functions for which legislative responsibility was reserved to Westminster. The most prominent examples were Scottish local authorities. There is, of course, no general reservation of local government by the Scotland Act, but local authorities do have some powers in relation to, for example, consumer protection, which are outside the competence of the Scottish Parliament. Although local authorities become defined as bodies with mixed responsibilities, they fall almost entirely within the competence of the Scottish

[76] Some public bodies are non-statutory in origin.

[77] National Parks (Scotland) Act 2000.

[78] Regulation of Care (Scotland) Act 2001. From 2011, that Commission has been replaced by Social Care and Social Work Improvement Scotland and Healthcare Improvement Scotland – both products of the Public Services Reform (Scotland) Act 2010, which also prepared the way for many further reforms.

[79] Housing (Scotland) Act 2001.

[80] See also the recent creation of the Electoral Management Board for Scotland and the Housing Regulator.

[81] Equality Act 2006.

[82] These are reservations reinforced by Scotland Act 1998, Sched. 5, Part III, para. 3.

Parliament and the Scottish Ministers except that the Scotland Act places restrictions on the Parliament's power to confer or remove local authority functions that relate to reserved matters.[83]

Secondly, in relation to the 'reserved' public bodies, legislative power remains at Westminster, it has been possible for certain executive powers to be transferred to the Scottish Ministers or to be made exercisable subject to consultation with the Scottish Ministers by Orders in Council under s.63 of the Scotland Act – for instance appointments to the Equality Commission (see previously).

Finally and most prominently, the Scotland Act also created the 'cross-border public authority' (CBPA). The point here was to make special provision for those bodies that could be identified as crossing the devolved/reserved divide *either* because they exercised powers both in Scotland and (in a territorial 'cross-border' sense) in other parts of Great Britain or the United Kingdom *or* because, while confined to Scotland, they exercised powers that were both devolved and reserved *or* because they had both these 'cross-border' characteristics. In relation to all these bodies, the legislative competence of the Scottish Parliament in respect of their operations which are both Scottish and within the non-reserved sectors remains entirely in place. This is specifically acknowledged in the Act, quite apart from the general provisions that determine the competence of the Parliament, in S.90, which provides for the consequential transfer of property and liabilities if the Parliament legislates for the functions of a CBPA to be no longer exercisable in respect of Scotland. In the meantime, however, the designation of CBPAs was intended to recognise that the responsibilities of ministers (for instance, in relation to appointments to the authorities, their funding and the issue of policy directions) and also the rights of the Parliaments (to receive reports on their functioning) have to be shared in a rational manner. This is achieved partly in the terms of the Scotland Act itself and partly in designation orders and adaptation orders made by the Secretary of State.[84] Such provision has been made (both to designate the bodies and to adapt functions) across a wide range of public bodies.

Against this background, it is possible to consider the ways in which subsequent statutory provision at Westminster has affected and may continue to affect the position of shared public bodies – not only in relation to Scotland but also in relation to other parts of the United Kingdom.[85] Although it may be necessary for some purposes to take full account of the extent to which provision for a new public body impinges on the competence of devolved bodies (above

[83] Ibid., para. 1.

[84] Ss.88, 89. Such orders require approval by affirmative resolution both at Westminster and at Holyrood.

[85] A special category of public bodies affected by devolution is that of administrative tribunals, see later.

all, perhaps, to determine the appropriate extent of a Sewel motion)[86] and this will be a guide in framing the substantive terms of a Bill, the considerations to be taken into account in the setting up of a new public body will be common to most types of body with a multi-territorial jurisdiction, regardless of their status on the reserved/devolved scale. These considerations may be fairly simply stated although, in ways that will be touched on later, the provision of answers has been one of the most problematic areas of post-devolution legislation. The issues for consideration include the territorial scope of the new body, its powers and any continuing rights and liabilities, rules as to appointments including required consultation of interests and arrangements for scrutiny by auditors, ombudsmen and parliaments.

The parliamentary handling of Bills establishing new cross-border bodies, as well as technical aspects of the Bills themselves, have been of some interest. Most prominent has been the Bill that became the Health Protection Agency Act 2004, which established the new Agency with powers exercisable across the United Kingdom.[87] Its functions could be divided broadly into two groups: health functions in relation to protection from infectious diseases, and radiation protection functions. Because this produced a combination of both functions mainly devolved to the territorial administrations and reserved functions, special provision had to be made in various respects. Appointments to the Agency were shared between the devolved administrations in Scotland, Wales and Northern Ireland and the Secretary of State.[88] The Agency was a CBPA under the Scotland Act 1998,[89] but only for the purposes of two provisions of that Act.[90] The three devolved administrations could make payments (as they thought appropriate) to the Agency, as could the Secretary of State (who had to take account of payments made by the other governments).[91] And the accountability of the Agency to ombudsmen and to auditors has had to be redistributed.[92]

The Bill that led to the Children Act 2004 raised a range of different issues in the proposals it contained for the creation of a new Children's Commissioner. With Commissioners already in place in Wales, Scotland and Northern Ireland, the principal question was how far the new Commissioner should be a Children's Commissioner for England or a Commissioner for the United Kingdom. Should the new Commissioner simply join those in the devolved areas, with a similar

86 Described later.

87 The Health and Social Care (Community Health and Standards) Act 2003 also raised similar questions in its establishment of the Commission for Healthcare, Audit and Inspection (CHAI) and the Commission for Social Care Inspection (CSCI), although these are mainly confined to England and Wales. From April 2013 the Health Protection Agency was closed down but its brief life is a nice illustration of the complexity of devolved practice.

88 Sched. 1, para. 1.

89 Ibid. para. 6.

90 S.23(2)(b) (Scottish Parliament requiring persons to give evidence); and s.70(6) (Scottish Parliament not to require preparation of accounts).

91 Ibid. para. 19. See also controversy at report stage in the House of Lords in relation to these provisions: HL Debs 6 April 2004 col 1737.

92 Ibid., Sched. 3, paras. 1, 18; Sched. 1, para. 23.

jurisdiction for the 'devolved' interests of children in England, as they have elsewhere? Or should the Commissioner combine those responsibilities for England with responsibilities in the 'non-devolved' fields across the United Kingdom as a whole? This principal question was further complicated in debate about what should be the proper field of competence of the Commissioner. The Government's preference was for a UK Commissioner with a largely strategic policy role while many parliamentarians favoured a much more 'rights-based' approach with a focus on the investigation of individual complaints. That latter question can be put on one side, however, as one that does not directly raise an issue of legislation for devolution, although it should be noted in passing that the existence and operation in practice of rights-based Commissioners in the devolved territories, especially Wales, made it easier to oppose the Government's proposals.

Dispute resolution

This is probably the area in which the conditions of relative political harmony between the two levels of government have most affected working relationships. As mentioned later, emphasis has been placed on achieving a relationship designed to prevent significant public disagreement or disputes. A combination of a wish to avoid conflict and procedures to achieve this has meant that there has been no devolution-related hostile litigation between governments. If the situation does ever arise in which the UK government challenges directly[93] the validity of an Act of the Scottish Parliament or of an act or decision of the Scottish Government, it may be assumed that this issue would be raised in judicial review proceedings in the ordinary courts. The same would apply if the Scottish Government wished to challenge the validity of hostile action taken or threatened by a UK minister.

Although these options for judicial challenge are not directly addressed by the Scotland Act itself, what the Act does provide is special procedures applicable to what it defines as 'devolution issues'. These include questions raised in any legal proceedings as to whether an Act of the Scottish Parliament is within the legislative competence of the Parliament or whether acts and decisions of the Scottish Ministers are within devolved competence.[94] A devolution issue must be brought to the attention of relevant law officers, enabling them to participate in the proceedings. Separately, a law officer (e.g., the UK Attorney General) may initiate proceedings for the determination of a devolution issue, including a power to direct it straight to the UK Supreme Court.

It has been a feature of the operation of devolution so far that, although there have been many 'devolution issues' raised in the context of human rights

[93] The UK Government has already intervened in proceedings initiated by others. See for example, *Martin v. HMA* 2010 SC(UKSC) 40; *AXA General Insurance Ltd, Petitioners* 2011 SLT 1061.

[94] Scotland Act 1998 s.98 and Sched. 6.

challenges in criminal trials (because of the involvement of the Lord Advocate – a member of the Scottish Government – as prosecutor)[95] and a handful of other challenges on Convention rights and EU grounds to Scottish Government decisions and Acts of the Scottish Parliament,[96] there has been very little activity at all on the reserved/devolved borderline.[97] Most prominent has been *Martin v. HMA*,[98] which raised, in the context of road traffic legislation, very complex issues about the relationship between Schedules 4 and 5 to the Scotland Act 1998. It was a case that found the two Scottish judges in the Supreme Court bitterly opposed on the validity of the Acts of the Scottish Parliament at issue.[99] There is a continuing uncertainty, however, as to the general interpretative approach to be taken by courts where Scottish Parliament or Government measures appear to straddle the reserved/devolved borderline. S.29(3) of the Act places some emphasis on a test of 'purpose' but the *Martin* case has left doubts about how that test should be applied. There are also continuing questions as to how far the courts will tend, where possible, to defer to the judgment on *vires* of the Parliament or Government. What presumptions of legality will they bring to the exercise?[100] In the case of the Parliament, how far it is to be treated differently, because of its parliamentary status, or on the other hand, in the same way as other statutorily created bodies? To an extent, the courts may be assisted by s.101 of the Scotland Act, which requires that where an Act of the Scottish Parliament (or subordinate legislation) *could* be read as outside competence it should nevertheless be 'read as narrowly as is required for it to be within competence, if such a reading is possible'![101] A revealing area has been the extent to which the courts regard the Scottish Parliament as reviewable on the ordinary 'common law' grounds such as 'irrationality'. Initially, it seemed that such review should not, in principle, be available[102] but then that position was reversed[103] only to be followed by a more restrictive view on appeal to the Inner House of the Court of Session,[104] since broadly upheld by the UK Supreme Court.[105]

95 See later.

96 ASP challenges have included, most prominently, cases involving anti-hunting legislation. See for example, *Adams v. Scottish Ministers* 2004 SC 665. Most recently, in February and March 2012, provisions in the Criminal Procedure (Scotland) Act 1995 (inserted by the Criminal Justice and Licensing (Scotland) Act 2010) and the Agricultural Holdings (Scotland) Act 2003 were held to be outside competence. See *Cameron v. Cottam* 2012 SLT 173 and *Salveson v. Riddell* [2012] CSIH 26 (upheld in substance at [2013] UKSC 22), respectively. But see also *Scotch Whisky Association, Petitioners* [2013] CSOH 70.

97 In *Al Fayed v. Lord Advocate* 2004 S.C. 568; 2004 SLT 319, one of the reasons for the rejection of the petition seeking a fatal accident inquiry was that an inquiry into a foreign death was not within the competence of the Lord Advocate but was a reserved matter. See paras. 29–30 and [2013] UKSC 61.

98 2010 SC (UKSC) 40. See also *Imperial Tobacco Ltd, Petitioner* 2010 SLT 1203.

99 See C. Himsworth, 'Nothing Special about That', Edin LR, 14 (2010), 487.

100 See *Imperial Tobacco Ltd v Lord Advocate* [2012] UKSC 61.

101 See *Salveson v Riddell* [2013] UKSC 22.

102 *Adams v. Scottish Ministers* 2003 SLT 366.

103 *AXA General Insurance Ltd, Petitioners* 2010 SLT 179.

104 *AXA General Insurance Ltd, Petitioners* 2011 SLT 439.

105 2011 SLT 1061.

Relations between parliaments and governments: the Memorandum of Understanding and Concordats

It has been an important feature of the operation of the UK arrangements for regional autonomy that, alongside the mechanisms put in place for the formal resolution of disputes, especially over competence issues, there has also been a reliance on informal methods.[106] Thus, while the court-based features just described may be the principal formal determinants of the relationship between the Scottish and UK governments, a significant investment has also been placed by the UK government in the creation of departmental 'concordats' under an overarching 'Memorandum of Understanding'.[107] The Memorandum of Understanding contained the main principles of co-operation and the general arrangements. A series of supplementary agreements established a Joint Ministerial Committee[108] and formulated a general concordat on European Union policy issues and others on financial assistance to industry, on international relations and on the shared use of statistics. These are joined by bilateral agreements between the Scottish Government (and the other devolved administrations) and the different UK departments, designed to ensure that, on matters of mutual concern – for instance proposed legislation in common areas of interest – there will be consultation and a degree of confidentiality of communication. The concordats are expressly stated to be not binding in law but in honour only. At a meeting in March 2010 a meeting of the Joint Ministerial Committee adopted a Protocol for Avoidance and Resolution of Disputes.

The concordats have been supplemented by a number of Devolution Guidance Notes (issued successively by the Office of the Deputy Prime Minister, the Department for Constitutional Affairs, the Ministry of Justice and now the Cabinet Office), which contain procedural guidelines on the handling of many aspects of the devolutionary relationships. Different views have been expressed on the overall constitutional and political significance of the concordats.[109] While acknowledging that there might be a case for giving the concordats a more formal status, especially if they are to withstand the greater pressures of a markedly different political complexion of the parties at some future point, the House of Lords Constitution Committee has also had to take account of the view that the process of their making in the first place was more important than their operation in practice.[110] Despite the rhetoric of the desirability of harmonious relations, it is certainly true that one effect of the concordats between

[106] Part 4 of the Calman report placed great emphasis on the need for the strengthening of co-operation between the Scottish and UK Governments and Parliaments.

[107] Cm 4444 (1999), subsequently reissued as Cm 4806 (2000) and Cm 5240 (2001).

[108] For a time, the Committee was dormant. See A. Trench, 'Devolution: the withering away of the Joint Ministerial Committee?' PL (2004), 513. Latterly, however, activity has been revived and a number of meetings have been held. A significant wide-ranging meeting was held on 8 June 2010, with a re-commitment to a 'respect' agenda and to future meetings.

[109] See Himsworth and O'Neill, *Scotland's Constitution*, 188–93.

[110] HL, 'Devolution: Inter-Institutional Relations in the United Kingdom', para. 40.

'partners' of such differing power and influence may be to constrain further the autonomy of the weaker (devolved) party. What the concordat regime does, at least, reflect is the overall political character of the relationship between the two tiers of government and it will be particularly interesting to see what the effect of the SNP majority government in Edinburgh will be upon the concordats of an earlier era. The assumptions of co-operation may, in time, cease to apply.

Legislation at Westminster on devolved matters and the Sewel Convention

As noted earlier, the UK Parliament remains wholly competent to enact legislation for Scotland not only in relation to the reserved matters for which it retains exclusive jurisdiction, but also in relation to those matters devolved to the Scottish Parliament. The UK Government was not prepared, at the time the Scotland Bill of 1997/98 was under consideration, to modify this formal position, and indeed defended the view that some UK-wide legislation would continue to be useful in the devolved areas in the interests of certainty and efficiency where there was a broad consensus that uniformity of regulation was desirable. What the Government did concede, however, was that such legislation should be enacted at Westminster only with the prior consent of the Scottish Parliament. This undertaking was given by Lord Sewel, a Scottish Officer minister, and he has given his name to the 'Sewel convention', which encapsulates the need for consent to be sought, and to 'Sewel motions' (subsequently 'legislative consent motions'), which initiate the resolutions in the Scottish Parliament to indicate its consent. The arrangements have been documented in one of the Devolution Guidance Notes, as mentioned previously.

In the practice of devolution so far, there has been quite frequent use of Sewel motions[111] and the criticism is often made by political opponents of the Scottish Government that consent has too often been given for legislation to be undertaken at Westminster on matters devolved to Scotland. The dozen or so Sewel motions per year have not authorised a big *quantity* of legislation, in comparison for instance, with the volume of legislation passed at Holyrood, and many Sewels have had a largely technical aspect to them. It has also to be remembered that the Scottish Parliament's consent to Westminster legislating on a particular issue does not remove the Parliament's future competence to legislate on the same issue. Most controversial have been the instances where the Scottish Government and Parliament have used the Sewel route to pass a political hot potato (e.g., the Bill that became the Civil Partnerships Act 2004) to Westminster. Such political controversy apart, some serious attention has been given to the procedural improvements that may be necessary at both

111 For a full account, see A. Page and A. Batey, 'Scotland's other Parliament', PL (2002), 501. See also Himsworth and O'Neill, *Scotland's Constitution*, 195–9, and B. Winetrobe 'A partnership of Parliaments?' in R. Hazell and R. Rawlings (eds.), *Devolution, Law Making and the Constitution* (Exeter: Imprint Academic, 2005).

Holyrood and Westminster to ensure that Scottish law passed in the devolved areas is subjected to adequate scrutiny and control.[112] Interesting phenomena in recent years have been (a) the continuing prevalence of legislative consent motions under the SNP governments that appear to have shown no particular reluctance to permit (in a general spirit of co-operation) Westminster legislation in devolved areas; and (b) the acknowledgement by the incoming UK coalition government in 2010 of the obligations of the Sewel Convention – again as an aspect of a continuing spirit of co-operation enduring despite political change.

On the other hand, the case of the Scotland Bill 2010–12 provided a revealing illustration of the Convention under some strain. Even before the Scottish elections of May 2011, the Bill was special. A committee in the Scottish Parliament had been formed to scrutinise the Bill prior to the formulation of a legislative consent motion and that motion was itself the product not of the Scottish (SNP) Government (the exclusive originator of such motions up to that point) but rather of the (unionist) majority of the Parliament itself.[113] The motion gave the Parliament's consent to the UK government's Bill but did anticipate the need for further scrutiny of the Bill and a further motion to take account of developments during the legislative process at Westminster. In due course, a legislative consent motion based on a detailed agreement between UK and Scottish government ministers was approved by the Scottish Parliament on 18 April 2012.

Devolution and the autonomy of Scotland's legal system

Although the separateness of the Scottish legal system and especially its differentiation from the English common law as a mixed/civilian system is a phenomenon which derives from the pre-devolution phase of Scotland's autonomy, it has not been unaffected by the new devolution arrangements. There have been three principal features:

First is the accommodation of the Scottish legal system within the legislative competence of the Scottish Parliament. One of the defining characteristics of the campaign for devolution in Scotland was that a Scottish Parliament would provide a Scotland-based legislature not just to make better provision for the distinctive aspects of Scottish government and administration already mentioned, but also to make better provision for the legal system itself. Scotland 'mixes' the Anglo-American common law and the civil law, as applied in the distinctive system of courts, headed, apart from civil appeals to the House of Lords (and now the UK Supreme Court), by the Court of Session and the High Court of Justiciary sitting in Edinburgh. That legislative devolution to

[112] There was a major review of the Sewel Convention by the Procedures Committee of the Scottish Parliament – see SP Paper 428 (2005). On Westminster, see for example, C. M. G. Himsworth, Appendix to HL Paper 192 (2003–4) 'Devolution: Its Effect on the Practice of Legislation at Westminster'.

[113] Scottish Parliament Official Record, 10 March 2011.

Scotland would entail a special competence in relation to the legal system was acknowledged in the (Kilbrandon) Royal Commission report of 1973[114] and in the proposals that followed in both the 1970s[115] and again in the 1990s.[116]

In the Scotland Act 1998, the need to accommodate the Scottish Parliament's responsibility for the special character of Scots law has led to some of the Act's most sophisticated and complex provisions.[117] The Act has to recognise two demands. One is the need for the Parliament to respect the reserved/devolved borderline it generally lays down. Secondly it has also to enable the Parliament to make general provision for the civil and criminal law of Scotland, the point being that such general provision may inevitably affect the law on both sides of the reserved/devolved divide. A 'legal system' competence, since it is based on quite different criteria from those that apportion competences on a functional basis, cuts across the initial divide in uncomfortable ways. The general rules of criminal procedure affect the prosecution of offences related to both reserved and devolved subject matter. The general rules of contract and delict similarly cut across the subject divide and may, for instance, reach into the reserved areas of consumer protection or employment as well as the areas devolved to the Scottish Parliament. Judicial review procedures can plainly affect both devolved and reserved matters.[118]

The principal device for policing these cross-cutting competences is contained in S.29(4) of the Act, which expressly permits the Parliament to modify Scots private law or Scots criminal law even where those modifications may relate to reserved matters, provided that 'the purpose of the provision is to make the law in question apply consistently to reserved matters and otherwise'. In other words, the legal system provisions have this necessary across-the-board characteristic. Additional, and more complex rules, are contained in Schedule 4 to the Act and, until recently, these provisions appeared to have operated in a trouble-free way. There had, at least, been no public challenge to a Bill or Act drafted in reliance upon them. It should also be noted that there had been no challenge in the courts at all on the grounds that the Scottish Parliament has illicitly trespassed into the territory of reserved matters.[119] In the case of *Martin v. HMA*,[120] however, the ambiguities of Schedule 4 were sharply revealed.

In the meantime, the reform of the law of Scotland – especially in the field of property law – has been a prominent part of the workload of the Scottish

[114] Report of the Royal Commission on the Constitution (Cmnd 5460, 1973) paras. 772, 1132, 1150.

[115] *Our Changing Democracy: Devolution to Scotland and Wales* (Cmnd 6348, 1975) paras. 144–51.

[116] *Scotland's Parliament* (Cm 3658, 1997) para. 2.4.

[117] Himsworth and O'Neill, *Scotland's Constitution*, 134; C. M. G. Himsworth and C. R. Munro *The Scotland Act 1998* 2nd edn. (Edinburgh: Greens, 2000). See also C. Himsworth 'Devolution and the mixed legal systems of Scotland', JR (2002) 115.

[118] Interestingly, judicial review, as an aspect of 'the law of actions', is defined by the Scotland Act s 126(4) as part of Scots private law.

[119] But see *now Imperial Tobacco Ltd v Lord Advocate* [2013] UKSC 61.

[120] 2010 SC (UKSC) 40.

Parliament since 1999, in quite large part attending to what had become a growing backlog of recommendations of the Scottish Law Commission. We have had, for instance, the Abolition of Feudal Tenure etc. (Scotland) Act 2000 and the Land Reform (Scotland) Act 2003, which have radically reformed the property law of Scotland.

The second feature relates to the appointment and dismissal of Scottish judges. An important indicator of the strength of the legislative powers conferred on the Scottish Parliament[121] and, consequentially, the powers of the Scottish Government has been the inclusion within their competences of not only the general body of Scots law but also the Scottish judiciary.[122] This is significant in that there is entrusted to the Scottish judicial system, subject to appeal to the Supreme Court in civil matters, the resolution of legal issues which arise in Scotland, whether in the devolved or reserved sector.

Except for the specific reservation to Westminster of law making on the 'continued existence' of the Scottish Court of Session and High Court of the Justiciary, matters regarding the remuneration of judges,[123] the structure of the system of courts in Scotland and appointments to those courts are devolved. The only exception to the general rule on appointments[124] is that the two top judicial posts in Scotland – the Lord President of the Court of Session and the Lord Justice Clerk – are to be made on the recommendation of the UK Prime Minister, on the nomination of the First Minister. The First Minister directly recommends appointments of other Court of Session judges and of sheriffs. The opportunity of devolution has been taken to supplement the framework of the Scotland Act with a package of statutory rules on the operation of the Scottish judiciary at all levels and to introduce measures broadly protective of judicial independence. The Judiciary and Courts (Scotland) Act 2008 created a new judicial appointments board and made further provision in relation to judicial dismissals and much else.

A third element involves the powers of the UK Supreme Court. The new role for the Judicial Committee of the Privy Council and then, with effect from October 2009, the new UK Supreme Court in dispute resolution under the devolution settlement has already been mentioned. One feature of this arrangement that did not go unnoticed in Scotland was that, for the first time since 1707, it enabled not only civil cases but also criminal cases to pass to a London-based court for decision. This, combined with the broader possibility that human rights cases, with the capacity to reach into all aspects of a legal system, might bring a greater tendency towards a convergence of Scottish and English rules, presented a new challenge to the autonomy of the Scottish system.

[121] In contrast with the weaker version under the unimplemented Scotland Act 1978.

[122] And also the system of (administrative) tribunals but only so far as these are within the devolved sector. For detailed consideration, see Chapter 11 'Devolution' in *Tribunals for Users – One System, One Service* (Report of the Review of Tribunals by Sir Andrew Leggatt, 2001). Devolved tribunals were excluded from the coverage of the Tribunals, Courts and Enforcement Act 2007 but steps are now being taken in the direction of an integrated (devolved) courts and tribunals service for Scotland.

[123] Scotland Act 1998, Sched. 5, Part II, S.L.

[124] Ibid., s. 95.

In addition, the debate leading to the establishment of the Supreme Court itself (as a general successor to the House of Lords) provoked further controversy. Although that new court would not be given a wholly new status as a 'constitutional court' but would instead largely take over the appellate functions of the House of Lords, its creation was a matter of very great sensitivity in Scotland.

There have been two further developments. In the first place, some quite measured steps have been taken by the SNP in the direction of a modification of the current arrangements for the handling of final appeals in Scotland. At the time of the pre-2007 coalition government a Bill was introduced into the Scottish Parliament designed to abolish appeals from Scotland to the (then) House of Lords. That Bill made no progress but, after the SNP minority government was elected in 2007, it appointed Professor Neil Walker to consider the area more systematically. His report offered a number of options for the reform of Scotland's appellate jurisdiction.[125] The second, more traumatic, development has been the furore raised by one particular category of appeals. An interpretation placed by the courts on particular provisions of the Scotland Act has produced a situation in which, because of the involvement of the Lord Advocate (a member of the Scottish Government) as prosecutor in all criminal trials, many trials can be held to raise 'devolution issues'. The resulting complications and delays prompted the UK Government to propose the introduction of amendments to the current Scotland Bill. Much more prominently, certain cases have been taken to the UK Supreme Court and that Court has controversially overturned the decisions of the (Edinburgh-based) lower courts. In particular, *Cadder v. HMA*[126] produced the need for emergency legislation in the Scottish Parliament[127] to amend the law on police questioning and then *Fraser v. HMA*[128] reversed the Edinburgh High Court to annul a very high-profile conviction. These cases prompted concern on the part of the SNP Government, especially since its elevation to majority status in May 2011, that Scots criminal law was losing its identity, under the influence of a court staffed in the main by English lawyers.[129] More recently the Scottish Government insisted, amidst much rancour, that all criminal appeals to the Supreme Court should be abolished and established its own panel of experts to consider the matter.[130] Eventually, a compromise was agreed and incorporated into ss.34–38 of the Scotland Act 2012.

[125] Final Appellate Jurisdiction in the Scottish Legal System (2010). [126] 2010 SLT 1125.

[127] Although not a criminal case of this sort, *Somerville v. Scottish Ministers* 2008 SC (HL) 45 had also required much-resented emergency legislation. On that case and on human rights issues generally, see C. Himsworth, 'Human rights at the interface of state and sub-state: the case of Scotland' in T. Campbell et al. (eds), *The Legal Protection of Human Rights: Sceptical Essays* (London: Oxford University Press, 2011).

[128] 2011 SLT 515.

[129] Although, in both *Cadder* and *Fraser*, the Supreme Court judgments were primarily the work of the Scottish judges on the Court.

[130] The final report of that Review Group was published in September 2011 as 'Examination of the Relationship between the High Court of Justiciary and the Supreme Court in Criminal Cases'. See www.scotland.gov.uk/Resource/Doc/254431/0120938.pdf (accessed 26 March 2013).

Relations between Scottish devolved institutions and others in the UK and the EU

There is little doubt that, as devolution gathers pace in other parts of the United Kingdom, the position of individual devolved governments (and parliaments) vis-à-vis the UK institutions will be greatly strengthened by the expanding of mechanisms of co-operation and solidarity between the devolved governments themselves. If the Joint Ministerial Committee acquires a stronger role, this would be one such mechanism and others might well emerge, whether at the political or official level. Already there are many signs of co-operation and collaboration, especially between officials, and these will doubtless expand now that Welsh devolution has strengthened and the Northern Ireland institutions have become fully operational. In addition to those meetings that include UK representation, First Ministerial meetings are also held to which UK ministers are not invited and matters of common concern to the devolved governments can be discussed.[131]

Sub-state solidarity of another sort is currently being established through Scotland's participation in conferences of European regions with legislative powers.[132] Added to Scotland's maintenance of a permanent base in Brussels, these external relationships must tend to strengthen the Scottish Parliament and Government's internal relationship with the UK institutions. The conduct of European Union business has been a frequent point of discussion at Joint Ministerial meetings and after the Scottish general election of 2011 it was an early demand of First Minister Salmond that Scotland should have more influence over European policy.[133]

Outcomes: has devolution made a difference?

This sub-heading invites a full chapter to itself! Multiple interpretations of the question would be followed by multiple answers.[134] And, because it is still early in the evolution of devolved government, those answers would be provisional. In brief and too crudely, two strands might be identified:

As to what might be broadly characterised as political and constitutional change, there can be no doubt at all that the creation and subsequent operation of the institutions of devolved government have had a substantial impact. The

[131] Following one such meeting in Edinburgh on 31 May 2011, it was said that a shared agenda across financial, constitutional and policy reforms was discussed. Separately, the British Irish Council (which also includes representatives of Guernsey, Jersey and the Isle of Man) meets to discuss matters of common concern. Its secretariat is in Edinburgh.

[132] A network of some seventy-three regions across eight EU states.

[133] Scottish Parliament Official Record, 26 May 2011.

[134] See A. Trench (ed.), *Has Devolution Made a Difference?* (2004). See also M. Keating, *The Independence of Scotland: Self-Government and the Shifting Politics of Union* (London: Oxford University Press, 2009), and *The Government of Scotland: Public Policy Making after Devolution* (Edinburgh University Press, 2010).

profile of government has been raised by the new forms of exercise of executive power and the public forum provided by the Parliament. As it has turned out, the profile of the SNP, in particular, has been very substantially raised. Whether devolution has advanced the cause of Scottish independence or, alternatively, strengthened the Union cannot yet be ascertained. Perhaps, paradoxically, both have made progress. It may be that a compromise, much looser Union is in prospect, as a fairly direct consequence of the experience of devolution.

As to more immediate policy consequences, it was mentioned earlier that the creation of the Scottish Parliament has enabled more law-making to be done – even if there have also been disappointments about progress made. A constant complaint before devolution was that many legislative recommendations from the Scottish Law Commission were left unaddressed by the UK Government and Parliament and it was assumed that the creation of the Scottish Parliament would rectify the situation. It has, therefore, been a surprise to have the Commission still complaining. Although things are said to have improved since, it was reported in 2009 that the number of Commission reports that remained unimplemented had risen significantly *since* devolution.[135] Rather separately, on the assumption that devolution provides the opportunity for difference, the monitoring of policy outcomes, how these are achieved and how they are subsequently handled over time become important to the monitoring of devolution as a whole. High profile issues have included the funding of personal care for the elderly, the funding of students at universities, free medical prescriptions, and the management of hospitals within the National Health Service, in all of which areas there have been quite sharp divergences from English policies – in part, at least, because of the different political configurations in the Scottish Parliament and Government as compared to the UK. Such developments will need careful scrutiny over time. Bearing in mind the opportunities for difference prior to devolution, it is, as yet, far from clear whether devolution will lead to greater divergence or whether this will be restrained to an extent by the pressures towards convergence that may come from financial limitations,[136] popular expectations of 'uniform' (more equal) service provision, the problem of disengaging 'devolved' differences from 'reserved' uniform provision, and legal challenges.

Conclusions

From an international perspective, the best known symbol of the autonomy of Scotland – the twin autonomies of Scotland – has been the release from prison

[135] Scottish Law Commission, *Annual Report 2008*, report 214 (2009), available at: www.scotlawcom.gov.uk/publications/reports/2000-2009/ (accessed 28 March 2013). For a more general assessment of the Parliament's contribution, see E. E. Sutherland et al. (eds), *Law Making and the Scottish Parliament* (Edinburgh University Press, 2011).

[136] There have, for instance, been signs that Scottish free personal care for the elderly is under financial pressure.

on 20 August 2009 of Abdelbaset al-Megrahi, the only person to be convicted so far of the bombing of the Pan Am aircraft over Lockerbie in December 1998. Megrahi was released not on the authority of a UK minister but on the decision of Kenny MacAskill MSP, Cabinet Secretary for Justice in the devolved Scottish Government and under the laws of Scotland. The substance of the decision caused different degrees of admiration and outrage worldwide but there was no doubting its iconic status in the unfolding of the devolution story.

But, as I hope has been revealed in this chapter, there is a broader and richer tale to be told of the ways in which, under the peculiar conditions of the United Kingdom's unwritten constitution, the operation of devolved government in Scotland as a model of non-federal asymmetric devolution has developed since 1998. Three features have been prominent. First, the period of devolution has provided another chapter in a much longer story of Scottish autonomy. Secondly, it has taken place in a very complex and sophisticated governmental and administrative environment. Scotland's overall autonomous condition has been meticulously carved out of but, at the same time, left integrated within the web of the United Kingdom's patterns of parliamentary, governmental and judicial institutions and procedures. And thirdly, Scottish devolution has, throughout, remained politically contested. If it has ever represented a 'settled will' of the people of Scotland, that 'settled will' has been to retain a continuing uncertainty as to ultimate constitutional destinations. The political battle for hearts and minds, although conducted under relatively ordered conditions of peace and civility, throws up conflicts – some, such as the arrangements for funding and for top courts, very high profile; others to be found in the interstices of day-to-day administrative relationships – which are framed by different visions of Scotland's constitutional future; but now, above all, in the campaign leading to the independence referendum to be held in Scotland in September 2014.[137]

Whether or not the outcome of that referendum will be independence or the emergence of a new settlement based on a stronger version of home rule and a looser relationship with a continuing but changing United Kingdom and European Union,[138] the greatest contribution of the autonomy years from 1998 may have been the provision both of the conditions under which a new settlement could be negotiated and, in the meantime, the continuation of an acceptable, if complicated, quality of transitional governance.

[137] See, amidst a large emerging literature, I. McLean, J. Gallagher and G. Lodge, *Scotland's Choices* (Edinburgh University Press, 2013).

[138] There is nothing new about this vision. For a particularly lucid account, see N. MacCormick, 'Independence and constitutional change' in N. MacCormick (ed.), *The Scottish Debate* (London: Oxford University Press, 1970).

12

Macau

Transformation of an historic autonomy

*Paulo Cardinal**

Macau, a tiny place in South China with an overwhelming majority of Chinese inhabitants, has existed for the last half millennium in a strange state of disconnection vis-à-vis China. Although China is the natural source of its *Imperia* and *Dominium*, it was attached politically and administratively to a small far away country, Portugal, in a relationship of autonomy.[1] It was variously considered a commercial outpost, a colony with special status, an extraordinary condominium, a territory artificially adjoined to other Portuguese possessions in Asia, a territory leased from China, a territory offered by China and, ultimately, a 'territory under (transitional) Portuguese Administration', all these formulas showing that Macau's status has never been a stable topic.[2] Now Macau is a Special Administrative Region of the People's Republic of China enjoying a 'high degree of autonomy'[3] as agreed in a bilateral agreement between Portugal and China and elaborated in a constitution *lato sensu*,[4] the Basic Law of Macau.

* The author is grateful to Professor Yash Ghai for his suggestions and to Sophia Woodman for improving the final text. The author is fully responsible for the final published text and the views expressed do not represent and in no way bind the entities to which the author is professionally associated.

1 For a summary, see Tereza Sena, 'Macau´s autonomy in Portuguese historiography (nineteenth and early twentieth centuries)', *Bulletin of Portuguese/Japanese Studies*, 17 (2008), 79. Also, Paulo Cardinal, 'The judicial guarantees of fundamental rights in the Macau legal system – a parcours under the focus of continuity and of autonomy', in P. Cardinal and J. Oliveira (eds.) *One Country, Two Systems, Three Legal Orders – Perspectives of Evolution –: Essays on Macau's Autonomy after the Resumption of Sovereignty by China*, (Berlin/Heidelberg: Springer-Verlag, 2009), 223.

2 Sena, 'Macau's autonomy in Portuguese historiography', 79.

3 This principle of a high degree of autonomy is central to Macau's current status. See Vitalino Canas, 'A extensão da autonocaumia de Ma na comunidade e na Lei' [The extension of Macau´s autonomy in the community and in the law], *Boletin da Faculdade da Universidade de Macau* (below BFDM), 12(2001), 225.

4 The Basic Law is the formal domestic legal instrument that details the constitutional organisation of the SAR, including its political system, its autonomy, as well as the non-organisational constitutional frameworks such as in the fields of fundamental rights, economy and social issues. Thus this legal document has the appearance and the structure of a formal constitution and has been called a 'mini-constitution' or a 'para-constitution'. The main point is that the Basic Law is, in the SAR legal system, the constitutional law. See Paulo Cardinal, 'Fundamental rights in Macau: from territory under Portuguese administration to Special Administrative Region of the PRC', in Jorge Godinho (ed.), *Studies on Macau Civil, Commercial,*

At the turn of the twenty-first century, the historic autonomy of Macau underwent a fundamental metamorphosis. The foundation of its autonomy changed from being exclusively domestic – based on the Portuguese Constitution and Organic Statute – to being international – based on the Sino-Portugese Joint Declaration. It changed from a transitory autonomy without a fixed term while under Portuguese Administration, to a transitory autonomy with a well-defined term – ending in December 2049; from a focal point of sovereignty situated far away in Lisbon, to one that is nearby in Beijing; from a colonial relationship with the centre to a long desired reunification with the motherland; from a situation of divided sovereignty, that is sovereignty residing in China but the exercise of sovereign powers resting in Portugal, to a status in which both aspects of sovereignty – title and exercise – are reunited in one State.

The tension inherent in the relations between the autonomous area and the centre is evident in the words of autonomy – treaties, constitutions, laws and, perhaps even more, in the persons of autonomy. Within the words proclaiming autonomy and setting its boundaries, we find those persons who have the authority to guide the autonomous entity and those who guide the larger entity. Ultimately the realisation of the autonomy and the balance between the autonomous and centralised powers will rest in their hands. In the specific case of the Special Administrative Regions of China (SARs), one can, using the principle of 'One Country, Two Systems', ask whether the practice of autonomy will stress the component of one 'country' or 'two systems'.

History

An historical account of autonomy in Macau is important not only for a better understanding of today's Macau but to explain why a miniscule piece of territory came to have such significant autonomous status in one of the largest states in the world.

According to the official Portuguese version,[5] a Portuguese naval victory over the pirate fleets on the southern coast of China was the decisive reason for the Chinese emperor authorising, in 1557, the establishment of the Portuguese in Macau as a reward.[6] It should be pointed out the Portuguese had already been

Constitutional and Criminal Law (LexisNexis, 2010), 4–7; Cândida A. Pires, 'The organization of justice in the legal system of Macau – statics and dynamics of the Macau SAR courts', in M. A. Espadinha (ed.), *Law and Social Sciences* (University of Macau Press, 2009), 117.

[5] See Jorge Oliveira, Jessica Leão, Paulo Cardinal and Paulo Vidal, 'An outline of the Macau legal system', *Hong Kong Law Journal*, 23:3 (1993), 358–94, Sena, 'Macau's autonomy', 81. For a brief summary of other *official* versions and critique of the Portuguese version see, 'Arguments on the Portuguese Settlement in Macau', in Blogmacau.info, http://macau.blogharbor.com.

[6] See Montalto de Jesus, *Macau Histórico* [Historic Macau] (Macau: Livros do Oriente, reprint 1990), 39; Almerindo Lessa, *A História e os Homens da Primeira República Democrática do Oriente* [The History and the Men of the First Democratic Republic of the Orient] (Macau: Imprensa Nacional, 1974) 12; and Jorge Noronha e Silveira, *Subsídios para a história do Direito Constitucional de Macau (1820–1974)* [Subsidiary material to the History of Macau

roaming this area for several decades, developing trade and looking for new havens in this faraway and lucrative part of the world.

For more than two centuries, the Portuguese established in Macau administered their interests autonomously. In contrast to India, Macau was too small, too far away and too difficult to communicate with. The administration of Portuguese interests was in the charge of the Senado, a body based on the medieval Portuguese local autonomous government tradition, composed of three 'councillors' elected for three years by the Portuguese population, two judges and one procurator. It was vested with political, administrative and judicial powers, but represented only the interests of the Portuguese population, who were sometimes called to a 'General Council' to solve some of the more delicate matters. The Senado was elected and composed of 'local' Portuguese people concerned with local interests, thus ruling Macau in a very autonomous fashion and with little impact on the global Portuguese imperial interests. This curious political structure gave Macau the reputation and the credit for being 'the first democratic republic of the Orient'.[7]

From the seventeenth century on, Macau became the target of several incursions by the Dutch. The defence of the city required the permanent presence of a military commander. For that purpose the Senado created, in 1615, the post of 'War Governor'; in 1623 this title changed to that of 'Captain-General' or 'Governor', appointment to which was made by the Viceroy of India, not directly by Lisbon. However, the Chinese continued to assert their authority, collecting certain land and customs taxes. The Portuguese paid rent to China until 1849, when they abolished the Chinese customs house and declared Macau's 'independence' from China.[8]

Throughout the seventeenth and most of the eighteenth centuries, the Governor of Macau had purely military powers and could not question the ruling powers of the Senado. However, in the following centuries, the Governor's powers gradually increased, along with a corresponding reduction in the Senado's powers. In fact, at the dawn of transfer of the sovereignty to China, the Senado was no more than a simple municipality vested with no significant powers whatsoever.

On 26 March 1887, the Chinese government recognised the Portuguese right of 'perpetual occupation' of Macau in an international agreement, the Protocol of Lisbon,[9] later reaffirmed in the Treaty of Friendship and Commerce between

Constitutional Law (1820–1974)] (Macau: Publicações O Direito, 1991), 9–19. And, in English, John Wills and Paul van Dyke, 'Strange shores: 442 years of anomaly in Macau, and counting . . .', *Harvard Asia Pacific Review*, summer (2000); G. W. Keeton, 'The international status of Macau before 1887', in G. W. Keeton, *The Development of Extraterritoriality in China*, Vol. II (New York: H. Festing, 1969).

7 Expression first used by Lessa, *A História e os Homens da Primeira República Democrática do Oriente*.

8 A year highlighted in any Macau chronology as it also saw strong Chinese retaliation and finally the assassination of Gov. Ferreira do Amaral.

9 This treaty was later branded as unequal, although for a long time China did not attempt to address the evident gaps in the agreement.

Portugal and China, and confirmed perpetual occupation and government of Macau and its dependencies by Portugal, like any other Portuguese possession, save for the condition that Portugal would never surrender Macau to a third party without China's permission (Arts. 2 and 3).[10]

Three phases can be identified in the evolving status of Macau. The first, from the Portuguese establishment in the territory until the end of the eighteenth century, saw a 'system of mixed jurisdiction,' with both Portuguese and Chinese authorities exercising jurisdiction over Macau. The Portuguese had jurisdiction over the Portuguese community and certain aspects of the overall territory's administration, but no sovereignty.

The second phase began at the end of the eighteenth century. The importance of Macau within the Portuguese possessions was growing and Portuguese sovereignty over the territory was strengthened. Macau became formally a part of Portuguese territory as a colony.[11]

The third phase followed the Portuguese Revolution of 25 April 1974. The Portuguese abandoned the former colonial policy and Portugal and China established diplomatic relations in 1979. Both countries expressed interest in finding a mutually agreeable solution to Macau's status; negotiations began in 1985, a year after the signing of the Sino-British Joint Declaration, and in 1987 the Sino-Portuguese Joint Declaration provided that Macau would become a 'Chinese territory under Portuguese administration'. This status was recognised in the Portuguese Constitution, which stated, 'While under Portuguese administration, the territory of Macau shall be subject to a statute that is appropriate to its special circumstances'.[12] The statute could only be amended or replaced on the proposal of 'either the Legislative Assembly of Macau or the Governor of Macau, who shall take the opinion of the Legislative Assembly of Macau, the Assembly of the Republic, which shall take the opinion of the Council of State'.[13] Portugal could not amend the proposal without the permission of the Macau institution that had initiated it.

The Constitution granted Macau 'its own judicial system that is autonomous and adapted to the particular circumstances of that territory, as provided by

[10] On these treaty clauses, see António Vasconcelos de Saldanha *O tratado impossível: um exercício de diplomacia luso-chinesa num contexto internacional em mudança, 1842–1887* [The impossible treaty: an exercise of Luso-Chinese diplomacy in a changing international context, 1842–1887] (Lisboa: IDI-MNE, 2006); and Lourença Maria da Conceição, *Macau entre dois tratados com a China* [Macau between two treaties with China] (Macau: ICM, 1988), 99. On the problem of geographical scope of Macau, see António Vasconcelos de Saldanha, *Negociações e acordos luso-chineses sobre os limites de Macau no século XIX* [Luso-Chinese negotiations and arrangements regarding the scope of Macau in the XIXcentury] (Lisboa: Instituto do Oriente, 2010).

[11] For instance, the 1822 Portuguese Constitution stated in Art. 20(4), that the territory of the United Kingdom of Portugal included Macau. In 1972, the PRC formally stated at the United Nations that it did not accept that Macau (and Hong Kong) were eligible to be included on the list of colonial territories covered by the declaration on the granting of independence and later, the 27th UN General Assembly adopted a resolution on the list that did not include Macau or Hong Kong.

[12] Art. 292. [13] Art. 292(3).

law, which shall give full effect to the principle of the independence of the judiciary'.[14] Further, that status, transitory by nature, inaugurated a new era for Macau, providing for the opening of negotiations between Portugal and China concerning the resumption by China of full sovereignty over the territory. From these negotiations a formal international agreement emerged in 1986, called the Sino-Portuguese Joint Declaration on the Question of Macau, which was deposited at the United Nations.

International foundations

China and Portugal agreed on the transfer of sovereignty over Macau (as a special administrative region, SAR) to China in the 'Joint Declaration of the Portuguese Republic and the People's Republic of China on the Question of Macau', signed in Beijing in 1987. This specifies that the SAR will enjoy a high degree of autonomy and that the basic policies stated in the Joint Declaration will be incorporated into a Basic Law to govern it. China resumed sovereignty on 20 December 1999. The preamble of the Declaration described the question of Macau as 'left over from the past'; an anomaly for both China and Portugal. It sets out the fundamentals of the process of transfer, including the legal and judicial system, political structure, public administration and fundamental rights. Prior to 19 December 1999, the Declaration gave China considerable influence on Portugal's administration of Macau.

The framework of the Joint Declaration varies; it fluctuates in rigour depending on the situation in which it is applied and to whom it is being addressed. Effectively, then, the obligations created by the Declaration vary according to whether they deal with Portugal or China. First and foremost is the obligation to transfer the exercise of sovereignty over Macau from Portugal to China. Other obligations arise as a result of this. These are provided for in the various sections of Point 2, in which the PRC government 'declares' that China 'will pursue the following basic policies regarding Macau'. There follows a list of eleven important 'policies' which will define the future Macau SAR, which 'will be stipulated in a Basic Law [. . .] and they will remain unchanged for fifty years'. There are also obligations that are directed simultaneously to both parties, such as the creation of a Joint Liaison Group.[15] One of Portugal's obligations consists of promoting economic development and preserving Macau's social stability.[16]

It is apparent that the obligations are not directed uniformly to both parties, whether in terms of subject matter or time. In fact, the obligations of the

[14] Art. 292(5). [15] Art. 4 and Annex II, point 1.

[16] For more on this package of obligations, see Alberto Costa, 'Continuidade e mudança no desenvolvimento jurídico de Macau à luz da Declaração Conjunta Luso-Chinesa' [Continuity and change in the juridical development of Macau in the light of the Luso-Chinese Joint Declaration], *Revista Jurídica*, 1 (1988), 54. For Hong Kong, Marius Olivier, 'Hong Kong: An exercise in autonomy?' conference paper delivered at One Country, Two Systems: Theory and Practice international conference, Hong Kong, 1997, 71–2.

PRC, and, indirectly, those of the Macau SAR, last throughout the fifty years following the resumption of sovereignty.[17] This is thus a second transition period.

One might well ask, transition to what? After fifty years China will be free of any obligations stated in the Joint Declaration and could, theoretically, for example, abolish the SAR, change its nature, eradicate the high degree of autonomy, transform it into a municipality, revoke the Basic Law, eliminate the use of Portuguese language, restrict fundamental rights, demolish the current social-economic system, get rid of independent judicial power, alienate Macau or grant independence.[18]

The guarantees for all these elements in Macau's current system are in the Joint Declaration and, in accordance with the *pacta sunt servanda* principle, none of that will be possible within the timeline prescribed in the Declaration. The Declaration contains no mechanism for its enforcement, but respect for that *jus cogens* principle is a strong element and Portugal and the international community should have something to say in case of a breach. Besides, the PRC has everything to gain in preserving the Macau format in order to solidify its status in the international arena.[19]

In a sense, the Basic Law 'does no more' than detail the policies stated in the Joint Declaration,[20] as foreseen in Point 12. Thus, Gomes Canotilho sees the Joint Declaration as playing a role in guaranteeing, directing, stimulating and interpreting the future Macau SAR.[21] For the fifty years that started on 20 December 1999, the Joint Declaration will be the genesis, the anchor and the guarantee of Macau's autonomy.[22] It presents a framework for Macau's

17 For example, Paulo Cardinal, 'O sistema político de Macau na Lei Básica – separação e supremacia do executivo face ao legislativo' [The Macau political system in the Basic Law – separation and primacy of the Executive vis-à-vis the Legislative], *Administração*, 19/20 (1993), 79; Eduardo Cabrita, 'International and constitutional limitations on the autonomy of the Macau Special Administrative Region', *Macau Law Journal*, special issue (2002), 159.

18 Jorge Godinho, *Macau SAR Business Law and Legal System* (LexisNexis, 2007), states, Macau 'is now in a period of Chinese Administration under the conditions agreed between Portugal and China (1999–2049), and from 2049 it will commence a period of unrestricted Chinese Administration' and 'The Sino-Portuguese Joint Declaration will then cease to apply and therefore the Chinese Administration of Macau will no longer have to follow its requirements', 2, 5.

19 See for example, Arnaldo Gonçalves, 'Les implications juridico-constitutionelles du transfert de la souveraineté de Macao a la Républic Populaire de Chine' [The juridical-constitutional implications of the transfer of sovereignty of Macau to the Peoples Republic of China], *Revue Internationale de Droit Comparé* (1993), 838.

20 Chen Zhi Zhong, 'The Joint Declaration and the International Law,' *BFDM*, 11 (2001), writes that the Basic Law codifies the twelve points in the Joint Declaration, 2, 92.

21 Gomes Canotilho, 'As palavras e os homens – reflexões sobre a Declaração Conjunta Luso-Chinesa e a institucionalização do recurso de amparo de direitos e liberdades na ordem jurídica de Macau' [The words and the men – thoughts on the Luso-Chinese Joint Declaration and the creation of the amparo appeal of rights and freedoms in the Macau legal system], *O Direito*, October (1994), 7–8.

22 That is, in my view, the appropriate conclusion. The assertion that Chinese institutions and the Chinese Constitution are the primary source of Macau's autonomy leads to the denial of any

autonomy that has two main characteristics: the autonomy is internationalized[23] and temporary, and for the duration of the fifty-year period covered by the Joint Declaration,[24] it operates under the principle of unchangeability.[25] 'Even after fifty years our policy will not change either. That is, for the first fifty years it cannot be changed', said Deng Xiaoping.[26]

However, this does not mean that the contracting parties intended the arrangements to be untouchable, they were concerned to prevent an undesirable sclerosis of the legal system. This characteristic of elasticity, though limited, is an added guarantee to the effective survival of the legal system since it allows it, without changing its essential characteristics,[27] to adapt to the natural and unexpected evolution of the social system in which it is embedded. If it is the *veritas* that the legal system will have to be maintained although not in

role post-transfer for the Joint Declaration. The PRC Constitution opens the door in Art. 31, the NPC may even be the key to that door, but the creators and delivers of the autonomy institution, or the parents, are the signatory parties, Portugal and China, through a bilateral agreement. Both states are the parents even though the guardian and the parent that directly cares for the child – [Macau SAR] – is China. Making the same point, Manuel Almeida Ribeiro, 'A Região Administrativa Especial de Macau e o Direito Internacional' [The Macau Special Administrative Region and international law], *BFDM*, 13 (2002), 203. Although the SAR is founded on the basis of the One Country, Two Systems policy, Zhu Guobin asserts, 'This political structure is, however, a result of the Joint Declaration' even if an invention of the Chinese government, see 'Redefining the central-local relationship under the Basic Law,' paper given at One Country, Two Systems: Theory and Practice international conference, 1997. Arguing that the HKSAR is a creation of international law, Roda Mushkat, 'Hong Kong as an international legal person', *Emory International Law Review* 6 (1992), 114, 110; arguing against this view, among others, Olivier, 'Hong Kong: An exercise in autonomy?' 88.

23 The case of South Tyrol is a point of reference and comparison for the autonomies of Macau and Hong Kong. Surprising as it may seem, that case shares more of the 'uniqueness' of the Macau and Hong Kong autonomies. In fact, they have in common a transfer of sovereignty – at least to a certain degree – from one sovereign state to another sovereign state; that transfer was agreed and laid down in an international legal agreement; those agreements were deposited at the UN; thus, the foundation of the autonomy is primarily internationally based; one finds that there are at least two official languages within the juridical boundaries of the autonomies, the language of the 'new' sovereign as well as the language of the previous one. On this, see Oskar Peterlini, 'The South-Tyrol Autonomy in Italy – Historical, political and juridical aspects', in Paulo Cardinal and Jorge Costa Oliveira (eds), *One Country, Two Systems, Three Legal Orders – Perspectives of Evolution –: Essays on Macau's Autonomy after the Resumption of Sovereignty by China* (Berlin: Heidelberg; Springer-Verlag, 2009), 143. On the internationalised origins of autonomy, see also Markku Suksi, 'Prosperity and happiness through autonomy: the self-government of the Åland Islands in Finland', Chapter 2 in this volume.

24 In other words, it 'is not open-ended', Xiaobing Xu and George D. Wilson, 'The Hong Kong Special Administrative Region as a model of regional external autonomy', *Case Western Reserve Journal of International Law*, Winter (2000), 11.

25 Francisco Gonçalves Pereira, 'Accommodating diversity: Macau under China's Constitution', in *Macau on the threshold of the third millennium* (Macau: Instituto Ricci, 2001), 107.

26 Deng Xiaoping, *On the Question of Hong Kong* (Hong Kong: New Horizon Press, 1993), 61.

27 Liuting Wang, 'Macao's return: Issues and concerns', *Loyola of Los Angeles International and Comparative Law Review*, 22 (1999), 180 states that the new sovereign must acknowledge the existence of a differentiated legal system in Macau and of the local social customs. See also Sun Wanzhong, 'A Lei Básica da RAEM e a construção do sistema jurídico de Macau' [The Macau SAR Basic Law and the Macau legal system construction], *BFDM*, 13 (2002), 54.

absolute terms, however, it is no less true that it may only be modified within the limits established by the Joint Declaration.

Of course there is the possibility that alterations may be made that are not permissible because they ignore fundamental changes.[28] The general principles that shape the Macau legal system cannot be disregarded, nor its diverse legal regimes – for example of fundamental rights in general and of each right in itself. Their basic rationale must be honoured. In other words, the essential content of a given juridical regimen will have to be respected and kept. On the other hand, even the Basic Law itself is subordinated to the twelve basic policies of the Joint Declaration in the event of amendment.

If after those fifty years autonomy remains unchanged – as I believe it will – it will have a different legal foundation guaranteed in a different way.

The genesis and the guarantee of Macau's autonomy: the Joint Declaration

While the Joint Declaration works as a *grundnorm* for the Basic Law, there are significant differences between them. Article 2 of the Basic Law states, 'The National People's Congress authorises the Macau Special Administrative Region to exercise a high degree of autonomy', with the inference being that the NPC is the source of the autonomy that is bestowed as a gift to Macau. As a proclamation of sovereignty to an audience that includes the Chinese diaspora and the Chinese inhabitants of the SAR this view has a certain appeal, but on purely juridical grounds alone, it is incorrect.[29]

In truth, its autonomous status in the PRC is possible only because Macau returned to the motherland, but this return occurred as a result of the international agreement and the reunification came with a package of prices, as described earlier. The establishment of a SAR endowed with a high degree of autonomy represented a bilateral will and not the single will of one of the parties. Saying that 'the NPC authorises' is legally untrue and unrealistic since it does not have the power to do this. At the most one can concede that the NPC is mandated by the parties to act in this fashion and acts, in a sense, within that internationalised mandate. Why the NPC? Because in the Chinese domestic order, it is the institution that is considered to be the most appropriate and the

[28] Lok Wai Kin seems to suggest a similar idea by proposing a difference between the spirit of the laws and their basic value in contrast to the specific wording of the normative rules. The latter would be changeable. 'Impacto da Lei Básica da RAEM na concepcção do Direito de Macau' [The Macau SAR Basic Law impact in the Macau law conceptualization], *BFDM*, 13 (2002), 61.

[29] See, for example, Isaac, 'The constitutional framework'. As Zhu Guobin puts it, 'The power of autonomy enjoyed by the HKSAR does not derive from a delegation by the Central People's Government, but from an international arrangement', 'Redefining the central-local relationship under the Basic Law', 6. Where the Joint Declaration is silent but the Basic Law grants powers to the SARs, it should be considered a situation of delegation, especially if they are not derived from general principles stated under the Basic Law.

Joint Declaration did not need to interfere in such domestic legal matters. But the NPC could only act after the Declaration, since if the NPC already had the power to give such authorisation one would have to conclude that the agreement was not necessary at all.[30] It is true that under Chinese Constitution, the authority to set up a special administrative region comes from Article 31 of the Constitution. However, the exact form that autonomy takes in respect of Macau is determined by the Joint Declaration, but not solely. Also the simple fact that Macau was previously under the dominion of Portugal, so a unilateral constitutional act by China would be void of efficacy as long as Macau remained under foreign dominion, a fact in law. Hence, the international agreement facilitated the operation of the Chinese domestic legislation and schemes.

The principle of autonomy applies to the people of the autonomy; as the Joint Declaration states that both the government and the legislature of the Macau SAR will be composed of local inhabitants.

'The current social and economic systems in Macau will remain unchanged, and so will the lifestyle. The laws currently in force in Macau will remain basically unchanged'.[31] All the rights and freedoms of the inhabitants and other persons are to be guaranteed by law in the Macau SAR. One of the main pillars of the transition is clearly proclaimed in this normative discourse, the principle of continuity, thus reinforcing the idea of it being based on the previous special identity of Macau. In other words, the contents of the autonomy should not be less than that enjoyed by the Territory of Macau under Portuguese administration.[32] The Joint Declaration points to this and, in addition, effectively serves to extend the Macau autonomy, such as by mandating a self-contained judicial system.

Thus a paramount principle is the continuity of the present social and economic systems. In order to secure this, the laws currently in force will remain basically unchanged.[33] This principle is reinforced in Annexes I and III of the

[30] It is virtually impossible to find any reference to the Joint Declaration in the relevant Chinese literature on the subject. Clearly there is an effort to downgrade, if not entirely erase, the Joint Declaration. Reading some published works, one may not be aware there ever was such a thing as the Joint Declaration.

[31] Point 2 (4) and see also points 1 and 3 of Annex I with some differences in the language of the latter.

[32] Canas, 'A extensão da autonomia de Macau na comunidade e na Lei', 226.

[33] On this, Jorge Oliveira, 'A continuidade do ordenamento jurídico de Macau na Lei Básica da futura Região Administrativa Especial [The continuity of the Macau legal order in the Basic Law of the future special Administrative Region], *Administração*, 19/20 (1993); Cardinal, 'Fundamental rights in Macau', 1–37; and Armando Isaac, 'Substantive constitutional restrictions on the limits to the sphere of jurisdiction of the Macau Special Administrative Region's Courts', paper presented to the fourth Comparative Constitutional Law Standing Committee Conference, Bangkok, May 1999, 46. For a different approach, considering the wordings *principle of continuity of the legal system* as only denoting the phenomenon and not the principle itself since 'the guiding principle for selection of existing legal rules and legal theories shall be "the theory of possession" (. . .) for a jurisdiction built upon legal transplant, existing legal rules and legal theories should be preserved unless they are proven to be not suitable for the society or not corresponding to the common norms of the human society', Tong Io Cheng and Wu Yanni, 'Legal transplants and the on-going formation of Macau legal

Joint Declaration, which states that following the establishment of the Macau SAR, all the normative acts[34] previously in force in Macau shall be maintained unless they contravene the Basic Law or are subject to any amendment by the Macau legislative body. The Joint Declaration states that all fundamental rights and freedoms will be guaranteed.

This apparently paradoxical relationship – transition versus continuity – can be defined as a political and diplomatic formula created to ensure some balance between the resumption of sovereignty by a sovereign state and respect for the history, culture (including the legal culture) and specific identity of Macau. It also acts as a vote of confidence in the future by respecting the past. So, if it is true that we faced a change in the landlord in Macau, it is also true that the transition will not eliminate what existed before December 1999, but on the contrary it will maintain it.

Another principle is autonomy of decision making. Macau will, 'on its own', decide policies in the fields of culture, education, science and technology and protection of cultural relics. This is among several areas on which the SAR is given the power to decide by itself.

Using the name 'Macau, China', the Macau SAR may on its own maintain and develop economic and cultural relations, and in this context, conclude agreements with states, regions and relevant international organisations. It may issue its own travel documents. The establishment of these guarantees are of a particular significance if comparisons are made between the SAR and other examples of autonomy around the world. In fact, even states in federations are not granted such a degree of independent interaction in the international legal order as the SAR.[35] It is expressly provided with an international legal capacity either to conclude international treaties or to join international organisations.[36]

Thus the limitations on autonomy concerning foreign affairs are, in fact, mitigated, making the autonomy in some ways more extensive than others elsewhere.[37] Where else are there formal borders and customs controls inside the same country as there are between the Macau SAR and the rest of China?

Moving to the economic and financial areas, the contracting parties to the Joint Declaration established complete autonomy, including the power to retain

culture', in Reports to the eighteenth International Congress of Comparative Law, *Isaidat Law Review*, Vol. 1, Special Issue 1 (2011), 50–2.

[34] This concept in civil law legal systems encompasses all juridical rules irrespective of their origins, whether law, administrative regulations and so on. The point to make is that all juridical rules previously in force shall be subject to the continuity principle, no matter the official form in which they are written.

[35] Wang Shuwen, 'As características da Lei Básica da Região Administrativa Especial de Macau' [The characteristics of the Macau's Special Administrative Region Basic Law], *BFDM*, 1 (1997), 46, concludes that some of the powers enjoyed by the SARs are not present in federal systems.

[36] Annex 1, VIII.

[37] Xu and Wilson, 'The Hong Kong Special Administrative Region as a model of regional external autonomy', 2–5, stress that Hong Kong arguably enjoys, in real terms, more far-reaching external autonomy than any other region in the world, historical or current.

Macau's own currency. Macau will remain a free port and a separate customs territory in order to develop its economic activities and there will be free flow of capital. The Macau Pataca remains the legal tender of the Macau SAR and will continue to circulate and be freely convertible. Again, such a power is now not seen even in some important sovereign states, such as those of the European Union. In addition, the Macau SAR continues to have independent finances and the Central People's Government (CPG) does not levy taxes on it.

Even the maintenance of public order in the Macau SAR is the responsibility of its government, despite the sensitivity of this issue in China.

Further features of the autonomy include the provision that after the establishment of the Macau SAR the socialist system and socialist policies shall not be practised in Macau. Also, judicial power in the Macau SAR is vested in its own courts, with the power of final adjudication exercised by its own Court of Final Appeal with, however, some limits of a strictly non-adjudication nature, as the mechanism of the interpretation of the Basic Law, which so far has not been used in relation to the Macau SAR, in contrast to what has been happening in the sister SAR of Hong Kong.

It has been proposed that Macau should be named an *Exceptional* Administrative Region, rather merely a 'special' one, since 'special' is insufficient to describe the nature of the SAR's status and the dimension of the powers that it enjoys.[38] This argument seems persuasive, given the nature of the autonomy outlined earlier, which does not fit into any category of existing autonomous entities or even states within federations.[39]

Thus the international treaty granted an unprecedented autonomy and incorporated a wide range of detailed guarantees. It resulted from the free will of two sovereign states that converged and were legally formalised in the Joint Declaration – not as a result of any unilateral will. On the other hand, and again in accordance with the Joint Declaration, it was necessary to further detail the contents of those policies and principles, thus the necessity of a domestic legal act – the Basic Law.

[38] Jorge Bacelar Gouveia, 'A Lei Básica da Região Administrativa Especial de Macau – Contributo para uma compreensão de direito constitucional' [The Basic Law of the Macau Special Administrative Region – A contribution towards a constitutional understanding], *BFDM*, 13 (2002), 195. As explained by Xu and Wilson, the problem was that the term 'autonomous region' had already been allocated in the Chinese system. 'The Hong Kong Special Administrative Region as a model of regional external autonomy', 7.

[39] In truth, one can find in the schematics of the SAR elements of territorial autonomy, federalism, statehood, confederalism and *less* than regionalism. See P. Cardinal, 'Continuity and Autonomy – Leading Principles Shaping the Fundamental Rights Constitutional System in the Macau Special Administrative Region', *La ciencia del derecho procesal constitucional. Estudios en homenaje a Héctor Fix-Zamudio en sus cincuenta años como investigador del derecho* [The science of constitutional procedure law. Essays in homage to Héctor Fix-Zamudio in his fifty years as law researcher], T. IV, E. Ferrer Mac-Gregor and A. Zaldívar Lelo de Larrea (eds.), (Mexico,UNAM, Marcial Pons, 2008), 169–231.

Macau's autonomy and the PRC Constitution

In the Preamble to its Constitution,[40] the People's Republic of China proclaims itself to be a unitary multi-national state, thus not allowing – at least from a formal point of view – any kind of federalism. It also prescribes socialism as the system practised by the PRC. Article 31 was enacted in order to enable the state to establish special administrative regions when necessary. The systems to be instituted in special administrative regions shall be prescribed by law enacted by the National People's Congress in light of specific conditions'.

Autonomous areas in mainland China were created in order to accommodate ethnic diversity. Therefore the autonomous areas are each connected to a certain minority or minorities, as the Constitution states that nationalities regional autonomy is practiced in areas where people of minority nationalities live in concentrated communities.[41] In these areas,[42] organs of self-government are established to exercise the power of autonomy. Unlike for the SARs, there are no international agreements to regulate this process.

The Chinese Constitution thus incorporates different approaches to regional autonomy, and even establishes different constitutional norms for the 'domestic' autonomies and for the SARs in Articles 30 and 31 respectively.[43] Article 30 lists the administrative divisions of the state, including the autonomous regions, but not the special administrative regions, which are provided for in Article 31. The PRC Constitution further elaborates the essentials of the domestic autonomy regimes in Articles 112 to 122,[44] while the framework for the SARs

[40] PRC Constitution 1982. [41] Art. 4.

[42] Currently, there are five provincial-level ethnic autonomous regions. They are the Inner Mongolia Autonomous Region, the Xinjiang Uygur Autonomous Region, Guangxi Zhuang Autonomous Region, Ningxia Hui Autonomous Region and Tibet Autonomous Region.

[43] Further emphasising the different constitutional origins of the two types of autonomy, in Art. 62 on the functions and powers of the NPC, approving the establishment of autonomous regions is para. 12 while deciding on the establishment of special administrative regions and the systems to be instituted within them is covered by para. 13.

[44] The rules applied to ethnic autonomous areas in general are provided in Arts. 112 to 122 of the PRC Constitution, and the Law of the People's Republic of China on Regional Ethnic Autonomy. The organs of self-government of ethnic autonomous areas shall apply the principle of democratic centralism, must guarantee that the Constitution and other laws are observed and implemented in these areas, shall lead the people of the various nationalities in a concentrated effort to promote socialist modernisation, shall place the interests of the state as a whole above anything else and make positive efforts to fulfil the tasks assigned by state organs at higher levels, shall rationally readjust the relations of production and the economic structure and work hard to develop the socialist market economy, under the condition of adhering to the principles of socialism. See Arts. 3, 5, 7 and 26 of the PRC Law on Regional Ethnic Autonomy. For further development in relevant issues such as the common comments that legislative power is not authentic or it is only semi-legislative power see, for example, Chen Shaofan, 'New Enquiries on Several Problems of the Legislation by Ethnic Autonomous Areas in our Country', *Research on Ethnics*, 1 (2005); Dai Xiaoming and Huang Mu, 'On the Legislation of Ethnic Autonomous Areas', *Journal of Southwest University of Nationalities*, 7 (2002).

is established in their respective Joint Declarations and Basic Laws.[45] One of the legal consequences of this formal differentiation is that the rules regarding domestic autonomies may be amended in any way the legislators see fit, thus the legal status of those autonomies is basically dependent on the constitutional rules and does not derive from other norms such as, for instance, laws governing each autonomous entity.

Besides this aspect, other important differences shape the nature of the SARs: their foundation in international agreements, their limited time-frame, and the set of twelve policies agreed bilaterally. Thus the difference between the autonomous power enjoyed by the SARs and the autonomous areas is not only one of degree, but of their nature.[46]

China took a highly pragmatic approach towards the questions of Macau and of Hong Kong:[47] the point was to resolve these issues and allow reunification, even if that meant actually disregarding the stipulations of the PRC Constitution to a certain extent. In formal terms, it created Article 31 as a sufficiently vague device to allow the incorporation of the SARs into the Chinese state as a 'second system' enjoying a 'high degree of autonomy'. Article 31 was the necessary step to accommodate the constitutional framework to the international binding obligations that were to come. In a somewhat similar fashion, Article 292 of the Portuguese Constitution was construed to accommodate Portugal's legally binding obligations toward Macau. Article 292 alone could not serve the purpose of returning Macau to China with all the necessary guarantees, just as Article 31 alone could not realise the return of Macau and establish the terms for its incorporation.[48]

[45] Other references to the SARs in the PRC Constitution are found in Arts. 59(12) and 62(13), one being a norm of competence and the other a norm of representation. For the autonomous regions there are several more norms, for example in Arts. 62(12), 67(8), 67(12) and 67(20) and 89(4) and 89(15), to mention a few. Some of these are of great importance in the configuration of the nature and level of the autonomy, such as those that allow the Natonal People's Congress Standing Committee (NPCSC) to annul regulations of the autonomous regions, Art. 68(8), and stipulate that the State Council exercises unified leadership over the work of local organs of state administration at different levels throughout the country, and to lay down the detailed division of functions and powers between the central government and the organs of state administration of autonomous regions, Art. 89(4).

[46] Zhu, 'Redefining the central-local relationship under the Basic Law', 6.

[47] Liu Gaolong, 'O estabelecimento das Regiões Adminsistrativas Especiais traduz-se num grande desenvolvimento estadual' [The establishment of the special administrative regions means a great state development], *BFDM*, 12 (2001), 93, writes that in a unitary country the position of the SARs enjoying such a high degree of autonomy is unique, thus it constitutes a new departure in the organisation of the state.

[48] The provisions of the two constitutions thus work in a similar inverted fashion, and were bridged by the Joint Declaration. Art. 292 allowed the special status of Macau as a non-Portuguese territory, thus permitting it to be alienated, while Art. 31 allowed the return of Macau with a special status. Then it is up to the Chinese domestic legal order to decide, under the framework dictated by the Joint Declaration, the method by which the Macau reunification is to be effected, as it was up to the Portuguese domestic legal order to decide how to proceed with the disposal of powers over Macau.

Autonomy and the Basic Law

The Basic Law is the formal domestic legal instrument that details the constitutional organisation of the SAR, including its autonomy. This legal document has the appearance, the content and the structure of a formal constitution and can be called, as mentioned previously, a Constitution *lato sensu*.

In fact, if one looks at the legal order of the Macau SAR, the Basic Law is the highest source for the domestic legal system. This role is clearly indicated in Article 11, in a fashion rooted in Romano-Germanic legal systems: 'No law, decree, administrative regulations and normative acts of the Macau Special Administrative Region shall contravene this Law.'

It is important to reiterate that the Basic Law must follow the provisions of the Joint Declaration, although in some cases it has failed to do so.[49] Hence, when analysing and interpreting the Basic Law, the first step must be to see how the subject in question is dealt with in the Joint Declaration.[50]

The features of autonomy

The Basic Law states that Macau is authorised to exercise a high degree of autonomy.[51] As in the Joint Declaration, this is to be realised through the Macau SAR's enjoyment of a range of powers: executive, legislative and independent judicial power, including that of final adjudication;[52] and many others as seen previously when analysing the Joint Declaration, such as in the social, legal, economic, financial and cultural fields and even in some external affairs.

To this end, the socialist system will not be practiced in Macau,[53] and the SAR is to keep its own system, subject to the Basic Law.[54] The Basic Law provides for the system to be used in Macau: 'The systems and policies practiced in the Macau SAR, including the social and economic systems, the system for safeguarding the fundamental rights and freedoms of its residents, the executive, legislative and judicial systems, and the relevant policies, shall be based on the provisions of this Law.'[55] In addition, the PRC's national laws will not apply, apart from those listed in Annex III to the Basic Law.[56] In order to protect Macau's autonomy, the Law specifies, 'No department of the Central People's Government and no province, autonomous region, or municipality directly under the Central Government may interfere in the affairs which the Macau SAR administers.'[57]

These stipulations are just some of the items from an enormous list that is presented in the chapters on the economy, culture and social affairs, and on

49 See for example Cardinal, 'O sistema político de Macau na Lei Básica'; for Hong Kong, Yash Ghai, *Hong Kong's New Constitutional Order* (Hong Kong University Press, 1999), 146.

50 For instance, a hypothetical revision of the Basic Law to eliminate the right to strike would not be possible since this right is directly protected by the umbrella guarantees established in the Joint Declaration. The same logic would apply if a revision of the Basic Law was proposed to abolish the high degree of autonomy.

51 Arts. 2 and 12. 52 Art. 2. 53 Art. 5. 54 Art. 8. 55 Art. 11(1). 56 Art. 18(2).

57 Art. 22.

external affairs. Since most of the substance has been discussed previously in relation to the contents of the Joint Declaration, here I will focus primarily on the limitations the Basic Law places on Macau's autonomy.

The Basic Law also contains the possibility of expanding Macau's autonomy. It states, 'The Macau SAR may enjoy other powers granted to it by the National People's Congress, the Standing Committee of the National People's Congress or the Central People's Government'.[58] Such powers, one would assume, would not be those included in the already existing autonomy, but ones that cross the boundaries of autonomy and deal with reserved subject matters such as external relations.

Another important feature of the scheme is that in the Macau SAR context, Chinese nationality is generally less important than residence in the territory.[59] This contributes to the effective autonomy of Macau since people of various nationalities can belong on (almost) equal terms.

The limits of autonomy

The autonomy envisaged by the Joint Declaration has certain natural limits, and the Basic Law also expressly provides for certain other limitations that were initially expressed in the treaty.

First of all, Macau is Chinese territory, and the government of the PRC has resumed the exercise of sovereignty over it. Sovereignty now resides solely in the Chinese state, both in its title and in its exercise,[60] and the form of the autonomous entity is that of a SAR while the domestic legal document is a Basic Law enacted by the central authorities and not by the autonomous entity itself. Under such a framework, it is not possible for Macau to achieve formal federated status, even less for it to win independence. Second, there is a temporal limitation: the principle of the internationalised autonomy will remain in force for fifty years, hence it is guaranteed only for that period of time. Finally, Macau will enjoy a high degree of autonomy, except in foreign affairs and defence, which are the responsibilities of the Central People's Government. However, as mentioned earlier, there are exceptions that allow for the SAR to exercise extensive autonomy in external affairs. The first and third of these limitations can be considered as inherent in any form of autonomy, while the second is directly connected to the internationalised nature of the granting process.

Several further limitations on Macau's autonomy that are specific to this instance are laid out in the Joint Declaration. The Chief Executive will be

[58] Art. 20. Canas, 'A extensão da autonomia de Macau na comunidade e na Lei', 244, makes this point despite considering the article an enigma.

[59] António Katchi describes this as a *population* separation feature, which is one among several aspects of separation, such as territorial, linguistic, patrimonial, monetary and political structure separation. *Governo e administração pública de Macau* [Government and public administration in Macau] (Macau: Instituto Politécnico de Macau, 2004), 13–16.

[60] On this point, Olivier, 'Hong Kong: an exercise in autonomy?'

appointed by the Central Government, although the selection will be based on the results of elections or consultations in Macau. Officials holding principal posts will be nominated by the Chief Executive of the Macau SAR but appointed by the Centre. The limits are stated in point 3 of the Joint Declaration and are further developed in Annex I.

The relationship between religious organisations in the Macau SAR and those in other parts of the PRC shall be based on the principles of non-subordination, non-interference and mutual respect. This arrangement of mutual restraint relates to the sensitive issue of relations between the PRC and the Vatican, and while it might be considered a limitation on autonomy, it also acts as a guarantee for the autonomy of religious organisations in Macau.

Additional limitations are imposed through the Basic Law. It is notable that the language used in the Basic Law – since the centre 'authorizes', Macau 'may' do certain things and 'shall' do others – implies that autonomy is a favour granted from on high. The following list of specific provisions is not exhaustive, but rather highlights the most prominent limitations on autonomy.

Chapter I of the Basic Law, 'General Principles', essentially reproduces what has already been stated in the Joint Declaration. The most notable exception is that the concept of 'local inhabitant' is changed to that of 'permanent resident'.

Article 15 states that not only the appointment, but also the removal, of the Chief Executive, the principal officials of the government, and the Procurator General are the prerogative of the Central People's Government. Note that no mention of the procedure for removal was made in the Joint Declaration.

Article 17 sets out a complex procedure for a political variety of constitutional review: the laws enacted by the legislature of the Macau SAR must be reported to the Standing Committee of the NPC for the record. The reporting shall not affect the entry into force of such laws. If the Standing Committee, after consulting the Committee for the Basic Law,[61] considers that any law is not in conformity with the provisions of Basic Law regarding affairs within the responsibility of the Central Authorities or regarding the relationship between the Central Authorities and the Region, the Standing Committee may return the law in question but shall not amend it. Any law returned by the Standing Committee shall immediately be invalidated. This imposes a clear limit on the

[61] On this consultative body, see, Decision of the NPC on Approving the Proposal by the Drafting Committee for the Basic Law of the Macao Special Administrative Region on the Establishment of the Committee for the Basic Law of the Macao Special Administrative Region under the NPCSC (adopted by the Eighth NPC at its First Session on 31 March 1993), and its Appendix. This body is a working committee under the NPCSC, its function is to study questions arising from the implementation of Arts. 17, 18, 143 and 144 of the Basic Law and submit its views thereon to the Standing Committee. Its composition is as follows: ten members, five from the mainland and five from Macau, including persons from the legal profession, appointed by the NPCSC for a term of office of five years. Macau members shall be Chinese citizens who are permanent residents of the Macau SAR with no right of abode in any foreign country and shall be nominated jointly by the Chief Executive, President of the Legislative Council and President of the Court of Final Appeal of the Region for appointment by the NPCSC.

capacity to enact laws in the name of defining the boundaries of autonomy. Although the effect is the invalidation of the law, we do not know if the result is the invalidation of the law in *toto* or solely of a specific norm that is in violation of these parameters. However, there is still some self-restraint since it is not within the powers of the central bodies to change or amend the law.

Although Article 18 states that the NPC Standing Committee may add to or delete from the list of national laws applying to Macau in Annex III, it can do so only after consulting the Committee for the Basic Law and the SAR government. This process attempts, at least theoretically, a certain balance between the centre and the autonomous unit. Furthermore, laws listed in Annex III are confined to those relating to defence and foreign affairs, as well as other matters outside the limits of Macau's autonomy, 'as specified by this Law'. Especially when read in conjunction with point 2, second paragraph of the Joint Declaration stating that Macau will enjoy a high degree of autonomy, except in foreign and defence affairs, this restriction appears to presuppose that the residual powers not expressly allocated to Macau or the PRC should be considered to be vested in the SAR, as the promised 'high degree of autonomy' will be only limited in foreign affairs and defence matters, leaving the rest, *all the rest*, in the hands of the SAR. That is to say, regarding limitations on subject matters, the mechanism is one of a closed list composed of only two areas, and notably the list is one of exceptions and not one of *devolved* matters as is the case in so many autonomies. Besides, if this is not so, how could one expect the SAR fully to explore the guarantees in the Basic Law[62] aimed at ensuring that the previous capitalist system and way of life shall remain unchanged for fifty years? Certainly that way of life and its maintenance over its several fields presupposes that action can be taken in all the areas specified in the Basic Law, but not only those. If there is no provision in the Basic Law concerning the protection of endangered wild life, or agriculture, fisheries, urban planning, weights and measurements standards, should that mean that the SAR cannot act, for instance by means of legislation, in those areas? Would the PRC have to take care of such matters? I do not think so, and I believe that the spirit and extent of a high degree of autonomy does not point that way either. Even if the

[62] Art. 5. Canas, 'A extensão da autonomia de Macau na comunidade e na Lei', 242–3. This view is challenged by political authorities in China. However, from a strict juridical stance, since the scheme used means that only two general domains (defence and foreign affairs) are removed from the SAR's jurisdiction (along with some expressly mentioned specific competences such as in the fields of appointing senior officials or interpretation), and not, as in other examples provided by constitutional comparative law, a method of enumerating the areas of autonomy, namely legislative autonomy, leaving the rest that is not listed to the central powers, the residual powers irrespective of not being a federated state fall to the SAR. For a different perspective, see among others, Ghai, *Hong Kong's New Constitutional Order*, 1997 edn., 146, with detailed analysis, examples and references to official Chinese doctrine against the allocation of residual powers to the SARs. The issue of sovereignty is a powerful one indeed but it cannot, alone and by itself, stand against the vesting of residual powers in the SARs and, it is important to note once more, sovereignty is limited in *pacta* by the Joint Declaration for the period of fifty years.

common rule in autonomous regions points in the opposite direction,[63] one must remember that the SAR autonomies do not fit into any classical autonomy model. This SAR autonomy is different and goes beyond traditional boundaries in many ways, even exceeding the level of autonomy of local units in federated states (for example, in having its own currency, establishing formal frontiers and customs control with the rest of the country, issuing autonomous passports, as mentioned previously), thus challenging the claims of those who would put a restrictive gloss on the powers of the SARs by citing the fact that formally they are not states in a Chinese federation.[64]

Article 19 seriously limits Macau's judicial autonomy: its courts have no jurisdiction over acts of state such as defence and foreign affairs. The issue of acts of state are a matter for the Chief Executive. The relevant section reads, 'The courts of the Region shall obtain a certificate from the Chief Executive on questions of fact concerning acts of state such as defence and foreign affairs whenever such questions arise in the adjudication of cases. This certificate shall be binding on the courts. Before issuing such a certificate, the Chief Executive shall obtain a certifying document from the CPG'. This procedure has the potential for allowing further erosion of the scope of autonomy in practice.

Article 23 requires that the Macau SAR,

> shall enact laws, on its own, to prohibit any act of treason, secession, sedition, subversion against the Central People's Government, or theft of state secrets, to prohibit foreign political organizations or bodies from conducting political activities in the Region, and to prohibit political organizations or bodies of the Region from establishing ties with foreign political organizations or bodies.

Although the power to enact the laws is vested in the local bodies, the central authorities have given a direct command to enact certain legislation thus not allowing the possibility for the autonomous bodies to decide otherwise.

Article 144 establishes that the power of amendment of the Basic Law shall be vested in the NPC. This is the corollary of the previously mentioned limitation on the form and the source of the domestic legal instrument that outlines the autonomy structure of Macau.

The NPC Standing Committee, the State Council, and the Macau SAR have the power to propose bills amending the Basic Law. Amendment bills from the Macau SAR shall be submitted to the NPC by the Macau delegation to the NPC after obtaining the consent of two thirds of their number, two thirds of all the members of the Macau Legislative Assembly and the Chief Executive. Although

63 Although not in all known examples. In Italy for example, also a non-federal state, after the 2001 revision of the 1948 Constitution, Art. 117 established several areas reserved to the State and areas reserved to the regions (besides areas of concurrent powers) and stipulated that the regions have exclusive legislative power with respect to any matters not expressly reserved to state law, Art. 117(4).

64 Art. 20 of the Basic Law should also be interpreted in this light.

the fact that the Macau SAR may propose amendments does reflect some degree of autonomy, in this specific aspect Macau enjoys less autonomy than before.[65]

Before a bill amending the Basic Law can be put on the NPC's agenda, the Macau Committee for the Basic Law must study it and submit its views to the NPC. No amendment may contravene the 'established basic policies' of the PRC regarding Macau. This last statement is of critical importance in the maintenance of autonomy, since these policies are those that were the object of agreement and were thus detailed in the Joint Declaration.

Finally, Article 143 could potentially serve either as a threat to autonomy or create possibilities for its expansion.[66] This provision established that the power of interpretation of the Basic Law is vested in an external body, the NPC Standing Committee. This is a political institution, not a judicial one, and thus this means the imposition of a method that is foreign to Macau. The new system goes against the idea of autonomy proclaimed for Macau.[67] Regarding provisions of the Basic Law that relate to issues within Macau's autonomy, the NPC Standing Committee 'shall authorize the courts of the Macau SAR' when adjudicating cases 'to interpret [them] on their own'. However, if the cases involved are within the scope of the autonomy the question arises why it is necessary for an external body to authorise the local courts to interpret these provisions. Since there is no express provision for judicial review, of course the power of interpretation vested in the Macau courts is potentially important in protecting fundamental rights,[68] as well as in guaranteeing other structural principles as the principle of constitutionality and the principle of legality and the respect for the separation of powers modelled in the Joint Declaration and the Basic Law. The system may be unbalanced in favour of the Executive, but is nevertheless rooted in a separation of powers doctrine.

The courts of the Macau SAR are also authorised to interpret other provisions of the Basic Law in adjudicating cases. However, if they need to interpret the provisions of Basic Law 'concerning affairs which are the responsibility of the Central People's Government, or concerning the relationship between the Central Authorities and the Region, and if such interpretation will affect the judgments in the cases, the courts of the Region shall, before making their final judgments, seek an interpretation of the relevant provisions from the Standing Committee of the NPC through the Court of Final Appeal'. While this mechanism begins by extending the scope of the courts'

[65] Although the revision of the Organic Statute was vested in the Portuguese parliament, it depended exclusively on the impulse of the local autonomy bodies, as mentioned previously.

[66] The latter would only be the case if there was a trend in interpretation friendlier to the autonomy. This may not be likely but, in theory, the potential for broadening is there.

[67] For example, Cabrita, 'International and constitutional limitations on the autonomy of the Macau Special Administrative Region', 184.

[68] Fernando A. Correia, 'A fiscalização da constitucionalidade das normas do ordenamento jurídico de Macau à luz da recente jurisprudência do Tribunal Constitucional' [The control of constitutionality of the norms of the Macau legal system in the light of the recent Constitutional Court judicial decisions], *Revista Jurídica de Macau*, 4: 3 (1997), 26.

interpretation power, it ends with more limitations.[69] The negative impacts of the use of this procedure in Hong Kong are already well known, and are described in this volume. In the case of Macau, the mechanism has so far not been activated.[70]

The courts are required to follow any interpretation made by the Standing Committee, but 'judgments previously rendered shall not be affected'. Before it makes an interpretation, the NPC Standing Committee is required to consult the Macau Basic Law Committee.

A feature of autonomy: the political system

The fact that there is a separate Macau SAR political system is in itself a rather important indicator of the existence of institutional autonomy. Another question is the scope and the extent of the powers allocated to the various bodies comprising it, as well as their *internal* interaction. The relative amount of power given to the body that acts as the representative of the central entity is another important measure of autonomy.

In terms of titles of posts, requirements for holders of political office, powers and the relationship between the executive and the legislature the current political system of the Macau SAR is different from the previous arrangements in a number of respects. This is despite the fact that the system briefly described in the Sino-Portuguese Joint Declaration[71] was supposed to be allowed to continue to operate. The Basic Law did not actually follow several of the solutions outlined in the Joint Declaration.[72]

The system is based on two principal institutions: the legislature and the executive, the latter consisting of the Chief Executive, the government and the Executive Council. This structure is basically similar to that which existed before. However, the division appears to be based on a balance which does not in fact exist. A heavier emphasis is placed on the Chief Executive (who heads

69 Yash Ghai, *Hong Kong's New Constitutional Order*, 1997 edn., 185.

70 However, as this manuscript was being finalised, such an interpretation was issued regarding electoral matters in the annexes to the Basic Law. See 'Interpretação do Comité Permanente da Assembleia Popular Nacional sobre o artigo 7.° do Anexo I e o artigo 3.° do Anexo II da Lei Básica da Região Administrativa Especial de Macau da República Popular da China', Aviso do Chefe do Executivo n.° 21/2012. However, compared with the interpretations of Hong Kong's Basic Law, this interpretation did not have such a controversial political and juridical impact on the Macau SAR.

71 Xiao Weiyun states that the provisions of the Joint Declaration concerning these matters are vague. 'A estrutura política da Lei Básica da Região Administrativa Especial de Macau' [The political structure of Macau Special Administrative Region Basic Law], *Administração*, 19/20, 1993, 61; Yash Ghai and Peter Wesley Smith, 'Constitutional and legal system', in Philip Smart and Andrew Halkyard (eds.) *Trade and Investment Law in Hong Kong* (Hong Kong: Butterworths Asia, 1993) note the minimalism of the Declaration on this topic in contrast to the developed and detailed provisions on economic and social policies, 9–10.

72 Changes were made, for example, in titles: Chief Executive and Executive Council are used instead of Governor and Consultative Council. Also, Chinese nationality was made a requirement for holding certain public offices and the executive became a plural body.

the government and the Executive Council) than on the Legislative Assembly.[73] Since the Chief Executive is designed to be the institution more connected to the central power, whereas the Legislative Assembly is more closely connected to the Macau SAR population, and thus more representative of the autonomy principle, in effect this means that in terms of the operation of the political system, autonomy is diminished by the strengthening of the powers of Chief Executive and the consequent downgrading of the role of the Legislative Assembly.[74] Some authors suggest that a different kind of balancing mechanism has been created by granting exclusive legislative power to the Legislative Assembly.[75] Although the meaning of the Basic Law on this matter is in dispute,[76] the removal of legislative powers from the Chief Executive was indeed a major change. However, once the SAR came into being the administrative regulations have been revealed as a strong source of law (they have even been used to repeal legislative acts enacted by the Governor), undermining the supposed impact of this new 'balance'. Besides this, it is important to consider the current system of legislative procedure. The Basic Law introduces a mechanism of allocation of powers that requires the Chief Executive's written consent for the introduction of bills relating to government policies.[77] Furthermore, members may not introduce bills[78] relating to the following subjects: revenue and public expenditure; the

[73] Cardinal, 'O sistema político de Macau na Lei Básica', 93–4.

[74] Ibid.; and Malheiro Magalhães, 'O princípio da separação dos poderes na Lei Básica da Região Administrativa de Macau' [The principle of separations of powers in the Basic Law of Macau Special Administrative Region], *Administração*, 41 (1997), 730–1. On the impact of the diminution of the power of the legislature in Hong Kong on its autonomy, see Tseng Yu-sek, 'La peau de chagrin du haut degree d'autonomie' [The magic skin of the high degree of autonomy], *Bulletin de Sinologie*, 45 (1988), 10. It is indeed curious to note that, before reunification, Chinese scholars argued the opposite, concluding that the Macau SAR system would involve a balance of powers. See Leong Fan, *Guia da Lei Básica de* Macau [Guide to the Macau Basic Law] (Macau: Associação das Ciências Económicas de Macau, 1995), 89; Xiao, 'A Lei Básica e a evolução política de Macau'. However, at present the Chinese political and legal literature acknowledges virtually without any exception that the system is an executive-led system.

[75] V. Canas, 'A Lei Básica e a evolução política de Macau' [The Basic Law and the political evolution of Macau], *Política Internacional*, 15/16 (1997).

[76] At least from the point of view of the practical application of the system envisaged in the Basic Law. On this see, Cardinal, 'O sistema político de Macau na Lei Básica', 89; Paul Fifoot, 'One Country, Two Systems – Mark II: from Hong Kong to Macao,' *International Relations* (1994), 4; Magalhães, 'O princípio da separação dos poderes na Lei Básica da Região Administrativa de Macau', 730; Leong, *Guia da Lei Básica de Macau*, 207–8. From a strictly formal point of view, only the Legislative Assembly can enact laws, although the Executive often exercises de facto legislative power by enacting administrative regulations that deal with subject matters that should be the preserve of the Assembly. Law 13/2009, Regime juridicio de enquadramento das fontes normativas internas [General Legal Regime on domestic normative sources], was enacted to address this issue.

[77] Art. 75. This could include virtually all the activities and policies of the Macau SAR not specified by the other similar clauses.

[78] The limitation is solely on the initiation of a legislative procedure and is not extended to the subsequent power to propose amendments to bills introduced by the Executive. That is what is laid down in the Basic Law and a possible attempt to enlarge that already substantial limitation should be deemed contrary to Macau constitutional law. In fact, both in the Macau and Hong

political structure and operation of the government;[79] and the method for electing members of the Legislative Assembly.[80] Thus by imposing an absolute or a relative reservation of legislative initiative, the legislative power of the Legislative Assembly is diminished.[81]

The Chief Executive also has other powers over the legislative process. These are the powers:

- to return bills to the Legislative Assembly for reconsideration they are 'not compatible with the overall interests of the Region';[82]
- to dissolve the Legislative Assembly if:
  i. it insists on passing a bill that has been returned by the CE;
  ii. it refuses to pass a budget; or
  iii. it refuses to pass any bill;[83]
- to refuse authorisation to members of the government, among others, to testify or give evidence when requested to do so by the Legislative Assembly;[84] and
- to decide on the priority of the issues to be submitted to the Legislative Assembly.[85]

There are a few mechanisms that provide more balance to the system and, in any case, these are ineffectual and difficult to put into operation. For example, the statement that the government is accountable to the Legislative Assembly is not accompanied by any sanctions for failure to do so;[86] and the special procedure for investigating the Chief Executive does not give the Legislative Assembly any real powers, given that the power to make this decision is held by the Central People's Government. In addition, it is an extremely complicated process.[87] The procedures for forcing the resignation of the CE due to irreconcilable differences with the Legislative Assembly may only be used in extreme situations.[88]

Given the former praxis is less centred on a single body, the system as envisaged might allow the emergence of a system comparable to other 'strong-arm democracies' in the region where such power arrangements accompany economies with a strong capitalist bent.[89]

Kong Legislative Assembly's rules of procedure the limitation in general operates only to the original introduction of bills – in Hong Kong the President of the LegCo may decide that an amendment that will signify a decrease of revenue or a rising of expenditure may be introduced only by the Executive.

79 Art. 75. 80 Annex II, Art. 2.

81 Cardinal, 'O sistema político de Macau na Lei Básica', 94, and Magalhães, 'O princípio da separação dos poderes na Lei Básica da Região Administrativa de Macau', 730, both consider this mechanism an assault on the separation of powers principle.

82 Art. 51. 83 Art. 52. 84 Art. 50(15). 85 Art. 74(2).

86 Art. 66. 87 Art. 71(7). 88 Art. 54.

89 It is interesting to note that in Hong Kong's case, the Basic Law system was less disruptive of the pre-existing order and even includes some mechanisms for remedying any imbalances that might occur, but these were not adopted for Macau where the initial system was already more balanced and democratic. Albert Chen, 'From colony to Special Administrative Region: Hong

An autonomous system to protect fundamental rights

Fundamental rights are a recognised aspect of the autonomy idea. The Basic Law contains a substantive catalogue of fundamental rights that is quite satisfactory given the type of instrument,[90] particularly when compared with provisions made in other legal orders in the region, such as that of Hong Kong.[91] As a general rule, external reports on human rights in Macau are rather positive on the legal provisions for fundamental rights in Macau, as well as regarding, its general approach to respect for rights.[92]

The general directive principle is stated in Art. 4: 'The Macau SAR shall safeguard the rights and freedoms of the residents of the Macau SAR and of other persons in the Region in accordance with law.' Such provisions are given force by means of Art. 11, the second paragraph of which states that 'no law, decree, administrative regulations and normative acts of the Macau SAR shall contravene this Law'. This makes the Basic Law function as the norm parameter, the domestic constitutional platform.

It is important to point out that the fundamental rights articulated in the Chinese Constitution do not extend into Macau's new legal order. Certainly some Chinese constitutional norms are applicable in Macau, namely Article 31. However, that is not the case in relation to fundamental rights[93] due precisely to

Kong's constitutional journey,' in Raymond Wacks (ed.), *The Future of the Law in Hong Kong* (Hong Kong: Oxford University Press, 1989), 112.

90 Gouveia, 'A Lei Básica da Região Administrativa Especial de Macau', 187; Frances Luke 'The imminent threat of China's intervention in Macau autonomy: using Hong Kong's past to secure Macau's future', *American University International Law Review*, 15 (2000), 2. See also Cardinal, 'Fundamental rights in Macau'; V. Canas, 'The general regime of fundamental rights in the Basic Law and in the international instruments', in *One Country, Two Systems, Three Legal Orders*, Cardinal and Costa Oliveira (eds.), 655; Jorge B. Gouveia, 'Fundamental rights in the Macau legal system', in ibid., 695; and Fong Man Chong, 'The ranking of the international law in the framework of The Basic Law of the Macao SAR of the People's Republic of China and the introspection on the perplexities of fundamental rights', in ibid., 593.

91 See, for example, Fifoot, 'One Country, Two Systems – Mark II', 51–2; James Cotton, 'The retrocession of Macau and the limitations of the Hong Kong Model', *Pacific Focus*, 15: 2 (2000), 50; P. Cardinal, 'The constitutional layer of protection of fundamental rights in the Macau Special Administrative Region', *Revista de Direito Público*, 3 (2010), 211–62.

92 For example, the US State Department Report on human rights in Macau 2009, states, 'The government generally respects the human rights of its citizens', adding 'however, some problems remained, most notably limits on citizens' ability to change their government, reports of official corruption, and trafficking in persons'. Also European Commission, Joint Report to the European Parliament and the Council – Annual report Macao 2010, states 'the fundamental rights and freedoms of Macao's people have in general been respected'. This assertion does not mean that there are no breaches of fundamental rights in Macau – for example, on freedom of demonstration or denial of entry to people from Hong Kong without apparent reasons – but overall the situation is indeed positive. In this respect, the principle of local (Macanese rather than Mainland) philosophy in the interpretation and integrative methods is of utmost importance.

93 As in many other areas. See, among others, Wu Xingping, 'O sistema jurídico da Região Administrativa Especial de Macau' [The Macau Special Administrative Region legal system], *BFDM*, 13 (2002), 75–7; Xu Qing, 'A Natureza e o estatuto da Lei Básica da RAEM – uma

the autonomous character of the SAR, therefore neither Chinese constitutional norms nor the nature and spirit of their interpretation in the PRC system may be used to enlarge or to reduce the scope and content of the rights system or of any given right in Macau.

This understanding is grounded in the Joint Declaration and in the Basic Law. As stated in Art. 11, '[T]he systems and policies practiced in the Macau SAR, including the social and economic systems, *the system for safeguarding the fundamental rights and freedoms of its residents*, the executive, legislative and judicial systems, and the relevant policies, *shall be based on the provisions of this Law.*'[94]

Thus on these matters the Basic Law shields Macau from the correlative norms of the PRC Constitution. As one author puts it, 'under Article 11 of the Basic Law, the systems and the policies in the Macau SAR, are based on the stipulations of the Basic Law. This means to say that the Constitution is applicable in the Macau SAR, except for the stipulations that refer to the socialist system as well as those matters identified in Article 11'.[95] Thus in order to comply with this autonomous fundamental rights system, there is to be no importation of rules, methods and theories of fundamental rights that are observed in the PRC. This is particularly important as these employ an extremely different general approach to the subject matter than that in the SARs.

In other words, the system of fundamental rights is self-sufficient and concedes to outside norms only to the extent properly allowed, such as regarding the international covenants and also to ensure concurrence with the stipulations in the Joint Declaration, namely by establishing a mandatory catalogue of fundamental rights and establishing several general principles.

This self-contained system constitutes one of the most important and distinctive features of the Macau autonomy. In truth, from the formal point of view this self-contained system of fundamental rights represents an augmentation of the autonomy of Macau as compared with the situation prior to 1999, since before the transfer of sovereignty, the system relied mostly on the importation of norms and principles from the Portuguese Constitution.[96]

This is an area that reveals some of the differences between the two sisters in autonomy, Macau and Hong Kong. Macau has a more comprehensive list of fundamental rights than Hong Kong as well as providing a better theoretical legal cushion and practical tools of implementation, by expressly impregnating

tentativa de abordagem' [The nature and status of the Macau Basic Law – an approximation attempt], paper presented at the seminar Linhas de Evolução do Direito da RPC – Reflexos em Macau (1994), 22 and 23.

94 Emphasis added.

95 Wu, 'O sistema jurídico da Região Administrativa Especial de Macau', 74 and 76.

96 The system of fundamental rights in the Portuguese Constitution is widely recognised as very liberal, extensive and comprehensive in its coverage. One author describes it as one of the most *perfected* in the world: Jorge Bacelar Gouveia, 'A Declaração Universal dos Direitos do Homem e a Constituição Portuguesa' [The Universal Declaration of Human Rights and the Portuguese Constitution], in *Ab Uno ad Omnes* (Coimbra: Coimbra Editora, 1998), 958.

the fundamental rights system with transversal principles of human dignity and non-discrimination.[97]

The words of autonomy . . . and their implementers

The focus so far has been on the words of autonomy, that is to say the norms that create and regulate it, both in the Joint Declaration and in the Basic Law. But a norm is not a proper norm solely as words, a juridical norm only becomes so when interpreted and applied. For these operations people are necessary.

I believe that the actual destiny of Macau's autonomy rests in the hands of the people who govern it. Given the regulatory construction, how it functions is then up to those who operate it, elaborate it and shape it. In this exercise the scope of autonomy will be constructed. The dialectic tension inherent in autonomy phenomena – the central entity and its leaders will tend to push back the boundaries of autonomy, while the autonomous entity and its leaders will tend to enlarge its boundaries – will inevitably come into play. Borrowing a curious formulation, one could see this as 'one countryers' on one side and 'two systemers'[98] on the other – the proponents of sovereignty versus the proponents of autonomy.

In the case of Hong Kong, it appears that sometimes it is the leaders of the autonomous entity – in both in the judiciary and in the executive – who have promoted the interests of the centre in this dialectic. A curious situation indeed and one that is not reassuring for Macau.

However, this analysis should have made clear that despite a degree of elasticity, the words set certain limits. The words of autonomy are the first step in identifying the scope of autonomy but also the last step in setting its outer parameters.

Based on the model of the autonomy as written, the SAR cannot be considered either a traditional autonomous region or as a division of a federated state.[99] There have already been attempts to apply the format to other realities.[100] Even

[97] For further elaboration, see Cardinal, 'Fundamental rights in Macau'; and Cardinal, 'The constitutional layer of protection of fundamental rights in the Macau Special Administrative Region'.

[98] Benny Tai, 'One Country, Two Systems: the two perspectives', *Macau Law Journal*, special issue (2002), 150.

[99] Canas, 'A extensão da autonomia de Macau na comunidade e na Lei', 240. See also, M. Olivetti, 'The Special Administrative Regions of the PRC in comparison with autonomous regions models', in *One Country, Two Systems, Three Legal Orders*, Cardinal and Oliveira (eds.), 777; G. Rolla, 'The development of asymmetric regionalism and the principle of autonomy in the new constitutional systems: a comparative approach', in ibid., 461; and P. Cardinal, 'Continuity and autonomy', 197.

[100] For example, UN officials proposed 'One Country, Two Systems' as a solution to the East Timor issue. It was also considered for problems in the Balkans. Deng Xiaoping foresaw the potential of the format, asserting that it might be useful for the resolution of international disputes, *On the Question of Hong Kong* (Hong Kong: New Horizon Press, 1993).

simply using quantitative analysis or measurement does not make it possible to place the SAR in either of these two categories, since it incorporates elements of both and then goes beyond them.[101] For example, it has elements that usually are found only in sovereign states such as its own currency, a degree of international legal capacity, particularly in maintaining its own emblems such as a flag,[102] its own economic system, an independent taxation system with all revenues allocated solely to the SAR, its own customs system and controls and its own legal system.[103]

Another aspect of the Macau model is the fact that it seems almost blindly copied from the legal framework designed for Hong Kong. In some areas, this has caused difficulties, particularly related to the legal system, since Macau's system is a continental one whereas Hong Kong uses the common law. For example, Article 40 of the Macau Basic Law on the International Covenants has created doubts about whether Macau continues to be a monist system in which the treaties are directly applicable, or has changed to a dualist one, as in Hong Kong, in which the treaties must be transformed into municipal law to become effective. Another example is the creation of the executive order, an act completely unknown before 1999 and one that could result in disruption in the process of production of legal norms.

However, in some other respects copying the Hong Kong SAR legal framework would have worked to strengthen autonomy, as certain rules that could have been imported were not, thus diminishing the scope of Macau's

101 See, for example, Canas, 'A extensão da autonomia de Macau na comunidade e na Lei', 24.

102 Although this issue was previously controversial, there is now a general consensus on it. See for example, Roda Mushkat, 'The international legal personality of Macau', *Hong Kong Law Journal*, 24 (1994), 328, and *One Country, Two International Legal Personalities – the Case of Hong Kong* (Hong Kong University Press, 1997); Cardinal, 'The constitutional layer of protection of fundamental rights in the Macau Special Administrative Region', 212; Susan J. Henders, 'Region-states and the world: China pushes the envelope', in 'Is Ontario a region-state?', *Policy Options*, January-February (2000), 88; James Crawford, *The Creation of States in International Law*, 2nd edn., (Oxford University Press, 2006), 244; Jorge Bacelar Gouveia, *Manual de Direito Internacional Público*, 2nd edn. (Coimbra: Almedina, 2004), 456–7; Filipa Delgado, *Liçdes de Direito Público* [Public International Law], (University of Macau, Faculty of Law), 221–2. Ren Yue, 'Hong Kong in the eyes of the international community', in Joseph Cheng (ed.), *The Hong Kong Special Administrative Region in its First Decade* (Hong Kong Press, 2007), 305: Michael Ramsden and Oliver Jones, *Hong Kong Basic Law – Annotations and Commentary* (Hong Kong: Sweet and Maxwell, 2010), 205.

103 Both Macau and Hong Kong have their own legal systems with their own principles, norms and methods and separate from the legal system of Mainland China, with only limited and listed intersections. On this see for example, Yash Ghai, 'The intersection of Chinese Law and the common law in the Hong Kong Special Administrative Region: question of technique or politics?', *Hong Kong Law Journal*, 37 (2007), 363, Carlos Blanco Morais, 'A organização do poder politico-legislativo no Território de Macau – durante e após a transição para a soberania chinesa' [The organisation of the political-legislative power in the Macau Territory – during and after the transition to Chinese sovereignty], in *Estudos em Homenagem ao Prof. Doutor Rogério Soares* [Essays in homage to Prof. Doctor Rogério Soares] (Coimbra Editora, 2002), 146.

autonomy. A good example is Art. 68 of the Hong Kong Basic Law, which states that the ultimate aim is the election of all the members of the Legislative Council by universal suffrage, whereas in Macau the corresponding article *only* affirms that the Legislative Assembly is to have a majority – not a totality – of elected members.[104]

By contrast, in some cases the words of the Macau Basic Law reflect the particular characteristics of Macau, thus enhancing its autonomy. The reinforcement of fundamental rights mentioned here is one such example. Others are that the Macau SAR 'shall protect, according to law, the interests of residents of Portuguese descent in Macau and shall respect their customs and cultural traditions', that it 'shall establish consultative co-ordination organisations composed of representatives from the government, the employers' organisations and the employees' organisations', and that policies on tourism and recreation should be made 'in the light of its overall interests', reflecting Macau's reliance on the casino industry.[105] Land and natural resources within the Macau Special Administrative Region are state property, except for the private land recognised as such according to the laws in force before the establishment of the Macau SAR.[106] There is no prohibition on the President of the Legislative Assembly or members of the Executive Council, among others, having right of abode in any foreign country, as is the case in Hong Kong.[107]

In terms of the world of leaders and politics, for the centre formally the key role will be played by the NPC Standing Committee through its power to interpret the Basic Law. Of course, the top leaders of the PRC will inevitably have the final say on such matters in practice. On the side of the autonomy, the members of Macau's government, its Legislative Assembly and the judges in its courts will be the decision makers. Civil society will certainly have a role to play as well.

A special mention should be made of the Chief Executive, since the holder of this post has a dual role, acting both as representative of the centre and as protector of the autonomy. Thus, the Chief Executive: (a) acts as the head of the Macau SAR government, the executive organ of the autonomy,[108] and (b) is accountable to the Central People's Government as the head of the Macau SAR and its representative.[109] This means that although the Chief Executive is the top leader of the autonomous region, the post holder also has primary and direct responsibility to the centre, including accountability for the autonomy.

[104] Yash Ghai writes, 'This conservatism is somewhat surprising, for Macau achieved a measure of direct elections in 1976 under the Organic Statute, well ahead of Hong Kong', 'The Basic Law of the Special Administrative Region of Macau: some reflections,' *International and Comparative Law Quarterly*, 49 (2000), 192.

[105] Arts. 42, 115, 118.

[106] The land and natural resources in the Hong Kong SAR are state property without exception.

[107] For more examples, see Ghai, *The Basic Law of the Special Administrative Region of Macau*, 192–5; Wang, 'As características da Lei Básica da Região Administrativa Especial de Macau', 46.

[108] Art. 62. [109] Art. 45.

The Chief Executive has the responsibility and the capacity to determine the scope of autonomy vis-à-vis the centre. In no other person is this dialectical tension so clear and so onerous. Then within the SAR political system the actions of the Chief Executive have enormous potential to reinforce autonomy or to damage it. Also, this person has the responsibility to accommodate the SAR's policies within the PRC, both in acting scrupulously according to the law and in *selling* these policies in Beijing. An act that advances autonomy will undoubtedly need to be explained well to central leaders, otherwise it could very well lead to misunderstanding and conflict.

This discussion leads inevitably to the comparison between the autonomy praxis of Macau and Hong Kong. There has been much criticism of Hong Kong's leaders who have been charged with downgrading the SAR's autonomy. By contrast, assessment of Macau's performance in this regard has been quite positive. Given that the legal framework is almost identical, the reasons for this difference may be found in the people implementing autonomy, rather than in the legal framework for it.

The fact that Hong Kong is much bigger in so many aspects than Macau certainly is one explanation for why China would pay more attention. But this factor can only explain some of the differences. Another issue to be considered is that in Hong Kong civil society – and its outspoken calls for democracy – is clearly stronger than in Macau, despite the fact that Macau enjoyed democratic representation much earlier than Hong Kong. This factor may make the PRC leadership more nervous about Hong Kong. But to fully explain this situation I believe it is necessary to analyse the implementation of policy and the people who implement it. It is commonly agreed that Macau's top leadership has been competent and effective, in contrast to that in Hong Kong.

This does not mean that Macau should not try to become a more important player or that democratisation should not advance there. In this respect, Macau has much to learn from Hong Kong. It is the responsibility of the leaders of the autonomy to solidify the autonomy, and democratisation is evidently important to this process. The impetus for democratisation must come from Macau, as otherwise the current peaceful relations with the centre could, over time, mean a de facto erosion of autonomy.[110] Provided Macau continues to manage to combine the written framework for autonomy with effective leadership, it is possible it can avoid the erosion of autonomy seen in Hong Kong as a result of poor governance.

There are two additional unwritten guarantees for the Macau autonomy that also apply in Hong Kong. One is international monitoring, either institutionalised or by the media in general, and the other is the Taiwan question. While the latter remains unresolved, it operates as a guarantee, in the sense that the success of both Macau and Hong Kong is a card to be played in the game of

[110] For a pessimistic assessment, see Ghai, *The Basic Law of the Special Administrative Region of Macau*, 195.

reunification, an important measure of China's willingness to accommodate different systems in its attempt to attract the compatriots on the other side of the Taiwan Straits. The success will have to be not only economic, but also the safeguarding of extensive autonomy in areas such as the political system and fundamental rights.

13

Autonomy and conflict resolution in Bougainville, Papua New Guinea

Anthony J. Regan

Autonomy – particularly asymmetrical autonomy – is often a response to secessionist conflict. Legal measures for the political reorganisation of space allow groups claiming distinct identity to gain direct control over matters of particular concern to them. The state's territorial integrity is preserved, allowing it to exercise in the autonomous region powers of common interest to all regions.[1]

Bougainville, in the Southwest Pacific state of Papua New Guinea (PNG) has experienced three sets of constitutionally provided autonomies since 1976. Although the first two involved symmetrical autonomy covering Bougainville and PNG's other eighteen provinces PNG's history of autonomy largely involves efforts to resolve conflict concerning Bougainville.

The third autonomy – the main focus here – is provided for under PNG constitutional laws passed in 2002 to implement the Bougainville Peace Agreement of August 2001[2] (the 2001 Agreement), which ended a bitter secessionist conflict in Bougainville that raged from 1988 to 1997. The Agreement provides for both constitutionally agreed asymmetrical autonomy (applicable only to Bougainville and not other PNG provinces), and a deferred referendum on Bougainville's independence. The degree of autonomy available tends to blur PNG's sovereignty, particularly the right to the referendum. The autonomy arrangements involve disaggregating powers and resources previously held by PNG's national government, and include processes intended to ensure they are transferred to the Autonomous Bougainville Government (ABG). Such processes tend to add to the complexity of autonomy arrangements.

At the time of writing (mid 2012) the new autonomy arrangements have operated for the seven years since the ABG was established, through elections in mid 2005 – long enough for a preliminary evaluation to be made of their

[1] Yash Ghai, 'Ethnicity and autonomy: a framework for analysis', in Yash Ghai (ed.), *Autonomy and Ethnicity: Negotiating Competing Claims in Multi-ethnic States* (Cambridge University Press, 2000), 1–26.

[2] Text available at www.c-r.org/our-work/accord/png-bougainville/key-texts37.php (accessed 30 October 2011), or www.usip.org/files/file//resources/collections/peace_agreements/bougain_20010830.pdf (accessed 30 October 2011).

effectiveness. Bougainville's rich experience offers insights into a number of overlapping controversies about autonomy and conflict resolution,[3] including:

- Whether asymmetrical autonomy tends to generate conflict by creating pressure for its extension to all parts of a country, or alternatively, whether conflict is avoided by the tendency towards uniformity across the country;
- Whether autonomy is more difficult to concede and less likely to succeed if state sovereignty is disputed when autonomy is being established;
- Whether the blurring of sovereignty often involved in asymmetrical autonomy is a cause of disputes, or part of solutions to them;
- Whether rather than ending secessionist conflict, autonomy merely defers it, and may even add to it, by encouraging secessionists to choose to progress to independence, or, alternatively, whether autonomy tends to reduce the likelihood of secession;
- Whether autonomy is more difficult to concede and less likely to succeed where the autonomous area is rich in resources;
- Whether international community involvement tends to ensure that autonomy is both accepted as a solution to a conflict and actually implemented, or alternatively, whether such involvement is often just a favourable factor when establishing autonomy, but not capable of ensuring its implementation and success;
- Whether autonomy is more likely to succeed if negotiated in democratic and participatory ways rather than imposed; and in states with established democracy and rule of law tradition, rather than with authoritarian and arbitrary systems of governance; and
- Whether autonomy is more likely to succeed if it includes mechanisms for consultation and negotiation; independent dispute settlement mechanisms; and built-in flexibility to respond to what is inevitably an evolving situation.

Bougainville's experience also illustrates the considerable difficulties involved in implementing and managing complex autonomy, especially where both the state and the autonomous region are weak. It also highlights the significance of the use of constitutional entrenchment to protect autonomy from unilateral change by the central state.

Limited international foundations

The foundations of autonomy under the 2001 Agreement were domestic rather than in international or regional law, treaty arrangements or guarantees. The international community did, however, play a significant role in facilitating the peace process that gave rise to the Agreement, as well as contributing to its

[3] For discussion of some of these, see Ghai, 'Ethnicity and autonomy', and Thomas Benedikter, *The World's Working Regional Autonomies: An Introduction and Comparative Analysis* (London; New York; Delhi: Anthem Press, 2007).

contents (Mainly through mediation).[4] Bougainville leaders envisage a continuing role for the international community in ensuring implementation of the Agreement, a matter of some sensitivity for PNG.

The local foundations of autonomy

Background to autonomy negotiations

Bougainville is a group of islands (two large and many small) several hundred kilometres east of mainland PNG. Bougainville's approximately 250,000 people comprise less than four per cent of PNG's seven million people; its 9,438 square kilometres represents about two per cent of PNG's land area. PNG is a country of unparalleled cultural and linguistic diversity, having well over 800 distinct languages. The same pattern is evident in Bougainville, with twenty-five distinct language groups[5] and considerable differences in culture and identity within larger language groups.[6] Under nominal German colonial control from 1884, with the first colonial station established in 1905, Bougainville came under Australia's control early in World War I.

During the twentieth century Bougainvilleans gradually developed a common identity, the black skin colour of most Bougainvilleans (darker than most people elsewhere in PNG) being the primary marker. A major factor consolidating and politicising identity was resentment about the colonial government's imposition in the 1960s of one of the world's largest copper and gold mines at Panguna in central Bougainville.[7] Bougainvilleans saw the mine, operated by a Rio Tinto majority-owned subsidiary, Bougainville Copper Ltd, as imposed for the benefit of the rest of PNG, with few benefits and high social and environmental costs for Bougainville.[8]

[4] Anthony Regan, 'The Bougainville Intervention: political legitimacy and sustainable peace-building', in Gregory Fry and Tarcisius Kabutaulaka (eds.) *Intervention and State-building: The Legitimacy of 'Cooperative Intervention'* (Manchester University Press, 2008), 184–208, and Anthony Regan, *Light Intervention: Lessons from Bougainville* (Washington, DC: United States Institute of Peace, 2010).

[5] Darrell Tryon, 'The languages of Bougainville', in Anthony Regan, and Helga Griffin (eds.) *Bougainville Before the Conflict* (Canberra: Pandanus, 2003), 31–46.

[6] Eugene Ogan, 'An introduction to Bougainville cultures', and Anthony Regan 'Identities among Bougainvilleans', in Regan and Griffin, *Bougainville Before the Conflict*, 47–56 and 418–46, respectively.

[7] On Bougainvillean identity and its politicisation, see Jill Nash and Eugene Ogan, 'The Red and the Black: Bougainvillean perceptions of other Papua New Guineans', *Pacific Studies* 13: 2 (1990), 1–17; Douglas Oliver, *Black Islanders: A Personal Perspective of Bougainville 1937–1991* (Melbourne: Hyland House, 1991); Yash Ghai and Anthony Regan, 'Bougainville and the dialectics of ethnicity, autonomy and separation', in Ghai, *Autonomy and Ethnicity*, 242–65; Regan, 'Identities Among Bougainvilleans'; and James Tanis, 'Nagovisi villages as a window on Bougainville in 1988', in Regan and Griffin, *Bougainville Before the Conflict*, 447–72.

[8] Much of the extensive literature on the impact of the mine is in the bibliography in Terrence Wesley-Smith, 'Development and crisis in Bougainville: a bibliographic essay', *The Contemporary Pacific* 4, no. 2 (1992), 407–32. More recent studies include James Griffin and Melchior Togolo, 'North Solomons Province, 1974–2000', in Ron May and Anthony Regan

Conflict 1975–6

With the approach of PNG's independence from Australia, Bougainville's sense of a separate identity and resentments about mining enabled educated leaders to mobilise support for enhanced political power and increased mining revenues for Bougainville. In the three years before PNG's independence in September 1975, there was a strong push for Bougainvillean political autonomy. While secessionist demands were initially made as a negotiating tactic rather than a serious claim, many Bougainvilleans came to see secession as the answer to many complex problems.

In 1974, anxious to preserve fragile national unity, PNG made concessions. Disagreements in 1975 over both Bougainville's share of the mining revenue and the unexpected exclusion from PNG's independence Constitution of provision for provincial government led to a unilateral declaration of independence for Bougainville on 1 September 1975, days before PNG's independence. Both sides exercised restraint, PNG largely because of limited coercive capacity, heavy dependence on Bougainville-derived mining revenues and concern about undermining national unity. Bougainville failed to gain any international support for its secession and its leaders recognised they lacked capacity to develop an independent state. So the dispute was resolved by the 1976 Agreement to amend the PNG Constitution to provide for elected provincial governments, which would receive mining royalties and other revenues. While Bougainville wanted to be treated as a unique case, PNG's fears of divisive impacts elsewhere saw provincial governments established in the other eighteen provinces.[9]

The first autonomy arrangements, 1976–90

The 1976 Agreement was implemented through amendments to the PNG Constitution, which also authorised the Organic Law on Provincial Government.[10] These laws provided for a provincial government system implemented uniformly across PNG, with little that was specific to Bougainville's needs. Each

(eds.) *Political Decentralisation in a New State: The Experience of Provincial Government in Papua New Guinea* (Bathurst: Crawford House Press, 1997), 354–82; Don Vernon, 'The Panguna Mine' and Melchior Togolo, 'Torau Response to Change', both in Regan and Griffin, *Bougainville before the Conflict*, 258–273 and 274–290, respectively; and Tanis, 'Nagovisi villages as a window on Bougainville in 1988'.

9 On origins and operation of the provincial government arrangements see Yash Ghai and Anthony Regan, *The Law, Politics and Administration of Decentralisation in Papua New Guinea*, NRI Monograph 30 (Port Moresby: The National Research Institute, 1992) and the literature cited; and May and Regan, *Political Decentralisation*; Yash Ghai and Anthony Regan, 'Unitary state, devolution, autonomy, secession: dialectics of state building and nation building in Bougainville, Papua New Guinea', *The Round Table*, 95: 386 (2006), 589–608; and Ghai and Regan 'Bougainville and the dialectics of ethnicity'. On Bougainville's provincial government, see Griffin and Togolo, 'North Solomons Province'.

10 The PNG Constitution provides for a system of organic laws, authorised to elaborate matters specified in, and entrenched in a manner similar to, the Constitution. Together the Constitution and organic laws are PNG's 'constitutional laws'.

province could, however, make its own sub-national constitution, with considerable room for variation provided basic criteria were met. Bougainville's constitution was unique, and worked well. Further, PNG's only large mine then being in Bougainville, its government alone received significant untied revenue through mining royalties.

Until 1988 provincial government appeared to have ended secessionist pressures. While Bougainville's provincial government had less power than anticipated, it performed reasonably well. As public service capacity was built from a low base, the focus was on basic services and infrastructure, there being limited policy development capacity. Nevertheless it was more effective than other provincial governments and most national level administrative bodies. There was, however, some resentment in Bougainville that the 1976 Agreement was not implemented in full, with PNG increasingly centralising powers as control of state resources quickly became the key to accumulation of personal wealth in PNG. Members of the PNG Parliament (MPs) resented sharing power and resources with elected provincial governments.[11]

At the same time mining brought rapid social and economic change in Bougainville, and its provincial government had little capacity to respond to problems related to breakdown of traditional social structures, high levels of migration from other parts of PNG (seen as resulting in criminal activity and the 'diluting' of Bougainvillean identity) and limited employment and economic advancement opportunities available to Bougainvilleans, especially young males. Despite growing social pressures and widespread but unfocused sympathy for independence, by the late 1980s Bougainville's provincial government still enjoyed strong support. But for the relative success of the provincial government, support for secession would likely have been far stronger in 1988–9 than was actually the case.[12]

Conflict 1988–97

Bougainville's violent conflict 1988–97[13] was not originally a separatist dispute. Initial catalysts involved tensions among some mining area land-owner groups over distribution among them of mining-related revenue, as well as general resentment about the inadequate share of mine revenues they were receiving and anger among young Bougainvillean mine workers about employment opportunities and working conditions. Rejection of such claims led to young land owners and mine workers destroying mine power-lines and other property, the main aim being to bring PNG and Bougainville Copper Ltd to the negotiating table. Poorly judged violent responses from police 'riot squads'

[11] Ghai and Regan, *Law, Politics and Administration*, 'Bougainville and the dialectics of ethnicity', and 'Unitary state'.

[12] Ghai and Regan, 'Unitary State'.

[13] On the origins and course of the conflict, see Regan, *Light Intervention*, 17, especially the references cited in footnote 1.

and the PNG Defence Force generated ethnic resentments, leading to the development of coalitions with other disaffected Bougainvillean groups. From early 1989, these trends encouraged the key leader of both the young land owners and mine workers, Francis Ona, to support independence as a goal, around which he mobilised broad popular support. A widespread separatist rebellion developed rapidly, with the dissidents grouped loosely under the Bougainville Revolutionary Army led by Ona. Violence against non-Bougainvilleans saw most leave Bougainville by early 1990, a form of ethnic cleansing. The mine closed in May 1989, and has not re-opened since. By late 1989 the Bougainville Revolutionary Army had the upper hand in an escalating guerrilla conflict. In March 1990 PNG Defence Force personnel left Bougainville under a ceasefire arrangement, with police personnel unexpectedly departing at the same time. In May 1990 Ona issued Bougainville's second unilateral declaration of independence, prompting PNG to impose a sea and air blockade and suspend Bougainville's provincial government.

With all formal government ceasing to operate, the loosely organised Bougainville Revolutionary Army was not equipped to take effective control, though it attempted to do so. A semi-anarchic situation developed. Localised conflict (usually involving such issues as land and personal disputes) saw local Bougainville Revolutionary Army elements divide in many areas. As early as September 1990 communities at risk in local conflict called on the PNG Defence Force to return. As armed groups opposing the Bougainville Revolutionary Army developed links they became known as the Bougainville Resistance Forces. Leadership of this armed grouping and the communities from which it emerged tended to oppose secession, fearing independence under the Bougainville Revolutionary Army. Hence the increasingly bitter and destructive separatist conflict developed two main dimensions – PNG versus Bougainville Revolutionary Army, and *intra* Bougainville conflict, with many localised conflicts within and between communities.

The second autonomy arrangements, 1999–2005

Growing opposition by MPs to the provincial government system came to a head in 1995. Under amendments to the PNG Constitution and a new Organic Law on Provincial Governments and Local-level Governments, elected provincial governments were replaced by new bodies comprising mainly the MPs and heads of local government in each province. Provincial government autonomy was reduced significantly – sub-national constitutions were abolished (uniform provisions on provincial structures were now contained in PNG laws), provincial powers were reduced and PNG control powers increased.

Shortly before these constitutional changes were made, Bougainville's provincial government, suspended since mid 1990, had been reinstated on the urging of moderate Bougainvilleans seeking to negotiate autonomy as the solution to the conflict. Recognising that the reduced autonomy available under the

1995 provincial reforms was inconsistent with these efforts, PNG delayed the 1995 Organic Law coming into operation in Bougainville until 1997, when it was expected that special autonomy arrangements would have been finalised. So the 1977 Organic Law continued to operate there (the 1995 Organic Law applying elsewhere in PNG). But when new autonomy arrangements had still not been agreed in 1997, the interim arrangements for Bougainville had to be extended temporarily. With a peace process under way from mid 1997 (outlined later) it was expected that they might continue to be extended from time to time until a peace agreement was finalised. Unexpectedly an attempt to make such an extension in late 1998 failed, and as a result the 1995 reforms operated in Bougainville from 1999 until 2005 when the ABG was established.[14]

There are several ironies in the story of the 1995 reforms. First, they were possible mainly because of the extended period of suspension of Bougainville's provincial government (1990–5) – for until its suspension the strongest support for a high level of provincial autonomy had always come from Bougainville. Second, despite severe misgivings that what had been agreed in 1976 was being abolished unilaterally, Bougainville's moderate provincial leaders did not oppose the 1995 reforms, because they were negotiating asymmetrical autonomy arrangements for Bougainville alone, and never expected the 1995 reforms to apply there. Third, while the operation of the reforms was accepted in Bougainville from 1999 as politically expedient (many aspects of the reforms were never implemented there) the reduced autonomy involved was resented and became one of the 'benchmarks' the Bougainville parties used when negotiating increased autonomy under the 2001 Agreement.

Peace process 1997–2006

A peace process began in mid 1997,[15] moderate leaders of opposing Bougainville factions taking the initiative with some PNG support. While the Bougainville Revolutionary Army had achieved military advantage over PNG, most of its leaders recognised that complete victory would take time and would be deeply divisive. A moderate leadership long committed to a negotiated settlement came into power in mid 1997 after 'hard-line' leaders lost office following failed efforts to use foreign mercenaries to defeat the Bougainville Revolutionry Army.[16]

In mid 1997 Bougainville factions met in New Zealand and agreed to negotiate jointly with PNG. Late in 1997 the Bougainville factions met representatives of PNG, beginning an extended process that produced the 2001 Agreement. From early 1998 the whole process was opposed by the original Bougainville

[14] Regan, *Light Intervention*, 50–2.

[15] On the origins and development of the peace process, see Regan, *Light Intervention*, 27–62 and the references cited.

[16] On the Sandline mercenary affair and its impacts, see Regan, *Light Intervention*, 32–4 and the references cited.

Revolutionary Army leader, Francis Ona, and the minority of the armed group's former members and supporters who continued to follow him.[17] Ona claimed Bougainville was already independent under his 1990 unilateral declaration of independence. His opposition added to the difficulties of a complex peace process, but with a clear majority of the Bougainville Revolutionary Army supporting peace, Ona was never strong enough to actively oppose the process.

The parties (PNG and Bougainville factions) invited an international community intervention – mainly an unarmed regional military group led by New Zealand and Australia, as well as a small United Nations observer mission – that played vital roles, including providing the secure environment in which mutually suspicious parties learned to work together; facilitating the process; truce and cease-fire monitoring; providing legal and other advisors to parties to the negotiations; implementing weapons disposal arrangements; and mediating divisive issues.[18]

While the process could not have succeeded without that intervention, in general the parties remained in control as it moved forward. Their commitment to it and to the goal of achieving a political settlement remained strong throughout, something critical to the subsequent record of implementing the 2001 Agreement being generally positive (though not without some problems, as discussed later). Further, on both sides, considerable efforts (through consultation and participatory processes) were made to develop broad-based support for negotiating positions and for what was agreed on in several stages of negotiations.[19]

The 2001 Agreement: challenging and blurring sovereignty

Ending the violent conflict through the peace process involved negotiations far longer and more difficult than in 1976. Although PNG was no longer dependent on Bougainville's mineral wealth (the mine had long been closed and other major resource projects elsewhere in PNG were by then providing significant revenues), there was still PNG concern that Bougainville, as a small part of PNG, should not retain all Bougainville-derived mining revenue. Fear of special arrangements for Bougainville setting precedents elsewhere in PNG was a major concern. On the Bougainville side, there were deep divisions between those committed to the earliest possible independence, and others committed to continued integration into PNG. Intra-Bougainville negotiations in May–June 1999 produced a compromise documented in a 'combined' Bougainville negotiating position demanding significant autonomy (almost confederal in nature), and a referendum on independence deferred for three to

17 Reuben Siara, 'The time is now', in Rebecca Adams (ed.), *Gudpela Nius Bilong Pis. Peace on Bougainville: Truce Monitoring Group* (Wellington: Victoria University Press, 2001), 125–30; Regan, *Light Intervention*, 47–50.

18 Regan, *Light Intervention*, 63–84 and the references cited.

19 Regan, *Light Intervention*, Chapter 3, 55–61.

five years.[20] In addition, Bougainville sought demilitarisation of the province, and a high level of protection for the package of arrangements through their constitutionalisation.

That position largely set the agenda for the more than two years of negotiations that preceded that Agreement. To a considerable degree that 2001 Agreement is consistent with the initial Bougainville position, despite numerous modifications agreed during the negotiations.

PNG saw both the autonomy and referendum demands as challenging its sovereignty. On the referendum issue, more than eighteen months of intense negotiations almost ended in stalemate before a compromise was reached through mediation by then Australian Minister for Foreign Affairs, Alexander Downer. Late in 2000 he persuaded the Bougainville leaders to agree both to an increased period of deferral of the referendum (ten to fifteen years after autonomy began) and to drop their demand for a constitutional right to move to independence if the referendum resulted in a vote in favour of independence. Instead the outcome of such a vote would be negotiated, with the PNG Parliament having ultimate authority. This, Downer advised PNG, would preserve state sovereignty. At the same time he reminded the Bougainvilleans that although the East Timorese had no constitutional right to independence from Indonesia at the time of their referendum of 1998, the international community had ensured that an overwhelming vote in favour of independence was honoured. The Bougainvilleans took that as an assurance that the international community would play a similar role in Bougainville, while PNG saw Downer as supporting its right to reject a vote in favour of independence. These starkly different views have not yet been resolved, giving rise to possibilities of conflict over the referendum outcome.[21]

In seeking to end the secessionist conflict by combining arrangements for both significant autonomy and a referendum on independence, the 2001 Agreement does more than blur PNG sovereignty (as is often the case with asymmetrical autonomy). In fact the Agreement keeps alive Bougainville's challenge to sovereignty, not only through the guarantee of a referendum on independence but also other provisions, notably those concerning effective demilitarisation of Bougainville (including significant limits on PNG troop deployments); vesting of some 'foreign affairs–type' powers in the ABG; and an ABG veto on amendments to constitutional provisions giving effect to the Agreement.

In the referendum that must be held between ten and fifteen years after the first ABG election Bougainvilleans will vote on the future political status of the

[20] Anthony Regan, 'Resolving two dimensions of conflict and division: the dynamics of consent, consensus and compromise', in *Accord*, 12 (*Weaving Consensus: The Papua New Guinea – Bougainville Peace Process*) (London: Conciliation Resources, 2002), 36–43; Regan, *Light Intervention*, 85–8.

[21] Regan, *Light Intervention*, 88–90.

territory,[22] with the choices offered including independence for Bougainville.[23] Thus the referendum will be between mid 2015 and mid 2020, on a date to be agreed between Bougainville and PNG, taking account of progress with weapons disposal and the ABG's standard of governance.

PNG's reluctant concession of the unusual combination of constitutionally guaranteed referendum and complex asymmetrical autonomy[24] was, in part, based on the hope that the benefits of autonomy would encourage Bougainvilleans to vote against separation.[25] For Bougainville, although PNG's fiscal crisis at the time of the negotiations saw PNG refuse generous financial commitments of the kind France was making under similar arrangements intended to resolve conflict in its southwest Pacific colonial territory of New Caledonia, it was expected that as economic circumstances improved, PNG would allocate greater resources in an effort to generate Bougainvillean support for continued integration into PNG.

Demilitarisation is provided for through complex and closely interrelated provisions requiring: withdrawal from Bougainville of PNG Defence Force and police riot squad personnel; limits on future Defence Force deployment without Bougainville approval; disposal of weapons by Bougainvillean factions; and immunity from prosecution for all combatants for conflict-related offences.[26]

Turning to constitutionalisation (details of which are outlined later), Bougainville's reasons for accepting constitutional entrenchment as the main protection of what was agreed require comment. Initially bitterness towards PNG and its Constitution, generated by the years of violent conflict, saw Bougainville secessionists reluctant to negotiate anything short of guaranteed independence, to be achieved as early as possible. It was two years into the peace process before they were convinced of the need for an accommodation with Bougainvilleans committed to integration into PNG, in the June 1999 compromise 'combined' Bougainville negotiating position. Secessionist leaders were eventually (though reluctantly) persuaded to accept constitutional guarantees, due to PNG's reasonable record of longevity of, and adherence to,[27] and its Supreme Court's positive record of interpreting and enforcing, the Constitution, often against the government of the day. In addition the Bougainvilleans

22 Constitution ss.338–43, and Organic Law, ss.52–63 and Schedule 1.

23 The ABG legislature can decide that the referendum shall not be held (PNG Constitution, s.338(7)).

24 Similar combinations were agreed in agreements for New Caledonia (1998) and South Sudan (2005).

25 Anthony Regan, 'The Bougainville political settlement and the prospects for sustainable peace', *Pacific Economic Bulletin* 17:1 (2002), 114–29.

26 Art. 329 (and Arts. 5 to 10 of the Plan it endorses); Arts. 62–4; and Art. 331.

27 There has been constitutional continuity for the more than thirty-six years since PNG's independence, in 1975. As discussed elsewhere in this chapter, however, a major constitutional crisis developing in PNG from mid 2011 raises serious concerns about constitutional stability in PNG and appears to have significantly undermined the role of the Supreme Court as constitutional arbiter, developments that could possibly have major implications for Bougainvillean support for the Peace Agreement.

expected the international community to remain engaged, monitoring adherence to any agreement.

Purposes of autonomy

Resolving conflict

The 2001 Agreement aimed to resolve both the ethno-nationalist secessionist dispute between Bougainville and PNG and divides among Bougainvilleans. The conflict had strengthened the pre-existing sense of a common Bougainvillean identity distinct from the rest of PNG, ironically even among pro-integrationists. In general Bougainvilleans agreed that they should manage their own affairs without external interference, either under high levels of autonomy (for the pro-integrationists) or independence (for the secessionists). Having reached an intra-Bougainville compromise on the package combining autonomy and referendum they held a common view of the purpose of autonomy being a high degree of separation, rather than integration into PNG, and the protection of their rights as a minority. But those supporting secession also saw autonomy as just a stage leading to independence.

Largely because Bougainvilleans comprise a small minority in PNG, in a defined and remote geographical area where they constitute an overwhelming majority, the 2001 Agreement focused on territorial autonomy rather than, for example, power sharing within PNG government, or proportionality in national public sector institutions. Further, while the influx of migrants from elsewhere in PNG contributed to ethnic tensions in Bougainville in the 1980s, the effective 'ethnic cleansing' of 1989–90 resulted in Bougainvillean negotiators seeing little need to consider ethnic minorities within Bougainville in the 2001 Agreement. The position has changed, however, since 2001, there being growing concern in Bougainville not only about people from elsewhere in PNG settling in Bougainville, but also increasing presence of foreign citizens, notably Chinese.

Reflecting the goal of ending a bitter civil war and resolving the divisions it caused, the autonomy was explicitly asymmetrical, for Bougainville only. PNG recognised that the Agreement was a necessary condition of ending violence, and part of a process of peace-building, as is explicitly recognised in the name of one of the implementing constitutional laws – the Organic Law on Peacebuilding in Bougainville: Autonomous Bougainville Government and Bougainville Referendum (the Organic Law).

Since 2001 some wealthier provinces elsewhere in PNG have demanded that aspects of the Bougainville autonomy arrangements be extended to them, demands reflecting not so much tensions over any unfairness of asymmetry – there is widespread recognition that Bougainville is a special the case – but rather dissatisfaction with reduced provincial autonomy under the 1995 reforms. These developments have generated concern in PNG about autonomy potentially being divisive, and tend to reinforce PNG concerns that too much may have been conceded to Bougainville in the 2001 Agreement. Such trends probably help to explain PNG reluctance to implement aspects of autonomy discussed elsewhere in this chapter.

Social structures, identities and local autonomy

Autonomy was also seen as creating room for other autonomies within Bougainville, especially for its many small-scale communities and identities. Issues of local autonomy were made acute by the bitter localised conflict of 1988–97.[28] When Bougainville's sub-national constitution was developed from 2002 to 2004, provision was made not only for recognition of such autonomies, but also possible autonomy for three main regional groupings – south, central and north of Bougainville.[29] These regional identities reflect the impacts of uneven colonial development. The better educated and more developed north, where there were the highest levels of economic and social integration of communities into PNG, had long had a particularly strong sense of a distinct identity. The preponderance of pro-integration sentiment in that region during the conflict contributed to some ongoing inter-regional tensions that were sometimes difficult to manage during the peace process.

Autonomies within Bougainville have in fact received little attention since the ABG was established, mainly because of a marked reduction in intra-Bougainville tensions associated with implementation of the Peace Agreement and the expansion of economic development in Bougainville.[30] There is, however, a pre-existing Bougainville system of local government (councils of elders) that seeks to integrate local traditional authorities into small-scale local government bodies,[31] which the ABG recognises and supports.[32] However, because of limits in both financial resources and capacity of personnel, the considerable potential of the councils of elders has not yet been realised.

Constitutional provisions for autonomy within PNG

Having decided to pursue a high degree of constitutional protection of the Agreement, the Bougainville negotiators argued for two main elements. First, as much as possible of the Agreement should be constitutionalised. Second, constitutionalisation had to involve protection of the arrangements from

28 Ogan, 'An introduction to Bougainville cultures', Regan, 'Identities among Bougainvilleans', and Anthony Regan, 'The Bougainville conflict: political and economic agendas', in Karen Ballentine and Jake Sherman (eds) *The Political Economy of Armed Conflict: Beyond Greed & Grievance* (Boulder, CO: Lynne Rienner Publishers, 2003), 133–66.

29 Regan, *Identities among Bougainvilleans*, pp 439–42.

30 There is a partial exception involving localised violent conflict in the far south of Bougainville. Regan, *Light Intervention*, 121–6.

31 Anthony Regan, '"Traditional leaders" and conflict resolution in Bougainville: reforming the present by re-writing the past?', in Sinclair Dinnen and Allison Ley (eds.), *Reflections on Violence in Melanesia* (Canberra: Hawkins Press/Asia Pacific Press, 2000), 290–304.

32 Bougainville Constitution, s.49(2).

unilateral change by PNG. Despite initial PNG resistance based on sovereignty, both elements were eventually agreed.

It was agreed, however, that some aspects would not be constitutionalised. For example, PNG regarded the limits on its defence powers as so sensitive that explicit provision was made not to include them in law.[33] Nevertheless, Bougainville was concerned that the non-constitutionalised parts should not be forgotten (as had occurred with aspects of the 1976 Agreement). Two main approaches were agreed.

First, the Agreement itself was made an aid to interpretation for courts interpreting both the PNG Constitution provisions giving effect to the Agreement and the new Organic Law.[34] Second, much of what is provided by those constitutional laws must be done 'in accordance with' the Agreement, thereby requiring that it must be read together with relevant provisions of those laws. Such requirements can have significant substantive effect. For example the legislative subject of 'defence' (in relation to Bougainville) is vested in PNG,[35] 'subject to [. . .] the Agreement',[36] which itself contains significant limitations on PNG exercise of such powers. For example, PNG Defence Force personnel carrying out the limited defence functions allowed in Bougainville can only be deployed (in most instances) after consultation with the ABG and are to be 'unarmed'.[37] The effect of s.289(1) is to import into the Constitution the restrictions in the Agreement.

Turning to the question of protecting arrangements from unilateral change, inclusion in the PNG constitutional laws of most matters provided for in the Agreement itself offers a high degree of protection from change, such provisions being both difficult to make and to change.[38] But because of suspicions resulting from the experience of the conflict, and Bougainvillean perceptions that constitutional provisions giving effect to the 1976 Agreement had been repealed unilaterally and invalidly in 1995, Bougainville insisted on a further level of protection. It came to be called 'double entrenchment'. No proposed amendment to constitutional laws implementing the Agreement becomes law unless approved by the ABG legislature.[39]

Relationship of Bougainville and national constitutions

Bougainville sought an autonomy that gave it both the freedom to choose its own government structures, reflecting local needs, and protection of those choices from unilateral change by PNG. Apart from protection from outside

[33] Arts. 62 to 67, the provision on limits on deployment being 65(b).

[34] Agreement, Art. 3, and PNG Constitution s.278(3). [35] PNG Constitution (s.289(2)(d).

[36] S.289(1). [37] Agreement, Arts. 65(a)(iv) and 64.

[38] They require special majorities and procedures, and two separate votes in the PNG Parliament separated by at least two months.

[39] PNG Constitution ss.345–6. The complex procedure for ABG approval is provided for in the Bougainville Constitution, ss.217–18.

interference, concerns here included symbolism and enhancing legitimacy of the autonomy arrangements for Bougainvilleans. With some limitations, PNG negotiators were open to such concerns.

It was therefore agreed that Bougainville should have its own sub-national constitution establishing its autonomous government. The PNG Constitution is the source of legal authority for the Bougainville Constitution, which is the 'supreme law' in matters over which Bougainville has jurisdiction.[40] Hence the PNG Constitution itself provides that the Bougainville Constitution prevails over national laws dealing with matters in Bougainville's jurisdiction. It is the PNG constitutional laws, however, rather than the Bougainville Constitution that provide for ABG powers and funding and its relations with PNG. In general the Bougainville Constitution is restricted to providing 'for the organization and structures of the government for Bougainville under the autonomy arrangements in a manner consistent with this Part [of the PNG Constitution] and with the [2001] Agreement'.[41] The Bougainville Constitution must meet basic requirements such as democracy and good governance. However, the main point where PNG could question adherence to such standards was when deciding whether or not to endorse the Constitution after it was initially made by Bougainville-controlled processes. Finally, although PNG must be notified about proposed amendments to the Bougainville Constitution,[42] and may require consultation on them, it has no authority to amend that law.

Constitution-making power of the autonomous region

Bougainville's negotiators saw the authority to make their own constitution as an essential aspect of autonomy that would ensure that the ABG reflected Bougainvillean concerns and interests. PNG's concern was to ensure that the constitution met the basic requirements of the Agreement. A multi-stage constitution-making process resulted.

A broadly representative Bougainville Constitutional Commission consulted the people of Bougainville and developed constitutional proposals,[43] beginning in September 2002 and completing a draft Constitution and explanatory report in July 2004.[44] A constituent assembly representing all sectors of the population considered the draft Constitution, and amended and adopted it (September to November 2004).[45] National government endorsement of the draft was required prior to it coming into effect, the only grounds for refusal being failure to meet the requirements of the 2001 Agreement.[46] To avoid disagreements, both the Constitutional Commission and the Constituent Assembly were required to

[40] PNG Constitution s.286(1). [41] S.280. [42] S.287. [43] S.281.

[44] Bougainville Constitutional Commission, *Report of the Bougainville Constitutional Commission: Report on the Third and Final Draft of the Bougainville Constitution* (Arawa and Buka, mimeo, July 2004).

[45] S.284. [46] s.285.

consult PNG as they developed their proposals.[47] That consultative process was difficult, as elements of the PNG bureaucracy sought to undermine the 2001 Agreement, and intervention by senior PNG ministers was required to avert such efforts. Endorsement occurred in December 2004.

The constitution-making process was well received in Bougainville. It enabled many thousands to participate, and generated extensive debate, all contributing to public knowledge, and legitimacy, of the constitution, as well as some unusual features.

Constitutional provisions ensuring implementation[48]

Bougainville's negotiators had a particular focus on implementation of the Agreement that resulted from their awareness of three main issues. One was the incomplete implementation of the 1976 Agreement, a repeat of which they sought to avoid. A second was the fact that parts of the PNG bureaucracy opposed autonomy and could be expected to seek to block implementation of what their political masters conceded. Another was PNG's unstable national politics, which could possibly bring a less sympathetic government to power after the Agreement was signed. Hence they sought not only measures likely to ensure that the Agreement would initially be implemented (through constitutional amendments and the establishing of the ABG), but also others intended to ensure that despite the difficulties inherent in establishing a disaggregating autonomy, implementation of the transfer of powers and resources would occur in the longer term. For its part PNG was open to the Bougainville concerns, but had its own interest in ensuring disarming of the Bougainville factions prior to the ABG being established. A complex package of provisions intended to encourage implementation at different stages emerged from these various concerns.

As for initial implementation of the Agreement, both sides were given incentives to implement obligations that they might otherwise have been reluctant to undertake. Creative linkages were provided between provisions for: disarming by Bougainville's factions; withdrawal of PNG security forces from Bougainville; and constitutionalising and implementing of the referendum and autonomy arrangements. In particular, obligations on armed factions to undertake the first in a three-stage weapons disarming process (storage in single-locked containers) arose only on PNG both making the constitutional amendments implementing the Agreement and withdrawing its forces from Bougainville.

[47] Ss.281 and 284.

[48] Some aspects of autonomy discussed here are analysed further in Anthony Regan, 'Bougainville/Papua New Guinea', KREDDHA Autonomy Mapping Project: www.kreddha.org/mapping/downloads/080212_Bougainville.pdf(accessed 26 March, 2013); and Anthony Regan, 'Resolving the Bougainville self-determination dispute: autonomy or complex power-sharing?', in *Settling Self-determination Disputes: Complex Power-sharing in Theory and Practice*, Marc Weller and Barbara Metzger (eds.) (Leiden: Martinus Nijhoff Publishers, 2008).

However, once passed by the PNG Parliament, the constitutional amendments did not come into operation until the UN observer mission verified completion of stage two of disarming (storage of weapons in double-locked containers, with one key held by the UN). Lack of substantial compliance with the agreed process would have empowered the UN mission to delay ABG elections at the request of either party to the Agreement.[49]

These linkages worked reasonably, providing powerful incentives to PNG to withdraw its forces and pass the constitutional laws giving effect to the Agreement (the latter step achieved by early 2002). A UN supervised disarmament process, 2001–5, removed a significant proportion of weapons held by the Bougainville factions. An unknown, but significant, proportion of weapons remained (a major factor in localised conflict in south Bougainville 2006–11).[50] Through the linking and sequencing, however, each side agreed to implement steps that were to some degree against its interests.

The Agreement also provided for direct Bougainvillean involvement in key aspects of its initial implementation. One involved participation in a joint PNG-Bougainville working group overseeing drafting of the constitutional laws. A second involved Bougainville's control of the processes for making its own constitution. There were also incentives for implementation through provision for a system of dispute resolution during the implementation period (the period leading up to the establishing of the ABG). This system involved referring disputes to a neutral third party, with action in court as a last resort. The international community also had roles in implementation. One involved a requirement that PNG table the Agreement in the UN Security Council,[51] which the Bougainvilleans saw as applying pressure to PNG to comply with the Agreement. Also significant in encouraging implementation was the continuing involvement of international bodies: the UN mission remained until mid 2005, and the regional Peace Monitoring Group until mid 2003.

Whilst most aspects of initial implementation took longer than expected, in general PNG's record to 2005 was good. Implementation was accepted as a joint process.

In relation to provisions intended to encourage implementation in the longer term, the Bougainvilleans envisaged that considerable pressure would be provided by constitutionalisation of the detail of arrangements. Further, oversight of implementation was made a joint ABG/PNG responsibility, vested in the Joint Supervisory Body, a body comprising equal numbers of Bougainvillean and PNG representatives. Required to meet at least twice per year,[52] the Joint Supervisory Body is also a dispute resolution body, a

[49] For more detailed discussion of these arrangements, see Anthony Regan, 'External versus internal incentives in peace processes: the Bougainville experience', *Accord*, 19 (2008), 44–9, and Regan, *Light Intervention*, 92–3.

[50] For discussion of these issues see Regan, *Light Intervention*, 95–9 and 127–32.

[51] Agreement, Art. 334.

[52] Agreement Arts. 263–4; Constitution s.332.

role with significant potential importance in relation to implementation. In practice, although it was established promptly in 2005 and met as frequently as required until 2011 (it met just once in that year, and to mid 2012 had not met, despite several attempts to arrange meetings), the Joint Supervisory Body has been little utilised by the ABG to deal with major concerns about implementation (e.g. slow progress in transfer of powers) or implementation disputes.

Interpretation of constitutional autonomy provisions

The dispute settlement provisions envisage a role for courts, and in the process of dealing with such disputes issues about interpretation of the constitutional provisions for autonomy may arise. Under the PNG Constitution any such issue must be referred to the PNG Supreme Court.[53] In addition, provincial governments and the ABG are among the governmental bodies able to refer constitutional issues to the Supreme Court.[54] Since the early 1980s, provincial governments in other parts of PNG in dispute with the national government over constitutional arrangements have used such references, the Supreme Court often playing creative roles, balancing the interests of the levels of government.[55] Although there have already been several disputes with PNG where the ABG has considered seeking constitutional rulings (most notably concerning PNG failure to pay the 2010–11 restoration and development grants), to date no constitutional references have actually been taken to the Supreme Court.

Institutions of autonomy

Bougainville institutions

The Bougainville Constitution provides for an autonomous government composed of a wide range of institutions, in some respects similar to the PNG government. They include its own legislature, executive, judiciary, electoral authority, ombudsman, human rights commission, audit institution, administrative bodies (public service, police, correctional service) and so on. The arrangements are in many respects innovative, but other than those concerning legislative, executive and electoral institutions, most have not been implemented, due mainly to severe financial and personnel limitations facing the ABG. Until Bougainville institutions are established, PNG equivalents retain their roles in Bougainville. In the process of establishing these additional institutions, the ABG is required to include PNG nominees in the appointment body (the Senior Appointments Committee) established under the Bougainville Constitution.[56]

[53] S.18 [54] S.19 [55] Ghai and Regan, *Decentralisation in Papua New Guinea.*
[56] PNG Constitution s.321, Bougainville Constitution s.102.

Special arrangements apply to the public service and police service, with members of the PNG public service and police being assigned to carry out ABG functions through a Bougainville Administration and a Bougainville Police Service under ABG control, with the autonomous powers of the ABG over these bodies intended to increase gradually in response to ABG requests to a point where it will have its own separate public service and police service. The head of the Administration must be an ABG appointee,[57] and the head of the police an ABG nominee appointed by the PNG Police Commissioner.[58]

The ABG House of Representatives and executive began operating as soon as the autonomous government was established in mid 2005. Called the President, the head of the executive is elected by a Bougainville-wide electorate as a symbol of Bougainville unity, and has similar powers to a prime minister heading a parliamentary executive. Ministers (who, with the President, form the Bougainville Executive Council) are selected by the President from within the legislature, subject to some limits to ensure representation of women and the three regions of Bougainville (north, central and south). Reflecting strong pressure for change in women's roles in public life, three women are elected for regional seats in the legislature, with all voters eligible to vote. Similar arrangements apply to election of three former combatants, reflecting concern that those who were directly involved in the secessionist conflict have a voice in government in the period until the referendum. There are also thirty-three single-member local constituencies. Voting is by the limited preferential system that has been applied to PNG national elections since 2002 (other than for the first election in 2005, when the 'first-past-the-post' system was utilised).

Arrangements for the legislature and executive have operated reasonably well. Two general elections (2005 and 2010) and a presidential by-election (2008) have been successfully conducted by ABG electoral authorities with PNG and donor support. Because of a combination of both slow progress in transfer of powers from PNG and limited policy-making capacity in the ABG, most laws so far passed by the House of Representatives have dealt with ABG structures and processes rather than policy initiatives. The legislature has established a system of committees, but has demonstrated limited capacity to hold the executive accountable.

An emphasis on calls made by Bougainvilleans during the consultative constitution-making process for democratic and accountable governance saw inclusion in the Bougainville Constitution of provisions for: recall of members of the legislature; plebiscites for popular consultation on major issues; citizen-initiated legislation; enforceable leadership code arrangements much strengthened by comparison with equivalent provision in the PNG Constitution; and the ombudsman and human rights bodies already mentioned. However, recognising the likelihood of limited ABG fiscal resources for some years to come, the Constitution provides that these and other arrangements should 'evolve'

[57] Organic Law s.14. [58] Organic Law s.26(1).

gradually, as resources become available.[59] There is little likelihood of such funds being available in the period before the referendum must be held (2020), unless large-scale mining resumes, a possibility that the ABG has been gradually exploring since about 2006.

Aspects of arrangements for shared responsibility over key ABG appointments have contributed to tensions between PNG and the ABG. A major dispute arose over ABG power to appoint its senior public servant. Although the Organic Law[60] clearly vests that power in the ABG, subject only to a requirement to consult the head of the relevant PNG agency, no appointment was possible for about thirty months, from mid 2007 to late 2010, due to PNG insistence that the constitutional laws were silent on the issue, making PNG the appointing authority. The issue was not entirely resolved by unilateral ABG action to make its own appointment. Another problem concerned the need for ABG nomination of the head of the Bougainville Police Service, which has been ignored in the two appointments made since the ABG was established. Yet another involved the failure of PNG to nominate its representatives on the ABG Senior Appointments Committee, despite numerous requests from the ABG. This has prevented the ABG from appointing its Bougainville Electoral Commissioner. Instead it has been forced to make several six-month 'acting' appointments to the office.

The extremely weak capacity of the Bougainville Administration reduces the ability of the ABG to make effective use of the provisions on institutions. The very limited funding made available to the ABG under the autonomy arrangements makes it difficult for the ABG to take practical steps to deal with the capacity deficit.

Relations between national and autonomous institutions

Concern about the extent of PNG control of provincial governments under the 1976 Agreement and the 1995 reforms saw Bougainville's negotiations insist on minimum PNG powers to intervene in ABG affairs. Despite initial controversy, it was eventually agreed that PNG would not have the powers to withdraw or suspend ABG powers; to veto, disallow, or review ABG laws; or to suspend the ABG itself.[61] PNG does, however, have limited authority to withhold ABG funding if audit of PNG grants discloses systematic abuse.[62] There have so far been no significant difficulties in the operation of these arrangements.

Intervention limits relate mainly to ABG exercise of legislative or executive authority, and are in contrast to more co-operative arrangements applying to any judicial or administrative bodies, or other independent constitutional offices that the ABG establishes. These arrangements reflect PNG interests in avoiding excessive costs for ABG institutions, and in maintaining key features of

[59] PNG Constitution s.208.

[60] s.14. [61] PNG Constitution, s.331. [62] PNG Constitution, s.329; Organic Law s.51.

a single national legal and administrative system, thereby reducing the centrifugal forces it was feared would emerge from the degree of autonomy Bougainville demanded. For Bougainville, co-operative arrangements were to some degree seen as the price for achieving key demands such as the referendum and limited PNG intervention powers.

The ABG is empowered to establish courts, operating either wholly under Bougainville law, or under a mixture of both Bougainville and PNG law.[63] Such courts can include an equivalent to the highest PNG court of unlimited jurisdiction hearing cases in the first instance (the National Court), with appeals going to the PNG Supreme Court. This degree of incorporation was agreed in part because of Bougainville's small size and limited revenues and capacity. Further, the fact that the PNG Supreme Court would exercise the interpretative jurisdiction concerning the constitutional provisions giving effect to autonomy meant there could be advantages in linkages giving that Court some understanding of the Bougainville situation.

Concerning administrative bodies, if the ABG chooses to establish separate public service, police or correctional institutions, then management, work value criteria, pay standards and classifications and so on must be compatible with equivalent PNG bodies. As for independent constitutional offices, as already discussed, PNG is guaranteed roles in Bougainville-controlled procedures for making appointments of the senior officers in all such bodies.

Division of powers

The 2001 Agreement and the laws giving effect to it provide for a complex scheme for dividing responsibility for powers and functions in relation to Bougainville between PNG and the ABG, but also for their transfer to the ABG. Before 2005, most of these powers were vested in PNG. The expectation was that only some time after its establishment would the ABG develop the resources and capacity required to exercise many of the functions and powers outlined in the Agreement.

Similarly to the situation under the 1976 Agreement, Bougainville negotiators pushed for the maximum level of powers to be vested in the ABG, initially insisting that only defence, foreign affairs and currency should be reserved to PNG. It took months of negotiations for them to accept that additional powers should be vested at the national level, rather than all Bougainville powers being vested in the ABG whenever Bougainville determined it wished to exercise them, and that instead there first needed to be attention given to assessing ABG capacity, plans for building capacity to be developed jointly with the national government.

This approach of demanding the vesting of the maximum level of powers in the autonomous region's government is a common experience in developing

[63] PNG Constitution s.306(2).

autonomies elsewhere in the world. On the basis of Bougainville's experience under both the 1976 and 2001 agreements, major factors here include the symbolism of the autonomous region having powers as close as possible to those of an independent state, and awareness that the initial negotiation of autonomy is likely to be a one-off opportunity for pressuring an otherwise hostile national government into making major concessions. There are, however, problems inherent in this approach, as making available significant powers can put obstacles in the way of the autonomous government developing realistic plans based on assessment of real levels of resources and capacity, and can raise false expectations of what can be managed under autonomy (as occurred with Bougainville's provincial government under the 1976 Agreement).

Seventeen powers in relation to Bougainville are vested in PNG, mainly concerning international relations or maintaining the integrity of the state and of a single economic system.[64] These include defence and foreign affairs, external migration, currency, central banking, customs, international trade, international shipping and international civil aviation. The vesting in PNG is subject to some reservations to the ABG.

Three main categories of powers are vested in, or available to, the ABG. The first is the functions and powers of the Bougainville provincial government immediately preceding the ABG, which were vested in the ABG as soon as it was established.[65] These are mainly the same functions and powers held by provincial governments elsewhere in PNG,[66] related mainly to service delivery (e.g., health, education, agriculture and livestock extension and capital works construction) and some additional powers, particularly local level government and some police powers delegated in 2003. There is considerable overlap between them and the powers available to the ABG listed in s.290(1) (discussed later).

Second, the ABG has the powers needed to establish and provide for the operation of institutions under the Bougainville Constitution, as well as various other powers that the PNG Constitution makes available to the ABG should the Bougainville Constitution so provide (including significant powers relating to criminal law, human rights, emergencies etc.). In making the Bougainville Constitution, full advantage was taken of these arrangements in order to ensure the maximum range of potential powers were vested in the ABG immediately, without the need to subsequently apply the mechanism for transfer of powers that applies to the third category.

That third category involves an extensive range of subjects included in a list of fifty-nine items not vested immediately, but rather made available to the ABG, subject to it meeting the requirements of a transfer process. They include land, mining, environment and local government.[67] They are available, not

[64] PNG Constitution s.289(1). [65] S.294.

[66] The main exception here is powers in relation to police, vested in the Bougainville Interim Provincial Government from late 2003.

[67] PNG Constitution s.290(1).

immediately vested, in recognition of the fact that existing PNG laws cover most of the subjects in question, and that in almost all cases there has never been any history of such powers being exercised by Bougainville governments and so no existing capacity in the Bougainville Administration. Reflecting Bougainville concern that considerations of capacity and resources should not constitute insurmountable obstacles to transfer, powers are transferred on ABG initiative (twelve months notice to PNG, allowing necessary arrangements to be made for budgets, staff, assets etc.) and the drawing up of joint implementation plans for capacity development.[68] These provisions, when combined with the limited guarantees of ABG funding outlined later, add to the complexity of implementing autonomy.

While each government can make laws on the subjects reserved to the other, such laws cannot be inconsistent with those of the government with primary responsibility for the power in question.[69] Responsibility for any subject not clearly vested in either government (in practice those not thought of at the time the vesting of powers was negotiated) is to be allocated between the two governments, when such a subject is identified, on the basis of the principles underlying the two existing lists.[70]

Although there is no specific category of concurrent or shared powers, in effect some could be so classified, a consequence of provisions aiming to protect interests of one government despite the vesting of a particular power in the other. Such provisions place limits on, or encourage co-operation between, the governments in the exercise of a power, effectively meaning such powers are shared. They include specific limits on the use of some powers vested in PNG, or provision for limited ABG roles in exercise of aspects of such powers. Thus while defence, foreign relations (including foreign aid), telecommunications and human rights are largely PNG powers, there are limits on future deployment of the PNG Defence Force to Bougainville; some foreign affairs–type powers are vested in the ABG; the ABG has some rights on development of telecommunications and to negotiate and receive foreign aid; and the ABG has powers to restrict and elaborate the human rights otherwise guaranteed under the PNG Constitution.

Conversely, there are a number of subjects where the ABG has powers subject only to specific limits, or to detailed requirements on co-operation with PNG. These include criminal law, human rights, regulation of foreign investment, judicial administration, police, the public service and prisons.

The ABG's 'foreign affairs–type' powers require brief elaboration, it being unusual to vest them in autonomous regimes, and they blur the boundaries of sovereignty. The ABG can enter into international agreements under PNG authority;[71] negotiate and obtain foreign aid, PNG being required to approve

[68] PNG Constitution ss.295 and 297, and Organic Law ss.4–6. [69] PNG Constitution s.296(2).
[70] PNG Constitution s.292. [71] PNG Constitution s.293(7).

such aid, though always 'subject to overriding foreign policy considerations';[72] with PNG consent, the ABG can send representatives or observers to regional meetings and organisations;[73] the ABG can 'participate or engage directly in the negotiation of international agreements of particular relevance to Bougainville';[74] it is to be represented in any PNG delegation negotiating agreements either with Solomon Islands on border issues or about access and other aspects of fisheries in relation to Bougainville maritime territory or areas of the PNG territorial seas beyond the three nautical mile limit of Bougainville maritime territory or in the area of the Exclusive Economic Zone and the continental shelf associated with it;[75] and the ABG can recommend to PNG names for inclusion or removal from its Visa Warning List.[76]

There are also limits on PNG's ability to exercise the foreign affairs powers otherwise vested in it. Although the exercise of all ABG powers is subject to PNG's international obligations,[77] PNG is required to consult Bougainville before entering into 'any proposed new obligations likely to affect the exercise by the Bougainville Government of the functions and powers available to it'.[78] Further, international agreements with a purpose of altering the autonomy arrangements take effect only with Bougainville's consent.[79] The ABG and PNG are to develop equitable arrangements for sharing revenues from fishing and other activities in the Exclusive Economic Zone associated with Bougainville.[80]

Several factors have contributed to slower than expected progress towards ABG exercise of functions and powers available to it. Although the transfer process just outlined does not apply to the ABG powers derived from the Bougainville Constitution (establishing ABG institutions, concerning criminal law etc.), the ABG has been able to exercise very few of them, mainly due to limitations of funds and staff capacity. In relation to the 59 powers listed in s.290(2) that are subject to the transfer process, slow progress in transfer results from factors such as: complexity of the arrangements; change of virtually all key PNG personnel since the 2001 Agreement was negotiated (resulting in very poor understanding of the Agreement and what was intended by it); limited ABG capacity and funds; and limited political commitment on the part of ministers in the PNG government. A few minor powers have been transferred, some significant powers (notably in respect of mining) are in the process of transfer, and a number of memoranda of understanding have been signed between PNG and the ABG providing for transfer of functions and powers listed in s.290(2) related to those 'inherited' by the ABG from the previous provincial government.

[72] Agreement Art. 175, PNG Constitution s.327. [73] Agreement Art.70.
[74] Agreement Art.73, PNG Constitution s.293(7). [75] Agreement Art.85.
[76] Agreement Art.80. [77] PNG Constitution s.293(2).
[78] S.293(3). [79] S.293(4). [80] Agreement Arts. 8 and 86.

Fiscal arrangements

These arrangements assume heavy reliance by the ABG on grants, at least until significantly increased economic activity in post-conflict Bougainville generates more internal revenues.[81] The Agreement and the PNG constitutional laws provide for payment by PNG of three main annual grants (inclusive of base amounts and annual adjustments). Further, the ABG receives the proceeds of PNG personal income tax and stamp duties collected in Bougainville, and has far wider taxing powers than existing provincial governments.

The main annual grant is the 'recurrent unconditional grant', calculated on the basis of the costs (inclusive of public service salaries) of any existing functions as well as PNG's costs in the year before transfer to the ABG of new functions. Two other main grants are payable, one for the cost of operations of police in Bougainville, and the other intended to contribute to the cost of 'restoration and development' in Bougainville. Amounts of the three grants are adjusted annually under the Organic Law. PNG is also empowered to make 'conditional' grants for 'specific purposes [. . .] proposed by [PNG] after consultation' with the ABG.[82] Because of grave problems caused for Bougainville's previous provincial government by unpredictable patterns of payments of grants (often involving long delays), the recurrent unconditional grant must be paid 'in such a way that it can be effectively and efficiently used and applied for the purposes for which it was provided in the year for which it was provided'.[83] In addition, PNG is required to make annual transfers to the ABG of the value of personal income tax, stamp duties and 30 per cent of goods and services tax collected in Bougainville.

The ABG's total budgeted revenue for 2011 was about K165mn[84] – about AUD66mn. In broad terms, the main sources are:

- About K115mn from grants and other revenue transfers from PNG;
- About K45mn from donors (notably Australia, Japan and New Zealand), this money funding most new capital works and maintenance (e.g., a trunk road and bridges, critical to agriculture);
- About K5mn from internal revenues collected by the ABG.

Very little of these funds are under real control of the ABG. In particular, of the three main grants, two meet the costs of the Bougainville Administration and police. Internal revenues mainly meet costs of the ABG political institutions. Donor funds are the subject of consultations with the ABG, but for the most part their expenditure is controlled by donors. So it is mainly the restoration

81 PNG Constitution ss324–9; Organic Law ss38–51.
82 Organic Law s.50. 83 Organic Law s.48(2)(b).
84 The PNG currency, the Kina (k) has had a value roughly equivalent to AUD0.40 for much of the period since the ABG was established.

and development grant (K15 mn, or AUD6.6mn in 2011) that has been available as ABG discretionary expenditure.

Alternative internal revenue options for the ABG are limited. Before the conflict, the Bougainville economy was dominated by the mine. There was, however, a significant agricultural sector, dominated by cocoa and copra production, with a significant large plantation sub-sector, but small scale Bougainvillean farmers contributing over 50 per cent of production by the mid 1980s. But during the conflict most infrastructure and production capacity was destroyed or severely damaged.

Since the conflict ended, the large-scale plantation sector has never been re-established. Some infrastructure has been restored, mainly through donor support, which has also helped re-establish the small-scale cocoa production, now valued at more than K100mn annually. The ABG has considered imposing an export tax on cocoa, but is reluctant to take money from the pockets of small farmers, especially if the tax were to encourage a black market in exports through neighbouring provinces in PNG. The other major economic activity involves small-scale gold extraction (both alluvial and hard-rock), which has taken off since about the year 2000, to a point where several thousand Bougainvilleans are involved, producing probably several kilograms of gold per week. The ABG would like to be able to tax this production, but the practical obstacles in the way of doing so are immense.

The grant provisions are in many ways the weakest part of the autonomy arrangements, in terms of limited base amounts and adjustment mechanisms. These weaknesses are mainly a result of a combination of the poor economic base in post-conflict Bougainville without the Panguna mine, and the ongoing fiscal crisis facing the PNG government during the 1990s and early 2000s, which limited its ability to guarantee significant funding for the ABG when the 2001 Agreement was being negotiated. On the other hand, at that time the senior PNG minister responsible for negotiating most aspects of the financial arrangements indicated that PNG was committed to ensuring adequate funding for Bougainville. Further, as already mentioned, the Bougainville negotiators assumed that PNG would follow the example of France in relation to New Caledonia in recognising the need to be generous.

In retrospect it was a mistake for Bougainville not to have insisted on provisions requiring grants to rise as the PNG economy improved, because from around 2005, PNG revenues rose rapidly as a result of the international resources boom, without any increase in ABG funding. It was not until 2011 that PNG showed interest in paying any more than the minimum – and until then significant disputes occurred about payment of the limited amounts under the grants PNG is constitutionally obligated to provide. The limited funding available causes considerable resentment in the ABG. Not only had more financial support been anticipated, but without much higher levels of funding the ABG has little ability to tackle critical deficits in administrative capacity and service delivery, nor to begin exercising the many powers available to it.

The ABG has been exploring ways of improving its fiscal position, initially the major focus being on attempting to get major mining projects established as quickly as possible, while at the same time moving to take over mining powers and develop its own mining policy (inclusive of new arrangements for mining revenue distribution). That has proved more difficult than expected, and under the President elected in mid 2010, has involved efforts to re-engage with Bougainville Copper Ltd with a view to exploring future options with the existing Panguna copper and gold mine. In addition, there are moves to expand the internal tax base, initially by imposing a sales tax on alcohol and tobacco products, expected to generate about AUD2mn annually from 2012.

Even when the 2001 Agreement was being negotiated it was clear that the main possible route away from ABG dependence on grants would be the establishing of major resource projects in Bougainville. The constitutional laws require that the amounts PNG collects in Bougainville from company tax, customs duties and PNG's 70 per cent share of Goods and Services Tax are assigned to a trust account established to meet the annual cost to PNG of the recurrent unconditional grant.[85] 'Fiscal self-reliance' is defined as the first year when the revenue from those sources is sustainably greater than the value of that grant.[86] At that point, the ABG is entitled to retain the amount equivalent to the annually-adjusted value of that grant. Any additional amount of tax revenue, over and above the value of the grant, will then be shared between PNG and the ABG, on the basis of 'an agreed revenue-sharing formula'.[87] Given the relatively low levels of revenue currently derived from sources such as company tax in Bougainville, the only point at which fiscal self-reliance is likely to be achieved is when a major resource project is established.

There are some important issues here. The first is that through these and other aspects of the fiscal regime PNG conceded the ABG's rights to a far more significant share of mining revenue than in the 1976 Agreement.[88] On the other hand, as yet no 'revenue-sharing formula' has been agreed, that difficult issue being deferred when the 2001 Agreement was being negotiated – basically left until a major resource project necessitates its negotiation. Of course, distribution of mining revenue in Bougainville is a sensitive issue, one that played a major role in the origins of the conflict, and there is the potential for considerable difficulty in reaching agreement. As with the referendum arrangements, this may be conflict deferred.

However, there has been some discussion of additional PNG funding to Bougainville. The first serious indication that PNG might be open to allocating

[85] Organic Law s.39.

[86] PNG Constitution ss.278(1), 324(a) and (b), 325, and 326(b), and Organic Law ss.39, 40 and 41(5).

[87] PNG Constitution s.324(b)(ii).

[88] Other aspects include the ABG's rights to revenues from PNG personal income tax, stamp duties and other taxes, likely to be significant if large-scale mining resumes.

significant additional funds to Bougainville on an ongoing basis[89] came early in 2011, apparently largely in response to ABG complaints about PNG's initial refusal and then long delays in paying the restoration and development grants for 2010 and 2011 and about the low levels of funds allocated to the ABG despite the heavy demands it faces. The then PNG Treasurer, Peter O'Neil, announced that K500mn (about AUD200mn) would be made available for 'high impact' projects over the following five years, the first tranche of K100mn expected before the end of 2011. Although O'Neil became PNG Prime Minister in August 2011, no payment was made in 2011 (even though PNG had a supplementary national budget in September 2011). K100mn was allocated in the 2012 budget. However, that was at the cost of non-payment of the restoration and development grant (regarded as being subsumed in the larger allocation). More important, the national government indicated that it intended to largely control prioritisation and management of expenditure of the funds, causing significant tensions between the governments. As of the time of writing (mid 2012) the funds remain under dispute, and the absence of the restoration and development grant for 2012 means that the ABG has almost no discretionary funding available to it.

There is already tension over several aspects of the fiscal arrangements caused by PNG reluctance to adhere to various requirements of the 2001 Agreement. As mentioned earlier, and for reasons that are quite unclear, its initial refusal to pay the restoration and development grant in 2010 and 2011 and had deleterious impacts on ABG planning, implementation and financial management. It took a series of confrontations in successive Joint Supervisory Body meetings and through the PNG press before the PNG government reluctantly paid the 2010 grant in February 2011, over fourteen months late, and the 2011 grant was not forthcoming until October 2011, almost ten months late. The amounts of the grant actually paid for both 2010 and 2011 were not calculated in accordance with the provisions of the Organic Law on annual adjustment of the grant,[90] resulting in significant underpayments for both years. Prior to PNG's reluctant concession in February 2011, the ABG came close to either invoking the dispute settlement provisions (described later), or referring the issues about the grants to the Supreme Court for a constitutional ruling. Issues about the K100 million allocated for Bougainville for 2012 and PNG failure to pay the 2012 restoration and development grant may need to be dealt with under the dispute resolution procedure.

Further, despite requirements that the PNG tax authorities pay to the ABG revenues from most PNG taxes collected in Bougainville,[91] PNG tax authorities have been unable to provide information on calculation of amounts payable to the ABG for the two main taxes in question (personal income tax and stamp

[89] Promises of 'one-off' additional payments for particular purposes were made in 2009 and 2010, considerably less being paid than was promised.

[90] S.49(2). [91] Organic Law ss.41 and 42.

duty), the ABG concern being that substantially more is payable than it is receiving. From 2011 there has been discussion of the ABG moving to exercise the authority that it is empowered to assume, 'after restoration', to 'impose, set rates of and collect personal income tax'.[92] Another serious problem has been the failure of PNG to pay the recurrent grant (as well as the other grants) in a predictable manner, causing the ABG all the same grave fiscal planning and management problems that the constitutional requirement for payment 'in such a way that it can be effectively and efficiently used'[93] were intended to avoid.

Shared rule

There are a number of issues concerning the extent to which provision needs to be made for participation of residents or institutions of the autonomous region at the national level. Bougainville negotiators originally envisaged essentially confederal arrangements under which Bougainville would have very limited involvement at the centre, their own institutions replacing most national institutions. Another issue concerned numbers of representatives in the PNG Parliament, it originally being proposed that Bougainville should have just one, who would be an ABG representative, rather than elected by Bougainville voters.

Ultimately Bougainville accepted a considerably higher degree of integration. The public service and other national institutions continue to be open to Bougainvilleans, even if the ABG does choose to establish separate institutions. Similarly, if such institutions are established, various provisions encourage co-operative arrangements, as mentioned earlier. In part Bougainville changed its position because of financial considerations, for in the process of negotiations it gradually became clearer that it would be many years before the ABG would have the resources needed to establish its own institutions.

Similarly, the proposals for a single Bougainville representative in the PNG Parliament were dropped in late 1999, not so much because of interest in integration, but rather due to the need to build unity among the diverse Bougainville factions at a time when three of the four sitting MPs were at odds with the coalition of Bougainvillean leaders by then already negotiating autonomy with PNG.[94]

There are, of course, some people from other parts of PNG still resident in Bougainville, and ten thousand or more Bougainvilleans live elsewhere in PNG. Their rights and interests are not the subject of specific protections. Rather, the human rights provisions of the Agreement – which ensure the continued protection of the quite extensive PNG human rights regime – were assumed to provide sufficient protection to both groups.

[92] Organic Law s.41(5). [93] Organic Law s.48(2)(b), earlier.
[94] Regan, *Light Intervention*, 50–2.

Methods of autonomy

Vesting of autonomy immediately changes the context for and the nature of relationships between the centre and the autonomous unit. Much more is likely to be at stake due to the increased powers and resources available to the latter, and differences in views about how the legal arrangements for the new relationship should be interpreted. In cases of asymmetrical autonomy, the change and possible tensions are likely to be greater, especially in a case such as Bougainville, where sovereignty is not only blurred by autonomy but also under continuing challenge. In these circumstances, any aspects of the arrangements dealing with relationships between governments can be of particular importance.

Co-operation and consultation between levels of government

Despite their interest in being as separate as possible, the Bougainvillean negotiators recognised the need for mechanisms for managing ongoing engagement between the governments, especially concerning initial implementation, transfer of powers, and allocation of resources. These mechanisms include those already discussed (initial implementation arrangements, the Joint Supervisory Body and requirements for joint implementation plans for transfers of powers). There is also provision for the establishment of mechanisms to discuss sensitive matters on which agreement could not be reached prior to the signing in 2001,[95] but so far there has been no move by the ABG to make use of such mechanisms, mainly because the ABG is struggling to manage the powers it has already assumed, and does not have the capacity to take major new initiatives.

ABG/PNG consultation is stated as a general principle of implementation.[96] The Joint Supervisory Body is envisaged as a primary point of consultation,[97] a role that overlaps its additional responsibility to act as a forum for consultation in the second stage of the dispute settlement procedure. Consultation is mandated at many points where decisions on potentially sensitive matters may be required, such as on the content of the Bougainville Constitution as it was being

[95] They include consultation both on extension of Bougainville's maritime territory beyond the limit of three nautical miles reluctantly agreed to by Bougainville (Agreement Art. 9); consultation on criminal law development by the ABG (Agreement Art. 297 and PNG Constitution s.291); ABG reference to the Joint Supervisory Body of concerns on aspects of telecommunications (Agreement Arts. 93–100); establishment of a joint commission on human rights and other implications of Bougainville proposals to to require clan-groups to meet customary obligations in relation to clan members convicted of criminal offences, and certain other issues relating to Bougainville powers over human rights (Agreement Arts. 128–33); and development of a mechanism for ABG participation in negotiating international agreements (PNG Constitution s.293(7)).

[96] PNG Constitution s.331(a). [97] S.332(3)(b).

developed;[98] on proposed amendments to that Constitution;[99] approval of foreign investment applications in relation to Bougainville;[100] where either PNG or the ABG wish to legislate on subjects not vested in either government;[101] where PNG proposes to enter into an international agreement likely to affect ABG powers or alter autonomy arrangements;[102] about the arrangements for transfer of a power that the ABG requests PNG to transfer;[103] various aspects of the referendum on independence;[104] proposed amendments to the PNG constitutional laws;[105] and other matters.[106] To encourage serious engagement there is an expansive definition of consultation setting out the kinds of exchanges required.[107] There is also provision for PNG and the ABG to hold 'annual wide-ranging consultations on the general operation of the autonomy arrangements', ordinarily to be conducted through the Joint Supervisory Body.[108]

So far, there has been virtually no use of the mandated consultation provisions, mainly because the circumstances where consultation is required have not arisen. The main exception is the process for transfer of powers, where consultation through the Joint Supervisory Body has occurred regularly, and with generally positive outcomes. With at least one area of mandated consultation, (appointment of the ABG's senior public servant, discussed earlier, where the ABG was required to consult the PNG Department of Personnel Management) PNG's refusal to accept that the ABG had the appointment power (subject to consultation) rendered the ABG consultative efforts nugatory. Further efforts to resolve the issue in the Joint Supervisory Body failed. Consultation in the Joint Supervisory Body did help resolve a serious conflict, when in February 2011 strongly expressed views of the ABG president on the non-payment of the restoration and development grant helped to persuade PNG to pay the grants due for the 2010 and 2011 fiscal years (later).

Methods of dispute resolution

Numerous aspects of the arrangements are intended to reduce the likelihood and scope of disputes. They include some already discussed, such as the constitutionalisation of details of autonomy (transfer of powers, grants etc.) and lack of PNG intervention powers. Constitutionalisation of detail has not been as successful as intended, as indicated by the difficulties with the appointment process for the Bougainville Electoral Commissioner, problems with other appointments, payment of the restoration and development grant, unpredictable payments of other grants and so on.

Provision is made for a multi-stage dispute settlement procedure, beginning with consultation between relevant government agencies, then consultation

[98] S.283. [99] S.287(3). [100] S.290(6)(e). [101] S.292(2).
[102] S.293(3). [103] S.295. [104] Ss.338 and 342. [105] S.345.
[106] Ibid. s.311(4)(a), 326(2)(b), 327(2)(b), and 328(1)(a), and Organic Law ss.4(1), 13(3), 14, 17(1), 21(4), 26(1), 36, 48(3), 50(a), 51(c), 54(1), 55(1), 56(1), 57(1), and 57(4).
[107] Agreement, Art. 269 and PNG Constitution s.278(2). [108] Ss.337(9), (10).

through the Joint Supervisory Body, then mediation and arbitration and finally reference to the courts (unless the parties agree to submit the matter to the courts at an earlier stage).[109] That process applies generally to any dispute between the governments, but in addition is required in relation to a number of specific areas.[110] As already discussed, the ABG has authority to refer constitutional issues to the Supreme Court.

There has so far been no explicit use of the dispute settlement procedure, except to the limited extent that the ABG has used the Joint Supervisory Body to raise concerns about matters such as delays in paying the restoration and development grants for 2010 and 2011.

A process for a five-year joint review of autonomy is also intended to reduce the likelihood of disputes. It includes assessment by independent experts of the operation of key aspects of the autonomy arrangements, including funding and personnel, judicial interpretations and distribution of powers.[111] The first such review should have occurred by mid 2010, but despite the Joint Supervisory Body discussing the issues involved, there had by the time of writing been no serious progress towards holding such a review.

The record of the use of the dispute settlement procedures to resolve problems with implementation and operation of the autonomy arrangements has been, at best, mixed. Arguably concerns raised by the ABG in the Joint Supervisory Body (one of the initial stages in the dispute settlement process provided by the PNG Constitution) helped to resolve problems over the payment of the restoration and development grant (and perhaps also contributed to pressures on PNG to make its February 2011 promise of K500mn for Bougainville projects over the next five years). However, the grant issues took a long time to resolve, and this could have been dealt with by invoking next steps in the dispute settlement procedure, or even by an immediate constitutional reference to the Supreme Court. A number of other failures by PNG to adhere to the autonomy arrangements have not been pursued through the Joint Supervisory Body, including disputes about ABG powers to appoint the senior administrator and police commander, failure to provide information about PNG collection of personal income tax and stamp duties in Bougainville and issues about how the proposed K500mn will be allocated and its expenditure managed.

Reasons for these various failures by PNG include the high turnover of senior bureaucrats and political leaders who were involved in negotiating the 2001 Agreement, a development that has contributed to growing ignorance about PNG obligations to the ABG; a view among some sections of the PNG bureaucracy that if Bougainville is likely to be moving towards independence it should not be assisted; and a tendency for the limited capacity in the PNG

[109] Ss.333–336.

[110] Ibid. ss.290(4)(g), 291(4)(b)(ii)(B), 293(5) and (6), and Organic Law ss.20(3), 30(3), 51(g), 55(3) and 57(5).

[111] PNG Constitution s.337.

government to be absorbed in aspects of development of huge liquified natural gas projects elsewhere in PNG. Factors contributing to ABG failure to use the dispute settlement procedures more actively include limited capacity, as well as personal and political links between ABG leaders and PNG leaders that sometimes contribute to a reluctance to confront (as do aspects of Melanesian culture). Whatever the various reasons on both sides, the lack of pressure from the ABG for PNG adherence to the arrangements almost certainly has itself contributed to a growing tendency on the part of PNG authorities to view implementation of aspects of the autonomy arrangements as optional.

A major political and constitutional crisis at the PNG national level beginning with the August 2011 replacement of long-serving PNG Prime Minister, Sir Michael Somare, by former Treasurer, Peter O'Neil has the potential to cause additional problems with the implementation of, and resolution of disputes about, autonomy. Enjoying majority support in Parliament, Mr O'Neil has ignored two Supreme Court decisions in constitutional challenges to the way he took office. In part he has been able to do so because the legitimacy of the Court as ultimate arbiter of constitutional issues has been undermined by perceptions that some members have been too close to the previous Somare government. In addition, the prior general acceptance by governments of the Constitution as the framework within which the state must operate has been significantly eroded. These developments raise concerns for Bougainville, given that the main protection for the provision of the 2001 Agreement was always envisaged to be its constitutionalisation.

Notions of parliamentary sovereignty

Throughout the negotiations for the 2001 Agreement, PNG struggled with the notion that the extensive legislative powers vested in the Parliament by the PNG Constitution should instead, in relation to Bougainville, be potentially available almost exclusively to the ABG. PNG negotiators succeeded in reducing the degree of separation that the Bougainvilleans had wanted. Nevertheless, the degree of power available to Bougainville is still potentially extensive. PNG has almost no coercive power over the ABG, and the constitutional arrangements are not open to change without ABG consent. Together, these and other features ensure that Bougainville enjoys virtually co-ordinate status with PNG, and thus notions of parliamentary sovereignty need to be re-examined.

Not surprisingly, the co-ordinate status is resented by elements of the PNG government and bureaucracy. In particular the ABG's 'foreign affairs–type' powers are a matter of great sensitivity, made more so by the ABG's clear intent to encourage ongoing involvement of parts of the international community in monitoring implementation of the Agreement. Both sets of sensitivities were evident in two incidents in 2011. In March the PNG Department of Foreign Affairs and Trade claimed that the ABG had breached protocol in relation to a visit to Bougainville by the Australian government Parliamentary Secretary for Pacific Island Relations. In August the same Department raised a range of objections about a seminar to mark the tenth anniversary of the signing of the 2001 Agreement being organised in Bougainville by a small team from the UN Department of Political Affairs.

Differing legal traditions

In general, there is as yet no real distinction between the legal traditions of Bougainville and those of PNG as a whole. On the other hand, it appears that the need to find an interface between modern law and the incredible multiplicity of customary systems of justice and dispute settlement that is part of the almost bewildering social diversity in PNG is taken more seriously in Bougainville than at the national level. When the Bougainville Constitution was being developed there was strong interest in gradual development by Bougainville of its own legal system based much more on custom than is the case in PNG generally, concerns reflected in the provisions of the 2001 Agreement in relation to criminal law and human rights, where later processes were provided to explore some constitutional issues involved.[112] To date a serious lack of capacity and resources in the ABG has been the main factor preventing exploration of the possibilities open under the Agreement and the Bougainville Constitution.

Concluding observations

What does Bougainville's experience tell us about relationships between autonomy and conflict resolution and peace-building? Before considering the questions identified in this chapter's introduction, some general observations are in order.

Autonomy under the 2001 Agreement has clearly contributed to conflict resolution in a situation where neither side was in a position to readily end violence through military victory, and so both were open to compromise solutions. But autonomy does not have limitless possibilities. In the wake of the intense conflict from 1988 to 1997, with its deepening of ethnic differentiation, and given the military advantage and considerable popular support achieved by the pro-secessionist Bougainville Revolutionary Army, as well as the deep divisions within Bougainville, more than autonomy was needed to resolve the situation. Hence, not only was the level of autonomy in the 2001 Agreement both much higher than in 1976 as well as asymmetrical, but in addition separatist sentiment could not be ignored. So autonomy had to be combined with a later process to take account of that support (the deferred referendum). Nevertheless, in the period before the referendum, autonomy is central to daily lives in Bougainville.

112 See, for example, Bougainville proposals reflected in the Agreement (Arts. 128–33) about Bougainville requiring clan-groups to meet customary obligations in relation to members convicted of criminal offences.

Hence it was expected that combining autonomy and referendum would give PNG the opportunity to work to make autonomy so attractive that Bougainvilleans would have a real choice in the referendum, between the benefits of an operating autonomy and the uncertain possibilities of independence.

By mid 2012, the record has been mixed. While initial implementation to the point of establishing the ABG was slower than expected, the record was generally positive. From mid 2005, however, Bougainvilleans have gained an impression that PNG is reluctant to implement autonomy in full. There is little evidence that PNG recognises the opportunities of autonomy. This is indicated in a number of ways: the limited funding made available to the ABG despite the significant improvement in the PNG fiscal situation since 2001; the struggle to get payment of the restoration and development grants for 2010 and 2011 and the underpayments due to failure to adhere to the annual adjustment provisions; the failure by PNG to account for collections in Bougainville of personal income tax and stamp duties; failure to pay the recurrent grant on time; failure to adhere to constitutional requirements about appointments of Bougainville's senior public servant and head of police; problems over appointment of the ABG Electoral Commissioner; and slow progress in transfer of powers.

Some reasons for these unexpected outcomes have been mentioned already. Of particular importance, though, are the perceptions by some in the PNG bureaucracy and political leadership that the likely referendum result will be a vote in favour of independence, and that in consequence there is little point in trying to persuade Bougainvilleans to support integration by strengthening autonomy. There are indications that some others argue that PNG has the constitutional right to reject a 'yes' vote in the referendum and will undoubtedly do so when the time comes, and as a result it matters little whether or not autonomy works.

PNG reluctance to implement autonomy in full is likely to consolidate Bougainville support for independence. In a situation where Bougainvilleans believe that the international community has an obligation to support implementation if the vote favours independence, the outcome could be a return to confrontation between PNG and Bougainville. Autonomy might then prove not to have been the solution to conflict, but merely an arrangement that has deferred it.

Turning to the specific questions, is there evidence here that asymmetrical autonomy tends to contribute to tensions and even conflict by creating pressure for extension of such arrangements to other regions? So far, the answer is 'no'. The wisdom and justice of resolving the Bougainville conflict through asymmetrical autonomy are widely accepted elsewhere in PNG. There is no generalised pressure to extend full autonomy elsewhere. Rather, resentment about the reduction of autonomy under the 1995 reforms still motivates some provincial governments to seek extension of some of the fiscal aspects of Bougainville's autonomy arrangements.

Does disputing state sovereignty make autonomy both more difficult to concede and less likely to succeed? The real challenge of 2001 was the Bougainville demand for a referendum on independence, and that challenge has since been maintained by the constitutional guarantee for such a referendum in the same laws that provide for autonomy. Undoubtedly the referendum demand was an affront to PNG sovereignty, making its negotiators even more uncertain than they might otherwise have been about aspects of the high level of autonomy Bougainville demanded. The referendum issue almost derailed the negotiations, and was only resolved by international mediation. But while it made autonomy more difficult to concede, PNG eventually accepted that there could be no settlement of the conflict without taking account of the depth of feeling on the part of Bougainville separatists, and so reluctantly made concessions. But as already discussed, the ongoing challenge to sovereignty is undoubtedly a part of more complex reasons for difficulties with implementation of autonomy.

Is the blurring of sovereignty through key aspects of Bougainville's asymmetrical autonomy a help or a hindrance to conflict resolution? As Ghai points out, anything perceived as undercutting sovereignty tends to be viewed as a hindrance by the state, while secessionists look for the trappings of sovereignty.[113] PNG found the Bougainville proposals for both the referendum on independence and high levels of autonomy very worrying, and naturally negotiated for as many modifications as possible. While PNG ultimately recognised substantial concessions were necessary, suggesting that a degree of blurring of sovereignty was essential to resolving the conflict, at the same time aspects of the arrangements are continuing affronts to parts of the PNG bureaucracy, in particular, and a source of tensions. At the same time, the blurring of sovereignty was essential to resolving violent conflict. So on balance, in the Bougainville case, it has so far been a factor more helpful to resolving conflict than a hindrance.

Does autonomy merely defer conflict, or make it worse, by encouraging secessionists to progress to independence, or does it tend to reduce the likelihood of secession? Bougainville's experience to 1988 might appear to support the proposition that autonomy encourages secession, given the fact that secessionist conflict re-emerged there just twelve years after the 1976 Agreement. But on closer examination, the situation is less certain. What re-opened the secessionist demands in 1988 was not autonomy – which had largely contained the politics of ethnicity in Bougainville since 1976 – but the combination of localised reactions to mining and violence on the part of PNG forces. Without autonomy from 1976, the violence beginning in 1988 would undoubtedly have been far worse.[114] All in all, the evidence suggests that the operation of autonomy limited the support for secession. As for the current autonomy arrangements, to date the evidence suggests that it is the failure of PNG to grasp the opportunities

113 'Ethnicity and autonomy', 16–17.

114 Ghai and Regan, *Unitary state, devolution, autonomy, secession.*

of autonomy (for example, in the way that France has done in relation to New Caledonia) that has the greatest potential to consolidate support for separation.

Is autonomy more difficult to concede and less likely to succeed where the autonomous area is resource rich? Bougainville's experience suggests that the key issue here may not be so much the extent of resource wealth, but the extent of the state's dependence on resource revenues. There is little doubt that that dependence was a major factor in the early resolution of the first separatist dispute through the 1976 Agreement. By the time the 2001 Agreement was being negotiated, a number of other large mines, as well as petroleum projects, provided additional PNG revenue sources. This change helps explain PNG's willingness to concede a greater share of mining revenues in 2001 than in 1976. On the other hand, deferral of negotiating arrangements for sharing mining revenues involved in the fiscal self-reliance concept clearly underlines the continuing sensitivity of sharing of mineral wealth for PNG.

Is an international community role needed for autonomy to be both accepted as a conflict resolution device and implemented, or is it merely important in ensuring initial acceptance but not the implementation and success of autonomy? It would have been difficult to achieve the 2001 Agreement without the international community, in terms of both enabling the peace process generally, and mediating the most divisive issues, especially the referendum compromise. The experience shows that this support can be critical not just in getting to initial agreement, but also in at least the initial phases of its implementation (e.g. passing the constitutional laws, establishing the ABG), as the roles played by the UN in Bougainville suggest. The subsequent difficulties experienced in the implementation of the complex autonomy provisions after the ABG was established, and the contribution that deferral of the decisions on both separation and sharing of mining revenues may make to tensions between parts of the PNG government and the ABG suggest a need for some form of ongoing international support in implementation. But there is considerable sensitivity about such involvement in parts of the PNG bureaucracy. Ultimate judgments about its contribution may have to wait until after the referendum, for only at that point will the efficacy of the 2001 compromise on the referendum issue become apparent.

Is a democratic and participatory negotiation of autonomy more conducive to its success than imposition of such arrangements, and are established state traditions of democracy and the rule of law more conducive to such outcomes than authoritarian and arbitrary governance systems? Bougainville experience offers some support for the importance of democratic and participatory negotiations, as the efforts committed to ensuring such processes were undoubtedly part of the reason for successful initial implementation of autonomy. Further, PNG's reasonably positive record with democracy and the rule of law (notably in relation to constitutionalism) were important factors in persuading Bougainville secessionists to accept constitutionalisation of the 2001 Agreement as a significant measure for protection of the Agreement.

To what extent are mechanisms for consultation and negotiation, independent dispute settlement mechanisms and built-in flexibility important to the success of autonomy? Concerning consultative and dispute settlement mechanisms, Bougainville demonstrates the value of clear roles for such mechanisms, the Joint Supervisory Body having proved a useful example. Consultation there has helped to resolve at least one serious inter-government dispute (over the restoration and development grants). Otherwise, the dispute settlement mechanisms provided for in the arrangements have been little used, even by the ABG in relation to the several PNG breaches of the arrangements, despite growing ABG frustration about such breaches, and the possibility that failure to confront PNG on the issues may be contributing to a PNG tendency to regard adherence as optional. These developments suggest that design of the dispute settlement arrangements is less the problem than the limited capacity of the ABG to utilise the arrangements effectively. As for the need for flexibility, while this may be desirable, it is also common for parties negotiating autonomy, usually in politically fraught circumstances, to seek certainty and clarity. Bougainville did just that, but at the same time pursued the goal of flexibility by inclusion of five yearly review provisions. But the limited progress in implementation of the arrangements is undoubtedly a significant factor in the lack of interest in the review arrangements, as there is so much that has not yet been tried.

Bougainville's experience shows that there can be grave implementation difficulties, especially in a situation involving gradual progress towards greater autonomy. Slower than expected progress can itself contribute to tensions and increase the risk of conflict. That was certainly a factor in relation to the limited implementation of the 1976 Agreement. The 2001 Agreement is still more complex and is being implemented by state structures with less capacity than in the late 1970s and 1980s. Frustration and misunderstandings over the issues involved in implementation are already creating tensions. On the other hand, making implementation a joint responsibility has had positive impacts.

Constitutional entrenchment has clearly been important in ensuring that secessionists had faith that what was agreed would not be changed unilaterally. Despite the problems of implementation, entrenchment continues to provide such a guarantee. This is likely to be especially important in cases where autonomy is intended to end secessionist conflict, where there is likely to be mistrust, but perhaps only where there is sufficient acceptance at the national level of basic standards of the rule of law. Entrenchment can offer a basis for establishing trust. There is also a variety in the levels of entrenchment, which can take account of such mistrust. The level of entrenchment that met Bougainville concerns in 1976–7 did not satisfy its concerns in 2001, when it insisted on 'double entrenchment'.

14

Comparative perspectives on institutional frameworks for autonomy

Sophia Woodman and Yash Ghai

The chapters in this book have provided a wealth of information on the genesis, institutional structure and functioning of autonomy systems around the world. Autonomy has frequently been studied as a solution to internal conflicts within the state. In this chapter, we look beyond autonomy's role in conflict resolution to consider the cases covered in this volume from a comparative institutional perspective, seeking to provide some insight into three related sets of questions. The first of these is: what are the circumstances that make a grant of autonomy likely? The second is: which of these conditions facilitates the creation of arrangements that enable autonomous operation of the unit created? What institutional frameworks are necessary for the successful operation of autonomy? Evidently, there is significant overlap between the first two of these sets of questions, and the distinction we draw between them is analytic. The third set of questions is: what are the consequences of autonomy and its effects on the kinds of problems, such as respect for minority rights, that led to the demand for autonomy in the first place? We begin with some remarks setting autonomy in its historical and global context.

Autonomy has been prominent among a repertoire of mechanisms for dealing with internal conflicts, particularly for implementing decentralisation in areas with a history of separate ethnic or regional identity. In particular, autonomy has been pursued in recent years as a solution to one of the most frequent causes of conflict, particularly internal wars, in the contemporary world – that of ethnic differences, with notable examples being Sri Lanka; Sudan; Kosovo and Bosnia in the former Yugoslavia; India; Indonesia; and the Philippines. Countries that have been bedevilled by ethnic conflicts rarely achieve their economic potential – conflict drives away investors, domestic capital is transferred abroad, land cannot be used productively (and sometimes not for years afterwards due to mining), skilled and educated people emigrate, many people suffer permanent injury, levels of education and literacy decline, large parts of the state revenue and private resources are wasted on arms and armies, people are traumatised. In a vicious cycle, ethnic conflict, and the state's responses to it, produce terrorism and wanton and massive violations of rights – and then more laws and policies restricting freedoms and liberties. Democracy is impaired or becomes impossible; free and fair elections can seldom be ensured.

Autonomy is no panacea, however: even where a certain degree of autonomy has been institutionalised, conflicts between such regions and the states in which they are situated may still break out as circumstances change. As we completed this book, in three well-established autonomous areas profiled here secession was again on the agenda as tensions around economic and social priorities in the wake of financial crises and neoliberal restructuring exacerbated long-standing disagreements between these areas and the central governments of the states of which they form a part. Following the victory of the Scottish Nationalist Party in elections to the Scottish Parliament, a referendum on independence for Scotland has been proposed. In Québec, secessionist sentiment rose following the election of the conservative government of Stephen Harper. Issues around the allocation of resources among Spanish regions have led to renewed calls for Catalonia to consider independence. However, these examples also highlight the contribution of robust autonomy arrangements to *resolving* conflict: in these cases, established institutions of autonomy meant that efforts to pursue secession were generally furthered through peaceful, even constitutional means, rather than through violence.

The practice of autonomy considered in this volume brings into focus the changing character of the modern state as well as the shifting climate of inter-state relations over time, which set the formation of autonomies on complex historical ground. The tolerance of autonomy and other asymmetrical arrangements within state structures has risen and fallen. The autonomy of the Åland Islands described in Chapter 2 of this book had its genesis in the ashes of a devastating war that owed its origins in large part to a moment when the ethnic nation-state became the dominant ideal. Just as colonial ventures across the globe challenged this model, the late nineteenth and early twentieth centuries saw the emergence of an ideal type of sovereignty as being uniform across national space, as well as based on ethnic homogeneity.[1] However, this was far from ever reflecting the actual practice of states, as de jure uniformity of citizenship and governance often concealed significant de facto asymmetry, both in terms of access of populations to the rights of citizenship mandated by the national state and in terms of the extent of powers exercised by local governments. In fact, in most of the world the nation-state form only became hegemonic for a short period from the end of World War II until the conclusion of the Cold War.[2] Yet even during this period when international institutions confirmed the nation-state as an ideal type, increasingly states had to find ways to institutionalise asymmetry as a way of dealing with the lack of fit between this ideal and the actual heterogeneity of governance regimes and ethnic landscapes

1 See for example, Susan J. Henders, *Territoriality, Asymmetry, and Autonomy: Catalonia, Corsica, Hong Kong and Tibet* (Basingstoke; New York: Palgrave Macmillan, 2010).

2 Kate Nash, *The Cultural Politics of Human Rights: Comparing the US and the UK* (Cambridge University Press, 2009).

within their borders. Such trends increased after the end of the Cold War, as challenges to existing boundaries came under new strain.[3]

At the international level, the development of transnational norms recognising minority rights and rights to self-governance promoted autonomy as a solution to these problems, especially in Europe, but also to a certain extent in the Americas and Africa. This has obviously accelerated with the gradual institutionalisation of the European Union, with its various dimensions of multi-level governance, as well as regimes of rights. These transnational regimes raise questions about whether the emergence of international norms on autonomy (and even scholarly work such as this book) further promote the concept as a tool for conflict resolution, sometimes even in circumstances where it may be difficult for it to work.

By contrast, few such regional norms or institutions have emerged in Asia, despite the multitude of problems left over from the creation of national states on territories formed by colonial empires comprising heterogeneous populations and regimes of rule. Many Asian states remain resistant to international norms that are perceived as potentially diluting their sovereign power over the territories under their control. Yet even in one of the principal sources of such resistance, the People's Republic of China, pre-existing traditions of indirect rule and asymmetric arrangements have allowed for flexibility in certain cases.[4] Also in the Asian context, the idea and practice of zoning, often associated with projects to attract global capital, such as special economic zones, has likewise introduced systematic unevenness in the territory of national states, formalised in contexts such as Hong Kong and Macau.[5]

A focus on the temporality of autonomy raises questions about the sequencing of autonomy institutions, and how this affects their impact. The Bosnia-Herzegovina and South Tyrol autonomies have many similarities in their stress on ethnic proportionality, yet the fact that these measures were brought in gradually in South Tyrol when some sort of state institutions were already in place and ethnic tensions had already diminished to a certain degree meant they have had very different outcomes. Also, the degree of historical and physical separation over time seems to matter – autonomy as a long-term cultural construction, that then functions better when enshrined in constitutional and legal norms because it already 'works' in some way, again, relating to the level of institutions available to be put into service for the purposes of realising autonomy. Thus a de facto sense of *territorial* autonomy – as opposed to a claim made on the basis of ethnic identity – makes formalising that autonomy as an asymmetrical arrangement within a state more possible.

[3] Ibid. [4] Henders, *Territoriality, Asymmetry, and Autonomy*, 8–11.

[5] Aihwa Ong, *Neoliberalism as Exception: Mutations in Citizenship and Sovereignty* (Durham, NC: Duke University Press, 2007), 97–118.

Table 14.1 Factors favourable to granting of autonomous status, at time of establishment. Weighting of conditions at time of establishment of autonomy (0 = not at all; 5 = absolutely)

	Factors positive to autonomy				Factors negative to autonomy		
Autonomous unit	Regime change	International engagement	Small unit, few resources	Tradition of democracy, rule of law*	Autonomy based on ethnicity	Disputed sovereignty	Total (positive factors minus negative factors)
Åland Islands	5	5	4	5	−4	−5	10
Bosnia-Herzegovina	5	5	3	1	−5	−5	4
Bougainville	4	4	3	4	−1	−4	10
Catalonia	5	0	0	1	0	−5	1
Hong Kong	4	5	3	0	0	−1	11
Kashmir	5	3	1	1	−4	−5	1
Macau	4	5	3	0	0	0	11
Norfolk Island	0	0	5	5	−1	0	9
Puerto Rico	5	3	3	5	−4	−3	9
Québec	5	0	0	5	−4	−5	1
Scotland	2	0	0	5	0	−1	6
South Tyrol	5	5	4	1	−5	−5	10
Zanzibar	5	0	4	1	−1	0	9

* Within the state in which the autonomy is situated.

The first part of this chapter considers conditions that have facilitated the granting of autonomous status to an entity or entities within the borders of an existing state. The second part explores what types of autonomy frameworks are most likely to result in asymmetrical governance structures that actually accord autonomous units significant powers of self-rule, as well as the capacity to resist encroachments on their autonomy by the state in question. The third section considers the consequences of the operation of autonomy for the resolution of the kinds of tensions that precipitated demands for greater self-rule. The primary examples are the cases used in the book, but we also include a few comments on other autonomies not profiled here.

Formation of autonomy

A product of regime change

The demand of a minority group or territory for autonomous status within a state is most likely to bear fruit in the context of an overall regime change in the state in question. This was the case in eleven of the thirteen autonomies covered in this book, as indicated in Table 14.1. Times when the architecture of the state, and its sovereignty, is under review present a moment of opportunity for challengers to arrangements under the previous ruling regime to assert a variety of claims, as well as for resolving issues relating to unevenness within national states left over from earlier historical arrangements. There are a number of reasons why regime change provides a climate that facilitates the foundation of autonomies.

Firstly, those who are in charge of the transition may have been opposed to the centralised system under the *ancien regime*. For example, the framers of the 1994 Ethiopian Constitution had fought against the centralisation of both Emperor Haile Selassie and his communist successors, both of which had refused to recognise the ethnic diversity of the Ethiopian people, and thus stifled minority groups. Local self-government was on the agenda in post-Mussolini Italy for much the same reason, and this general decentralisation facilitated a rethinking of the long-standing South Tyrol question.

Secondly, the end of the old regime may usher in a new balance of forces that may necessitate or facilitate the restructuring of the state, as in democratisation in post-Franco Spain in the 1970s. The new or aspiring leaders may need to find allies, to be secured by the promise of autonomy, as with the rise of the communist regimes in the Soviet Union and China. After the collapse of the Soviet Union, Russia tried to maintain its territorial integrity by promising greater autonomy to its constituent parts. The Philippines conceded the principle of autonomy for the indigenous people and the southern Muslims after the overthrow of autocrat Ferdinand Marcos both because autonomy was more consistent with notions of 'people power' and because the new regime needed to consolidate its hold on power. In Nepal, it became possible to discuss and lobby for autonomy after negotiations concluded the civil conflict there and the monarchy was dissolved. Democratisation in Indonesia facilitated the resolution of long-standing conflict in East Timor, and in Aceh, the effects of the 2004 tsunami combined with this to bring about the end of an insurgency there through a grant of substantial autonomy.

Achievement of independence, largely as a result of decolonisation, has provided an opportunity for a fresh look at the apparatus of the state and the establishment of institutional structures designed to accommodate previously excluded or suppressed social and political forces. Imperial rule produced many multi-ethnic colonies; centralised rule established during colonial domination was unacceptable to many communities on independence. A large number of autonomy arrangements were established at the time of independence, including in India, Nigeria, Ghana, Kenya, Uganda, Papua New Guinea, Vanuatu and Indonesia. The integration of territories held by colonial powers but historically part of China created opportunities for the establishment of autonomies in Hong Kong and Macau. The end of British sovereignty over Hong Kong was facilitated by Beijing's willingness to countenance 'a high degree of autonomy' for the territory within the People's Republic, and this model was also adopted to bring Macau into the PRC soon after.

Sometimes autonomies have been established following a compromise among local groups; on occasion, the withdrawing colonial power has insisted on such arrangements in the decolonisation settlement. The latter has been more common, and a version of such attempts at continuity is apparent in Kashmir, where British efforts to incorporate the princely states into the new India were apparent. Incorporation under pressure is less likely to ensure the successful implementation of autonomy, because the majority resents the imposition. For that reason few autonomy regimes in Africa have survived for any length of time after independence. Continuing tensions over the status of Kashmir – as well as its divided status, with part of its historic territory going to Pakistan – have meant that the autonomy it was granted in the early years of the Indian Republic has remained elusive.

The weakness of a new regime may be seized upon by groups that have long had secessionist aims. There was considerable optimism in East Timor that the crisis of the Indonesian state would facilitate its independence or at least a high degree of autonomy. Similarly Tibetan leaders considered that the end of the Cultural Revolution was propitious for the realisation of 'genuine autonomy' in Tibet; and for a time the prospects looked promising.[6] Experience does not suggest, however, that regime change will always lead to autonomy when a group is demanding it.

The establishment of autonomy involves a major reorganisation of the state. Those who enjoy positions of power in the apparatus of the state are unlikely to give up their control of power willingly. They may of course be compelled to re-negotiate the structure of the state if irresistible or strong pressures build up for reform or their own position becomes weaker (as when autonomy was provided for Southern Sudan).

Re-organisation of the state may also follow a less radical regime change, as was the case in the UK following the Labour victory in 1997 after a long period of Conservative rule. Autonomy for Scotland was one of a number of elements of a constitutional reform package proposed by the Blair government following its election, and, as Himsworth notes in his chapter, the arrangements for Scotland (as well as Wales and Northern Ireland) are premised on and supported by these wider reforms.

International agreements facilitate autonomy as option

The involvement of other states and inter-governmental agencies clearly makes it more likely that the option of autonomy will be considered as a form of resolution to long-standing tensions around self government or ethnic self-determination. Significant international involvement characterised six of the thirteen autonomies studied in this book (see Table 14.1), while two more (Scotland and Catalonia) have clearly been affected by emerging norms that

[6] For a recent assessment, see Yash Ghai, Sophia Woodman and Kelley Loper, 'Is there space for "genuine autonomy" for Tibetan areas in the PRC's system of Nationalities Regional Autonomy?' *International Journal of Minority and Group Rights*, 17 (2010), 137–86.

encourage greater participation by regional governments in the European Union.

The formation of the autonomy in Åland, with the involvement of the League of Nations, provided an instance of such international engagement that has been seen as a model for resolving issues of ethnic and linguistic diversity in national states. Yet this case also makes clear the limits of such engagement: the baseline of the League of Nations settlement was that a solution should be found that did not alter the existing borders of states. This emphasis on maintaining existing boundary lines goes along with a general reluctance to intervene in what are seen as the internal affairs of states that has consistently been an international norm.

More recently, the OSCE and other international actors have deployed forms of autonomy with strong international involvement in efforts to resolve conflict in Eastern Europe, with very mixed results, as the case of Bosnia-Herzegovina and the Dayton Agreement make clear. In the case of Bougainville, too, a group of interested states contributed to brokering an agreement to resolve conflict between insurgents there and the government of Papua New Guinea. The parameters for EU accession have acted as a form of pressure on states with significant minority populations to resolve long-standing issues of lack of representation of such groups in order to improve their chances of being accepted as members.

In some cases considered in this book, autonomy has been established following the formulation of a bilateral treaty that has outlined the terms of the autonomy, and served as a yardstick for measuring the compliance of the state granting the autonomy with the original promises made. This was the case for the autonomies established in South Tyrol, Hong Kong and Macau. These bilateral treaties made re-incorporation into the state in question acceptable to the affected communities. Yet as these cases also show, the record of such bilateral arrangements in influencing the actual legal and political structure of the resulting autonomy frameworks, as well as their operation, has often revealed the limitations of such treaties, in that once the agreement is concluded, the outside state (Austria in the case of South Tyrol, Britain in the case of Hong Kong and Portugal in the case of Macau) has limited leverage (and possibly interest) in ensuring that the autonomy functions well, and may be more concerned with maintaining good relations with the incorporating state than with ensuring the agreement is followed to the letter.

A key element in all of these examples is the extent to which the structure, institutions and operation of the autonomy remain a concern of outside states after the involvement in an initial agreement to grant autonomy. An important element here is the interests and policies of powerful states at global and regional levels. As mentioned previously, once the commitment to autonomy has been made, there is a general reluctance to intervene in what are subsequently seen as matters of domestic governance. In the case of the European Union, broader emerging regional norms and standards, as well as the lure of accession, have provided some support for the claims of those seeking to make autonomy work. However, it is also apparent that the various types of international engagement in the case studies cannot guarantee the success of the resulting arrangements, an issue dealt with in more detail in the next part of this chapter.

Established traditions of democracy and rule of law facilitate autonomy

Autonomies have undoubtedly been most successful as a form in states that already operate within a liberal framework. However, many autonomies have been formed in states which do not provide such conditions, and in such cases there have often been significant obstacles to realising the promises in an initial grant of autonomy. Evidently, this element speaks both to the conditions for the formation of autonomies and the potential that they may result in real self-governance, and thus the analysis here addresses both elements. Specific manifestations of such arrangements are outlined in part two of this chapter.

The reason that liberal societies have the best record on autonomy is that they have established traditions and institutions of rule of law and democratic governance. On the whole, pluralism is valued and there is respect for cultural and religious differences. Autonomy arrangements require give and take; they depend on frequent negotiations for adjustments of relationships or the implementation of the law. Elected representatives at the centre and regions enjoy the support of their people and are respected as such. The law provides the framework for relations between the centre and regions and defines the powers of the respective governments. The success of autonomy depends on adherence to the law. Disputes on the meaning of the law are resolved ultimately by the courts, whose decisions have to be respected by all parties concerned.

Nordquist's research found a strong relationship between the level of democracy at the centre and the durability of autonomy. He has found that democratic countries were most hospitable to autonomy and that Europe was the most successful region in the practice of autonomy.[7] Even within such conclusions, different versions of democracy and rule of law provide distinctive climates for autonomy. The centralised, unitary character of the state in the United Kingdom, for example – with its doctrine of parliamentary supremacy – means that autonomy arrangements, such as those in Scotland, can always be at risk.

Our case studies support a strong correlation between liberal states – and what might be termed 'democratic moments' in non-liberal ones – and the formation of autonomy. Six of the autonomies under study in this book were formed in states with traditions of rule of law and democracy (see Table 14.1), while a further two, South Tyrol and Catalonia, were formalised at moments when the states involved were undergoing democratisation after the end of a period of

[7] Kjell-Åke Nordquist, 'Autonomy as a conflict-solving mechanism – an overview', in Markku Suksi (ed.), *Autonomy: Applications and Implications* (The Hague: Kluwer Law International, 1998), 69–71.

authoritarian rule. In Hong Kong and Macau, autonomy arrangements were worked out during a period of significant liberalisation of the Chinese communist state, including constitutional revision and economic marketisation. The institutional frameworks for Kashmir and Bosnia-Herzegovina were formulated in the wake of devastating wars when efforts were being made to constitutionalise political arrangements and deal with ethnic conflicts through a combination of legislative frameworks and institution-building.

By contrast, although non-liberal states may grant autonomy, the future of the units created as self-governing entities is uncertain at best. The durability of autonomy arrangements can be analysed in three categories of states: liberal societies, communist states and Third World states.[8] The worst of these in realising autonomy in practice have been communist states. In both the Soviet Union and China, provisions for autonomy in areas dominated by a titular nationality were negated by the overall control of the Communist Party, which had little commitment to pluralism. Yet the examples of Hong Kong and Macau show a record of a relative degree of autonomy within the People's Republic of China when some mechanisms to support the autonomy are in place, as well as the impact of local traditions of rule of law that contrast with a lack of such arrangements in the larger state.

The effects of local rule of law traditions may be considered by comparing Hong Kong and Macau, with basic laws that are largely similar.[9] The role of the legal and judicial system in Hong Kong in upholding autonomy has been stronger than in Macau. Is that due to the fact that Hong Kong's underlying law is the common law, while Macau follows the civil law tradition? The common law links Hong Kong to legal systems derived from Britain, while Macau is connected to Portuguese legal traditions and those of its former colonies. Is the greater assertion of Chinese authority in Macau due to the more robust character of the common law as compared to the civil law? The question is not easy to answer, for there are many other factors that could explain the dissimilar influence of China: the smaller size of Macau, closer contact between Macau and China during the colonial period, Hong Kong's greater integration in the international economy, a more passive legal profession in Macau and the presence of highly talented and influential foreign judges in Hong Kong. The traditional resistance of the common law to the invasion of other legal systems through the type of legal reasoning, grounding in facts, the specificity of doctrine and the theory and practice of precedent may also be a factor. Other features of legal arrangements may also contribute to differences between the two Chinese autonomies: the relative dominance in Hong Kong public life of lawyers and the strength of civil society there, as noted later. The international

[8] Yash Ghai, 'Decentralisation and the accommodation of ethnicity', in Crawford Young (ed.), *Ethnic Conflict and Public Policies* (London: Macmillan Press, 1997).

[9] In fact, as Cardinal points out, the Macau Basic Law is modelled on the Hong Kong version, to the extent that in some ways it fails to take Macau's institutional history and framework into account.

community and global corporations have shown less interest in Macau, due to its relative lack of importance to the world economy; and British economic interests are more extensively engaged in Hong Kong than Portugal's in Macau.

Other examples question the extent to which a particular legal tradition supports autonomy. Whether derived from common law or civil law, legal institutions in Third World states are often weak and unable to hold executive authorities to the discipline of the law.[10] Thus for autonomy, in the Third World the record is mixed, with some successful examples but also spectacular failures. Numerous autonomies in this category atrophied because the central government, normally in a commanding position, showed scant respect for the law or judicial institutions. Examples are plentiful in decolonising states in Africa and Asia.[11] Ghai highlights the difficulties of power sharing in Third World states due to the centrality of the state to accumulation and as a means to personal and group aggrandisement.[12]

Autonomy is easier to grant in small and marginal areas

A state finds it easier to accommodate the aspirations of small communities for autonomy. Small communities may not be strong enough to pose the threat of secession. Autonomy for them may not involve a substantial re-organisation of the state. Indeed it may involve hardly any re-organisation, as forms of local government can be used for their self-government. The impact of small communities or the territories they inhabit on the larger political or economic system is often negligible; and for that additional reason a large measure of autonomy can be granted them. Typically these autonomies also exist on the geographical peripheries of the state – another factor which may minimise their impact on the state. Some of the most successful autonomies are in this category: Åland Islands (Finland); Faroe Islands (Denmark); Azores and Madeira (Portugal); the Channel Islands (Britain); and the Saami in various Nordic states.

These uncontroversial autonomies can be compared with, for example, the autonomies of Buganda and Southern Sudan. Both these regions were central to the politics of their states. Buganda was also physically central. Both had rich resources that were then or could potentially be of great significance to the economic well being and development of the state. In neither case could the authority of the central government be effectively consolidated as long these autonomous areas were not brought under a greater measure of national control.

[10] Ghai, 'Decentralisation and the accommodation of ethnicity'.

[11] These include Uganda, when Obote attacked the Palace of the Kabaka of Buganda and thus brought Buganda's autonomy to an end in disregard of the constitution; Sudan, where Numeiry effectively tore up the instrument for the autonomy of Southern Sudan; the illegal annexation of Eritrea by the Ethiopian Emperor, bringing to an end the federation ordained by the United Nations; and the total disregard by West Pakistan of the constitutional autonomy of East Pakistan (now Bangladesh).

[12] Ghai, 'Decentralisation and the accommodation of ethnicity'.

The experiences of the autonomy of Bougainville within Papua New Guinea serve to remind us that an island, although geographically separated from the other parts of Papua New Guinea and containing only a small proportion of the national population, can be caught up in the maelstrom of national politics if it is rich in resources, as was the case in Bougainville, with its wealth of minerals.

Even when autonomy initially seems uncontroversial, tensions may emerge. In the case of Norfolk Island described in this book, granting autonomy to a remote island community may have seemed an unproblematic solution to the set of strange historical circumstances through which the community of people who call themselves 'Pitcairners' came to be formed, as Irving discusses. Yet the Island elite's desire for continued self-rule has posed repeated challenges to norms of governance in Australia, particularly those that set common standards for individual rights and social provision. This case reveals some of the tensions between small scale autonomies and regimes of rights even in liberal states.

Autonomy is easier when sovereignty is not challenged

Autonomy has been a cause of great contention because it is associated with assertions of or qualifications on state sovereignty. Autonomy thus becomes less problematic if it can be dissociated from sovereignty. But challenges to sovereignty that emerge after autonomy has been established can result in tensions; whether or not this is the case is related to the character and history of the particular territory involved, as discussed earlier.

In a sense, autonomy can be seen as inherently a response to an overly rigid notion of sovereignty exemplified in the ideal type of the nation-state. While it may be true analytically that sovereignty is performed by states, rather than being a possession that can be cut up in chunks,[13] the symbolic struggle over sovereignty conceptualised in precisely the latter sense is alive and well. And where autonomies involve significant law-making power – sometimes even constraining the actions of the sovereign through legislative enactments of the autonomous area, as in Åland – they certainly impact on a conception of sovereignty as having the 'last word'.[14] Yet as many contemporary theorists of globalisation point out, there are actually many such constraints on sovereigns.[15] The question is, then, in which contexts sovereignty is mobilised by state and non-state actors as a field of struggle over power.

One way of understanding these divergent perceptions of sovereignty is to focus on its territorial aspect, both from the perspective of groups with secessionist ambitions and from the perspective of states.[16] In their contemporary

[13] See for example, Nash, *The Cultural Politics of Human Rights.*

[14] Ibid., 72, citing Carl Schmitt.

[15] See for example, Saskia Sassen, *Territory, Authority, Rights: From Medieval to Global Assemblages* (Princeton University Press, 2006).

[16] Monica Duffy Toft, *The Geography of Ethnic Violence: Identity, Interests and the Indivisibility of Territory* (Princeton and Oxford: Oxford University Press, 2003).

form, a predominant concern of states is maintaining the integrity of their territory within the boundaries they assert. Since the majority of states are multi-ethnic, most are concerned that division of their territory through secession could set off a chain reaction as a precedent for the remaining ethnic groups. States are thus concerned to prevent such claims, viewing their territory as indivisible. By contrast, groups that identify a specific homeland constituting a part of a state over which they have a particular claim may also view this territory as indivisible, in the sense that the territory itself is perceived as co-terminous with their identity as a group. When such perceptions of indivisibility come into conflict, ethnic war may be the outcome.[17] In such circumstances autonomy can be a key compromise as it incorporates both the group's sense of its territory as a separate entity and the maintenance of existing state borders, thus fulfilling the state's desire to avoid dividing its territory.

A case in point is China's statements in recent years that it would be prepared to discuss autonomy for Tibet if the Dalai Lama acknowledged that Tibet was an inalienable part of China's 'sacred territory'. China's leaders agreed to negotiate Hong Kong's future only after Margaret Thatcher committed to relinquishing UK sovereignty over the territory. And China was able to accept autonomy for Hong Kong in part because its leaders realised that it was inconceivable that the residents would ever try to secede. After Franco's death, his followers were prepared to discuss regional autonomy in Spain once agreement was reached on what is now Article 2 of the 1978 Constitution, 'The Constitution is based on the indissoluble unity of the Spanish Nation, the common and indivisible country of all Spaniards'. In the case of Bougainville, although the autonomy arrangements effectively 'blurred' sovereignty, according to Regan's case study in this book, agreement to move towards this framework for resolving the conflict could only be reached once the insurgents had agreed to accept Papua New Guinea sovereignty over the area, even if only on a temporary basis. In some countries, pre-emptive steps have been taken against the concession of large measures of autonomy by declaring the unitary nature of the state, as has been the case in Papua New Guinea and Sri Lanka.

Autonomy becomes easier to countenance either because the autonomists are not claiming independence or the national government is not concerned with maintaining sovereignty. The classic example of the latter situation is the attitude of the 'metropolitan' state to its 'associated states'. The decolonisation of Cook Islands and Niue was accomplished by their transformation as associated states of New Zealand. Cook Islands enjoys a considerable amount of autonomy; over the years its autonomy has increased, under encouragement from New Zealand. New Zealand would not be upset if Cook Islands wanted to secede completely from New Zealand sovereignty. In fact links to that sovereignty are more important to the Cook Islands, for it entitles Cook Islanders the right to enter and reside in New Zealand (and derivatively Australia).

[17] Ibid.

Relations between Åland and Finland are relaxed and cordial because Finland has not perceived a threat to its sovereignty over Åland, whereas the Ålanders have seen significant benefits from their connection with Finland. Suksi characterises the creation within Finland of a second law-maker in Åland as a 'devolution of internal sovereignty', which significantly constrains actions of the sovereign. Even though sovereignty is no longer contentious, a small minority in the Islands still favours independence. Italy was able to contemplate extensive autonomy for South Tyrol with a substantial majority of Austro-Germans once the proportion of Italian-speaking residents had increased, principally through the merger with Trentino. The autonomy of linguistic provinces in India, which have no separatist ambitions, has been much less problematic than in Kashmir, the status of which has been more controversial, divided as the region is between two powers, India and Pakistan, often in a state of de facto war. Regional autonomy in Sri Lanka has become so difficult because of the secessionist claims of the Tamil Tigers. Also potential beneficiaries reject autonomy for Tamil areas precisely because the acceptance of autonomy is seen to compromise their claims for independence.

This last point highlights the relationship of ethnic cleavages within the population of a state to whether or not autonomy is considered as a viable option. Where the population of an existing state is composed primarily of two main ethnic groups, granting some form of autonomy to the territory associated with one of these groups, as in the Sri Lanka case, inevitably raises questions about the future cohesion of the state. As international law identifies a 'people' as the unit that may exercise self-determination, the potential of an autonomous unit to become an independent state poses a continual challenge to state unity, and the maintenance of sovereignty over the existing territory.

In Bosnia-Herzegovina, an imposed solution bracketed disputes over the sovereignty of the joint entity established to join the Serb, Bosniac and Croat areas. Yet these disputes have continued, and threaten the operation of the federal level, as the Serb and Croat areas constantly raise the prospect of seceding from the joint entity, and question the legitimacy of its rules. The continuing involvement of the international community in making rules at this level, breaking deadlocks between the parties to reach settlements, has contributed to the legitimacy deficit of the federal unit that joins the three areas.

Yet the question of when a group with different cultural characteristics becomes 'a people' is far from fixed; in some of the autonomies covered in this volume, linguistic differences are constituted as ethnic, thus potentially identifying the group in question as a separate 'people', whereas in others they are not, for example. Much depends on how ethnicity is conceived by the state and the populations that constitute it, and whether any tensions between dominant majorities and subordinated groups are conceived in ethnic terms. Strong identification with a territory does not necessarily mean that this identity becomes ethnic, as, for example, in the case of Scotland.

Autonomy may be hard to operate when there are basically two communities, or when, as in Canada now, the founding assumption of the federation of two communities has been outlived. Federations with two communities of about equal population size have greater potential for the emergence of conflict, as well as more limited scope for trade-offs. When the two communities are unequal in size, the federal arrangements become merely a form for the domination of the smaller by the larger – and thus a negation of the federal principle, as is often claimed by the Francophones in Canada, and was claimed by the Slovaks in the days of Czechoslavia. This is more evidently the case in the relation between Zanzibar and Tanzania.

For these reasons, autonomy has generally been seen as a more viable option in ethnically diverse countries. A larger number of groups allows for flexibility in arrangements and the establishment of a degree of balance, a point well demonstrated by the Indian experience. A larger constellation of interests have a stake in the success of federal arrangements, and collectively, the clout to achieve this. Catalonia is a key example here, where frameworks for regional autonomy have been advanced by policy innovations in some regions that have then been taken up by other areas. South Tyrol has also benefitted from similar dynamics in Italian regions. Yet these relatively successful integrations of minority groups can also be explained through the emergence of formal or proto-federalism, and thus a general distribution and devolution of state sovereignty, rather than as a function of ethnicity per se.

The conclusions of the analysis laid out in Table 14.2, based on weightings of various factors favourable or unfavourable to the formation of autonomies, may at first seem paradoxical. Higher scores should reflect more propitious conditions for autonomy. Yet some of the autonomies seen as models, such as Québec and Catalonia, score very low. These cases highlight the importance of federal systems to the formation of autonomies even in unpromising circumstances, as we discuss further in the next part of this chapter.

Factors contributing to effective autonomy

Continuing international involvement

The importance of engagement and monitoring by parties outside the state within which the autonomy is established does not cease once the entity is formally set up, although it has often been the case that pressure has effectively decreased following such a settlement. Yet one of the features of autonomy arrangements that have worked over the long term – particularly when they involve marginal or fairly small areas that lack significant political clout at national level within the state – is continuing international involvement.

South Tyrol is a case in point. Despite the drafting of an agreement between Austria and Italy in 1948 in which the former renounced its claim to the territory in return for Rome agreeing to establish a framework for autonomy, little was

Table 14.2 Factors facilitating exercise of autonomy. (0 = not at all; 5 = absolutely)

Autonomous unit	Continuing international involvement	Participatory and democratic negotiations*	Built-in consultation mechanisms	Constitutional entrenchment	Independent dispute resolution	Clear division of powers	Total score high = 30 low = 0
Åland Islands	2	1	5	5	5	5	23
Bosnia-Herzegovina	5	0	3	4	4	3	19
Bougainville	4	5	4	5	4	4	26
Catalonia	1	4	4	4	4	3	20
Hong Kong	2	1	2	3	1	4	13
Kashmir	1	2	2	3	3	2	13
Macau	2	1	2	3	1	4	13
Norfolk Island	1	2	2	0	2	2	9
Puerto Rico	3	1	2	1	1	4	12
Québec	1	4	5	4	5	4	23
Scotland	1	4	4	2	3	4	18
South Tyrol	4	2	3	3	4	4	20
Zanzibar	0	0	1	2	0	1	4

* At the time of formation of the autonomy.

achieved until a combination of internal unrest and Austrian complaints at the United Nations forced Italy to take action. Austria did not ask for the resolutions it had tabled to be withdrawn until the required legislative framework was in place, and real efforts had been made to implement it.

Agreement on the Bougainville autonomy was brokered by several other interested states, with some UN involvement. International engagement remains crucial to the continuing implementation of the autonomy arrangements, both in terms of monitoring compliance by both parties, but also in providing technical support and training to Bougainville so that it can develop the institutional capacity to take on the powers the agreement envisages.

Evidently, the inclusion of Puerto Rico on the list of colonial territories following the formation of the United Nations put pressure on the United States to resolve the anomalous status of the islands as 'unincorporated territory'. Its name was removed from this list at the request of the United States after Puerto Rico enacted its own Constitution in 1952. Pressure was off the United States until the formation of the UN Committee on Decolonisation in 1960, which repeatedly raised the case of Puerto Rico. The right of the Puerto Rican people to self-determination has been widely recognised, yet a final settlement of the territory's status has still not been reached.

In the cases of Hong Kong and Macau, although both involve bilateral treaties – with the UK and Portugal respectively – the importance of these as normative sources for the autonomy arrangements has been subsequently downplayed by the Chinese side. A form of international pressure can be seen in the regular reporting conducted by the UK on the state of autonomy in Hong Kong, and under the 1992 US-Hong Kong Policy Act, which requires that the executive branch provide annual reports to the US Congress on Hong Kong's autonomy arrangements. The effect of such pressure, however, has been limited; partly due to the fact that some of the more obvious inroads into Hong Kong's autonomy have taken the form of requests from the Hong Kong government for intervention in the form of legal interpretations by the National People's Congress Standing Committee, as described by Ghai.

However, in the case of Bosnia-Herzegovina, continued international involvement is indicative of a stalemate and the failure of autonomy to resolve the tensions left over from the war. Here a fractured and fractious 'international community' cannot withdraw, as its intervention is constantly needed to break the political deadlock created by a political framework that both reinforces ethnic divides and creates few incentives for compromise among the local parties. This case is a cautionary tale about the effects of a hasty settlement forced through by international parties, as well as the effects of competing visions *among* hegemonic powers following the settlement.

More limited and sensible international involvement should represent a potential for unwelcome consequences to the state if it interferes with, or fails to deliver on, the autonomy arrangements. Such a possibility of 'harm' has been found to be crucial in making negotiated settlements following civil wars work well for both parties, and in building better institutions.[18] Yet it is this longer-term international engagement that has often been lacking in such agreements.[19] Autonomy usually requires that the community involved compromise on their desire for secession; for such a spirit of compromise to prevail at state level, too, sometimes continuing pressure from third parties may be essential.

Participatory and democratic negotiations

Earlier, we discussed the ways in which liberal democratic systems in which rule of law is respected create a favourable ground for the formation of effective autonomies. In such conditions, negotiations are more likely to involve consultation with affected parties. The character of the process through which autonomy is negotiated, and the extent to which this involves popular participation, clearly has an impact on the outcome.

Participatory and negotiated settlements are more likely to have dealt with pressing problems, avoiding the superficiality of settlements produced under heavy external pressure. They are likely to represent a balance of interests, with different parties holding a stake in their success. The least successful of India's autonomies is Kashmir, which was not negotiated but provided for in response to a complex international situation, with Kashmiris not having been involved, and the other Indians resenting what they regard as unfair privileges for Kashmir, as Cottrell demonstrates.

Many systems of autonomy that were established in the dying days of colonialism were imposed rather than negotiated; they were the price that nationalist leaders had to pay for independence. These leaders resented them and dismantled them as soon as they had the opportunity to do so. In most instances, members of the groups for whose benefit autonomies were established had little understanding of the frameworks that had apparently been worked out for their benefit; at best the arrangements were inter-elite bargains. Although not imposed, the agreement on the merger of Tanganyika and Zanzibar was not only opaque but also failed to specify many elements of the relationship between the two, making domination by the larger and more powerful Tanganyika and the diminution of Zanzibar's autonomy virtually inevitable.

Some contemporary settlements suffer from similar kinds of difficulties. The case of Bosnia-Herzegovina is an example, with hurried agreements produced under pressure from hegemonic powers eager to end the bloodshed in the former Yugoslavia involving discussions behind closed doors without any kind of public consultation. This particular agreement, as Marko describes, also inscribed particular assumptions about ethnic separation and representation

[18] Duffy Toft, *The Geography of Ethnic Violence*.

[19] Monica Duffy Toft, 'Peace through security: making negotiated settlements stick', conference paper, 2006.

that have proved inimical to reconciliation among the warring parties and to the formation of effective institutions in Bosnia-Herzegovina.

Yet participation is not a sine qua non of success. Ålanders were not only *not* involved in the negotiations for their autonomy, but were initially opposed to it (as representing a lesser degree of recognition than they wanted). The only form of consultation involved in the settlement was a visit by representatives of the League of Nations to the Islands that heard from some representatives of the population there. As a consequence, while the Islands' Legislative Assembly was formally created in 1920, it did not meet at all until 1922, as initially the Ålanders resented it as an imposed institution. However, subsequent changes to the system of autonomy involved their full participation and now Ålanders have a strong sense of 'ownership' of autonomy. Hong Kong's autonomy also owes little to the participation of its residents, being an agreement between the incoming and departing sovereigns. However, the autonomy is valued greatly by these residents, because they realise that the alternative would be complete assimilation into the Chinese political and economic system. Autonomy, and the particular institutions it enables, has become a means for Hong Kong people to distinguish themselves from mainlanders.

Another caveat is presented by the case of Catalonia, which is certainly a positive example for the impact of democratic and participatory processes. However, this case also highlights that reaching consensus meant a lack of clear rules, with multiple possible interpretations. While this might be seen as creative ambiguity on the one hand, it is also a source of continual friction, since Catalan leaders and their counterparts in Madrid have varying perceptions of what these vague rules should mean.

Mechanisms for consultation and negotiation

In any system of devolution of power, disputes about the proper relationship between different levels of government are likely to arise. When disagreements come up, it is extremely important to have mechanisms that promote dialogue between the parties so that co-operation can be pursued and disputes resolved. When all else fails, ultimately judges may have to decide the matter in question, but it is sensible to try to resolve them by political means first. Some disputes are unsuitable for judicial resolution, and are best dealt with through political settlements.

A spirit of consultation and negotiations in good faith is vital for autonomy systems. It is also vital to a democratic system – a point on which the Canadian Supreme Court placed a particular emphasis in its 1998 decision on whether Québec had a right to secede from Canada, discussed by Simeon and Turgeon. Indeed Canada has pursued this strategy for several years now in its search for a constitutional settlement that satisfies the aspirations of the Francophones and First Nations – and a host of other interests. Not all the problems have been resolved, yet these efforts have kept Canada from dividing and have lent to the participants a sense of common enterprise. Switzerland's success is often attributed to habits of consultations and negotiations. The integrity of India as a state can also be attributed to the willingness to negotiate differences: so often when a region has been on brink of a breaking away, negotiations have been initiated and disaster averted.

It is important, as the Canadian Supreme Court has pointed out, that negotiations be conducted in good faith. If they are not, negotiations can be counterproductive. This point is well illustrated by the experience of Papua New Guinea. The relevant constitutional instruments provided for various mechanisms for consultation and mediation – particularly important as they also provided for the phased transfer of powers to provinces. Meetings were indeed regularly held, but the central government equally regularly disregarded agreements reached or recommendations made. This created great resentment in the provinces, particularly in the eastern island provinces, including Bougainville.[20]

Permanent institutions for consultation are a feature of a number of well-established autonomies. For Catalonia, the State-*Generalitat* Bilateral Commission provides a forum for negotiation, which has been essential, given the vagueness of the original settlement, mentioned earlier. Scotland and the UK hold regular meetings in the Joint Ministerial Committee, as well as at departmental level, to work out divisions of responsibility between ministries in Scotland and in Westminster. The Åland Delegation is a joint expert body with representation both from the state and from the autonomous area. The Finnish system requires that Åland be consulted on acceptance of EU provisions that would affect Åland's legal order, and on Finnish policies towards the EU more generally. The Bougainville Agreement established a Joint Supervisory Body composed of representatives of the state and the autonomy, designed to be a forum for negotiating their ongoing relationship and issues arising from the operation of the autonomy arrangements.

By contrast, in the absence of such mechanisms tensions can be left unresolved, threatening the future of the autonomy arrangements. During one-party rule in Tanzania, the ruling party was supposed to be a forum for working out political matters, including the relationship between the mainland and Zanzibar. But in practice mainland forces were dominant in the party, and a one-party structure is hardly amenable to recognising differences of interest.

Where single parties govern, policies are generally worked out in these closed fora prior to being introduced into formal political institutions. Given the fact that the Chinese Communist Party does not operate openly in Hong Kong and Macau – a peculiar situation, to say the least, that the dominant party of the state of which they are a part should be an underground organisation in the

[20] Yash Ghai and Anthony Regan, *The Law, Politics and Administration of Decentralisation in Papua New Guinea*, NRI Monograph 30 (Port Moresby: The National Research Institute, 1992).

two special administrative regions[21] – negotiations between Beijing and the autonomous governments in Hong Kong and Macau have to be conducted entirely informally, as there are no established mechanisms for them. The one partial exception, the Basic Law Committee, has singularly failed to present the position of Hong Kong people. In part this absence of discussion mechanisms may be because despite granting these special administrative regions a 'high degree of autonomy', the idea of negotiations between the two sides implies a parity that is contrary to the vertical hierarchy of state organs envisaged in the Chinese Constitution. Despite China's leaders' repeated rejection of calls for movement towards formal federalism – raised during drafting of the 1954 and 1982 Constitutions – some commentators consider the degree of decentralisation in the PRC to have made it into a de facto federal system,[22] yet the bargaining between centre and provinces is entirely informal.

In multi-party systems, political parties may provide a forum for reaching informal agreements on issues relating to the autonomy arrangement. However, this depends on whether the national party structure extends into the autonomous area. In Åland, for example, there is little correspondence between Åland political parties and national parties in Finland, although there are some connections between the social democratic parties in both. Rule of a national party with strong roots in an area seeking greater autonomy may help in formulating such arrangements. For example, formal autonomy for Scotland was worked out during a long period of dominance of Labour governments in the UK, with the party's historical strength in Scotland facilitating an arrangement that seemed likely to entrench that position, although as recent events have made clear, in fact the autonomy has served to strengthen the Scottish National Party, which was previously fairly marginal. Connections between Catalan parties and the Spanish Social Democrats provided favourable conditions for the solution of some of the problems arising in the autonomy frameworks in Spain.

Despite the importance of structures that promote ongoing dialogue over the terms of the autonomy, smaller units may be wary of institutional forms that appear to incorporate them into the state structure, and more interested in maintaining distance than talking. For example, the lack of representation of Norfolk Island in federal institutions in Australia is not resented by residents there; on the contrary, Islanders are concerned to block what they see as unwanted 'integration' into federal arrangements to preserve their autonomy, as Irving describes. Efforts to increase their representation were rejected by 80 per cent of Islanders voting in a non-binding referendum on these grounds. There are other examples too where the autonomous region wants to be left alone.

[21] Christine Loh, *Underground Front: The Chinese Communist Party in Hong Kong* (Hong Kong University Press, 2010).

[22] Yongnian Zheng, *De Facto Federalism in China: Reforms and Dynamics of Central-Local Relations* (Singapore: World Scientific Publishing, 2007).

Built-in flexibility essential for autonomy to work

The conditions that led to the claims for autonomy are dynamic and changing. They are affected by economic circumstances, international developments, changing expectations of groups and by the manipulation of ethnic sentiments by political or religious leaders. Solutions that may have been acceptable at one time are no longer acceptable at a later date. Also not all groups desire the same solutions; some groups may want greater autonomy than would satisfy other groups. It is therefore useful to have arrangements for autonomy that can respond to changing situations.

Autonomy arrangements based on overly rigid legal frameworks can encounter difficulties when such new conditions arise. This is especially the case when independent mechanisms for resolving disputes are absent (discussed in the next section) and when established mechanisms for consultation have not been set up. Both of these conditions are apparent in Hong Kong and Macau, where the autonomies were essentially created through formal legal frameworks that specify the institutional arrangements, but lack flexibility to respond to changing circumstances. In Hong Kong, these arrangements have led to continuing tensions and disagreements, where the local government has repeatedly sought intervention of the centre to resolve problems it claims to face arising from the legal framework, diminishing its autonomy as a result. By contrast, Macau has had fewer such problems. A cynical view would be that this difference is the result of Macau's less active civil society and greater willingness to go along with what the Mainland wants without being told. A more positive view is advanced by Cardinal, who points out the importance of leadership in Macau, and the way the leaders there have worked to maintain good relations with their Mainland counterparts through informal channels.

Classical federations provide one model for such negotiations. Changes in the relationship of a unit with the centre require constitutional amendments. India has created several new states since independence; but they have to fit into the existing model of federal states – with a major exception for Kashmir and minor exceptions for a few other states. In recent years, however, constitutional arrangements provide considerable flexibility. Both Spain and Papua New Guinea set up frameworks for negotiations for autonomy in their original constitutional design. Provinces desiring autonomy could request it, subject to procedures in the province or unit to ensure that the request has the support of the majority of its people. In these cases there is also built-in flexibility about the powers that a province may acquire; they can choose from a menu of powers, but have to satisfy certain tests before they can get more than a prescribed minimum. Powers can be phased in over a period of time, as the province demonstrates its ability to take on additional responsibilities and institutions for this purpose are established. The arrangements under the Charlottestown Accord would have provided for negotiations by various groups for their autonomy or rights, but this settlement was later rejected by other provinces in Canada.

While flexibility (and the habits of negotiations it generates) has positive consequences, it has also attracted significant criticism. From the point of view of a group wanting autonomy, there is an advantage in getting what it wants in one go; there are critical moments in history when the group is in a strong negotiating position, such as when it is willing to bring a revolt to an end, or there is international pressure on the central government. If the autonomous unit does not capitalise on that moment, it may be unable to secure transfers of further power. This was very much the experience in Papua New Guinea; no province was able to secure further powers than were conceded on the establishment of autonomy.

There are other reasons as well that militate against flexibility. Too much time can be spent on negotiations. Negotiations can become acrimonious. The centre can drag its feet, or impose additional preconditions for the transfer of new powers. This was the experience in Spain; it seemed at one point as if the whole scheme might collapse. The degree of flexibility in the original arrangements for Catalonia were a compromise in which the two sides agreed to leave various aspects open for future resolution; but this has led to continuing efforts by Catalan elites to expand their powers, which have been much resented at national level. Flexible arrangements require good faith on the side of all parties; if this is forthcoming, there is much to be said for flexibility.

Independent dispute settlement mechanism is essential

Disputes inevitably arise during the operation of autonomy, given changing circumstances and inevitable disagreements about what provisions worked out in advance are supposed to mean in practice. The most common form of dispute resolution is to allow adjudication of some kind by independent courts. Where certain courts are empowered to determine knotty constitutional issues, and courts are generally well established, competent and respected by both the state and the autonomous communities, such dispute resolution can be essential to the continuing viability of autonomy.

As discussed earlier, direct political negotiations are also essential, and courts certainly cannot be the forum for resolution of all kinds of disagreements between the state and autonomous units. Many issues are better resolved through direct negotiations, as they require compromises on both sides that judicial solutions may not provide. However, independent courts are crucial in maintaining constitutional parameters, providing authoritative settlements of long-standing issues of dispute and sometimes, breaking political deadlocks. For example, the Canadian Supreme Court's deft handling of the secession reference, and its mapping out of a means of secession through peaceful means, to a certain extent relieved tensions between the two parties. The perceived impartiality and independence of the Papua New Guinea Supreme Court, and its role in dispute resolution regarding the autonomy arrangements, has been central to the acceptance of the people of Bougainville of autonomy. The experience in Spain has been somewhat similar; a key decision of the Constitutional Court was necessary to break a logjam and to restart the process of transfer of powers to the regions.

However, when political elites in an autonomous unit politicise court decisions, damaging the image of impartiality of legal judgments in the eyes of the public, this may be dangerous for autonomy. In recent years, this has been the case in relation to the Constitutional Court's judgments on issues relating to Catalonia. States too may politicise law, damaging the independent status of courts; this has been the case in Italy in recent years, where extreme pressure on the judiciary has led to a series of rulings that regions find overly partial to the interests of the centre, reversing a trend for the Constitutional Court to act as a protector of autonomy.

In some of the autonomies studied in this volume, independent mechanisms for dispute resolution are entirely absent. This is notably the case in Hong Kong and Macau. Despite the extensive autonomy granted to these units – in some cases going beyond the powers usually accorded to units in a federation, for example, independent representation in inter-governmental organisations – when disputes arise, the ultimate authority for ruling on interpretations of the relevant instruments is China's National People's Congress or its Standing Committee. This system reflects the PRC's rejection of the doctrine of separation of powers; as the apex of formal power in the PRC system, the Congress represents the concentration of political power. Such an arrangement for dealing with disputes can result in the negation of the autonomy. It is ironic that the interpretations the Standing Committee has issued in respect of Hong Kong have all been at the request of the unelected government of the Special Administrative Region. By contrast, Macau only requested one interpretation on electoral rules in 2012.

Courts are also crucial in the case of small autonomies that have very limited political clout at national level. The case of Åland and the actions of the Finnish Supreme Court are a case in point. This Court has the power to decide cases in which disputes between the two parties arise in relation to division of powers, among other matters. Papua New Guinea provided a limited and residual role for courts in inter-governmental relations. But the political processes it envisaged did not produce harmony or progress, because the centre had little interest in autonomy. When the existing autonomy was invaded by the centre, it was the judiciary that came to the assistance of provinces.

Where an international agreement specifies this as a dispute resolution mechanism, recourse may be had to the International Court of Justice. Such a mechanism was established in the case of South Tyrol, but has never been used, as Austria has not been willing to take such action, even in the years when it sought to internationalise the autonomy arrangements through referring the case to the United Nations.

Constitutional entrenchment is a key guarantee

As discussed in section one, the rule of law is crucial to autonomy arrangements. A key feature of such frameworks is the entrenchment of autonomy in constitutional provisions that ensure that the autonomy cannot be altered without the consent of the autonomous area. Various versions of such arrangements are evident in the cases covered in this book.

Federal structures inherently entrench the rights of their constituent parts, with the centre deriving its powers from the agreement of the provinces that make up the federation. Québec's autonomous status is inherent to the confederal design of the Canadian federation, which is seen as deriving from the consent of the provinces that compose it. However, the degree of asymmetry allowable for Québec within that federal structure has continued to be controversial, and has remained a source of significant tension to date. As Simeon and Turgeon write, 'De facto asymmetry is widely accepted; formal asymmetry opposed'.

Although passed by the autonomous area, Catalonia's Autonomy Statute has protected status in that amendments require consultation between the state and the autonomy, and no changes are possible without the consent of both. In addition, Catalonia's power in the national *Cortes General* means that its representatives could block constitutional changes that were seen as inimical to Catalonia's status.

Yet when a federation is inherently asymmetrical, involving unification of a smaller, weaker partner or partners with a larger one, there is always the danger that any constitutional guarantees may be overridden by the centre without the consent of the autonomy. This has been the case in Tanzania, where the powers of the Union have been used to diminish those of Zanzibar. In part, this is due to the weak tradition of rule of law and the long dominance of a one-party system in Tanzania, which gave Zanzibar few opportunities to assert its case against the overwhelming power of the central authorities.

However, certain forms of constitutional entrenchment have been successful in protecting the rights of smaller units, even in non-federal systems. The relationship between Finland and Åland is a case in point. The latter's autonomy is entrenched in several ways: agreement is needed both by the Finnish Parliament and the Åland Legislative Assembly for any changes to the constitutional order. The Åland Legislative Assembly can reject any alteration to which it does not agree. Within Åland, certain changes to the legislative order that affect the 'internal constitutional order' may only be made with a super-majority vote.

A similarly strong form of entrenchment is part of the Agreement that was reached between Papua New Guinea and the insurgents in Bougainville. This Agreement incorporated what Regan terms 'double entrenchment' by requiring the assent of Bougainville to any changes in the constitutional arrangements regarding the autonomy at federal level. In addition, explicit provisions in the federal Constitution state that Bougainville's own Constitution prevails over national law in the autonomous area. Furthermore, the Agreement specified that a referendum on independence could be held in Bougainville after the settlement had been in place for three to five years. This latter provision set in place strong incentives for the state to respect the autonomy arrangements, although in practice this has not been unproblematic.

A form of constitutional entrenchment may operate without being formalised in law: although Australia has the power to amend or repeal the Norfolk Island Act, it has politically been unwilling or unable to do so, despite repeated assertions that changes should be made, often related to Australia's responsibility to ensure that human rights are protected throughout its territory. Such constitutional conventions can act as an unwritten constraint even on unfettered sovereign powers.

Likewise, in the UK, parliamentary sovereignty leaves Scottish autonomy on apparently shaky ground. Yet the unwritten features of the constitutional order in the UK, and the Treaty of 1707 that originally incorporated Scotland into the United Kingdom, impose effective constraints on actions of the sovereign that would serve to limit or reduce Scotland's autonomy. At the same time, however, the constitutional order in the UK gives Scottish institutions little effective control over the formal constitutional arrangements from which their powers derive.

The system of ethnic power-sharing and the associated constitutional veto available to constituent units in the Bosnia-Herzegovina arrangements might be considered a form of constitutional entrenchment. However, in this case, it has proved to be a recipe for governmental paralysis, a situation that has required repeated international intervention through the office of the High Representative to the UN Secretary General to move forward on the formation of institutions at federal level in the face of a lack of political will among entrenched political elites at the level of the ethnic Entities that constitute the confederation.

Explicit division of power facilitates the exercise of autonomy

Clear divisions of powers between autonomous units and the states of which they form a part are an essential part of successful autonomies. However, changing circumstances often require revisiting such divisions as new situations arise that call existing arrangements into question. One key distinction has been between federal or federal-like frameworks, in which powers are viewed as inherently resting with the constituent provinces, as is the case in Spain and Canada; and asymmetrical frameworks in which autonomy is seen as a grant of powers from above, such as in the cases of Åland, South Tyrol and Scotland. Then there are anomalous cases, such as Puerto Rico, which is attached to a federation, the United States, but is not formally a unit of the federation, but an 'unincorporated territory'.

In the case of states that are formally federal, such as Spain and Canada, powers exercised by the state are those granted to it by the provinces, and thus the latter retain residual powers. However, even within these arrangements disagreements around divisions of powers still arise. Such disputes have been endemic to the autonomy arrangements for Catalonia, as the original compromise that launched the current framework was reached at the cost of leaving key areas fairly vague. This complexity applies not only to Catalonia, but is inherent in the general system of division of competences between state and regions in Spain. The system is one which allocates functions rather than subject matters among the parties. In recent years, Catalan institutions have sought to expand the Community's powers into areas that have been found by the Constitutional Court to be the exclusive domain of the state.

While vesting residual powers in the autonomous area is common in federal arrangements, in certain cases it can operate as a centripetal force, pushing constituent units apart and hollowing out the federal level. This is the case in the constitutional design imposed in Bosnia-Herzegovina in the Dayton Agreement, where key powers that are usually held by the federal level remained with the ethnic Entities. In the case of Zanzibar, despite residual powers remaining with the constituent units of the federation in the original design, the overwhelming powers of the Union and the lack of clear arrangements for deciding on changes to the structure have meant a great expansion of the powers at the centre, at the expense of the autonomy of Zanzibar.

Clear divisions of power have facilitated the exercise of autonomy in smaller non-federal units. For example, there is a clear division of powers in relation to Åland, with specified competences to legislate for the state and the Åland Legislative Assembly. The Agreement for the Bougainville autonomy likewise incorporates a clear division of powers, with provisions allowing for certain powers to be phased in once the autonomous area has the capacity to exercise them. The scheme of division is thus both specific and flexible, accommodating the initially weak institutional framework of the Bougainville autonomous government.

The basic laws for Hong Kong and Macau enacted by China's National People's Congress have allocated some powers to the two special administrative regions that go well beyond those usually exercised by autonomous areas, including independent membership of some intergovernmental organisations, immigration-related powers and the use of their own currencies. In the areas of economic life, although many powers are specified, these are constrained by a particular vision of the economic role of the two regions as centres of trade and finance, thus serving to limit the *way* these powers may be exercised. Furthermore, as Ghai points out, the basic laws failed to specify the powers of the state and the autonomies in a definitive list, despite proposals for this. This refusal reflects an unwillingness on the part of the central authorities in the PRC to countenance formal measures that divide sovereignty, thus calling their ultimate commitment to autonomy into question.

Social and political consequences of autonomy arrangements

Autonomy has profound consequences, shaping the identities and characteristics of the territories where it is practiced and the people who live in them – as well as the states in which they are situated – in distinctive ways. In this section we consider some of the effects of autonomy, as well as considering cross-cutting issues that have been raised in the chapters in this book, but are not considered in the discussion earlier. These are outlined in Table 14.3. The first part of this section examines some questions relating to ethnicity arising from our comparative analysis of the institutional characteristics of autonomies. It also examines how forms of local citizenship serve to bolster the identity of the autonomous area, and the effects of these forms on ethnic tensions in the larger state. The second part considers the extent to which these cases support the proposition that states that allow asymmetrical arrangements to be formed within their territory are likely to move towards federalism in the longer term. Finally, some of the downsides and tensions arising from autonomy systems are considered.

Ethnicity: a complex and variable factor in autonomy

Much has been written about ethnicity and autonomy; indeed this has been a primary focus of much of the literature on the topic.[23] By contrast, this book concentrates more on institutional factors; yet this approach too brings into view certain questions about the relationship between ethnicity and autonomy, particularly the effects of particular institutional arrangements on ethnic tensions, ethnic consciousness and identity more generally.

As markers of minority status, ethnic identities have often been central in the processes leading to the formation of autonomies and the institution-building that follows formal establishment. Yet questions around whether identities are mobilised as ethnic and in opposition to each other are complex and difficult, and much research has failed to provide adequate answers. Our focus in this book on institutional frameworks for autonomy has concentrated on how ethnicity works within the autonomies themselves, and has inevitably left much unsaid about the larger context for ethnic politics both within the states in question and in their regional environments.

The overwhelming majority of the world's states are multi-ethnic.[24] Within such states, claims for self-governance on the basis of an ethnic identity raise the possibility of setting precedents for other groups. While formally federal

[23] See for example, Marc Weller and Katherine Nobbs (eds.), *Asymmetric Autonomy and the Settlement of Ethnic Conflicts* (Philadelphia: University of Pennsylvania Press, 2010); and Yash Ghai (ed.), *Autonomy and Ethnicity: Negotiating Competing Claims in Multi-ethnic States* (Cambridge University Press, 2000).

[24] According to Duffy Toft, *The Geography of Ethnic Violence*, 90 per cent of the world's states have two or more ethnic groups within them.

Table 14.3 Social and political consequences of autonomy

Autonomous unit	Forms of ethnic identification	Degree of tension over ethnicity	Character of local citizenship	Shifts towards federalism	Secessionist tendencies	Areas of tension
Åland Islands	Language	Low	Formal, residence	No	Minimal	EU rules
Bosnia-Herzegovina	Religion/nationality	High	Dual citizenship (state and autonomy)	Failure of federalism	Yes	Ethnic divisions
Bougainville	Racialised difference	Medium	Residence	Somewhat	Yes	Resources
Catalonia	Language	Low	Linguistic	Yes	Yes	Resources
Hong Kong	Language	Medium	Formal, residence	No	Minimal	Autonomy, inequality
Kashmir	Religion	High	Formal, residence	Existing federalism	Somewhat	Security
Macau	Language	Low	Formal, residence	No	No	Inequality
Norfolk Island	Heritage	Medium	Formal, heritage and residence	Yes – but little effect	Somewhat	Rights of minorities
Puerto Rico	Language	Medium	Dual citizenship (state and autonomy)	Yes	Somewhat	Inequality
Québec	Language	Medium	Linguistic	Existing federalism	Yes	Language
Scotland	Heritage	Low	Residence	Somewhat	Yes	Social policy
South Tyrol	Language	Medium	Linguistic	Yes	Low	Constitutional reform
Zanzibar	Religion, heritage	Medium	Formal, residence	Yes – but little effect	Somewhat	Inequality

systems provide a framework for maintaining the borders of a state while concurrently recognising the aspirations of particular groups to self-governance, in the absence of such institutional structures to manage them, states may be concerned about setting off a cascade of similar assertions of a right to asymmetrical arrangements. As Duffy Toft argues, a key differentiating factor here is the patterns of settlement of ethnic groups within a state, and the extent to which existing administrative boundaries within a state reflect these.[25]

Given that the type of autonomy studied here is by definition territorial in character, it involves an identification of a group with a particular territory. As highlighted in Table 14.3, language is the most prominent form of ethnic identification in the autonomies studied in this book, and in many cases, protecting the language of the group that forms a majority in the areas has been a key aim of the autonomy. In some autonomous areas, such as Québec and Catalonia, language remains an issue of continuing tension with the speakers of the majority language in the larger state of which they form a part.

Basing autonomy on common language groups appears to lead to relatively stable and well-functioning autonomy. Despite its diversity in linguistic and religious terms, Switzerland is a key example, with each canton having a majority of one or other linguistic community. Autonomy in Indian federalism is based primarily on language, but different linguistic groups have many cross-cutting identities, in terms of religion, caste and traditions. The relative success of these autonomy arrangements has been explained in terms of cross-cutting identities, yet this book makes clear that rules that institutionalise preferences for one or other language in the autonomous area can operate in a way that appears fairer than other types of ethnic preference. For example, people of Italian extraction living in South Tyrol may be treated the same as native German speakers, provided they develop a certain degree of fluency in German.

This is not to say language is trouble-free as a basis for autonomy; tensions may certainly arise over linguistic issues. This has been particularly the case where a minority language group perceives their cultural distinctiveness to be under threat from demographic change towards the dominant language. In Québec, Francophones feel their language is threatened by the dominance of English in the Canadian federation, and their cultural distinctiveness appears to be in danger of disappearing in a demographic tide due to combined factors of immigration, lack of population growth among Francophones within Québec itself and the diminishing strength of French-speaking communities elsewhere in Canada.

The contrast between these cases and Bosnia-Herzegovina is instructive, however. There ethnic distinctions that are based on religion and historical communities are built into the governance framework in a way that cements these identities and does not allow movement from one group to another. An Anglophone may become a Francophone, and a Finn might eventually become

[25] Ibid.

an Ålander if he/she learns Swedish and fulfills the residency requirements; but a Bosniac may have much more difficulty becoming a Serb, in particular because doing so would likely necessitate giving up his/her previous identity.

Local citizenship

Thus the extent to which autonomy serves to reduce ethnic tensions may depend in part on the terms in which local citizenship is framed. Table 14.3 outlines the different bases of local citizenship in the thirteen autonomies in this book. Local citizenship is relatively exclusive and restrictive in Hong Kong, Macau, Kashmir, Norfolk, Zanzibar and Åland. All of these incorporate some version of formal membership through versions of the *jus domicili* (right of residence), a form of citizenship generally neglected in scholarly work on the subject.[26] These schemes either block settlement of citizens of the state from other regions in the autonomous area, or prevent them from enjoying the rights of local citizens until they have been resident for several years. In the case of Hong Kong and Macau, Mainland residents have to obtain permits for visits to the special administrative regions. Although Australian citizens can travel freely to Norfolk Island (but must show their passports on entry), they are not permitted to settle there without permission from Norfolk authorities.

Even autonomous areas with more open terms of citizenship, such as Scotland, Catalonia, Québec and South Tyrol, maintain some restrictions on granting rights to non-resident citizens of the same state. For example, the Scottish government decided to maintain free university tuition for residents in the face of recent tuition rises in England, yet students from England who go to study in Scotland must pay the same rate of tuition there as they would at home. Québec sets rules that the children of settlers from inside and outside Canada must be educated in French-medium schools.

A factor that has contributed to the trajectory of some of the autonomies covered here is the possibility of exit, and the way that may relieve pressure on a metropolitan power to resolve the status of a territory. In the case of Puerto Rico, residents were granted the right of entry to and citizenship in the United States, despite the fact that in Puerto Rico itself they were often not eligible for the same types of benefits enjoyed by US citizens in states recognised as full parts of the Union, and those resident in Puerto Rico do not have the right to vote in US federal elections there. It is now almost 100 years since US citizenship was extended to people in Puerto Rico, but the expectation that this grant of citizenship was a precursor to full incorporation as a state of the Union has still not been fulfilled. Voters chose this option in a 2012 referendum on the future of Puerto Rico – but only a minority of residents actually voted for statehood.[27]

[26] Yishai Blank, 'Spheres of citizenship', *Theoretical Inquiries in Law* 8:2 (2007), 411–52.

[27] In the November 2012 poll, a majority of voters (54 per cent) said they did not want to maintain Puerto Rico's current status, but a significant proportion of those who voted (24 per

Local citizenship is about more than formal status, however. The strong sense of local identity apparent in Hong Kong – often expressed as opposition to the values of the authoritarian Mainland – reflects a civil society committed to liberal rights and freedoms. It remains to be seen whether the formal rights provisions in Macau, which are stronger than those in Hong Kong, as Cardinal points out, will result in better protection of rights there despite weaker civil society support. In tiny Norfolk Island, strong pressures for social conformity are reinforced by local self-governance, leaving little space for the expression of divergent interests among Islanders. As Irving highlights, a failure of Norfolk to guarantee the equality of rights to which all Australian citizens should be entitled has been a common feature of arguments for greater intervention by Australia in Norfolk's affairs, much to the chagrin of the ruling elite in Norfolk. In Bosnia-Herzegovina the space for civil society is constricted by the dominance of political identities based on ethnic groups, reinforced by the legal and constitutional framework, as Marko describes. Here non-sectarian forces have little space to work against divisive politics, or advance different conceptions of what it means to be a citizen. Bosnia-Herzegovina's system of 'dual-dual' citizenship – which means each person is simultaneously granted citizenship of the Entity in which they reside and the federal state – has actually served to hollow out federal level citizenship and entrench ethnic divisions.

So while it is apparent that autonomy serves to reinforce a local sense of identity, the actual effects of this on inter-ethnic relations within the autonomous area itself or between an ethnic group identified with the autonomy and groups from elsewhere in the state are dependent on the particular institutional forms local citizenship takes. Certainly, autonomies generate a political elite that often has an interest in promoting a sense that the identity of residents of the territory is separate and different from others within the state. But this may or may not take the form of mobilising ethnic hostility – the recent moves towards referenda on independence in Scotland, Catalonia and Québec have not been accompanied by a rise in *ethnic* tensions, despite the wars of words these aspirations have provoked between rival political elites. It remains to be seen whether the voters will be persuaded by these campaigns for political independence, in the absence of any sense of urgency for separation.

Asymmetric arrangements are likely to move towards uniformity/federalism

Examining the temporal sequence of the autonomies studied in this book highlights the fact that such forms of asymmetry are increasingly being used as a way of dealing with the unevenness of diversity within states. However, it could be

cent) did not vote at all on the second question, on the form of status they preferred. Of those who did choose an option, 61 per cent opted for statehood, 33 per cent for Puerto Rico to become a 'sovereign free associated state' and 6 per cent for independence. 'Puerto Ricans favour statehood, poll shows', *The Guardian* (8 November 2012), available at: www.guardian.co.uk/world/2012/nov/08/puerto-ricans-favour-statehood (accessed 26 March 2013).

argued that over time, states that institutionalise asymmetrical arrangements will tend to move towards making them apply uniformly, particularly by adopting a federal structure. The cases considered here also show that even when conditions for the formation of autonomy might not seem propitious, the prior establishment of federal structures makes asymmetrical arrangements more possible. This explains the formation of autonomies in Québec and Catalonia despite the presence of many factors that in other contexts might have made this impossible, as shown in our analysis in Table 14.1.

Asymmetrical forms make management of centre-region relations and public affairs complex. Autonomy arrangements in Papua New Guinea adopted in 1976 provided for any province that wanted autonomy to negotiate with the centre and agree on the range of powers for devolution. It was assumed that the more developed provinces, with better educated persons and greater resources, would ask for and be granted more autonomy. This may not have been what the less developed provinces wanted, but the move away from asymmetry came from the national government itself, on the advice of management consultants who were concerned with the bureaucratic difficulties of the national government managing its relations with nineteen provinces, varying in their status and powers.

Setting up asymmetrical arrangements raises serious political problems in a state with a democratic system. Setting up the legal arrangements for a 'high degree of autonomy' for Hong Kong and Macau within the PRC might have been much more difficult if the minority groups that have only titular autonomy, and have not even been able to use the powers granted to them fully[28] – including the Tibetans and the Uyghurs – had been able to debate publicly why similar conditions should not apply in their regions.

If the national government is inclined to support autonomy, it may have to generalise the conditions for the grant of autonomy. In Papua New Guinea in 1976, negotiations for autonomy were conducted between the national government and the representatives of Bougainville. The assumption was that the arrangements under negotiations were for Bougainville only; and in fact Bougainville leaders insisted that only their province should be entitled to them, in order to recognise their distinctiveness. However, the government realised that parliamentary support for these arrangements could not be guaranteed unless all provinces were given similar options, and so the law provided. Similar developments occurred in Spain, where all provinces or groupings of provinces were given roughly the same options as the 'historic territories'. Increasingly Spain takes on the appearance of a federation, and a symmetrical federation at that. The devolution to provincial councils in Sri Lanka followed a similar trajectory, diluting the special claims of Tamils to autonomy. Canada is moving in the same direction to the chagrin of the Québec Francophones. In Britain,

[28] Yash Ghai and Sophia Woodman, 'Unused powers: autonomy legislation in the PRC', *Pacific Affairs* 82:1 (2009), 29–46.

following the formation of autonomies for Scotland and Wales through 'devolution', there has been agitation for the establishment of 'English regions'. Several Italian regions now have 'special statutes' and the powers of even ordinary regions have expanded.

The push towards generalising the powers that have been granted to an autonomous area in asymmetric fashion may be related to the relative power of the autonomous unit in question in the national arrangement. Catalonia plays a strong role in national institutions, with the second largest number of representatives in the national parliament, and has had enormous influence in shaping the trajectory of central-local relations in Spain. Québec too has shaped the terms of federalism in Canada to a large extent. Such dominance may elicit resentment of other sub-national units, and thus, ironically perhaps, act as a driver towards uniformity.

Such moves towards federal style arrangements are not necessarily against the interests of the original claimants of autonomy. They should temper their pride in being 'distinctive' and having this recognised by consideration of the benefits they obtain by generalisation of autonomy. They would likely cease to be the object of envy and resentment. A greater number of beneficiaries would produce a more balanced state. A greater number of beneficiaries would also increase the capacity of regions to negotiate with the centre and extract higher benefits.

Such a calculus apparently does not apply in the case of small units, such as Åland, the Faroe Islands in Denmark and Norfolk Island. In these cases, the autonomous units have little influence at national level, and are relatively marginal to the form and character of the state more generally.

Again, Bosnia-Herzegovina provides a contrary case to these trends. The confederal system established under the Dayton Agreement is so weak and lacking in powers that its operation has repeatedly been called into question. The Agreement failed to centralise the powers that are usually monopolised at federal level: military and police powers in particular. Thus the Entities, as the constituent units are called in this arrangement, maintain their own coercive forces, and block the development of collective solutions to common problems, continually raising the prospect, as Marko puts it, of whether the 'constitutional design and politics in [Bosnia-Herzegovina] have become the means for continuation of the war by other means'.

Potential downsides of autonomy

As highlighted by many of the chapters in this book, while they can provide for significant self-government, asymmetrical arrangements such as autonomy are not without their problems. The extent to which these become acute, or actually diminish the rights of the inhabitants of autonomous areas, depends in large part on the specific form of autonomy institutions and local citizenship. Areas of specific tension relating to each autonomy profiled in this book are outlined in Table 14.3.

In the case of small and marginal units, asymmetry may represent an abdication of responsibility on the part of the state in question. As Irving writes of individual rights in Norfolk, autonomy 'masks abdication or neglect on the part of national government' for the realisation of rights that should be guaranteed to all citizens of Australia. The Norfolk system allows for the interests of a small dominant elite to override the rights of the majority in the name of protecting Norfolk's 'heritage'. Puerto Rico's situation has some similarities to this, in that the anomalous status of the islands has allowed the United States to pick and choose which elements of federal law should apply there.

A similar abdication of responsibility – in this case, for the harms of past policies of what might be termed a form of cultural genocide through forced assimilation – is apparent in the current round of treaty-making with some First Nations groups in Canada. Here autonomy has been used as a device for severing any possibility of future claims for historical restitution, as well as a way of essentially forcing aboriginal communities into making deals with resource extraction companies due to lack of other resources for development.[29] In these cases, autonomy appears to be a strategy that distances the national state from responsibility to address historical wrongs, or to be held responsible for environmentally hazardous development policies.

Bosnia-Herzegovina is an example of how entrenching ethnic divisions in the name of resolving ethnic tensions has actually had the opposite effect, creating a situation where the elements of common citizenship in the federation are being strangled by the lack of agreement between elites divided along ethnic lines. This 'war by other means' has meant that provisions giving displaced persons a right of return have proved to mean little in practice.

These cases highlight the inherent tensions between the group rights that are implicit in autonomy arrangements, and respect for and realisation of individual rights. Conflicts of this sort are inherent in schemes that entrench the rights of any particular group. As the discussion of ethnicity and local citizenship has shown, balancing such competing imperatives requires establishing institutional frameworks for group rights that do not entrench ascribed characteristics, and permit exit and change by individuals. Achieving such balance also entails commitments to human rights frameworks in the institutional design of autonomies. The question of the protection of the rights of groups that become minorities within the autonomous areas has yet to be resolved satisfactorily, although it has been addressed in various cases.

Another area of tension has been around questions of resources, and by extension, social policy. In the cases of Québec and Catalonia, this has been

[29] See for example, Colin Samson and Elizabeth Cassell, 'The long reach of frontier justice: Canadian land claims "negotiation" strategies as human rights violations', *The International Journal of Human Rights* (2012) available at: http://dx.doi.org/10.1080/13642987.2012.695860 (accessed 30 November 2012).

particularly the case around issues of what is called in Canada the 'spending power' of the centre. One of the main reasons for the Catalan elite's efforts to push for a referendum on independence has been a sense that Catalonia's rich resources have consistently benefitted the centre more than the Catalan Community. Divergent perspectives on social policy between the Conservative-led government in Westminster and the government of Scotland are also a dispute about resources and how they should be used, as well as a question of priorities. In Québec too, a more generous social state is under threat from a trend towards reduction in social services from the perspective of Ottawa.

Issues of control and distribution of resources are related to the extent of inequality within autonomous areas, as well as between their populations and those of the states to which they belong. Autonomy can entrench inequalities, as in the case of Puerto Rico, where disparities both within the islands and between them and US states are notable. In Hong Kong and Macau, maintaining existing economic relations – laissez-faire capitalism – is a central meaning of autonomy from the perspective of Beijing. This has meant gross disparities in wealth within these small city states, even though resources for addressing inequality are readily available, particularly in the case of Macau with its booming casino industry.

Finally, security concerns – actual or perceived – can block the implementation of autonomy frameworks and the realisation of self-government. In the case of Kashmir, concerns about security in this province divided between Pakistan and India have led to the effective disappearance of autonomy arrangements, as again and again, direct rule from Delhi in various forms overrides local governance arrangements. Hong Kong's autonomy has repeatedly been under threat from local efforts to impose the restrictive definition of 'security' used in the Mainland. The vocal populace of Hong Kong, aided by a strong civil society, have held off such threats – for now.

Autonomy not a panacea

While it may provide for a significant measure of self-government and serve as a form for the resolution of long-standing disputes, autonomy is no guarantee that the issues it was created to solve will be addressed. As this book has shown, to function well autonomy frameworks require a great deal of work to form and develop effective institutions within the autonomous area, as well as mechanisms for debating and resolving differences that arise between the autonomy and the state. Under pressure from international interlocutors, the autonomous region often secures more powers than it is able to use effectively, creating another kind of vacuum, to the disadvantage of the regional population. However, the outcome is not only to do with the capacity of the autonomy itself to develop such institutions, but also the larger institutional landscape of the state in which it is situated.

Table 14.2 provides scores for some of the main factors relating to autonomy institutions covered in the chapters. The autonomies considered as models, such as Åland, an example of an autonomy in a non-federal system, and Québec, in the federal category, score high on our measures. However, Bosnia-Herzegovina is also in the high-scoring category, yet can hardly be considered as an example of successful autonomy. Bougainville also scores high, but there have been significant difficulties in realising the promise of the strong institutional framework for the autonomy in practice. Thus institutional design is certainly a necessary condition for autonomy that works, but it is far from sufficient for that purpose.

The scores in Table 14.2 need to be read together with those in Table 14.3 to give a fuller sense of how autonomy works and why. Our discussion has emphasised the importance of the specific forms taken by local citizenship, and the extent to which these provide neutral terms that allow the people of the state and the autonomy to move freely and take on the identities that they choose in the process. However, the case of Puerto Rico points to the dangers for *autonomous* citizenship of a regime that enables exit to a more privileged form of citizenship in the larger state (the United States in this case), since this lessens the pressure from within to make the terms of rights and freedoms apply equally to those within the autonomous region. The case studies also highlight how, as an attribute that can be learned and layered on other forms of identity, language has proved to be a fair basis for local citizenship that does not preclude either exit or entry.

The cases discussed in this book show that autonomy is always a work in progress. Even established autonomies can find their powers under threat from the vagaries of politics within and beyond the autonomy and the state. The expanded autonomy enjoyed by South Tyrol may well be affected by the 'centralising wind' in Italy, which has recently even affected the rulings of the Constitutional Court, previously seen as an institution supportive of autonomy. While flexibility may be essential for autonomy to function effectively, this feature can also work against it when conditions change. Democratic politics is unpredictable; and politicians aiming to speak in the name of 'the people' at national level may sometimes choose to sacrifice minority rights when these are presented as conflicting with 'national interest'.[30]

Conclusion

The Introduction to this volume pointed to the importance of autonomy in the organisation of a large number of states and urged scholars of law and politics to pay more attention to the rationale, structures and consequences of autonomy. The aim of this book is to add to our knowledge of autonomy systems, through a focus on institutions. As this chapter shows, institutions are critical, but a number of factors affect the working of institutions, including history, international pressures, attitudes of political parties and their leaders. Similar institutions in different countries thus do not have the same results;

[30] Nash, *The Cultural Politics of Human Rights.*

social, political and economic contexts influence the dynamics of institutions in important ways. The study of institutions has to be supplemented by an understanding of these contexts. Nor do we have much understanding of how autonomy affects the larger constitutional and political systems of the country – the studies in this book provide some indication, but further research is needed on these issues.

The future of autonomy as a constitutional device to solve internal problems of the co-existence of different communities and regions is uncertain. Due to the newness of many autonomies and the paucity of research, we have limited understanding of the long-term effect of autonomy on state structures or group relations. This book has noted some apparent contradictions in autonomy regimes. Autonomy is a response to marginalisation, or oppression, but can itself all too easily become an instrument for the marginalisation of others. Based on claims of human or group rights, it has denied sections of the community or other groups their rights. Starting as a response to discrimination, it sets up its own orthodoxy. Justified in the name of diversity, it tends to entrench boundaries between cultures. Instead of defining identity as a composite of different values and multiple affiliations, identity is perceived as made up of a singular and exclusive affiliation. Supported by international and regional communities, the dynamics of autonomy tend towards the denial of universal values. In reality the case for autonomy is generally pragmatic: the cessation of violence, the resolution of long-standing claims for greater self-government, preventing a break-up of a state, or incorporating territories previously under colonial rule. An important element in achieving autonomy in many cases has been the ability to deploy weapons against not only the armed forces of the state but also against civilians. There are of course examples of autonomy that not only brought peace but also upheld human rights and justice. In recent cases when autonomy was negotiated, considerable emphasis was placed on human rights of all and the participation of regional minorities in the institutions and affairs of the region.

The growing acceptance of autonomy as a solution to ethnic and other regional differences raises fundamental questions about the nature of the state. As the Introduction shows, some elements considered until recently to be central to formation of an effective state (undivided sovereignty, nationalism, individual rights and common citizenship) are challenged by autonomy. An illuminating example is the negotiations for a new constitution that have been underway in Nepal in recent years, with the collapse of the monarchy and the questioning of Brahminic hegemony.[31] Various marginalised groups, particularly Dalits, indigenous peoples and Madhesis, argued for autonomy of one kind or another; in the case of the indigenous peoples, influenced by the ILO Conventions on Indigenous Peoples and the UN Declaration on the Rights of

[31] Yash Ghai, 'Ethnic identity, participation and social justice: a new constitution for Nepal?' *International Journal on Minority and Group Rights* 18:3 (2011), 309–34.

Indigenous Peoples. However, numerous indigenous peoples have moved out of traditional communities and are pursuing different kinds of lifestyles. There are few areas where indigenous peoples are a majority and attempts to carve out autonomous areas for them led either to minute pieces of territory or the denial of full rights of other people living in what were claimed to be their traditional domains. In either case a meaningful autonomy would be elusive. Such issues are highly salient also for indigenous people in North America.

In Nepal, the alternative to a massive fragmentation of community and territory was a centralised but inclusive state committed to an agenda of social justice. The ruling class, while firmly opposed to fragmentation and autonomy, was reluctant to give up its control of the state and the privileges it derives from those (the most significant political parties, even the Maoists, were under the dominance of the upper castes). There could not have been a sharper contrast in the approaches to the formation and structure of the state. It seemed that autonomy, while second best, was the only real option for the disadvantaged and the marginalised. The ruling class, while desirous of a united nation, was not prepared to make concessions and limit the scope of its authority, which might have made unity a meaningful and realistic option. This is a poignant example of the kinds of dilemmas facing autonomy.

Index